MARRIAGE FOR MODERNS

Henry A. Bowman

Department of Sociology
The University of Texas, Austin

MARRIAGE FOR MODERNS

seventh edition

McGRAW-HILL BOOK COMPANY

New York   St. Louis   San Francisco   Düsseldorf   Johannesburg
Kuala Lumpur   London   Mexico   Montreal   New Delhi
Panama   Rio de Janeiro   Singapore   Sydney   Toronto

234567890 MUBP 7987654

Library of Congress Cataloging in Publication Data
Bowman, Henry Adelbert, date
  Marriage for moderns.
  Includes bibliographies.
  1. Marriage. I. Title.
HQ734.B76 1974   301.42   73-12188
ISBN 0-07-006800-3

*This book was set in Electra by Black Dot, Inc. The editors were David Edwards,
Ronald Kissack, and Susan Gamer; the designer was Janet Durey Bollow; and the
production supervisor was Joe Campanella. The drawings were originally done by
BMA Associates, Inc., and adapted for use in this edition by Judith McCarty.
The printer was The Murray Printing Company; the binder, The Book Press, Inc.*

*Cover photographs and photography by Susan Ylvisaker, except for photographs on
pages 3 (top), 4, and 112 by Roger Lubin, and a photograph on page 339 by Gary
Freedman.*

To L.B.B.

contents

Preface   ix

PART 1   SEX AND THE SEXES ON THE AMERICAN SCENE

one   The Sexes: What They Are and Why   11
two   The Sexual Revolution   37
three   Marriage and Alternative Life-styles   81

PART 2   MARRIAGE IN PREPARATION

four   Preparation through Choice   119
five   Choices Involving Contrasts: Mixed Marriage   147
six   Launching Marriage   179

PART 3   MARRIAGE IN PROCESS

seven   Marriage and the Social Climate   223
eight   Making Marriage Meaningful   267
nine   Sex in Marriage   301

PART 4   FROM MARRIAGE TO THE FAMILY

ten   Pregnancy and Childbirth   347
eleven   Conception Control and Abortion   395
twelve   Child Rearing and Family Living   451

References   475
Indexes   503
     Name Index
     Subject Index

Since the first edition of this book was published in 1942, a tidal wave of change has swept over American life and culture. Inundated by this wave of change have been marriage and family life, sex and the relationships between the sexes, reproduction and the control of conception, and a host of related areas. Results have been mixed. Many old attitudes and standards have been shaken. Some have been washed away. Others have been eroded and will never be the same again. Some attitudes and types of behavior have turned out to be solidly founded and have withstood the force of the waves and currents, while the protective covering of others has been diluted and their visibility has thus been increased. As in any flood, debris has floated to the surface. There is sediment to be cleaned up. There is need for reinforcing and rebuilding where weaknesses of structure have been revealed.

The overall result is that this is not only a time of change but also a time of confusion. Perhaps never before in our history has the individual been badgered by so many conflicting points of view, with so few guideposts, so little pressure toward conforming to any given point of view, and so much freedom of choice. Even since the sixth edition of this book appeared four years ago, there has been an "explosion" of publications of varying merit presenting the individual with a multiplicity of alternatives from which to choose in determining his life-style. Change which was formerly looked at askance by large segments of society is now accepted, even encouraged, as experimentation in seeking new and better ways of life.

The reader of this book is addressed, not as a scientist seeking an objective understanding of institutions, social processes, and human behavior to which he will remain an outsider. He is addressed as an individual seeking to steer a personal course through the crosscurrents in order to further his own understanding so that, from his own point of view, he may more fully and effectively participate in the cluster of activities which do and will continue to constitute his life-style.

To this end he needs facts. But facts alone are not enough. He needs also food for thought in the form of presentation of alternatives, raising of questions, and suggested possibilities and probabilities. This is not a book of recipes for happy marriage. At no point will the reader be told what he ought to think or even how he ought to think. He will, rather, be given points and issues about which to think. If he is willing to digest what he reads, no matter what the degree of his agreement or disagreement, he can further his preparation for marriage.

In the preparation of this seventh edition, both deletions and additions have been made in order to tailor it more appropriately to the contemporary scene. The title suggests this: *Marriage for Moderns.* Among the additions are discussions of the following:

preface

The sexual revolution, presenting research data on premarital intercourse and an analysis of those data, but also presenting a variety of points of view with the emphasis that the central issue in the sexual revolution, in the new morality, is freedom of choice

Marriage and alternatives to marriage, including communes, group sex, extramarital intercourse, trial marriage, serial marriage, marriage in two steps, repudiation of marriage, and related topics

Recent developments in contraceptive methods and devices, oral contraceptives and questions regarding their safety, intrauterine devices and their effectiveness, voluntary sterilization of male and female

The women's liberation movement and changes in the roles of men and women

Abortion, especially abortion on request and the issues associated with it, and recently developed methods of inducing abortion

New developments relative to pregnancy and childbirth

Sex in marriage, utilizing the studies of Masters and Johnson and others

Developments relative to black-white marriage and Catholic–non-Catholic marriage

Statistics have been updated, and the most recent available research data are presented. Since no one book can be "all things to all men," at the end of each chapter is a list of selected readings. These readings have been chosen for their interest and timeliness. Wherever appropriate, paperbacks have been indicated. Students who want still further material on given topics may supplement these lists with titles suggested by the instructor.

This book contains core materials that the author believes students need to know in order to further their understanding of marriage and thus make marriage more meaningful. The conclusion regarding these materials has been reached after many years of teaching a marriage course and of contact with thousands of students both in the classroom and in counseling, plus careful attention to the suggestions, reactions, and criticisms of both students and instructors regarding the six previous editions.

HENRY A. BOWMAN

MARRIAGE FOR MODERNS

Society has always had a hand in determining the relationships of the sexes, a situation referred to as a "cultural universal" [Murdock, 1960]. One of the universal determinants is some form of marriage. Thus, marriage is an ancient and venerable institution. It has survived all the ups and downs and has weathered all the vicissitudes of mankind's long existence. It is not likely soon to become obsolete. Marriage changes slowly, but it does change. It changes because the various elements of a culture are integrated—change in one is reflected in change in others. Marriage changes in response to basic social and economic conditions. It changes as new ideologies emerge, as new opportunities arise, as new demands are put upon it, and as a culture produces new kinds of people to participate in it. As marriage changes, elements of the old are carried along as new elements develop. On the one hand, this contributes to the strength of the institutional structure. On the other hand, it produces problems.

Marriage in modern America exhibits both old and new elements. Some of the reasons for which present-day Americans marry—for example, division of labor by sex—are as ancient as marriage itself. Other reasons—for example, romantic love—are relatively new arrivals on the cultural scene. As new reasons for marriage emerge in the process of cultural change, new questions arise: What is the "nature" of the two sexes? How may an understanding of their similarities and differences be utilized for mutual betterment? What should the roles of the sexes be? What is meant by "love," and how may love be recognized? What is involved in the choice of marriage partner? Is it possible to prepare for marriage? If so, how? How may successful marriage be achieved? Are there feasible alternatives to monogamous marriage in this country? In this section we shall consider the nature of the sexes, the cultural changes which are occurring regarding their relationships, and the life-styles among which they may choose in relating to each other.

part 1

SEX AND THE SEXES ON THE AMERICAN SCENE

Sometimes people say Jael and I look alike, and sometimes we dress alike, but as people we're really very different.

Hob and I moved to the country because we like the seclusion, and living here gives us a sense of being more in tune with ourselves and with the universe.

On Tuesday nights Bill and I go to the studio. Bill plays and I dance. There we're away from everything else in our lives, and we can just be alone together.

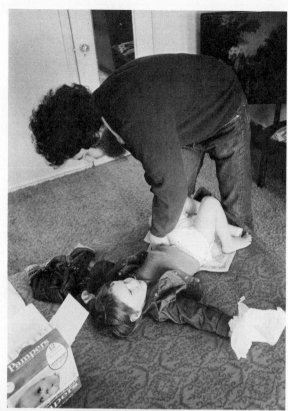

Karen and I have switched roles. I stay home to take care of our son Zachary; Karen works.

Ever since Tiffany was born, things haven't been so smooth between Mark and me.

Almost every night Linda and I and Tara go for a walk to watch the sunset.

Raising kids by yourself isn't easy, especially when you're caught up in your job, but I try to spend as much time with the children as I can. And I like flying kites, too.

I want my sons to grow up to be good, strong men, and I hope I can guide them, even though their father isn't living with us now.

The four of us share a house. Laurel and I are a couple. Jamie and Roslyn are both single.

Dinner in our commune is a time for sharing food and the day's experiences, and for talking out problems.

Here we all are—Clifford, Cindy, Clifford Jr., and me, Bianca—in our living room.

The family doesn't get together very often, but Mom's birthday is one time we always do. It's fun.

The Sexes: What They Are and Why

That the human race is composed of beings of two types—male and female—is one of the fundamental facts of life. It is a fact that at first glance may seem too obvious to mention. Yet it is often ignored or overlooked in our efforts to raise the plane of satisfaction in living. Out of this fact of sexual *dimorphism* (two forms) grows much of the world's beauty in art, literature, drama, and human relations. Out of it, also, grow some of life's most trying problems, bitterest disappointments, deepest hurts, and most distasteful ugliness. Human beings can choose to utilize the potentialities of sexual difference as one of the most fruitful means of overcoming the essential aloneness of the individual life, or—instead of establishing meaningful, enduring relationships—they can choose to use sexual difference to widen the gulf between self and others. There is no wider gulf between individuals than that created when one considers the other a thing. Sexual difference is one of the inescapables which everyone must face and to which everyone must in some way orient himself. Members of the opposite sex, with their attributes, their roles, and their expectations, are part of the environment in response to which personality develops. Each of these two types of beings, male and female, must in some way take into account the existence of the other.

POSSIBLE REACTIONS AND ATTITUDES

"Take into account" in the preceding paragraph implies both attitudes and behavior. The latter we shall discuss later. Attitudes exhibit a wide range of variation. Some are traditional and resistant to change. Some are cultural and in a state of transition. Some are individual, reflecting a person's reaction to his own sexual classification; his experience; the concomitant classification of others; role expectations; and similar factors.

A not uncommon attitude today is that expressed by Kate Millett [1970], prominent in the women's liberation movement, who says that "the sexes are inherently in everything alike, save reproductive systems, secondary sexual characteristics, orgasmic capacity, and genetic and morphological structure." The implication in such a statement is that all other apparent differences between the sexes are the products of culture and experience and could, therefore, be altered. There is truth in such an implication. But it leaves unanswered the question of how far and how readily, granted the inherent similarities, the characteristics of the sexes can be changed to individual and societal advantage.

one

11

Nevertheless, some persons today are proceeding on the assumption that behavior, roles, status, interpersonal and intersexual relations, marriage—in short, everything thought to be changeable—should be changed. Change in the sexual sphere is, indeed, needed. But it is important that it occur with understanding and perspective.

Another not uncommon attitude is that the sexes have always been in conflict and will continue to be so. This conflict often takes the form of exploitation, each sex assuming that in one way or another, at one time or another, it is the victim. An assumption of perpetual, unresolved conflict—a defensiveness against the possibility of exploitation—keeps members of either sex alert to threat by the other and is a potential barrier to meaningful relationships. Granted that the facts of the situation and the personalities involved in given circumstances may make such a threat more than imaginary, this defensiveness—this suspicion of one another—is a common ingredient in the attitudes of the sexes toward each other.

Some years ago the psychologist Alfred Adler coined the term *masculine protest.* He was referring to women who resent their femaleness, with its attendant roles and status, and wish they could be male. Some of them strive in a way to be male. Some set out to surpass men in one way or another. Some demean men. Some encourage affection from men, only to humiliate them, never forming enduring emotional attachments with any man.

There are more females who are to some degree dissatisfied with their femaleness than there are males who are dissatisfied with their maleness. For example, in two studies of university students, of 185 and 286 males, 12 and 15 per cent respectively and, of 148 and 265 females, 55 and 40 per cent respectively reported that at some time they wished that they had been born of the opposite sex [Katz, 1968]. Whether women should feel as some of them do, whether they have justifiable reasons for their attitudes, is partly a matter of individual judgment. Of course, the women who are dissatisfied feel that their reasons are sound. There are, on the other hand, women who are wholeheartedly enthusiastic about being women [see Bardwick, 1971]. Men rarely question the desirability of being male. The result is that women, some of whom are discontented and question the desirability of being women, and men, who rarely question the desirability of being men, are expected to work out an adjustment in marriage as if there were no difference in attitude toward roles and status. Hence, men who lack insight into this difference, or those whose attitudes and behavior accentuate the very difference women resent, contribute to the maladjustments both seek to avoid. Women who assume that being male means the absence of all problems make a similar contribution.

Even the most ardent feminists cannot avoid admitting that there are some differences between the sexes. Disagreement arises on what those differences are, what causes them, whether they are changeable, and what to do about them. It would seem that the most potentially productive attitude is one which recognizes that (1) some differences are innate, some are acquired; (2) those which can be changed for the better should be changed, while others should be

SEX AND THE SEXES ON THE AMERICAN SCENE

understood and accepted; and (3) social change is often slow. Thus, a young person looking forward to marriage might most profitably accept differences and adjust to them rather than wishfully demanding and expecting favorable change at an unlikely early date. A person also might keep in mind that he or she may marry someone whose characteristics and habit patterns, at least to an appreciable extent, bear the imprint of experience within a culture. On the other hand, he or she may not marry such a person, and attitudes will reflect this choice. Whether inborn or acquired, if differences between the sexes exist—and obviously they do—they are part of the world of reality in which we live. In such a world satisfaction in living is promoted by understanding and intelligent adjustment. It is furthered by the acceptance and utilization of those things which, for personal or social reasons, cannot readily be changed. At the same time, rather than making marriage a microcosm of societal turmoil, adjustment implies working for possible change, but in a way that will permit satisfactory living in the present as well as progress toward future betterment.

ADJUSTMENT

All this suggests that the need for adjustment exists in marriage or in any other relationship in which human beings are associated. Whether or not males and females have identical possibilities is an academic question. They are different both because they were born that way and because they have been made that way. In human relationships the question of nature versus nurture is not primary. Adjustment occurs among people as they are, not as they are hypothetically thought to be.

Adjustment is the fundamental thread running through the relations between men and women. It is the fundamental thread running through marriage; it is the very essence of marriage. It is the point of departure, the springboard, for the discussion in this book.

Throughout this discussion two words, "adjustment" and "problem," will be used frequently. It is important that the first be interpreted not as implying something static and the latter not as implying only something negative. Human life is replete with problems—situations in which individuals are confronted with possible alternatives and hence face a need for making choices, decisions, and judgments which may be made more effectively on a basis of information, understanding, and insight than on a basis of ignorance, irrationality, and obtuseness. But these choices, decisions, and judgments are also made with relation to goals, values, attitudes, and assumptions which may not be established on a factual basis. They often have a strong individual emotional coloring. They are also tinted by the cultural climate in which the individual lives. Complete objectivity, however essential to scientific understanding, is not possible in many aspects of day-by-day living. Facts alone cannot tell an individual what alternatives to choose. Facts can tell him, so to speak, how the gun operates; but they cannot tell him what target to shoot at or motivate him to pull the trigger. Hence he is called upon to consider possible flaws in his assumptions, the extent of his biases, and the possible limitations of his factual data. In the last analysis, however, he must make choices, decisions, and judgments in order to continue to live—unless, of course, someone makes them for him, as in the case of an infant, an incapacitated person, a person subjected to physical force. As he goes through this process of choosing alternatives, the individual seeks to move toward a type of adjustment that will, from his particular point of view, make his life more satisfactory—not necessarily more pleasant or happier, but more acceptable. Because life conditions are in a state of constant flux and the human individual is in a state of continuous development, whatever equilibrium is achieved is unstable. Adjustment is never complete, and we may think of it as dynamic rather than static.

SOME DIFFERENCES BETWEEN THE SEXES

We shall not attempt a complete inventory of all the differences between the sexes. In fact, at the present stage of knowledge, such an inventory is impossible because so much remains to be learned, and there are numerous items on which research studies do not agree. We can, however, indicate some of the more apparent and more commonly assumed differences in order to make a point.

One of the most obvious differences is that of size. Taken as a group, men are larger than women. This is a matter not only of common observation and statistical fact but also of expectation. Men are expected to be larger than women; husbands are expected to be larger than their wives.

It is important to note, however, that though men as a group are larger than women as a group, some women are larger than some men. There is a good deal of variation within each group; individuals range from relatively tall to relatively short, with the majority clustering around the average. If the sizes of the two groups were plotted on graphs, these graphs would overlap. Size, then, though constituting a rather obvious difference between the sexes, does not make possible the drawing of a hard and fast line between them, and so it is with other traits.

Man's skeleton is not only larger than woman's but also more heavily constructed, and various parts have different relative proportions. In man the areas to which the muscles are attached are rougher and hence can accommodate larger muscles. In woman the pelvis is broader and shallower, so her legs are inclined to form a V while a man's are inclined to be more nearly parallel, a difference that is important in athletics. Furthermore, the shallower pelvis makes the woman better adapted for childbearing than she would be if her bony framework were like man's.

Men are more pugnacious than women; they are not only more prone to fight but are more inclined to enjoy fighting. They express this pugnacity in sports, in business, in warfare, and in other ways. It is said that women are more adaptable to new situations; that women are better "domesticated" in the sense that they have less tendency to form gangs and are less likely to feel the "call of the wild." Men consider women vain, and women consider men conceited.

Probably they have equally sensitive egos but manifest them differently. Men have a tendency to bellow and beat upon their chests, so to speak, while women are less vociferous in exhibiting their self-esteem. The demand in present-day American culture that a man must be demonstrably successful in what he undertakes or in whatever society expects of him places the male in a position that renders his ego very sensitive and easily threatened.

Women tend to be more subtle, more indirect in their methods and in achieving their objectives. Perhaps this technique has been forced upon them through centuries of dealing with men, who throughout history have had more power. It was and is the most effective way to gain their ends for persons whose inferiority was taken for granted until only yesterday and still is taken for granted in many quarters. Women have become adept at it.

In courtship men tend to assume the role of pursuer while women tend to assume the role of pursued. Women respond favorably to pursuit by men; men usually respond unfavorably to pursuit by women. This difference is probably the result of both biological and cultural factors. When one sex attempts a reversal of role, the other is inclined to resent it. Women almost unconsciously assume the role of the pursued, but not actually to the point of escape. They know that, with custom and men being what they are, to seem to run away invites pursuit. Men's interest in women, on the other hand, is exhibited more directly, more aggressively, and more obviously.

There are, however, indications that women are losing their traditional reserve and are becoming more direct and aggressive in their approach to men. Whether this is temporary or represents a permanent change in the folkways remains to be seen.

In spite of this change in female aggression in approaching the male, American culture still sustains a male-female differential with respect to a felt need to be chosen. Actually, although they travel different routes to reach the same destination, male and female both choose and are chosen. Traditionally, however, the male's selection of a dating or marriage partner has been assumed to involve more active, more apparent choosing, while the female's has been assumed to involve more acceptance, less apparent choosing. She has not had the same freedom as he to decide whom she will attempt to choose; she has had to wait until he took the initiative, except in so far as she brought herself to his attention or made herself attractive to him. This differential is focused in the traditional assumption that it is the male who finally asks the female to marry him; the reverse has only recently become more common, but it is not yet universally approved. Because of this differential there is a difference in the reaction of the sexes to failure to date or to marry. An example of this is what is termed *senior panic* or *senior slump* [Bardwick, 1971] in some colleges. The term refers to the anxiety with which some unattached senior women approach graduation, hesitant to leave a source of "man power" without having been chosen. Such a reaction is seldom, if ever, found among male students.

It is often said that women are more emotional while men are more intellectual and more logical, that men reason while women feel. When one witnesses some of the intellectual achievements of modern women, however, and observes some of the mass blunders and primitive expressions of modern men, one is prone to doubt this assumed difference in intellectual and emotional behavior. The difference between men and women is not that the former reason while the latter feel; it is one of type of emotion expressed and degree of freedom in expression.

The common and uncritical assumption is that men have greater freedom than do women. In some respects this is true. Men have greater freedom of activity and are less subject to restriction and direction. They may move about more freely, are supervised less carefully, and are in some ways freer to determine their own behavior. In other ways, however, men have less freedom than women do. As Bardwick [1971] says, "Women have role freedoms that men do not have and restrictions that men do not experience." There is some tendency for women to compare their own lot to the more superficial aspects of men's. Some women formulated their attitudes toward freedom in their adolescent years and have not since reexamined them from a more mature point of view. Others do not see both sides of this issue with equal clarity.

There are standards of manliness to which men are in a measure expected to adhere. Women are freer to express such emotions as fear, pity, sadness, and affection for persons of the same sex. A man may feel like crying, but he may not do so for fear of being called "sissy." He may be petrified with fright, but he must put on a bold front to avoid being classified as a coward. In some respects, also, men are so overlaid with traditional restrictions and inhibitions as a result of training that they not only do not express such emotions freely but often come to experience them to a lesser degree.

Men are subject to a traditional code of chivalry which, though fading, is still extant and is directed toward standardizing men's behavior. According to this code men must show women courtesies, protect them, assist them, and accept their verbal or physical attacks without retaliation. There is no similar code for women.

Most men have no choice as to whether or not they will become breadwinners and support their families. Women may or may not have gainful employment after marriage, as they choose. In some cases, to be sure, that choice is forced upon them, but not in the same way as it is upon men. Men may have more freedom as to choice of type of gainful employment, but they have less freedom as to whether they will make that choice. When a married woman is employed, it is through voluntary choice or because of the exigencies of her individual situation. A man works partly for the same reasons but also partly because of the pressure exerted by the traditional cultural pattern. He must work to prove that he is a "real man." A woman can be a "real woman" and never earn a dollar.

There is a tendency for men to be more interested in facts as such or facts and their general, impersonal significance, while women are inclined to be more interested in relationships, especially the personal aspects of those relationships [see Bardwick, 1971]. It is for this reason, among others, that communication between the sexes is sometimes difficult. If one says to a group of women, "Women are inclined to take things personally," someone in the group will probably retort, "I don't."

It may be, as is commonly assumed, that men are more predictable to women than women are to men, but this does not mean that women are never baffled by men's behavior. They are. Traditionally, men's way of life has imposed upon them a certain expectation of predictability. Women, on the other hand, have not only not had the same social pressure in the direction of predictability but assume that being unpredictable is a woman's prerogative. The "average man" is likely to throw up his hands and say, "She's only a woman; you can never tell what a woman will do next." Of course he cannot, because he has made so little effort to understand her. By his words "she's only a woman" he implies that he believes her somewhat inferior and probably not worth understanding. Women have been forced through centuries of subjection to understand men, at least in some ways. If they have not been able to control men by the direct methods that men use on women, they have been able to exert considerable influence, often without men's being aware of it, because they have learned to understand men, at least in some respects, and therefore can to a certain degree predict their behavior.

Sex Drive

Generally speaking, a man's sex drive is characterized by greater urgency than a woman's. A woman's sex drive may be as strong as a man's when circumstances are favorable and she is aroused; but sex drive does not have the same priority in a woman as in a man. Men are more compulsive with regard to sex; and sexual interest is more nearly ever-present. Women's interest is less compulsive and more likely to be periodic; and women are more likely to have inhibitions. As a group, women can get along more comfortably with less sexual release than men can. There are more women than men who have little or no interest in sexual intercourse.

In their ability to respond sexually, women vary over a wider range than men do. Men tend to cluster around the average. Bardwick [1970] mentions the "all-or-none phenomenon in males." Women exhibit more extremes. "There is great variation in both the intensity and the duration of female orgasmic response, while the male tends to follow standard patterns of ejaculatory reactions with less individual variation" [Masters and Johnson, 1966]. There is a natural brake put on the male in that his ability to repeat ejaculation of seminal fluid within a brief time span depends upon the rapidity with which his glands can secrete that fluid and he can be resensitized to sexual stimulation. Since a woman's response is not dependent upon any such secretion and ejaculation, she may, in some cases, have a series of climaxes far surpassing the number of her husband's climaxes. This means that the most responsive women are more responsive than the most responsive men. Woman's "physiological capacity for sexual response infinitely surpasses that of man" [Masters and Johnson, 1970].

But this is not the same as the timing of women's response in individual acts of sexual intercourse. Men's response in intercourse is more rapid and more spontaneous. Women's response is slower and less spontaneous. These two differences between the sexes—one, rapidity of arousal and spontaneity of response; the other, capacity for repeated response—are often confused. The latter will be discussed more fully in a later chapter.

It is possible for a woman to enjoy sexual intercourse without having orgasm. Some women do regularly. Others do occasionally. It is also possible for a woman to pretend to have orgasm, to fake it. Some women do so for the sake of their partners. A woman's ego is not threatened by lack of orgasm in the same way that a man's is, and by faking orgasm she can avoid judgment by her partner. A man, on the other hand, is under an ever-present threat of possible sexual failure. He can enjoy sexual intercourse, at least to some degree, whether or not his partner experiences orgasm. But he is considered a failure by both himself and his partner if she does not. He cannot have sexual intercourse at all without erection of the penis. Erection cannot be pretended, simulated, or faked. If he does not achieve erection, he has failed in both his eyes and those of his partner. He cannot avoid judgment for such failure. We shall return to these points when we discuss sex in marriage. Herein is an important difference between the sexes which needs both to be understood and to be kept in mind when the relative freedoms and pressures of the sexes are compared.

Men more readily separate sex and love, while women are more inclined to combine them [see Bardwick, 1971]. This is one of the important differences between the sexes. It means, among other things, that men and women approach sexual behavior from somewhat different points of view or orientations. We shall discuss this difference more fully later. Failure to understand and appreciate it is a frequent contributor to unsatisfactory sexual relationships.

Puberty

At puberty a child's sex organs, which have remained more or less quiescent, begin to function in more nearly adult fashion. During the same period, secondary changes take place.

A boy's voice changes. His muscles increase in size. His shoulders broaden. Pubic hair appears. What was previously only an unimpressive fuzz becomes a shaveable beard.

In a girl, the breasts develop. Owing to fat deposits, what were angularities become more aesthetic lines. Pubic hair appears. The pelvis broadens, and the girl is prepared for childbearing. But, although there are instances of extremely early motherhood, there is evidence to suggest that in many cases a girl does not immediately become fertile when she reaches the *menarche*, that is, when she begins to menstruate [Montagu, 1946; Riley, 1959; Wilkins, 1965; Wharton, 1967]. Some investigators, however, question this and believe that in many girls fertility typically is established just prior to the first menstrual period [Greenhill, 1960]. The earliest authenticated case of motherhood is that of Lina Medina of Peru, who began to menstruate at age eight months; became pregnant at age four years, ten months; and had a 6½-pound boy by Caesarean section at age five years, eight months [Jolly, 1955].

In addition to adjusting to the physical changes that occur at puberty, the child must adjust to emotional changes and learn to live with the new attitudes and new subjective experiences that spring up within him. Also, since girls on the average reach puberty earlier than boys, there is a period in which many girls are both more mature and taller than boys of the same chronological age. The situation creates problems for both sexes. It is at this period that some girls begin to lean in the direction of older boys.

In both sexes the production of sex cells begins (sperms in the male, ova in the female). In the boy there is the secretion of seminal fluid which is stored in the seminal vesicles and constitutes an internal stimulus or readiness to respond to sexual stimulation. Puberty is announced in part by the discharge of this fluid during sleep. These nocturnal emissions, or "wet dreams," are a normal occurrence in the male. Typically they are marked by pleasurable sensations and are accompanied by sexually colored dreams (as compared to romantic dreams). In such a dream the boy sees a girl's body or parts of girls' bodies or has contact with a girl's body, or something similar. In the girl puberty is marked in part by the first menstruation.

Most children reach puberty at about their twelfth to fourteenth year, but in exceptional instances girls have menstruated much earlier. Some girls do not begin to menstruate until their late teens or early twenties. A few never do, and their condition is termed *amenorrhea.*

At puberty the sexes meet a fork in the road of development that is the point of departure for some of the later differences in attitude toward, and behavior regarding, sex. The changes which occur at this time further sharpen the differentiation between the sexes, lead to increased intersexual attraction, and establish more firmly the individual's identification with his own sex. To some degree these processes are already under way before puberty is reached, not only through anatomy but also through names, clothes, social groups, and differential treatment and expectations. Generalizing and recognizing the fact of variation in both groups, the sexes may be described as follows. Whether these differences are culturally or biologically determined is not our immediate concern.

MALE	FEMALE
1 Considerable interest in sex.	1 Less interest in sex, but not zero interest.
2 Much discussion of sexual activities, less of romantic activities.	2 Less discussion of sexual activities, more of romantic activities.
3 Sexual sensitivity and response spontaneous.	3 Sexual sensitivity and response less spontaneous.

a Little or no learning needed for response.

b Accumulation of seminal fluid constitutes internal stimulus.

c Tend to cluster around mean; less variation; relatively few unawakened or unresponsive.

4 Pleasurable sexual experience:
a Frequent.
b Tends to be "continuous"; regularly repeated.

c Typically starts early in life.

d Extends through greater part of life.

e Practically all have some such experience at some time.
f Reaches peak of frequency and physical responsiveness in teens.
g Experiences orgasm plus ejaculation.
h Lesser orgasm capacity; can achieve orgasm and ejaculation less frequently in limited time span.

5 Nocturnal emissions practically universal; pleasurable, frequent.

6 Masturbation practically universal, especially among younger males.

7 Premarital sexual intercourse:
a More males engage in.
b More frequent by those who engage in.
c Usually pleasurable.

d More males initiate.

8 Active imagination relative to sex.

a More learning needed for response.

b Nothing equivalent to accumulation of seminal fluid.

c Wider range of variation; many unawakened or unresponsive; some more responsive than males.

4 Pleasurable sexual experience:
a Less frequent.
b Tends to be "discontinuous"; often long periods between instances of sexual activity.

c In some cases, starts late in life.

d Often experienced during brief part of life; sometimes only once.

e Some never have such experience during entire life.
f May not reach peak comparable to male until months or even years after wedding.
g Experiences orgasm; nothing equivalent to ejaculation.
h Greater orgasm capacity if responsive; can reach orgasm more frequently in limited time span.

5 Nothing equivalent to nocturnal emissions.

6 Masturbation at some time by perhaps two-thirds, often extending through brief part of life.

7 Premarital sexual intercourse:
a Fewer females engage in.
b Less frequent by those who engage in.
c Often not pleasurable, disappointing, painful.
d Fewer females initiate.

8 Less active imagination relative to sex.

a Nocturnal sexually colored dreams common; typically accompanied by orgasm and ejaculation.
b Sexually colored daytime fantasies more common.
c Romantically colored daytime fantasies common.

9 Much interest in tactile sensations.
a Readily responds to being touched by opposite sex.
b Seeks to touch opposite sex; interested in "exploring" female body.
c Because of interest and experience, more inclined to think of reproductive organs as "sexual" organs.

10 Much interest in visual experience.
a Interested in seeing female body.
b Interested in seeing pictures of female body; may have pictures of identified, conventionally clothed females, but also interested in pictures of unidentifiable, nonconventionally clothed or unclothed females.

11 Is reared with less emphasis upon modesty.

12 Nothing equivalent to menstruation.

13 More readily separates sex and love.

a Nocturnal sexually colored dreams less common; sometimes accompanied by orgasm.
b Sexually colored daytime fantasies less common.
c Romantically colored daytime fantasies common.

9 Less interest in tactile sensations.
a Some response to being touched by opposite sex.
b Sometimes seeks to touch opposite sex, but ordinarily not interested in "exploring" male body.
c Because of less interest and experience, more inclined to think of reproductive organs as merely genital organs.

10 Little interest in visual experience; often no interest.
a Little or no interest in seeing male body.
b Little or no interest in seeing pictures of male body; may have pictures of identified, conventionally clothed males but usually sees no point in having pictures of unidentifiable, nonconventionally clothed or unclothed males. Likely to be aware of male's interest but not likely to understand why he has this interest.

11 Is reared with considerably more emphasis upon modesty. (Modesty is a matter of convention, not a simple matter of yardage.)

12 Menstruation: never pleasurable, always inconvenient, sometimes painful.

13 More inclined to combine sex and love.

21

As a result of these differences between the sexes, which are in part an outgrowth of changes that begin or are accentuated during puberty, at the time of the wedding a couple may represent significant contrasts in their experiences up to date and their approaches to the sexual aspect of marriage. Their problem is not one of determining the statistical probability of the other person's exhibiting certain traits or reflecting certain experiences. Their problem is recognizing the possibility of such, thus opening the way to greater understanding. For example, assuming that the wedding occurs some years after puberty, the bridegroom, through one or more forms of sexual release (nocturnal emissions, masturbation, premarital sexual intercourse), may have had hundreds of separate instances of pleasurable sexual experience, and perhaps more than a thousand. The bride, on the other hand, may approach her wedding without ever having had even one such instance. The question is not, "How many brides and bridegrooms are like this?" The question is, "What is the condition of this particular couple?" If neither individual is aware of the typical difference between the sexes relative to interest in visual experience, tactile sensations, or modesty, unintentional offense may be committed [see Kinsey *et al.*, 1948, 1953].

One of the differences between the sexes very difficult for both to understand is the difference in interest in visual experience. Males are interested in seeing females—the more the better, both numerically and anatomically. They want to see female bodies with as little concealment and as much exposure as possible. They are interested in pictures of female bodies, as evidenced, for example, by the multiplicity of magazines devoted to such pictures to be found on newsstands. Millions of copies of such magazines are sold monthly. The females in the pictures are simply females; male readers are not concerned about their identity.

Females, on the other hand, are ordinarily not interested in seeing the nude male body. They are not interested in seeing pictures of the nude male body. They not only see no point in looking at pictures of nude males, but also see no point in males being interested in pictures of nude females. There are magazines containing pictures of males to be looked at by females, but the males are usually conventionally clothed romantic figures, movie stars, singers, or similar persons. There are also magazines containing pictures of scantily clad male athletes. There are magazines containing pictures of nude males to be looked at by male homosexuals. But until recently there has been no widely read publication for females similar to the many for males devoted to pictures of nudes of the opposite sex. In 1972, one of the national women's magazines for the first time featured a photograph of a nude male. Following this, several wide-circulation magazines featuring pictures of nude males were launched. Whether this will prove to be an experiment or the beginning of a new trend remains to be seen.

This difference in interest in seeing the nude body of a member of the opposite sex is important because obviously two persons of opposite sex go on the same honeymoon. The combination of this difference plus the difference in modesty plus the difference in urgency of sexual drive may create a problem for a

SEX AND THE SEXES ON THE AMERICAN SCENE

couple unless understood by both parties. We shall return to this point when we discuss sex in marriage.

Birth and Death Rates

There are more males than females among babies born alive. Over a long period in this country the rate averages about 105 boys to 100 girls [U.S. Bureau of the Census, *Statistical Abstract*, 1972]. Fluctuations occur from year to year, but there are always more boys than girls at birth.

There are also more males among babies born dead. More males die in infancy. In fact, the death rate for males exceeds that for females for all ages [U.S. Department of Health, Education, and Welfare, Aug. 30, 1972]. "This sex differential for mortality is not limited to the United States. . . . Excess mortality for men is almost universal" [U.S. Department of Health, Education, and Welfare, September, 1971]. Men are more subject to hazardous occupations and leisure-time activities and to warfare. Most major diseases strike down more males than females. There are two and one-half times as many male suicides as female suicides and four times as many male as female homicide victims [U.S. Bureau of the Census, *Statistical Abstract*, 1972]. The average expectation of life is more than seven years greater for women than for men [U.S. Department of Health, Education, and Welfare, July 25, 1972].

This is a rather interesting situation in view of men's traditional claim that they are the stronger sex. When it is a question of muscular strength, men are undoubtedly the stronger. When it is a question of living long, living well, and withstanding the vicissitudes of existence, men must yield the place of honor to women. Men are stronger, but women are more durable.

The result of the combined operation of these birth-rate–death-rate factors is that at younger ages there are more males than females in the population. In the middle twenties the sex ratio—that is, the number of males per 100 females—drops below 100 and remains so for every older age [U.S. Bureau of the Census, Mar. 19, 1970].

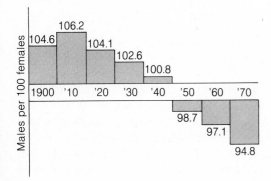

Figure 1.1 Sex ratio, 1900 to 1970. [U.S. Department of Commerce, Bureau of the Census, 1970 U.S. Census of Population.].

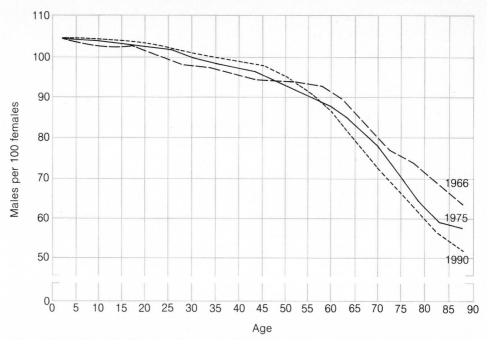

Figure 1.2 *Estimated and projected sex ratios for the United States.* [*U.S. Bureau of the Census,* Current Population Reports, Projections of the Population of the United States by Age, Sex, and Color to 1990, with Extensions of Population by Age and Sex to 2015, *ser. P-25, no. 381, 1967.*]

As indicated in Figure 1.1, the sex ratio of the entire population has shown a steady decline since 1910 and is now 94.8 [U.S. Bureau of the Census, *Statistical Abstract,* 1972]. (See the projection indicated in Figure 1.2.) Out of each 100,000 of each sex born alive, approximately 51,000 males as compared to 70,000 females survive to the proverbial "three score and ten years." By age eighty there are almost twice as many female as male survivors [U.S. Department of Health, Education, and Welfare, 1968]. The longer life expectancy of women, combined with the tendency of women to marry men older than themselves, results in the fact that there are almost five times as many widows as widowers [U.S. Bureau of the Census, *Statistical Abstract,* 1972].

Conclusion

We might go on discussing numerous differences between men and women, differences in physical traits, in interests, in attitudes both toward things other than themselves and toward each other, in expectations which the sexes set up for each other and which are set up for them by culture. As we intimated above, however, our purpose is not to present a complete inventory of differences but rather to provide a springboard for a discussion of relationships. We have said enough to show:

1   That men and women are different.

SEX AND THE SEXES ON THE AMERICAN SCENE

2 That, since they are different, they are called upon to adjust to one another. The achievement of this adjustment involves not only a general recognition of sex differences but also the observation of the person with whom the adjustment is to be carried out.

3 That, although there are important differences, these differences overlap, so that for almost every trait some men exhibit it more clearly than do some women and vice versa. In some instances there are men who, for a number of traits, are more feminine than average women and women who, for numerous traits, are more masculine than average men. Furthermore, though there are important differences, there are also important similarities, so that every individual represents a blend of male and female characteristics. This blending extends even to the primary genital organs, men having not only the developed organs of males but also the rudimentary organs of females and women having not only the developed organs of their own sex but also rudimentary male organs. This blending is apparent, for example, in the presence of rudimentary breasts in the male. "There are two sex-sides to being human" [Lal, 1966]. Allowing for diagrammatic oversimplification, a comparison of the characteristics of males and females as groups would appear as in Figure 1.3, while a comparison of the characteristics of one male and one female would appear as in Figure 1.4.

In relatively rare cases an individual has the genital organs of both sexes more or less well developed. Such an individual is termed *hermaphrodite* or *pseudohermaphrodite.* However, there never has been an authenticated human case in which the same person could be both a mother and a father, although such instances occur in certain lower animals. There are cases in which an individual starts life as one sex and later lives as the other. This may be the result of surgical correction of a misinterpretation of the person's sex at the time of birth due to "confused" anatomy. There are other individuals who feel that they are "trapped in the wrong body." They have the anatomy of one sex but feel that they have the psyche of and should be the other sex. Through hormone therapy and surgery some of these persons "change" sex. Such individuals are termed *transsexuals.* A transsexual actually wants to be of the opposite sex. A transvestite wants only to *appear* to be of the opposite sex, and it is to this end that he cross-dresses.

Figure 1.3 Diagrammatic representation of the overlap of the characteristics of the sexes as groups.

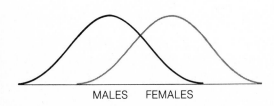

MALES   FEMALES

Figure 1.4 Diagrammatic representation of the characteristics of the sexes as individuals.

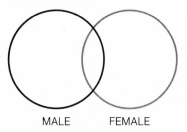

MALE   FEMALE

In addition to the differences between men and women taken as groups, there are individual differences regardless of sex. One might think of the sex differences as sweeping currents, while individual differences are waves rising here and falling there, superimposed but not necessarily dependent upon the currents underneath. Except for the genetic identity of one-egg twins, there are no two persons exactly alike either as to innate potentialities or as to experience. Habits, tastes, attitudes, ideas, ambitions, and a host of other things make for individual differences, which must also be taken into account in adjustment.

We have suggested that there are also important similarities between the sexes. There is no measurable difference in intelligence. Both men and women have sensitive egos which they seek to protect in one way or another. Both appreciate being respected as persons and resent being used as objects. Both have a desire for self-determination and have objectives for the pursuance of which they demand freedom of judgment and choice. Both are faced with the necessity of fitting their natural attributes into a cultural pattern and accepting roles which involve both opportunities and limitations. Both have a need for self-assertion and self-expression, approval, security, love, and affection. Both have sexual needs. Men and women have physiological processes in some ways conspicuously different but in many ways basically similar. Their psychological processes are basically similar, and observable differences are largely a reflection of cultural expectations rather than the product of dissimilarity of neural function. Their emotional responses exhibit many similarities in spite of the cultural framework within which emotions are expressed and in spite of presumably basic differences, as, for example, in the case of mother love. In the mutual adjustment that marriage entails it is just as essential to be aware of these similarities as it is to recognize the differences. Problems may be caused by failure to understand similarities (for example, when a man does not understand his wife's desire for self-determination) just as they may be caused by failure to recognize differences (for example, when a wife does not appreciate her husband's attitude toward his job).

WHAT CAUSES THE DIFFERENCES?

Several factors operate together to produce the differences between men and women taken as groups and to make individuals what they are.

Determiners in the Cells

Each human being begins life as a single cell. This cell is the result of the fusion of two other cells—one from the mother, one from the father—and contains within it the determiners (*genes, chromosomes*) of the individual's hereditary traits as well as the determiners of sex.

When the original cell divides into two, these two into four, and so on until in the fully grown person there are trillions of cells, the determiners of sex pass into each of the new cells in the same combination as was found in the first one.

The only exception to this is the sex cells of the new individual, in which only one of the pair of determiners of sex is found. In a sense, a person is male or female through and through. All the body cells are male or female, as the case may be.

This fact is actually not so all-important as it may seem at first glance. As Money says [Winokur, 1963], ". . . The presently observable chromosomal differences between male and female are such that by themselves and in isolation from other variables of sex they bear no relationship at all to the development of gender role and identity." Many factors operating after the new individual is formed and while he is developing may alter his development by affecting the way in which his inborn characteristics, his physiological processes, and his experience within his environment react upon one another. But the fact remains that all his cells, with that one exception, have the same genetic constitution, the same determiners; and because of this he has a tendency to fall on one side or the other of the sexual fence.

Physiological Processes: Glands

Both sexual and individual differences are produced in part by the way one's body functions, by the physiological processes that occur, and by the way one reacts to stimuli. One of the chief factors in determining such processes is one's glandular setup. In many important respects we are what our glands make us.

One pair of glands the secretions of which play an important role in making us what we are is the *sex glands* (gonads—testicles or testes in the male, ovaries in the female). Early embryos are sexually undifferentiated; they develop similar structures. The combination of chromosomes producing male or female is the first link in a chain reaction. If the combination is such that it produces a female, the embryo develops ovaries. Embryonic ovaries are inactive and secrete no hormones. If, however, the combination produces a male, testes will be developed. Embryonic testes are active and secrete *testosterone* (male hormone). Evidence suggests that, no matter what the chromosome combination, if ovaries develop or if neither ovaries nor testes develop, the individual will be female. The individual will develop into a female unless there are active testes secreting testosterone, which causes the individual to develop into a male. In other words, "Male features appear only if testicular masculinizing factors impose masculinity and push back femininity" [Jones, Jr., and Scott, 1971]. It is for such a reason that an occasional individual has the body structure of a female but with nonfunctioning testes or ineffective testes located inside the body cavity [Dewhurst and Gordon, 1969; Goldman and Milman, 1969; Page, Villee, and Villee, 1972]. The above is not the same, however, as saying that all embryos are female, as some persons assert.

Usually only experienced horsemen ride stallions (normal males). Less expert horsemen ride mares (females) or geldings (castrated males, that is, males with testes removed). The gelding behaves more like the mare than like the stallion. Both gelding and mare are more tractable, more easily controlled, and more readily predictable. To ride in a cart hitched to a team of bulls would be almost suicidal. Not so with a team of oxen (castrated males). The difference between the behavior of the bull and that of the ox has become proverbial—"like a bull in a china shop," "mad as a bull," "dumb as an ox."

When by accident or for medical reasons the sex glands are removed from a human male, profound changes occur. Such a person is termed a *eunuch*. If the person is young at the time, he fails at the age at which puberty normally occurs to develop the typical characteristics of men. Voice remains high-pitched. Beard and body hair do not appear in normal amount. Muscles have a tendency to be flabby and weight usually increases. The primary genital organs fail to develop normally, and, of course, the person is sterile. Male aggressiveness often fails to appear. If the glands are removed later in life, masculine traits change somewhat, and characteristics such as those mentioned above appear. In addition, the sexual impulse and interest in the opposite sex decrease considerably or disappear entirely [Bremer, 1959; Charny, Suarez, and Sadoughi, May, 1970]. In short, the person becomes "neuter," or, perhaps more accurately, he assumes a role partway between masculine and feminine but not entirely either. Equally important changes occur when the ovaries are removed from females (the operation is termed *ovariectomy* or *oophorectomy*), but such females are not referred to as "female eunuchs." The difference between the stallion and the gelding, the stallion and the mare; between the bull, the ox, and the cow; between the normal man and the eunuch or the normal man and the normal woman is caused in part by the presence or absence of the hormones secreted by the sex glands.

Caution needs to be exercised in reasoning from lower animals to human beings. On the other hand, equal caution needs to be exercised in assuming that human beings are a conspicuous exception among mammals, since they are mammals with similarities of anatomy and physiology. Human beings are biological as well as psychological and cultural organisms. No individual is reared without the influence of culture. Nor can he entirely escape his biological nature.

"Presence or absence" does not necessarily imply "all or none." Here again, we must think in terms of blending. The hormones which play so important a part in masculinizing the male are normally found in smaller quantity in the female. On the other hand, the hormones which play so important a part in feminizing the female are normally found in smaller quantity in the male. Thus, masculinity or femininity is in part a result of hormonal balance and may vary in degree as that balance varies.

The effects hormones produce are relative to the character of the tissues and organs on which they act, and these, in turn, are basically male or female. There is even evidence suggesting that "part or parts of the central nervous system are masculine or feminine, depending on the sex of the individual" [Young, Goy, and Phoenix, Jan. 17, 1964; also Money and Ehrhardt, 1972].

Maleness and femaleness, masculinity and femininity constitute a continuum. A continuum connotes differences of degree rather than simply "all or none." Maleness is not the same as masculinity, nor femaleness the same as femininity, though there is an overlap of terms as well as an overlap of anatomy and behavior. Generally speaking, "maleness" and "femaleness" refer to genetic constitution (determiners in the cells) and to primary sex organs, while "masculinity" and "femininity" refer to secondary sexual characteristics and, as discussed below, to learned behavior. "Maleness," "femaleness," "masculinity," and "femininity" all connote something positive; none represents merely a lack of its paired opposite.

An individual having ovaries, a uterus, and other typically female elements of genital anatomy is classified as female. If the individual also has a deep voice, the voice may be referred to as being masculine; but it will be *she* who has the masculine voice. An individual having testes and other typically male elements of genital anatomy is classified as male and referred to as *he*; but if *he* has scanty facial hair and small features he may be described as having a feminine appearance. If the individual exhibits a number of secondary characteristics ordinarily attributed to the opposite sex, he or she may be referred to as a feminine or masculine person, as the case may be. As a sidelight on our traditional attitude toward the two sexes in this connection, it is interesting to note that there is a special term, *effeminate*, applied to males as an expression of disapproval, with no similar special term applicable to females, for whom the term *masculine* does not connote quite the same type or degree of disapproval.

Masculinity and femininity also connote a certain relativity. Neither could exist were it not in contrast to the other, just as there could be no long without short, no up without down, no good without evil, no light without dark. Neither masculinity nor femininity would be possible if there were one sex instead of two. Masculinity and femininity also connote not only the objective existence of a combination of attributes, but also a degree of reciprocity, a relationship. A woman is feminine not only because she exhibits certain characteristics per se, but also, and perhaps more importantly, because she has the ability to make men interpret her and respond to her in a certain way. The converse is true of a man and masculinity. Masculine and feminine characteristics vary with individual and societal expectation. But the one thing which transcends culture and cannot be permanently removed is that aspect of complementarity which provides the sexes with a mutual look in each other's direction.

Culture and Experience

"Masculine" and "feminine" also apply to learned behavior, as suggested above. Because of genetic constitution (the determiners in the cells), anatomy, physiology, and hormones, typically each individual, as indicated earlier, begins life more or less "leaning" in the direction of masculine or feminine behavior. " . . . Owing to prenatal genetic and hormonal influences human beings are definitely predisposed at birth to a male or female gender orientation" [Diamond, 1965]. But with a few possible exceptions, biological differences do not by themselves determine such behavior. Biological differences do present possibilities for, and impose limitations upon, learning.

Each individual is born into a cultural framework which from birth onward determines to a considerable extent the manner of his life, the direction of his development, and the definition of what he is expected to do and become, depending upon his sexual classification. ". . . Sexuality is a dimension of personality (being male or female) expressed in every human act" [Masters and Johnson, 1970].

It is because of this fact of cultural framework within which the individual develops and the fact that culture varies among peoples, and even among groups within a people, that males or females do not exhibit identical behavior the world over or through time among a given people. Definitions of masculinity and femininity differ as culture varies and changes. For example, in this country slenderness for women is considered to be more attractive than larger size, but in some countries a buxom woman more nearly meets the ideal. In the United States feminine modesty demands that in public a woman conceal her genital anatomy; in some countries she must cover her face. When life conditions change, alterations in behavior may ensue. For example, during the Second World War the balance between the sexes was upset because so many young men were in military service and hence unavailable to women in their home communities. As a result, many women became quite "unfeminine" in the degree to which they became aggressive in taking the initiative in arranging dates and lowered their standards as to acceptable appearance and manners of men. In present-day America the population is so large and so varied, and our culture is changing so rapidly (though not at a uniform rate in all respects or in all subgroups), that there is considerable difference of opinion as to what standards of masculinity and femininity are acceptable.

But whatever the differences developed or permitted, in every known culture there are generally understood and expected means, such as clothing, hair styling, ornamentation, names, and terms of address, for readily distinguishing between the sexes. Deliberately to conceal sexual classification, intentionally to use misleading insignia, or effectively to disguise oneself as a member of the opposite sex so that others are deceived (as the transvestite does) is considered a serious offense or a symptom of maladjustment. Anything which produces only superficial camouflage rather than true disguise, as, for example, costuming in a masquerade or in a play, does not fall into the same category.

In short, one of the factors making us what we are and contributing to the development of differences between the sexes is experience within a given culture. But "experience within a given culture" implies more than merely experience within a given environment which leaves the individual largely the same personality that he was before the experience, as, for example, an experience in the mountains, in another city, or in a foreign country. "Experience within a given culture" implies the molding of the individual within a framework, the formation of habits, attitudes, conditioned responses, beliefs, values, and patterns of behavior which together determine in large part the individual's way of life. The culture becomes *internalized*; it becomes, so to speak, part of the individual's personality.

Some experience is sexually colored; some is not. From infancy boys and girls are subjected to different educative processes. Their games and toys are different and reflect their future adult roles. The stories they read or hear tend to have a masculine or feminine coloring. The standards set for them by their parents and by society at large differ. There is a selection of experience so that different environmental factors act upon the two sexes. Each is encouraged to do certain things and prohibited, or at least strongly discouraged, from doing others. Each has restrictions on freedom but in different ways. Girls are given more protection, and they grow to expect it. Boys are allowed more independence, and they grow to take it for granted as a masculine prerogative. As the individual grows older, this process of selection, like other aspects of culture, becomes increasingly internalized; each experience conditions him further so that his screening of new experiences becomes more and more a matter of his own choosing rather than having to be left to the discretion of others, as in the case of the young child.

When we think of the development of social life through a long period of time, we see that certain fundamental, unchangeable differences between the sexes could constitute forks in the road leading to the emergence of different patterns of life, different standards, different expectations, and different attitudes of each sex toward the other. Take, for example, the fact that women are physically vulnerable, not only because of their size and strength, but also because their structure permits the possibility of imposing sexual intercourse upon them against their will, something for which there is no parallel in men; ". . . male genitals invade; female genitals are invaded" [Gray, 1967]. Some would say that a parallel in men is found in the fact that the male can have homosexual anal intercourse forced upon him. But whether this is sexual intercourse in the strict sense of the term is open to question. On the other hand, men's vulnerability lies in the urgency of their sex drive and their susceptibility to sex appeal. Take the fact that pregnancy and childbearing encumber women but there is no similar encumbrance among men. Consider the cyclical nature of women's reproductive functions as compared with men's. Or take the fact that maternity is subject to proof but paternity is not. In the light of such differences and others equally important, it is not surprising that there are somewhat different patterns of life that constitute the mold into which individuals are not only squeezed but also assumed to fit "naturally."

> Apparently certain inherent sex differences may condition the members of each sex toward the learning of specific skills and the assumption of certain roles which become institutionalized in occupational roles and other cultural prescriptions. The latitude of these sex roles and their variations are, to some extent, determined by the norms and values of the society and the status accorded each sex within it [Garai and Scheinfeld, May, 1968].

The differences in standards of behavior set up by the group are expressed in exaggerated fashion in the old nursery rhyme: "What are little boys made of? Snips and snails and puppy-dog tails. And what are little girls made of? Sugar and spice and everything nice." "He's a real boy," says the proud father, implying that there is a standard of "boyness" and that his son is living up to that standard. The half-shocked mother who says, "Boys will be boys," implies that being a boy is different from being a girl. The words "tomboy" and "sissy" show that there are rather well-defined roles of behavior even for children and that deviation from those roles is not socially approved. In short, each sex tends to learn to act as it is expected to act. Masculinity and femininity are cores around which the structure of personality develops. "In reality there is no such thing as a human being— 'human being' is only a general concept, a fiction. Wishes and expectations are always centered somehow around the quality of being of a different sex . . ." [Giese, 1970]. An individual is born male or female, but he or she learns to be masculine or feminine, as the case may be, according to the cultural patterns of society. Sex is genetic, but gender is acquired.

In assessing the contribution of various factors to the sexual development and behavior pattern of the individual and in classifying individuals of confused sexuality, seven criteria or "variables of sex" [Hampson, J. L., 1964] are employed:

1   Chromosomal sex—the genes and chromosomes.
2   Gonadal sex—the presence, structure, and function of testes or ovaries.
3   Hormonal sex—the quantity and proportion of "male" and "female" hormones.
4   Internal reproductive structures—the presence or absence of internal organs other than testes or ovaries.
5   External genital morphology—the structure of external genital anatomy.
6   The sex of assignment and rearing—the designated sexual classification of the child at birth and whether the child was reared as a boy or as a girl.
7   Gender role or psychologic sex—the individual's sexual behavior and his attitudes toward his classification and expected role; everything he says, thinks, or does to indicate his status as a male or a female. ". . . Gender role is not an innate endowment, but rather is built up gradually during the course of growing up as a consequence of the planned and unplanned life experiences which a child encounters and transacts. The earliest years of life appear to be the most critical ones. . . . Of all the variables of sex . . . the best predictor of the gender role of an individual is the *sex of assignment and rearing*" [Hampson, J. G., 1964].

In short, this means that sexual differences develop before birth. At birth, so far as gender role and identity are concerned—that is, whether the individual will be masculine or feminine—the individual is "bipotential." The final, but not the only, determiner of gender role and identity is experience within a given culture, especially the way an individual is reared owing to that individual's classification at birth. Gender identity is established very early in life; some investigators say within the first two or three years. As suggested earlier, the individual is born male or female but becomes masculine or feminine. Gender role is learned, but this does not mean that either the masculine or the feminine role can be learned equally readily by either sex. Being born male or female, the stage is set for the selectivity of an individual's experience and, to some degree at least, the predisposition of his response to cultural expectations [Hampson, 1965; Sears, 1965; Young, 1965; Stoller, 1968; Dewhurst and Gordon, 1969; Green and Money, 1969; Josselyn, 1970]. Culture "condenses already existing tendencies into authoritative guiding images; it does not freely invent them without regard to reality" [Bednarik, 1970].

There is another aspect of the problem, however. It is true that the child is faced with two more or less distinct patterns of life—masculine and feminine—and is expected to adopt one of them. But masculinity and femininity are not entirely distinct; they overlap. Some individuals have more difficulty than others in living up to the standard set for their sex. Polk and Stein [1972] mention the "pressure on an individual to conform to the cultural stereotypes even in those respects in which his personality is incongruent with the social expectations." A confusion in roles may result, and the integration of personality sometimes becomes difficult. On the other hand, because learned differences do change, and because masculinity and femininity do overlap, in some respects our society is becoming more tolerant of the overlap. Increasingly in this country we accept with approval—even at times expect—the exhibition by either sex of characteristics and types of behavior which have been traditionally associated with the opposite sex. Take, for example, women's increased directness in their approach to men, as already mentioned, women's engagement in competitive occupations, men's increased interest in children and increased participation in child care.

Besides the sexually colored experience to which a person is subjected there are innumerable experiences that are entirely individual. They are so obvious as to need no further explanation, but they play an ample role in making us what we are.

No one of these three types of factors—inborn traits, physiological processes, or experience—is sufficient alone to determine individual or sex differences. They all react one upon the other, making the individual as well as the group the product of nature plus nurture.

ARE MEN AND WOMEN EQUAL?

One often hears the questions: Are men and women equal? If not, which is inferior; which, superior? Taken as it stands, the first question is unanswerable. Equal in what respect? Two things cannot be just equal; they must be equal with respect to a given set of qualities. Even then, the answer depends in part on the connotation of "equal." Men and women are equal as to number of hands. They are unequal as to muscular strength. They are equal in intelligence, though unequal in brain size. Do they have equality of opportunity for self-determination? Some would answer in the affirmative, others in the negative. Certainly they do not have identical opportunity for self-determination. Are the roles of husband and wife equally important? They are; but this does not make them interchangeable. When either men or women talk of wanting equality with the opposite sex, what they both usually mean is equality of opportunity rather than identity of role or of responsibility.

To speak of one sex as being inferior to the other is nonsensical unless some standard of superiority-inferiority is set up. If a masculine standard is used, women become inferior by definition. If a feminine standard is used, the reverse is true. We have a strong traditional tendency to set up a masculine standard; therefore, for centuries there have seemed to be more respects in which women were inferior to men than in which men were inferior to women.

Actually, each sex should be judged in terms of its own attributes and functions, not in terms of the attributes and functions of the opposite sex. One sex may be considered superior to the other not when it performs its own functions better than the other can perform them, but only when it can perform the functions of the other or common functions better than the other can perform them. If, for example, one were to compare the men and women engaged in a given occupation, one might set up a standard of proficiency in that occupation and determine whether one sex was superior or equal to the other. But to say that women are inferior to men because there have been more male than female geniuses is absurd because in fulfilling their traditional role women have had neither the need nor the opportunity to exhibit the particular type of genius that men exhibit in science, inventions, and the arts [see Sherman, 1971]. It would be just as sensible to reverse the definition and say that men are inferior to women because throughout history men have been inferior homemakers.

THE SEXES ARE COMPLEMENTARY

Together a lock and key that fit form a functioning unit. Together they can accomplish something that neither acting alone can accomplish. Nor can it be accomplished by two locks or two keys or a lock and key that do not fit. Each is distinct; yet neither is complete in and of itself. Their roles are neither identical nor interchangeable. Neither is superior to the other, since both are necessary. They are equally important. Each must be judged in terms of its own function. They are complementary. A lock and a key that do not fit, or two locks, or two keys represent a simple sum—one plus one equals two. But a lock and a key that fit add up to more than two because they represent one plus one plus function.

So it is with men and women; together they form a functioning unit. Either alone is in a sense incomplete. They are complementary. Though separate with the possibility of independent existence, they are at the same time mutually dependent parts of a functioning whole. This complementarity is not 100 per cent complete and does not apply to all traits, functions, drives, or goals. When men and women engage in the same occupations or perform common functions, this complementary relationship may break down. The sexes are not complementary for such things as number of appendages, need for food, and so on, but in many important respects they are.

"Complementary" connotes more than merely quantitative difference. It is not the same as "supplementary." It connotes completion, a combination of differences that creates a new entity rather than simply an additive process. For example, a wife's earnings might be thought of as supplementing her husband's income. But if he is the breadwinner and she is the homemaker, they complement each other, since their relationship represents a combination of role differences to form a functioning unit.

One aspect of complementarity is simultaneity and reciprocity. A complementary relationship does not arise automatically, though the ingredients for it are in part natural attributes and in part characteristics produced by culture and uncritically accepted. Such a relationship is established only when individuals of opposite sex are simultaneously and reciprocally interested in accepting and utilizing their differences, this interest being conditioned by the cultural pattern within which they live. Thus complementarity is not only observed and recognized but also created.

A complementary relationship is reciprocal in another sense, also. "Supplementary" may connote interest by, or advantage to, only one person. "Complementary" connotes reciprocal interest and advantage on the part of two persons who simultaneously derive benefit from their differences.

To live together in a complementary relationship implies cooperation. In many cases, when a woman enters the business or professional world, she must learn to compete with men. If she marries and becomes a homemaker, she needs not to compete but to cooperate. She and her husband need to establish not a competitive but a complementary relationship. The woman who leaves her temporary occupational pursuit when she marries but who carries with her the competitive attitude that she has learned and that she needed in her occupation, the gainfully employed married woman who cannot successfully exhibit a cooperative spirit at home, the husband who carries competition into his relationship with his wife—these persons prevent the development of that complementary relationship in marriage.

To speak of the sexes as complementary does not suggest that one be a satellite of the other, that they be diametrically opposite in all traits, that one merely correct the deficiencies in the other's personality, or that the wife direct all her energy toward furthering the occupational success of her husband. It implies merely a recognition of difference between men and women and a utilization of this difference for the furtherance of common ends.

SELECTED READINGS

Bardwick, Judith M.: *Psychology of Women*, Harper & Row, Publishers, Incorporated, New York, 1971. (Paperback.) The author says that "there are fundamental psychological differences between the sexes that are, at least in part, related to the differences in their bodies" and that "these constitutional dispositions are responded to differently by a particular culture according to the values of that culture."

——— (ed.): *Readings on the Psychology of Women*, Harper & Row, Publishers, Incorporated, New York, 1972. (Paperback.) The development of sex differences, sex roles, the "motive to avoid success" in women, critical analysis of writing of one of the women prominent in the women's liberation movement.

————, Elizabeth Douvan, Matina S. Horner, and David Gutmann: *Feminine Personality and Conflict*, Brooks/Cole Publishing Company, Belmont, Calif., 1970. (Paperback.) Each chapter is written by a psychologist and addressed to some problem associated with the status of women. Discusses the nature of female sexuality, women's conflicts over their sexuality, relationship between femininity and achievement, masculine and feminine ego styles.

Lewis, Edwin C.: *Developing Woman's Potential*, Iowa State University Press, Ames, Iowa, 1968. (Paperback.) Sex differences in personality, abilities, and roles; and factors causing them. Cites numerous studies.

Money, John, and Anke A. Ehrhardt: *Man & Woman Boy & Girl*, The Johns Hopkins Press, Baltimore, 1972. (Paperback.) A comprehensive discussion of the nature and development of gender identity.

Montagu, Ashley: *The Natural Superiority of Women*, rev. ed., Collier Books, The Macmillan Company, New York, 1970. (Paperback.) Discusses the traditional subjection of women, sex differences, women's creativity and genius, etc.

Sex Information and Education Council of the United States: *Sexuality and Man*, Charles Scribner's Sons, New York, 1970. Sex similarities and differences, premarital sex standards, masturbation, sex education, and a variety of other topics.

Sexton, Patricia Cayo: *The Feminized Male*, Random House, Inc., New York, 1969. Sex differences as they are influenced by and create problems in schools. Author believes that schools in particular and American culture in general tend to devalue masculinity and to feminize males.

The Sexual Revolution

It does not require very astute observation or very sensitive perception to be aware that something is happening in this country relative to sex. Sex is freely discussed. Censorship of movies has relaxed to the vanishing point. Nudity, sexual intercourse, and masturbation are shown on the screen. Television programs, even commercials, include reference to sex. Popular magazines heretofore devoted to other subjects—for example, women's magazines—devote considerable space to it. In 1972, as mentioned earlier, one of the national women's magazines for the first time featured a photograph of a nude male. Publications showing nude females are too numerous to count. Books and articles on a great variety of sexual experiences and techniques, from bona fide serious educational materials to extremes of inaccuracy, poor taste, irresponsible assertions, and depictions of the rawest types of sex, are plentiful and readily available. Kephart [1972] says that "we are living in an era of publicized passion." Bednarik [1970] mentions "conspicuous sex consumption." Extramarital sex, mate swapping, and bizarre sexual practices and positions in intercourse are not only accepted but recommended. Homosexuality is increasingly accepted; and homosexuals freely admit their preferences, form organizations, and even "marry."

There are, however, still persons and organizations which insist upon traditional "no-no" morality, oppose sex education in schools, would if they could remove sex from all public discussion and give no one but themselves the right of judgment or freedom of choice. And there are myriad persons of all ages who are poorly informed about sex.

two

IS THERE A SEXUAL REVOLUTION?

Whether or not we conclude that there is a sexual revolution depends not only on fragmentary data and all-too-common broad generalizations but also, and very importantly, on the answers to a number of questions. When the term *revolution* is employed, what is being compared with what? Is the reference to changes in attitudes, behavior, incidence of premarital sexual intercourse, numbers of persons involved in group sex, living arrangements such as co-ed dormitories and communes, freedom of discussion and publication, legal restrictions, homosexuality, acceptance of activities such as oral-genital sex, censorship, moral standards, use of contraception, legalization of abortion—what? What time period is implied? When did the revolution begin? If we are thinking of changes that have occurred since Puritan days, that is one thing. If we are thinking of changes that have occurred since the Second World War, that is another. Are we thinking of a long, slow, evolutionary process such as the industrial revolution? Or are we thinking of a sudden occurrence such as a political or military revolution during which one power group takes over control from another power group? What proportion of society must be involved to constitute a revolution?

American society is in a state of flux, and changes relative to sex are part and parcel of overall social change. Concern about such changes has been expressed for decades, suggesting that they began some time ago. Notice the dates of the following newspaper headlines. The similarity among the headlines is so great that any one of them could be attributed to another year.

SEES MORAL DECAY IN AMERICAN LIFE (1925); COLLEGE LOOSENESS BLAMED ON CO-EDS (1926); STAGG BLAMES DRINKING MOTHERS FOR THE LAPSE OF MODERN YOUTH (1927); COLUMBIA SENIORS HELD UNHOLY FOR ATTACKING THE MORAL CODE (1930); PEALE DEPLORES IMMORALITY RISE (1945); MORAL LAPSE LAID TO KINSEY REPORT (1950); SOCKMAN DEPLORES 'LOW EBB' OF MORALS (1952); SURVEY DEPLORES DECAY OF VALUES (1960); MORALS TERMED TOP SOCIAL ISSUE (1962); HARVARD'S STUDENTS CAUTIONED ON SEX (1963); NEW MORAL ISSUE IN SEX PRESENTED (1965); GIRLS ENTERING COLLEGE ASK ABOUT BIRTH CURBS (1965) [*The New York Times Magazine*, 1965].

Undoubtedly there has been, and there still is, an ongoing sexual revolution. (Some would say "sexual evolution.") It is on a broader base and permeates farther into our total way of life than sexual freedom per se might suggest. It involves everything we think or know about sex and the sexes and what we do about sex. But there is no conclusive evidence that the revolution has occurred in all areas at the same rate or to the same degree. Various groups and types of people adhere to, accept, or resist a multiplicity of ideas, standards, and ways of life. Ours is a pluralistic society. This is no more apparent in any aspect of American life than it is in the area of sex. Perhaps one of the most important results, if not the most important result, of the sexual revolution is the growing, but not yet universal, acceptance of this fact of pluralism. Diversity rather than uniformity is expected. Difference is tolerated, even encouraged. Experimentation is looked upon not as a threat to established ways, but rather as a seeking after new and better ways.

In this sense there is a "new morality." It is a morality of freedom of choice rather than a morality of conformity. Of course, freedom of choice necessarily involves definition, limitation, and responsibility, for unless everyone's freedom of choice is prevented from injuring others and from depriving others of their freedom of choice, ultimately freedom of choice ceases to exist; no one has it. Perhaps this is the crux of the problem of the new morality. The solution cannot be found in law, moralizing, preachment, rebellion, rule making, forceful restraint, or indoctrination. The solution can be found only through awareness of available facts, carefully thought-through personal values, and the acceptance of responsibility for one's individual behavior. Unless freedom of choice is based on an understanding of the alternatives from which choice is to be made, it cannot be truly free. The fact that American society is pluralistic does not imply that the individual is without a point of view. It implies only that he works out his own point of view; he does not accept it ready-made from others.

PREMARITAL SEXUAL INTERCOURSE

As mentioned earlier, something is happening in this country relative to sex, and one does not require very astute observation or very sensitive perception to be aware of it. But there is one area, namely, premarital sexual intercourse, where something more than observation and perception is needed, because, of necessity, both observation and perception are limited. What is needed is facts. Are there any known facts? If so, what are they? It is sometimes assumed that the major aspect of the sexual revolution is an increased incidence of premarital intercourse. Is such intercourse more widespread, more common than it used to be? What do available research data indicate?

Various studies arrive at different conclusions relative to the incidence of premarital intercourse. With considerable condensation and oversimplification to permit presenting them in tabular form, the findings of available research in premarital sexual intercourse are summarized in Table 2.1.

If at least part of the conclusion regarding the incidence of premarital intercourse is to be based on studies such as these, it behooves us to take a very close and critical look at the statistics reported. It must be admitted, of course, that in the area of sexual activity, getting facts is extremely difficult. Investigators who have laboriously gathered the reported statistics have made a genuine contribution to understanding. But these statistics do not constitute the last word on premarital intercourse.

In looking at the table, the reader will immediately note the wide variation in the figures. If the figures represented a trend toward greater incidence of premarital intercourse, one would expect some degree of consistent increase. But such is not found. This is not to say that there has been no trend toward a higher incidence of premarital intercourse but only that these statistics do not indicate it.

Sometimes a trend is "established" by selecting and combining studies made at different times, sometimes with incomparable samples or methodology, and often with disregard of the findings of other studies conducted at about the same time. For example, Blaine [1964] mentions surveys conducted in various colleges and concludes that they show a trend toward an increase in premarital intercourse in the college group. In the first study mentioned, one reported in 1929, 35 per cent of the women and 50 per cent of the men had had premarital intercourse. "By 1938 the figures had risen a little" to 37 per cent of the women and 61 per cent of the men. In 1953 two studies "showed" that the percentages "had risen" to 50 for females and 67 for males.

Blaine does not identify the studies, give the size of each sample, or explain the methodology employed by each researcher. Yet he twice refers to rates that "had risen," as if a trend had been established. In the interpretation of sexual phenomena such errors are not uncommon. Such statements are often accepted by uncritical readers as fact without question.

If we select and combine studies in this way, we can "establish" even opposite "trends." For example, suppose from Table 2.1 we select studies giving the following percentages for premarital intercourse for females:

1929	Hamilton	35
1938	Terman	37
1953	Kinsey	60

Has a trend toward nonvirginity been established? Now suppose we select three other studies from the table as follows:

Table 2.1 Incidence of premarital intercourse as reported by various investigators. Dates in most cases, except where two studies by the same researchers are compared, are those of publication of the data, since in some cases the research extended over several years. Abbreviations: m.—males; f.—females; c.—college; st.—students; l.—level; hs.—high school.

DATE	INVESTIGATOR	NATURE OF SAMPLE	PER CENT OF SAMPLE REPORTING INTERCOURSE	
			MALES	FEMALES
1915	Exner	518 c.st.	36	
1923	Peck & Wells	180 c.l.	35	
1925	Peck & Wells	230 c.l.	35	
1929	Davis	1,200 c.l.		11
		1,000 c.l. & hs.l.		7
1929	Hamilton	100 m.c.l., 100 f.c.l.	54	35
1934	Dickinson & Beam	350 c.l. & hs.l.		12
1938	Terman	792 c.l. & hs.l. (couples)	61	37
1938	Bromley & Britten	470 m.c.st., 618 f.c.st.	52	25
1938	Peterson	419 c.st.	55	
1940	Landis et al.	109 c.l. & hs.l.		23
		44 c.l. & hs.l.		27
1946	Porterfield & Salley	285 m.c.st., 328 f.c.st.	32	9
1947	Finger	111 c.st.	45	
1947	Hohman & Schaffner	1,000 c.l.	68	
1948	Kinsey et al.	5,300 (total)	92	
		3,471 c.l.	67	
1950	Ross	95 c.st.	51	
1951	Gilbert Youth Research	c.st.	56	25
1953	Kinsey et al.	5,940 (total)		50
		4,457 c.l.		60
1953	Burgess & Wallin	580 m., 604 f.	68	47
1953	Clark	113 f. given pelvic exam		60
1953	Landis & Landis	600 m.c.st., 1,000 f.c.st.	41	9
1954	Reevy	139 c.st.		7
1958	Christensen & Gregg	94 m.c.st., 74 f.c.st. (Mountain states)	39	10
		213 m.c.st., 142 f.c.st. (Midwestern)	51	21

1953	Kinsey	60
1967	Elias	53
1968	Packard	43

Shall we now conclude that there has been a downward trend in premarital intercourse for females? Or shall we seek another explanation for the variation in the figures?

Some researchers have used the same inquiry form with similar samples at two different times in order to detect change if there has been any. For example, Christensen and Gregg studied college students in 1958 and again in 1968; Bell and Chaskes in 1958 and 1968; Robinson, King, and Balswick in 1965 and 1970. These studies show some increase in the percentage of females who report

Table 2.1 Continued

DATE	INVESTIGATOR	NATURE OF SAMPLE	PER CENT OF SAMPLE REPORTING INTERCOURSE	
			MALES	FEMALES
1958	Bell & Chaskes	250 c.st. (dating)		10
		(going steady)		15
		(engaged)		31
1959	Ehrmann	841 c.st.	65	13
1960	Kanin	177 wives of c.st. with future husband		44
1965	Yankowski	245 m., 255 f.	81	57
1965	Robinson et al.	129 m.c.st., 115 f.c.st.	65	29
1967	Freedman	49 c. (seniors)		22
1967	Elias	5,001 m.c.l., 4,514 f.c.l. (white)	72	53
		1,075 m. non-c.l., 1,247 f. non-c.l. (white)	60	79
		499 m., 494 f. (nonwhite)	94	82
1967	Kaats & Davis	239 m.c.st., 319 f.c.st.	60	41
1968	Christensen & Gregg	115 m.c.st., 105 f.c.st. (Mountain states)	37	32
		245 m.c.st., 238 f.c.st. (Midwestern)	50	34
1968	Bell & Chaskes	205 c.st. (dating)		23
		(going steady)		28
		(engaged)		39
1968	Packard	665 m.c.st., 728 f.c.st.	57	43
1968	Katz	47 m.c.st., 39 f.c.st.	36	23
		41 m.c.st., 39 f.c.st.	39	26
1969	Peretti	298 m., 367 f.	50	20
1970	Robinson et al.	137 m.c.st., 158 f.c.st.	65	37
1970	Merit	10,560 m.hs.st., 11,440 f.hs.st. (jrs.-srs., high achievers)	18	15
1971	Merit	11,730 m.hs.st., 11,279 f.hs.st. (jrs.-srs., high achievers)	22	19
1971	Fujita et al.	163 m.c.st., 283 f.c.st.	46	31
1972	Eastman	98 m.c.st., 88 f.c.st.	55	49
1972	McCance & Hall	1,552 f.c.st. (Scotland)		44

premarital intercourse, with the percentage of males remaining fairly constant. The studies are provocative. They may get closer to the facts than comparison of studies of different groups relative to the indication of trend. They suggest the need for further research.

The samples in such studies, however, are too small to project any national trend. How can we be sure whether the figures indicate increased incidence of premarital intercourse or increased freedom to report such intercourse? Both would be aspects of the sexual revolution. College "climate" has changed in the past few years. A few years ago attitudes were such that it was more difficult, especially for females, to admit having had premarital intercourse. Nowadays it may be more difficult to admit virginity. Some people answer inquiry forms in terms of what they believe to be the expected answers. Students are sensitive to peer-group expectations, and this could play a part in their giving different answers. On the other hand, the percentages may actually indicate a change in sexual behavior. If we assume greater freedom in reporting premarital intercourse, as mentioned above, the figures in Table 2.1 should reflect this greater freedom in increased percentages with the passage of time. But such is not the case.

The figures presented in these studies represent *cumulative incidence*, that is, lifetime incidence, the percentage of a given sample that *ever* had premarital intercourse. Compared with this there is *active incidence*, that is, the percentage of a given sample *currently* having premarital intercourse. To aid in clarifying the distinction between cumulative and active incidence, let us apply the concepts to the occurrence of measles. If a large number of people, say, a good-sized college class, were asked whether they had ever had measles, the great majority would probably report that they had. But this being cumulative, lifetime incidence would not indicate that there was a current measles epidemic (active incidence). In a similar way the cumulative incidence (lifetime figures) for premarital intercourse cannot tell us what is currently going on.

Cumulative incidence includes more and is therefore higher than active incidence. For example, Ehrmann [1959] found that 65 per cent of the male students and 13 per cent of the female students in his study reported that at some time in their lives they had had premarital intercourse, but only 38 per cent of the males and 9 per cent of the females reported that they were currently having it.

If students in a college class were asked whether they had ever smoked, a certain proportion would answer in the affirmative. But how could we ascertain from these figures how many were still smoking and how many had quit?

Cumulative-incidence percentages make no allowance for individual frequency. For example, a woman had premarital intercourse once at age sixteen. She has not repeated it and, of course, is no longer a virgin. As a college student she is included in a study of premarital intercourse. In answer to the question, "Have you ever had premarital intercourse?" she answers, "Yes." Another woman during her high school and first two college years had intercourse numerous times with fifteen men and had two pregnancies, both terminated in abortion. But she reconsidered her behavior and stopped having intercourse about a year ago. She is in the same college class as the first woman and, in answer to the same question, she too says, "Yes." Another woman in the same class remained a virgin until she entered college two years ago. She too answers, "Yes." All three affirmative answers are included in the statistics as if there were no differences among them.

Let us again use a comparison for clarification. If a group of people were asked whether they had attended college, of those answering in the affirmative, there might be one who went $3^1/_2$ years and dropped out to get married, one who went 3 years and was expelled for poor grades, one who went 1 year, one who went 4 years to one college, one who went 1 year to each of four colleges, one who registered and attended classes for one semester, and one who registered and attended classes the first day only. Yet they could all say that they had attended college.

Many of the incidence statistics do not include certain qualifying considerations that are important in evaluating sexual behavior. Such behavior for females, for example, cannot be measured simply by counting the number who report that they are no longer virgins. Ascertaining the percentage of virgins tells us little, if anything, about current sexual practices. Suppose every postpubertal female in the country had intercourse just once, so that there were no virgins left. What would be indicated in regard to current sexual activity?

Some studies indicate characteristics of the sample such as age of subjects, class differences, race, whether the subjects were students or nonstudents, what proportion were married, and so on. Other studies do not make these distinctions. College students are not a completely homogeneous group. Those in large urban universities, small colleges, religious schools, private colleges, and so on may exhibit different behavior. Note, for example, the differences indicated by Christensen and Gregg in Table 2.1 for Midwestern and Mountain-state students. Considerations such as the following are important: How long ago did the intercourse occur? What was the couple's attitude toward it? How many partners did each individual have? Was the intercourse casual or were the couple in love? Was there pressure from the peer group, from the other person? Had one or both of the parties used drugs or alcohol? What was the mental health of the persons involved?

Male and Female Orientation

In interpreting the statistics for premarital sexual intercourse, one of the most important considerations is the difference in male and female orientation. This is taken into account in some of the studies but does not, of course, show up in tabulated figures. There are similarities as well as differences between the sexes, too, and the following are generalizations. We cannot, however, assume that all females are like the minority who claim that there are no differences.

If the male is able to have sexual intercourse at all, he practically universally derives pleasure from it. There may be reasons other than pleasure for which he has it—for example, to prove himself a man, to meet a challenge made by associates, or some similar reason. But by and large he finds intercourse to some degree enjoyable regardless of how he feels about the female. This pleasure is usually one of his basic motivations. He has intercourse for the sake of intercourse.

There are females who enjoy intercourse for its own sake, just as males do, but there are fewer females who do so than males. Still generalizing, the female is more likely to be interested in intercourse when she has a meaningful relationship with the male, especially if she believes that she and he are in love. Studies indicate this. For example, as a result of his research Reiss [1970a, 1970b] says, "The factor that most decisively motivated women to engage in coitus and approve of coitus was belief that they were in love." "Romantic love led more women than men to be permissive. . . ." [Reiss, 1970b]. Ehrmann [1959] says that females are more concerned with romanticism, while males are more concerned with eroticism. He states that the difference is "so marked that there are distinct male and female subcultures." Bardwick [1971] says that females tend to engage in sex for love and for the sake of the male. A woman's primary motive for having sexual intercourse "is not the gratification of her own genital sexuality but the gratification of the male and the securing of his love" [Bardwick, 1970]. Bernard [1972a] says that females want caresses, tenderness, sexual appreciation, and the interested attention of men, and that "if they had their own way, most would not feel compelled to seek genital sex relations." Reiss and Ehrmann are men; Bardwick and Bernard are women.

Masters and Johnson [1970], in their research and in their therapeutic program through which they seek to help married couples with sexual problems to improve their adjustment, ordinarily work with husband and wife conjointly. In a few cases they have worked with men only, providing these men with "partner surrogates," that is, women who served temporarily as "wives" in helping the men solve their sexual problems. But they did not provide "partner surrogates" for women, because for women "security of an established man-woman relationship, real identification with the male partner, and warmth and expression of mutual emotional responsivity are all of vital concern . . . in promoting effective sexual functioning." They speak of "woman's justifiable, socially enhancing need for personal commitment."

Of course, not all females have an inclination to combine sex and love, but there are fewer females than males who have no such inclination. Ultimately, the female needs to learn to combine love and sex, while the male needs to learn to combine sex and love. Some males learn this sooner than others. We might say that the male is interested in intercourse regardless of his partner, while the female is interested in her relationship with her partner regardless of whether they have sexual intercourse.

For the male, sex tends to be an end in itself, while for the female sex tends to be a means to an end, that end being popularity, acceptance, love, and perhaps marriage. As a result, the female may be disappointed when she has intercourse and finds that it does not express the male's love and will not lead to marriage, while the male may be surprised when he finds that the female is thinking in terms of love and marriage. In fact, he may be frightened to the point of dropping her to avoid an entanglement he had not anticipated.

Females as well as males take the initiative in instigating intercourse, although less frequently [Ehrmann, 1959; Kirkendall, 1961]. Females more frequently than males engage in intercourse unwillingly [Ehrmann, 1959]. Of course, the decision to have intercourse may be mutual. Whereas the male practically always enjoys intercourse, if he can have it at all, the female may find the experience distasteful, uncomfortable, even painful. This may be more often true at first intercourse but is not unknown at other times if the male is hasty and thoughtless and insufficient time is allowed for the arousal of the female. For many women premarital intercourse is less than an overwhelming orgasmic experience. More than a few women have reported to the writer that they "got nothing out of" intercourse and did it because the man suggested it. One wonders whether there is such a person as a college male who could honestly say that he "got nothing out of" intercourse and did it only because a woman suggested it.

Still generalizing, we may conclude that, with some exceptions, the statistics, such as those in Table 2.1, for males represent a fairly consistent and uniform experience, while those for females represent a variety of experiences associated with the primary sexual experience, and that females who report premarital sexual intercourse are not all equally "sexy" merely because they have had sexual relations.

Methodological Problems

All studies of premarital sexual intercourse to date entail methodological problems of one sort or another. This is not necessarily an indication of carelessness on the part of the researcher but is in many instances a built-in limitation on the study of sexual activity. Sampling is a perennial problem in statistical research. Reference to Table 2.1 will readily indicate the wide range of sample size; the fact that some samples, for example, were college classes while others were people living in a given community; and the overweighting of college students and college-level individuals. College classes are "captive" groups and are hardly random samples, since selection has already occurred when students enter college. They are not even random samples of the college population, since selection also occurs when students register for a given course.

Some samples are composites; for example, three to six students from each of 100 colleges are combined to form a total of five hundred. Which three to six students can be assumed to be representative of an entire student body? Packard [1968] sent 100 questionnaires, to be distributed to students by students, to each of twenty-one American colleges and universities. Of these 2,100 questionnaires, 1,393 (67 per cent) were returned. How careful could supervision be under such circumstances? How much research error accumulated through such a method? Were the students who responded volunteers, chosen at random, or pressured by friends? Were there effective safeguards to prevent error or misrepresentation?

A special type of sampling error may creep into this kind of research procedure. One might term this "skimming" or "horizontal" sampling. Unless great caution is exercised in supervising this method of research, there is the possibility that students most amenable to answering a questionnaire on sex will be those contacted or those who most readily volunteer. Hence, in a general but significant way, the sample from each college is taken from the same type of students instead of being a random sample or a "scattered" sample. Oversimplifying, suppose in each school there are students of types A, B, and C. Type A are those most likely to answer a questionnaire on sex. Therefore, when the returns from several schools are combined, instead of representing all three types of students, they are overweighted with type A. The returns represent neither a random sample nor a cross section nor all the various types of students, and the returns do not describe any school population or the total college population.

Are studies based on a series of interviews and studies based on questionnaires comparable? Are those done at widely different times comparable? Can one done a half century ago and one done last year be compared when there has been so much change in attitude toward sex and willingness to discuss it freely?

Even the most carefully conducted research studies of premarital sex are unavoidably based upon recall, that is, on the ability and the willingness of individuals questioned to remember and accurately report previous sexual activity. Some individuals are inclined to overreport, some to underreport.

How much credence, for example, can be given to the following report sent to the author by a male student? Shall we interpret it as a statement of fact, a tongue-in-cheek attempt to shock a professor, boasting by an insecure male who substitutes wishful thinking for reality, or an expression of the delusions of a sick mind?

> I am a twenty-one year old senior. I belong to a social fraternity and maintain a B average. I participate actively in intramural sports and some campus activities. To the best of my knowledge, I have dated 97 girls. (I am excluding those I may have dated only once.) I have had sexual intercourse with 64 of these. Of the 33 others, I have dated 17 of them only twice, 8 three times, 1 four, 3 five, 3 six, and 1 seven times. I had sexual intercourse the first time when I was fourteen years old. The total number of times since then ranges between 950 and 1100. Frequency has been relatively the same for the past five years, namely, three or four times per week. In the past year, however, intercourse has been limited to the same six girls. I have been pinned during this time; consequently I have not been dating in the general sense of the word. I have generally dated girls from better families. Most of them have been popular students. The most numerous incidents of sexual intercourse with one girl is about 100; the least is eight. I have never had intercourse with a prostitute.

There is not always consistency between what we say we believe we should do, what we actually do, and what we report we do. Years ago C. Wright Mills [November, 1940] pointed out that discrepancies between talk and action constituted the central methodological problem in social science. "Often there is a disparity," he said, "between lingual and social-motor types of behavior." In the last analysis, all studies of premarital sexual intercourse are based on subjective reports, not objective facts. Objective data are not produced by the alchemy of quantifying subjective data.

The studies provide very useful insights. They present a more helpful picture of cumulative incidence than of active incidence. The result is that though the picture of cumulative incidence is incomplete, the picture of active incidence is sketchy indeed. Some of the studies document and corroborate what experienced counselors have long suspected.

There is no incontrovertible proof that there has been a recent trend in the direction of more frequent premarital intercourse, as some persons assert. "Since approximately the time of World War I there is no strong evidence that the rates of premarital coitus have been increasing. Therefore the belief that premarital sexual experience is much more common, especially for girls, since the end of World War II is not supported by available research evidence" [Bell, 1966]. "The popular notion that America is undergoing a sexual 'revolution' is a myth. The belief that our more permissive sexual code is a sign of a general breakdown of morality is also a myth. These two myths have arisen in part because we have so little reliable information about American sexual behavior. . . . In short, today's more permissive sexual standards represent not revolution but evolution, not anomie but normality" [Reiss, 1970a]. "The idea of sexual revolution regarding non-marital coitus is . . . documented and perpetuated by the mass media, not the research data. . . . The so-called revolution may be viewed as one of attitudinal change rather than behavioral changes on the coital level" [Elias, 1969]. "The greater change, actually, is in sexual attitude, rather than in behavior. If behavior has not altered in the last century as much as we might think, attitudes *have*—and attitudes and behavior seem closer today than for many generations" [Reiss, 1970a].

Why Is An Increase in Premarital Intercourse Assumed?

If research data do not indicate an increase in premarital sexual intercourse, why is there a common belief that an increase has occurred? It cannot be categorically denied that there has been an increase. All that can be said with certainty is that the research data do not indicate it. It is possible that there has been an increase but as yet no way has been found to measure it. But this possibility does not justify a categorical assertion that an increase has occurred.

There are a number of possible factors that may explain the belief that an increase in premarital intercourse has occurred. One of these is visibility. "When there are more people doing the same thing, one is prone to believe that something new is happening. When twice as many people do something, it becomes more noticeable even though the percentage remains the same" [Reiss, 1969]. The population of the United States has increased. In the past three decades the college enrollment has multiplied about ten or eleven times. Let us imagine a college with an enrollment of 1,000. There is one student who exhibits behavior X. He is hardly noticed by the rest of the students and the faculty. He presents no problem; he is no threat. He is tolerated but not a subject of concern.

In contrast, imagine a university with an enrollment of 50,000. There are fifty students who exhibit behavior X, the same proportion, namely 1 per 1,000, as in the college. But fifty individuals are not so readily ignored or absorbed. They begin to recognize each other, group together, organize, have meetings, demand rights, ask for a meeting room and concessions. Though the percentage has not changed, the visibility has.

An illustration of increased visibility that has led to a belief in increased incidence is homosexuality. There is no way to prove that homosexuality has increased in this country. To do so we should not only have to have accurate statistics on the incidence at present, when homosexuality is more readily acknowledged, but also equally accurate statistics on earlier periods, when homosexuality tended to be denied. Such statistics we do not have. But there is no doubt that homosexuality is more visible than it used to be. Other similar illustrations are group sex, extramarital sexual relations, and oral-genital contact.

Other factors that tend to reinforce the belief that the incidence of premarital intercourse has increased are as follows:

The assumption that changes in attitude toward sex must necessarily reflect changes in behavior. Sometimes changes in attitude follow changes in behavior. Sometimes changes in behavior follow changes in attitude. Sometimes attitude changes without any changes in behavior, and vice versa. As mentioned above, attitudes toward homosexuality have changed without any demonstrable change in the incidence of homosexuality. Acceptance of a given type of behavior may neither reflect nor produce changes in that behavior.

Freedom of discussion of sex has increased public awareness of various types of sexual activity. But freedom of discussion measures freedom of discussion, not the phenomena discussed. This is another aspect of visibility. As Reiss [April, 1966b] says, "What has been going on less openly for some decades becomes known and is thought to be new."

The mass media have done their share to contribute to the belief that premarital intercourse is increasing. Sex is a marketable commodity, a salable product. It is the "in thing." The media have not failed to notice this. Kennedy [1972] says, "This is the best-reported revolution in history." The mass media often function like a lens, dissecting out and magnifying small groups and making them appear to be entire populations. Some popular writers are knowledgeable and sincere and endeavor to present the facts. Others are more articulate and assertive than they are informed. Some are not aware of many of the studies that have been made or what they may indicate, and as a result are prone to make broad generalizations and draw premature conclusions. Some will write almost anything that will assure sale of their wares.

There has been a marked rise in the venereal disease rate, especially among young people; the number of illegitimate births is increasing, with the rate showing a decline except among younger women; reform of abortion legislation has already occurred, as we shall see later; and a growing number of women are requesting oral contraceptives from student health centers—all suggesting the *possibility* of an increase in premarital intercourse but not establishing that increase as fact.

The coining of new terms gives an impression of newness relative to the phenomena they describe. For example, "generation gap," "credibility gap," "search for identity," "identity crisis," "now generation," "gay society," and similar terms attach new labels to phenomena with historical roots. The same may be said of "sexual revolution" and "new morality."

There is a special source of possible error in impressions expressed by older persons, even social scientists, journalists, counselors, and similar personnel. As an individual grows older, he observes more of what is occurring around him and his observations become cumulative, since they occur repeatedly. He becomes aware of behavior of which he was unaware in his earlier years or toward which his attitude was then different. Then he compares what he "sees" with what he "remembers," when neither may be completely clear or accurate. Hence, he may assume that there has been social change when the actual change has been in himself. This generalization is not, of course, true of all older persons. But in a particular case there is the possibility of the error's creeping in. Sometimes even younger persons coming into contact with, say, premarital pregnancy for the first time will assume that something new is occurring.

Students sometimes make generalizations based on limited observations or hearsay. For example, a student says, "All my friends have had premarital intercourse," as if he had a sound basis for his generalization, when what he "knows" about his friends' sexual activity is more likely to be what they have told him than what he has observed.

There are several other assumptions that play a part in reinforcing the belief that the incidence of premarital intercourse has increased:

The assumption that criticism of past standards is equivalent to living by new standards. Many students criticize the standards of the past but think in terms of freedom of choice—that each person may do as he wishes—while they themselves do not have intercourse.

The assumption that an individual who is an expert in one area will be equally expert in another. Competence is allowed to spill over into areas in which the individual is a layman. For example, a nuclear physicist is asked what he thinks about present-day sexual practices. He makes a statement which is no more valid than that of any other intelligent layman, but it is accepted as having authority as a statement in the field of science.

The assumption that the number of individuals who consult counselors is a measure of the incidence of a given activity. It may indicate only the availability of counselors.

The assumption that with freer behavior in other areas, for example, the use of drugs, drinking, protests, or dress, there must of necessity be freer sexual behavior.

The assumption that the behavior of small minorities, for example, students who live together in co-ed dormitories or people living in communes, is indicative of the behavior of people in general.

The assumption that "everybody's doing it."

There is also the matter of the will to believe. Some persons refuse to accept evidence unless it supports their position. They hold on to their biases regardless of research data. Also, "If people believe they are in the midst of a sexual revolution they will try to act as if this was true" [Kennedy, 1972].

While there is no incontrovertible evidence that there has been an increase in the incidence of premarital intercourse, there is some evidence to suggest a shift in the type of female involved. Available evidence suggests that males in this country have about as much premarital sexual freedom now as formerly. In earlier times, however, the females with whom the males had their premarital experience more often belonged to a group, such as prostitutes, from which the males did not choose their wives. Nowadays, there is a tendency for the females to belong to the group from which the males do choose their wives, for example, co-eds. Many present-day females have premarital intercourse only when they have some emotional involvement, or the hope of such involvement, with the males concerned. Some girls have intercourse only with fiancés.

FREEDOM OF CHOICE

Where does all this discussion leave the reader? Analysis of research findings and of common assumptions may inform him, give him food for thought, or motivate him to reexamine his own assumptions. But so far as his own sexual behavior is concerned, he is still where he started—he has to make judgments in terms of his own values and objectives. Even if it were accurately known how many people have premarital intercourse, the reader would still have to make his own decisions. If he concludes that there are forces at work that are beyond his control and that will shape his attitudes and determine his standards for him and that, therefore, he cannot determine these for himself; if he concludes, as some professional writers do, that control of sexual behavior is not only impossible but undesirable, that such behavior cannot be related to values and objectives except by changing the latter to conform to the former, he has relinquished his freedom of choice. Any choice, any decision made, represents a value judgment; it cannot be completely objective. Research may be value-free, but a decision never is. An individual who feels he must do something because others are doing it has sacrificed his freedom of choice just as much as the individual who refrains from doing something because others have prohibited it.

"It's up to you" is not enough. True, it is up to the individual. He has freedom of decision. But how can he make a sound decision? What does he need to take into consideration? He is bombarded on all sides by a great variety of points of view. The crosscurrents of opinion within which he seeks to steer a course are enough to confuse anyone. It is easy to rationalize, especially under the stimulus of sexual arousal or the impetus of love. In fact, at a critical moment, it is easy not to think at all, just to feel.

If there is to be freedom of choice regarding premarital intercourse, it must be a choice *among* alternatives, not simply the choice of a given alternative. Some persons think that freedom of choice means only the freedom to *do* something. They forget that it means also the freedom *not* to do that thing. So, when it is suggested that the individual have freedom of choice regarding premarital intercourse, such persons conclude that everyone will choose to have intercourse. But individuals who choose not to have intercourse have exercised freedom of choice, too. This is a source of confusion relative to premarital sex.

When it is said that there should be freedom of choice relative to premarital intercourse, does this mean that everyone should have such freedom? Should any lines be drawn on the basis of age or maturity? If so, how? Who decides whether a couple are old enough and mature enough? Sometimes the most immature are most confident of their maturity. Some speak of "consenting adults." What definition of adulthood is implied? Who may be considered an adult—a twenty-one-year-old who can sign a valid contract or marry without parental consent, an eighteen-year-old who can vote in a national election, a sixteen-year-old who can get a driver's license, a college freshman who is three months older than a high school senior, a girl physically mature enough to become pregnant (say, twelve years old)? In the last analysis, is an adult someone like "me," the user of the term? If one uses the criterion of consenting adults, he must draw a line between adults and nonadults. Otherwise the term is meaningless. Then what does he say to persons who, by his own definition, are on the nonadult side of the line? Does he fall back on the "no-no" arguments that he reacted against in the first place? Or does he say, "It's up to you," in which case he vitiates his argument concerning consenting adults. It is easy to make general statements but difficult to apply generalizations to the specifics of decision making.

DECISION MAKING

What issues are relevant to decision making? What are some of the things an individual might take into consideration in reaching a sound decision regarding premarital intercourse? What are his reference points? He might consider first the nature of intercourse itself.

Nature of Sexual Intercourse

Sexual intercourse is not merely a quantitative extension of petting, different from it only in degree. It is true that when an attempt is made to distinguish between "heavy" petting and intercourse, they are found to be separated, not by a sharp, clear-cut boundary line, but rather by a boundary zone, since the distinction may depend upon details of anatomy and fine-spun definition. Intercourse involves a very special relationship between two personalities and a very special use of their anatomy. It involves a relationship in which the complementarity of maleness and femaleness is brought to a unique focus. Two individuals of the same sex can pet as intensively as two of opposite sex. But, in the strict and accurate sense of the term, two individuals of the same sex cannot have sexual intercourse. They can stimulate each other genitally or have "anal intercourse" as some homosexuals do, but this is hardly sexual intercourse. The fact that intercourse is related to the possibility of conception, even though contraception may be employed to thwart that possibility (but not always successfully), suggests a qualitative difference between intercourse and petting.

Sexual behavior is an integral part of life activity. It is subject to the same kind of logic as other human behavior. Hence, premarital intercourse is not an isolated phenomenon unrelated to the rest of life. Whatever an individual's premarital sexual behavior may be, it is part and parcel of the fabric of his life, not a patch upon that fabric which may be applied or removed as whim suggests or circumstances permit.

Man is an idealizing mammal. It is part of his nature to believe in something. One of his continuing problems is to interpret life in terms of meaning. Hence, the individual has the problem of imputing some kind of meaning to premarital intercourse. Sex per se is neither good nor bad, beautiful nor ugly, moral nor immoral. Whether it becomes one or the other of each of these pairs of attributes depends upon how it is used and the meaning imputed to it. The individual has the freedom to choose the type of sexual behavior that he deems most suitable for himself. Hence, he can commit himself to a given pattern of sexual activity. Indeed, he must commit himself to some pattern of sexual activity because it is humanly impossible to live by all possible patterns simultaneously.

The University Situation

If the individual is a member of a simple, uncomplicated society which has been isolated for a long time and which, therefore, represents a homogeneous population with uniform patterns of behavior universally accepted within the group and exhibiting little or no change from generation to generation, his problem is easy. In fact, he may have none, since he takes for granted the culture in which he has been reared. But if the individual is a college or university student living in the highly complex, urbanized culture of present-day United States, his problem is at the opposite extreme. Patterns of behavior vary according to class, region, generation, and the myriad subgroups and cross-classifications that constitute modern America. The population is mobile and heterogeneous. There are no unquestioned norms for many things, including sexual behavior.

A large university, and to some extent even a small college, exhibits many of the characteristics of an urban community. Whatever its location, it represents, in a sense, an urbanized population. The student body is heterogeneous and is composed of secondary rather than primary groups. The phenomena of large numbers are observable. As the size of a population increases, the individual's concern and felt responsibility for the total group decreases. It is difficult for the individual to form a strong loyalty to the total group. Impersonality and anonymity increase. Standards of the secondary groups within the total population are varied and sometimes conflict. Hence, there is less pressure to conform because there are no universal norms to which to conform. There is a degree of individual freedom of action and belief not found in smaller groups. Outside control of the individual tends to come not from the entire group, but from specialized sources. Hence the need for control from within the individual is increased. Family pressure tends to be replaced by pressure from nonfamily organizations. The university population, like an urban population, is mobile. It is even more temporary. The individual is often judged on the basis of impressions and externals rather than on the basis of thorough and intimate acquaintance. He is appraised less as a total personality and more as a specialized performer in a particular, temporary group.

In such a situation, how does an individual decide which standards and practices to accept and which to reject? How can he exercise the freedom of choice that is the prerequisite of decision making relative to premarital intercourse? Whatever decision he makes will rest on one or a combination of the following items, some of which overlap.

1   The assumption that what seems to be new is preferable to what seems to be old. (Sexual freedom should be unrestrained. Conventional sex is obsolete. There should be a single standard—the male standard. Virginity is out of date.)
2   The assumption that what seems to be old is preferable to what seems to be new. (Sexual intercourse should be postponed until marriage. Chastity is preferable to unchastity. Men want to marry virgins.)
3   Choosing what he wants to do because it is pleasurable or advantageous. (Sex is fun—sex for its own sake unrelated to love or marriage. There is nothing wrong with exploiting a girl, using her as a sex object, or with leading a man on for the sake of popularity or marriage.)
4   Choosing what he thinks is best for others or for one other. (Sexual intercourse may possibly "hurt" a woman. It may damage her self-worth. There might be a pregnancy. A woman should have intercourse because of a man's sexual need.)
5   Choosing what is felt to be for the general good in the long run. (Complete sexual freedom would be bad for society. If everyone tries to have unrestricted freedom, all freedom is destroyed.)
6   Doing uncritically what he believes to be general practice, what "everybody's" doing. (The sexual revolution gives everybody a green light. "All my friends have intercourse.")
7   Considering the relationship. (The relationship is more important than physical sex. Mutual respect is more important than intercourse. Intercourse should occur only when it is an expression of genuine love. Intercourse makes a couple closer and contributes to their relationship.)
8   Relating behavior to principles and ideals. (Do not believe in premarital intercourse. It is better to wait until marriage. Want intercourse in marriage to be special. Love is more important than marriage; do not need marriage.)
9   Evaluating behavior in terms of objectives. (Premarital intercourse takes meaning away from sex in marriage. Premarital intercourse contributes

nothing to marriage and may detract something. Why wait until marriage—we may not live that long.)

10 Relating behavior to moral and/or religious precepts. (Premarital intercourse is immoral, sinful.)

11 Doing what will avoid unpleasant consequences. (Having no intercourse avoids possible pregnancy. Premarital intercourse, if it became known, might damage one's relationship with a husband or wife.)

12 Rationalizing behavior. (Why not have intercourse, since sex is not that important? The chance of pregnancy is very slight.)

13 Acting on impulse. (Become aroused in petting. Can't help it. It just happens.)

14 Acceding to group pressure or the influence of one other person. (All my friends say virginity is out of date. My friends say I am undersexed. Friends say intercourse proves I'm a man.)

15 Something can be learned through premarital intercourse that can be applied to marriage. (A premarital test of responsiveness is necessary.)

16 Curiosity. (Wanted to see what it was like.)

Some of these items deserve further elaboration because they continue to be issues relevant to decision making.

INDIVIDUAL FREEDOM AND SOCIETAL GOOD

How and where is the line to be drawn between individual freedom and societal good? To illustrate, a man with his wife and baby in his car is driving at night on the open highway at 100 miles per hour. Is such a man committing a dangerous, unwise, unlawful, antisocial, or immoral act? A man draws a gun and shoots toward a crowd of people "just for fun." Must we wait to judge his act until he shoots someone? Or may we judge his act by its potentialities as well as by its consequences? An individual is arrested while selling narcotics to high school students. He argues that the students purchase voluntarily, that this is a free country, that we protect freedom of enterprise, and that, therefore, society is unjust in depriving him of his chosen means of livelihood. How much weight should his argument be given? On the one hand, we protect the sanctity of the home. On the other hand, we permit the state, by its right of eminent domain, to force a family to sell its home so that the state may use the land in connection with a public works project. Is this consistent? An individual has no living relatives. He is dying of an incurable disease. The pain is excruciating. There is no known means of helping him. He asks his physician to administer a drug that will quickly and painlessly end his life. Should the physician be permitted to accede to his patient's request? An individual sees a person about to commit suicide. Should he let the person go ahead on the assumption that the person has a right to do as he wishes with his own life? Or should he try to stop the person on the assumption that there is a societal element involved? A hopelessly deformed baby is born but does not breathe spontaneously. Should the obstetrician let it die or try to get it to breathe?

Hypothetical cases such as those mentioned above point up the pertinence of the issue: How and where is a line to be drawn between individual freedom and societal good? Could something be good for the individual and not good for society, or good for society and not good for the individual?

How much responsibility, if any, does the individual have for the welfare of society? There is no answer to this question that will be acceptable to everyone. It is interesting to note, however, how much concern for societal welfare students have exhibited in recent years. They have protested against war. They have taken a part in the solution of urban problems. They have become involved in racial issues. They have exercised the right to vote. Ecology has become a focus for both attention and action. Poverty and overpopulation have become issues of great concern. Some young women who have never been either married or pregnant have requested sterilization as their contribution to the achievement of zero population growth [Garcia, June, 1972]. Is premarital intercourse entirely a matter of individual freedom of choice or is a question of societal good somehow involved in it? If the latter, where is a line to be drawn between individual freedom and societal good?

DOUBLE STANDARD

In many aspects of life in this country we are moving toward equality of the sexes. In the specifically sexual sphere, however, there are remnants of a double standard. Infidelity is considered to be more serious for a wife than for a husband. In cases of premarital pregnancy there is more severe criticism of the woman than of the man. The assumption that males should have more premarital sexual freedom than females should have is made by numerous members of both sexes. Some males set up a "double double standard"—a standard of premarital sexual freedom for themselves, a similar standard for females with whom they have their premarital intercourse, and a standard of premarital chastity for the group of females from which they will choose their wives. Such a position is logically untenable because, if it were universalized, it would result in all females being virgin, in which case no males could have premarital intercourse, or else in all females having premarital intercourse, in which case there would be no virgins to marry. The double standard is so deeply ingrained traditionally in this country that our language contains no word for the equivalent of virginity in the male. This lack implies cultural acceptance of premarital sexual freedom for males in much the same way as the lack of a word applicable to wives that would be equivalent to "henpecked" implies an acceptance of the husband's domination of the wife and a resistance to the wife's domination of the husband.

Some males set up a "double double standard" in another way. They advocate premarital sexual freedom for all males and all females—except their sisters. Such males support on one hand the values which they repudiate on the other.

Some individuals interpret present-day practices as movement in the direction of a single standard of premarital sexual freedom for both sexes. Some persons advocate such a standard. Others insist that there should be a single standard of premarital chastity. There is much confused thinking and still more confused assertion on this issue. At some place in the formulation of his own point of view, each individual must come to some conclusion on this issue if his philosophy is to be integrated and consistent.

GOAL ORIENTATION

In spite of the fact that some students claim that marriage is no longer necessary or even desirable, and in spite of the fact that some persons choose alternative life-styles, some of which do not involve marriage, most college students expect someday to marry or are already married. We may assume that they want marriage to be successful. What constitutes marital success is determined in part by cultural standards but also in part by the attitudes of the persons involved. At any rate, as already mentioned, it is reasonable to suggest that, in making a decision regarding premarital intercourse, the individuals evaluate it in terms of the almost universal objective of marriage which students set for themselves. When this is done, such questions as the following arise: Is premarital intercourse a contribution to the achievement of this objective? Or is it neutral? Or is it an impediment?

Research findings are far from conclusive with regard to the effect of premarital intercourse on marital adjustment [Davis, 1929; Hamilton, 1929; Terman, 1938; Kinsey, Pomeroy, and Martin, 1948; Locke, 1951; Burgess and Wallin, 1953; Kinsey, Pomeroy, Martin, and Gebhard, 1953; Hamblin and Blood, Jr., October, 1956; Kanin and Howard, October, 1958; Kirkendall, 1961]. The reasons for this inconclusiveness are the difficulty of getting the data and of separating the variables involved. Premarital intercourse can affect a marriage only in so far as the two persons with their particular attitudes react to it. It is also difficult to determine cause and effect. For example, if more women who have had premarital intercourse than women who have not had such intercourse are sexually responsive in marriage, does this indicate that premarital intercourse increases responsiveness or that responsive women are more likely to have premarital intercourse [Kinsey, Pomeroy, Martin, and Gebhard, 1953]?

Whatever the research findings may or may not be, only the individuals involved can decide whether premarital intercourse fits into the pattern of attitudes and values upon which they expect to build their own marriage. Both successful and unsuccessful couples are to be found among those who had premarital intercourse as well as among those who did not. So the fact of intercourse alone cannot be considered a determining factor. But we might guess that a discrepancy between what a couple did premaritally and what they expect of each other and how they evaluate each other after the wedding might play a part in their mutual acceptability as husband and wife.

Provided that he does not victimize another person in the process, and provided that he does not violate the law, each individual is free to decide what kind of marriage, if any, he wants. If he can find a partner with a point of view similar to his own, they may work out what they consider to be an acceptable relationship even though it may be of a type that would not be acceptable to the great majority of people.

However, many present-day Americans are endeavoring to work out a type of marriage somewhat new in history. It is new in its emphasis on interpersonal relationships, on love and mutuality, on function rather than structure. As the divorce rate shows, this type of marriage is not achieved in all cases. But as the marriage rate and remarriage rate show, Americans keep trying to work it out. It must have great potential or it would have lost its popularity long ago. Many persons feel that, instead of emphasizing its shortcomings and suggesting other alternatives, we should give our attention to improving it.

As already mentioned, the individual does not have to choose this kind of marriage. But if he does choose this kind of marriage, if this is the kind of marriage he wants, it behooves him to evaluate premarital activities in terms of this objective. He cannot afford merely to stumble along without ever raising any questions regarding premarital attitudes and behavior, as if these were entirely separate from marriage, as if a wedding could magically create "out of whole cloth" the ingredients this sort of marriage requires. On the other hand, if this is not the sort of marriage the individual wants, it still behooves him to evaluate his premarital attitudes and activities to see whether they are likely to contribute to the sort of life he expects to live.

DO MALES NEED SEXUAL INTERCOURSE?

It would be ludicrous to phrase the question, "Do males want sexual intercourse?" The answer to that one is apparent. But do they *need* it? The word "need" has a variety of definitions. Sometimes it is used to mean "require," for example, "I need food." Sometimes it is used to mean "want urgently," for example, "I need a new car." Which meaning describes the male's sexual drive? Masters and Johnson [1970] say that "sexual functioning . . . has a unique facility that no other natural physiological process . . . can imitate. *Sexual responsivity can be delayed indefinitely or functionally denied for a lifetime*" (Masters and Johnson's italics). This would seem to put it into a class with "need" for a car rather than "need" for food, in short, to consider it as an urgent want rather than a necessity, a "felt need" rather than an actual need.

Whether a male believes that he has an actual need or a felt need (an urgent want) for sexual intercourse, his belief is likely to affect his decision making. If he believes he has an actual need and that unless this need is met there will be dire consequences, then from his point of view seeking intercourse becomes a sort of form of self-preservation. Pressuring a female to have intercourse reluctantly because he needs it becomes, to him, acceptable procedure. If he believes he has an urgent want and failure to satisfy it will not result in dire consequences, then pressuring a female to have intercourse takes on a different coloration.

A male who insists that he has an actual need for intercourse can "paint himself into a corner." Suppose he is married. His wife is pregnant and miscarriage is threatened. Her obstetrician advises no intercourse until after the child's birth. Or suppose for some other reason no normal intercourse can occur for an extended period. What will this man do? Will he assume that the sexual need of a married man is less demanding than that of a single man? Will he seek another woman with whom to satisfy his need? Will he relieve his sexual tension through masturbation? Will he live with frustration until normal intercourse can be resumed? When men who say that males *must* have intercourse are asked what will happen if they do not, they have no answer. Perhaps the basic questions are: What controls whom? Who controls what? Does sex control the male or does the male control sex? What is more important, what is less important, than intercourse?

EFFECT ON THE RELATIONSHIP BETWEEN MAN AND WOMAN

When intercourse occurs with a prostitute or when it is promiscuous, the relationship between the male and the female is already defined. When the intercourse is over, the relationship is terminated. The relationship is not meaningful and holds little, if any, possibility of becoming so. But when intercourse occurs between two persons who are eligible as marriage partners or who have an emotional response to one another or an emotional investment in each other, the possible effect of the intercourse on the relationship, present or future, becomes a consideration.

In spite of the fact that there is increasing acceptance of premarital intercourse, there are also people who do not accept it. Some men still insist on virginity in the women they marry. Some women accept instances of premarital intercourse with other women in the lives of the men they marry only with reluctance and the somewhat cynical attitude that that is the way men are and women cannot do anything about it. The question is not whether it is justifiable for people to maintain such attitudes. The realistic question is "Can a person be happy in marriage with an individual who does maintain such attitudes?" Withholding knowledge of premarital intercourse from the other person until after the wedding or having that person learn of it indirectly has been known to be more traumatic than the fact of the intercourse itself because of the reflection on mutual trust. This possibility, however, does not justify confession in which a burden of guilt is merely transferred from one person to another without solving anything.

Kirkendall [1961], in doing research on college males, found that some of them had a poignant regret for having intercourse with one woman and in so doing felt they had let another woman, for example, a fiancée, down. Sometimes premarital intercourse tends to separate a couple when they assumed it would strengthen their relationship. In some cases the relationship seems to be strengthened by intercourse. This may actually occur or it may be, as Kirkendall [1961] suggests, that the intercourse does not damage a relationship that is already strong.

Sometimes the relationship is one-sided because the male seeks only his own sexual release with little, if any, thought for the female and her feelings and frustrations. For her it seems to be all give and for him all take. This depersonalizes a relationship that should be very personal. It seems to the woman that, instead of being wanted for all her personal qualities, she is wanted only because she is female. As one woman said after a fourth man had invited her to spend the night in his apartment, "I was beginning to think that nobody cared about *me*." Some women contribute to this situation by making femaleness so conspicuous that they obscure femininity.

The relationship may also be one-sided if the male seeks intercourse to "prove" that he is a "real man." If he actually believes that intercourse is a valid test of manliness, he may feel better after he passes the test, even though he has had no concern for the girl and has considered her only as a means to an end. Surely being a "real man" includes more than the ability to copulate.

We may safely assume that premarital intercourse is more often initiated by the male than by the female. Therefore, the male is more likely to be ready to respond. His preparation is well under way before intercourse begins. In fact, we may go a step farther and assume that the young, healthy male is almost always ready to respond. The female's readiness may not be under way in advance. Because of the male's haste or his ignorance of female responsiveness or the difficulty of arousing her if she is having intercourse under pressure and reluctantly, the woman may not be prepared to respond. The result may be that intercourse is incomplete, unsatisfactory, disappointing, even uncomfortable. It is not difficult to understand why some women conclude that men are interested primarily in their own sexual satisfaction and that sex holds little promise of mutuality.

As mentioned earlier, females are more apt to combine sex and love, while males more readily separate them. Hence, the female may have intercourse because she feels she loves the male. Therefore, ipso facto, since he suggested intercourse, it must indicate that he loves her. She mistakenly assumes that his thinking is the same as hers.

Such a trap is even more serious when the male deliberately misleads the female into believing that he loves her, knowing that she feels she loves him, and in this way persuades her to have intercourse. This is illustrated in the following case. The woman thought she was in love, though the time element involved would make this unlikely. The woman was virgin. The man had had frequent intercourse with numerous women. The couple met on the fourth of the month. On the sixth the man told the woman that he loved her. She felt that she was falling in love with him and agreed to intercourse. No contraception was used. On the ninth he asked her to marry him a month later. She agreed. Intercourse without contraception occurred again. That was the last time she ever saw the man. Fortunately she did not become pregnant.

There is still another way in which the relationship may be one-sided. The argument is often advanced that, if a woman does not want to have intercourse, a man who loves her and respects her will not expect her to do so. To this a counterargument is sometimes expressed to the effect that, if a man wants intercourse, a woman who loves him and respects him and is aware of the male's sexual drive will have it with him for his sake rather than her own. What is overlooked in the counterargument is the fact that the man's restraint and the woman's yielding may involve different "costs" which cannot be equated. The situation is similar to that in which a man asks a woman to drop out of school in order to marry him immediately but she insists upon postponing marriage in order to complete her education. His cost in waiting and her cost in giving up her degree cannot be equated.

"Virginity" has a more or less specific meaning, even though at times it is confused. That meaning is part of the cultural climate in which women are reared. A woman can lose her virginity only once. Of course, a man can have his first intercourse only once, too. But before he has that intercourse he has had numerous instances of orgasm and ejaculation through masturbation and nocturnal emissions. When he has his first intercourse, there is no change in his anatomy. Not so with the woman. Her anatomy is changed. She passes a milestone in her life. For this reason a woman may develop a strong attachment to the male with whom she passes this milestone. This attachment may be accentuated if she feels that, being no longer virgin, she would be unworthy of another man. Not all women have this belief, of course, but some do, and no one can predict in advance which ones will. Therefore, any male who has intercourse with a virgin woman assumes a responsibility for her as a person. It is not unknown for a woman to have an unpredictable loss of a sense of self-worth after her first intercourse. Again this gives the male with whom she has that intercourse a responsibility. Responsibility is, after all, one of the prerequisites of freedom.

If a woman fears that she will lose a man unless she agrees to intercourse, she may have it, in a sense, voluntarily, but she does not have it freely. Such a woman might ask herself whether losing the man would really be as bad as she first thought. If he would give her up as a person because he cannot have her as a sexual partner, how highly does he regard her as a person? How much respect does he have for her feelings? Does he have the sort of attitude toward her that she would want in a husband? After the wedding would he have more concern for himself than for her? To establish a sound marriage she must have a husband she does not fear losing every time he and she disagree on something. If the woman can lose the man over the matter of premarital intercourse, she may well be glad to lose him, having discovered in time the kind of person he is. It might be said, on the other hand, that through her refusal he discovers what kind of person she is and might be glad to lose her. Perhaps. But as indicated above, there are two quite different sets of considerations underlying his demand and her refusal.

The anticipation of male sexual demands may put a woman so on guard that a barrier is put in the way of what otherwise might develop into a sound relationship.

Some women express appreciation for a sense of security in dating. They dislike spending a date uneasily wondering when the man is going to make a suggestion regarding intercourse. They prefer to be able to trust the man so that they may relax, knowing that no such suggestion will be made. That a woman might appreciate this sort of security is something that has escaped the attention of many a college male.

The idea that the man might take some responsibility in this respect seems incredible and ludicrous to many male college students. On numerous occasions, in groups of male students and in mixed classes, the author has asked the question: Why don't men draw sexual lines? The question is invariably greeted with laughter. Of course, some college males do draw sexual lines. But many males have the attitude that any woman who will agree to intercourse is fair prey. They interpret their own responsibility as being limited to going no farther than the woman wants them to go. They push her to determine where she draws the line, and then usually they abide by it. But if she is willing to have intercourse, they feel no responsibility. In other words, they feel no responsibility for her as a person regardless of what her limits are. It is a secondary or tangential responsibility that they feel, since it is the woman, not they, who sets the definitions, establishes the limits, and makes the value judgments. Their objective is to "get" as much as possible. This is an interesting situation in view of the fact that American men deplore domination by women; yet some turn to women for the definition of the limits on their sexual behavior. One wonders what attitudes such males will carry into marriage.

WHAT IS LEARNED IN PREMARITAL INTERCOURSE?

It is sometimes assumed that premarital intercourse is a useful, perhaps necessary, learning experience in preparation for marriage. This is too broad a generalization. Of course, an individual capable of learning at all can learn something through almost any experience. But this does not mean that premarital intercourse involves a learning experience that will contribute to preparation for marriage. Before it can be evaluated in such terms the reasons for the experience have to be established. A voluntary act cannot be separated from the motives, attitudes, and conditioning factors that lie back of it. If premarital intercourse is due to immaturity, lack of standards, an exploitive attitude, a neurotic personality, insufficient self-discipline, an effort to "prove" something such as manliness or liberal thinking, a rebellion against the system or tradition, pressure by the peer group, meager understanding of sex, an inclination to act on impulse without thought of consequences, lack of appreciation for the other party, an attempt to provide a solution for the problem of insecurity, a remedy for loneliness, or a means of satisfying a hunger for affection, then it is apparent that what the individual may learn may not contribute to preparation for the sexual aspect of marriage. It may not help him integrate sex into a satisfying pattern of life. Marmor [June, 1969] refers to "sex for nonsexual reasons." Such reasons thwart the possibility of learning something about sexual intercourse as a two-sided relationship.

Some persons maintain that a woman may find advantage in being initiated into sexual experience by a man who is not her husband so that the first steps are associated with an impersonal relationship and dissociated from her marriage. This can occur only if the experience does not cause her to react unfavorably. Furthermore, this argument disregards women's inclination to combine sex and love, as mentioned earlier. To argue, as some do, that intercourse before marriage enables a woman to avoid the risk of psychological shock during the honeymoon is mistaken, since shock is dependent upon her relationship with some man, not upon a wedding ceremony or her marital status.

Some women express the desire that the men they marry will have had premarital intercourse on the theory that through the experience the man will have learned something that can be applied to the wife's initiation into the sexual side of marriage. This could happen only if the man had an enduring and meaningful relationship with a woman with whom he was emotionally involved, but this is usually not what a wife has in mind when she says she wants her husband to have had intercourse. She assumes that he can learn what he needs to know in a few transient episodes, in which he may have no thought for the woman, being concerned only with his own reactions. It cannot be said categorically that he will not learn something useful. On the other hand, it can be said that he may possibly learn what he will later need to unlearn. Masters and Johnson [1970] point this out. Golden [May, 1971], to whom we shall refer later because of his study of honeymoon couples, says that premarital intercourse "teaches little. It does not condition to a fuller adjustment to the orgasmic level, particularly for the female."

Premarital Testing of Responsiveness

If sexual responsiveness is important in marriage, why not test it out before the wedding? Why enter marriage blindly? University males sometimes put questions concerning premarital testing in rather blunt form. "Would you buy a suit of clothes without trying it on?" "Would you buy a pair of shoes without trying them on?" One must answer such questions in the negative but add that there is a difference between a woman and a pair of shoes. What happens to a pair of shoes is inconsequential. What happens to a woman is of great consequence. One would not expect a pair of shoes to have any attitude toward him. A woman is certain to have an attitude. One does not consider establishing a lifelong relationship with a pair of shoes. There is no chance that by accident a pair of shoes will have little shoes. So the comparison breaks down and becomes meaningless.

A male university student who had been arguing in favor of a premarital sexual test was asked what he would do if he loved a woman and they were engaged to be married but she refused to submit to the test. He replied that he would "go along with her" provided that she would agree to having intercourse two or three times just prior to the wedding. But what if, being inexperienced and knowing that she was being tested, she proved to be unresponsive; what would he say to her? What would he do? Would he reject her as a person because of one element in the total situation, her physical responsiveness? Would he say, "We were to have been married in a few days. You failed the test. The engagement is hereby called off"? Would he marry her in spite of what the test showed, in which case they would be in a no more favorable, and perhaps in a less favorable, position than they would have been without the test? Would they both not have been better off if he had assured her that, since they loved each other so deeply, no sexual test was necessary and that they could be confident that their sexual adjustment could be worked out successfully even though this might take a bit of time?

Sexual responsiveness is not something to be tested. It is something to be developed, through time and experience. This can be done most readily in a setting of love and security. Sexual adjustment is something to be "built."

The idea of testing disregards the sexual nature of women, that is, as women are to be found in our culture regardless of whether this "nature" is inborn or acquired. Many women are not spontaneously responsive. They must learn to be responsive. Therefore, sexual responsiveness is not something which a woman either does or does not have, as she has or has not blue eyes or a certain blood type, which may be ascertained by means of a simple test or by direct observation. If a couple have premarital intercourse with the idea of testing and the woman is responsive, admittedly they have learned something. But if, for any one of a number of reasons, personal or circumstantial, the woman proves to be unresponsive, what will they conclude about her probable responsiveness in marriage? In such a case, the couple have learned nothing. They may even be worse off than they were before the test if they leap to conclusions on the basis of it.

When a man suggests a premarital sexual test, he is assuming that he has "what it takes" and that the woman may or may not have what it takes, that only she can fail. If in the test the woman proves to be unresponsive, does it prove that she lacks something? Since females are not as spontaneous as males in their sexual responsiveness, her lack of responsiveness during the test may be the result of his failure rather than her own. Through ignorance of sex and sexual difference, through emphasis on a quick test and corresponding lack of emphasis on love, tenderness, and a growing interpersonal relationship, through creating tension by putting the woman under the stress of a test rather than putting her at ease by creating an atmosphere more conducive to her responding, through implying some lack of confidence by the very suggestion of a test, through implying that there is one aspect of their relationship, the sexual, that can outweigh all the rest in importance in his estimation, that it can outweigh even his love for her as a person, through making the sexual relationship one-sided (*You* are being tested by *me*), he fails to help her succeed and then concludes that the failure is hers, not his. ". . . Fear of inadequacy is the greatest known deterrent to effective sexual functioning . . ." [Masters and Johnson, 1970].

Once in a while an extreme consequence such as that in the following case emerges. A young woman said she was interested in sex, seemed to have normal desire, and often became stirred up when her fiancé caressed her. The couple decided not to wait until after the wedding to have intercourse. An attempt was made. Despite her other feelings favorable to sexual adjustment, the woman subconsciously feared the consequences. The result was that intercourse was impossible because of involuntary contraction of some of the muscles associated with her genital organs, a reaction termed *vaginismus*. Further attempts were followed by like results. The woman at length became much concerned over her continual failure, worried about it, and became upset emotionally. She feared that she was unfit for marriage and that she could never be a wife to the man she loved. This worry cast her into a vicious circle: the more she worried, the more she failed; and the more she failed, the more she worried. She felt that it would be unfair to marry unless she proved her adequacy, and this could not be proved without marriage. She finally learned from a counselor that her solution was to marry. The probability was that, as soon as the risks entailed in premarital intercourse were removed, her adjustment would make rapid progress. If, however, she had not sought counsel and had broken her engagement, she would have brought great unhappiness to herself and her fiancé. If, on the other hand, her premaritally generated fears had become so firmly established that they carried over into marriage, adjustment might have become difficult, if not impossible.

It takes time to develop a full sexual adjustment in marriage. For many couples the gates of heaven do not swing wide at the first experience. If this first experience is based too largely on physical appeal, the gates may remain closed and locked. One cannot learn all there is to know about sex in a fleeting, abbreviated episode. Since there is so often no time in premarital sexual experience to develop adequate adjustment, premarital intercourse is not a test of sexual responsiveness or of fitness for marriage.

If through the test the couple find that the woman is sexually responsive they have learned something; but they have not proved that they could live together happily in marriage, because in marital adjustment more is involved than physical responsiveness. Such a couple may develop a false sense of security because they base their prediction of marital success on only one factor in the total situation. Cases come to a counselor's attention in which a couple have a satisfactory sex relationship but are contemplating divorce.

IS LOVE ENOUGH?

Promiscuity, exploitation, mere voluntary consent, reluctant intercourse under pressure, irresponsible "hit-and-run" episodes, rationalizing infatuation and sex drive, even deceit and misrepresentation are not uncommon. Forming a point of view regarding them is relatively easy. Some students say that just wanting sexual intercourse for its own sake is enough, and, assuming two consenting adults, that love is not necessary. So why ask, "Is love enough"? Some students redefine "commitment" and speak of having intercourse with someone to whom one is "committed" for a weekend. All that some students of both sexes ask is that they be free to have intercourse when, as, and with whom they choose, provided that the couple like each other and do not mislead one another. They speak of giving each other "security" in a relationship lasting two or three days.

On the other hand, there are students who do not subscribe to the assumption that intercourse without love is acceptable. Yet they wonder whether love is an adequate reason for intercourse. Premarital intercourse by mutual consent, by young people who accept responsibility for their behavior and for each other, who feel that they are in love and want to express their love as fully as possible, and who in many cases expect someday to marry each other, is emerging as a special kind of permissiveness.

Suppose it is said, "Yes, love is enough." Joseph Fletcher, in his book, *Situation Ethics* [1966], argues for a "law of love" and for judging the rightness or wrongness of premarital intercourse by the presence or absence of responsible love between the participants. That still does not solve the problem for the individual couple. "Love is enough" is an abstract, generalized statement. When applied to a given couple, it leaves related questions to be answered before a decision is made. Love per se does not necessarily make a decision sound. A couple could be in love and still act impulsively. It is easy to rationalize.

The "love is enough" argument is based on a hypothetical assumption that the love is genuine. It does not take into account the possibility that the couple may believe they are in love when actually they are only infatuated or they have a strong feeling about each other amplified by their eagerness to have intercourse. If a couple are genuinely in love, they are willing to commit themselves to each other and to trust each other's commitment, to take responsibility for one another not only sexually and in case of pregnancy but also in connection with mutual respect, concern, and welfare. They are not afraid of commitment. If circumstances do not permit their getting married, they still are not hesitant to think in terms of "standing up to be counted" as a final expression of their love and commitment.

IS ENGAGEMENT ENOUGH?

Couples who raise this question must be thinking in terms of marriage, or they would not wonder about engagement. They consider engagement as an expression of commitment, a sort of "standing up to be counted" short of the wedding, a transitional state between falling in love and marriage. Engagement is sometimes thought of as "almost but not quite" marriage, thus justifying intercourse. Studies show that many engaged couples do have intercourse. On the other hand, not all engaged couples marry. Many engagements are broken. Occasionally unforeseen circumstances make necessary the postponement of the wedding. A recent newspaper notice, accompanying a photograph of the bride, announced the wedding as having occurred the previous day, described the bride's gown, listed the attendants, and indicated where the couple were spending their honeymoon. In the same issue of the paper there appeared an article with the headline PAIR CALLS OFF WEDDING, saying that the wedding had not taken place as announced and that owing to the necessity of printing parts of the paper in advance, the information was published before the cancelation of the wedding was announced.

An engagement is only as substantial as the two people in it. It may have the approval of families and friends. Society at large approves the fact of engagement as a social process. But society does not give an engagement the degree of support and protection that it gives a marriage. Engagement involves folkways, but marriage involves mores. This is shown by the fact that a couple may enter an engagement through no more than mutual agreement; it may be broken either by mutual agreement or by the decision of one person. There are no legal or societal demands in connection with either process, except in so far as there may be almost obsolete legal remnants of bygone days, such as seldom-used provisions for breach of promise. Hence engagement does not provide a couple with the complete framework within which to engage in an activity which may eventuate in a condition, namely, pregnancy, which needs societal support. Consequently cases like the following are possible.

The couple were engaged. The man had given the woman a ring. Parents and friends were informed of the wedding date. The couple attended universities some distance apart. During vacations they returned to the same home town. On one of these vacation visits the woman became pregnant, but the pregnancy was not diagnosed until after she and her fiancé had returned to their respective campuses. When she became aware of the pregnancy, the woman notified the man. A few days later she received the following note:

Dear Jane:
   I am terribly sorry to hear the news that you are pregnant. My advice to you is to see a doctor and get some pills to get rid of it. Don't try to force me to marry you because I am already married. How far along is it? If you can't get the pills, get the boy who is responsible for it there to get them. Sorry. A blood test won't prove anything.

Yours respectfully,
Bill

Investigation showed that the man was serious. After receiving word of the pregnancy, he hastily married a woman he had dated a few times at his university. They were both of legal age for marriage. Nothing could be done about it. The pregnant woman had her baby at term and placed it for adoption.

It is true, of course, that had this couple been married before the woman became pregnant, her husband might not have taken responsibility for her and the baby and might even have divorced or deserted her. Yet the difference in her status and that of the child, the degree of societal support accorded her, and the alternatives available to her in the two situations are obvious.

Conclusion

In a word, all this suggests that the issue facing people today is not only one of freedom versus restriction or of preventing pregnancy but also one of deciding upon what meaning they want to express through sex and how this may best be accomplished. Without meaning, present-day freedom is no better than traditional restriction and makes no greater contribution to human personality or happiness. Nowadays whatever meaning is imputed to sexual intercourse comes from the persons involved, with, of course, cultural coloration; it is not imposed by the cultural pattern. Freedom undirected toward carefully thought-out goals and devoid of meaning can in the "long run" be disappointing. The consequences of freedom unseeingly used can be as binding as the results of restriction blindly applied.

PETTING

A discussion of premarital sexual freedom would be less than complete without some mention of petting. There are many terms that apply to physical contact that stops short of sexual intercourse. Without difficulty and without attempting to make a formal study, the author has collected more than five hundred such terms from his own students. None of them is specific. Some are picturesque. Some are geographically so highly localized that they are meaningless to persons from other parts of the country. Take, for example, making out, grubbing, hinking, goat roping, Russian hands and Roman fingers, watching the black Christmas tree lights, making like crickets, lip lapping, ivory clanking, bubblegum tag. The great variety of such terms is one side light on the widespread distribution and frequency of the activity they are designed to describe and indicates, too, the casualness with which this activity is currently accepted. We shall use the term *petting* because it is probably the most widely understood. Many students insist that it is obsolete and "for the books"; but they use other, more recent terms that are not widely intelligible.

Physical contact between the sexes may extend from holding hands to sexual intercourse. It is difficult to draw an arbitrary line on one side of which will fall contact that one would not define as petting and on the other side of which is petting. Surely hand holding or a single good-night kiss would not be considered petting. Some persons distinguish between necking and petting on the basis of intensity, areas of anatomy involved, and extent of fondling or bodily exploration in addition to kissing. Such distinctions have value, but there is another side to the problem. Different criteria may be used in differentiating among terms for the purpose of discussion on the one hand and for the purpose of evaluating the activities to which the terms apply on the other. An individual reacts as a whole, not as an agglomeration of disconnected parts. His behavior must be evaluated in terms of what happens to him as a person, not merely in terms of the parts of his anatomy involved. This suggests that necking and petting are phases of the same process, that they are variations of degree rather than of kind. We shall define "petting" as physical contact for pleasure as an end in itself, involving some degree of bodily exploration, arising from sexual desire in one or both parties but stopping short of intercourse, and of such nature that in one or both there is produced an increased sexual sensitivity and response, a stirring up of sexually colored emotions, and an increased tension that can be relieved immediately only by intercourse or some substitute therefor. In the absence of relief, the tension has a tendency to persist for a time. When a couple's petting includes parts of their bodies ordinarily not exposed in campus dress, they not only increase the stimulation of one or both, but they redefine their relationship. In a sense, every bodily contact is a definition of a relationship.

It is unlikely that anyone is seriously hurt by petting per se, though women are sometimes disturbed. It is so common that, if it were hurtful, there would be a continuous epidemic. This does not mean, however, that there are no questions to be asked about it or that there is nothing to be taken into consideration in making decisions regarding the relationships between the sexes. Also, in the mind of many a woman the man's insistence on petting reinforces her attitude that males are interested only in sex and not in women as persons.

Petting involves strong emphasis on physical stimulation and response. This can lead to sexual arousal to the "point of no return." The couple may have intercourse without having intended to do so. They are like a man whose rowboat is caught in the irresistible current at the brink of the falls. If such a man would row to shore, he must start to do so upstream while he can still pull against the current. A woman previously unaware of her responsiveness who became aroused to the point of no return and had intercourse with no contraceptive protection is a not infrequent visitor to a counselor's office.

In a study of approximately five hundred college females and four hundred college males from two large Midwestern state universities, Kanin [September, 1970] found that when "mutually consented erotic involvement has progressed to the genital petting stage" the male may exert "a forceful attempt to bring his companion to coitus." In other words, when there is genital petting, "college men sometimes use physical force" to get intercourse.

Most dates are relatively brief and time limitations necessitate centering attention on few activities. If attention is centered on petting, a false focus is created. Other activities that would help the couple get better acquainted may be neglected. Overemphasis on the physical may lead them to appraise each other too much in terms of physical attributes and response. This may make distinguishing between love and infatuation difficult and lead to premature marriage.

It is not uncommon for the sexual tension generated in petting to be relieved by orgasm for the female and orgasm plus ejaculation for the male, instead of its eventuating in intercourse. This sexual tension may also result in pain in the region of the testes in the male, a condition referred to as *orchialgia* or *testalgia*. It is probably referred pain due to congestion in the prostate gland [Cawood, February, 1971]. Such pain is uncomfortable but it is not dangerous. It tends to disappear in a short time after the stimulation causing the tension ceases, even in the absence of orgasm-ejaculation. Knowledge of the possibility of such pain on the part of the male who has the prospect of it sometimes is used as a lever to persuade a woman to have intercourse for his sake, especially if she does not understand the nature of the pain and fears that it will be harmful to the male. Under similar circumstances of stimulation without release, some females, too, have discomfort due to congestion and tension in the pelvic region.

We may guess that with their different orientations toward sex, males more often than females initiate petting (using the term as we have defined it, namely, as involving bodily exploration). Of course, some women initiate petting but probably not as frequently as some men claim. College women—even in these days of presumed sexual freedom—sometimes ask how petting may be prevented. Why do men always want to pet? Why do women always have to fight men off? Why do men always want to put their hands under a woman's clothing? Why do men always want to unfasten a woman's bra? Such questions asked by women are common. Some women consider such activities, when initiated by men, a violation of their privacy. The kind of behavior that women may consider a problem men do not have to contend with, or if they do confront it, they consider it not a problem, but an opportunity. But the different attitudes of the two sexes is something that might be taken into account in a particular situation.

In this discussion, we have assumed that decision making implied a conscious, thoughtful process. Such a process is less likely to occur if the couple, or one of them, are under the influence of alcohol or other disorienting drugs. Some persons, of course, use such drugs in order to lower their inhibitions. Others discover that lowered inhibitions are a result although not an intentional objective of the use of such drugs, and that problems may thus be created. Many women have found that combining drugs with petting and sex is like driving a car without brakes. In one case, for example, a woman who attended a party where everyone, including herself, drank considerably and where petting and intercourse were indiscriminately free found herself with only the vaguest memory of what had happened for part of the evening. There was evidence that she had had intercourse, but with which men and how many she did not know. She spent some weeks worrying about pregnancy, which fortunately did not occur.

THE PROBLEM OF RISK

Serious questions could be raised about an individual who confused freedom to drive a car with freedom from the possibility of accident while driving. One would hesitate to ride with him if he assumed that accidents happen to other people but could not happen to him or that accidents happen only when they are planned. It is as shortsighted to disregard the risks in premarital intercourse as it is to build a case against it primarily on the basis of risk, as was done so often in the past and is still done by some persons.

Life entails risk. Some risk is unavoidable, for example, the risk of inhaling harmful bacteria while breathing. Some risk is practically unavoidable in our type of living, for example, that involved in travel. Some risk is avoidable, for example, that involved in drug abuse. Each individual has, on the one hand, the problem of reducing necessary risk and, on the other hand, that of deciding how much unnecessary risk he is willing to undergo. In doing this he must reach some conclusion as to what possible price he is willing to pay for what possible gain. Since neither the gain nor the price of premarital intercourse can be accurately predicted in advance, one could prove to be out of proportion to the other—like burning a cathedral to fry an egg. Would the end result be the purchase of complex problems with the currency of pleasure or the purchase of an enriched relationship with the coin of risk? Or would the risk element not be great enough to be given serious attention?

Risk may be considered in two ways: (1) What is the statistical risk; that is, how frequently is it incurred relative to the frequency of premarital intercourse? (2) What is jeopardized if the consequence does occur, and what can be done about it? The individual's problem is not merely the achievement of the scientist's objective understanding of a statistical analysis of a situation. His problem is also the subjective one of evaluating and assimilating what may be for him a world-shaking, life-encompassing experience, even though he may be only one inconspicuous statistic in the over-all picture.

Each individual also has the problem of deciding how much avoidable risk he is willing to impose upon another person and for what reasons. If a person wants to play "Russian roulette" with the gun pointed at his own head, that is one thing. If, however, he wants to play "Russian roulette" with the gun pointed at someone else's head, it becomes an entirely different issue. In premarital intercourse, who plays "Russian roulette" with the gun pointed at whose head? Let us imagine that a study is made of the restaurants most frequented by students at a given university. The study reveals that the most popular restaurant serves 10,000 meals per month. It also reveals that on the average 2 persons per month who eat at that restaurant contract ptomaine poisoning and die. That is 1 death per 5,000 meals. Would you eat there? Would you take your fiancé, husband, wife, or parents there? If, each month, the restaurant held a drawing and one of its customers won a sum of money, how large would that sum have to be to make you willing to eat there or take a person meaningful to you there? What about premarital intercourse, which involves a risk greater than 1 in 5,000?

In premarital intercourse, then, both parties assume risk. For the man the risks are as follows:

Accusation of Rape by Force

Cases are not at all unknown in which a woman voluntarily has premarital intercourse, and afterward, because she feels guilty, or to get attention, or because the fact is discovered, or for some similar reason, she claims rape. Usually there are no witnesses to premarital intercourse. Hence it is the man's word against the woman's. She may not succeed in making her accusation hold up in court. But even after the fire is put out, so to speak, the odor of smoke remains in the air, and there may be people who still wonder whether the man was guilty and justice miscarried. There may be others who wonder what the woman's ulterior motive was. "There is hardly any accusation so easily made and yet so hard to disprove as that of rape" [Graves and Francisco, April, 1970].

Accusation of Statutory Rape

Typically, state law specifies an "age of consent." This is the minimum age which an unmarried girl must have reached in order legally to give consent to sexual intercourse. If she is below the age of consent, she cannot legally consent to having intercourse even though she voluntarily says the words agreeing to it. A comparable situation is found in an individual's inability to sign a valid legal contract before age twenty-one even though he writes his name on the contract form.

Let us assume that in a given state the age of consent is sixteen. A physically well-developed fifteen-year-old girl claims to be seventeen. A twenty-one-year-old man takes her at her word. She voluntarily has sexual intercourse. Her parents discover this fact and make known her correct age. The man with whom the girl had intercourse is liable to prosecution for statutory rape, which constitutes a felony.

Accusation of Paternity

If a woman becomes pregnant, any man who has had intercourse with her within a given time span is a possible candidate for an accusation of paternity. Cases such as the following have come to this writer's attention:

1 The man admitted intercourse but disclaimed paternity, saying that the woman had confessed to intercourse with other men. His family paid a considerable sum of money to the woman's parents on their promise not to institute a paternity suit and not to put pressure on their son to marry the woman.
2 A pregnant woman tried to force a man to marry her after they had had intercourse. The man resisted. The woman finally admitted that she knew that this man could not be the father of her child because she was already pregnant when the intercourse occurred; but he was a more desirable candidate for marriage than any of the other men with whom she had had intercourse.
3 A woman claimed pregnancy and almost succeeded in forcing a man to marry her. Before the wedding she admitted that she was not pregnant. They had had intercourse and she was using the "pregnancy" as a means of exerting pressure because she wanted to marry this particular man.

Contrary to common assumption, paternity cannot be unequivocably ascertained by means of blood tests. It is true that blood types are hereditary. Blood tests made upon man or men, mother, and child can ascertain whether a given man could or could not be the father. That is not equivalent, however, to determining that a given man is the father. For example, suppose Miss X has a child. She admits having had intercourse with three men, namely, A, B, and C. Blood tests are made on all five persons. The tests indicate that Miss X could not have had that child, with its particular blood type, with A or B. She could have had that child with C. That still does not prove beyond all doubt that C is the father. Miss X may not have mentioned D, with whom she also had intercourse and whose blood type is the same as C's.

Pressure to Marry in Case of Acknowledged Paternity

Pressure to marry in such cases may be "external" or "internal." It may come from parents, fear of gossip, or concern for reputation. Or it may come from a sense of honor and responsibility.

If the couple are engaged, there may be no pressure in the usual sense of the term because they plan to marry anyway. Their problem is relatively simpler, involving only actual or asserted change of wedding date. In some cases, however, marrying earlier than they had expected is a serious upset to a couple's families and to their educational and occupational plans.

If, on the other hand, the couple had not planned to marry or would not be good choices as marriage partners for one another or do not know each other well enough or are not in love, marriage to camouflage a pregnancy or to give a child a legal father and a name may be damaging to all three persons.

For the Woman There Is the Risk of Pregnancy

At the present stage of knowledge there is no 100 per cent perfect contraceptive. Employed with care and intelligence under circumstances conducive to their most efficacious use and based upon the advice of a physician, the better contraceptives assure a reasonable degree of control of conception. Under circumstances not conducive to careful use, for example, where there is haste, inadequate knowledge, or lack of responsibility; when the contraceptive methods used provide a low degree of effectiveness; or if the contraceptives are purchased on the recommendation of drugstore clerks or magazine advertisements, the risk of pregnancy is ever present.

Neither contraceptive information nor contraceptive devices alone can prevent conception. Information must be applied. Devices must be put to use. There is a not uncommon assumption, even among professional writers, that with the ready availability of effective contraceptives, especially the pill, the risk of premarital pregnancy is no longer a threat. Assuming that all students know about contraceptives is unrealistic. Assuming that, if they did know about contraceptives, they would all put that knowledge to work, is equally unrealistic, as we shall see.

Knowledge of effective methods of contraception has been available in this country for some time. Yet American women continue to have hundreds of thousands of unwanted pregnancies each year; and as we shall discuss in a later chapter, there is widespread approval of the liberalization of abortion laws. Why is there approval of more liberal abortion laws if contraceptives are being used as widely and as effectively as is so often claimed? There is no more guarantee that contraceptives will be used responsibly in the future than there has been evidence of responsible use up to date. Technological advance is not a substitute for human responsibility. One indication of this is the number of college and university couples who have premarital intercourse without, or with inadequate, contraceptive protection.

Premarital Intercourse with Inadequate Protection

In one study [Crist, November, 1971] of 393 "sexually active" college females it was found that 65 per cent used no contraceptive or one of the least-effective methods, namely, rhythm, withdrawal, or douche. We shall discuss these methods in a later chapter. They are methods that require no preparation in advance, and the first two entail the use of no equipment. In another study [Fujita, Wagner, and Pion, Mar. 1, 1971] it was found that, of 163 college males and 283 college females, 30 per cent of the former and 22 per cent of the latter reported no contraceptive use except rhythm or withdrawal in some cases. In a study [Bauman, August, 1971] of 98 college males and 88 college females it was found that 40 per cent usually used no contraceptive or one of the three least-effective methods mentioned above. Another report growing out of the same study [Eastman, W.F, 1972] mentions that 59 per cent of the males and 64 per cent of the females had their first intercourse with no contraceptive or used a method of "limited reliability." During a four-year period between 1967 and 1971 Kuchera [Oct. 25, 1971; October, 1972] studied the administration of a "morning-after pill" to 1,000 co-eds at a state university. Each co-ed had had "one unprotected or inadequately protected sexual exposure since the patient's last menses" [Kuchera, October, 1972]. In a study [McCance and Hall, June 17, 1972] of 684 nonvirgin undergraduate women at the University of Aberdeen, Scotland, it was found that 53 per cent had used no contraceptive at the time of their first experience. Of those who had had intercourse up to twelve times, only about half used contraceptives on every occasion. Of 486 students of the 684 mentioned above who had had intercourse in the six weeks prior to the study, 26 per cent had relied on withdrawal or rhythm.

Reasons for Inadequate Protection

Studies [Lehfeldt, May, 1971; Sandberg and Jacobs, June, 1972; McCance and Hall, June 17, 1972] have brought to light a variety of reasons for which premarital intercourse occurs without adequate contraceptive protection. Among them are ignorance of what contraceptive methods are effective and where to get them; nonacceptance of a method prescribed by a physician because it is thought to be unsafe; objection to contraception on religious or moral grounds; denial that contraception works; irresponsibility; immaturity; willingness to take a chance; emotional disturbance; desire for evidence of fertility or virility; enhancement of sexual pleasure by the thrill of taking risks; availability of abortion; rebellion against society or parents; hostility toward the other sex; diminishment, by contraception, of the possibility of controlling or manipulating the relationship; equation of love with self-sacrifice; a belief that intercourse is sinful and pregnancy is the punishment; a feeling that pregnancy is a gift of love; the belief that sex is for procreation only; unwillingness either to deny oneself or to delay intercourse; a desire of the female to become pregnant to force marriage; an unconscious desire to become pregnant; the feeling that it can't or won't happen to me; and the belief that intercourse is a demonstration of love.

In addition to these reasons there are others that we might guess are not uncommon in a college population and that deserve special mention. Some college students believe that intercourse should be unplanned, that it should occur on impulse—on the emotion of the moment. They believe that using contraceptives makes intercourse premeditated, detracts from its spontaneity, and debases sex. The female's use of a contraceptive—for example, the pill—is synonymous with preparedness, and many girls do not want either to give the impression or to admit to themselves that they anticipate intercourse. It would seem that they could work out some balance and either prepare for the possibility of intercourse or refrain from intercourse if they are unprepared.

Tietze [1960], after careful mathematical analysis, wrote, "The probability of conception resulting from a single unprotected coitus would . . . appear to lie between 1 in 50 and 1 in 25." These figures do not suggest that a woman may have intercourse between twenty-four and forty-nine times without the risk of conception. Every pregnancy results from one act of intercourse. Each time a woman has intercourse without adequate contraceptive protection she assumes not a part of the risk, but the entire risk of conception. Yet some students think that infrequent intercourse is only a partial risk. Co-eds have been known to say, "I didn't do it very often—how could I get pregnant?" [Fujita, Wagner, and Pion, Mar. 1, 1971].

Neubardt and Schulman [1972], in a book on the techniques of abortion addressed to physicians, say, "Unplanned pregnancy in both married and unmarried women occurs most often in those who have the least sexual activity. If there is any chance that a patient is counting on infrequency of exposure to provide some protection, please do not settle for that." Women having infrequent "exposure" often make the same assumption as that made by the co-ed mentioned above. But it does not follow that the converse is sound, namely, that the way to avoid pregnancy is to have frequent intercourse.

Frequency of Premarital Pregnancy

There is no way at present to get a complete and accurate picture of premarital pregnancy. But there are useful studies giving some indication of frequency. These studies include such items as the number of babies born alive to unmarried mothers, the number of unmarried women who have abortions, the number of babies conceived before the wedding but born in marriage, the number of women who report premarital pregnancy regardless of the termination of such pregnancy.

In studies made by Gebhard and his associates [1958] in a sample of 5,940 women, it was found that among girls who had reached age 15, *including all girls who had reached this age disregarding whether or not they reported that they had had premarital intercourse,* 1 in a thousand had already become pregnant; among those who had reached age 20, 33 in a thousand; among those who had reached age 25, 75 in a thousand; and among those women who had reached the thirties and forties and were still unmarried, 100 in a thousand, or 10 per cent, had become pregnant. The above figures are for all the women and make no allowance for differences relative to educational level. By age 25, 8 per cent of those who had attended college and 11 per cent of those who had attended high school had become pregnant. By age 30, 10 per cent of the college group and 13 per cent of the high school group had done so. Among the women *who had had* premarital intercourse, 25 per cent of the high school group and 17 per cent of the college group had become pregnant by age 25, almost 29 per cent of the former and more than 20 per cent of the latter by age 30. Generalizing, these investigators assert that among women who have premarital intercourse, 1 in 5 becomes pregnant at some time before marriage. Of the women in the sample who had become pregnant before the wedding, 13 per cent had done so twice, 5 per cent three times, 2 per cent four or more times. In one study of 96 unmarried fathers and 222 unmarried mothers it was found that 12 per cent of the former and 28 per cent of the latter had been involved in two or more pregnancies [Pannor, Massarik, and Evans, 1971].

In 1968 there were 339,200 illegitimate births in the United States. These constituted almost 10 per cent of all live births. The *illegitimacy rate* (the number of illegitimate births per 1,000 unmarried women fifteen to forty-four years of age) was 24.1, almost 3½ times the rate for 1940 [see Figure 2.1] [U.S. Bureau of the Census, *Statistical Abstract,* 1972]. The rate has been declining for all age groups except the fifteen- to nineteen-year-old group for both whites and nonwhites and the twenty- to twenty-four-year-old group for whites. Over-all, the rate for nonwhites has been decreasing while the rate for whites has been increasing [Ferriss, 1971]. Even if the illegitimacy rate remains constant, the number of illegitimate births may be expected to increase to 403,000 by 1980 [U.S. Department of Health, Education, and Welfare, February, 1968].

Not all the reasons for the increase in the number of children born out of wedlock are known. One, of course, is the increase in population. This would affect the number but not the rate. Another may be that the improved health of young people results in fewer stillbirths and spontaneous abortions [Cutright, April, 1972]. Still another reason is probably the fact that today, in cases of premarital pregnancy, there is less pressure put upon couples to marry than there used to be. On the other hand, there are many illegitimate pregnancies

Figure 2.1   Estimated illegitimacy rates, 1940 to 1968, per 1,000 unmarried women aged fifteen to forty-four years. [*U.S. Department of Health, Education, and Welfare,* Facts of Life and Death, *1970.*]

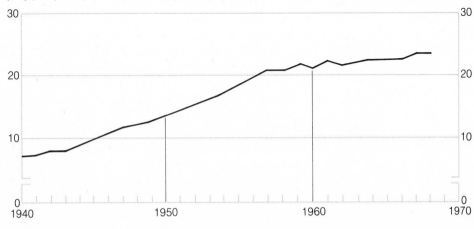

legitimated by marriage, since a child born after a couple marry is considered legitimate even if the parents marry on the day before its birth or even after the mother begins labor. It has been estimated that more than one-fifth of first babies are born to women married less than eight months [U.S. Department of Health, Education, and Welfare, March 27, 1970]. When babies born out of wedlock are added to these, the estimate is that about one-third of all first babies born were conceived outside of marriage [U.S. Department of Health, Education, and Welfare, March 27, 1970]. It is also estimated that of the women bearing babies within the first eight months of marriage, about one-fourth had attended college for one to four or more years [U.S. Bureau of the Census, Apr. 16, 1971]. In a study of 175 unmarried fathers and 179 unmarried mothers [Pannor, Massarik, and Evans, 1971] it was found that about 42 per cent had attended college.

In studies of marriages in the Middle West, Christensen [February, 1953, August, 1963] used the method of "record linkage"; that is, he compared dates for first births with wedding dates of parents of these children, making an allowance for premature deliveries. In this study he found that one-fifth of all first births within these marriages were the outcome of conceptions that must have occurred before the wedding. Approximately one-third of all live births, or currently more than one million annually, are first births. Hence, Christensen's findings suggest that each year more than 200,000 babies are born within marriage after having been conceived before the wedding. This figure corresponds very closely to the estimate of 218,000 babies born to women married less than eight months [U. S. Department of Health, Education, and Welfare, Mar. 27, 1970]. Vincent [October, 1967] estimates that each year there are 400,000 pregnant brides.

Premaritally pregnant brides are not distributed evenly throughout all age groups. In one study, Lowrie [February, 1965] found that ". . . the proportion of pregnancies varies inversely with the age of the bride—or groom." He found that 70.9 per cent of the premaritally pregnant brides were 18 years old or younger; 95.3 per cent were 21 or younger. Among the nonpregnant brides in this study, 28.8 per cent were 18 or younger, 75.9 percent were 21 or younger.

Figures such as those above are subject to question because there is no way of being certain that findings emerging from a study of a sample of the population are descriptive of the entire population. But if we assume a reasonable degree of validity in the studies mentioned and others like them, and we combine and generalize upon the figures for births recorded as illegitimate and children born within marrage but conceived before the wedding, assuming the addition of an unknown number of premarital pregnancies terminated by abortion before or after the wedding (Kinsey reported that among the women in his sample from 88 to 95 per cent of the premarital pregnancies were terminated by induced abortion before marriage) [Calderone, 1958], an unknown number of such pregnancies ending with a stillborn child, and an unknown number of illegitimate infants killed immediately after birth (some of which are discovered, and in some cases the mothers are apprehended), we arrive at approximately three quarters of a million. If there are anywhere near three quarters of a million premarital

SEX AND THE SEXES ON THE AMERICAN SCENE

pregnancies in this country each year, this constitutes a problem of major proportions and suggests a risk in premarital intercourse that is not to be ignored.

The number of children born out of wedlock does not by itself present the entire picture of illegitimacy. In one study made in New York City it was found that more than 20 per cent of the unmarried mothers had no prenatal care until the seventh or eighth month, and 17 per cent (as compared with 3 per cent of married mothers) had no prenatal care at all. In another study, also made in New York City, it was found that the maternal death rate among the unmarried was almost twice as high as among the married. The infant death rate was more than twice as high for children born out of wedlock as for those born in wedlock. Among children born out of wedlock the death rate for those born to mothers who had no prenatal care was $3^1/_2$ times as high as for those born to mothers who had such care. Almost twice as many children born to unmarried mothers, as compared with those born to married mothers, were premature [Oettinger, 1962].

When a woman has a premarital pregnancy, there are relatively few alternatives open to her.

1 She may marry. If she was engaged when the pregnancy started and her fiancé is the father of the child, the situation is as favorable as it could be under the circumstances. If she marries a man whom otherwise she would not marry, the marriage gets an inauspicious start. If she marries a man she knows is not the father of the child and does not apprise him of the fact of pregnancy, in some states the man has ground for annulment or divorce should that fact become known after the wedding. At best such a procedure is a serious form of misrepresentation. A woman may, and in some cases does, marry a man who accepts the child even knowing that he is not the father. In one case the woman had already become pregnant before she met a certain man. On their first date she told him about the pregnancy. He became so enamored of her and had such a compulsive desire to protect her that he married her within a month after their meeting in order to legitimate the child.

If a couple have premarital intercourse because they are not ready to marry, will they be more ready to marry if a pregnancy leads them to marry earlier? There is evidence to suggest that marriages entered into in order to camouflage a premarital pregnancy are more than ordinarily unstable. In one study it was found that the divorce rate was more than twice as high for those marriages in which conception occurred before the wedding (with the child born after the wedding) as it was for those marriages in which conception occurred after the wedding. Of the latter 8.95 per cent ended in divorce; of the former 18.54 per cent ended in divorce [Christensen and Meissner, December, 1953; see also Christensen, August, 1963].

2 The woman may remain unmarried and have the baby at full term. Some women keep their babies. Others place them for adoption. One estimate places the number of such cases at 50,000 per year [Oettinger, 1962]. Some girls sell their babies illegally on "black market." Because of antagonistic public opinion some women who keep their babies disguise their situations

through "white lies" regarding marriage. A few women destroy their babies after birth. Such an act is, of course, a felony.

3 The woman may have an abortion. We shall discuss abortion in a later chapter.

Risk of Venereal Disease

There are several venereal diseases. The ones that are most serious and that will concern us are syphilis and gonorrhea. Space does not permit going into detail regarding the organisms that cause these diseases or their symptoms, cures, and effects. Our point of focus will be the risk of contracting one of these diseases in premarital intercourse. Syphilis and gonorrhea are both very contagious. Of reported cases of syphilis, 95 per cent are contracted through intercourse, and the other 5 per cent are contracted through kissing when there is a cut or scratch in the mucous membrane of the lips or mouth, by oral-genital contact, by prenatal transmission, by transfusion, or by accidental direct innoculation [Wallace, June, 1971b]. Gonorrhea is almost always contracted through sexual intercourse. Reports of contagion by means of bath tubs, swimming pools, and toilet seats are without foundation in fact.

It is difficult to get accurate statistics on the incidence of syphilis and gonorrhea because only a small proportion of cases are reported. Private physicians report only about one case in eight or nine [ASHA, 1971; Galton, January, 1972; Schroeter and Lucas, February, 1972]. This fact must be kept in mind in interpreting figures indicating changes in incidence. It is possible that part, although by no means all, of any apparent increase in incidence is due to better reporting.

In 1971, 573,000 cases of gonorrhea were reported and it is estimated that 2,000,000 cases occurred [Brown, February, 1972; Schroeter and Lucas, February, 1972]. In that same year 20,000 cases of syphilis were reported and it is estimated that 70,000 to 75,000 cases occurred [Brown, February, 1972]. In short, every fifteen seconds around the clock an American is infected with venereal disease [Galton, January, 1972; Brown, February, 1972].

Until about 1969 there seemed to be a downward trend in the rate (cases per 100,000 population) of reported cases of syphilis. Many people were optimistic that the disease was being brought under control. Then in 1970 the American Social Health Association (ASHA) [1971] reported an unexpected upturn in the rate, as if a smoldering fire had burst into flame. There is now an "expanding epidemic of serious proportions" [ASHA, 1971]. Reported cases of gonorrhea have shown a steady increase. The number of cases reported annually has almost doubled since 1965, and the rate has more than doubled since 1957 [ASHA, 1971]. The present rate for syphilis is about 10 per 100,000 and for gonorrhea about 285 per 100,000 [ASHA, 1971].

This situation is serious any way it is considered. But there are three facts that further complicate it relative to premarital intercourse. For both syphilis and gonorrhea the highest rates occur in the twenty- to twenty-four-year age group [ASHA, 1971; Brown, February, 1972]. Reported cases of males with syphilis outnumber infected females about two to one, and with gonorrhea, about three to one [Brown, February, 1972; Schroeter and Lucas, February, 1972]. About 80 to 85 per cent of females and a smaller percentage of males (variously estimated to be 5 to 50 per cent) with gonorrhea are asymptomatic, that is, they have the disease and can transmit it to another person but they themselves show no symptoms of it [Galton, January, 1972; Brown, February, 1972; Schroeter and Lucas, February, 1972]. Of course, the presence of the disease can be ascertained by laboratory tests. Some asymptomatic individuals are not even aware of the fact that they have gonorrhea.

At one time it was thought that penicillin would prove to be the ultimate cure for syphilis and gonorrhea. It is still effective for syphilis and, when combined with other drugs, for gonorrhea. But some gonorrhea organisms are becoming partially resistant to it. Other antibiotics are being used with some success but the final answer has not yet been found [Neumann and Baecker, Jan. 24, 1972; Schroeter and Lucas, February, 1972; Rudolph, June 19, 1972].

Most cases of venereal disease are contracted through sexual intercourse, and the rate is rising and is already at the epidemic level. The highest incidence rate is in the twenty- to twenty-four-year-old group. Two to three times as many males as females reportedly have either syphilis or gonorrhea, but 80 to 85 per cent of females and some males who have gonorrhea are asymptomatic. With more than eight million college and university students coming from a variety of backgrounds and having a variety of life-styles, regardless of how one may feel about the desirability or undesirability of having premarital intercourse, such intercourse involves a potential health hazard for the college group. This hazard cannot be removed simply by refusing to face it.

The only contraceptive that is even partially effective in preventing venereal disease contagion is the condom. Fiumara [October, 1972] mentions conditions (some of which would be likely to make intercourse less than satisfactory) to be met before the condom is effective against gonorrhea: There must be no preliminary sex play, no kissing, no fondling, no intercourse before putting the condom on; the condom must be intact both before and after use; it must be put on and taken off correctly. Even if all these conditions are met, the condom is inadequate protection against syphilis because it does not cover all the areas of the couple's bodies that may come into contact.

Men have never liked the condom, because they believe it reduces sensation. But many men have used it, nonetheless. At present it is the only means of contraception available to men (except, of course, vasectomy, which would have no effect on venereal-disease contagion and is not likely to be sought by young, unmarried males). With the increasingly widespread use of contraceptive methods (especially the pill) used by women, a reasonable guess would be that more men will leave the responsibility for contraception to the woman, and consequently fewer men will use the condom. Some investigators believe that this is now happening and that it is one of the reasons for the rising incidence of venereal infection. Fiumara [October, 1972] also says that a man whose female partner is using the pill, or says she is using the pill, would not dare to use a condom because it would suggest that he thought she had venereal disease.

SELECTED READINGS

Banowsky, William S.: *It's a Playboy World*, Fleming H. Revell Company, Publishers, Westwood, N.J., 1969. Critical analysis of the playboy philosophy, not only as it is expressed in the magazine *Playboy*, but also in the context of what is happening socially, sexually, and morally in America, where, the author believes, the playboy philosophy is widely accepted as a way of life.

Bertocci, Peter A.: *Sex, Love, and the Person*, Sheed & Ward, Inc., New York, 1967. The author claims that the basic argument against premarital sexual intercourse is "untouched by medical advances" and that questions concerning premarital sex cannot be answered without considering related issues.

Calderone, Mary Steichen: "How Young Men Influence the Girls Who Love Them," *Redbook*, July, 1965, pp. 45ff. Discussion of the role young men play in the sexual development of girls.

Hettlinger, Richard F.: *Living with Sex: the Student's Dilemma*, Seabury Press, Inc., New York, 1966. Addressed primarily to college men. Discussion of premarital intercourse, "the girl's point of view," masturbation, the playboy philosophy.

Hofmann, Hans: *Sex Incorporated*, Beacon Press, Boston, 1967. "A positive view of the sexual revolution." Discusses "how sex can be incorporated into a total life-awareness."

Kennedy, Eugene C.: *The New Sexuality: Myths, Fables, and Hang-ups*, Doubleday & Company, Inc., Garden City, N.Y., 1972. Analysis of sex in present-day America, premarital intercourse, extramarital sexual relations, homosexuality, masturbation, pornography. Author says American culture is "desperately preoccupied with sexiness and so blinded to real sexuality."

Packard, Vance: *The Sexual Wilderness*, David McKay Company, Inc., New York, 1968. (Paperback.) A study of sexual attitudes and behavior. Contains numerous references to other studies and quotes numerous investigators, writers, and commentators.

Reiss, Ira L.: *Premarital Sexual Standards in America*, The Free Press, New York, 1960. Analysis of sexual standards rather than a statistical analysis of sexual practices; what the future trend will be.

Schur, Edwin M. (ed.): *The Family and the Sexual Revolution*, Indiana University Press, Bloomington, 1964. (Paperback.) A book of readings designed to "bring together some highly provocative materials relating to three hotly disputed topics that lie at the center of key changes affecting the modern family—sex standards, women's roles, and birth control."

Marriage and Alternative Life-styles

What does the term *alternative life-styles* suggest? In a heterogeneous population, a pluralistic society such as ours, not every person or group subscribes to the same way of life. This has been true in the United States for some time. Communal societies; polygamous marriage; group marriage; males having wives and mistresses simultaneously; extramarital sexual relations; prostitution; homosexuality; premarital sexual freedom; unmarried persons living together (either with or without the intention of establishing common-law marriage); the repudiation of marriage; nudism; and other life-styles all have historical precedents. Although they have received increased attention recently, none of these is new. What is new, perhaps, is a growing acceptance—at least a tolerance—of these life-styles and sometimes a recommendation of them as a solution to certain problems of living. What is also new is the term *alternative life-styles*, which puts a variety of forms under one caption as one broad category.

The term *alternatives* could imply that certain life-styles are substitutes for conventional marriage or that there are various choices, one of which is marriage. There is a shade of difference in these two interpretations. The former sets up conventional marriage as a base from which other alternatives are variations. The latter suggests freedom of choice among all alternatives. At this point in American social development the former interpretation is probably more widely applied.

We have long accepted intercultural differences in life-styles. If the Scandinavians want to have sexual freedom, that is their affair. If the Eskimos want to have wife lending, that is their right. If a given people want to have polygamy, that is their privilege. Now, perhaps, we are coming to a similar acceptance of intracultural differences. We have become more flexible in interpreting possible threats to the established mores. "Live and let live" is increasingly characterising our approach to life.

It is obviously not possible for all life-styles to become universal or even majority practice. All but one must remain minority practices for the simple reason that there can be any number of minorities but only one majority.

Among the alternative life-styles which we shall discuss are conventional, monogamous marriage and variations on such marriage. These variations fall into three categories: the absence of marriage; supplements or adjuncts to marriage (a

three

couple having both marriage and an alternative simultaneously); and modifications of marriage.

We cannot assume that the practices of the majority necessarily meet the needs of a specific minority. Neither can we assume that the practices of a specific minority will necessarily eventually meet the needs of the majority. Whether a given life-style represents a step toward general practice or whether it represents the meeting of the needs of a small, temporary, peripheral group or whether it is an experiment, only time will tell. It is sometimes assumed, not only by the individuals involved but also by outside observers, that every seeming innovation in a small group represents the point of the wedge of social change. If we learn anything from history, we learn that many such apparent innovations either remain as the life-styles of small minorities or are gradually phased out.

Sometimes it is assumed that it is the form of a given life-style that determines its success or failure, that the solution to the problems of one style is the adoption of another. It is not the form, but rather the people in it, that determines whether a given way of life will succeed or fail. People who are failures in, or discontented with, one type of relationship will not automatically become successes in, or contented with, another just because it is different.

In the following discussion we shall use the term *marriage* to mean marriage as it is ordinarily understood in this country, unless the term is preceded by a qualifying adjective. Since the focus of this book is preparation for marriage, only brief attention will be given to alternatives to marriage. The reader is referred to the Selected Readings at the end of this chapter for further discussion of these alternatives.

ABSENCE OF MARRIAGE

Factors, in Effect, beyond Conscious Control

The fact that there are more females than males in the population, the type of community in which one lives, responsibilities which prevent meeting eligible persons, occupational isolation, ignorance of ways of approaching the other sex or too-long delay in earlier years, lack of interest, distorted ideas, disinclination to assume the responsibilities of marriage, disappointment in love, death of a fiancé, parents, fear of sex or of one's own capacity to "measure up," guilt, falling in love with a married person, and similar factors not uncommonly prevent marriage.

Factors Subject to Conscious Control

The deliberate choice of celibacy—that is, singleness due to religious vows, as in the case of a priest or nun—is such a factor.

Homosexuality

Homosexuality itself is, of course, beyond the individual's conscious control. He does not decide by simple choice to be homosexual or heterosexual. An individual who is homosexual may choose to change his orientation and cease to be homosexual and, to that end, seek counseling help. Homosexuality is not an either-or state. There are degrees and gradations. Some persons are as nearly 100 per cent homosexual and others are as nearly 100 per cent heterosexual as it is possible to be. But in between the extremes there are many individuals who exhibit a combination of characteristics. Some of these individuals marry. But most individuals with homosexual preference remain unmarried by choice. In recent years, since homosexuals have become freer in identifying themselves and in seeking an end to discrimination, some homosexuals have demanded the right to "marry" each other and a few have had "wedding" ceremonies. Such arrangements are not marriages in the customary sense of the term and do not have the same legal status, although for some homosexuals they apparently do meet a need.

Repudiation of Marriage

A reason for not marrying which has gained prominence in recent years, especially among students who are rebelling against the "establishment," is the repudiation of marriage as an unnecessary and undesirable relic of a Puritan past, an outmoded and dysfunctional attempt on the part of society to limit the freedom and dictate the life-style of the individual. The feeling is that people should be free to live together without marriage if they so desire. It is claimed that, in the last analysis, a marriage license or certificate is only a piece of paper. It is not so important as the couple's relationship. In fact, marriage may detract from, rather than contribute to, the completeness of the couple's commitment, since marriage places limitations on their love. It is said that the wedding is only an outward form which establishes another outward form, marriage. True meaning is found not in forms but in a relationship. A wedding may satisfy the demands of society, but it does nothing for the couple. If a couple love each other, they do not need a wedding. If they do not love each other, a wedding will not help.

One of the outgrowths of this point of view is the co-ed dormitory. In some colleges a co-ed dormitory is merely a dormitory with separate wings or floors for male and female students, with rules regulating visiting in each other's rooms and with common recreational and dining rooms. In other colleges a co-ed dormitory is one in which intervisiting rules have been relaxed. In still others a co-ed dormitory is one in which male and female students live together as couples without marriage and without administrative restrictions. The last arrangement is recommended by some students as being better than dating as a way of getting acquainted. They say that it is more natural and less artificial than dating. Many such students eventually marry, but not necessarily each other.

Any arrangement such as the last above, in which students live together as couples, is selective. Students choosing it would be those with special needs or with attitudes—at least at the outset—that would make them less likely to be disturbed by such an arrangement. Students living in this way often feel that their arrangement is equivalent to marriage without the restrictions of marriage. They have sexual freedom, may share expenses and housekeeping tasks, and are at liberty to terminate the relationship at will. Yet, by the nature of the situation, their commitment to each other is less than complete. They have taken no stand on responsibility for each other. Their freedom could lead to as great a trauma as a broken marriage if their sexual relationship led to an emotional involvement, say, for the woman, and the man terminated the arrangement. Some students think of such co-ed living as a form of trial marriage. There are limitations on such a point of view. Many students do not enter such an arrangement as a trial of marriage to each other, and, by definition, there cannot be a trial of *marriage* without *marriage* because such a trial involves only certain aspects of marriage rather than a total life plan. One student, who had argued in favor of such trial marriage, said he was afraid to marry because of the financial problems and responsibility. There seems to be here a contradiction in terms between *trial marriage* and *marriage*.

SUPPLEMENTS (ADJUNCTS) TO MARRIAGE

Extramarital Sexual Relations (Adultery)

Such relations are, no doubt, as ancient as marriage itself. It is difficult to get accurate statistics, but apparently such relations are common. In American society adultery has been condemned on moral or religious grounds by the majority of the population—even by some who have engaged in it. At the same time there has been a "closed-eyes" policy in some quarters. Adultery is a ground for divorce in all states, even in those which do not specify grounds in the law. Most Americans enter marriage with the expectation of sexual exclusiveness, and the discovery of adultery on the part of one spouse is deeply traumatic to the other.

In recent years, however, an attitude that may not be new but is newly articulated and publicized theorizes that, since monogamous marriage no longer meets the needs of its participants, extramarital sexual relations are desirable. Such relations are recommended as a means of giving husband and wife freedom, providing sexual variety, being a test of love because they remove all restrictions on love, meeting a human need to love more than one person at one time, and having a bolstering and therapeutic effect on a marriage which has lost its zest or "gone stale." Terms such as *beneficial experience* and *healthy adultery* are used.

Group Sex

Other terms for group sex are *co-marital sex*, as suggested by William Genné [Roy and Roy, 1969], *swinging, mate swapping,* and *wife swapping.* The term *husband swapping* is never used, although of necessity "swapping" is a two-sided process; this suggests that males have more interest than females do in this type of arrangement. Reiss [1971] refers to group sex as an "egalitarian form of adultery," since most of the persons involved are married, and both partners participate simultaneously and by mutual consent. At times, however, the "mutual" consent is one-sided. The husband initiates participation to which the wife gives reluctant consent. In some cases, however, after she has tried it, the wife finds that she is more favorably inclined toward the arrangement than she thought she would be. In other cases the wife participates and finds that it continues to be unattractive to her. Instances have been known in which a wife became ill at the prospect of participating the first time.

There are many types of people involved in "swinging"—professional people (physicians, teachers, engineers, scientists, etc.), white-collar workers, blue-collar workers, and others. On the whole, groups tend to be somewhat homogeneous but not completely so. This is due to a selective process through which new participants are invited to join a group and are approved by members. Groups vary from small circles of friends to large numbers of people, many of whom were not acquainted before their first get-together. Some groups have been associated for years. In other cases the group is continuous, but the membership is fluid and constantly changing; there are many dropouts. Disillusionment is not uncommon.

Swingers contact each other and possible new recruits through a variety of channels. Friend-to-friend communication is not uncommon. "Feeling out" likely individuals at bars and social gatherings takes place. One of the common channels is placing advertisements and answering the advertisements of others in magazines. One organization issues specially numbered car stickers so swingers can identify each other on the highway [Grold, October, 1970]. Often there is a good deal of drinking at group get-togethers. There may be dancing, game playing (for example, strip poker), or similar activities.

Although sex for the sake of sex is the primary objective of swinging, a secondary objective is socializing, and get-togethers are not invariably unrestricted debauchery. There are rules and mutual understandings governing group activity. At a get-together sexual relations are free and are not restricted to intercourse. Partners may be exchanged at will, but it is expected that married couples will not have intercourse with each other. No woman is obligated to have intercourse with any particular man; she may refuse, and he is obligated to accept her refusal. A woman may attend and refrain from participating if she is menstruating. A couple who pair off to have intercourse may have privacy or semiprivacy if they so desire. At some gatherings there are a number of people in the same bed at the same time in semidarkness and often somewhat foggy from drinking. Under such circumstances it is considered a faux pas for a married couple, who did not recognize each other, to have intercourse. There are rules governing bodily cleanliness and means of bringing disregard of these rules to an individual's attention. Ordinarily groups are composed of married couples, and unmarried persons are not invited, although there are other groups composed of singles only. Sometimes two unmarried persons of opposite sex may attend a predominantly married group, especially if the man brings an extra woman. Sometimes a married couple bring an extra woman. Bringing an extra man is discouraged. Typically, homosexuals are not welcome in a swinging group, although some swingers do engage in homosexual relations during a get-together, not necessarily because they are homosexuals but because they find such relationships stimulating. In swinging groups there is some *voyeurism*, that is, there are individuals, especially men, who attend partly just to see other people unclothed or engaging in some form of sexual relations. There is also some exhibitionism. Generally it is assumed that the woman will take responsibility for contraception. Most swingers are hesitant to let their children know about their swinging. They resort to careful planning and subterfuge to prevent their children from finding out.

Inevitably there is competition, or at least comparison, in swinging groups. How can an individual have intercourse with a number of persons and not form some image of them as more or less effective sexual partners? How can an individual fail to compare other persons with husband or wife, as the case may be? Hence, jealousy is not uncommon.

One of the universal, or near-universal, rules among swingers and one that raises serious questions about swingers' philosophy and activities, however free sexual intercourse may be, is that there are to be no emotional attachments formed between partners as a result of swinging. In other words, sexual intercourse is depersonalized and is required to occur without love, affection, or meaning. Swinging might therefore be considered a genital life-style, although there is an attitude among swingers and others that swinging strengthens marriage. Such an assumption is not, of course, to be interpreted as a general prescription for marriage problems. If swinging does strengthen marriage—an assumption questioned by some knowledgeable persons—it is relative to the kind of individuals in the marriage, their personalities, expectations, and the nature of the situation for which such strengthening is considered a remedy. The very assertion that swinging is a strengthening factor is an implication that the marriage is not entirely satisfactory, else it would not need strengthening.

MODIFICATIONS OF MARRIAGE

Communes

One of the alternative life-styles that has been given considerable attention in recent years is the *commune,* or community, as the members themselves (the communalists, communards, or communitarians) often refer to it. It is difficult to generalize on communes because they represent such a broad spectrum of differences. Some of them exhibit life-styles such as those mentioned above. We shall mention these styles again as necessary.

Communal societies have been organized at various times throughout a good part of American history. Most of them have been short-lived. A few have continued in greatly altered form. Still fewer, if any, have persisted in approximately their original form.

Below are described some of the characteristics of present-day communes. These characteristics may be found in various combinations except, of course, a combination of opposites; for example, a commune could not be organized and disorganized at the same time.

Some communes welcome everybody who comes to them; anyone who wants to stay may do so and share what the members of the commune have. Other communes are selective, either on theory or because they have found through experience that the group cannot continue to function effectively if all types of persons are permitted to join it regardless of what those persons are, what they are seeking, or how they fit into the group.

Some communes are composed principally of persons whose primary motive is escape from the "establishment," the "mass society." Others are composed of individuals whose motive is to leave one type of life in order to seek another they consider better. For example, their motivation may be strongly religious.

A commune may include a variety of types of persons, some well educated and, in some cases, having professional degrees or professional training and others less educated, as well as individuals of different personality types and conditions of mental health. A commune may be organized or may lack organization. The members may feel not only that organization is unnecessary but that its lack is a source of pride.

There may be one or more persons in the commune representing authority or leadership either through being chosen for such a function or through having personal qualities and charisma that lead to the emergence of such a role. In other communes there is no one who has any more authority than anyone else. Decisions are made by vote of the entire group, a process that sometimes proves laborious and time-consuming but is democratic, although at other times it leads to inactivity when no decision can be reached.

In some communes there is a plan for work—for doing chores, for cooking, etc. Persons are assigned to jobs according to a schedule. In other communes there is no planning, no scheduling. Everyone is free to do as he wishes, to "do his thing." There are no requirements, the assumption being that everyone will want to do his share and the work will get done. In reality such an arrangement often results in work being left undone.

Some communal groups own the property on which they are situated. In some cases they purchased it. In others the land originally belonged to one member of the group. In still others a group member owns the land and buildings and lets the commune live there.

Some communes are productive and self-sustaining. They raise a good part of their own food, construct buildings, repair equipment. Some members may be gainfully employed and contribute their earnings, or a portion of them, to the group. In some cases the commune or certain members manufacture salable products. In other communes attempts at productivity have been only partially successful or have failed completely or the production of salable items has not been tried. Even in producing food and other products for the use of the commune some groups have had difficulty because the members have not had training in the skills necessary for survival under meager and harsh conditions. In some cases communalists receive allowances from parents or receive public welfare checks and in that way contribute to the group. They often rationalize this as temporary dependence on the establishment during a transition period until the commune becomes self-sustaining. In any case, a commune depends for its existence on the mass society which it repudiates. Cars, telephones, electricity, medical services, protection, equipment, fabrics, and a host of other products and services come from sources other than the commune itself.

Lack of skills in maintenance often results in the commune members' living under unsanitary conditions and in poor housing, with inadequate diet and with a low and harsh standard of living.

Some communes get along well with their neighbors and consciously seek to improve public relations. Other communes are in constant conflict with their neighbors and are looked at askance by the police.

In some communes there is emphasis on esoteric, perhaps Oriental, religious beliefs and practices. In others there is no emphasis on religion. In still others the emphasis is on traditional Christianity.

Just as there is a variety of points of view and practices in communes relative to the above items, there is a variety of points of view and practices relative to sex and marriage. In some communes there are both married couples and single members. In some, sex is entirely free and twosomes may pair up as they wish, whether or not one or both are married. In others there is "group marriage" by mutual understanding, although such an arrangement has no status within the law. Some communes are felt by their members to be large "families." In some there is sexual freedom but it is regulated by the group; that is, a schedule is drawn up to make known who will sleep with whom on a given night.

In some communes children are cared for by their natural parents. In some, care of children is scheduled as other tasks are scheduled, while in others the assumption is made that all members of the group are responsible for all children. If, for example, a mother leaves for the day, her children will be cared for without previous planning. Not uncommonly children are neglected under such an arrangement. On the other hand, in some groups males as well as females take an interest in child care.

In some communes each member is free to do as he wishes regarding the use of drugs and alcohol. In others the use of drugs, especially, is discouraged or even prohibited.

Yaswen [1970], writing a "post-mortem" after his experience in a commune, mentions the common assumption that the "hang-ups" of individuals are due to the "mass society" rather than to the individuals themselves and that, therefore, these "hang-ups" will be straightened out in the community. He adds, however, that such assumptions are naive. He explains further that "when people set out to build a utopian community, they are starting out with an image constructed mainly of ideas of what they do *not* want the community to be, rather than what they *do*." They are overreacting to societal norms that they are seeking to escape. This overreaction, he explains, may be therapeutic for the reactor but may be ruinous for the community because the individual may be willing to sacrifice the entire group in pursuit of a single ideal. He says, ". . . Communities of people who come to community in pursuit of something *other* than community seem to have a better chance of survival than those where community itself is the goal. . . . No wonder communities fail; *they are consumed by the fires they set, to fight the fires they flee*" (Yaswen's italics).

Some say that communes are a step in the direction of social change. Roberts [1971] says that "the majority of Americans will never participate in communal experiments." Many agree with him. He says further that "complete abolition of sexual restraint and repression makes lasting communities and societies impossible." In some communes there is modified sexual restraint but it is not fully comparable to monogamous marriage.

As pointed out earlier, members of a commune typically are reacting against the "establishment," the "mass society." Their children, however, not having lived in the mass society, will react to the deprivations and low standard of living (in many instances) of communal life, and this may make the "grass on the other side of the fence" look much greener. Groups of all types and motivations have found that adherence to the ways of the group becomes diluted among the children, and one of the major problems of continuance is that of holding the younger generation to the objectives and ideals of the founders.

On the whole, communalists are young people. Communes are youth-oriented. But youth is obviously impermanent. What will happen as communalists grow older and fall into the age group of the generation which represents the establishment? Communalists are not preparing for life in the mass society as they know it. They are preparing for a continuation of life in a commune or for life in a new society which the commune will introduce and whose initiation will require rapid and widespread social change within the life-span of present-day communalists. One wonders whether such change can occur.

Society has to be affluent, as American society is today, to sustain an unproductive minority, unless the members of the minority are incapacitated. People may, of course, be productive in ways other than manufacturing material goods, as for example in the arts, in government, and in a multitude of services. At their present stage of development, many communalists are not productive and are not preparing to become productive. One wonders where this will eventually lead, and what enduring form of marriage and family life will emerge from these experiences.

Group and Multilateral Marriage

Group marriage is not limited to communes. Such marriage may involve two or more already married couples or several single persons who decide to live together as a married group, with sexual relations free and with the sharing of expenses and household tasks. It may involve a threesome, sometimes termed *trio marriage* or *triad* or *troika*, consisting of one male and two females, or, probably less frequently, one female and two males. *Group marriage* suggests an understanding within the group; it is not a legal status.

Opinions differ on the possibility of making group marriage successful and what its future may be. Kilgo [March, 1972] says that "the problems encountered in group marriages are probably too great for most people to overcome."

Trial Marriage

Trial marriage is sometimes referred to as "apprenticeship marriage." Bernard [1972b] mentions "renewable marriage." In 1927 Judge Ben Lindsey wrote about "companionate marriage." Margaret Mead [July, 1966] discusses "marriage in two steps." She mentions "individual marriage," a licensed union with only an ethical, not an economic, obligation. The male would not be required to support the female. "Individual marriage" would be binding on the couple's being committed to each other as long as they wished to remain together but it would not apply to them as future parents. "Parental marriage," with its own license, ceremony, and kinds of responsibility, and always preceded by individual marriage, "would be explicitly directed toward the founding of a family." This would be marriage that "looked to a lifetime relationship." Individual marriage would be a serious commitment, entered into in public, and validated and protected by law and in some cases by religion, in which "each partner would have a deep and continuing concern for the happiness and well-being of the other." It would give two young people a chance to know each other better than in a brief love affair and "would help them grow into each other's life—and allow them to part without the burden of misunderstood intentions, bitter recriminations, and self-destructive guilt."

"In contrast to individual marriage, parental marriage would be hard to contract." In parental marriage, "each partner would know the other well, eliminating . . . any one of the thousand shocks that lie in wait for the person who enters a hasty marriage with someone he or she knows little about."

Mead's marriage in two steps is very similar to Lindsey's companionate marriage. Mead recognizes this but suggests that the time is more ripe for the acceptance of this concept now than in the 1920s. The idea of marriage in two steps is intriguing, but one wonders whether it is feasible with only the advantages mentioned by Mead and no serious disadvantages. If two young people enter an individual marriage before they are well acquainted, what is to guarantee that there will not be complex problems of adjustment, with disappointment and disillusionment, as is possible in any type of marriage? If they dissolve the individual marriage, it could be as traumatic as the breakup of any marriage, especially if one partner wants to dissolve it and the other does not. Mead says that an "individual marriage" would allow a couple "to part without the burden of misunderstood intentions, bitter recriminations, and self-destructive guilt." But by the time such parting occurs, original logic may become dissolved in emotion. If they enter individual marriage knowing that it may be considered tentative, would this be a real test of marriage? Mead assumes that a couple in an individual marriage will not have a child simply because they do not plan to have it. What if they have a child during that marriage and one or both of them do not want to go on to the next stage, parental marriage? Will they then have a parental marriage against their will and be ill prepared for it? Will the child be a trap? Is there any basic difference between an individual marriage and the first, childless phase of any marriage? Mead says that parental marriage "would be hard to contract," implying that individual marriage would be easy to contract. Would this not be an invitation to what amounted to a purely sexual arrangement for young people vulnerable because of infatuation or sexual attraction?

Serial Marriage

"Serial marriage," as predicted by Toffler [1970], is an extension of the concept of what is sometimes termed *serial polygamy* as we shall discuss it in Chapter 7. It implies that an individual may have a series of spouses, one at a time. It also involves the concept of trial marriage. But persons who think of serial polygamy are usually seeking to describe our system of frequent divorce and remarriage, a system possible within the law, generally accepted unless blatantly abused, but withal considered a regrettable necessity. Toffler, on the contrary, presents serial marriage as the marriage pattern of the future.

Toffler, like many others today, believes that conventional American marriage is becoming increasingly less well adapted to human needs. As this maladaptation continues to increase, "we can anticipate open public acceptance of temporary marriages." The present-day divorce rate suggests that there is already acceptance of temporary marriages, but again as a regrettable necessity. Toffler goes on to say that couples will enter marriage "knowing from the first that the relationship is likely to be short-lived. . . . They will know, too, that when the paths of husband and wife diverge . . . they may call it quits—without the shock or embarrassment, perhaps even without some of the pain that goes with divorce today. And when the opportunity presents itself, they will marry again . . . and again . . . and again."

He goes on to say that serial marriage is the "mainstream marriage of tomorrow." As it becomes more common, we shall characterize people, not by their marital status, but by their marital "career" or "trajectory." In this trajectory there will be four stages: first, trial or probationary marriage; second, at the end of the trial marriage the couple would either formalize their relationship or seek new partners and may choose to have or adopt children; third, when the children leave home, the couple will enter a "real marriage," perhaps the most enduring of all; fourth, at retirement they may or may not continue marriage, may remarry, or may remain single.

Temporariness will be at least a standard feature, and perhaps the dominant feature, of marriage in the future. Of course, there will be some people lucky or skillful or intelligent enough to make long-lasting monogamous marriage work. As others try a series of partners, there will be a slow but relentless rise in the number of marriages per capita. Still other people will try numerous experiments. The over-all result will be a "rich variation in the types of marital trajectories that people will trace, a wider choice of life patterns, an endless opportunity for novelty of experience."

As in the case of Margaret Mead's marriage in two steps, Toffler's prediction leaves unanswered questions. How can there be commitment in marriage on a tentative basis? To recognize as an outsider that many marriages will be short-lived and to enter a given marriage with the conviction that it will probably be short-lived are quite different. Such a conviction of probable failure could in itself be a factor contributing to failure. It is easy to theorize that marriages will be dissolved without shock or pain, but how can trauma be avoided if there is emotional involvement? If the two people in a probationary marriage do not simultaneously want to discontinue it, how is hurt to be avoided for the one who wants to remain married? "No change in either the form or the contents of the commitments which people make to one another mollifies the pain and suffering of a broken relationship. It hurts. It hurts if both welcome the break. It hurts even more if only one does" [Bernard, 1972b]. It is easy to say that new marriage partners will be sought later in life and after preliminary trials, but would all ex-spouses at a given point in their trajectory be prepared for this? For example, Toffler makes no allowance for many older men's preference for younger women.

MARRIAGE

Why People Marry

Marriage is not something that "comes naturally." It is not the product of inborn behavior patterns, sometimes called "instincts." It is an institution. It is a cluster of mores and folkways, of attitudes and ideas, of social and legal definitions. One of its focal points is the "sex instinct," but marriage is much more than that. It is more than mating. If marriage and mating were the same, there could be no illegitimate children. Human beings mate, but they also marry. In their marrying, instinct plays a relatively minor role. If, then, they do not marry instinctively, why do they marry?

People marry for a combination of reasons. Such reasons as love, economic security, home and children, emotional security, parents' wishes, escape from loneliness or from a parental home or other disagreeable situation, money, companionship, sexual attraction, protection, notoriety, social position and prestige, gratitude, pity, spite, adventure, and common interests are obvious. Law and custom play a part.

In some cases in which a person has been disappointed in love, had an engagement broken, or suffered some similar painful experience, he transfers his affection from the first love object to a second, feeling toward the second as he felt toward the first even though the second may be a quite different sort of person and even though he has not known the second long enough to be in love with that person. He makes a choice before he has sufficiently regained his emotional balance to make a wise one. This is marriage on the rebound.

There are still weddings resulting from pressure—"shotgun weddings"—but there is less pressure than formerly. There is a growing feeling against forcing a couple to marry, even if there is a premarital pregnancy. A forced marriage gives a child a legal father but cannot give him a loving father or the advantages of having happily married parents. Sometimes when there is neither love nor social pressure a man feels honor bound to marry the mother of his child. But such a feeling is hardly a substitute for love and is difficult to sustain throughout marriage.

In some cases the more parents object to a marriage, the more determined the young couple become and the more attractive they seem to each other. They marry not so much because they want to marry as to assert themselves. Many a person marries because others in his circle of friends are marrying and he does not want to be the last one to do so. In recent years this reason for marriage has become frequently apparent as the age at marriage has declined and an increasing number of adolescents of high school age, sensitive to the pressure of the peer group, have become involved.

In the last analysis, people marry because marriage is the most widely accepted social pattern for relationships between the sexes. Monogamous American marriage involves a cluster of values which goes far toward meeting the needs of the majority of the people. It is not perfect, but neither is any other social arrangement. Many fail in attempting to work it out, but failure is not uncommon in any human endeavor. Whatever its shortcomings may be, American marriage contains the possibility for combining two complementary sexes in a mutually rewarding relationship. Enduring love; companionship; the security of mutual commitment and concern; that special understanding, closeness, and acceptance that humans can receive from one other person, especially a person of opposite sex; "the profoundly reaffirming experience of genuine intimacy" [Kennedy, 1972]; sexual exclusiveness; cooperation in the maintenance of life; parenthood and family living; and similar values continue to attract people to marriage and motivate them to seek to work it out. This cluster of values of which the individual becomes aware as he internalizes the culture in which he is reared is the basic reason for which Americans marry. Many persons achieve what for them is completely satisfactory marriage. Many fail to achieve a marriage that they can continue to tolerate. But in between these extremes there are millions of Americans who achieve a type of marriage which, though less than ideal, for them is more acceptable than an alternative.

LOVE

If you were to ask a group of married people why they married, it is unlikely that they would enumerate the values mentioned above. Probably the majority of them would say, "Because we were in love." They "married for love." No doubt they would be at least partly correct. They did marry because they experienced a feeling that they interpreted as love. It is difficult, however, to state with any great degree of precision just what the feeling is. We use the term *love* in a great many different senses. You say, for example, "I love my parents," "I love my fiancé," "I love God," "I love my country," "I love animals," "I love nice clothes," "I love to hunt." It is obvious that you cannot love your mother in the same way that you "love" hunting. You do not have the same emotional experience with your country that you have with a fiancé.

We might qualify the term *love* by such adjectives as "filial," "parental," "conjugal," "romantic"; but that would still not explain precisely what we mean when we say we "marry for love," or we "fall in love." Furthermore, love means different things to different people, depending upon their background and experience, and it has various meanings at different periods of life.

What distinguishes the love into which we "fall" from the other types of love is the obvious sexual element, the fact that it grows out of a recognition of sex differences. This is not the same as saying that love is entirely on a physical basis, for it is not. Sex is more than physical; it ramifies all through an individual's life. But in romantic love, the love into which we "fall," the love that leads up to and over into marriage, there is a centering of attention on the other person as a focus of biological urges and a means of relief from biological tension.

Misconceptions Concerning Love

There are a number of common misconceptions concerning love that play a part in our thinking about it and add to the confusion of the individual who is attempting to determine whether what he is experiencing is genuine love or one of the counterfeits that often pass for it. Some of these misconceptions are as follows.

We say that we "fall in love," but it is difficult to know precisely what connotation of "fall" is implied. "Fall" is a word of many meanings. To mention a few: Be careful that you don't "fall" on the stairs. A soldier "falls" in battle. Temperature "falls." Night "falls." A government "falls." A city "falls" to the enemy. A person "falls" ill. An event "falls" on Sunday. A man "falls" heir to a fortune. Her eyes "fall" when he looks at her. Certain items "fall" into three classes. An individual "falls" among thieves and is robbed. It is the "fall" of the year. A boy sees a beautiful girl and "falls" for her. One "falls" back on a previous argument. A couple "fall" behind in the payment of their bills. The soldiers "fall" upon the enemy. Two friends quarrel and "fall" out. A plan "falls" through. The animal "falls" into a trap. The student "falls" in line.

It is commonly assumed that "fall in love" connotes something unexpected, something precipitous, something over which the individual has no control and for the results of which he therefore has no responsibility. But it is worth noting that the phrase is not "fall into love" with the implication of "fall into a trap." It is "fall in love," suggesting that the meaning is more like that of "fall heir" or "fall in line," implying "become heir" or "get in line," a less headlong process.

We assume that we "fall in love" only with our "hearts," but that is not true. We do "fall in love" with our "hearts" but also, it is hoped, with our "heads." In addition, the process is colored by the traditions, customs, standards, ideas, and ideals of the group in which we live and out of which our attitudes spring.

It would be much better to say that we grow into love. That would be nearer the truth, but it sounds unromantic. Although one may fall precipitously into a condition of violent infatuation, it takes time for love to develop. Love is a complex sentiment. It does not strike suddenly or fall unexpectedly like manna from heaven. It comes only when two individuals have reoriented their lives, each with the other as a new focal point. "An individual is in love when meeting the emotional needs of his beloved becomes an ultimate emotional necessity for him" [Klemer, 1970].

Some persons believe that when an individual is experiencing what he interprets to be love, his immediate experience outweighs all other considerations. He is sometimes almost expected to lose his perspective. There is also an assumption that what an individual feels at a given moment cannot and will not change and that therefore it must be love. These misconceptions go hand in hand with the uncritical assumption that love is largely a physical experience.

Some persons attribute to love an almost unlimited power of offsetting or eradicating individual shortcomings. The assumption seems to be that, if feelings are sufficiently intense, personality traits will affect neither the couple's relationship nor their marriage, or else that undesirable traits will be molded to fit the ideal merely through the healing balm of love.

There exists a similar misconception relative to love's ability to solve problems. Individuals supposedly in love often blithely disregard problems connected with parents, income, possible babies, employment, the completion of their education, and so on.

Some individuals believe that somewhere in the world is *the* one, the only person with whom they could fall in love and with whom they could find happiness. They are depending upon a kind fate, plus a certain amount of seeking on their own part, to bring the two predestined lovers together. This is a very romantic conception, but it cannot be squared with the facts. The assumption that only people suited to each other will fall in love is false. Since Americans are born at the rate of one about every ten seconds, it would be somewhat difficult to keep one's seeking abreast of the population.

What happens to make it seem as if the above theory were true is probably this: Two persons have certain ideas concerning an ideal marriage partner. They meet and fall in love. During this process each revamps his ideal to fit the other person, and consequently each has fallen in love with the ideal partner. But before that happened, they might as readily have fallen in love with any one of a number of persons. After the ideals have been revamped and centered on given individuals, however, this fact colors their attitude toward other persons and might make it difficult to fall in love with anyone else.

There is a misconception that when love does come it can be instantly recognized. One case illustrates this point clearly because it is extreme. A serviceman wrote to a college woman whose picture he had seen in a newspaper. She responded. Through correspondence they presumably became acquainted, fell in love, and became engaged. On his first leave, the man came to meet his fiancée for the first time. He was scheduled to arrive on Thursday. The wedding, for which the woman had made all arrangements, was to take place on Friday. On Wednesday the woman was asked how she could be sure that she was in love with a man whom she had never seen. She answered, "As soon as he steps off the plane, I'll know."

There is a common assumption that a person marries only another individual and that therefore only his feelings toward this individual are important; other considerations may safely be disregarded. In one sense, of course, a person does marry only an individual. In another sense he "marries" that individual plus that individual's family, background, social status, occupation, financial condition, moral standards, friends, and past, and everything connected with him.

The above misconception leads to another with which it overlaps, namely, that love is the only and entire basis for marriage. Yet associated with this misconception is another, contradictory, one. There are persons who believe that falling in love is the only prerequisite for getting married, but at the same time they believe that most couples fall out of love sooner or later after the wedding and settle down to a more or less humdrum marital existence in which each takes the other for granted.

How Can One Tell Whether One Is Really in Love?

There is no simple formula for determining the presence of love. One cannot say, "$a + b = c$; therefore, I am in love." Hence, with the possibility of their overlapping, we have chosen to do two things: first, to present a brief series of contrasting attributes of love and infatuation; second, to present a series of questions to aid in self-analysis. The items mentioned below represent tendencies. One cannot say consistently, "Love is always like this, while infatuation is always like that." These items are intended only to help the individual reach a conclusion regarding his own experience.

Love and infatuation   Love grows, and all growth requires time. Infatuation may come suddenly. The question of whether or not there can be love at first sight is often raised. What usually happens in "love at first sight" is that the couple are strongly attracted to each other, perhaps infatuated, from the very beginning. Then this strong attraction develops into love without any break in the process. It seems as if it were love at first sight; but that does not prove that it was.

"Love at first sight" may also be compulsive in nature. The individual has a strong urge to love someone, and this urge becomes focused on a particular person. What should be expressed as "This is the individual I must love" is expressed by the person concerned as "This is the individual I do love." Such an urge to love is not uncommon in adolescence, when new emotions, with which the young person has not yet learned to live and which are largely the result of his own physiological development rather than of his experience, begin to well up within him.

Such "love" may also be an outgrowth of an individual's insecurity or his fear that because of personal unattractiveness or inability to meet members of the opposite sex he may never marry. Seizing upon the first opportunity to be attractive when someone exhibits interest in him, he convinces himself that it must be love at first sight.

Usually an individual reaches a sound conclusion that he is in love after seeing the other person under a variety of circumstances. An individual may become infatuated after seeing the other person in relatively few situations or even in only one and reach a premature decision about love.

Love grows out of an appraisal of all the known characteristics of the other person. Infatuation may arise from an acquaintance with only a few or only one of these characteristics.

When an individual is genuinely in love, he is in love with the other person as a total personality; his feelings grow primarily out of his relationship with that other person and a total estimate of him. An infatuated individual may be "in love with love." His feelings are primarily self-generated and grow only in part out of his relationship with the other person. The other person is a hook on which these self-generated emotions are hung.

Love is other-person-centered. It is outgoing. It results in sharing. Infatuation is self-centered. The other person is a means of self-gratification. An individual in love feels identified with the other person; they seem to be a team or pair. An infatuated individual is inclined to think of the other person as separate from himself but to be used for his own satisfaction.

Genuine love is centered on one person only. An infatuated individual may be "in love" with two or more persons simultaneously. These persons may be quite different as to personal qualities. The following is a not unusual situation. A woman is "in love" with two men and cannot choose between them. One is relatively mature, stable, ambitious, thrifty, responsible, and reserved. The other is irresponsible, fun-loving, and a free spender. At times she likes to be with one, at other times with the other. When she thinks of marriage, neither man seems to have all the qualities that she would want in her husband. What is the explanation of this seemingly incongruous situation? It is unlikely that a woman could be genuinely in love with two men who are so different. One possible explanation is that the woman is relatively immature and is in the midst of emotional transition between late adolescence and early womanhood. In so far as she is a woman, she seeks the qualities represented by the first man. In so far as she is still adolescent, the qualities of the second man appeal to her. She is "on the fence" emotionally, and her experience has not yet permitted her to find one man who exhibits all the qualities she seeks. To get what she wants she must combine the qualities of two quite different men. Hence she is "in love" with both. Many such individuals eventually marry persons whom they had not yet met at the time the above problem arose. In counseling, the author has talked with students who claimed to be in love with even more than two persons simultaneously. One woman claimed to be in love with four men and said she could not choose among them because she loved them all equally. Another woman insisted that she was in love with five men, from each of whom she had received a ring or pin. Finally she married, and later divorced, a sixth man whom she had not yet met at the time of the counseling.

An individual in love tends to have a sense of security and a feeling of trust after considering everything involved in his relationship with the other person. An infatuated individual tends to have a blind sense of security based upon wishful thinking rather than upon careful consideration, or he may have a sense of insecurity that is expressed as jealousy.

An individual in love works for the other person or for their mutual benefit. He may study to make the other person proud of him. His ambition is spurred, and he plans and saves for the future. He may daydream, but his dreams are reasonably attainable. An infatuated person may lose his ambition, his appetite, and his interest in everyday affairs. He thinks of his own misery. He often daydreams, but his dreams are not limited to the attainable. At times the dreams become substitutes for reality, and the individual lives in his world of dreams.

Love leads to idealization, but because the ideal is partly an outgrowth of understanding of and appreciation for the other person, it may be checked against reality without loss. In infatuation there tends to be idealization accompanied by a disregard of reality. A certain amount of idealization may be desirable, for none of us can look at a love object with complete impersonality; but the idealization should be continually checked with reality and not depart so far from it that sight of the real person is lost and a true appraisal is impossible.

A couple in love face problems frankly and attempt to solve them. If there are barriers to their getting married, these barriers are approached intelligently and removed. Those that cannot be removed may be circumvented, but with the knowledge that what is done is deliberate circumvention. In infatuation, problems tend to be disregarded or glossed over. Barriers to the couple's getting married may be lightly set aside, and circumvention may be confused with solution. If, after the wedding, these same problems again arise to harass the marriage, the couple may not have foreseen that this would occur. A couple in love intelligently anticipate such problems.

Love tends to be constant. Infatuation often varies with the "distance" between the couple. There may be greater attraction when they are separated because they overidealize each other but less when they are together because they see each other as they are and are more critical. Or there may be greater attraction when they are together because of physical appeal that beclouds judgment and less attraction when they are separated because physical responses are less intense and they see each other from a different point of view. There may be less attraction when the couple are apart because each sees the other in total perspective and the situation becomes more complex, but when they are together physical presence seems all that is necessary and the situation appears simpler.

Physical attraction is a relatively smaller part of their total relationship when a couple are in love, a relatively greater part when they are infatuated. Allowing for diagrammatic oversimplification, in Figure 3.1 the square representing physical attraction is the same in both diagrams. It is a relatively greater part of the square representing infatuation, a relatively smaller part of the square representing love. The reason for this is that infatuation is largely physical

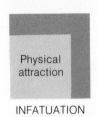

Physical attraction

INFATUATION

Physical attraction

LOVE

Figure 3.1 Diagrammatic representation of the relationship between physical attraction and infatuation and love.

attraction, while love is founded on a broader base; the couple in love have a more inclusive relationship of which physical attraction is only one facet.

When a couple are in love, any physical contact that they have is likely to have meaning as well as to be a pleasurable experience in and of itself. It expresses what they feel toward each other. In infatuation, physical contact is typically an end in itself. It represents only pleasurable experience, devoid of meaning.

In love an expression of affection may come relatively late in the couple's relationship. In infatuation it may come earlier, sometimes from the very beginning.

Love tends to endure. Infatuation may change suddenly, unexpectedly, unpredictably. When love changes, the reasons are usually more or less apparent. Infatuation may change for no apparent reason, and the cause of the change is to be found in the physiological and psychological processes of the individual in whom the change first appears rather than in what the other person has done or become.

An infatuated individual may have learned nothing through previous experience. A person in love uses his previous experience to increase the probability of wiser judgments. For example, a woman claimed to be in love with and was planning to marry a man she had dated for about two weeks. She said that three times before she had thought she was in love after a very brief acquaintance but each time had found that she was not and had terminated the relationship. But she insisted that this time it was "different." This was real love, and she could be sure of that because of its difference from the other times. She was confident that she could ascertain this after only two weeks. A person ready to be in love would see what had happened earlier and realize that "this time" could be proved different only by waiting longer to discover how the relationship developed.

Love is "tough"; it is resilient. It can absorb personality conflicts and adverse circumstances without being unduly threatened. Even when there is conflict, the individual in love accepts the other person and is concerned about that person as well as about himself. Hence a person who is in love is not readily provoked to impulsive rejection or to impatient lashing out with criticism designed to demean the other person in order to protect himself. Infatuation is more brittle. An interpersonal relationship based upon it, though intense, hangs by a slender thread. It is easily threatened. Relatively minor events or bits of personal behavior can upset it. Since infatuation is so largely a type of self-gratification, the infatuated individual is inclined either to gloss over or to be blind to the other person's faults or to attempt to change for his own increased comfort even relatively insignificant traits of the other person. Love is not blind, contrary to the old adage. It is infatuation that is blind. Love sees but accepts. "A friend," someone has said, "is one who knows all about you and loves you." If this be true of friends, how much more true it is of persons in love!

A person who is genuinely in love is concerned about his relationship with the other person. His concern is about the relationship, not just about the contribution of the relationship to his own pleasure. He does not deliberately do anything that might damage that relationship. He is alert to possible means of strengthening it, preserving it, and furthering its development. An infatuated individual is more likely to lack awareness of the role he can play in furthering the relationship. He may do things to please the other person, but these things are designed to increase the other person's acceptance of him and therefore to increase his own self-gratification rather than to strengthen the interpersonal relationship.

A person who is in love seeks to please the other person but also has the concern, insight, and courage to do what is best for that person even when that person himself does not understand what is best for him and demands only what is pleasant to him. This is not intended to imply making another person's decisions for him but making one's own decisions on the basis of love-induced concern. For example, take the case of a woman who, in spite of a man's impatience and in spite of her desire to be married, refuses to agree to an early wedding date in the face of the man's need to prove himself occupationally before assuming the responsibilities of a family.

A couple in love are not indifferent to the effects of postponing their wedding and do not prolong the period of postponement unduly, but they can wait a reasonable time; they do not feel an irresistible urge toward haste. They may think of the period of postponement as one of further preparation so that when it does occur their marriage will be on a sounder basis than if they married immediately. An infatuated couple often feel an urge toward immediate marriage. Postponement is intolerable to them, and they interpret it as deprivation rather than as preparation. When a couple feel that marriage is so important to them that they cannot wait, they only prove what they do not see, namely, that marriage is too important to be hasty.

Questions for self-analysis   The questions listed below are intended as an aid in self-analysis. They are for the person who has doubts; they are not meant to undermine the confidence of anyone who feels sure. The reader may answer each question for himself. In many instances no one can tell him what the answer should be. He must determine the significance of an affirmative or a negative answer in his own case and weight each answer in the light of his own personality, the other person's personality, and the whole situation. Not all the questions necessarily apply to every person, and there is no single criterion by which he can solve his problem. One might answer all of them and still be in doubt if in his case there were special considerations that are not included.

Above all, these questions are not to be scored as a test, as in the case of a list of similar queries that appeared in a popular magazine. The questions were useful, but the author of the article suggested that each "yes" answer count $5^{1/2}$ and that the total score would indicate the degree of infatuation or love. Such a suggestion is absurd. Who can say that a "yes" answer means the same for everyone? Moreover, not all "yes" answers would necessarily be of equal value; and the configuration of answers, that is, which ones were answered "yes" and how they were related, as well as the number of them, would be significant.

"No" answers are not necessarily undesirable in the light of a total situation. Being in love cannot be expressed by a mathematical average. Furthermore, a person cannot make himself be in love by "going through the motions" of the things suggested in the questions. Following, then, is the list of suggestions to aid the individual in analyzing himself to determine whether or not he is in love.

1   Do you like to be in the company of the other person? Do you prefer that person's company to anyone else's?
2   Is the individual personally attractive to you? Do you feel inclined to apologize for his or her appearance, manners, ideas, conversation, or language? Are you confusing admiration with love and assuming that your relationship is the platonic variety, involving no physical elements? It is as unwise to attempt to rule out physical attraction as it is to permit such attraction to be the entire basis of your relationship.
3   How do you make up after a quarrel or difference? How do you go about reestablishing your relationship?
4   As you look back over your relationship from the first meeting, how has it changed? Which of the diagrams in Figure 3.2 most nearly describes it, and what does this mean in your case? Notice that all the possibilities may show considerable resemblance to one another in the earlier stages. Only increasing acquaintance over a period of time makes it possible to distinguish among them.
5   Do you have common interests? Did you have these interests before you met? Or did you develop them together? Or did you become interested in the other person's interests? If the last is the case, are your interests sincere, or are they a means of being attractive to the other person?
6   Has enough time elapsed to tell? The sooner after meeting the couple consider themselves in love, the greater the probability of infatuation.
7   Is there anything more than physical attraction in your relationship? How soon after your acquaintance began did you begin to be affectionate? If you feel strong attraction toward the other person, become stirred up when you are together, dream about him or her constantly when you are separated, even though you have known the individual only a very short time, there is a

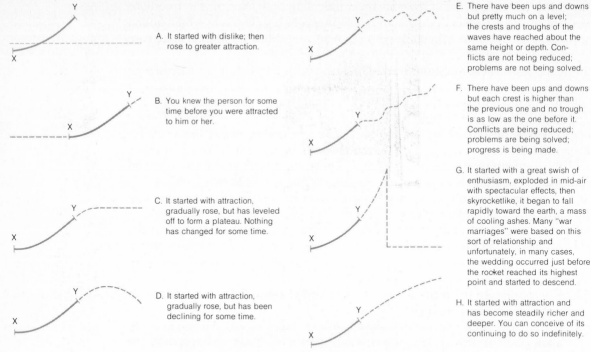

A. It started with dislike; then rose to greater attraction.

B. You knew the person for some time before you were attracted to him or her.

C. It started with attraction, gradually rose, but has leveled off to form a plateau. Nothing has changed for some time.

D. It started with attraction, gradually rose, but has been declining for some time.

E. There have been ups and downs but pretty much on a level; the crests and troughs of the waves have reached about the same height or depth. Conflicts are not being reduced; problems are not being solved.

F. There have been ups and downs but each crest is higher than the previous one and no trough is as low as the one before it. Conflicts are being reduced; problems are being solved; progress is being made.

G. It started with a great swish of enthusiasm, exploded in mid-air with spectacular effects, then skyrocketlike, it began to fall rapidly toward the earth, a mass of cooling ashes. Many "war marriages" were based on this sort of relationship and unfortunately, in many cases, the wedding occurred just before the rocket reached its highest point and started to descend.

H. It started with attraction and has become steadily richer and deeper. You can conceive of its continuing to do so indefinitely.

Figure 3.2 Possible changes in a couple's relationship to be considered in diagnosing love. The X-Y *portion of each line may look the same as that portion of the others, disregarding the oversimplification. The direction the line will take after point* Y *can be determined only over time.*

possibility that the attraction is largely physical. At least the possibility is great enough to consider postponement of marriage until you can be more sure. What proportion of your time is taken up with close physical contact? How intense is such contact? Does it dominate your relationship? Is it characterized by such urgency that it leads you to disregard time, place, circumstances, other people, or appropriateness? Is it preventing the two of you from getting to know each other in a way conducive to the development of love? Is it furthering your total relationship, or are you letting one aspect of your relationship get out of perspective?

8 Do you love the individual as a person, or do you like merely your feeling about him or her? Are you in love with a personality or "in love with love"? The boy or girl in early adolescence is inclined to be attracted to persons of the opposite sex in general. Almost anyone passably acceptable will serve as the focal point for the new emotions that have sprung up within the child. At that stage the child is "in love with love." Some persons develop beyond this stage sooner than others. Where do you stand? Are you still in the stage of being "in love with love"?

9 Are you attracted to the individual for what he or she is or for what you read into him or her? Have you overidealized the person to the point of blindness

so that you pick out those traits that seem to fit your picture of an ideal spouse and close your eyes to others? Is the individual like an oil painting, attractive because of what is on the canvas, or like a motion-picture screen, reflecting only what is projected onto it?

10 Does the person "wear well" with your friends and family? You may see qualities that your friends do not appreciate or have not had opportunity to observe. On the other hand, your friends may be more objective and unbiased; they are not likely to be blind to shortcomings. Your parents may not know the person as well as you do; they may be biased in their appraisal; and they cannot weigh all the subjective elements involved in your choice. On the other hand, however, it is highly likely that your parents have had more experience with marriage than you have.

11 Are you attracted to the person for what he or she is or for what he or she can give you or do for you?

12 Over what matters and how frequently do you have conflict? Is the conflict open or suppressed? Is it superficial or fundamental?

13 Are you willing to make concessions, or do you always expect the other person to do the pleasing, agreeing, and adjusting?

14 Do you have any doubts about your love? A certain amount of doubt while love is developing is not unusual. When, however, the question is whether or not to marry, the old adage, "When in doubt, don't," is apropos. Marrying to escape a doubt-ridden situation does not resolve doubts; it merely puts them out of mind temporarily.

15 How do you weather a crisis together?

16 Do you feel that you want to love the other person or that you have to resist it? Is yours a case in which strong physical attraction tends to draw you toward the other person at the same time that careful appraisal of personality makes you resist the physical appeal?

17 Do you feel that, if you "let yourself go" and loved the other person as much as you might, you would become submerged in his or her personality and lose your individuality?

18 Are you sufficient stimulus for each other when you are together, or do you require external stimuli, such as movies, dancing, or a group of people, to prevent boredom? To what degree is your stimulus for each other limited to physical appeal?

19 Do you love the person in your calmer moments, or do you seem to be in love only when your temperature and blood pressure are high and your heart is palpitating?

20 In your mind, how does the individual fare in competition with others? As comparisons are made with others, is he or she always at the top of the list? Or are you constantly looking for "greener pastures"?

21 How readily and how frequently do you publicize what ought to be private? Calling attention to the other person's weaknesses, recounting embarrassing experiences, or disclosing confidential information may indicate a disregard of the feelings of the other party. Overly conspicuous "necking" may indicate

an overabsorption with sex rather than an expression of love; or it may be a rebellious rejection of traditional standards.

22 What is the relationship between your enthusiasm and the presence or absence of the other person?

23 Do you feel that your relationship hangs on a very slender thread and could be easily broken? Does it seem to be constantly threatened?

24 Do you willingly permit the person to date when you are separated for an extended period? What is the reason for your answer and what does it mean with regard to your relationship with the other person?

25 Do you forgive, tolerate, accept, overlook, or resent faults and shortcomings? Do you love the individual "faults and all," or are you holding yourself in check pending the other person's reform?

26 What is the effect of separation after it is over?

27 Have you seen the individual in enough different types of situations and observed enough different facets of personality to know that you are in love? An individual may base his judgments of another person upon words rather than upon direct observation of behavior. Take, for example, the matter of an individual's family and his relationship to it—so important because in a real sense, as suggested earlier, when a person marries he marries a family as well as a spouse. If an individual has not been observed in his family, is it safe to base one's judgments upon what he says about family when what he says must of necessity be biased and incomplete? Do you see each other primarily during vacations or week-end visits when the holiday spirit may generate attitudes and behavior that may be misleading, since each person "puts his best foot forward" and his "true self" may be obscured?

28 Do you see the person's faults *and* their significance? Or do you merely see faults in a distant, detached way, without realizing what those faults would mean in marriage?

29 When you are with other men or women without this person present, do you think more or less of him or her, as to both frequency and intensity?

30 If he has told you in no uncertain terms that he is sure he loves you and will love you forever, what part does this certainty play in making you feel that you love him? If she seems indifferent, has it caused you to confuse love with the "spirit of the chase"? Are you under the pressure of some "test" of love, such as "If you love me, you will do thus and so"?

31 Do you feel that you love the other person even though he or she does not love you, has mistreated you, has rejected you, or has exhibited qualities clearly unfavorable to marriage? If so, why? What does it mean? Is your "love" compulsive, as discussed earlier? Are you strongly infatuated? Do you fear an admission of failure? Are you afraid that, if you lose this person, you will never find another? Is your personality such that you need to be hurt? If you are a woman, do you have an attachment for this person because you had sexual intercourse with him?

32 To what extent do you feel identified with this person? Do you think of

yourselves as a pair or as isolated individuals? How much do you voluntarily share with each other?

33   How much are you concerned about the individual's welfare and happiness?

34   Is there anything or anybody in life that you consider more valuable to you than this other person or that you love more than you love him or her? If so, what or who is it, and what does that fact mean?

35   Do you have a desire to escape an unhappy home, school, or work situation? Such a desire to escape often "makes the grass on the other side of the fence look greener." Marriage looks like the way out. Under such circumstances, it is easy to confuse infatuation and love.

36   What has been your reaction to these questions? Have you found it difficult to be honest with yourself? Have you rationalized any of your answers? Have you dismissed the use of such analysis on the assumption that questions cannot help you anyway? Have the questions put you on the defensive, as if you were afraid they would undermine something not fully secure?

The reader may wonder whether there can be genuine love. Doubts about his own feeling may have increased. Let him remember that love that cannot stand the test of thirty-six questions could never stand the test of thirty-six years of marriage or, for that matter, even thirty-six months of marriage.

In many cases, try as he will, an individual cannot reach a conclusion as to whether or not he is in love. Sometimes the more he tries the more confused he becomes; and the more confused he becomes, the more he feels impelled to reach a conclusion, until the vicious circle into which he has been precipitated absorbs a large portion of his time, energy, and attention. There is no simple prescription that may be administered to such a person to rid him of the problem that plagues him. Probably the answer is time and the explanation of his plight is this: He is trying to reach a conclusion by intellectual processes alone, when that conclusion must be based at least in part on a growth process, and growth requires time. His experience up to date in his relationship with the other person has contributed certain "data" that form part of the basis upon which a conclusion will eventually be reached. But the "data" are incomplete and, although the individual goes over them, examines them, "digests" them again and again, he arrives nowhere. What he needs is more experience, more contact with and observation of the other person, more "data." This will require time. Since it is indecision that is plaguing him, and since any decision will aid him in breaking the vicious circle, the individual may "make a decision to make no decision"; that is, he may definitely make up his mind to suspend judgment until he has more "data" and for the time being stop trying to reach a conclusion.

Putting all that we have discussed up to this point into a nutshell, we may say that two individuals are in love not only when they have certain strong emotional responses to one another and have a particular type of regard for each other. They are in love when their mutual relationship fosters the growth of each individual and is itself likely to increase in depth. They are in love when they begin to merge their patterns of life into one common pattern that will eventually represent a new entity of which each individual is a complementary part. Love "is a total emotional response and requires an echo" [Ackerman, 1958].

In discussing love, we may well raise one further question. Upon what basis shall I assume that I shall be loved by my marriage partner? Is it because I do so many things for that person? Love in marriage cannot be forced, earned, or purchased. If I think that it can, I am likely to assume that the other person has an obligation to love me and that the more that I do the more I should be loved. In the last analysis, love in marriage is a free gift. Shall I be loved by my marriage partner because I am so lovable? If I make that assumption, I express such conceit that I would be unlovable. Besides, people do not love only lovable persons. I may expect to be loved by my marriage partner because that person is so loving. Then I do things selflessly to make that person happy not *in order to* be loved but *because* I love and am loved. In a successful marriage the process is two-sided and works both ways. The result is that each person makes a continuous and growing contribution to the happiness of the other without expectation of return except in the deep, abiding joy that comes from giving. With commitment to this principle goes ego surrender. With ego surrender goes a reduction in the number and type of things that can be interpreted as threats to self or to marriage. To be loved is a great privilege. To be loved is also a great responsibility. When an individual allows himself to be loved, he holds in his hand the happiness, perhaps even the destiny, of another person.

THE MARRIAGE RATE

How Many Marry?

The marriage rate (the number per 1,000 population who marry in a given year) fluctuates from year to year. It decreases during a depression, for instance, and tends to increase at the beginning and at the end of a war. More than a year before the United States entered the Second World War, when Selective Service was under consideration, the marriage rate rose [see Figure 3.3]. After Pearl Harbor the rate reached another peak. Then, while millions of men of marriageable age were in military service, many of them abroad, the rate decreased. It rose again after the surrender of Germany and Japan, reaching an all-time high in 1946. After that it declined for a while only to rise again as the young people of the "baby boom" of the 1940s reached marriageable age. In 1970 the marriage rate reached 10.7, the highest postwar point reached since the late 1940s [U.S. Department of Health, Education, and Welfare, Sept. 21, 1971]. In 1971 the rate was 10.6 [U.S. Department of Health, Education, and Welfare, Aug. 30, 1972].

In 1971, there were 2,196,000 weddings [U.S. Department of Health, Education, and Welfare, Aug. 30, 1972]. This was the highest number in any year since 1946. It marked an increase for the thirteenth consecutive year, an increase due to the growth of the young marriageable population during the sixties. It is

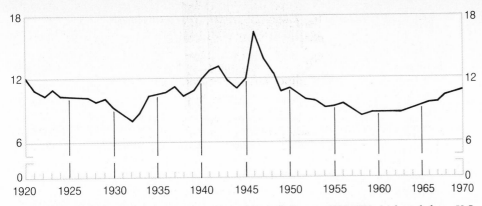

Figure 3.3 Marriage rate per 1,000 population: United States, 1920-1970. [Adapted from U.S. Department of Health, Education, and Welfare, Monthly Vital Statistics Report, *July 22, 1971].*

estimated that after 1975 the annual number of weddings will exceed 2,500,000 [*Statistical Bulletin,* June, 1970].

About 95 per cent of the population marry at least once. Of those who marry, about one-sixth marry twice and a small percentage three or more times [U.S. Bureau of the Census, September, 1972]. In 1970 there were more than 45 million married couples as compared with 40 million in 1960 [U.S. Bureau of the Census, July 13, 1970]. Such figures do not support the assertions of some persons that marriage is becoming passé. Carter and Glick [1970] point out that since 1940, "for every unit of increase" in the proportion of the population who are divorced "there have been five units of increase in the proportion married. With prospects already pointing to a mere 3 or 4 percent of persons who never marry, the main issue regarding bachelors and spinsters becomes increasingly one of when, rather than whether, they will eventually marry."

Age at First Marriage

When the ages at first marriage for all persons who marry in this country are arranged in order from lowest to highest, the middle, or median, age is about twenty-three for males and twenty plus for females. In other words, half the males who marry do so at age twenty-three or younger, and half the females who marry do so at about age twenty or younger. As indicated in Table 3.1, the median age at first marriage has shown an over-all decline since 1890, but there has been relatively little change in recent years. "Caution should be exercised in the interpretation of small changes" [U.S. Bureau of the Census, Jan. 25, 1967] because limitations of sampling and estimating techniques may produce errors larger than annual changes.

There must of necessity be some point past which the median age at first marriage cannot decline. It appears that that point may have been reached, but whether this is true remains to be seen.

Table 3.1. Median age at first marriage

YEAR	MALE	FEMALE	YEAR	MALE	FEMALE
1972	23.3	20.9	1956	22.5	20.1
1971	23.1	20.9	1955	22.6	20.2
1970	23.2	20.8	1954	23.0	20.3
1969	23.2	20.8	1953	22.8	20.2
1968	23.1	20.8	1952	23.0	20.2
1967	23.1	20.6	1951	22.9	20.4
1966	22.8	20.5	1950	22.8	20.3
1965	22.8	20.6	1949	22.7	20.3
1964	23.1	20.5	1948	23.3	20.4
1963	22.8	20.5	1947	23.7	20.5
1962	22.7	20.3	1940	24.3	21.5
1961	22.8	20.3	1930	24.3	21.3
1960	22.8	20.3	1920	24.6	21.2
1959	22.5	20.2	1910	25.1	21.6
1958	22.6	20.2	1900	25.9	21.9
1957	22.6	20.3	1890	26.1	22.0

Source: U.S. Bureau of the Census, November, 1972.

As indicated above, the median represents the midpoint of a distribution. Half the people who marry do so at an age lower than the median. It is inevitable, therefore, that the lower half of the distribution will overlap with the ages of high school and younger college students, many of whom are married. This very early marriage is not the result only of young people's immaturity, impetuousness, and caprice. It is also a reflection of tide-like social changes that are sweeping over Western culture.

The percentage of people who get divorces is approximately twice as high for males who marry at ages fourteen to twenty-one years and for females who marry at ages fourteen to nineteen years as for persons who marry at later ages [U.S. Bureau of the Census, Oct. 7, 1971]. In a study published in 1972 [U.S. Bureau of the Census, September, 1972] it was found that, for women whose first marriage had ended in divorce, the median age at first marriage was two years higher for those married once than for those married twice and three years higher for women married once than for those married three or more times. Generalizing, getting married below the median age seems to be more hazardous than getting married above the median age. However, such a generalization cannot be applied to individual cases. There are numerous factors involved in addition to age per se (for example, pregnancy, immaturity, rebellion against parents). Some individuals are more ready to marry at earlier ages than others are at later ages. Nevertheless, the fact remains that many very young people are ill-prepared to make the decisions and assume the responsibilities that getting married unavoidably entails.

SELECTED READINGS

Bartell, Gilbert D.: *Group Sex: A Scientist's Eyewitness Report on the American Way of Swinging*, Peter H. Wyden, Inc., New York, 1971. (Paperback.) A study of swinging and the people who swing.

Bernard, Jessie: *The Future of Marriage*, The World Publishing Company, New York, 1972. How each spouse sees marriage differently, the "housewife syndrome," "renewable marriages," changing concepts of extramarital relationships, communes and cooperative households, swinging, group marriage, serial polygamy, the women's liberation movement, the future of marriage.

DeLora, Joann S., and Jack R. DeLora (eds.): *Intimate Life Styles*, Goodyear Publishing Company, Inc., Pacific Palisades, Calif., 1972. (Paperback.) A report on interviews with swingers and how swinging affects the participants; discussion of communes and the people in them.

Fairfield, Richard: *Communes U.S.A.: A Personal Tour*, Penguin Books, Inc., Baltimore, 1972. (Paperback.) Author visited communes in Europe and the United States. Discusses various types of communes.

Fitzgerald, George R.: *Communes: Their Goals, Hopes, Problems*, Paulist Press, New York, 1971. (Paperback.) Discusses the people who join communes and why; hopes and objectives; life in communes; sex, marriage, family relationships, child rearing; strengths and weaknesses; future of communes.

Fromme, Allan: *The Ability to Love*, Farrar, Straus & Giroux, Inc., New York, 1965. This book "is designed to help you enhance your ability to love." Discusses what love is, the sexual expression of love, romantic love, ability and inability to love, love and marriage.

Hart, Harold H. (ed.): *Marriage: For and Against*, Hart Publishing Company, Inc., New York, 1972. (Paperback.) Fifteen views of marriage, its functions and dysfunctions in the United States; alternative life-styles; a criticism of Margaret Mead's "marriage in two steps."

Houriet, Robert: *Getting Back Together*, Coward, McCann & Geoghegan, Inc., New York, 1971. Author visited and reports on a variety of communal groups, including one group marriage.

Magoun, F. Alexander: *Love and Marriage*, rev. ed., Harper & Row, Publishers, Incorporated, New York, 1956. Definitions, nature, and expressions of love; choosing a marriage partner; emotional adjustment; in-laws.

Melville, Keith: *Communes and the Counter Culture: Origins, Theories, Styles of Life*, William Morrow & Company, Inc., New York, 1972. (Paperback.) Author "investigates the communal movement as a form of rebellion against the American middle class" and looks at American culture through the communes. Says that "valuable ideas are being tested in the communes."

Neubeck, Gerhard (ed.): *Extramarital Relations*, Prentice-Hall, Inc., Englewood Cliffs, N.J., 1969. (Paperback.) A symposium presenting various points of view.

Otto, Herbert A. (ed.): *The Family in Search of a Future*, Appleton Century Crofts, New York, 1970. (Paperback.) Alternatives to the American family structure, "progressive monogamy," group marriage, the tribal family, marriage in two steps.

In some cultures in which young persons have little to say about choice of marriage partner, the prerequisites for marriage may be relatively simple and consist chiefly of arrangements made by parents after the young persons have reached marriageable age, sometimes even earlier. In this country today, on the other hand, young persons have great freedom in selecting a marriage partner, and their choice is prefaced by an unprecedented freedom of contact and communication in premarital activities as well as an unprecedented lack of parental control of eventual choice.

Hence, questions such as the following arise: What is involved in making a choice of marriage partner? What may be said about choices involving special circumstances—for example, a difference in race or religious faith? How long should two people know each other before they make a choice? Why do some people make poor choices? What about engagements? What is the meaning of a wedding? What transitions are people called upon to make between singleness and marriage?

These and other questions we shall now consider.

part 2

MARRIAGE IN PREPARATION

Hank and I only met two weeks
ago . . . so, we'll see.

Being with Jael feels good.

Wendy and I have decided to live together.

For us being together is the most natural thing.

We've had a lot of hassles to work out—and they have.

Sometimes I just need a hug.

Sharing a front porch makes us all closer.

We wanted to be married in the house where we found each other.

Preparation through Choice

DATING

In this country today marriage is typically preceded by a period of dating during which young people presumably become acquainted and gradually narrow down the possible choices of marriage partners until a final choice is made. In spite of this, however, there is some tendency to divorce dating activities from preparation for marriage and to think of them as incidental and, to some extent, as ends in themselves. In dating, not only does each person "put his best foot forward" but often each sees everything, including the other person, through rose-tinted spectacles. There is much idealizing and wishful thinking. Sometimes, because of this, promises are made that cannot be kept, and expectations are built up that cannot be fulfilled. Marriage then seems like a "letdown." The reason is not that marriage is less interesting or exciting than dating but that in marriage there is inevitable impact with reality; and in dating reality may be temporarily obscured by imagination. Much is said about how people change, often for the worse, after they marry. The greater change is in dating. Before marriage the persons put on a false front, and each sees the other from a favorably biased point of view. Then, after the wedding, each returns to the real self and the spouse sees that self as it is, not as it was thought to be.

Much is written and said about failure in marriage. Relatively little is mentioned concerning dating failures except in connection with failure to date or to have a good time. Yet, in a significant sense, many "marriage failures" are in reality "dating failures." These include the failure to allow sufficient time to become acquainted, failure to make intelligent decisions, failure to correlate values with behavior, failure to make wise choices—they occur before the wedding but become apparent only afterward. Lack of recognition of this fact makes for a disregard of the problems and processes of dating and a somewhat uncritical attitude toward the activities involved. This tendency is accentuated by the fact that never before in history have so many persons dated so much through such a long period in their lives with so few recognizable guideposts, such ill-defined social patterns, such a wide variety of standards, and so few socially imposed controls.

The automobile, commercialized amusements, the growth of cities, the shrinkage of dwelling size, the increased use of apartments, the changed status of

four

women, new expectations with regard to marriage, greater freedom of association among young people, and a myriad of other factors are making dating something that it used not to be. As noted already, today there is less social and parental control; this fact puts a new responsibility upon the shoulders of the young persons making their own plans and choices.

We have reached a period of national development when the old is no longer adequate and the new is in the process of being established. There are confusion, transition, and lack of clear-cut definition. Standards are ill-defined. Young people must rely upon their own judgments, their own conclusions, their own definitions of objectives, and their own self-discipline more than before. Many of the admonitions of their parents are of the "don't" variety and have their roots in a cultural period somewhat different from the present. Survivors of a previous era cannot be expected to set the standards for this one. If modern young people want successful marriage, they will have to work for it and through intelligence adapt their dating to the exigencies of the day. Abandoning the old without substituting an improved new, rushing blindly through an open gate just because it is open and without ascertaining where it leads, cannot help playing a part in making the marriages of the future no better than those of the past.

Qualities of a Date

The qualities desirable in a husband or wife and those desirable in a date are not necessarily identical. In dating, some of the more superficial and inconsequential qualities play a prominent role. For example, a date is expected to be a free spender, but he need not be occupationally ambitious. In dating it is more important for a woman to be attractive than to know how to keep house. When students are asked to list the qualities that they like in a date, and those that they desire in a husband or a wife, heading the first list are likely to be such things as ability to carry on a conversation, good manners, consideration, pleasing personality. In the other list the qualities most frequently mentioned are likely to be such things as companionship, ability to provide, understanding, love, ambition, intelligence.

Somewhere in the welter of each individual's personal attributes are those traits that will contribute most abundantly to his success or failure in marriage. They may not be fully developed in the earlier part of the dating period. A youthful individual must be judged by his possibilities as well as by his achievements, provided that one does not confuse observation of possibilities with wishful thinking and the other person does not expect possibilities to substitute permanently for actualities. Like saplings, the traits and potentialities of a husband or wife may be partially shaded and hidden by the already grown trees and underbrush of more readily apparent traits of dates. To seek them out and clear the land around them so that one may see the nature of the growth that will form the new forest, as well as the components of the present one, is the process of intelligent choice of a marriage partner.

Typically, people do not marry until they have dated each other for a more or less extended period. This would suggest that, as dating progresses and it becomes increasingly marriage-oriented, the standard of what constitutes desirable traits in a date may well be reappraised. An individual may consciously begin to ignore those aspects of our dating system that are temporary and unrelated to successful marriage and begin to give more attention to those qualities of a date and those aspects of our dating system that are related to successful marriage. In this way a person may have a more functional dating experience. When the need for such a transition is not recognized, an individual may base his choice of marriage partner on an inappropriate set of qualities.

LENGTH OF ACQUAINTANCE

How long should two people know each other before they marry? There is a relationship between length of acquaintance and success in marriage, longer periods of association being related to more successful marital adjustment. There is a qualitative as well as a quantitative aspect to this matter, however. It is not only how long but how well a couple have known each other.

When two individuals marry after a relatively brief acquaintance, they learn things about each other after the wedding that they might better have learned before. They learn them in a new atmosphere with a different "freedom" of choice. There is greater pressure toward either acceptance or conflict. They may be called upon to revise their expectations regarding one another, especially with respect to each person's role in marriage. Inability to revise such expectations and to accept the other person as he is rather than as he was thought to be is one of the factors commonly contributing to marital failure. Putting it another way, they marry before they know each other well enough to reject each other as marriage partners.

Although no one can say with any reasonable degree of definiteness precisely how long acquaintance should be, of some cases it may be said with certainty that the period is too brief. In student groups, instances of whirlwind romances continually come to light. The following cases illustrate this point. A couple had a "blind date" on June 9. On June 16 the man proposed marriage; on June 22 the woman talked with a counselor, wondering whether she should marry immediately. In another instance a woman's parents arranged to have her meet a man of whom they strongly approved. With some reluctance she had a date with him. She found that she liked him better than she had anticipated. On their fourth date he gave her a ring. The wedding followed shortly thereafter.

At a dance two students met for the first time. The man had had a quarrel with his fiancée on the evening of the dance. A few days before, the woman had had a serious quarrel with her fiancé. After the dance some of the students decided to go to a nearby restaurant. By the time this couple arrived at the restaurant they were married. They had gotten the license clerk out of bed to get a license and a jeweler out of bed to purchase a ring. A woman whom they had taken along as a witness remonstrated with them, and the jeweler tried to dissuade them. But the bridegroom was insistent, and they married after only about three hours' acquaintance. They lived together several years, had two children, and were then divorced. In such cases it is obvious that the period of acquaintance was too brief before commitments were made.

Occasionally, one of these abbreviated acquaintances prefaces successful marriage because the two persons are highly compatible and their relationship expands and deepens after the wedding. But the chance element is greatly increased, and they are successful in spite of, not because of, the brief acquaintance. Their rare experience is a very precarious basis upon which to rationalize one's own desire for haste.

Let us perform an imaginary experiment. We shall choose at random 1,000 college men and 1,000 college women, none of whom is married. We shall blindfold these 2,000 individuals and let them mill about in a large enclosure. At a given signal they will stand and take off their blindfolds. Then each man will marry the woman standing nearest his right hand. It is highly probable that in this group of a thousand marriages there would be some successful, just by chance. There would be persons who married without ever having seen each other before but who, nevertheless, would have fallen in love and married if they had met. By chance some individuals would make a good "choice" of marriage partner. How many people, however, would want to acquire a spouse by such a process? They would argue that the chances were against a good choice and that it was a mistake to give too much weight to the exceptions. Yet when similar exceptions occur in day-to-day life, some persons use them as a basis for broad generalizations, unfounded assumptions, and wishful thinking.

A type of acquaintance that is frequently deceiving because it gives a superficial appearance of sufficient length is that which depends largely upon correspondence. The following is a typical example. (Similar cases may readily be discovered in any school in which a large proportion of students are living away from home.) On a trip in April the woman in this case met a man with whom she spent about two days. After separating, they corresponded for some fifteen months. During that period their letters became more personal and amorous until the couple thought they had fallen in love. By correspondence, too, they became engaged. In one way they had known each other for more than a year. In another way their acquaintance was of only two days' duration. When the man spent two weeks at the woman's home the next summer, they found that they scarcely knew each other. Their letters had completely misled them. Before the man departed, they had broken their engagement.

A variation of this type of acquaintance is the one in which the couple are separated most of the time and see each other only during brief vacation periods, when there is a holiday atmosphere. Each "puts his best foot forward," problem "solving" is limited to discussion, and the objective is to have as good a time as possible in the few days available. In one case, for example, the couple were together for a total of only forty to fifty days in four years, never more than three days at one time. Yet they planned to marry soon.

Another type, deceiving because it gives a superficial appearance of sufficient length, is that which begins relatively early in life. For example, a student says, "I have known her for five years and gone with her for three. That ought to be long enough." But they are both eighteen years old. Thus, they became acquainted when they were thirteen and started dating each other when they were fifteen. Certainly this five-year period should not be given the same weight as the period, say, from eighteen to twenty-three.

CHOOSING A MARRIAGE PARTNER

A wise choice is "half the battle." One person cannot tell another whom to choose or even how to choose. But the importance of choice can hardly be over-emphasized. Of all the choices an individual is called upon to make, the choice or lack of choice of marriage partner can go as far as any, and farther than most, toward determining the quality of his life. It is safer and easier to choose well than to attempt to alter personalities after the wedding. It is better to match than to patch. Change may occur through experience, self-effort, or the influence of one's spouse; but it can take place only on the foundation of personality traits present before it began.

Personality traits are types or aspects of behavior. They are abstractions deduced from observation of concrete, overt acts. Traits themselves have no actual existence within an individual. His behavior does not express his traits; his behavior *is* his traits. Changing those traits is not a process like that of changing one's clothes, taking off one garment and putting on another. It is, rather, a process of change in behavior, which entails the development of new habit patterns. As a rule people do not like to be changed, especially when the suggested alteration implies inferiority, and they are made the subject of a reform program concocted by someone else.

Each of a person's traits is relative to all others and is manifested against the background of his total personality. None ever stands alone, isolated from the rest of the individual. Each is also relative to the attitude of every individual who makes a judgment of it. Besides, traits are not always constant. A person may exhibit a given trait under one set of circumstances but not under another. He may, for example, be honest when he is trusted but dishonest when subjected to suspicion. He may control his temper at home but lose it on the golf course.

The same trait may appear in different light as circumstances vary. If a man has fought his way to the top in business, we must expect him to be aggressive. Aggression, however, is more acceptable at a meeting of the board of directors than at the family dinner table. Absorption in his work may be commendable in a man; but if he cannot escape it long enough to spend some time with his wife, it becomes an annoyance rather than a virtue. An individual cannot be two personalities simultaneously—one with his family, another with other persons. If he seems to be so dually constituted, it is because the traits in his personality appear different under different circumstances.

Qualities of a Marriage Partner

It would be an interesting and perhaps provocative exercise to attempt to list all the qualities desirable in a marriage partner. The end result would probably be an inventory of all the virtues and some of the vices, depending upon one's point of view, of which the human race is capable. Our difficulty in presenting such a list would be that we should be attempting to catalogue the desirable traits to be found in marriage partners in general. Actually, there is no such thing as a generalized husband or wife; there is only some particular woman's husband, some particular man's wife. It is useless to talk about the qualities of a spouse until we answer the question, "Whose spouse?" The qualities held to be desirable are variable and depend upon the personality and expectations of the individual making the choice. Qualities are not absolutely desirable or undesirable. They are relatively so and are weighted according to the attitudes of the maker of the list.

One author asked a thousand couples to state types of behavior that they felt contributed to the success or failure of their marriages. In the published list of those items most frequently mentioned are to be found such things as "She always has meals on time. She sews very well. She always has clean clothes for me to wear. She washes my back. He helps me with the dishes. He loves nature. He does not overtell old jokes. He gladly rubs my back." The list contains many items more commonly desirable than the ones quoted here. These are cited to show how weighted by individual points of view the qualities considered desirable in a husband or wife may become. It is apparent at a glance that for one man whose marital happiness rests to an appreciable degree on the washing of his back there must be thousands who are quite content to make their toilet single-handed.

It is suggested, therefore, that the reader do the following: Under each pair of vertical bars in the chart in Figure 4.1 write a personal trait or aspect of behavior that you consider important in a marriage partner. Shade in the left bar to indicate the degree that represents you, the right bar to indicate the degree that represents the person being considered, as in the example at the left. How do you compare with respect to the most important considerations?

Choice is two-sided, and an individual should not expect his choice of partner so to counterbalance his own shortcomings that he interprets preparation for marriage only in terms of search, to the exclusion of self-improvement. The better choice one is, the better choice he can make. The use of personality rating scales may be helpful if administered and interpreted by an expert, but they are not to be used indiscriminately by amateurs.

In choosing a marriage partner further considerations are also important, such as the following: (1) The type of person one wants. This person may be either a reflection of an ideal or the individual to whom one has already developed an emotional attachment. (2) The type of person one needs—that is, the person one can best get along with, who will complement one's own personality, who will afford emotional and economic security, to whose life one can make a contribution, and with whom one can maintain a desirable standard of living and life-style. (3) The type of person one is likely to be able to get. In this connection we are making no implication of superiority or inferiority but only of difference, and we do not mean that one's standards should be low. Individuals who fall in love with married or engaged persons, who in hero-worshipping fashion fill their daydreams with visions of movie stars or other celebrities to the exclusion of more mundane

Trait
x

Figure 4.1

contacts, who seek to attract persons who are obviously not interested in them, who refuse to consider any but a very wealthy person—these and numerous others are thinking only in terms of what they want and overlooking the important question of what they are probably able to get. One person cannot choose another unless that other person is available. Availability is determined not only by existence, proximity, and acquaintance but also by interest in and inclination toward the individual hoping to make the choice. There must be reciprocal attraction, which in its turn increases attractiveness. One cannot make a choice without simultaneously being a choice.

A good choice may be "half the battle," but it is only half; it is the beginning, not the end, of marital adjustment. The situation is not dissimilar to that found in choosing an occupation. No matter how wise one may be in making an occupational choice, no matter how well he is adapted or prepared, there still remain many adjustments to be made and much work to be done before success in that occupation is achieved.

Choice involves not only the personality of the other person but also things associated with him, the circumstances under which the couple will live, the demands of the husband's or wife's occupation, the place of residence, and the type of in-laws. This is in some ways more true of a woman's choice of husband than of a man's choice of wife, because, probably in the majority of cases, even today when rapid social change is occurring, the nature of the husband's occupation, the "long arm of the job," reaches so far into their family life and plays such a large part in determining the wife's role and the kind of personal qualities she needs to fulfill that role successfully. The husband's occupation also plays a large part in determining the couple's place of residence and status in the community. There is a tendency for the wife to assume the social position of the husband rather than vice versa. The divorce rate varies according to occupation, tending to be higher for men who are away from home a good part of the time and lower for men whose occupations permit them to spend more time with their wives. In thinking of marriage to a particular man, any woman would find it well worth while to make a careful analysis of the circumstances under which she would live and the demands that would be made upon her and then frankly to ask and sincerely answer the questions, "Can I adapt myself? Have I the personal equipment to succeed under these circumstances? Will I be happy in this type of life twenty years after my wedding?" A man, thinking of the demands that his occupation would put upon a wife, would do well to ask himself whether a particular woman was prepared to meet those demands successfully.

When a person chooses a marriage partner, he chooses "an area of operation." This "area of operation" defines, at least in part, the opportunities that will be presented by, and the limitations that will be imposed upon, his marriage. In a sense, he puts himself in the position of a creative artist. Through what steps does such a person go in creating a work of art? First, he gets an idea. Second, he chooses a medium of expression by means of which he can express the idea. Third, he uses the medium to create the work of art. Once he has chosen his medium of expression, he has the potential for creativity which his material affords. But he is also limited by the limitations of his medium. No matter how great the artist's skill, no matter how far-reaching his vision, no matter how penetrating his insight, no matter how high his hopes, he still cannot make wood do the work of stone or make paint behave like clay. In like manner an individual approaching marriage goes through several steps. First, he gets the idea—marriage. Second, he chooses the person, his medium of expression, through whom and with whom he will work out in reality his idea of marriage. This person will provide the marriage with certain potential for success. He will also impose upon the marriage certain limitations depending upon his personality and concept of the relationship. The individual choosing a marriage partner, like the artist, cannot make wood do the work of stone or make paint behave like clay. He is limited by the limitations of his material. Naturally, this is two-sided, and the marriage represents a combination of the "pluses" and "minuses" of the two parties.

"Limited by the limitations of the material" becomes clear when, for example, there is a discrepancy between actual role and expected role. If a man wants his wife to be very domestic but marries a woman who neglects homemaking because of her career interests, if a woman wants a husband interested in participating in shared family recreation but marries a man who prefers strictly masculine pastimes "with the boys," if a woman expects a husband to participate in housekeeping and marries a man who shuns "woman's work," there is almost sure to be antagonism. Conflict in marriage is normal. In some marriages, of course, there is more than in others. Some conflicts are at least hypothetically resolvable. For example, a couple might resolve conflict over money by earning more, spending less, or making alterations in the handling of funds. On the other hand, conflict growing out of a difference in religious faith, moral standards, age, or cultural background may prove to be unyielding. When an individual chooses a marriage partner, to a considerable degree he chooses the conflicts that his marriage will entail.

One particular situation in which an individual is "limited by the limitations of the material" is that in which the person chosen is a psychopathic personality (psychopath, sociopath). Such a situation may approach as closely as any known to a completely one-sided relationship, a marriage doomed from the beginning. The possible choice involved in such a situation will bear careful thought, especially in those cases in which the individuals have known each other only a relatively brief time and in only limited circumstances.

The psychopath is more easily discussed than diagnosed in advance, and, of course, there are varying degrees of psychopathology, and not all psychopaths exhibit all the characteristics described in the following general statement. In retrospect the psychopathic personality may readily be distinguished. What makes him such a misleading choice as marriage partner is his "false front." He may be very intelligent. He may exhibit superficial charm and savoir faire. He may be attractive in appearance, a generous spender, a courteous guest, a glib conversationalist, and an affable companion. In reality, he is unable to understand human relationships. Insight into self and others is lacking. He cannot learn the difference between moral and immoral, lawful and unlawful, or socially accepted and socially disapproved behavior. He lacks ambition, industriousness, foresight, self-discipline, and persistence in what he undertakes. He does not have the ability to follow a carefully thought-out life plan. He makes the same errors and has the same failures again and again. He feels no regret, remorse, or shame for what he does to hurt others. He uses others for his own ends and then wonders why they resent being used, as if he had done nothing blameworthy. He tells untruths, sometimes apparently without realizing that they are untruths (the so-called "pathological liar"), at other times with full awareness that they are untruths but with no compunction about telling them anyway. Although he may be brilliant academically, he does not learn by experience. He is unreliable, untrustworthy, egocentric, unresponsive to personal feelings, and excessively pleasure-seeking. His sex life tends to be impersonal, trivial, and poorly integrated. He is incapable of love.

The psychopathic personality is only incompletely understood, and causation is obscure. There is no known "cure." An individual who marries such a person may have the impression at the time of the wedding that the chosen one is just what he had been seeking and had always hoped for, only to discover soon after the wedding that the other individual had "put on an act" in order to get married and is incapable of fitting into the role expected. Because there are such individuals—more than one would like to think—and because they are chosen as marriage partners (only to make marital adjustment impossible no matter how hard the other person tries), allowing time for adequate acquaintance before the wedding is strongly indicated. (For a thorough discussion of the psychopathic personality see Cleckley, 1964.)

Background Factors

Undoubtedly, factors in an individual's background play a significant part in making him what he is. Whether he comes from a happy or an unhappy home; his relationship to his parents, and their treatment of him as a child; whether he developed relative independence or emotional overattachment to his parents; the degree of his socialization, his sibling relationships, and what he learned in his early years regarding human sexuality—factors such as these affect the development of his personality, and this in turn makes him a relatively good or a relatively poor "marriage risk." Each such factor needs to be understood and evaluated in each individual. Broad generalizations are of little help except in calling attention to the importance of such factors. Research studies are, of necessity, based upon groups (samples). Their findings give a picture of a group but may not apply with equal vigor to each individual in the group. Caution in interpretation is, therefore, indicated.

If, for example, we studied a thousand persons who came from very happy home backgrounds, and another thousand who came from very unhappy home backgrounds, we should find more unsuccessful marriages among the second group than among the first group. But we should also find some unsuccessful marriages among persons coming from happy backgrounds and some successful ones among persons coming from very unhappy backgrounds. Whether a given individual being considered as a marriage partner falls into the majority or the minority of either group can be ascertained only by understanding that individual. Hence, background factors may be given attention but need not be considered deterministic in making a final choice.

Sexual Attraction

Sexual attraction is naturally important in choosing a marriage partner. There are exceptions, of course, as in the case of two very old persons, but in choices made by persons of student age it may not safely be disregarded. Students sometimes speak of "platonic love." Nevertheless, sexual attraction is very obtrusive, overshadowing other considerations more often than being overshadowed by them. In choosing a marriage partner, one cannot depend upon sex appeal alone or too much or for too long. There are so many aspects of marriage besides the sexual, and it is important that perspective not be lost. A couple are married for 168 hours per week. If they spent 7 of these hours in specific sexual activity, this would probably be above average. This would leave them 161 hours per week for other-than-sexual activities. What they do during these 161 hours is as important as what they do in the other 7.

American culture today is so permeated with sex—activity, discussion, pictorial representation—that sex is being made more prominent outside of marriage than it actually is in marriage. This does not mean that sex is less important in marriage than out of marriage. It means only that most married persons consider it one of several important aspects of their total relationship. Outside of marriage, sex is often made to seem the primary aspect of a couple's relationship, with other aspects subordinated to it; but there is a difference between prominence and importance.

Physical Health

Health is an important consideration. Although one may not choose another *because* of a healthy body, he may refrain from choosing someone because of lack of health. At any rate it is important for both persons to know what they will have to face in marriage so far as health is concerned. For this reason each one may have a premarital medical examination more extensive than that required by state law. There are six functions of such an examination: (1) to ascertain the state of general health and to point out, if necessary, any symptoms that might affect the couple's choice or their future conjugal relationship; (2) to discover details of anatomy that might affect the couple's sexual adjustment; (3) to discover, if possible, any anatomical characteristics that would make it inadvisable for the woman to become pregnant; (4) to test for the presence or absence of the Rh factor in the couple's blood; (5) to give the couple an opportunity to talk over their marriage and their initiation into it with the physician and to have questions answered; (6) to permit the couple to get advice, if they so desire, on some method of controlling conception that would be acceptable to them. Criteria for an adequate premarital examination are indicated in Figure 4.2.

The purpose of the premarital medical examination is not to ascertain whether the couple can have children. The physician may make observations that suggest possible relative infertility, but many of the conditions contributing to infertility are not taken into account in the premarital medical examination at all. At the present stage of knowledge there is no way that a physician can tell that a given couple can have a child, unless, of course, they have already had one. Nor is the purpose of the medical examination—as is often supposed—entirely negative, that is, to prevent the marriage of the unfit and perhaps to make it advisable for two persons who are in love to relinquish the idea of marrying. Its chief purpose is to assist marriage in getting a better start and to enable couples to make the best possible adjustment.

Hereditary Traits

In choosing a marriage partner, one chooses not only an individual and his relatives but also, in a sense, his more distant ancestors in so far as he exhibits hereditary traits or carries the determiners of them with the possibility of passing them on to his children. Consequently, the question of heredity is important. This matter not infrequently comes to the attention of the counselor via the worries of some person in love who is concerned about the advisability of marriage or parenthood, because of either his own hereditary constitution or that of the other person.

Reliable data on human heredity are not so plentiful as one might wish. Those that are most uncontestable apply to such traits as eye color, skin color, supernumerary fingers or toes. The typical person, however, wants to know about the inheritance of such things as insanity, feeble-mindedness, cancer, tuberculosis, syphilis, and criminality. Sometimes the data are conclusive, sometimes inconclusive. There are frequent apparent exceptions. The whole matter of human heredity is more complex and less well understood than the arithmetic ratios of coat type in guinea pigs or color in peas, often employed to illustrate Mendelian laws to the beginning student, might lead one to suppose. So many human "traits" are not simple. They are complex combinations of traits that

A

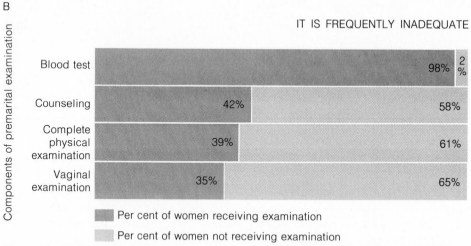

Complete physical examination:
  General medical history
  Routine studies including chest X-ray,
  blood tests, and urinalysis
  Examination of heart, lungs, head, neck,
  breasts, abdomen, and extremities

Pelvic examination:
  Assurance that genitalia and reproductive
  potential are normal
  Evaluation of rigidity of hymen; hymenal
  dilatation if necessary and desired
  Visualization of cervix and Papanicolaou smear
  Palpation of uterus, adnexa, and cul-de-sac
  Contraceptive advice and instruction, when
  desired

Psychosexual and marital counseling:
  Discussion of possible fears, anxieties,
  and guilt feelings associated with coitus
  Discussion of realistic expectations of
  sexual responses of each partner
  Discussion of personal adjustments in
  marriage and avoidance of some of the pitfalls

B

IT IS FREQUENTLY INADEQUATE

Components of premarital examination

Blood test	98%	2%
Counseling	42%	58%
Complete physical examination	39%	61%
Vaginal examination	35%	65%

▓ Per cent of women receiving examination

░ Per cent of women not receiving examination

Figure 4.2 (A) What should be included in the premarital examination; (B) what actually was included in the premarital examination among a group of 2,000 women. [Sylvester W. Trythall, "The Premarital Law," Journal of the American Medical Association, vol. 187, no. 12, pp. 900–903, March 21, 1964.]

result from multiple hereditary determiners acting together, and they are eventually manifested in a social environment. The problem is so complicated and ramifies in so many directions that in this book we can do no more than touch upon a few broad generalizations and then make a suggestion.

Although some investigators are reopening the question of the inheritance of acquired traits, for our purpose we may assume that such traits are not inherited. In order to be inheritable a trait must be carried in the genes. If an external influence, such as X ray, affects the genes of a given individual, mutations may be produced and the traits of his offspring affected. External influences that affect only the body tissues of an individual do not affect inheritable traits.

Hereditary traits and congenital traits are often confused. Hereditary traits are those produced by factors carried in the genes. Congenital traits are those present at, or immediately following, birth, whether or not they are inherited. "Hereditary" refers to causation. "Congenital" refers to time. This distinction is important because it is sometimes assumed that, because a trait is present at birth, or occurs soon after birth, it must be inherited. For example, a student is worried because his fiancée's brother is mentally retarded. Inquiry reveals that the retardation is due to a birth injury and is, therefore, not inheritable.

Hereditary traits are passed down to us not only from our immediate ancestors but from all our ancestors. Many of us would probably find wormy fruit on our family trees if we examined them carefully and traced back far enough. The purpose in saying this is not to minimize the importance of heredity or to pass lightly over those cases in which it is a serious consideration with regard to a given marriage. Our purpose is rather to remove some of the unnecessary fears with which persons looking forward to marriage are sometimes plagued.

In deciding whether or not to marry an individual in whose family line there are known to be defects which may possibly be inheritable, or in case there are such defects in one's own line, a distinction may be drawn between the advisability of marrying and the advisability of having children. If the individual with whom marriage is contemplated is himself free of the defect, then marriage may be safely planned. If the individual manifests the defect, then the decision may be made with this knowledge in mind. If he does not manifest it but there is reason to believe that he carries it in his genes and may pass it on to his children, then marriage may occur, with the possibility of taking adequate steps to prevent conception.

In any case, the solution to the problem lies in knowledge and intelligent planning, not in worry. Worry over the inheritance of defects sometimes causes more damage than the defects themselves. It is conceivable that worry might precipitate mental illness which is not inherited and which the individual would not have acquired if he had not worried about inheriting it. Worry that a defect will be exhibited by one's children often leads to expecting that it will be manifested and to such continual "reading into" the child's behavior that the environmental stage is set for his developing the trait one hopes he will avoid.

If there is reason to believe that one party has in his family line a questionable hereditary trait that might make marriage or parenthood inadvisable, there are four things to be done before a final decision is made. (1) Gather all available information about the individual's background. (2) Submit the data to the best authority available, telling the whole truth in so far as this is possible. Students are especially fortunate in this connection because they may submit the data to an instructor in a marriage course, in biology, in genetics, or in psychology, or to a college physician who is likely either to know the answer himself or to know where it can be found if it is known at all. In some cases, such as with certain types of mental deficiency, our knowledge is such that the couple may be assured that the likelihood of their children's inheriting the trait is no greater than that of children in general. In other cases a less favorable answer would have to be given, but it could be given with reassurance. In still other cases, the possibilities are not so clear-cut, so it would be advisable to get the judgment of more than one expert. (3) Draw a careful distinction between traits that would make marriage inadvisable and those that would make parenthood inadvisable. (4) When the judgment of the experts has been communicated to the couple and accepted by them, the couple should consider it carefully, to be sure that they understand it and all its possible implications and ramifications, then draw their own conclusion, make a plan for the future, adhere to it, and stop worrying.

Common Interests

In one sense the term *common interests* connotes such things as hobbies; interest in sports; and taste in music, art, and drama. It is important that the couple have some such interests in common. It is also important that they have individual interests. In addition, each person needs to have understanding of, tolerance of, and appreciation for, the other person's interests, that is, "an interest in the other's interests." It is desirable that each one's interests be compatible with and acceptable to the other. When such interests are not mutually acceptable, they may wedge a couple apart instead of drawing them together. A hobby may be an intruder instead of a binder.

The term *common interests* also connotes common purposes and sense of purpose, common goals, similar ideas concerning the couple's activities, similar expectations concerning the role of each, similar interpretations of life in general and of their own life-style, similar attitudes toward children, home, religion, values, sex, people, money, and property. It is apparent without explanation how significant such common interests are in marriage. Yet many young people assume that recreational interests are the only common interests they need.

The more enduring common interests are, the more important they are likely to be in marriage. Pursuit of them must also be sincere and well founded. Sometimes, in order to advance the courtship process, one individual will superficially take up the interests of the other, only to drop them again after the wedding and thereby dissolve what the other person had assumed would be a bond between them. This temporary pursuit of an interest is not always insincere, as the individual may confuse interest in the other person with interest in what that person does. One of the best tests of supposedly common interests is to compare them in retrospect—that is, before the two individuals met, as well as after. Common dislikes as well as common likes may draw a couple together, but dislikes are too negative to take the place of common interests in marriage.

Standards of Behavior

It is important to consider a disparity in standards of behavior because it indicates a difference in attitude toward something that at least one of the couple considers a value. Difference in attitude is often accompanied by difference in behavior, and this may be fertile soil in which to grow the seeds of friction.

Honesty, broadly interpreted, connotes not only truth telling and refraining from stealing and cheating but also integrity, the degree to which an individual "holds together." In turn this connotes a predictability that is important in the establishment of enduring interpersonal relationships. Given a set of circumstances, one can be confident of what an honest person will do. On the other hand, the behavior of a dishonest person is shifty because it rests not on oneness of personality but on multiplicity, depending on whim, selfish interest, the misleading of others, shady deals, partial truths, broken promises, and lack of correlation between what is affirmed and what is done.

In contemplating a marriage in which there is a difference in standards of conduct, an individual might well answer one important question to his own satisfaction: What does this difference mean to me? If he lets judgment become clouded by romance, he may make an unwise choice that will not stand the test of time. If he rests his decision on a verbal promise to reform made in response to a request to change or an expression of disapproval, when the other person's intent is merely to remove a barrier to getting married, his decision may be precarious indeed. If he depends upon reforming the other person after marriage, he is falling into the trap of wishful thinking. It often happens that the person with the lower standard pulls the other down rather than that the person with the higher standard raises the other.

Economic Elements in Selection of a Partner

At no known period in history, among no known people, has marriage succeeded without some degree of cooperation, through division of labor by sex, in the maintenance of a way of life. In present-day United States this involves the husband's occupation and earning, the wife's homemaking, and sometimes her earning as well. But between earning and the maintenance of a way of life there is the intermediate step of spending. This involves a complex of attitudes, objectives, knowledge, choices, and activities that do not come naturally to a young couple when they fall in love and contemplate marriage. The effective handling of this intermediate step requires the development and focusing of skills and processes on objectives that have been mutually agreed upon. Hence it would seem appropriate for two individuals considering each other as possible marriage partners to begin to explore this intermediate zone together.

Such exploration might include a consideration of such questions as the following: At the time of marriage will the man's income be sufficient to maintain a home and provide for the arrival of a possible child? If not, how will his income be supplemented? Will the woman continue employment? Would she be able to do so if she became pregnant? Will they receive a subsidy from their parents? Is the man interested in, and does he have aptitude for, the occupation which he has chosen? Is he industrious and ambitious? Does the woman have the interest and skills necessary for effective homemaking? How important do the couple consider homemaking? How do the two persons use their present incomes? For what does each spend beyond necessities? Do they manage to save anything? Is either wasteful? Do they budget their money and stay within the budget? Do they spend without plan until their money is exhausted and then borrow, go into debt, or appeal to their parents? Do they exhibit similar degrees of generosity? What is their attitude toward home ownership? Toward cars? Toward insurance? Toward installment buying? Do they agree on how and by whom the family income will be handled? Do they know how to shop wisely? If they have had ample allowances from parents, would they be prepared to take a possible step down in their standard of living when they marry? Have they worked out trial budgets based on realistically projected family income and a realistic understanding of the cost of living? If in attempting to do so they ran into snags, did this motivate them to get further information or to sidestep the problem and say, "We'll find a way. We'll cross that bridge when we come to it"?

"Likes" and "Opposites"

Proverbially, "Likes repel, opposites attract," as if human beings were the poles of a magnet and their behavior were governed by relatively simple forces. Such a broad generalization might easily be carried to ridiculous extremes. If opposites attract, then the intelligent should marry morons, large persons should marry small ones, and college students should marry illiterates. If likes repel, similar interests, values, temperaments, or backgrounds would produce discord rather than harmony. Husband and wife should have complementary rather than clashing characteristics, enough similarity to be mutually agreeable and enough dissimilarity to be mutually stimulating. Even this is a broad generalization. In the last analysis all depends upon the two personalities involved. In some cases likes, in others unlikes, have happy marriages.

There are combinations of traits, however, that merit caution. We may mention a few by way of illustration. A meticulously neat individual and one who carelessly leaves his clothes and other things lying about, a person who is punctual and one who disregards time, two individuals whose tempo of life is different, a person who pays particular attention to manners and one whose manners are crude, a person who is affectionate and one who does not like to touch or be touched, a person who is interested in acquiring things and one who would like to sacrifice things for travel and states of mind, an individual whose rhythm of life makes him nocturnal and one whose rhythm makes him diurnal, one who is gregarious and one who does not like to be with groups of people, a very modest individual and one who is uninhibited, a person with a sense of humor and one lacking it, a conventional individual and one inclined to be conspicuously unconventional, an individual who has enthusiasm for living and one who is bored with life, an optimistic person and a cynic, an individual who functions more effectively under pressure and one who "goes to pieces" under stress, a sexually "warm" and responsive person and one who is sexually "cold" and unresponsive—such combinations can, of course, be successful when the differences are accepted or are offset by other traits and circumstances, but such combinations can also contribute to perennial conflict, especially when the differences crystallize as focal points of irritation.

With human nature so variable and so complex and with the final judgment to be made by the reader anyway, we might never strike upon exactly the combination of traits that is in his mind as he thinks of his possible union with some particular person. We cannot even go so far as to say that it is always essential that the husband be masculine and the wife feminine, although this is the most commonly accepted and expected type of "opposites" that attract. It is better to suggest to the reader that he make his own careful analysis than to give him the impression that a short list of generalizations will pigeonhole his particular problem and yield a ready-made judgment. Furthermore, it is not only the difference or similarity in one or a few particular traits that counts but all the traits of each person, the constellation of traits which constitutes his total personality. A sense of humor may offset a quick temper; a lovable disposition may counteract the impracticality of the dreamer.

Choosing a Partner Like One's Parent

Not uncommon is a tendency to seek a marriage partner like one's father or mother, as the case may be, the parent of opposite sex having been an adolescent ideal. It may be well to desire that a husband or a wife possess some of the admirable qualities of one's parent, and the parent's qualities may form a good basis upon which to found an ideal that will grow as time goes on. But to set up one's parent as an ideal and to insist that one's spouse conform is to establish an impossible expectation and to set an unattainable goal, for several reasons. There are no two persons exactly alike. Parents and future spouse were born in different cultural eras. Typically, the former are also some twenty to thirty years ahead in their development. Twenty-five years from now one's husband or wife may be more like one's father or mother, but at the moment it is impossible to eradicate the age difference. Furthermore, an individual does not know firsthand what his parent was like when the parent was the age of the future spouse. Because parents love one another and have a happy marriage does not prove that the child could duplicate their experience with one of them. In order to live with one of the parents as the other does, the child would have to be that parent rather than himself. In many cases, it is not the actual qualities of the real person that are set up as the standard but rather the idealized image of the parent. Actually, not even the individual himself completely attains this unreal standard. Naturally, then, no other person could be expected to attain it.

If a child's relationship with the parent of opposite sex has been unpleasant, he may seek a marriage partner having quite different qualities. This is understandable and not unreasonable, as long as he allows for difference of degree in various personality traits and realizes that traits may be exhibited differently under varying circumstances, judges by the whole individual, and knows at least in part which of his parent's traits were present at the time of marriage and which developed because of the marital situation.

REASONS FOR POOR CHOICE OF MARRIAGE PARTNER

Some of the factors making for poor choice of marriage partner have already been implied. Confusing infatuation with love; hoping to reform the other party; judging by too few qualities; marrying before tastes and attitudes are well developed; overemphasizing money; acting under the stimulus of rebound, spite, habit, pity, and similar attitudes—these obviously contribute to errors in judgment. Among other factors are those that follow.

Some persons make a poor choice of partner because they marry in haste—to repent at leisure and perhaps in misery. Less care and intelligence may be exhibited in choosing a husband or a wife than in choosing an occupation, registering for courses, or even selecting new garments. Marrying the first person who is willing, without waiting for experience broad enough to give ground for comparison and contrast, sometimes makes for poor choice. This does not mean that the first person is invariably a poor choice. It suggests only the exercise of caution and judgment and a clear understanding of the fact that it is false to assume that, if the first person is not accepted, there will be no other.

There are individuals who are not sufficiently conversant with the requirements of marriage. They do not understand what marriage involves, do not realize that it is a most intimate relationship and that there are responsibilities as well as pleasures. Some go so far as to think only up to, rather than beyond, the wedding or even to think of marriage as if it were a lifelong date. Some persons gloss over problems or irritating personality traits because they do not recognize the difference in the time element in dating as compared with marriage. Suppose, for example, a couple have personality traits that cause them to annoy one another. In dating, they are aware of this annoyance; but dates are limited in time, and after each date there comes a period of temporary separation, after which another date is voluntary. In marriage there is no similar separation with similarly voluntary reunion; therefore there is no respite from the annoyance, and repetition of the annoyance is anticipated as inescapable. Also, because of the nature of marriage and attitudes toward it as compared with dating, a greater feeling of "ought" is read into the behavior of the marriage partner—"She ought not do this to me, because I'm her husband"—and this makes the annoyance two-pronged: there is the annoyance produced by the trait itself plus the annoyance produced by her continuing to do it when she "ought" not do so. The result is that the annoyance tends to be cumulative unless, in time, the couple immunize themselves against it. A personality trait that is annoying may be like a pebble in one's shoe. If you walk across the room with a pebble in your shoe, you will notice it, but it will not be either excessively painful or injurious. If, however, you walk 20 miles with the same pebble in the same shoe, at the end of your trip you will have either an open wound or a callus. Dating is like walking across the room. Marriage is like taking a 20-mile hike.

Marrying to please one's family rather than oneself is risky, since the individual rather than the family has to live with the person chosen. In some cultures where more emphasis is put upon institutional factors in marriage, such as support, protection, and reproduction, and less upon personal factors, such as companionship and love, families may make better choices than individuals, since what is sought is stability rather than personal satisfaction. In our culture, where the personal factors are held in such incomparable esteem, only the individual himself can make the final choice, although he may, of course, give weight to his family's opinions.

The marriage of childhood sweethearts does not always turn out so satisfactorily as storybooks lead one to suppose. The common assumption is that, if persons have liked each other since childhood, they must know each other well enough to marry successfully. In some cases this is true. The couple have developed along parallel paths and, in spite of contacts with other persons, they find each other most attractive.

In other cases, however, childhood sweethearts marry because they have been afraid of people and have lacked social experience. They cling to their earlier choice because their fear or lack of contacts prevents their making another. Such persons are emotionally immature and, in a sense, theirs is a child marriage. Since marriage is for adults rather than children and should be the outgrowth of adult experience, and since it succeeds or fails to the degree to which it can survive in an adult world, the marriage of such childhood sweethearts is sometimes a precarious one. It may not fail in the sense of ending in divorce; but it may fail in the sense of falling short of the possibilities of which marriage is capable. For a similar reason, marriage of cousins may be ill-advised. Disregarding for the moment the biological and legal considerations in connection with consanguineous marriage, if relatives are attracted to each other because they have been thrown together, have known each other from child-hood, and are too shy or too fearful to make wider social contacts, their marriage falls into a class similar to that discussed above.

In one sense, everyone who marries does so to escape something as well as to achieve something. He wants to escape various unpalatable elements in his unmarried state. But to marry to escape circumstances that are unusually unpleasant, such as an unhappy home situation, the irksomeness of earning one's own living, or the demands of a school program that is not to one's liking, when the factor of escape carries more weight than the relationship with the other person, is a precarious basis upon which to make a choice of marriage partner. One case will serve to clarify the point. The parents of the woman in this case were divorced when she was an infant. When she was ten years old, her mother married an alcoholic. The daughter never got along with him. There were frequent quarrels, especially when he had been drinking, and there was perpetual ill feeling. The woman had for some time felt a desire to leave home. At the age of seventeen she became engaged to two men and accepted a ring from each. Because she could not make up her mind as to which she loved more, she wavered between them. Usually she was partial to the one who was present. Her decision was made for her when one of the men left town. Soon afterward, she married the other. An impersonal observer could recognize almost immediately that the woman was deeply infatuated with both men and not ready to marry either. Her desire to escape from home was so great that she could not resist and blindly made her choice. Two years later she obtained a divorce.

Marrying merely to satisfy an urge to marry rather than a desire to marry a particular individual may lead to poor choice because requirements are relaxed. If it appears to a woman that she may be the last one in her group of friends to marry, she may become more than ordinarily anxious. Some women reach a point in their development that is sometimes referred to as the "nest-building stage." They simply want to get married. Because of the different orientations of the two sexes—women toward homemaking and motherhood, men toward masculine occupations—men are not so likely to manifest this "nest-building stage," although some reach a stage where they want their own home, security, and family, and this is equivalent to "nest building."

Parental Objections

Parents' approval and successful marriage adjustment tend to go hand in hand, while in cases in which there is parental disapproval, there is a higher percentage of poor adjustment. When there is parental disapproval, it is essential to ascertain first the nature of the objection. Do the parents insist upon lifelong celibacy, or do they object to the child's marrying immediately or in the near future? They may later approve of a marriage to which they now object because of the age element involved. Or is opposition due to the fact that they do not approve of the individual chosen?

When parents object to a child's ever marrying, there are only two alternatives. One is for the child to acquiesce in his parents' wishes and remain celibate for life. This is too much for parents to expect. Sometimes they sincerely believe that the child will avoid unhappiness by remaining single. They assume that the child will have the same marital disappointments that they had. At other times their wish to have the child remain celibate is entirely selfish, although they may not be aware of that fact. They want the child to remain with them, to keep the family intact, or to take care of them in their old age or infirmity. The other alternative is for the child to marry against his parents' wishes. Before he does so, however, he should be sure of his decision and know that he is mature enough to take a step so drastically affecting his relationship with his family.

If the parents object to their child's marrying immediately or soon, it may be worthwhile to wait a bit longer, especially if the child is of student age. It means so much to a young couple to have their parents on their side that a brief wait may prove a good investment in future happiness.

If the objections are not directed against marriage as such or the time of marriage but apply only to a particular individual chosen, they should not be disregarded until one is certain that he understands the reasons behind them. If the objections are the outgrowth of prejudice or incomplete knowledge, they may be given little weight if the parents remain immovable, or they may be altered by arranging contacts between the parents and the individual in question so that the former will see the latter in a different light. Sometimes parents see things that their children, in the throes of romance, overlook. Older persons are often better able to judge those qualities that will further and those that will impede marital adjustment than is the younger person, who has no first-hand experience of marriage. In such cases objections should be given weight and the opposition should not be lightly dismissed on the basis of wishful thinking or attributed to prejudice when the disapproval is actually the outgrowth of careful, balanced observation. It is easy to describe a person as biased when his only fault is disagreement with us. Children who term their parents prejudiced often do so because they themselves are strongly prejudiced in the opposite direction. Two persons in love are never completely unbiased.

When parental disapprobation is directed toward a specific individual, the child in love sometimes exhibits negativistic behavior. The objections have an effect opposite to that intended; instead of making the love object seem less attractive, they make him seem more so. The young person may confuse his attitude toward the other individual with his reaction against his parents. Since many an ill-advised choice is made for this reason, it might have been included among the reasons for poor choice listed above.

Overattachment to Parents

Students often ask what an individual may do if he is in love with a person who is overattached to parents or whose parents are overattached to him. Such a student must realize first of all that there is no simple thing to be done to remedy the situation and that he himself is probably in the least advantageous position to do anything. He may, however, understand the other person, and that is part of the solution. There are several considerations to which he may give serious attention in deciding whether or not marriage would be advisable.

How old is the parent who is overattached to the child?

Where will the young couple live with relation to the parents of the spouse with the fixation?

Does the parent use subtle means to hold the child?

Is it a case of parent being overattached to child, child being overattached to parent, or mutual overattachment? With regard to the reader's marrying the person in question, the three situations are mentioned in order of increasing seriousness.

Will the individual have to contribute to the support of the parent after marriage?

Will the couple live with the parent or vice versa?

Has there been any appreciable change in the parent-child relationship? Is the child making progress toward independence, or has his development apparently ceased on a definitely immature level? Has his falling in love had any effect on his relation to his parents?

How old is the child in question? What appears to be overattachment at eighteen may be delayed maturity rather than fixation. On the other hand, there may be fixation at this age.

Is either child or parent aware of this situation? Is either attempting to do something about it?

Are there other children to whom the parent may turn if the child in question marries and leaves home?

Is the parent a widow or widower, or is the other parent living?

Who makes the child's decisions for him?

Is the person dominated by the parent, or is he squirming under the parental thumb?

Is the child afraid of the parent? Is he afraid to hurt the parent's feelings by getting married or by disagreeing with the parent?

Is the child able to adjust himself to life away from the parent?

Persons contemplating marriage with individuals who are the victims of parent fixation naturally wish that something could be done about this condition. Sometimes something can be done. But there are limitations, as follows:

A parent fixation is a pattern of behavior that crystallized in childhood and is used inappropriately to meet adult situations.

Because the pattern is one of habitual responses in the child, not in the parent, time, distance, or even the death of the parent will not necessarily remove the fixation.

An intellectual understanding of fixation will not necessarily change the individual's emotional reactions, though the former may be a step toward the latter. Because intellectual understanding and emotional reactions may be in "watertight compartments," so to speak, verbal discussion of the problem may not solve it.

An act of will alone is not the solution to the problem. The individual cannot say, "I will no longer have a parent fixation," and thereby remove it, though here again such determination may be a step toward solution.

Threat, force, shame, shock, and similar factors will not remove the fixation.

A wedding is not an automatic solution. It does not suddenly change the participants' emotional reactions to parents. In one case coming to the author's attention, a bride's mother telephoned her while she was on her honeymoon and told her to return home. The bride did so. When the husband appeared at his mother-in-law's house and asked to talk with his wife, he was not allowed to enter. He never saw his wife again and, after several months of fruitless effort to save the marriage, he finally got a divorce.

The solution to the parent-fixation problem requires time, further maturation, reeducation, insight, a desire to remove the fixation, and the provision of life circumstances that encourage or call for the formation of new and more mature habit patterns. But in many cases no solution is possible, because the fixation is of too long standing, is too "deep-set," and involves too large a proportion of the individual's personality and behavior.

ENGAGEMENT

Engagement affords added security of choice during the period prior to the wedding and provides the couple with opportunity to make final plans and to announce their intention to marry. It affords opportunity for the first, or perhaps for further, steps in the assimilation of each person into the in-group that constitutes the family of the other person, a preparatory excursion into "in-lawness."

How Long Should Engagement Be?

The question, "How long is too long for an engagement?" is a reasonable one but difficult to answer. Much depends upon personalities, propinquity, the reason for the delay in wedding plans, how often the couple see each other, whether they date other people while engaged, and other similar factors that vary in individual cases. The opinion commonly expressed among students to the effect that on the basis of a few months' acquaintance a couple may safely enter upon an engagement of several years' duration is open to serious question indeed.

Should Engagement Mean Monopoly?

An engagement may be broken, but while it lasts it should signify what might be called emotional monopoly; otherwise it becomes meaningless. There should be no doubt in the mind of either party that the other is his final choice of marriage partner. If there is doubt, there should be no engagement.

There is a practical problem met by engaged persons, particularly when they are students attending colleges in widely separated towns. Should they or should they not date other persons? Much depends upon how far separated they are, how often they see each other, how remote marriage is, what their individual attitudes are, what frequency of dating is anticipated, and what sorts of dating activities would be involved.

Engaged students frequently complain that they do not enjoy dating. The probable reason for their dissatisfaction is that, instead of accepting other individuals as people, they continually compare them with the fiancé. Naturally, in most cases the others then do not make a brilliant showing. Such students could have an enjoyable time if they ceased making comparisons.

Other engaged students express apprehension because they do enjoy dating. They conclude that if they can find pleasure in the company of a person of opposite sex other than the fiancé or if they can be interested in the activities of mixed groups without the fiancé's being present, their enjoyment is an indication that they are not in love. Again, they have failed to realize that it is possible to like other people without thinking of them as competitors with one's chosen partner.

Students may object to the idea of an engaged person dating during a prolonged absence because they think of every date, even an occasional one or a first one, as a possible step toward the altar or as involving an inevitable threat of petting and/or sex. Apparently they do not believe that a date could have any other definition or purpose.

In the last analysis, the question is not whether engaged persons date. The question is whether they are free to date if they want to do so. Who tells whom what he or she may or may not do? Do the couple have confidence in each other's judgment and trust each other? Or does one seek to control the other's behavior by imposing his own will upon that person? "I love you so much I can't stand the thought of your dating while I'm away. If you date, I'll be very unhappy." In other words, "I don't want *you* to date, because if *you* date, *I'll* be unhappy." Apparently whether *you* are unhappy is not a consideration. Is such a demand an expression of love and trust upon which marriage can be built or an indication of immaturity, insecurity, and self-centeredness that suggests that the individual is not ready for marriage?

Our references above have all been to dating for pleasure and convenience, without serious interest in the other person and without petting or sexual intercourse, and to dating no one person exclusively. "Going steady" with one individual would give a fiancé justifiable reason for distrust and for assuming that the engagement no longer had meaning. Dating without the fiancé's knowledge and consent involves certain risks. Under most circumstances, that is scarcely fair play.

Rings, Pins, and "Drops"

An engagement ring has a standardized meaning which is generally agreed upon. The meaning of a pin or "drop" (something a woman wears on a chain around her neck), however, is not clearly defined. (In some schools being "dropped" is referred to as being "lavaliered.") Because of this lack of clear, commonly accepted and understood definition, a pin or "drop" may vary in significance from group to group and even from individual to individual. The man who gives it may give it a meaning different from that given to it by the woman who accepts it. There may be agreement upon meaning when the pin or "drop" changes hands; but as time goes on the meaning may become altered for one person while it remains constant for the other. The symbol remains the same, but the significance has shifted. It is for this reason, among others, that a reasonable degree of caution in giving and accepting pins and "drops" is indicated. It is easier to give or accept such a symbol than it is to return it or have it returned, as the case may be. Shifting meaning of which the individual himself is unaware but which is increasingly clear to the other party is the cause of many a hurt.

Questions to Be Discussed during Engagement

When a couple are contemplating marriage, there are several questions which they might well consider during the engagement at the very latest—preferably before. (1) Are they going to plan to have children? If so, when and about how many? What is each person's attitude toward control of conception and abortion? (2) Where will they live after the wedding? (3) What type of wedding will they have? When will it take place? Whom will they invite? (4) Will they have a honeymoon? If so, where will they go? How long will it be, and how much will they let it cost? (5) What are their attitudes toward the sexual side of marriage? Are there any facts that they should obtain from reading or a counselor? Will they have a premarital medical examination?

The reader may think that such questions are too trite to be mentioned, that every couple naturally discuss such topics and reach mutually acceptable answers before the wedding. By and large this is probably true; but it is not universally true. In counseling, the writer has had persons come to him with marital problems emerging from a failure to answer one or another of these questions.

Telling about Oneself

How much of one's past should be revealed to one's fiancé? No universally applicable answer to this question is possible. It depends upon a number of factors which vary in individual cases: the other person and his attitude toward oneself and one's behavior; what he volunteers about himself; what the incidents are that cause the question to be raised; how long ago they occurred; how much possibility of continuation or repetition there is; one's own present attitude toward the past; what has happened between the incidents and the engagement; how much danger of discovery there is or how much risk of information reaching the fiancé through indirect channels; how much each wishes to know about the other; the reason for which the individual feels he should tell.

One generalization is apropos: By and large it is better to let the other person volunteer information, and to accept what he volunteers as the whole truth, than it is to pry through curiosity into experiences which the other person long ago buried and does not want to disinter, especially since prying is likely to imply lack of trust.

No one is under obligation to bring all the skeletons out of the closet just because he has become engaged. It is only fair play, however, to reveal anything that has bearing on the couple's future relationship; for example, the presence of disease, previous marriage, hereditary or other defects, debts, imprisonment, and similar items should be told. Anything that may readily be learned through a third party is better told in advance.

Whatever is revealed is better told before the wedding. If it is told after the wedding, the other person may feel trapped. It is important to avoid overstressing the facts for the sake of feeling that one has made a confession. Because of the hypersensitivity of both persons during engagement, it is easy to exaggerate either the revelation or its interpretation. What is told should be told as information that will further the marital adjustment of the couple. It should not be told only to obtain emotional release, important as this release may be. The effects on the other party, as well as the effects on oneself, should be taken into consideration.

Many young people struggle painfully with this question of revealing the past. They feel guilty when they think of keeping some fact secret. They feel fearful when they think of making it known. They are torn by conflict and indecision. Such persons may find help in discussing the problem in confidence with a counselor, either to bring a plan to a focus or to confirm a plan already determined upon.

Broken Engagements

Engagements entered with best intentions and sincerest motives are sometimes broken. Those entered without careful thought and after very brief acquaintance are especially ephemeral. The younger the couple are at the time of engagement, the more likely they are to change their attitudes toward one another and, consequently, the greater the probability that the engagement will not endure.

Many an engagement is broken because a couple "put the cart before the horse" and expect the engagement to do something it cannot accomplish. They are insecure in their relationship and fear they will lose each other. They become engaged in order to create the security they desire. But an engagement cannot produce security. It can only express security that already exists.

Of 1,151 college sophomore women, 287 said they had been engaged once; 66, more than once. Since most of the women were still in their teens, the probability is that many of these engagements have since been broken. In a study of 1,000 engaged couples, at least a third of the men and about half the women had had one or more broken engagements [Burgess and Wallin, 1953].

In a study of 8,000 women who had been married, more than one-fourth (26.8 per cent) had been engaged at least once before becoming engaged to the men they married; about 10 per cent (included in the 26.8 per cent) had been engaged twice before.*

A broken engagement is distressing, to say the least, but it is not so painful as a broken marriage. It is better for the couple to learn before their wedding that they are incompatible than to marry blindly and discover this later. The purpose of the engagement is to enable them to make the final adjustments before the wedding. It is inevitable that some of these attempts at adjustment will fail.

As a rule, the time to break an engagement is as soon as either party wishes to break it. This does not mean that it is to be broken and remade each time they

---

*In this study, 20,000 questionnaires, were sent to former students of Stephens College; 9.526 questionnaires were returned. Of these 9,526 women, 8,001 reported themselves as having married. Since some of the women were recent graduates and may have married later, these figures do not suggest a marriage rate.

have a quarrel and then patch up their differences. When either one after careful thought decides that he cannot go on with the wedding plans, the other person should be notified. This notification will be unpleasant for both parties and may be extremely galling to the one notified. Once a couple have become enmeshed in a relationship as permeating as an engagement, it is usually impossible for one to get out without hurting the other unless by uncommon coincidence both desire release. The longer the break is postponed, the greater the hurt is likely to be, and during the delay the one who is going to make the break must "put up a false front" and misrepresent himself to the other party. To marry a person against one's better judgment is only to increase the injury. It is neither a favor nor a charity to marry a person against one's will. Neither pride, the opinions of family or friends, the fact that wedding plans are under way, nor the embarrassment of facing the other person is sufficient reason to postpone the effecting of one's decision.

Another not infrequent deterrent to making one's decision known is the fear that the disappointed individual will commit some rash act as a result of the break. Consider such cases as the following.

After a brief acquaintance and on the basis of what later proved to be infatuation, a college woman became engaged to a man who soon afterward joined the Army. When the woman discovered that she was not in love and did not want to marry him, the man threatened to desert the Army and do something desperate. His mother tried to prevail upon the woman to marry her son, insisting that a broken engagement would result in the ruination of his future. The woman was confused and did not know what to do.

A couple had been going together for several years. The man was sure he loved the woman and was very persistent about their marrying. For some time she had felt that she was no longer in love with him and was convinced that she would never marry him. She had repeatedly tried to explain her attitude, but he refused to listen. The man had periods of depression and moodiness. Once after she had told him she could not marry him he became very depressed. He went for a walk, met a friend, and the two men decided to go hunting. When the man in question took his gun from its rack, it went off and the bullet penetrated his chest just over his heart. At the time, it was reported as an accident and the woman accepted that explanation. Later, however, when they had talked of marriage again and once more she had told him she could not marry him, he then told her that what had passed as an accident had been an attempt at suicide. After that she was afraid that if she persisted in her refusal he would make another attempt to take his own life.

What should an individual do under circumstances such as these? There is only one feasible plan of action: break the engagement as painlessly as possible, take a firm stand, and tenaciously adhere to the decision. If the engagement was seriously entered and the break is founded upon a sincere change of heart, what the other person does, even if it be self-destruction, is not the fault of the one making the break. This may seem like a heartless statement; but it is not so heartless as it would be to suggest that the future happiness of two persons be jeopardized by plunging them into a loveless, incompatible union. Again, a counselor may be able to help the student work out a plan.

In the great majority of instances, suicide threats in this sort of circumstance never get any further than the self-pity stage, and relatively few are ever carried out. If an individual seeks alcoholic escape from problems or threatens suicide, he exhibits an instability of personality which in itself might be ample reason for breaking the engagement, even if love had not died or reason had not intervened. If he threatens vengeance, he demonstrates a type of immaturity that would be highly undesirable in a marriage partner. Most people recover from the shock of a broken engagement more readily than either of the two fiancés imagines possible at the time of the break. In a state of emotional upset it is easy to exaggerate possible consequences, most of which never occur.

Some individuals recover slowly. A few never recover. But such cases do not constitute sufficient reason for entering an undesired marriage, though they do constitute weighty argument for avoiding insincerity, shortsightedness, and premature commitment in becoming engaged.

It is to be expected that both parties, and especially the unwilling participant, in a broken engagement will be temporarily upset and disillusioned. For the latter to do something to prevent permanent bitterness and frustration is not easy. In so far as possible he may face the facts, and, after allowing for a period of adjustment, start over. To assume a "her-or-nobody" attitude spells defeat. As soon as feasible he may begin to date and may from the beginning associate with persons of both sexes in mixed groups. In addition to permanent disillusionment, perhaps his most imminent danger and the trap into which he is most likely to fall is "rebound."

SELECTED READINGS

Montagu, M. F. Ashley: *Human Heredity*, 2d ed., The World Publishing Company, Cleveland, 1963. Discussion of heredity with special emphasis on human heredity. Included is a "census of inherited disorders which should enable the reader to look up any condition in which he is interested."

Scheinfeld, Amram: *Heredity in Humans*, J. B. Lippincott Company, Philadelphia, 1972. Nontechnical. Genetic risks of drugs, chromosome abnormalities, racial differences, inheritance of certain diseases, genetic engineering, genetic codes governing male and female. Answers many questions.

Choices Involving Contrasts: Mixed Marriage

MIXED MARRIAGE

Let us define as mixed a marriage in which there is a considerable, obvious, significant, and unusual difference between the spouses. This excludes sex difference. In all marriages there are some differences. Many of these if accentuated to the point of being contrasts, either actually or in the judgment of one or both of the spouses, would be sufficient to classify the marriage as mixed. Sometimes in a mixed marriage there is more than one element of mixture. Take, for example, a case such as the following. At the time of the wedding the man was twenty-five years old, the woman was thirty-two. He had never been married before. She had been married twice before, the first time at age fourteen, and had a son aged seventeen. The man was Protestant, the woman Catholic. He had had two years of college. His father had a college degree; his mother had attended high school. The woman had completed only elementary school, and her parents were uneducated. The couple dated for three weeks before they married. Within two weeks after the wedding the wife started dating other men. Before the two weeks had elapsed the couple began to talk of divorce; but somehow the marriage lasted for two years before the husband finally obtained a decree.

Usually there is little hope of changing the elements of difference in a mixed marriage. The couple, to make their marriage successful, must adjust to them. Too often the young person in the throes of romance forgets the first point and assumes that the second is easier than is actually the case.

Theoretically there is no *type* of marriage that contains within itself the germs of its own inevitable failure. Any *type* can be made successful if the couple face and solve the special problems involved. This is not the same as saying that any marriage can be made successful. At times the *if* is insurmountable. There are individual marriages that may be hopelessly doomed from the beginning.

In a sense, what was just said about mixed marriage is true of marriage in general. There is no single element that is always present in successful relationships and always absent in unsuccessful ones, or vice versa. Success or failure depends upon one whole personality reacting with another whole personality and both reacting to the whole marital situation.

In mixed marriage, too, success or failure depends upon total adjustment rather than merely upon the elements of difference. For example, in an interfaith

five

marriage, success or failure depends not only upon the religious difference as such but also upon the husband's attitude toward the wife's religion and her attitude toward his; upon their personal qualities; and upon numerous other elements—such as sex, money, in-laws, children, recreation—which compose the total situation. A mixed marriage presents the problems of regular marriage plus those due to the fact of mixture. In a mixed marriage, as in any other, differences and similarities must be weighed one against the other. In every marriage there are both; success depends upon the relative proportion between them, the weighting given to them, and the degree of sharing that they permit.

Although the success of mixed marriage depends upon the total situation and the two personalities involved, rather than upon only the elements of mixture, those elements sometimes become the focal point for conflict or are blamed for conflict which is due to other causes. Suppose, for instance, that there is conflict between a husband and wife because their personalities are incompatible. Suppose that to this situation there is added a disparity in religion. Unconsciously the couple seek an explanation of their poor adjustment. From their point of view the most obvious explanation is the religious difference. Consequently, they fasten upon that. They feel that if they could resolve the conflict over religion their problems would be solved. As a matter of fact, the religious difference is only one among many contributing factors playing a part in their marital disharmony. In almost every case, disharmony, discord, and failure in marriage are the result of multiple causation. There is seldom only one single cause, although there are cases—such as that in which one partner is a psychopathic personality, as mentioned earlier—which are so one-sided that they cannot be worked out by the other partner, no matter who he is or what he does.

Let us examine several types of mixed marriage and attempt to ascertain the special problems that each type may add to marital adjustment.

AGE DIFFERENCE

Recent news articles mention a bridegroom of 78 and a bride of 26, a man of 82 with a 21-year-old wife, a woman of 62 who seeks a divorce from her 30-year-old husband, and a man of 24 who married a woman of 75. In this country in 1959, in 29 reporting states, there occurred 15 marriages in which the groom was 70 or over and the bride was 20 or under, 6 in which the groom was 15 or under and the bride was 20 to 30, 139 in which the groom was 20 or under and the bride was 30 to 39, 16 in which the groom was 20 or under and the bride was 40 or over, and 1 in which the groom was 19 and the bride over 65 [U.S. Department of Health, Education, and Welfare, vol. 1, 1959]. Another report [Bureau of the Census, February, 1972] mentions a woman of at least 75 who married a man under 25. In 1 marriage in 40 the wife is 5 or more years older than the husband [Dublin, 1965]. There are many other instances in which the age difference is not so great as some of those mentioned above but in which the motives and problems are similar. It is difficult to draw an arbitrary line separating marriage with typical age difference from that classifiable as mixed. Some difference, especially toward the seniority of the husband, is not only accepted but usually expected. Let us say only that (1) the greater the difference, the more likely it is that there will be problems; and (2) the greater the difference is in proportion to the ages of the two persons, the more likely it is that these problems will be accentuated. A wife of 20 and a husband of 35 would probably find adjustment more trying than a wife of 40 and a husband of 55. In either case, the absolute difference is 15 years; but fifteen is larger in proportion to 20 and 35 than it is in proportion to 40 and 55. In some instances in which there is considerable, or even extreme age difference, the marriage appears to be happy. This is because the couple have particular needs which such a marriage can meet. Their experience and judgment cannot be taken as a basis for generalization. In other cases the attitudes and behavior of the two persons are more nearly alike than their calendar ages [see Cuber, May, 1971].

In connection with marriage mixed as to age, there are four questions to be answered: (1) Why does the younger person want to marry the older one? (2) Why does the older one want to marry the younger one? (3) What special problems may they face? (4) Will this kind of marriage meet their individual needs better than one with less age difference?

Many of the reasons for which people in general marry will, when given special emphasis, serve as answers to the first two questions. The desire for emotional or economic security, love, money, inheritance, social position and prestige, the satisfaction of making a conquest, pity, gratitude—these may motivate the younger individual. Parent attachment and emotional immaturity of such nature that a parent substitute, rather than a husband or a wife, is sought may play a part. If a woman fears sex or childbirth, she may feel that there is less chance of having her fear realized if she marries an older man. Hero worship may be confused with love. A woman may rationalize infatuation by stating reasons why she believes a husband should be a good deal older than the wife.

Either person may have failed to meet an eligible mate of an age more nearly comparable with his own. Either may be subject to flattery. A young woman may be flattered by the attentions of an older man because she assumes that he has chosen her from among many alluring women whose hearts he might easily have captured. Either may be motivated by a desire to dominate. The younger may accomplish this because of the elder spouse's gratitude for having a young person marry him. The older individual may accomplish it because of his age and experience. Such a person may have a parental attitude toward the youthful spouse.

There is sometimes a desire to regain lost youth. This desire may be the rationalization of emotional regression. There may also be fixation. The older person may have stopped his emotional development at the stage at which he was interested in very young persons of the opposite sex.

In the case of an older man and a younger woman, there may be a special sexual element. Some older men find younger women physically more attractive than they do women of their own age. Men do not experience a menopause; only a person who has *menstruated* can have a *menopause*. Among investigators, there is no unanimous opinion regarding a male climacteric, or change of life [Oliven, 1965]. One writer [Riley, 1959] says, "There has been fairly general acceptance of a syndrome in males that resembles the menopausal syndrome in females." Another [Lloyd, 1964b] says, "The . . . male climacteric probably exists, but it is rare." Still another [Weaver, October, 1970] says that "there is no anatomic or physiologic evidence to support the theory" of a male climacteric. Men do, of course, pass through a process of aging. But if there is a male climacteric, the symptoms are not so clear-cut as those in women and are far from universal. Nevertheless, in later life some men do exhibit a flare-up of interest in sex, as if they were making one last grasp at youth before settling down to older age. In such cases, however, there is reason to suspect that marriage is not so satisfactory as it appears on the surface and that the presence of deep-set problems, especially sexual ones, is highly probable.

What Special Problems May the Couple Face?

The greater the age difference, the greater is likely to be the disparity in the couple's patterns of behavior. There may be variation in tastes, in interests, in recreational pursuits, and in attitude toward life. This book is directed to students, and in this section we are assuming that one of the persons is of student age. We are not discussing the marriages of older couples.

There is likely to be a difference in degree of "habit set" The younger person will probably be more flexible and adaptable than the older. This may necessitate more adjustment on the part of the younger person, because the older one persists in his habitual ways.

An older husband may assume a paternal attitude toward his wife If there are plans or decisions to be made, he makes them because she is too inexperienced and he feels that he knows what is good for her. He may be impatient with her because of her inexperience. He is not seeking a wife who will be a partner in all respects. He expects her to fulfill only part of the wifely role. Sharing is incomplete. Consequently, he does not anticipate her taking responsibility for things financial. In some cases she is in a measure an outsider who steps into an already functioning establishment and is accepted partly as wife and partly as permanent guest. Some women find this situation difficult to adjust to; they do not want to be patronized. They are likely, too, to feel the sting of public opinion because they realize that friends are aware of their equivocal position.

An older person may have reduced physical capacity An older husband may be unable to meet the sexual expectations of a young wife; but there is no such reduction in sexual capacity in women with increasing age as there frequently is in men. If the younger person is interested in active sports, the older one may not be able to keep up. An older man may not be able to get enough life insurance to protect his family.

While still in the prime of life the younger person may have to care for a senile spouse. As stated in an earlier chapter, on the average women live longer than men; wives tend to outlive their husbands. In a marriage in which the wife is considerably younger than the husband, she is almost sure to face years of widowhood. On the basis of 1968 death rates in this country, it has been found that a woman of 45 whose husband is 20 years older has a 90 percent chance of becoming widowed after her husband has reached the age of 65 [*Statistical Bulletin,* July, 1971]. If the couple have children, they may be left fatherless at a critical stage in their development.

If the husband is considerably younger than the wife, their problem of adjustment during the wife's menopause may be accentuated At that period some women become nervous, change in appearance, and put on weight. With the traditional masculine affinity for feminine youthfulness, it is not difficult to see how adjustment in such cases might become complicated.

The family of each spouse may have difficulty in accepting the other spouse In one case, for example, a girl of twenty married a widower of fifty. This gave her parents a son-in-law older than themselves and gave the girl stepchildren older than she was. When the couple had a child, it was younger than its nieces and nephews.

There may be a problem with regard to common friends The very young wife trying to assume a matronly role in order to fit into a group of women of her husband's age may have difficulty because the older women do not readily accept her as one of their company. She may appear younger and more inexperienced than is actually the case. The older husband trying to keep pace with the friends of a very young wife may have an equally difficult problem. They can scarcely accept him as one of their own companions, and he must often force upon himself interest in their recreations. Instead of his appearing more youthful, his age is accentuated. In many cases there is no group into which both husband and wife readily fit as a couple.

Since tradition is more favorable to the marriage of an older man and a younger woman than to one in which the age difference is reversed, an older wife and a younger husband have the problem of adjusting to an attitude that places their marriage in the category of the unusual People look askance at them, wonder why they did it, and become overcurious.

There is the necessity of the couple's assuming a well-balanced attitude toward their own marriage They should, of course, face and solve as objectively and as rationally as possible the special problems involved. But there is danger of putting too much emphasis on the problems and of exaggerating them beyond the limits indicated by the facts.

A seniority of six years on the part of the wife is worth considering; but it is not serious enough to damage a marriage if considered intelligently and without exaggeration. One couple exhibiting such an age difference had known each other for some time, were in love, were both well-educated and apparently well-adjusted persons, and had similar interests and backgrounds. The husband, however, started on the wrong course of action. Immediately after the wedding he began seeking information as to how to surmount the obstacle in the path of their happiness. He searched through books for suggestions. He asked physicians what to do when his wife reached the menopause. Before two months of marriage had passed, he visited a counseling agency to ask for advice. Fundamentally his attitude was sound. He wanted to attack the problem with as much knowledge as he could accumulate. But he was exaggerating the problem and worrying about it out of proportion to its importance, until his attitude, rather than the age difference, was rapidly becoming the obstacle to happiness.

In contemplating marriage to an older person who has never married before, there are some important questions to be answered by the younger individual before the final decision is made. Is there something about him that makes him an undesirable choice? Has he lacked interest in marriage? Is he well adjusted? Has singleness been due to economic, educational, or military factors or to factors involving his personality and emotional maturity? Is he overattached to his parents? How and why did he get so far along in life without marrying? If these questions cannot be adequately answered, then marriage may be a risk.

DIFFERENCE IN NATIONALITY

Nationality difference implies variation in customs, standards, and points of view. The greater the contrast in the backgrounds of the two spouses, the greater the possibility of there being special problems of adjustment. If there is also a language difference, the situation is rendered even more complicated.

In some ways difference as to nationality and difference as to family background are similar; but the latter is a difference that occurs in a single matrix of custom, while the former involves the more basic ways of life. Every people believes its accepted way of life to be superior and right. It is more or less intolerant of other peoples' ways. In their dealings with each other, people set out with preconceived ideas and prejudices. When an individual reflects the attitudes of the group, these may have a direct bearing on the marital relationship.

One of the most pertinent differences between this country and some other nations, as far as marriage is concerned, is the dissimilarity in attitude toward women, in their status, in their role, in the degree of restriction placed by custom upon their behavior, in women's attitude toward their own position and toward men. Attitudes toward authority in the home, toward the organization of the family with respect to relatives and in-laws, toward morality and aesthetics, and toward many other things may vary. Such differences may make a contribution to marriage. On the other hand, they may make adjustment difficult, depending upon which spouse is American and where the couple live.

The problem of deciding whether or not to marry a person of another nationality is not uncommon among students who are in a position to meet men and women from other countries. If an American meets a foreign student who is taking college work in this country, knows the language, is partly assimilated through his school experience, and plans to live here permanently, the problem of adjustment in marriage is one thing. But for the American who plans to marry a foreign student and reside permanently in the latter's homeland without first having experience in that country, it may be quite another. Let us remember, however, that the potential problem is relative to the degree of difference between the two nationalities. One would scarcely consider the marriage of a citizen of this country and an English-speaking Canadian to be "mixed."

It is exciting and romantic to fall in love with someone whose foreign extraction casts a halo and stimulates the imagination. If residence abroad is contemplated, the thrill of travel is added. In cases that have come to light in conferences with college students, the thrill, excitement, and glamor have often tended to becloud judgment and to make the wedding the limit of foresight. Furthermore, there is usually no way of checking on the credentials of one whose roots and attachments are abroad. Like everyone else, he is biased. He may make exaggerated claims about himself or his family; the American can judge only by his word and his own attitude toward his own importance. In rare cases there is deliberate falsification. For illustration let us consider a specific case.

The woman was an American college student who fell in love with an Iranian. They planned to marry when he graduated and to return to Iran to live. The thought of travel and residence in a foreign land seemed like a thrilling adventure to the woman and, as subsequent events proved, the glamor camouflaged her infatuation and made it seem like love. About Iran, about the man's family, and about his way of life she knew nothing except what he had told her. There was no reason to doubt his sincerity, but even sincere persons can look at life only through their own eyes. He saw Iran and his people through the eyes of an Iranian, not through the eyes of a young American woman thousands of miles away from relatives, friends, familar scenes, and customary ways of life.

In the discussion of her contemplated marriage, it soon became apparent that there were several questions that she had never sought to answer. Would the day-by-day existence of an Iranian wife be agreeable to her? What is the position of women in that country? Would her relatives-in-law accept her? Would she like them? Could she learn the language quickly enough to prevent the beginning of an unbridgeable gap between herself and her husband's people? Would she become homesick? Would she be satisfied to see her children reared as Iranians? Would the economic structure and her husband's place in it be exactly as he had described them? Would the Iranian standard of living be acceptable? Is there any prejudice in Iran toward Americans?

The answers to these and similar questions she did not know. To marry without knowing them would be to take a plunge in the dark. The more she thought about it, the more she realized that there was little in favor of her plan and much against it. At length she decided to break her engagement, and she has not regretted doing so.

We do not mean to imply that a marriage such as this can never succeed. However, the problems are complex. Not everyone is equipped to solve them.

DIFFERENCE IN RACE

Until very recently in this country there has been more racial intermixture than interracial marriage. This has been due in part to the intermixture which occurred between white males and black females before the abolition of slavery. It is thought that, because of this intermixture, a large proportion of American blacks have some white ancestry. As mulatto-white and mulatto-mulatto intermixture continued, many instances of gradual lightening of skin coloration from generation to generation have occurred, until some mulattoes—though they carry black genes—have become as light as whites. Mulattoes are classified as blacks, but many of these very light mulattoes "pass," that is, they cross the color line and pass as white. On the other hand, there are many very light mulattoes who could readily pass but who choose not to do so. No one knows exactly how many persons there are in the general population who pass or have passed. Estimates vary widely. Through the years the cumulative effect of passing would be considerable. Hence, interracial marriage has become complicated by the fact that a special group is involved in it; and this may be the fact in a particular marriage without its being known by either or both spouses, their children, or society at large.

There has also been more racial intermixture than interracial marriage because of laws in some states prohibiting marriage between a white person and a member of another race. Only recently have such laws been declared unconstitutional.

The greatest barrier to interracial marriage lies in the mores, the established customs of the group that are deemed essential for societal welfare, together with the attitudes and prejudices to which such mores give rise. But mores and attitudes are subject to change. There is no natural, inborn, instinctive, biological aversion to interracial marriage, as some persons assume. This is shown, for example, by the acceptance of interracial marriage in some countries. It is also suggested by the fact that, if there were a natural aversion to it, legal and social efforts to prevent it would be unnecessary.

Although not so clear-cut and rigorously prescribed as in some cultures, our mores do sustain a degree of exogamy and endogamy. *Exogamy* defines the group outside of which an individual is expected to marry. *Endogamy* defines the group within which an individual is expected to marry. We are, for example, exogamous relative to family (at least within certain degrees of consanguinity). We tend to be endogamous relative to race and religion. We do not penalize people for crossing endogamous lines as severely as some cultures do. But there is an underlying attitude—and although this attitude is now changing, it is still more or less uncritically accepted—that people should "marry their own kind."

In recent years in this country there has presumably been an increase in interracial marriages—"presumably" because in 1960, for the first time, the census included data on the race of the husband classified by the race of the wife [Carter and Glick, 1970] and because, given the methods of enumerating such marriages, the data compiled do not present the complete picture. The proportion of all marriages that are interracial is very small, probably 1 per cent or less. There are more cases in which the husband is white and the wife nonwhite than vice versa, in part because of the fact that many men in military service during the Second World War married Oriental women [U.S. Department of Health, Education, and Welfare, September, 1968; Carter and Glick, 1970]. Other factors contributing to this increase in interracial marriage are urbanization, with its attendant indifference and impersonality relative to individual behavior so long as such behavior does not encroach directly upon the freedom and welfare of others; the influx of foreign students and other visitors; the extension of American business and political interests throughout the world; the increased intermingling of peoples; and a growing feeling that people should be free to make their own choices. To these factors may be added two others. One is the "racial revolution" which has been proceeding apace. The other is the cause-and-effect relationship between social change and acceptance of it. Repeated exposure to a phenomenon and increased familiarity with it tend to further acceptance of it. In turn, growing acceptance facilitates increased frequency. To some degree, then, a social phenomenon is the cause of its own proliferation: the more interracial marriage occurs, the more it is likely to occur.

There is still another factor that has entered the picture of interracial marriage, specifically, black-white marriages. There have long been whites who have made black-white marriage the ultimate reason for continuing insistence upon racial discrimination—"Would you want your daughter to marry a Negro?" There is now beginning to emerge a small number of whites who are going to the opposite extreme and making such marriage the ultimate test of their own racial acceptance—"My greatest contribution to racial equality is to marry a Negro" [see Hernton, 1965]. In either case perspective is lost. Marriage to a particular individual is confused with dedication to a "cause" involving a group. Entering any type of marriage to "prove" something is not likely to accomplish anything; the individuals marry for a reason that is difficult to sustain and that is unrelated to the factors which contribute to marital success. A black-white marriage, like any other marriage, should be entered because two people want to marry and to make a free choice, regardless of their race.

A gradual increase in interracial marriage of various types may be anticipated. But numerical increase will not automatically remove possible problems and make success easier to achieve. The racial revolution is only in progress; it is far from complete. During the period in which the reader of this book will make his choice of marriage partner, and for some time thereafter, interracial marriage will entail problems with which many mixed couples will be ill-prepared to cope and which only some will be able to solve successfully [see Pavela, May, 1964]. A sociologist examines social change objectively and describes his observations impersonally. But a young couple contemplating marriage must work out a highly personalized relationship within the undercurrents and crosscurrents of a social milieu. They are not called upon to use their marriage as a contribution to the solution of a complex social problem.

Interracial marriage, like all types of marriage, does not occur in a vacuum. It occurs within a societal matrix. Many persons other than the couple are involved. No matter what the couple's attitude toward each other may be, the attitudes of family, friends, and members of society at large seep into their marriage; they cannot be completely walled out and disregarded. One of the criteria of success or failure in marriage is the degree to which a given marriage facilitates or erects barriers to the association of people. In present-day America, even in the light of recognized social change, interracial marriage perhaps more than any other type contains stone and mortar for the building of walls between people. In many communities a racially mixed couple have difficulty in finding friends who are sufficiently unprejudiced to accept both spouses without hesitation or discrimination. Many families are not prepared to accept a child-in-law of another race [see Washington, 1970]. The spouse belonging to the majority race may find himself the target of prejudice and discrimination directed by segments of society toward the minority race. The situation is, of course, changing. But we are discussing the reality of the immediate future, not a hypothetical, more-distant future in which contemporary problems will have disappeared.

There is the matter of the child born to interracially mixed parents. The child's associates are inclined to relegate him to the status of one of the two racial groups he represents—the one that is held in lower esteem. Often the child is torn by conflicting loyalties. A very small admixture of yellow, brown, red, or black "blood" can cause an individual to be classified with the minority race. Usually no amount of white ancestry is considered potent enough to counteract this imbalance. Hence we may find an interracially mixed child who holds the same aspirations as white peers and who does not understand why he is shackled by social pressure and public opinion to an inferior status.

Racial difference per se is not the basic problem in interracial marriage. The basic problem is one of degree of acceptance or rejection of each other on the part of the two races involved and hence the degree of acceptance or rejection of the interracial marriage in a given community. For example, in one part of this country a marriage between a white and an American Indian may be fully accepted, even glamorized. In another part of the country such a marriage may be considered anathema or "lower class," and the couple may be ostracized.

There are instances of marriage which, strictly speaking, are not interracial. Yet, by the general public in some communities, they are treated to some degree as if they were. In some parts of the country where there is a large Latin-American population, a marriage of a Latin-American and an Anglo-American may be put into such a quasi-racial category. The false assumption underlying such classification is that all persons of darker skin belong to non-Caucasian races. Actually skin color is only one criterion of racial classification, and a not-too-accurate one at that. There are darker-skinned peoples, such as Latin

Americans, who are "white," and lighter-skinned people, such as light mulattoes, who are classified as black.

DIFFERENCE IN FAMILY BACKGROUND

As everyone knows, there are superior individuals who have sprung from seemingly poor family backgrounds and inferior persons who have derived from apparently good ones. The basic question in this connection is not only the nature of the family background of the person with whom marriage is contemplated but also how much it has affected him. Not all persons are affected to the same degree by similar circumstances; but in many cases environment leaves its mark, and an individual's family experience is carried into his marriage.

Difference in family background may seem relatively innocuous to college students who are temporarily isolated from such background and are in circumstances conducive to making judgments of other people somewhat unrelated to family circumstances and extraction. But difference in family background may imply dissimilarity in any number of things taken for granted as part of an acceptable and appropriate way of life by one or the other spouse—for example, food tastes and levels of quality in cookery; degrees of neatness and cleanliness; table manners; English usage; types of recreation; definitions of husband and wife roles; attitudes toward arguing, quarreling, or a husband's striking a wife; standards relative to the use of alcohol, tobacco, or even coffee; scales of values; the celebration of holidays; definitions of authority within the family; and prejudices and biases of one sort or another.

Consider two examples. In the first, the wife was an only child in whose parental family birthdays and holidays had always been days of special celebration and gifts. The husband was one of eight children in a family that was too poor to give special attention to any holiday except Christmas. On the couple's first wedding anniversary, the wife surprised the husband with an attractive, expensive gift. The husband gave the day no thought and bought nothing for the wife. His reaction to her disappointment was, "I felt so small that I could have left the room through the keyhole."

In another case the husband came for counseling with a written list of thirty-eight complaints against his wife. One of the major complaints was that their sexual adjustment was unsatisfactory. Another was that when they married she had agreed to continue working until he received his degree. These two problems proved to be related, in that continual bickering over the wife's employment, housekeeping, and money had seriously cooled the wife's interest in sexual intercourse with her husband. The husband assumed that the wife was breaking a bargain in wanting to give up her job. In a sense she was. But the basic cause of her attitude was not personal; it was cultural. It was a reflection of a family background deeply ingrained in her personality. Her parents were native-born but of European stock. The family lived in a small community of families of similar extraction, so that attitudes were subject to relatively little change. In the wife's family it was taken for granted that women did not have gainful employment after they married. It was "simply not done." By a devious route, then, the family background of this wife had crept into the couple's sexual adjustment.

In some cases a problem arises because one of the couple "bends over backward" in an effort to get as far as possible from his family background. For example, a husband whose mother was a careless housekeeper demands that his wife be meticulous, or a wife whose parents used poor English continually badgers her husband because of his careless speech.

Another pertinent reason for taking background into consideration is that, whether we like it or not, the wedding delivers to each spouse free of charge a complete set of in-laws. These in-laws will visit and be visited, will make demands of one sort or another, and in many cases will try to hold the child to their own pattern of life, even though he has departed from it. Much depends upon proximity of residence; but geography does not always eradicate family bonds or extricate a child from the cultural pattern that has been woven around him.

DIFFERENCE IN EDUCATION

The question of whether to marry anyone of considerably different educational experience is not uncommon, in the public at large or among college students who are away from the home town, where the fiancé, who is not planning to attend college, has remained after graduation from high school. The answer is not simple, because there is a distinction to be made between real and formal education. Usually these two types overlap; but they are not necessarily identical. There are many self-educated persons who have never attended college; and there are many poorly educated men and women who have been awarded degrees.

A distinction must also be made between technical, specialized, occupational, professional training and education for living. A woman with a bachelor of arts degree has three or four years less formal schooling than a man with a medical, engineering, or law degree; but so far as education for living is concerned, they have approximately equal amounts. Two high school graduates may have about the same amount of education for living, even though one of them goes on after graduation and takes several years of specialized business training.

When there is considerable disparity of education between husband and wife, there are in general four possible courses that their marital life may take. (1) They may make a satisfactory adjustment, with little actual change on either side. (2) There may be formed between them an unbridgeable chasm. (3) The one with the better education may assist the other to raise himself to the higher level. (4) The one with the lesser education may drag the other down to the lower level. The last is the path of least resistance and is not infrequent in actual experience.

DIFFERENCE IN INTELLIGENCE

Difference in intelligence and difference in education are not necessarily concomitant. Some individuals, by good fortune, devious means, or misplaced charity, zigzag through the maze of hurdles that better students jump, escaping academic elimination and receiving degrees that are insignia of neither ability nor achievement. On the other hand, there are persons of high intelligence whose interest is not stimulated by a college program and who drop out.

In uncommon cases couples of noticeably different intelligence get along well in marriage because, as we have said, success is in part relative to expectations. A genius and a dullard may make a mutually satisfactory adjustment if the former is not unhappy in intellectual isolation, enjoys a pleasant home, and has his emotional needs satisfied, and if the latter finds it agreeable to serve the superior spouse and bask in reflected brilliance with hero-worshiping admiration. Still, such marriages of genius and dullard are not common enough to furnish the basis for generalization.

In more ordinary unions in which there exists a difference in intelligence between the spouses, there is danger that the two may grow apart. Intellectual isolation may prove irksome and unsatisfying to the superior individual. They may both discover that in marriage mental stimulation is as important as emotional satisfaction, that exchange of ideas and contact of minds are as essential as exchange of caresses and contact of bodies. Intellectual isolation may result on the one hand in withdrawal, so that the superior spouse becomes less and less a part of the total marital situation, or on the other hand in his seeking elsewhere for the stimulation and intellectual contacts that the other spouse cannot supply. Either condition may produce a loneliness that makes marriage disappointing.

The less intelligent spouse, if he is keen enough to sense the real situation, may develop a feeling of inferiority. If he is not so keen, he may aggravate the difficulty by his very apathy and blindness. If the former occurs and he does grow to feel inferior, that too may produce loneliness that will eventuate in withdrawal or the seeking of companionship upon a more acceptable level. A feeling of inferiority may produce unhappiness, insecurity, and frustration. The inferior spouse aspires to keep pace with his superior partner but comes to realize that his mental legs are not long enough to maintain the stride. A satisfactory adjustment may be achieved, however, if the husband and wife find areas in their relationship which represent common ground and put them on a more nearly equal footing, or if each spouse is encouraged to use his or her special abilities, or if they both recognize and accept their differences.

DIFFERENCE IN PREVIOUS MARITAL STATUS

Although the divorce rate is higher in marriages in which one spouse has been married before than it is in those which represent first marriage for both persons, among the remarriages that do endure the level of success is about the same as in first marriages that endure. Yet marrying a widowed or a divorced person is not the same as marrying one who has always been single, no matter how similar the external conditions may seem to be. When such a union is contemplated, answers to a number of important questions might well be ascertained to the satisfaction of the person to whom marriage will be a new experience. Again, we are assuming that the reader is of student age. If the other individual's previous marriage was happy, that fact is likely to affect his attitude toward his new relationship. If it was unhappy, that experience will have left a mark. There is also the fact that marriage gave him a social status that cannot readily be eradicated from the memories of those who know him, especially if they also know or knew his spouse. It is inconceivable that anyone with normal human sensitivites could be completely indifferent to a marital experience.

Whether the previously married person was widowed or divorced, there is the question of rebound. Is he marrying in an attempt to fill a void in his emotional life and doing so before he has become sufficiently readjusted to make a wise choice based upon sound judgment? Is he marrying in desperation? How much time has elapsed since his divorce or bereavement?

What is his attitude toward his first spouse? Is there any possibility of that person's coming between you, either actually or in the imagination of one or both of you? In particular, why is he contemplating marriage with you? Is it because you are you and he loves you for yourself, or because you are so much like the previous spouse with whom he was happy, or because you are opposite in type and personal qualities from the person with whom he was unhappy? Does he love you or his first spouse in you? Does he continually compare you with the other person? Is the comparison favorable or unfavorable? How do you react to this comparison? Could you tolerate it over a long period in the close contacts of wedded life? Does he continue to display reminders of his past experience; if so, might they become barriers between you or make you self-conscious in your new relationship?

Will you, when you marry this person, step into a home already furnished and established by the previous spouse? Or will the two of you begin a new home together? Could you make an adjustment if the former were the case?

After the wedding, where will you stand in the estimation of his friends and relatives, especially those of the former who were friends of both husband and wife? This problem becomes more than usually complicated if the friends and relatives feel that he remarried too soon.

What are his knowledge of and attitude toward sex as compared with yours? Some individuals are so abysmally ignorant of sex, even after marriage, that their marital experience makes no appreciable difference in their attitudes. In other cases marital experience, especially when coupled with some ignorance and lack of consideration, leads a person to make demands that the uninitiated, inexperienced spouse cannot meet. In still others, it produces deeper understanding, fuller appreciation, and greater consideration.

There are further special questions applying to marriage with a divorced person. One of the most important considerations is the real situation out of which the divorce grew. Unless he understood that situation, one could scarcely marry a divorced person without risk. Yet such marriage in darkness is sometimes contemplated.

Knowledge of the grounds for divorce alleged in court is not sufficient, because causes and grounds are seldom identical. The grounds are worked out to satisfy the requirements of the law and may have little relation to the couple's actual relationship. Furthermore, there is a tendency for more divorces to be sought by and granted to wives. To ascertain who sued for divorce would not render the information desirable in contemplating marriage to one of the divorced partners.

Whether or not the other person was more at fault than his first spouse, there is the possibility of a problem's developing. If he was more at fault, he may repeat his mistakes. He may also still be in love with the former spouse. There is reason to believe that some divorced persons fail in completely overcoming their fixation upon the former mate. If he was less at fault, he may be bitter and disillusioned. He may even marry for revenge. In either case, he may regret the divorce. It is important to know whether he has become soured and pessimistic about marriage or is still optimistic and looking for the best that marriage has to offer.

It is essential to know, too, whether he has readjusted himself after the divorce crisis. The concept of successful divorce is provocative in this connection. Was he at odds with his former spouse, with marriage, or with life in general? If the first is true, then marriage to another person may prove successful. If the second is the case, previous maladjustments may again develop, or a new start may make for better adjustment because the first marriage and its termination, though painful, were instructive. If the individual was and is at odds with life, of which marriage is only one maladjusted part, a second marriage will in all probability eventuate in some such way as the first unless those personality traits or circumstances that set him at odds with life are readjusted. This is not a simple, quick process. A divorced person may also develop an attitude of self-protection inconsistent with freely outgoing love for a second spouse, so that his capacity to love another person wholeheartedly is impaired.

Another pertinent question is the number of former marriages and divorces. One may be more hopeful of a person who has been divorced but once. When the process is repeated over and over again, that is fair evidence that the individual is seeking something that goes against his personality or the nature of married life will not let him attain. Take, for example, a student's mother who has been divorced fifteen times, or another student's father who has been divorced seven times and is contemplating an eighth marriage with a woman so much like the others that the student predicts another failure, or the "parents" of another student who has had eight "mothers" and seven "fathers." Jessie Bernard [1956] speaks of the "divorce prone." Marriage to such a person would probably be a temporary affair.

For obvious reasons, in marriage to a divorced person the possibility of the former spouse's becoming a disrupting factor is greater than in widowhood. There is not only a possible emotional bond but the very real possibility of appearance or communication. The former spouse may be met at social gatherings. News is spread through common friends. The person may have trouble and ask for assistance, as in one case in which the husband did not hear from his former wife until several years after his second marriage, when she wrote for money. There may even be an attempt to rewin the divorced spouse who has remarried. Whether or not a marriage can withstand the pressure of such circumstances depends upon the personalities of the two spouses.

If a divorced man pays alimony to his former wife, this fact may serve either to maintain the tie with the earlier marriage or to keep alive bitterness and disappointment. In either case, the economic problem of living on a reduced income may be irksome, especially since it is easy to project the blame for it onto the recipient of the alimony.

If the divorced individual had children by the first spouse, they may serve as a tie to the past, even though they live with the other person. A marriage may be so unhappy that divorce is a release and the two persons are gladly rid of each other. But one can scarcely be divorced from his children. Seldom do they contribute to the cause of marital failure. Parental attachment is usually too strong to be severed by court decree. If there are children through the new marriage too, the whole situation becomes complicated, as the relationships between the two sets of offspring become tangled, equivocal, and sometimes hypersensitive.

In cases of marriage to a widowed or a divorced person whose children live with him there is the problem of determining whether one has been chosen chiefly to become a husband or a wife or mainly to become a stepparent. In either case, there is stepparenthood with its ensuing adjustments. In general, the younger the children are, the less difficult the adjustment becomes. If they are very young, little difficulty is encountered unless the stepparent resents them. If they are old enough to have known both their natural parents, there is not only the problem of the mutual adjustment of new parent and children and the latter's acceptance of the former but also the problem of the children's adjustment to the new relationship between their natural parent and the stepparent. In many cases, the children are on the defensive. The new parent is an outsider intruding into a hitherto closed family group, and acceptance is difficult. In other cases the children are eager for the parent to remarry.

The stepmother, like the mother-in-law, has been subjected to a great deal of suspicion and caricaturing. Some of it has been deserved. Much of it has not. There are stepmothers who show favoritism, who resent the children of some other woman, and who use them as focal points for all the pettiness and cruelty of which their personalities are capable. But there are also others who courageously and with self-abnegation assume the arduous task of rearing the children of the men they love and do as well by them as their personal resources would permit their doing by their own offspring. Some women eagerly desire stepchildren. In one case a plan was evolved by which a prospective stepmother made frequent visits to the home of the child's grandparents for the express purpose of winning the child's confidence and affection and of gradually weaning it away from the unofficial guardians who had kept it for so long that they were reluctant to give it up.

In attempting to overcome the one-sided "stepmother image" and also the possible prejudice of the children toward her, the woman may overstress care and attention. If she disciplines the children, she may feel that she will be blamed for doing it because they are not her own. This may make her feel awkward and self-conscious toward them, even jealous of them. The woman may feel that she gives the impression of loving the children too little, and this may lead her to indulge them too much.

DIFFERENCE IN RELIGION

Religion is more important in marriage than some persons in love are inclined to think. It may be a uniting force or a disrupting influence. It may be the prop that supports a couple during a crisis, or it may precipitate a crisis. It may make for peace and happiness or for dissension and ill will. It may serve as a means of dissipating potential conflict or as a focal point upon which incipient conflict may crystallize. It may be a common interest orienting husband and wife in the same direction, or it may produce a divergence of interests, drawing husband and wife toward opposite poles. It may make possible a profound sharing or it may militate against sharing.

Younger persons sometimes fail to realize the importance of religion in marriage because their relatively short time perspective does not permit a final judgment. College students often abandon religion and the church temporarily, only to return to them later in life, when the responsibilities of marriage and parenthood awaken them to a new sense of religious values. When this occurs, early training often reasserts itself. The apple seldom falls far from the tree. If the religious backgrounds of husband and wife are basically different, that difference may again come to the fore, especially in time of crisis, even though in earlier years it was somewhat overshadowed by romance. Religion often plays relatively little part in dating. The result is that young people may become emotionally involved with each other before questions of religious difference arise, since such questions assume importance in their thinking only when marriage is contemplated. People in love often fail to realize, too, that it is not only religion as such that is important but also what is done in connection with it. If religion involved only faith, entirely separate from life activities, religiously mixed marriage would present few problems. But differences in faith entail differences in practice, in verbal expression, and in attitudes toward children, foods, holidays, and numerous similar things. They also involve families and other people with divergent attitudes and patterns of behavior. These can result in tugs, pressures, and conflicts as each family attempts to hold one member of a couple to the pattern which the family has set.

When there is a difference in faith and church affiliation, there may be not only a negative effect on the marriage but a lack of positive effect. If religion means something to a couple, then their having common experiences through participation in the activities of the same church will mean something. If their religious difference deprives them of these common experiences, a bond which strengthens many marriages is lacking.

When marriage to anyone of different religious background and affiliation is being contemplated, there are several questions to be answered.

How much does religion mean to you? Is it something of little importance, in which your interest is superficial, or is it something so vitally important that you could not conceive of living without it? Do you believe that your particular faith is the only right one, or are you tolerant and broad-minded? Do you have a driving zeal to convert others to your belief, or are you willing to let each adhere to the belief of his choice?

How great is the religious difference between you and the other person? Is it a Catholic-Protestant difference, Jewish–non-Jewish, Christian–non-Christian (such as Buddhist or Mohammedan), fundamentalist-liberal, religious-nonreligious, denominational (such as Baptist-Methodist), or a matter of degree, one of you being more religious than the other but both adhering in general to the same faith? How tolerant and broad-minded is the other person? Would either or both of you make religion a bone of contention? How did you deduce your answer to this question? Have you ever discussed religion together? Do you argue about it and find yourselves emotionally wrought up and unable to find any common basis for agreement? Do you contemplate avoiding an interfaith marriage by having one person accept the faith and join the church of the other? Would she expect you to change your religion, or did you offer to do so? Would you expect him to change his, or did he suggest it? Has either of these alternatives been discussed? If so, when you discussed them, did you mean change in religion or change in church affiliation? It is easy to talk glibly about the latter when romance casts a rosy hue upon problems. But is the former really, at least readily, possible? If one changed, would it be because of conviction or to remove a barrier to marriage? Is your plan for the eradication of the religious difference the choice of a compromise church which both persons will join? For two persons who are affiliated with somewhat similar Christian denominations this may not be too difficult. But for the Catholic–non-Catholic, Jewish–non-Jewish, or Christian–non-Christian couple a mutual compromise is another matter. There is no church "between" Catholic and non-Catholic, for example. Each church is either one or the other or neither. The other types mentioned are similar. Hence in some cases what is suggested as a compromise is actually a somewhat one-sided concession. Have you planned that each will retain his own faith and affiliation? If so, have you carefully thought through the problems that this might involve in later life, when there are children to be reared?

Children can scarcely adhere to two divergent faiths; some choice must be made. To plan to let the child make his own choice when he reaches the age of discretion is more easily said than done. Either he must be subjected to some religious influence in early life and thus have his choice colored or he must be allowed to grow to the age of discretion without having any religious influence exerted upon him, and thus be expected to make a choice with no foundation upon which to make it. Frequently the husband and wife who are tolerant of each other's religion find themselves unable to agree upon the training of offspring. The child may be pulled simultaneously in two directions; if, then, he goes the way of one parent, the other may feel resentful. The problem can be worked out, but a satisfactory solution requires all the personal resources that the two parents possess.

This is a discussion of marriage, not of theology. We are interested in the role of religion in marital adjustment, especially in the part that religious difference may play and in the problems that such difference may create or accentuate. Our discussion is not to be interpreted as a criticism of any religious group. In this discussion all faiths are considered of equal merit and are on an equal footing. "Many are the paths which lead in shadow up the side of the mountain; but from the cloudless summit all who climb behold the selfsame moon." So says an old proverb, and such will be our attitude toward religions in the discussion that follows.

In the United States today there are almost 300 Christian denominations and sects, plus several varieties of Jews, plus miscellaneous non-Christian–non-Jewish groups, plus a great body of unaffiliated believers and nonbelievers. Within such heterogeneity, differences range from one extreme to the other relative to the authority of the clergy, theology, ritual, demands upon members, attitudes toward life, and day-by-day behavior. Even within a given group differences may be noted; for example, Missouri Synod Lutherans differ from other Lutherans, Southern Baptists are not identical with American Baptists, "high" and "low" Episcopalians exhibit considerable variation. It is, therefore, a mistake, except within very broad limits, to lump subgroups together as if they were alike—for example, to compare Christians with Jews as if all Christians and all Jews were alike, to compare Catholics with Protestants as if there were no range of variation within these groups.

It is a mistake, too, to overlook the fact that every group is composed of individuals who also exhibit a range of variation. Some are more devout, some less. Some are liberal in their point of view, some conservative. Some attend religious services regularly, some are like "Christmas-Easter Christians." Some claim to believe but do not participate in the activities of a religious organization, while others participate but are not sure what they believe. Some are tolerant, some intolerant. And so it goes.

Almost anything can become a problem of interfaith marriage if one or the other party somehow relates it to "faith." For example, in one case coming to the writer's attention, both husband and wife were members of the same very conservative denomination but before marriage belonged to different church congregations, one a bit more liberal than the other. They came for counseling on a problem that they considered "interfaith"—she liked to roller skate and he felt that roller skating savored of the immoral because of the type of people one met at the rink. Most people would consider roller skating about as innocuous as any activity in which an individual could engage.

People seldom have friction over true religion, but they are continually at odds over all sorts of dogmas and practices. Suppose, for example, one spouse believed that Jesus was the product of natural reproductive processes and had a natural biological father, while the other spouse believed that his birth was unique in that he was the child of a virgin. To many persons this is a fundamental theological contention, and it could be the source of endless argument and perennial friction. The theory of evolution has proved its power to generate dissension and ill will. Women's smoking may by devious route be brought under a religious-moral banner and become a thorn in doctrinal flesh. Even the quantity of water necessary to initiate a convert into the company of the elect may be permitted to separate believers who ought to be united in common purpose. Some churches frown on such commonly accepted things as movies, instrumental music, and drinking coffee. A couple may easily run their marriage aground in the shallows of denominational difference.

Persons of different faith have at least a minimum common orientation in that they are both religious and are likely to have some appreciation of the importance of religious values, although they disagree on particular items of belief and practice. But a religious and a nonreligious person do not have even this minimum common orientation. A nonreligious individual, by definition, could hardly be expected to appreciate religious values. Therefore, the marriage of a religious and a nonreligious person may provide fertile soil for conflict. On the other hand, two tolerant individuals who are willing and able to give each other freedom of both thought and action may well work out a faith–no-faith marriage.

The point of all this is to suggest that "interfaith marriage" is not a simple uniform entity and therefore subject to the same arguments pro and con as if all such marriages were alike and generalization were easy. In contemplating interfaith marriage, the broad, over-all differences between the two faiths in question, plus the differences represented by the subgroups to which the two parties belong, plus the particular personalities and points of view of the two individuals, are all worthy of serious consideration. In short, then, Catholic-non-Catholic marriage, Jewish–non-Jewish marriage, even Protestant-Protestant marriage must be particularized. "Interfaith marriage" is only a term. The problems, if there are any, are found in "interfaith marriages," and the distinction between the concepts represented by the singular noun "marriage" and the plural noun "marriages" is the point of departure for working out such marriages successfully.

Catholic–Non-Catholic Marriage

No one book would have space to discuss all the possible forms that "interfaith marriage" might take. There is one form, however, that is common and involves considerations often overlooked or not understood, namely, Roman Catholic-non-Catholic marriage. Granted that this type of interfaith marriage must be particularized, as must others as mentioned earlier, there are points to be understood before a particularized judgment can be reached in a given situation, partly because the Catholic Church establishes a framework for its members within which a valid marriage with a non-Catholic may be contracted. In so doing, the Church does not take individual differences into account in all respects. "There are 'good practicing Catholics' and some careless ones. But in canon law what counts is whether or not one belongs to the Catholic Church" [*A New Catechism*, 1967].

The Catholic Church is a world-wide organization with levels of authority which are ultimately vested in the College of Bishops, among whom the Pope, the "Vicar of Christ," is considered the "first among equals." The bishops, with the Pope as their head, constitute the Magisterium, the teaching authority, of the Church. Under certain well-defined circumstances, and then only in matters dealing chiefly with doctrines of faith, the Pope is considered capable of making infallible pronouncements binding on all Catholics. Thus far, only one such pronouncement has been made in this century. But even when pronouncing a dogma infallible, the Pope must consult the bishops and the faithful. Not all religious decrees have the same binding force so far as obedience is concerned. Not even all the clergy agree with the bishops on everything. Nor do Catholic laymen always agree with the clergy. But most will accept, and often if necessary obey, official pronouncements, even though there may be some disagreement with them. Many individuals, both lay and clerical, make their disagreement known [Noonan, 1966]. Catholic laymen exhibit a range of belief and behavior but within certain limits, since to remain Catholic they must accept some things in common.

The Catholic Church has always been subject to change. In recent years, partly in response to scientific discovery, new thinking, and evolving life conditions, a number of changes have occurred in a relatively brief time and more are being demanded by both clergy and laymen.

Because of these changes, some students have gotten the idea that the problems of Catholic–non-Catholic marriage have suddenly disappeared. Such is not the case. They have been eased, but they have not been eradicated. One major change has been the discontinuation of the written "Ante-nuptial Contract and Promises" to be signed by both the Catholic and the non-Catholic party, a document which until recently was a "thorn in the flesh," especially for non-Catholics. The Catholic party now promises, either orally or in writing, to "do all in my power to share the faith I have received with our children by having them baptized and reared as Catholics." Before the wedding, "the non-Catholic must be informed of the promises and of the responsibility of the Catholic. . . . No formal statement of the non-Catholic is required" [Foy, 1972]. To promise that children "will be" reared as Catholics and to promise to "do all in my power" to have them reared as Catholics do not seem to carry the same weight of obligation. "Parents . . . have the right to determine, in accordance with their own religious beliefs, the kind of religious education that their children are to receive." But his faith is "the source of a serious obligation in conscience on the part of the Catholic, whose conscience in this regard must be respected" [Foy, 1972].

Students sometimes express the belief that the Catholic Church approves of the couple's rearing boys in the faith of the father and girls in the faith of the mother. Such a belief is erroneous. One of the chief reasons for which the Catholic Church disapproves interfaith marriage is the danger that the children will be lost to the faith and to the Church. The influence of the non-Catholic parent may prove a hindrance to the child's acceptance of Catholic doctrine and his devotion to Catholic ideals unless this influence is counteracted by the Catholic parent, the Church, and the parochial school. Another reason is that the faith of the Catholic and/or the non-Catholic party may be compromised.

Even though the children are reared as Catholics, the problem is not automatically solved. It is one thing to agree to a plan for the training of one's future children, who are not yet born; it is another to carry out such a plan without reluctance or regret. One of the sources of problems in a Catholic–non-Catholic marriage is the difficulty, if not the impossibility, of predicting whether an "understanding" reached in one set of circumstances before the wedding will meet expectations after the wedding in another set of circumstances, which were beyond comprehension when the "understanding" was reached. Non-Catholics usually do not want their children to be Catholics any more than Catholics want theirs to be non-Catholics. Suppose, however, that the children are reared as Catholics without either reluctance or regret on the part of the non-Catholic parent. There still remains the matter of the children's reconciling themselves to having a non-Catholic parent, who cannot participate fully in their church activities on an equal footing with themselves.

"Where there are serious difficulties in observing the Catholic canonical form in a mixed marriage"—for example, when there is a special need to preserve family harmony or prevent family alienation, when it is necessary to obtain parental consent, when there is a special friendship with a non-Catholic clergyman, or when there is a desire that the wedding occur in a church that has special importance to the non-Catholic—permission may be obtained to have a non-Catholic wedding in a non-Catholic church. In exceptional cases, for example, in certain Catholic-Jewish marriages, permission may be obtained to have a civil ceremony. The Catholic Church does not permit two religious ceremonies or a single ceremony in which both Catholic and non-Catholic rituals are used jointly or successively. With permission, a non-Catholic clergyman may participate in a Catholic ceremony or a priest may participate in a non-Catholic ceremony by giving additional prayers, blessings, or words of greeting or exhortation or by reading a lesson or preaching—provided the wedding is not part of the Eucharist (communion, Lord's Supper) [Foy, 1972].

The Catholic Church does not approve divorce in the case of a valid, sacramental, and consummated marriage. In case of a marriage declared null and void by the Church from the beginning, divorce for civil reasons—to satisfy state law—is acceptable and is considered a "civil ratification of the fact that the marriage bond really does not exist" [Foy, 1972]. Under certain circumstances the Church permits the "innocent or aggrieved party," with permission from Catholic authority, to obtain a civil divorce "for the purpose of acquiring title and right to civil effects of divorce, such as separate habitation and maintenance, and the custody of children," but such divorce does not ". . . break the bond of a valid marriage" [Foy, 1972]. Excommunication is automatic if a Catholic attempts to remarry after a divorce from a valid marriage [Foy, 1972].

In recent years there have been hopes and demands on the part of both Catholics and non-Catholics that the Church change its stand and approve the use of contraceptives, especially the pill. The use of the "safe period" or "rhythm" for serious reasons was fully sanctioned for the first time by Pope Pius XII in 1951 [Noonan, 1966]. These serious reasons, or indications, fall into several categories [Clemens, 1957; Thomas, 1957; Tobin, 1962]:

Medical; for example, the process of childbearing involves unusual difficulties for the wife; the wife is unable to carry pregnancies to term; the mother suffers unusual strain in rearing her children; there is prolonged illness among the children or the presence of a defective child requiring special care.

Eugenic; for example, a child is likely to exhibit inherited defects; in a case of demonstrated Rh incompatibility a physician advises that subsequent children may be seriously affected.

Economic; for example, the father is unemployed; the father is incapacitated and unable to fulfill his role as breadwinner; the couple desire to avoid indebtedness by spacing pregnancies.

Social; for example, the couple are faced with a long separation due to the husband's military service; the husband and wife are students; the couple cannot find adequate housing; the couple want to space their children.

In the absence of such serious reasons, "The determination to avoid habitually the fecundity of the union while at the same time to continue fully satisfying their sensuality, can be derived only from a false appreciation of life and from reasons having nothing to do with proper ethical laws." Pius XII [1951] went on to say that, in cases where conditions are such that pregnancy absolutely must be avoided because of the risk to the woman, and dependence upon the "safe period" would not give her "sufficient security, . . . there is but one way open, that of complete abstinence" from sexual intercourse.

Before 1951 approval of "rhythm" had been limited and cautious. In *Casti connubii,* in 1930, Pope Pius XI said, "Since . . . the conjugal act is destined primarily by nature for the begetting of children, those who in exercising it deliberately frustrate its natural power and purpose sin against nature and commit a deed which is shameful and intrinsically vicious. . . ." But later in the same encyclical he said, "Nor are those considered as acting against nature who in the married state use their right in the proper manner although on account of natural reasons either of time or of certain defects, new life cannot be brought forth" [Freemantle, 1956]. In his statement in 1951, Pius XII said, "We have affirmed the lawfulness and at the same time the limits—in truth quite broad—of a regulation of offspring. . . . Science, it may be hoped, will develop for this method a sufficiently secure base" [Noonan, 1966]. The Second Vatican Council (1962–1965) in its published documents [Abbott, 1966] mentioned that "certain conditions often keep couples from arranging their married lives harmoniously, and that they find themselves in circumstances where at least temporarily the size of their families should not be increased. . . . To these problems there are those who presume to offer dishonorable solutions." But the Council did not refer to any specific methods of contraception. "This is a different standpoint than that taken under Pope Pius XI, some thirty years ago, which was also maintained by his successor. We can sense here a clear development in the Church, a development which is also going on outside the Church" [*A New Catechism*, 1967]. These were significant steps forward.

The Catholic Church does not approve the use of coitus interruptus (incomplete intercourse) or chemical or mechanical contraceptives, including the pill. The reason is ". . . the fact of an established design which God Himself has written unchangeably into the natural structure of the conjugal act and which cannot illicitly be interrupted" [Cavanagh, 1965]. In other words, contraception is an interference with natural moral law.

While some Catholic clergymen and laymen want to see the use of contraceptives, especially the pill, approved [Foy, 1968], others speak strongly against contraception. For example, in "The Government and Birth Control," adopted by the National Conference of Catholic Bishops in 1966, there is mention of ". . . blameworthy solutions to problems connected with birth regulation" [Foy, 1967]. "Contraception is wrong because it is a fictitious symbol of love, a substitution of what, in truth, symbolizes shared selfishness for what symbolizes utter self-giving" [Quay, 1961]. The use of the pills directly as contraceptives has been referred to as "a grave sin" [Noonan, 1966].

In "The Government and Birth Control," the National Conference of Catholic Bishops in 1966 mentioned ". . . the freedom and responsibility of spouses to make conscientious decisions in terms of nuptial love, determination of family size and the rearing of children. . . . Basic to the well-being of the family is freedom from external coercion in order that it may determine its own destiny. . . . Primary responsibility for decisions in this area belongs to parents, . . ." but they should be guided in their choice of means of "birth regulation" by the ". . . divine law itself and should be submissive to the Church's teaching office . . ." [Abbot, 1966; Foy, 1967]. "The last word lies with the conscience, not with the doctor or the confessor" [*A New Catechism*, 1967].

Then in July, 1968, Pope Paul VI issued an encyclical, *Humanae vitae*, in which he emphatically and unequivocally reiterated and upheld the Church's traditional position on contraception and other practices related to reproduction. There was an immediate storm of protest and the Church was thrown into a state of turmoil so apparent that shortly after issuing the encyclical Paul published a plea to Catholics for understanding, acceptance, and obedience. These two pronouncements not only sharpened the controversy in the Church relative to contraception but also complicated the issue of papal authority and threw into a new dilemma the clergy who do not agree with the Pope's point of view but are nonetheless expected to obey his injunction in giving counsel to married couples both inside and outside the confessional. Whether change will be brought about during the lifetime of the present Pope remains to be seen. While there are many Catholics who disagree with the Pope, there are also, as indicated above, many whom his encyclical vindicated, and their position has been strengthened by his decree. Hence change is not impossible, but it is probably unlikely, and the problem regarding contraception in some Catholic–non-Catholic marriages continues to be what it has been for some time, while in others it will be solved as it has been in the recent past, namely, by the couple's making their own judgments regardless of official Church teachings.

While the Church does not approve the use of the pill for contraceptive purposes, it does approve its use for medical, noncontraceptive purposes, for example, to treat a disease such as endometriosis [Cavanagh, 1965]. The Church does not approve of direct sterilization (such as vasectomy or salpingectomy) but does approve of indirect sterilization [see Pope Paul VI, July, 29, 1968]. For example, if a woman has malignant tumors of the ovaries and the only treatment to save her life is surgical removal of the ovaries, the removal of the ovaries will result in sterilization. But such sterilization is indirect and not intended. Therefore it is acceptable [Pope Pius XII, 1951; Fremantle, 1956; Thomas, 1957]. The Church does not approve of therapeutic abortion ". . . even to save the life of the mother" [Pope Pius XII, 1951; see also Pope Paul VI, July 29, 1968]. "Direct abortion is not justifiable for any reason, e.g., therepeutic, for the physical and/or psychological welfare of the mother; preventive, to avoid the birth of a defective or unwanted child; social, in the interests of family and/or community" [Foy, 1972]. If, however, a woman has a tubal pregnancy and the tube is likely to burst, in which case she may have serious infection and hemorrhage, the physician may remove the tube surgically. This results in the unintentional death of the fetus and is not considered the same as the intentional destruction of the fetus in therapeutic abortion [Noonan, 1966]. The cases mentioned, in which something disapproved by the Church is accepted as an incidental and unintentional consequence of something approved, illustrate the principle of double effect [Noonan, 1966].

In spite of its emphasis upon the importance of reproduction, the Catholic Church condemns artificial insemination, whether the donor of the seminal fluid is the woman's husband or an anonymous male chosen by a physician, or both. The reasons given for such disapproval are that children should be the product of a loving relationship between husband and wife rather than the result of a laboratory procedure; that artificial insemination involves the perversion of a natural faculty, since sexual intercourse is naturally a cooperative act; and that such insemination typically involves the collection of the seminal fluid either through the use of a contraceptive device or through masturbation, which is considered to be grievously sinful [Good and Kelly, 1951; Pope Pius XII, 1951]. The Catholic Church is not alone in disapproving artificial insemination. Many non-Catholics assume it to be a matter of personal decision. But some Protestant clergymen have vigorously expressed objections to artificial insemination involving a nonhusband donor on the ground that such a procedure savors of adultery. Some courts have raised questions regarding the legitimacy of a child when the father is a nonhusband donor. The question of whether the woman's husband should be required to adopt the child in order to make it his legal heir has still not been answered to everyone's satisfaction.

As we pointed out at the beginning of this section, a group such as the Catholic Church is composed of individuals who exhibit a range of variation. Hence we must not be surprised when some Catholics do things not approved, or at least not encouraged, by their Church, especially since not all Catholic clergy agree on certain issues, and on one major issue, contraception, Pope Paul VI has made a pronouncement strongly questioned by many clergy. ". . . Abstract polemics concerning Catholic teachings," say two Catholic scientists [Duffy and Wallace, 1969], "cannot always be directly translated into uniform behavior patterns among Catholics throughout the world. The individual conscience is more meaningful to people who value individual responsibilities and the respect for the rights of others."

An increase in interfaith marriages in which one party is Catholic may be anticipated. "The trend toward more mixed marriages will undoubtedly continue to gain momentum, propelled by the ecumenical spirit and the relaxation of Church regulations. It is predicted that before long one out of two valid Catholic marriages will be mixed. The number of invalid mixed marriages, also on the rise, will increase the figures even more" [Wakin and Scheuer, 1966]. It is estimated that at least 25 per cent of parents and children are lost to the Church because of mixed marriages, and this loss tends to be cumulative because the children are less likely to be reared as Catholics and more likely to intermarry [Wakin and Scheuer, 1966].

Catholics are becoming more like non-Catholics in their approval of contraception, although there are still differences between the two groups. Many Catholics use contraceptives and visit birth control clinics or raise no objection when a non-Catholic spouse does either of these. In 1965, in a study of 655 married women, it was found that nearly two-thirds of the Catholic women who had used some form of contraception had at some time employed methods not approved by the Church [Westoff and Ryder, 1967]. One study of 2,713 white married women revealed that Catholics did not use contraceptives so freely as non-Catholics. Catholics, as compared with others, more frequently relied on the "safe period" only and tended to begin to use contraception later in married life. It was found that in mixed marriages the religion of the wife tended more often than that of the husband to determine whether any method was used and, if so, which. Altogether, however, 30 per cent of all the Catholics, and 50 percent of those Catholics who used any type of contraception, had adopted methods considered unacceptable by the Church. In some cases of mixed marriage the issue of contraception was found to be a source of serious marital conflict [Freedman, Whelpton, and Campbell, 1959]. A survey made by the *Catholic Digest* found that about half the persons questioned ". . . did not accept their Church's teaching on the morality of contraceptive practices." "Indeed, the present ban on artificial contraception may be to American Catholicism what prohibition was to American society: honored more in the breach than in the observance. One conclusion appears painfully clear. The more Catholic couples conform to the pressures of America, the more they will move away from traditional and religious ideals. The Americanization of the Catholic attitude on birth control is unmistakable" [Wakin and Scheuer, 1966]. These are revealing and significant statements, especially since they are made by a Catholic sociologist (Father Joseph Scheuer) and a Catholic journalist (Edward Wakin).

Even in the light of all that has been said, it would be a mistake to conclude that since the Church is changing and since many Catholics do not follow the teachings of their Church in all matters, problems of Catholic–non-Catholic marriage are a thing of the past. Much depends, of course, on the two persons involved. But the fact remains that with the still-existing differences between the framework of Catholic and of non-Catholic approach to marriage, reproduction, and sex, there is still fertile ground in which conflict may readily grow. Such conflict is not inevitable, but its prevention and resolution require special prerequisites in the way of personal qualities and philosophy of life [see Simon and Simon, 1967].

Preparing for Catholic–non-Catholic marriage If Catholic–non-Catholic marriage is seriously contemplated, there are two things to be done. These are the *sine qua non* of common sense and successful adjustment. (1) As much as possible should be learned about the other person's religion. This may be done through reading, church attendance, and conference with both the non-Catholic clergyman and the priest. (2) The couple should agree upon a practical, workable plan, which should be more than an easily entered and equally easily broken compromise. This plan should be discussed with both clergymen and, if possible, with both sets of parents. We are assuming, of course, that both parties are the type who will adhere to agreements once made.

In cases in which students have fallen in love, or what they momentarily diagnose as love, and are more or less definitely thinking in terms of Catholic–non-Catholic marriage, there is often a tendency to talk glibly but understand slightly, to make broad statements of intention or ability that pass beyond the limits of practicality and probability. Such students agree so readily to become Catholic or to believe that the other person can do so that it is obvious that the difficulty, if not the impossibility, of this process has entirely escaped them. The conversion of the Catholic to a faith other than his own is usually unlikely. The conversion of the non-Catholic merely in order to avoid interfaith marriage technically rather than through conviction is not likely to solve anything, because such "conversion" is difficult to sustain. "A request for a purely opportunistic 'conversion' to the other confession without inward conviction can never be entertained. Such a step, even if it leads on the surface to a new entry in the Catholic register, is no gain to the Church, it is a loss; not a conversion but a perversion; a seduction and an aberration, for one may only give assent to faith with an upright conscience" [Häring, 1966]. Students are inclined to discount or overlook the influence of bias, to forget parents and their role after the wedding, to minimize the problem of child rearing, or even to have a sort of temporary amnesia with regard to the fact that reproduction is still a part of human life.

Jewish–Non-Jewish Marriage

Among the problems to be confronted in Jewish–non-Jewish marriage are many of those met in the Catholic–non-Catholic type, and we shall not elaborate upon these again. The reader may readily make his own inferences. There is, however, no well-organized, centrally controlled, world-wide church hierarchy to bring pressure to bear upon the individual Jew and to mold his thinking, as there is in the case of a Catholic. This leaves the Jew freer and also permits a wider range of variation among Jews than among Catholics. Officially, the latter tend to be perhaps more nearly uniform, and those who do deviate from the commonly accepted tenets of the Church do so without the Church's sanction. With Jews there is a variety of points of view, each represented in one or more organizations, ranging from the strictly orthodox group, who adhere closely to ancient Hebrew belief and custom, through the conservative, to the most liberal or reform Jews, who dispense with ancient ritual and freely reinterpret the Scriptures. As a group, Jews hold marriage and family life in very high esteem. Their attitude toward contraception is similar to that found among Protestants. Among Jews there is no celibate priest class. Rabbis may marry as Protestant clergymen do. Among some Jews, Jewish–non-Jewish marriage is prohibited. Some rabbis will not officiate at a Jewish–non-Jewish wedding but, nevertheless, do recognize the marriage as valid.

Perhaps no group of people is more carelessly lumped together than are Jews in the thinking of the average white, non-Jewish American, unless it is blacks. To him a Jew is a Jew, and he makes little or no allowance for individual differences. He is all too prone to let prejudice color his feeling toward the whole people, whereas he does not fall into the same trap and as thoughtlessly generalize where non-Jews are concerned. Furthermore, he is not aware of the social stratification that Jews recognize among themselves, just as all groups do.

Prejudice does form one of the important elements in the background against which Jewish–non-Jewish marriage takes place. This problem is not one-sided, however. Jews are often prejudiced against non-Jews, just as the latter are often prejudiced against the former [Gordon, 1964]. Prejudice, no matter who exhibits it, is unfortunate enough. But prejudice on the part of members of the majority group against members of the minority group contains the seeds of greater hurt. Try as he may to prevent it, and sincere as he may be, the non-Jew in a mixed marriage does in some cases find himself subjected to anti-Semitic prejudice because of his Jewish spouse and in other cases is put on the defensive.

In some of the more orthodox Jewish families a non-Jewish child-in-law is not readily accepted. There is, also, the often disheartening problem of rearing children who, because of their mixed ancestry, are subjected to the same prejudice as Jews.

Prejudice and discrimination are painful to Jews. But somehow through the centuries they have learned to live with them and even to survive persecution. Hence, when the mixed child of a Jewish–non-Jewish marriage is the victim of prejudice and discrimination, the Jewish parent is not surprised. The non-Jewish parent, on the other hand, never having had to learn to live with this sort of social pressure, is ill-prepared to meet the situation when his child is the target of such hurt. This parent, being a member of the majority group, takes his privileges for granted. Often he assumes that his child will have the same privileges. When the child is classified as a member of a minority group and is treated accordingly, the non-Jewish parent may be at least nonplused and at most may be deeply and perhaps permanently hurt.

CONCLUSION

As was said at the beginning of this chapter, theoretically any *type* of marriage can be made to succeed if the special problems involved are faced and solved. We have attained some slight insight into the possible magnitude of this *if* and should have reached the conclusion that in real life the problems are more obtrusive than a brief written exposition might seem to indicate. It is trite to say that the problems of mixed marriage are most readily avoided by avoiding mixed marriage. Yet this is true; and it may be well to impinge this platitude upon the thinking, unmarried, unengaged reader who is still free to make his choices without hurting anyone or causing himself pangs of conscience. In many cases mixed marriages turn out to be happy and successful. But the reader should be sure that he has taken a careful personal inventory of himself and the other person before he blithely assumes that they will fall into the category of the favored.

Mixed marriage may be approached in one of two ways. Looking at it from the point of view of the sociologist, it is apparent that whenever groups of people are brought into contact over a long period of time there will be intermixture and in many instances intermarriage among them. If they are groups within a highly mobile population, such as that in the United States, this process will be accelerated. But the process itself appears to be inevitable [Gordon, 1964].

On the other hand, mixed marriage may be approached from the point of view of the couple contemplating such marriage within a given social milieu, with its attendant pressures, expectations, customs, attitudes, and prejudices. The couple are concerned about the success or failure of one marriage, not about a sociological process. They have no obligation to contribute to social change. Therefore, what the sociologist assumes is inevitable a given couple may decide is for them unwise.

SELECTED READINGS

Baer, Jean: *The Second Wife: How to Live Happily with a Man Who Has Been Married Before*, Doubleday & Company, Inc., Garden City, N.Y., 1972. Discusses many aspects of second marriage; based on 220 interviews plus personal experience.

Besanceney, Paul H.: *Interfaith Marriages: Who and Why*, College and University Press Services, Inc., New Haven, Conn., 1970. (Paperback.) A Catholic sociologist discusses reasons for various types of interfaith marriages, their frequency, and the people involved. Also includes discussion of interethnic marriage.

Callahan, Sidney Cornelia: *Beyond Birth Control*, Sheed and Ward, Inc., New York, 1968. A critical analysis of the Catholic Church's position on sex and birth control by a Catholic woman who concludes that "the acceptance of birth control proves that, like the Sabbath, sex is made for man; man is more important than his own reproductive functions."

Downs, Joan: "Black/White Dating," *Life*, May 28, 1971, pp. 56–67. Discussion of interracial dating, especially among university students, and their reactions to it.

Furlong, William Barry: "Interracial Marriage Is a Sometime Thing," in William J. Goode (ed.), *The Contemporary American Family*, Quadrangle Books, Inc., Chicago, 1971, pp. 136–151. (Paperback.) Discusses some of the problems of interracial marriage and presents specific cases.

Gordon, Albert I.: *Intermarriage*, Beacon Press, Boston, 1964. (Paperback, 1966.) Discussion of interfaith and interracial marriage. Includes statistical material not readily available elsewhere, summary of opinions of some five thousand college students, and seventeen recorded interviews with the intermarried. Author is a rabbi.

Hathorn, Raban, William H. Genné, and Mordecai Brill (eds.): *Marriage, An Interfaith Guide for All Couples*, Association Press, New York, 1970. The editors are a Catholic priest, a Protestant minister, and a rabbi. They say, "This book is *not* directed to those who unite two different faiths in a religiously mixed marriage. Rather it is a compendium of insights from our three traditions which we believe will enrich any couple. . . . We have tried not to gloss over our differences."

Heer, David M.: "Negro-White Marriage in the United States," *Journal of Marriage and the Family*, vol. 28, no. 3, pp. 262–273, August, 1966. Also in Ira L. Reiss (ed.), *Readings on the Family System*, Holt, Rinehart and Winston, Inc., New York, 1972, pp. 234–253. (Paperback.) The increasing rate and rising trend of black-white marriage. "It is hard to imagine a set of conditions under which Negro-White marriage rates would increase so rapidly as to achieve any large intermingling within the next 100 years."

Kreykamp, A. M. J., L. Schellevis, L. G. A. van Noort, and R. Kapstein: *Protestant-Catholic Marriages: Interpreted by Pastors and Priests*, translated by Isaac C. Rottenberg, The Westminster Press, Philadelphia, 1967. (Paperback.) A constructive, cooperative effort by Protestant and Catholic clergy to help couples in mixed marriages understand the meaning of marriage and each other's faith.

Larsson, Clotye M. (ed.): *Marriage across the Color Line*, Lancer Books, Inc., New York, 1965. (Paperback.) Discussion of interracial marriage presenting both favorable and unfavorable reactions to such marriage and including statements by persons who have such marriages. Also includes a discussion of the history of racial intermixture in the United States and of persons who have "crossed the color line."

Rock, John: *The Time Has Come*, Alfred A. Knopf, Inc., New York, 1963. The author is a Catholic gynecologist who, through his research on infertility, contributed to the development of oral contraceptives. He makes proposals for ending the controversy over birth control and considers the possibility of reconciling oral contraceptives with the Catholic point of view.

Simon, Paul, and Jeanne Simon: *Protestant-Catholic Marriage Can Succeed*, Association Press, New York, 1967. A Protestant husband and a Catholic wife discuss how they solved various problems in their marriage.

Washington, Joseph R., Jr.: *Marriage in Black and White*, Beacon Press, Boston, 1970. Author feels black-white marriage must become a matter of free choice with support for either choice. "Marriage in black and white is . . . the ultimate criterion of an open society." Discusses the children of black-white marriages.

Launching Marriage

Launching marriage in present-day America involves not only what a couple do to begin their marriage but also the circumstances under which they do it. Ordinarily what they do includes a wedding, a honeymoon, and a series of transitions from singleness to the married state. The circumstances under which they do these things vary somewhat from couple to couple, and we cannot discuss all the possibilities. There is one set of circumstances, however, under which an unprecedented number of couples are launching their marriages, namely, the combination of marriage and higher education. Because these circumstances have arisen only in relatively recent years in appreciable numbers of cases, there are still aspects of such marriages that call for special understanding. In these cases "launching" has something of a double meaning. It implies a beginning in the usual sense of the term, but it also implies a two-stage beginning, a transitional state from which a couple will eventually emerge into marriage that more nearly fits the customary pattern. Hence we shall discuss campus marriage as one of the elements in the background within which present-day marriages are being launched.

THE WEDDING

Even in these days of rapid social change in this country, most people marry. Only a minority live together on a permanent or semipermanent basis without marriage. Some of these people have a mutual agreement which, from their point of view, is equivalent to marriage. By and large, weddings are still very much a part of the American way of life.

The purpose of the wedding is publicity in the better sense of the term. It is not notoriety, as some couples apparently assume when they have the ceremony performed in theaters, on horseback, at the bottom of the sea, on roller skates, or in blocks of ice. Notoriety puts the emphasis on the *how*; publicity puts the emphasis on the *fact that*. It is the announcement of a new relationship in which society, as well as the two individuals themselves, is interested. For this reason there are a ceremony, public records, an open expression of willingness on the part of the couple, witnesses, sanction of the state and frequently of the church, and an impartial representative of the state or of both church and state. There are exceptions made for some religious sects, for example, the Quakers.

There is a demand today for the legalization of the "marriage" of two homosexuals. There is reason to doubt (as many persons do), however, that such a "marriage" would actually constitute a valid union, since elements long accepted as an integral part of marriage are absent—for example, a relationship between male and female, sexual intercourse in the strict sense of the term, and the possibility of procreation.

The wedding does not have as its purpose the creation of personality traits that are not found in the two persons before the ceremony. It contains no magic. There is no administering of a love potion, no laying on of hands to remove evil spirits. No oracle speaks on the wedding day to communicate to the bride and groom the divine will or to teach them how to "live happily ever after." Whatever happiness they achieve is the result of intelligence, knowledge, love, effort, and commitment.

The wedding creates status, rights, and opportunity. It gives the couple the opportunity to achieve a new degree of mutuality; it does not provide the wherewithal to make that achievement. It does play a part in crystallizing and focusing the meaning of the couple's relationship. The wedding is a major vehicle for the couple's expression of mutual commitment, a setting in which each person may publicly "stand up to be counted" relative to responsibility and concern. Therefore, it has a personal as well as a social function.

Interest of State and Church

Society, the state, is interested in weddings for several reasons: (1) To safeguard moral standards. Society is anxious that no one shall depart from the mores, the accepted norms. (2) To protect property rights. The state is interested in knowing what belongs to whom. Whether or not the ceremony contains the phrase *with all my worldly goods I thee endow,* property rights are redefined at a wedding. According to the law of the state, husband and wife have various rights to each other's property and to property acquired jointly during the marriage while they both live, when one spouse dies and there are no children, or when one dies and there are children. The wedding is a way of showing that the couple acquiesce in the laws of property. (3) To determine the legitimacy of children. Society is interested not only in biological parenthood but in what might be termed "social parenthood," that is, the assumption of social responsibility for children, their support, name, and inheritance of property. Although there is no way of guaranteeing legitimacy or proving paternity—as we pointed out in an earlier connection, fatherhood is based largely on faith—society operates on the assumption that, unless there is evidence to the contrary, the children of a given wife belong also to her husband, especially when he accepts them as such. (4) To protect persons from abuse and exploitation. The state is anxious to guarantee status to those who marry. Hence measures are taken to prevent bigamy, fraud, the use of force, and the marriage of children and of persons seriously incompetent. When prevention fails, the state may punish the person whose infraction makes it impossible to guarantee status to the other party. (5) To guarantee the legality of contracts. The wedding ceremony is not a contract in the strict business sense; but there are similarities, and in some cases wedding agreements do involve contracts. (6) To guard against marriages within prohibited degrees of relationship. All states, for example, prohibit marriage between close "blood relatives." Some extend the prohibition to include close relatives-in-law.

The church is interested in weddings for some of the above reasons and also because in some faiths marriage is considered a sacrament. Even when marriage is not counted strictly a sacrament, it is often considered to be ordained by God, and the ceremony contains an important religious element. For this reason a representative of the church is often the officiant. This representative has another function, too, however. The state must, of necessity, depend upon people to see that its requirements are carried out. A clergyman is a person to whom this responsibility may be entrusted.

Size of the Wedding

It is impossible to generalize or to state specifically just how large a wedding should be. A wedding, like a garment, should fit. It should be appropriate to the standard of living and social position of the couple. As is true of a garment, there is no point in having the largest one possible.

The wedding day tends to be more the bride's day than the groom's. The bride is the center of most attention. The change in her life and status brought about by the wedding is greater than that to which the groom is subjected. In most cases she changes her name, follows the groom as to place of residence because his occupation is considered more important than hers, becomes economically dependent upon the husband, assumes the responsibility for homemaking, and prepares—socially, at least—to have children. Furthermore, she is more likely than the groom to be sentimental about the wedding. She wants something to remember and wants a ceremony that will be remembered by her friends. Since this is true, the bride's wishes may within reason take precedence over those of the groom, who may want a simple ceremony, quickly performed. To have friction over wedding plans because the groom seeks to impose his ideas upon the bride is a poor way to start a marriage. On the other hand, however, it is important that the bride be sensitive to the feelings and wishes of the groom.

Cost

Size and cost are usually closely correlated, but this is not necessarily the case. Cost, too, should be appropriate to the couple's standard of living. An expensive wedding that is out of proportion to income seems top-heavy and may mean the spending of money that the couple could better use for some other purpose, such as house furnishings. There is no value in a "big splash," as such. A too expensive, too spectacular wedding tends to put the emphasis in the wrong place, namely, on the wedding instead of on the marriage. The former becomes an end in itself.

Most of the wedding expenses are borne by the bride and her family. Nevertheless, as the cost increases, the groom's expenses increase also. It is true of many college students that the bride's family is well established and can afford a relatively expensive wedding, but the groom is still in school or just recently out of school, has a small income, and in many cases has debts. A large wedding would be a burden that he could not readily bear. This situation may well be taken into consideration when plans are being made.

Preparation

Preparation for a wedding involves innumerable details and activities. The more orderly this preparation is, the more foresight and planning are applied, the less will be the fatigue and tension. Under the best circumstances there may be some fatigue, and it is sensible to make every reasonable effort to minimize it. To put off wedding preparations until the last minute, as some students do their academic work, is to invite the same sort of flustered haste in the former as is found in the latter, with an additional element of nervousness in the case of the wedding, which leads to increased irritability.

If we accept the premise that the marriage is more important than the wedding, then we may seriously question the wisdom of the social schedule which precedes and accompanies the wedding in the case of many couples. The success of marriage does not depend solely on honeymoon attitudes and experiences. Yet, at best, the couple's first days together after the wedding, and especially their first night together, are often supercharged with emotion, sentiment, romantic expectation, and sometimes apprehension. This last is more often experienced by the bride as she contemplates her new sexual role, but is not limited to brides.

If the couple do not plan carefully and instead approach their first days of marriage "worn out" from numerous parties, receptions, receiving lines, and so on, it is not unknown for them to "get off on the wrong foot" on their honeymoon. They are victimized by well-meaning parents and friends who sometimes use the bride and groom to further their own social ambitions. Of course, they themselves may encourage this social orgy. This is not meant to imply that there should be no prewedding social events involving the prospective bride and groom. It is meant to suggest only that perspective not be lost.

Date

The wedding date is ordinarily set by the prospective bride, taking into consideration, of course, the wishes of the fiancé and his occupational or other responsibilities. She has to make more preparation than he and can more accurately determine how much time she will need and when her family will be able to carry out their responsibilities. Also, she will, if possible, want to set the wedding date so that it will not fall during her menstrual period, not only because of sexual relations but also because during that period many girls tend to be depressed, tired, or irritable. If, however, the groom is understanding and well informed, if he gives the bride's happiness and the success of the marriage precedence over the immediate satisfaction of his sexual impulses, if he is not dominated by an outworn tradition that dictates inevitable consummation of the marriage on the wedding night, the problems attendant upon menstruation are not insurmountable.

With increasing frequency physicians are prescribing contraceptive pills several months in advance of the wedding for girls about to be married. The objective is to establish effective conception control from the very beginning of the marriage. Since the pills also regularize the menstrual cycle, the girl can predict her period and avoid it in setting the wedding date.

THE WEDDING CEREMONY

The wedding may vary from the barest minimum with a brief statement before a civil official, on the one hand, to an elaborate church affair, on the other. It varies from church to church. It may vary within a given church. If they include statements to meet the requirements of the law, a couple may write their own ceremony. It would be impossible to reproduce here all the forms of the service in which readers may participate. Since, however, so many readers will have a religious ceremony, we have chosen to present certain statements or concepts connected with a typical Protestant, Roman Catholic, and Jewish wedding.* We cannot, of course, expect universal agreement on meaning, and the following is intended to be suggestive rather than definitive. During a religious wedding ceremony a couple utter some of the most profound intentions and acknowledge some of the most far-reaching responsibilities of which human life is capable. Yet circumstances are often such that their attention is directed toward what is happening rather than toward the meaning of what is said.

"Dearly beloved, we are gathered together here in the sight of God" is a commonly used opening statement in the Protestant ceremony. In the exhortation before marriage, the Catholic priest says, "You are about to enter into a union which is most sacred and most serious, a union which was established by God himself." At the beginning of the Jewish ceremony there is this invocation: "Blessed may you be who come in the name of the Lord; we bless you out of the house of the Lord. May He who is mighty, blessed and great above all, may He send His abounding blessings to the bridegroom and the bride." Such statements affirm the religious nature of marriage and serve to remind the couple of the fundamental orientation of their new life together.

The phrase "and in the face of this company" usually follows the statement mentioned above in the Protestant ceremony. This is more than a courteous nod in the direction of the assembled guests. It is more than a speaker's beginning with

*Statements from the several ceremonies are taken from the following publications: Protestant: William H. Leach, *The Cokesbury Marriage Manual*, rev. ed., Abingdon Press, Nashville, Tenn., 1961. Roman Catholic: *The Mass on the Day of the Marriage*, according to the text in the *Collectio Rituum 1964* by the National Catholic Welfare Conference, revised in accordance with the directive of May 4, 1967, Sacred Congregation of Rites, Leaflet Missal Company, St. Paul, Minn., 1968. Jewish: Lilly S. Routtenberg and Ruth R. Seldin, *The Jewish Wedding Book*, Schocken Books, Inc., New York, 1968.

"Mr. Chairman, friends." It is a reference to the importance of marriage as a basic social institution. Because society has always been deeply interested in and concerned with marriage, it is taken for granted that representatives of society will witness a wedding. All three ceremonies include such witnesses, and in the Jewish ceremony they are to be unrelated to the bride and groom. This same societal interest in marriage is also implied in a later statement in many Protestant ceremonies, "If any man can show just cause why they may not lawfully be joined together, let him now speak, or else hereafter forever hold his peace." Such interest is indicated, too, in the publication of the banns before a Catholic wedding.

Is the Wedding or Marriage a Sacrament?

A sacrament is defined as "an external, visible sign of internal, invisible (or spiritual) grace." Most of the major Christian churches define at least baptism and communion (the Lord's Supper) as sacraments. Two exceptions are the Baptist church (or churches) and the Disciples of Christ, in which such rituals are referred to as ordinances rather than as sacraments. The Catholic Church frankly uses the phrase "The Sacrament of Matrimony" and usually combines the wedding with the nuptial Mass.

Phrases such as "holy matrimony," "instituted of God signifying unto us the mystical union that is betwixt Christ and His Church," "holy estate," "God's holy ordinance" which are found in many Protestant ceremonies raise the question of whether the wedding or marriage is a sacrament in Protestant churches, too. Answers to this question among Protestants reflect considerable divergence of opinion. Some hold that marriage is a sacrament. Others hold that marriage is not a true sacrament but is sacramental; that is, it is the symbol of and means for the spiritual union of two persons. Such a view suggests that marriage may become a means by which God's love is made manifest in human life but that this does not of necessity occur at the time of the wedding. The wedding offers the couple an opportunity to participate in the sacramental possibilities of marriage. Through the wedding they indicate their readiness to do so. The wedding does not, however, force these possibilities upon them or make their participation automatic.

Who or What Marries a Couple?

A couple may marry without a license if they can find an officiant willing to perform the ceremony. In such a case the penalty, if any, falls upon the officiant; but the marriage is usually valid. A valid marriage may occur without a ring. Except in cases of common-law marriage and in those involving the adherents of certain religious sects, there is an officiant. If the couple believe that their wedding was bona fide, only to learn that the officiant was an imposter, their marriage is usually still valid. It is not necessary to include any religious element

MARRIAGE IN PREPARATION

in the ceremony in order to fulfill the requirements of the law. It is impossible to escape the influence of the state. But the state merely sanctions; it does not marry people. The state, for instance, could not marry two persons against their will. Witnesses, by definition, merely observe. It is not required that the bride be "given away." In the last analysis, then, the element without which there can be no valid wedding is found in the couple's mutual agreement, their "I do's" or "I will's." This mutual agreement is termed *consensus*. This it is that marries them, with the sanction of church and/or state. This statement cannot be taken too literally, however. A couple could not marry themselves simply by saying that they had agreed to be husband and wife, though in some states such an agreement is a legal consideration in determining their status at common law.

It is important to note that when "I will," "Wilt thou have this woman to be thy wedded wife," "Wilt thou love her, comfort her, honour, and keep her," or "Wilt thou take (Name) here present" is used, it implies an act of will, not the future tense of the verb. If it did imply the future tense of the verb, it would have to be followed by another question, "When?" This act of will is expressed in the Jewish ceremony simply as "Do you (Name) take (Name) to be your wife (husband)? . . ." All this is indication that at the core of marriage there is a deliberate, voluntary commitment to a new relationship.

A New State of Being

Toward the end of the Protestant ceremony the clergyman says, "I pronounce that they are man and wife." In making this statement he is not marrying the couple. He is announcing the fact that they are married and that their marriage falls within the framework defined and approved by church and state. In some Protestant ceremonies "declare" is used in place of "pronounce." Before the clergyman makes the above pronouncement or declaration, he summarizes what has happened with such phrases as "having consented together in holy wedlock," "have witnessed the same before God and this company," "have given and pledged their troth," "have declared the same by giving and receiving a ring and by joining hands." The use of the word "pronounce" in this connection is similar to the use of the same word by a physician when he says, "I pronounce the patient well" or "I pronounce the patient dead." This does not imply that the physician has healed or killed the patient. It is an announcement of a recognized state of being.

In the Catholic ceremony, after the bride and groom have expressed their commitment, the priest says, "By the authority of the Church I ratify and bless the bond of marriage you have contracted." The priest does not marry the couple at this point any more than a Protestant clergyman does, as mentioned above.

What is this state of being that the clergyman recognizes? Is it merely a new social relationship? A partnership? A cooperative pair? A new opportunity for two people to share a common life and to have children? A common responsibility? A union of two persons in love—within the law and approved by the church? It is all these—but also more. It is a relationship in which two individuals may find possibilities for sharing in a spiritual and, some would hold, a sacramental union. They become "one flesh."

On a certain occasion in answer to a question, Jesus quoted a statement from the book of Genesis (Gen. 2:24) as follows: "For this cause shall a man leave his father and his mother and cleave to his wife; and they two shall be one flesh" (Mark 10:7–8). The term *one flesh* implies more than sexual union. It implies that a new "body," a new oneness, has been created—an entity that is more than the mere sum of two separate and distinct units. Even the law in its most critical application recognizes that there is something unique in the husband-wife relationship and that they are not two entirely distinct persons when it provides that in court a wife cannot be forced to testify against her husband or a husband against his wife when one is accused of a felony. It would be too much like a person's testifying against himself. As suggested earlier, some churches go farther and recognize this uniqueness as the establishment of both a sacramental union and a new spiritual entity described by comparing it to the "mystical union" of Christ and the Church.

A Single Standard

The statement to which each person says "I do" or "I will" typically is the same for both. There is no double standard of intent or responsibility. In the light of the equality implied in this statement, it is interesting to note that some ceremonies make allowance for the woman to be given in marriage, usually by her father or some relative or close friend. There is no corresponding procedure by which the man is given in marriage. Does this suggest inequality? This practice may be a carry-over from very early times when a woman passed directly from the control of her father to the control of her husband with no intermediate state of relative independence. Or it may be an indication that women are accorded more protection than men. Assuming greater vulnerability and therefore a greater need for protection of women, it is considered important for somebody besides the woman herself to approve of her marriage. If this approval can be expressed through a public act, the marriage may be given some added element of security by being tied in with the woman's parental family.

Taking of Hands

At some point in the ceremony it is common for each to take hold of the other's right hand. This adds a new element, namely, personal contact. Whenever two persons bring parts of their bodies into contact in an acceptable, favorable way, they tend to break down some of the barriers that ordinarily exist between them and to begin to share one another. To some degree, however slight, a community, a union is set up between them. For example, a kiss is an expression of affection. Shaking hands is an expression of friendship. In the wedding ceremony we find community and union implied through a symbolic form of physical contact. In the Jewish ceremony such community is symbolized by the bride and groom twice drinking from the same cup of wine.

Marital Adjustment Implied

In the commitments which a couple declare, there are statements that both implicitly and explicitly suggest the nature of marriage adjustment. For example, Protestant: "Wilt thou love her (or him), in sickness and in health; and, forsaking all others, keep thee only unto her (or him), so long as ye both shall live?" and "To have and to hold from this day forward, for better for worse, for richer for poorer, in sickness and in health, to love and to cherish, till death do us part." Catholic: "I, (Name), take you, (Name), for my lawful wife (or husband), to have and to hold, from this day forward, for better, for worse, for richer, for poorer, in sickness and in health, until death do us part." Jewish (Reform): "Do you (Name) take (Name) to be your wife (husband), promising to cherish and protect her (him), whether in good fortune or in adversity, and to seek together with her (him) a life hallowed by the faith of Israel?"

These statements suggest (1) that the couple will accept one another as they are; (2) that they will both love and respect each other in spite of possible shortcomings; (3) that they will exert continued effort to make the marriage succeed; (4) that they may well anticipate problems; (5) that marriage is an exclusive relationship; (6) that they commit themselves to it.

Following the statement of commitment, there is an exchange of a ring or rings. We shall discuss rings and their meaning later in this chapter. Suffice it to say here that in the modern wedding ceremony the ring is a token, a symbol of the pledge made and of the hope that the marriage will be permanent.

Is Marriage Dissoluble?

In one form or another, the Christian ceremony typically contains the following statement made by Jesus: "Those whom God hath joined together let not man put asunder." This statement plus the phrases "so long as ye both shall live" and "till death do us part" raises a basic issue. Is marriage dissoluble? Is divorce ever justified? We know, of course, that divorce is possible within the law. We know, too, that the great majority of Americans regret the occurrence of divorce but, nevertheless, accept it. But how does divorce harmonize with religious teachings? Here, again, we find far from universal agreement. Divorce is possible within the Jewish faith. The Roman Catholic Church holds that valid marriage once established and consummated is indissoluble because it is under the jurisdiction of God and not within the jurisdiction of any human agency. By and large, Protestant churches permit divorce, and the following is broadly representative of a Protestant point of view.

It is true that in a typical ceremony the couple say "I will" or "I do" to a question that ends with the expression "so long as ye both shall live." This may be interpreted as expressing their solemn intent to the best of their ability at the time of making the commitment. It need not be interpreted as the irrevocable welding of eternal bonds merely through the saying of words. "So long as ye both shall live" does not follow a promise merely to stay married. Ordinarily it follows a commitment to "live together after God's ordinance in the holy estate of matrimony," a commitment to love, comfort, honor, protect, and be faithful to the other party. If a couple find that their marriage has ceased to be what the first part of this statement suggests, and if we recognize that no amount of insistence or force can re-create and reestablish such a marriage, then it would seem that rigid adherence to "so long as ye both shall live" is a preservation of the body after life has been destroyed. In the expectation of society and in the thinking of the couple entering it, marriage is taken to be a permanent relationship. The great majority of marriages are such permanent relationships, at least until the death of one of the parties. Some persons would hold, therefore, that marriage in intent and in essence is indissoluble, and that dissolubility suggests a passive process. On the other hand, marriage is destructible, destructibility suggesting a sundering of a relationship that, by its very nature, should not have failed but somehow did.

Since the Roman Catholic Church does not recognize divorce in the case of a valid and consummated marriage, it cannot approve of remarriage after divorce. Such remarriage is accepted within the Jewish faith. Protestant churches vary in the degree of their acceptance of remarriage. Some raise no issue. Some accept the remarriage as valid but do not permit the wedding ceremony to be performed in the church. Some oppose remarriage. Among the last there is often an inconsistency. They deplore divorce, even though they may accept it, on the basis of children's need for two parents and whole family life. But in opposing remarriage they deprive children of the possibility of having such whole family life. Thus the children are penalized for the mistakes of the parents and become unwitting victims of doctrine.

WEDDING CUSTOMS

Many contemporary wedding customs are so old that their origins are lost in antiquity. In numerous cases we can only speculate as to how they started. Such customs are *survivals*; that is, they have maintained their form but have lost their original meaning and endured beyond the time when they had a function in connection with the ceremony. They might be called social fossils or be compared to vestiges, such as the appendix.

When we know nothing of the origin of one of these survivals, or when the original function, though known, is no longer acceptable, we rationalize the custom and convince ourselves that we carry it out for good luck. When doing something for luck savors too much of the superstitious, we are inclined to continue to do it "for fun." In most cases we carry it out because it is traditional and we accept tradition uncritically.

Marriage is a very ancient institution. There are no peoples known today, no matter how primitive, and no peoples known in history without some form of marriage. We can assume that marriage is almost as old as the human race. When a twentieth-century couple marry, they step into the stream of cultural history and link themselves with one of the oldest, most venerable, most tenacious, and most durable institutions known—an institution that has persisted in one form or another through all the vicissitudes of mankind's varied experience and in the face of innumerable theorists and reformers because it is the most effective means thus far discovered or evolved for ensuring the values maintained by marriage. Marriage is not the outgrowth of modern state legislation and romantic love alone. It is the product of the ages. One simple, concrete way of showing this is through a brief discussion of wedding customs.

The term *wedding* itself is a carry-over from ancient times. Originally the *wed* was the money or goods that the prospective groom gave to the father of the girl to secure or pledge the purchase of the bride.

The throwing of rice is common in this country. According to one theory, the rice constitutes a symbol of fertility. Throwing the rice is an expression of a wish that the new couple will have many children or is an offering to the spirits with this end in view. It is apparent that this custom has lost its original meaning, since having many children is not an immediate objective sought by most newlyweds. According to another theory, the rice was originally an offering to appease evil spirits bent on doing harm to the bride and groom. Or the throwing of the rice may be an outgrowth of the ceremonial eating of it.

To show how saturated with tradition we are, how we accept tradition uncritically, and how anything different from the customary is likely to seem ridiculous, let us suggest for illustration that navy beans be substituted for rice at weddings. They are small and inexpensive. They make as much or as little impression when they strike. They have the advantage of being more readily discovered and located in one's clothing. Yet such a substitution seems preposterous. The reader's reaction to it shows how he looks at life through the colored glasses of the mores and folkways and how the use of rice has become conventionalized.

Old shoes are sometimes thrown after the couple or tied to their vehicle as they leave the scene of the ceremony. Why old shoes? In many parts of the world the throwing of shoes has been considered a means of bringing good luck [Brasch, 1965]. In Scotland and Ireland shoes were thrown after anyone starting a new enterprise. When Queen Victoria first went to Balmoral Castle, shoes were thrown after her for good luck. In ancient Germany, after the ceremony the bride threw one of her shoes. The person who caught it would not only be the next to marry but would have lifelong good fortune.

A commonly accepted theory is that the shoe signifies the sealing of a bargain or the transference of authority or property ownership. This was true among the ancient Egyptians, Assyrians, and Israelites [Eichler, 1925]. In the Old Testament story, when Ruth and her mother-in-law, Naomi, returned to Bethlehem after the death of their husbands, Naomi set about planning the remarriage of the younger woman. According to the law of the levirate, it was the duty of the man nearest of kin to the deceased husband to marry the widow, the children of the union becoming the heirs of the dead man. Boaz was related to

Ruth's former husband, but there was one man whose kinship was nearer. Boaz wanted to marry Ruth. So he went to the city gate and waited for the other man to appear. Then he called together ten of the town's elders and in the presence of these witnesses stated that Naomi wanted to sell some land and whoever bought the land would have Ruth as his wife.

> And the kinsman said, I cannot redeem it for myself, lest I mar mine own inheritance: redeem thou my right to thyself; for I cannot redeem it. Now this was the manner in former time in Israel concerning redeeming and concerning changing, for to confirm all things; a man plucked off his shoe and gave it to his neighbor: and this was the testimony in Israel. Therefore the kinsman said unto Boaz, Buy it for thee. So he drew off his shoe. And Boaz said unto the elders and unto all the people, Ye are witnesses this day, that I have bought all that was Elimelech's. . . . Moreover Ruth . . . have I purchased to be my wife, to raise up the name of the dead upon his inheritance . . . [Ruth 4:6–10].

If the throwing of old shoes after a bridal couple is, as it seems, a carry-over of a means of sealing a bargain, one may readily see how a wedding links the couple to the past, for the story of Ruth is supposed to have occurred more than three thousand years ago, and the custom was already established at that early date.

The bride often wears "something old, something new, something borrowed, and something blue." The origin of this custom is not known. Part of it may again be attributed to the ancient Israelites, who were bidden to wear blue upon the borders of their garments, blue signifying purity, love, and fidelity.

The bride may wear a veil, or part of her costume may be what might be considered a remnant of a veil. It seems strange that on her wedding day, when she should be proud of her appearance, the bride should wear what is ordinarily a face covering. The veil may originally have been a means of indicating difference in status between an unmarried and a married woman. Typically peoples in some way indicate this difference. It may be a carry-over of the canopy held over the bridal couple during the ceremony among the ancient Hebrews and sometimes still used in the Jewish wedding. Or it may have originated as a means of disguise from evil spirits. All our remote ancestors believed in such spirits. On her wedding day a girl was considered especially vulnerable to their influence, and in many parts of the world today a bride is disguised as a means of protection. Originally the veil may have indicated the woman's submission to her husband or her change of identity [Brasch, 1965].

The use of a ring as a token or pledge is ancient. After Joseph had interpreted Pharaoh's dreams to the latter's satisfaction, the ruler said to Joseph, "See, I have set thee over all the land of Egypt. And Pharaoh took off his ring from his hand, and put it upon Joseph's hand . . ." [Gen. 41:41–42]. Other early peoples used rings in a similar manner. Eichler [1925] says that the ancient Egyptians were the first to use the ring in connection with marriage vows. In hieroglyphics a circle represents eternity, and the ring probably symbolized the eternal nature of marriage ties. Among the early Anglo-Saxons a ring was included in the *wed* mentioned above. This ring was worn on the bride's right hand until the time of the wedding ceremony, when it was transferred to her left hand. Wedding rings were employed by the Christians as early as A.D. 860.

There are several theories as to why the ring is worn on the fourth finger of the left hand. It is said that in early times the right hand signified power and authority, while the left signified subjection and submission. The ancient Greeks believed that there was a vein extending directly from the ring finger to the heart, the seat of love. It may be that the ring is worn on this particular finger merely because it is the least used of all fingers and ornaments worn upon it cause no inconvenience [Brasch, 1965].

In many wedding ceremonies, both bride and groom have attendants. With the possible exception of the best man, these attendants no longer have any save a decorative function. This custom may have its origin in the ten witnesses required in ancient Rome, the witnesses usually being friends of the bride's family. Or the custom may be a carry-over of marriage by capture. It is thought that in very early days wives were stolen or captured and that parties of friends and relatives to protect the woman or assist the prospective husband gave rise to the custom of having attendants. Among some peoples today there is still mock capture at the wedding ceremony [Sumner and Keller, 1927].

Until recently the bride promised to "love, honor, and *obey*." Nowadays *obey* is commonly omitted. The status of women has changed, and the relationship of husband and wife has been considerably altered. Hence, there is no use in including superfluous words in the ceremony. It is significant, however, that the word "obey" was until recently commonly employed and is still sometimes used and also that at no time did the groom promise to obey; he promised to "love, honor, and *cherish*," or something similar.

The custom of the bride's throwing her bouquet to the young unmarried women after the ceremony is still not uncommon, although bouquets are now sometimes composed of numerous sections wired together and ready for convenient distribution. When the bride does throw her bouquet, the belief is that the girl who catches it will be the next to marry. It is said that in the early fourteenth century in France it was considered good luck to procure one of the bride's garters after the ceremony—a custom rather inconvenient for the bride. From this grew the custom of throwing a stocking, a practice that was common during the fifteenth century. This, too, was inconvenient and gave way to throwing the bouquet [Eichler, 1925].

It is believed to bring ill luck if the groom sees the bride in her wedding dress or sees her at all before the ceremony on the wedding day. The origin of this custom is uncertain. It may be that it began when parents feared elopement and consequently being cheated out of the bride price. It may have originated in the belief that the groom could direct evil spirits or the evil eye to the ever-vulnerable bride.

In many cases noisemakers are used before or after a wedding. A bell is rung, tin cans are tied to the couple's vehicle, or other cars follow the bridal car with horns sounding. We accept the wedding bell without question, and the other two types of noisemaking are rationalized as "fun." But one wonders what the origin of this custom was. It may have begun with the belief that noise frightens evil spirits, as many peoples still hold. It may be only a means of publicity.

Often there is an element of slight promiscuity introduced into a wedding. After the ceremony proper the men are free to kiss the bride and the women to kiss the groom. The commonly accepted line drawn between those who have such freedom and those supposed to exericse restraint and to lack interest in such osculatory indulgence breaks down. There is reason to wonder whether this slight promiscuity is reminiscent of the complete license found at weddings among some of the peoples of the world whose beliefs and customs have remained unaltered for centuries.

It is not unusual for the groom to carry the bride over the threshold of their new home. In ancient Rome the threshold was considered sacred to Vesta, the goddess of virgins, and it was thought to be an ill omen if the bride stumbled over it. To prevent her stumbling, the young husband carried her into the house. What happens if he stumbles with her is not clear.

The custom of "belling" or charivari (often pronounced colloquially as if it were "shiveree," with the accent on the last syllable) is current in some communities. The practice has many local variations. In each case the twofold function seems to be the same, namely, publicity plus community acceptance of the marital status of the newly-wed pair. Newspapers and other modern means of publicity and communication make a demonstration superfluous in most communities, but the custom persists in part as a survival.

SECRET MARRIAGE

There is a difference between a secret wedding and a secret marriage. The former is an elopement and the fact of marriage is made known after the ceremony. In the case of the latter, the secret is kept for an extended period and neither the ceremony nor the new relationship is made known. An elopement may also be a "runaway" wedding which is not necessarily performed secretly but is performed in a manner and in a place that carry it beyond the influence and observation of relatives and friends.

In the case of either wedding or marriage, there are various degrees of secrecy possible. The secret may be kept from everyone except the license issuer, the officiant, and the legally required witnesses. It may be kept from parents, from friends, from an employer, or from the public at large. The degree of secrecy and the persons from whom the secret is kept constitute variables that affect the arguments pro and con listed below.

There are few valid arguments in favor of either secret wedding or secret marriage, and those few apply to relatively rare circumstances. In cases where there is *unreasonable* and *unfounded* opposition, where parents insist upon lifelong celibacy, where there has been a recent death in the family that upsets wedding plans and preparation, or where similar unusual conditions exist, secrecy may be justifiable. But such cases are relatively uncommon. Nothing is gained by reading into the situation elements that are not there in order to rationalize secrecy.

There are secret weddings and secret marriages that work out well, but in general the arguments against them are weightier than those in their favor. There is no opportunity for the couple's enthusiasm to be either counterbalanced or reinforced by the judgment of relatives and friends. Secrecy is all too often the outgrowth of haste; and hasty marriage frequently ends in failure. Married life is started with deception and concealment. It is not only a matter of deceiving those who might object to the marriage but also a matter of keeping secret something that one wants very much to make known. One young woman who had married secretly and kept the secret for some time explained that after the ceremony she was very happy. She loved her husband and they planned eventually to marry anyway, but they married secretly in order to do so earlier. She wanted very much to tell her family and friends how happy she was, and her emotions seemed to accumulate as time went on. But because of the administrative situation in the school that she was attending, she could not mention it. When the time came that she could tell her secret, her original burst of enthusiasm had waned somewhat, for she had then been married for several months; much to her regret, she had missed one of the great experiences of a woman's life.

Secrecy is likely to offend parents and friends and often makes for enmity with in-laws. Parents are usually hurt, not only because their child has married but because their pride has been injured by their being kept ignorant of plans and events. Often, too, the bride's parents have for years dreamed of wedding plans for her. Her secrecy seems like an affront, since it has the appearance of a refusal to accept what they are eager to give or a lack of gratitude for what they would willingly have done. Secrecy may also seem to parents an indication of lack of trust, in that it appears as if the son or daughter did not feel free to confide in them.

Then, too, suddenly to find that they have a new son-in-law or daughter-in-law without having gradually come to an acceptance of this state of affairs is frequently something of a shock to parents and necessitates readjustment more rapid than they had anticipated.

Marriage is important enough to make it worth while to start out under the best possible auspices. Parents and parents-in-law may do much to make marital adjustment easier or more difficult. Unless it means the sacrificing of one's happiness, the cultivation of their favor is an investment that pays ample dividends.

There is sometimes a cloud of suspicion cast over a secret wedding or secret marriage. When at last the facts are made known, people naturally wonder about the reason for the secrecy. Was she afraid she would lose him? Did she not get along well with her family? Was it a forced marriage? Did they really marry when they say they did, or did they marry later and then say that they had been secretly married earlier in order to camouflage a premarital pregnancy?

The best secrets sometimes leak out, and then seemingly well-laid plans are disrupted. If the marriage as well as the wedding is kept secret, the couple find difficulty in living either as single or as married persons. If they try to live in the latter way, their behavior will be subject to question by their families and friends. If they attempt to seem unmarried, there frequently ensues a problem of dating, especially if the couple attend different colleges. It is all very well to make ambitious statements about letting each other date, but because of our expectation of exclusiveness it is difficult to work out smoothly. Husband or wife may not be able to accept in practice what seems acceptable in theory when marriage is being contemplated, and it appears that whether or not they will marry soon and secretly depends upon their willingness to be liberal and broad-minded. There is also likely to be criticism when the dates discover that the person they thought single is married and that they have been duped. Public opinion is unfavorable to such dating. In one case a co-ed secretly married went steady with a man for several months. She was a frequent visitor in his home and accepted by his family as a "girl friend." The man spent many hours coaching her in academic subjects in which she had difficulties. At the end of the college semester, when his help was no longer needed, she told him that she had been married some time before. His disillusionment and his family's resentment may be imagined.

If the marriage is secret and the wife becomes pregnant, explanation is made most difficult. Friends and relatives may or may not believe that she was married at the time of conception. A person does not usually carry a certificate stating the date of the wedding so that he may show it to friends the moment their doubt and suspicion become manifest. Such a certificate, even if one did carry it, could not be made available to everyone who might have an inclination to pick up and pass on a tempting bit of gossip.

This section on secret marriage is intended for the single, not the married. We should be the last to implant doubt, apprehension, or regret in the mind of a reader already secretly married. What is done is done. Such a one needs a practical plan for the future, not criticism of the past. Our purpose has been to provide food for thought. No one needs to marry secretly unless he chooses to do so; he is never forced to do it. Our hope is that those contemplating secret marriage will weigh the pros and cons before making a decision.

THE HONEYMOON

Originally the term *honeymoon* referred to the period immediately following the wedding, during which the couple's affection was thought to wane like the moon. Nowadays, the term usually refers to a wedding trip. Not every couple has a wedding trip, of course, and there is no reason to assume that married life cannot have an auspicious beginning without one.

The function of the honeymoon is to enable the couple to make the transition from single life to married life with greatest facility and fewest handicaps. Whatever furthers this transition may be promoted. Whatever impedes it may be avoided. Since in some respects the honeymoon is an artificial situation, it need be only long enough to fulfill its function. Customarily the groom's financial condition determines cost.

Since the function of the honeymoon is to facilitate the couple's transition to married life, a leisurely schedule rather than an overcrowded program is more conducive to this end. The honeymoon is not a travel-bureau, prearranged, all-expense tour on which the traveler has little to say about time schedules and feels that, unless he sees every monument and witnesses every spectacle, he is not getting his money's worth. Dashing here and rushing there may lead to excessive fatigue, and fatigue may lead to irritability which, in turn, during the hypersensitive days of the honeymoon, may give rise to disillusionment.

The couple may not make their destination known to all their relatives and friends because they want to avoid possible intrusion. But to leave addresses with someone so that they may be reached in an emergency will put them at ease. One would expect it to "go without saying" that both persons would be aware of honeymoon plans, but this is not always so. In one case, the man planned the honeymoon and built it up to the woman as a surprise and an exciting trip, refusing to give her any details. Imagine her disillusionment when the honeymoon turned out to be a one-night stay at a second-class local motel.

THE TRANSITION FROM SINGLENESS TO MARRIAGE

We have referred to the honeymoon as a period of transition. Actually, of course, it represents only part of such a period. The transition from singleness to marriage begins at least with the engagement and extends through the wedding and honeymoon and into marriage itself [see Lopata, 1971]. To make their marriage succeed a couple must pass through a number of transitions. To the degree to which they fail to do so, the marriage is likely to suffer. Some of these transitions are as follows.

From independence to interdependence; from independence to a "team" relationship This "team" relationship is, in a sense, unique because it involves two persons of opposite sex. When two complementary equals are united in common purpose, a new oneness, a new entity, is created. Their relationship extends not to a part of life but to a fundamental way of life. Such a transition entails concessions on either side. It requires a new perspective in that the relationship is in some ways considered more important than the individuals in it. Obviously, a person who cannot make this transition and who consequently continues to think, act, make demands, and set expectations as if he were still single is an impediment to the success of the "team."

From a premarital sexual pattern to a marital sexual pattern For many persons, especially but not exclusively women, this involves a transition from premarital chastity or infrequent, often incomplete, sexual relations to unrestrained marital sexual experience. For some women this expected about-face is not easy, and the full transition takes time. But certainly it is appropriate to expect a woman who marries to redefine her sexual objective and shift it from premarital self-protection and reluctance to marital acceptance and enthusiastic sharing. A woman can hardly be married and single simultaneously. If she insists upon protecting herself from her husband, what did she mean in the wedding ceremony when she said, "I take this man"?

Depending upon his premarital experience or lack of it, the man may be called upon to make a transition from giving first consideration to his own sexual satisfaction to giving first consideration to the satisfaction of his wife, through which his own satisfaction is increased. He is called upon to think of sex as a mutual rather than only as a self-oriented experience.

The couple are called upon to make a transition from thinking of sexual intercourse as having no place in their premarital behavior pattern, from treating it casually, from being subject to premarital limitations, or from the woman's reluctant acceptance for the sake of the man's pleasure, to integrating it into the totality of their common life.

From the relative irresponsibility of romance to the responsibilities associated with establishing and maintaining a home and family For this transition many young people are not well prepared. The man may fail to understand that homemaking and family living today put demands upon him other than in his role as breadwinner. He may expect his wife to continue to wait upon him as his mother did or to perform without reciprocation on his part the personal services for which in his premarital days he was accustomed to pay and for which, therefore, he felt no call to express appreciation. The woman may be unprepared to carry out housekeeping duties with efficiency and dispatch. Her attitude toward gainful employment may lead her to resist or even to reject the role of homemaker to which, she feels, there is attributed too little prestige.

From the responsibility of carrying out assignments to the type of responsibility that makes assignments unnecessary College students who may be considered "good students" in the sense of carrying out assignments and conforming to faculty expectation are in some cases ill-prepared to make and carry out plans without outside pressure. They fritter away time and energy and sometimes do only the minimum necessary to "get by"—or less—because in marriage they have no one to tell them what to do.

From premarital food preparation to family feeding This applies particularly, but not exclusively, to women. Many a girl who is skilled at preparing party foods finds herself confronted with quite a different problem in preparing a balanced diet for a husband who eats 1,095 meals per year or in feeding two persons on a meager income.

From student purchasing to family purchasing With some exceptions, college students may usually do the bulk of their purchasing in a small number of stores of relatively limited type adjacent to the campus. Family purchasing presents a somewhat different problem because of the greater variety of items to be purchased and because of the resulting greater complexity of the budget. With the exception of gifts, student purchasing involves largely items for oneself. Family purchasing requires knowledge of buying items for a home, for a member of the opposite sex, and for children.

From a single-person spending pattern to a "double-person" spending pattern In some cases the man continues to think in terms of "my money," a portion of which he reluctantly doles out to his wife when her need is clearly apparent or her pleas are sufficiently convincing. Cases are known in which such an attitude is so ingrained in a man that he even thinks of her income as "my money." In one case, in which the wife was working to put her husband through school, he would accompany her to the bank when she deposited her paycheck and then give her a small allowance from her salary. The woman, in some cases, continues to spend family income as if she were still single and receiving an allowance from her parents and her own desires were the only ones to be considered.

From premarital identity to marital identity This transition is more conspicuous for the woman than for the man, since in most cases she assumes her husband's surname preceded by "Mrs." A few women combine their maiden name with the husband's surname into a hyphenated "married name" and a few are beginning to use "Ms." rather than "Mrs." as suggested by women's liberationists. Nonetheless, the woman comes to be thought of, and, perhaps more importantly, comes to think of herself, as the wife of so-and-so. This shift in identity is difficult, even traumatic, for women who fear a loss of individuality. Other women accept it as part of getting married and are not threatened by it.

Men, too, change their identity at marriage but not to the degree that women do. Married couples come to be thought of as pairs. Unless a man is dishonest about it, he comes to be thought of as the husband of so-and-so. The wearing of wedding bands by both sexes is an outward indication of this shift in indentity, and men are increasingly accepting rings.

From being a child of one's parents to being husband or wife This raises the question, "Who will be put first in one's scale of values, spouse or parents?" The individual who cannot put spouse first is not ready to be married.

From being a child of one's parents to being a child-in-law of the other person's parents This transition takes time and calls for understanding and effort on the part of all concerned, as we shall see in a later chapter.

From marriage to the family, that is, from having no child to having a child For obvious reasons the arrival of the first child is most critical so far as this transition is concerned. "A marital relationship undergoes irreversible change with the arrival of the first baby" [Ehrlich, 1972]. A question arises as to the spouse's and the child's relative position in one's scale of values. In a successful family there is an integration of such nature that spouse and child are not thrown into competition for the attention of the other parent. In some families, however, the arrival of the first child means that husband or wife, more frequently the latter, allows attention to the child, in a sense, to squeeze the other party out of the marriage relationship. In other words, the woman becomes so much a mother that she is correspondingly less a wife. In occasional cases the situation is vice versa. For example, in one case the couple got along apparently happily until the birth of the first baby. Then the husband refused to go out with his wife in the evening because he would not leave the child with a baby-sitter. He objected to his wife's shopping, visiting friends, or attending church for the same reason. He would not go out or let her go out and take the child along because he feared it would contract some contagious disease. The wife felt that she was virtually a prisoner in her own home because of her baby.

From personal appearance to attract to personal appearance to please Actually the above distinction is not complete; the two processes overlap. But although there are many young people today who are very casual in their dress, there are also many who give time and attention to making themselves attractive during their dating days only to let their appearance rapidly deteriorate after the wedding. Not everyone can be beautiful or handsome; but everyone can, if he will, make the most of his possibilities. Neglect of appearance is sometimes a reflection of disappointment with marriage.

Even persons most attentive to personal appearance cannot be equally attractive at all times. No one is so attractive upon getting up in the morning or while doing certain types of work as he may be at other times. Marriage involves understanding and accepting this fact—which in itself is a transition for many persons with limited premarital contacts. The critical point here is the individual's attitude toward personal appearance after the uncertainty of the premarital search for a spouse is ended and the security of marriage makes attracting another person no longer necessary. The transition involved is that between attraction, on the one hand, and attractiveness, on the other.

CAMPUS MARRIAGE

In appraising campus marriage, broad generalizations become meaningless. To be helpful the appraisal must be particularized. The question is not, "Can such marriage be made to work?" The question is, "Can this particular couple, with their particular objectives, assets, and liabilities, in their particular situation, make such marriage work?" Much depends upon the quality of persons involved. Here, for example, is a young man who is unmarried. He has a high IQ. His parents subsidize him so generously that he does not have to earn money during his college days. He is in excellent health. Yet he is on scholastic probation because he does not maintain a required grade level. Here, on the other hand, is a young couple both of whom are employed because they are completely on their own financially. They have two children and are expecting a third. The wife is concerned lest labor start during the final examination period. They participate in campus activities, are very happily married, and are both maintaining a commendable grade level.

A few decades ago only an occasional college or university student married and remained in school. This was especially true of undergraduates in liberal arts colleges. There was widespread skepticism, and some outright opposition, relative to both students' ability to handle successfully the education-plus-marriage situation and the advisability of letting them attempt it. Some administrators were convinced that an appreciable proportion of married students in an undergraduate student body would somehow constitute a threat, a disrupting influence. In some schools there was discrimination as well as skepticism. For example, married students were not permitted to participate in school-sponsored athletic events, could not live in dormitories or fraternity or sorority houses, or were not allowed to hold offices in campus organizations.

Today much of this earlier resistance to campus marriage has disappeared. Only traces of it remain. Administrators have found that many students can successfully combine marriage and college education and that married students are not only not a source of campus disruption but may contribute to campus stability. Yet in some schools married students are relegated to inferior housing, and there is a sort of unexpressed attitude to the effect that "You married of your own free will. Therefore, if you have any problems due to the fact that you're married, don't expect us to help you solve them."

Number of Married Students

In 1971, there were 8,087,000 students enrolled in institutions of higher learning. Of these about one-fourth were in two-year colleges and three-fourths in four-year colleges [U.S. Bureau of the Census, March, 1972]. In 1971, one-fourth of all college students were married and living with their spouses [U.S. Bureau of the Census, October, 1972]. This figure does not, therefore, include students who were married but whose spouses were absent, for example, in military service. Half again as high a percentage of male students (29 per cent) as female students (19 per cent) were married and living with their spouses [U.S. Bureau of the Census, October, 1972].

There are several possible explanations for the difference in the percentage married between the two sexes. As a group, males are more likely than females to go through college. Males are also more likely to work for advanced or professional degrees. Male students, as a group, are older than female students. There are some married male students whose wives already have their undergraduate degrees. Many married women drop out of school because of childbearing or in order to contribute to family support while their husbands are students.

This is not the entire picture, however. In 1971, about 25 per cent of the students in two-year colleges were married and living with their spouses as compared with 12 per cent in the first two years of four-year colleges [U.S. Bureau of the Census, June, 1972]. See Table 6.1 for a comparison of married students with other first- and second-year students relative to full-time and part-time enrollment. The figures suggest that one of the "costs" of campus marriage is that it takes a longer period to get a degree. It is estimated that by 1980 total college enrollment will reach 10 to 11 million [U.S. Bureau of the Census, February, 1972]. Thus, the number of married students may be expected to increase accordingly.

Since present-day college education is so closely tied in with occupational training for many students, males and females are subjected to somewhat different social pressure toward getting degrees. There are males who drop out of college because they cannot handle satisfactorily the combined task of marriage, study, and earning. On the other hand, there are males whose motivation toward completing a degree is increased with marriage. Generalizing, this increased motivation is more likely to be seen in the male than in the female because the male is subject to the social expectations associated with family support and standard of living.

In contrast, after her wedding, many a girl loses her motivation for getting a degree. She may see a less apparent connection between her college work and her new role as wife-homemaker than her husband sees between his studying and his occupational objective. She may become absorbed in her new responsibilities. She may feel that her husband's burden would be lightened if she got a job. She may find it inconvenient to get to classes at times when she would prefer to be doing something domestic. Since she is under neither social nor occupational pressure to get ahead in the sense in which her husband is expected to get ahead occupationally, she may fail to see the importance of continuing her education. She may feel that when she married, she "arrived." Overlooking the relationship between education and satisfaction in living, she may feel that it is pointless to continue to work for a degree when she is already where she wants to be. Her motivation gradually slips away. She drops out. If her dropping out means that eventually her husband will continue to grow while she marks time, an educa-

Table 6.1. First- and second-year students: marital status and enrollment.

SEX, MARITAL STATUS, AND FULL-TIME AND PART-TIME ENROLLMENT	PERCENT DISTRIBUTION	
	TWO-YEAR COLLEGES	FIRST AND SECOND YEAR OF FOUR-YEAR COLLEGES
MALE	100.0	100.0
Married, wife present	28.6	15.0
Enrolled full time	9.3	6.4
Enrolled part time	19.3	8.6
Other marital status	71.4	85.0
Enrolled full time	57.5	78.9
Enrolled part time	13.9	6.2
FEMALE	100.0	100.0
Married, husband present	20.5	8.5
Enrolled full time	5.7	4.9
Enrolled part time	14.8	3.6
Other marital status	79.5	91.5
Enrolled full time	58.0	85.7
Enrolled part time	21.5	5.8

Adapted from U.S. Bureau of the Census, *June, 1972.*

tionally mixed marriage may develop, though it was not such a mixed marriage at the time of the wedding.

The girl may also overlook the importance of her education as a type of insurance. Typically a man sees a point in carrying life insurance to protect his wife and children in the event of his death. He purchases the life insurance with money which he receives in return for effort and time. If a husband dies, usually his wife must take employment. If a wife dies, on the other hand, the husband's employment goes on. So her means of protecting her children, should her husband die, is not through life insurance, as such, but rather in having occupational training, which is attained through effort and time just as is the money used by a man to purchase insurance. Says Margaret Mead, "A girl's education today is her dowry."

This matter of dropping out gives concern to school administrators as well as to students. Precisely how common it is cannot be ascertained because, when students drop out of college, the reasons for their doing so are not always readily apparent, and precipitating causes may be confused with basic causes. But we may be sure that, among students who might otherwise receive their degrees, a higher dropout rate, like reduced academic load and hence a longer period required for a degree, is one of the costs of the increase in the number of campus marriages. A degree is a worthy objective. Marriage is also a worthy objective. The concept of cost arises when one such objective is sacrificed for the achievement of another such objective.

Dropping out is sometimes followed by projection of blame in later life. For example, suppose a woman drops out in order to get a job so that her husband may graduate. In later life, when she has forgotten how eager she was to leave school but feels different from the wives of her husband's professional associates because she has no degree, she may project the blame onto him. Or suppose a male student drops out because his wife becomes pregnant and must give up her job and there is no way for the family to be supported except through his efforts. He gets an immediately well-paying but blind-alley job. As the years go on the men who would have been his professional associates move ahead in the field in which he would prefer to be working. He begins to feel like a "might-have-been." It would not be difficult for him unintentionally to project blame for his failure onto the wife and child. The accusation "if it hadn't been for you" can be devastating for a person to live with.

Other considerations in connection with campus marriage are as follows.

Age and Maturity

After the Second World War, when the great influx of veterans into the colleges occurred, a rapid increase in the frequency of campus marriage took place. The arrival of veterans on the campus was not the only factor causing this increase, but it was undoubtedly one contributing factor. Many of the veterans were older than the previously typical undergraduate. Hence many of the married students were older. No figures are available for comparing the ages of married students then and now. But it would be safe to guess that with the increase in the number of campus marriages the picture has changed somewhat. Many current campus marriages involve relatively young students. Some of them are immature. It goes without saying that the age and maturity of the persons participating in a marriage, campus or otherwise, play an ample role in the success or failure of that marriage.

Status

An individual's or a couple's place in the college scheme is an important consideration so far as marriage is concerned. Contrast these two cases with respect to the advisability of marrying. One case involves two seniors who plan to marry in March and who graduate in June. The other case involves a seventeen-year-old freshman woman and an eighteen-year-old sophomore man who plans to go through medical school. They met in September and plan to marry during the Christmas vacation. Both of these would be considered campus marriages.

Grades

When the increase in campus marriages began, grade studies made in certain schools suggested that, as a group, married students earned higher grades than unmarried students [Riemer, February, 1947]. In evaluating such studies one might well wonder whether sufficient weight was given to two factors, namely, the ages of the students studied and the fact that grade studies must of necessity be made on students who are in school rather than on ex-students who for one reason or another dropped out of school or on persons who might have become students had there been nothing in their situations to prevent their doing so. There are cases in which marriage has provided a student or a couple with a sense of security, motivation toward study, and time free from pressures of dating, and thus contributed to the improvement of grades [Schroder, November, 1963]. On the other hand, there are students whose grades suffer because of marriage. The research data are not conclusive [Samenfink and Milliken, August, 1961]. Certainly no one would seriously suggest marriage as a way to raise one's grades.

Husband's Mobility

In some occupational fields a beginner, even though he has a professional degree, is expected to be able to move about from one location to another. It is a method used by large companies to find the proper niche for promising young men and to train them in the intricacies of the organization. In some instances an unmarried man may be moved about more readily than a married man, and the former is more amenable to such mobility. A married man may give more weight to income, housing, schools, and similar items than to the opportunity presented when moving is suggested. In some cases wives object to moving because they want to remain near parents, or they just get one apartment arranged to their liking when they are called upon to leave it and start over on another, or they do not like the prospect of living in the community in which the husband's new job would be located, or for any of a number of similar reasons. Hence, a woman contemplating a campus marriage might well give serious consideration to the question of whether she would help her husband or hinder him in the crucial early days of his career.

There may also be a problem of academic mobility. Even when a mistake has been made, a married male student may not feel free to change his major or his field of professional training, especially if such change would involve loss of credit and his wife or economic need puts him under pressure to get his degree as soon as possible.

Attitude of Parents

Parental approval and good will are assets to be preserved, if possible, in any marriage. Campus marriage is no exception. In many cases parents disapprove of a marriage when one or both of the couple are students, whereas these same parents would be more likely to approve if the young couple were not students. No matter how this may be explained—as cultural lag, failure to understand present-day trends, conservatism, fear of dropping out, insight, concern, love—it is part of the reality of the situation within which campus marriage occurs. This is not meant to imply that, no matter how old or how mature the young couple may be, the judgment of their parents must be the final determining factor in whether or not they marry. It is meant to imply that parental judgment is not to be lightly disregarded as if it had no bearing on the marriage.

Here again there is the problem of possible cost as one worthy objective is weighed against another worthy objective. Some couples confuse the importance of the time of marriage with the importance of the fact of marriage and in so doing sacrifice parental good will that might have been preserved if the wedding had been postponed to a later date.

Finances

In a campus marriage there is not only the problem of sufficient income per se but a correlative, and sometimes more sensitive, problem of who depends upon whom for what and for how long. We shall discuss this latter problem later.

Many campus couples exist upon minimum financing. Some have learned how to economize, how to stretch their income, how to do without things they want but do not need, how to budget, how to have recreation at low cost, and how to make some of the things they cannot afford to buy. To arrive at such a solution to the problem of finances requires the cooperation and understanding of both husband and wife. It cannot be achieved by one spouse while the other continues to act as if he or she were still single.

In any discussion of the financial problems of campus marriage the question of parental subsidy is certain to be raised. Should or should not parents contribute to the support of the campus couple? Should they be expected to do so?

Parents who willingly subsidize a son or daughter as a single student may refuse to continue such subsidy after the student marries. Others equally willingly continue subsidy after the wedding. Some increase it. In a few cases the two sets of parents and the campus couple work out a cooperative plan.

In those cases in which parents refuse to contribute to a child's support after the latter marries, one wonders whether there is merely bias expressed or a principle involved. They draw the line of support very sharply at the wedding— "When you marry, don't expect any more help from us."

On the one hand, the parents have a point. A couple should, if possible, be independent when they marry. On the other hand, the attitude that suggests the drawing of such a sharp line of demarcation at the wedding is one that emerged from social conditions of the past. It does not take fully into account the new phenomenon represented by the extension of higher education which parents themselves approve and encourage. It is easy to assert that young people should wait to marry until they have completed their formal schooling. One might more hopefully have expected this assertion to be a deterrent in earlier days when few attended college. But when one is discussing more than 8 million college students who represent almost a cross section of the population rather than a select elite, and who constitute a democratized student body whose objective is largely education for immediate practical use, occupationally or otherwise, rather than intellectual pursuit for its own sake, one must expect life to go on. One cannot expect all 8 million students to postpone marriage until they have completed their degrees when for some this means four to eight years of training beyond an undergraduate degree. This is in no way intended as meaning that parents should subsidize every campus marriage. It implies only a new evaluation of an old assumption. A similar new evaluation would be appropriate for those husbands who accentuate the problem of family financing by resisting a subsidy which the wife's parents are able to afford and willing to continue.

Parental subsidy does not necessarily mean regular allowance. It may take the form of special gifts, aid in time of financial stress, such as at the birth of a child, or payment of special costs, such as insurance premiums. It must also be noted that in any case of parental subsidy, no matter what form it takes, the gain is not worth the cost if the subsidy is accompanied by parental interference in the young marriage, if the subsidy is so generous and can be anticipated for so long in the future that the young couple grow to depend upon it and therefore lose their ambition and in a sense become pauperized, or if the young husband cannot accept the subsidy without a feeling of resentment or inadequacy yet the wife's parents insist upon continuing it.

Whether parental subsidy of campus marriage is desirable or undesirable is still an open question. No universal generalization can answer the question. In some cases it has worked out well; in others, poorly. In many cases it has not been tried. Whether it is good or bad, whether it should be more common or less common, the fact remains that at present not all parents favor it. The young person contemplating campus marriage must face the reality of the present, as well as the hopes of the future. Unless he is sure of his own parents' willingness and ability, and the willingness and ability of his fiancée's parents, to subsidize a contemplated marriage, the reader would be buying a grab bag if he married and depended upon the continuation of allowances for support.

Planning

Whether or not campus marriage succeeds depends in large part on the quality of planning with which it is inaugurated. Some students make plans which "look good on paper" but which cannot function effectively under any circumstances other than those anticipated at the time of the planning. There is no allowance made for the unexpected. There is not enough flexibility to permit the plan to be adapted to altered conditions. The plan is such that, if one element breaks down, the entire plan collapses. Only part of the marital situation, rather than all of it, is taken into account; the couple do not foresee the total job to be done. There is no reasonable assurance of the couple's attaining all of their objectives; there is the likelihood of their having to sacrifice one objective—marital success, academic degree, parental good will, or having children—for another, as mentioned earlier. For example, the couple's income will depend largely upon the wife's continuing to earn. If she becomes pregnant and has to give up her job, the plan collapses because no allowance is made for such an eventuality. Or the couple do not take into account the total job to be done, namely, earning, housekeeping, possibly child care, and academic work. They assume the same sort of division of labor that they could safely assume if the husband were a full-time breadwinner and the wife a full-time homemaker-mother; but such an assumption in their case is invalid.

A good plan is one which (1) is realistic and includes a critical appraisal of the couple's assets and liabilities; (2) takes into account the total job to be done and includes a mutually agreeable means for doing the job; (3) is flexible enough to be adapted to changing circumstances but sufficiently rigid and strongly enough motivated to withstand the ups and downs of day-to-day trials and errors; (4) is not so critically vulnerable at one point that the success of the entire plan rests upon the achievement of one part of it; (5) gives the couple some assurance of getting what they want; (6) at least to a reasonable degree eliminates conflict among their objectives so that these objectives, as mentioned above, are not set in opposition to each other in a way which permits one to be jeopardized by another. Most students enter college with serious intent. They hope to obtain an education, including for most of them occupational training. Their occupational ambitions ordinarily are geared to a high level of expectation. At the same time they hope someday to marry and establish a new family. Some consider the possibility of meeting a possible future marriage partner through campus contacts. Most of them are interested in maintaining a happy relationship with their own parental families and are hopeful of establishing an equally happy one with their new families-in-law when they marry. They want the social experiences which ordinarily accompany campus life. None of these objectives becomes any less important merely because a couple fall in love.

Security

Marriage can provide a unique type of security, but it cannot provide such security unless there already exists a sound and secure relationship between the two persons before the wedding. In other words, marriage cannot transmute insecurity into security; it cannot make security "out of whole cloth." It is not per se the solution to the problem of the couple one of whom does not want to return home or the couple who are afraid that during summer vacation or after the graduation of one of them they will drift apart. Marriage also provides the possibility of a solution to the problem of sexual tension. But it is not to be thought of merely as a solution to this problem. Some persons recommend early marriage as a means of solving the problem of premarital sexual intercourse. Such a recommendation is oversimplified and is often based on a disregard of other important considerations.

Special Stresses

One of the reasons for which campus marriage presents a problem to many persons, both to the individuals in it and to others, is that they make the erroneous assumption that campus marriage is merely young marriage that happens to occur in a college milieu. This assumption leads to expectations that may be appropriate for ordinary marriage but are not appropriate for campus marriage. There is a discrepancy between expectation and reality. The result is special stress, special pressure.

Campus marriage is young marriage, but it is not merely young marriage that happens to occur in a college milieu. In some respects it is a new type of marriage because it entails factors hitherto relatively unknown to the degree to which they are now found. The sooner this fact is recognized, the sooner progress will be made in improving campus marriage. We shall stop trying to fit the square peg of stereotype into the round hole of social change. Counseling has revealed some of the special "pressure points" in campus marriage, and the following are among them.

Reversal of role In many campus marriages the wife is the primary, sometimes the only, breadwinner. In some cases the husband resents this reversal of role and is uneasy under it. He may feel guilty. He could accept support from his wife if he were incapacitated. Such support would be socially approved. But he is able-bodied; and commitment to getting a degree does not carry the traditional weight carried by physical need. Under the circumstances it might appear logical for him to give a good deal of time to housework, but this he is not necessarily able or willing to do. His wife resents this because she has to carry a double load. There are also cases in which conflict arises because of the wife's resentment of the fact that the husband is not earning enough. Being less appreciative than he of the importance of his degree, she would like him to leave school and get a job so that she may stop working. This he will not do. In short, role reversal may be a problem for either or both spouses.

Because of role reversal, there have arisen a new "species" of wife and a new "species" of husband. The new species of wife is the woman who works to "put her husband through school." At commencement time some colleges and universities, half seriously, half facetiously, award such wives the P.H.T. degree (putting husband through). The new species of husband is the man who not only accepts but demands his wife's continued employment. In one case coming to the author's attention the wife had decided to divorce her graduate-student husband. When she told him of her plan, he said, "When we married, you said you would work until I finished graduate school. All right. Work until I get my degree. Then, if you want to get a divorce, it'll be OK with me." Reprehensible as such an attitude is, that husband could not have justified, even to himself, either such an assumption or such a statement a few decades ago.

Aspiration level   When an individual compares where he is with where he thinks he ought to be relative to standard of living, his definition of the latter will naturally affect his degree of acceptance of the former. The unmarried student thinks of his present standard of living as temporary, not entirely of his own making (although of his own choice because of his subordination of standard of living to academic achievement), the best that he and/or his parents can do under the circumstances, and something that will change when he gets his degree. His standard of living is not radically different from that of many students about whom he knows. A considerable amount of minimum living on limited income is commonly accepted among students.

The married student, on the other hand, when comparing his present standard of living with that which he feels he ought to have, is sometimes less likely to fit himself into the general college picture and more likely to compare what he has with the standard of living of the general married group in his socioeconomic class. He operates within a different framework. His present situation, then, seems full of limitations and deprivations and is less likely to be accepted without stress and strain. For example, an unmarried woman who would get along well on a minimum standard financed by her parents or her own employment may be discontented with the same standard when financed in part by a husband because being married gives her a different aspiration level on the basis of which she appraises her present standard and finds it wanting. Similarly, a male student may get along well with minimum income while he is unmarried but shift his basis for comparing where he is with where he thinks he ought to be when he marries and is called upon to provide a standard of living for a wife and perhaps children in a way which reflects upon him as a man. These are broad generalizations, to be sure, by no means applicable to all married students, but such cases do come to light.

Parental expectations When there is reversal of role as suggested above, the wife's parents sometimes contribute to family conflict by continually nagging their daughter with the insinuation that her husband "is not doing enough." This may be an expression of their disapproval of their daughter's having contracted a campus marriage, or it may be an indication of their lack of understanding that campus marriage is different from the type of marriage to which they are accustomed.

Wife's responsibilities Many a campus wife carries an unusually heavy load of responsibility. She may be a student herself, have employment, do housekeeping, and take care of one or more children. Even when she herself is not a student, her load may be heavy. In some cases this one-sidedness stems from lack of cooperation on the part of the husband. But in other cases it is not entirely his fault. If he is a poor or average student and has to struggle to maintain his grades but is determined to get a degree, he may literally not be able to help his wife as much as either of them would like. It is difficult for some campus wives to understand this and to accept a heavy load of responsibilities and yet have so little in the way of material goods and comforts to show for it. In some cases the total load is more than one person can carry successfully. If, in such a case, the husband criticizes the wife for neglecting part of the load, say certain aspects of housework, her resentment may be bitter indeed.

Child care Many campus couples are faced with the necessity of providing care for very young children while the parents are in class or at work. Sometimes this results in relatively unprecedented arrangements which emerge from the ancient truth that "necessity is the mother of invention." For example, one couple arranged their two class schedules so that one could be at home while the other attended class. But the college provided only ten minutes between classes. So one of the spouses would take care of the baby while the other went to class. Then the parent-sitter would take the baby to a halfway point on the way to class to be met by the other parent who was on the way home from class and took the baby back to the apartment.

In the country at large, many gainfully employed married women who have children drop out of employment while their children are very young and return to work after the children have entered school or become somewhat independent. In 1967, of married women living with their husbands, 23 per cent of those with children under 3 years of age were employed as compared with 32 per cent of those with children 3 to 5 years old and 45 per cent of those with children over 6 years old [U.S. Department of Labor, *1969 Handbook on Women Workers*]. Comparative figures are not available for campus wives. But it would be safe to guess that here may be found one of the pressure points in campus marriage. When the husband is a student, the wife's income is most needed, and this is often the very time that her children are of preschool age. In other words, some campus wives must of necessity cope with a situation which the great majority of wives have found reason and means to avoid, namely, gainful employment during the early years of their children's lives.

Parental subsidy This point will bear a second reference. Many a conflict in campus marriage arises from some situation positively or negatively associated with parental subsidy. No amount of theorizing on the part of the young couple to the effect that they ought to be independent of their parents increases their income. No amount to the effect that parents ought to help reduces the couple's financial needs. No amount of similar theorizing on the part of the parents decreases the young couple's expenses. The campus couple may be caught between the pressure of tradition and customary expectation—on their own part as well as on the part of others—on the one hand, and the struggle for existence, on the other. But in their case the struggle for existence is not imposed upon them in the ordinary sense of the term. It arises from their own decision to marry and at the same time attend college. There are two hypothetically escapable elements in the situation, namely, the determination to continue their education and the determination to marry. They could, if they would, leave school, have a customary marriage, and live "normally." Or they could postpone marriage. Neither, of course, will they do. Yet these hypothetically escapable elements color the problem of parental subsidy, both in the giving of subsidy and in the receiving of it. In some cases they make the parents more than usually reluctant to give it. In other cases they make the campus couple reluctant to accept it. If the young couple were actually reduced to a simple, elemental struggle for existence, and both they and their parents recognized it as such, the problem of parental help would be greatly modified, if indeed it did not disappear.

Academic pressures There are pressures involved in breadwinning, but they have been recognized and accepted since time immemorial. Family life is adapted to them. For example, the meal schedule, reacreation plans, vacation trips, place of residence, and similar things are determined in part by the requirements of a man's and/or a woman's job. The pressures imposed by academic work, when compared with those above, are both atypical and irregular. They are not universally understood and accepted. As a result, there are campus wives, who are themselves not students, who are irritated by and come to resent the husband's attention to study. If the couple have no children and the wife is gainfully employed, she may want to leave the home for social contacts and recreation in the evening, which is the only time the husband has for study. When final examinations, bar examinations, and similar pressures enter the picture, the wife may fail to understand the husband's increased preoccupation, tension, irritability, and fatigue, and interpret his behavior as an indication of lack of interest in her.

Similarly, there are wives who have as great determination to complete their education as their husbands have. Yet some husbands fail to understand this. If the husband also depreciates the importance of a woman's education, thinking of it as something casual which she can readily give up without regret, the stage is set for his misunderstanding the effect of academic pressures upon her.

A problem may arise when a husband spends a good deal of time studying with friends at night. He may do this because he finds it helpful. Yet the wife may fail to understand. On the other hand, the husband may rationalize as necessary spending time studying with friends when actually it provides a means of escape from his wife.

In cases in which the husband is a student and is employed and the wife is a student and/or is employed, their schedules involving times of arising and retiring, times of greatest busyness and preoccupation, and leisure time may coincide so infrequently that they seldom talk together at length without a feeling of pressure or without distraction. Communication suffers. Sometimes even their sexual adjustment is affected.

In some cases, when husband and wife are both students, there is competition for grades. This is often intensified if they are both in the same course or class; at times it becomes especially acute when the wife receives higher grades than the husband. Some husbands accept the wife's higher grades with admiration for her. Others, however, find her success more than they can tolerate, and conflict ensues. In one case, such competition was brought to an unusually sharp focus when the husband took a given course the first semester and the wife took the same course with the same instructor the second semester. She deliberately set out to get a higher grade than her husband had gotten—and she did, a fact of which she kept her husband reminded, much to his annoyance. Of course, with the attitudes underlying this sort of behavior, there would no doubt be conflict no matter which spouse deliberately set out to get and then received higher grades.

Temporariness   Much that is included in the experience of the campus couple is temporary. For example, they struggle for an education, knowing that when they have completed it they will start again, perhaps "at the bottom." Young couples like to establish homes, to accumulate household goods, to improve or even to buy their place of residence. The campus couple often have substandard housing. They cannot afford to purchase many household items both because they do not have the money and because they know that they will have to pay for moving them later. They often take little interest in improving their place of residence because they know they will not live in it very long. Young couples like to begin building a circle of friends. But the campus couple know that any friends they make will in all probability be left behind, or will leave them behind, when education is completed. But as we shall see, this temporariness, though it may constitute a problem, may also suggest one approach to a solution of a problem.

Deception   There are no figures available relative to frequency, but instances of deception in campus marriage do occur. Cases come to light in which a male student marries a woman presumably for love (at least she thinks so) but actually for financial support, only to divorce her after getting his degree. Of course, there are also cases among non-students in which a man marries for economic reasons. But in the college situation the male has a specific, immediate, time-limited need—a special problem of support while a student. This makes it easier for an exploitive male to rationalize being in love (since he assumes no responsibility for the relationship) or deliberately to mislead the woman. The wife works to make an investment in their common future but makes the devastating discovery that she has been used, unloved, and finally rejected.

Making Campus Marriage Successful

Assuming maturity, an adequate period of acquaintance, a wise choice of marriage partner, the absence of deception, and similar items that play a part in the success of any type of marriage, the first step in making campus marriage successful is to recognize it for what it is. This implies that the couple understand that there is a discrepancy between the stereotype of young marriage and campus marriage. There is a difference between common expectations and actual reality. Campus marriage entails special stresses, special "pressure points."

The next step is to accept the fact that campus marriage involves such special "pressure points" and plan and act accordingly. This may be more easily said than done in some cases, but it is possible for a couple to do it, too. In doing it one of the most helpful factors is an understanding of the relative temporariness of many of the special problems involved. In appraising their marriage and each other, the couple may differentiate between the permanent and the temporary in their situation and by the same token decide which aspects of their marriage call for permanent decisions and which for tentative ones. If they can hold on until education is completed, then they may emerge into a more nearly conventional type of marriage in which roles are more nearly customary, traditional expectations are more nearly within reach, and their temporarily thwarted hopes may more readily be realized.

SELECTED READINGS

Golden, Boris A.: "Honeymoon Sexual Problems," *Medical Aspects of Human Sexuality*, vol. 5, no. 5, pp. 139–152, May, 1971. Niagra Falls, New York, and Ontario, Canada, attract some 35,000 honeymoon couples annually. Dr. Golden has practiced in this area for twenty-three years. He interviewed twenty-one other physicians in preparing this report on honeymoon sexual problems.

Marriage is not merely a part of life; it is a way of life for which the current term is life-style. As such, for its success, it requires a continuous process of adjustment on the part of the persons in it. Such adjustment is not static. It does not imply the couple's reaching a "dead level" of equilibrium. Rather, it implies dynamic change, continuing "growth" on the part of both the couple and their relationship. In order for such "growth" to be achieved, the couple need to have an understanding of various aspects of marriage—psychological, interpersonal, social, sexual, and reproductive—as well as an understanding and acceptance of each other as persons. They need to have an awareness of possible problems plus a commitment to the solution of the soluble ones and the acceptance of the insoluble ones. In short, they need a will to succeed. As a marriage becomes a family, with the arrival of a child, both new problems and new opportunities arise.

WHAT IS SUCCESSFUL MARRIAGE?
Successful marriage is a dynamic, growing relationship in which the personalities of both partners continue to develop. It reaches a relatively high level of personal satisfaction. Both parties get at least what they expected from marriage. The couple achieve relatively full use of their personal resources and draw freely upon environmental resources to further their adjustment. There is no unusual amount of conflict, overt or covert, and the marriage endures so long as both parties live. Joint enterprises and intimate relationships are not only acceptable but attractive and are carried out not only willingly but enthusiastically. The essential elements in the marriage are assimilated into the personalities of both parties; no essential element is permanently encysted and shut out of the life of either partner. In such marriage each individual is permitted to approach as near to his objectives as his capacities will allow. There is nothing in the relationship to impede him. Neither spouse is a threat to the ego or individuality of the other. Each spouse gives the other freedom, confident that that freedom will never be abused.

Since marriage involves persons other than the couple themselves, social as well as personal criteria of success must be taken into consideration. A successful marriage meets the requirements of the law. It is consistent with the expectations set by the mores. The relationship of the marriage partners produces a "climate" conducive to the healthy emotional development of children. A successful marriage is conducive to the free association of people. An individual marriage is not an isolated phenomenon. It is an integral part of a social mosaic. It is a focus for the crisscrossing of innumerable human relationships.

part 3

MARRIAGE IN PROCESS

One thing Larry and I have found is that we can really be ourselves with each other.

We bought a small house in the suburbs, and it's all right for now.

We can all grow with each other.

At times it seems we stay together only because of Nito.

Sometimes we just have to talk things out.

Being alone together really completes us.

Marriage and the Social Climate

ROLES EXPECTED AND ROLES PLAYED

In an earlier chapter the point was made that men and women are complementary but that this complementarity is not manifested uniformly throughout their numerous and varied characteristics and relationships. The complementary nature of the sexes is most clearly apparent in connection with affectional, sexual, and reproductive behavior. Except in the case of deviants with regard to the first two and except in the case of hypothetically possible experimental parthenogenesis with regard to the third, this aspect of complementariness may be considered universal and permanent.

In other respects, however, the complementary nature of the sexes is more flexible and more sensitive to cultural influence. It is, therefore, subject to change. Nowhere is this more apparent than in the roles of the sexes in present-day American social and occupational life and in marriage and family living. The roles of the sexes, both as expected and as played, exhibit variations relative to socioeconomic class and educational level. However, since this book is addressed primarily to college and university students, most of whom are either members of the middle class or aspirants to it, a discussion of roles with, at times, some degree of middle-class orientation is not entirely inappropriate.

AMERICAN MARRIAGE IN EARLIER TIMES

seven

In earlier times in this country the family exhibited more prominently than it does today what are termed its *institutional aspects.* Such elements as the support of the family by the husband-father, the maintenance of the home and the bearing and care of children by the wife-mother, mutual protection, and the production of goods were considered criteria for evaluating the success or failure of marriage and family life. The man was accepted as the head of the family. He had considerable authority over both his wife and their children. This authority was supported by the mores and to some extent by the law. There was a clear-cut division of labor by sex both in the home and in the occupational world outside the home. One could accurately speak of "men's work" and "women's work."

There were couples who developed deep conjugal love and devotion. But love, especially love with a romantic coloring, was not considered the *sine qua non* which it has approached today [see Gordon and Bernstein, November, 1970]. The sexual aspect of marriage was tolerated by women as essential to childbearing and as unavoidable in fulfilling the function of wife. We may safely assume that fewer women than at present either achieved or were aware of the possibility of achieving satisfaction in their sexual relations. We may be sure that fewer women expressed such interest and awareness and that still fewer demanded such satisfaction as an essential criterion for the evaluation of marriage.

In their activities leading up to the wedding, young people had, of course, to get acquainted. But their contacts were restricted both by the mores and folkways and by the common practice and probably universal acceptance of chaperonage. There were at least some rules governing propriety relative to discussion, so there were restrictions not only on the topics a young couple might discuss but also upon the content and extent of their discussion. Undoubtedly young people made some appraisals of each other in terms of personal attractiveness and had romantic inclinations toward each other. There was a place for romantic love, but it was not allowed to overshadow other considerations.

Under such circumstances, the answer to the question "What are the qualities of a good husband or a good wife?" would reflect the emphasis upon the institutional aspects of family life. One might well imagine that many an American woman in the early days set up criteria not dissimilar to those expressed by a Boer woman who lived on the African frontier. Said she, "I am sick of all this talk of choosing and choosing. . . . If a man is healthy and does not drink, and has a good little handful of stock, and a good temper, and is a good Christian, what great difference can it make to a woman which man she takes? There is not so much difference between one man and another" [Leyburn, 1935]. Such an attitude makes choice of marriage partner relatively easy because the criteria of choice are readily observable and do not depend largely on personal taste. It therefore permits both more help in making the choice and more control of the choice on the part of the young couple's families.

In those early days many a couple considered their marriage to be successful in the absence of love. Because of this and also because of the widespread opposition to divorce and the division of labor which made husband and wife economically necessary to each other, the divorce rate was low. In a sense, in earlier times the marriage was considered more important than the persons in it. The couple were expected by society to perform duties, make sacrifices, and accept circumstances, unless extreme, for the good of the marriage. Now the marriage is considered less important than the persons in it, dissolvable when it ceases to meet their personal expectations. When the marriage is considered less important than the persons in it, this appraisal is the outgrowth of individual judgment and voluntary perspective rather than the result of law and custom.

To a considerable extent, education, religious worship, recreation, and manufacturing were carried on in or through the family. Because communities were small and travel to and communication with the outside were both slow and difficult, the pressure of primary group control was considerable. That is, the same group lived together, worked together, traded with one another, worshiped together, played together, and banded together for mutual aid in time of crisis. Hence each family was an integral unit in a face-to-face society. Therefore, whatever the conditions and relationships within a marriage, the marriage was held together in part by forces exerted from the outside.

CHANGES IN AMERICAN MARRIAGE

Present-day American marriage still entails an ample economic element, and the institutional factors in family living are far from absent. Division of labor by sex, support, protection, mutual aid, childbearing, and child rearing still exist. Manufacturing activities, education of children, recreational pursuits, and religious worship are still carried on in the home or through the family. But the picture is changing. Many of these activities, at least to a considerable degree, increasingly center on nonfamily agencies, as shown diagrammatically in Figure 7.1. The increase in urban and suburban living has broken down the primary face-to-face groups, thus removing some of the societal support from marriage, not in the sense of reducing societal approval of marriage but rather in the sense of there being fewer external, societal, and institutional forces acting to keep marriages structurally intact. There is increased emphasis upon how persons of opposite sex feel about one another and what kind of interrelationships they establish. In short, in present-day America, there is much less emphasis upon the institutional aspects and much more upon the personality aspects of marriage and family life. This change is manifested in numerous ways. It is important to note, however, that at no known period in history, among no known people, has marriage succeeded on the basis of emotion alone. There is always found some degree of cooperation, through division of labor by sex, in the maintenance of a way of life. American marriage is no exception.

In the activities and events preceding the wedding, young persons have a degree of freedom not so great as that found in some cultures but conspicuously greater than that which existed in this country in earlier days. Some degree of physical contact between individuals of opposite sex is widely and casually accepted, although there is far from universal agreement on the matter of premarital sexual intercourse. Discussion is almost, but not quite, unrestrained. There are young persons of college and even high school age who discuss topics such as sex and reproduction more freely and with less embarrassment with dating partners than married couples of yesteryear discussed such topics with each other after the birth of their first baby.

In marriage and in choosing for marriage, that element given greatest prominence is love. "Marrying for love" implies a primary emphasis upon emotion, upon how two individuals feel about one another, and upon personal satisfaction, and a corresponding reduction in emphasis upon the institutional aspects of marriage. Hence, new criteria of success in marriage are established. New qualities desirable in a husband or wife are highlighted. New opportunities are presented for richness of living and completeness of sharing in marriage. But along with those opportunities go new problems, for when people do not find in marriage the personal satisfaction that they anticipated, they feel justified in seeking escape. Other social changes have made such escape easier than it used to

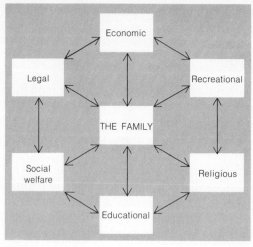

(a)

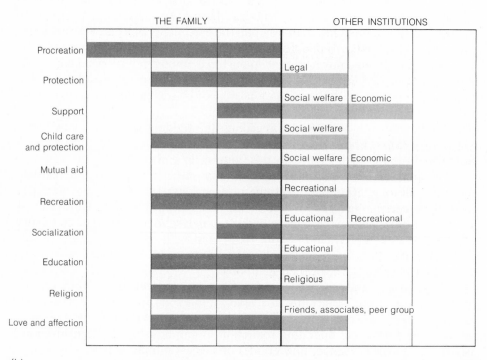

(b)

Figure 7.1 Diagrammatic representation of the interrelatedness of social institutions: (a) the family as an integral part of the social structure; (b) the way in which nonfamily agencies have taken over family functions (the proportions indicated are not intended to be exact). One problem of the present-day American family is to develop personality functions to replace those lost to institutions.

MARRIAGE IN PROCESS

be. One of the side effects of "marrying for love" is an increase in marital instability and hence of divorce. This is not meant to imply that more marriages are unhappy today than in earlier times, for there is no known way of making such a comparison. "Unhappy" and "unstable" are not synonymous.

When marriage is based upon love and when personal satisfaction is given more weight than institutional factors, the responsibility for wise choice of a marriage partner rests upon the shoulders of the individuals making the choice. Today they can and do get little help from their families. Often the help that is volunteered is rejected. In a way this makes choice of a marriage partner more difficult than it used to be because the elements upon which it is based are less readily observable, depend upon personal taste rather than a cultural standard, rest upon an appraisal of another personality largely extracted from that individual's background, and are so variable that each individual who makes such a choice assumes it to be unique. One can hardly imagine a young American college student of today saying anything even remotely approximating the statement of the Boer woman quoted earlier.

As contrasted with marriage of the past, present-day American marriage presents both sexes with a changed and expanded concept of the roles expected of husband and wife. Put another way, each sex is expected to play a greater multiplicity of roles, to do a wider variety of things. In a sense, each individual is expected to be a larger number of different persons.

The Role of the Husband

American society gives evidence of moving toward an equalitarian type of family life [Goode, 1963]. But not all groups and subgroups are moving toward this end at the same rate. There are differences among the various segments of society; and within groups families are not necessarily uniform. The result is that, while many men are assuming the new husband-father role as described below, there are other men whose roles are more nearly traditional and whose wives, with themselves, accept a patriarchal or semipatriarchal type of family life. Hence, the generalizations below are not universally applicable. They do, however, represent a trend.

The male is still expected to be the primary provider for the family. In some states his wife may sue for divorce on the ground of nonsupport should he fail to do so. However, he is not necessarily the only provider. There is a rapidly increasing number of families in which that role is shared by both spouses.

According to census definition the husband-father is head of the family. But functionally he is not head of the family in the traditional, authoritarian, patriarchal sense. The power structure of the family is changing. His expressed judgments relative to family behavior and welfare may be given considerable weight, but they are not necessarily considered the last word. He has the legal right to determine domicile for his family, and in some states he may sue his wife for divorce on the ground of desertion if she refuses to join him in the residence he has established. To a considerable extent the demands of his occupation take precedence over those of the wife's occupation or desires in determining where the couple will live and to what socioeconomic level their common life will be geared. There is an increasing inclination for family decisions to be made by husband and wife, or even by all family members, jointly rather than by strictly masculine decree. Yet there are many males who still assume that the husband has some natural or inborn right to a majority of the family votes. They sometimes express this as "If a husband and wife cannot agree on a particular issue, shouldn't the husband, because he is the male, have the last word, the right to make the final decision?" Such a statement reflects a traditional assumption taken for granted rather than insight into the new sort of interrelationship toward which American marriage is moving. It also suggests entering marriage with the objective of getting one's own way, assuming that one is naturally better qualified than someone else to make decisions, imposing one's will upon another person rather than making a mutual contribution through acceptance, and the recognition of variation in competence depending upon the issue under consideration. Masculine dominance is a point of view to which many modern wives do not subscribe.

In his role as father, the present-day male is more than a biological parent, a provider, and a disciplinarian. Many a man shares the lives of his children, understands them and openly shows affection for them, plays a part in their rearing, and participates in infant care. He may attend classes for prospective fathers, read books on child psychology, participate in the PTA, and force his growing bulk, softening muscles, and queasy stomach through the "survival test" of a boy scout hike and cook-out in order to prove that he is a pal to his son. He not only does not expect his children to be "seen but not heard" but is more likely to resign himself to being neither seen nor heard when his children reach adolescence and begin to date. He is often unashamed to be seen carrying a baby or hanging out a baby's laundry which he himself has done. If his children attend college, he may willingly continue their financial support beyond the point at which they have become emotionally and socially independent of him and resistant to whatever remnant of paternal authority he has sought to retain. In some cases such financial support continues after the wedding. In earlier times financial independence and personal independence were more likely to occur simultaneously, thus drawing a sharper line of demarcation representing the termination of parental control. Nowadays that line of demarcation is often ragged, and the parent-child relationship is equivocal, making for problems with which neither side is well prepared to cope.

There is a growing feeling that the home is no longer only a place of comfort and refuge for the male; it is becoming an area of participation. This means that there is not only sharing of family life on the part of the husband-father but also more participation in the tasks of housekeeping. Clear-cut division of labor by sex within the home is breaking down. We can no longer speak of "men's work" and "women's work" with the simple accuracy of earlier days. The shift is far from complete. There are still many males who resist housekeeping and participate reluctantly, if at all, or participate only in emergencies. Their resistance is often

MARRIAGE IN PROCESS

most apparent when the task in question is symbolic and doing it regularly might seem to indicate acquiescence in a change in masculine status or authority. For example, preparing breakfast is for many a man such a symbolic task. In earlier times when a man did predawn chores on the farm, he could well expect his wife to have a substantial breakfast ready for him when he returned to the house. Nowadays breakfast tends to precede work rather than follow a part of it, and is often light, requiring little or no preparation. Yet, not because of inability to do it or because of time or energy limitations but rather because a carry-over of attitude has made breakfast symbolic, many a man insists that it be prepared by his wife. In his estimation, "getting up to get my breakfast" is an indication of wifely commitment and effectiveness. There are some women who do not want their husbands to take any part in housekeeping. On the other hand, however, there is an increasing number of husbands who willingly do household tasks.

Exactly how much housekeeping a particular man will do must be determined by a number of factors: the time available to each spouse; how much of the total housekeeping job must be done after regular work hours; how the job may best be done, given the skills and interests of the husband and wife; the attitude of each person toward his own role and toward the other person and that person's role; what kind of marriage the couple expect to achieve; and how much they appreciate leisure time together. Too broad generalizations as to what responsibility a modern husband should assume are likely to be less than helpful. What is needed is not generalization but rather particularization. The question is, "What is the best arrangement for this couple with their personalities and abilities and their specific situation?" A problem often arises when an attempt is made to impose in advance a traditional pattern of family living without taking into account emerging and shifting variables.

The husband of today is expected to be a companion to his wife, to share leisure time with her and to engage with her in social activites and recreational pursuits. This creates a problem for both marriage partners, since it implies not only sex-limited interests on the part of each but also common interests. With the present-day awareness of women's affectional and sexual nature, the male is expected to be both a lover and a sexual partner in a sense somewhat different from that of earlier times. The difference emerges from a new insight into female sexual responsiveness and the possible means through which it may be evoked. This recognition that women may achieve, and in increasing numbers seek, sexual satisfaction presents the male with a new problem of understanding and a new orientation for his sexual drive, for it is no longer a simple matter of directing his efforts to his finding sexual release himself through the use of a female partner who derives no comparable release herself, but rather one of his finding his greatest satisfaction both through and simultaneously with the sexual satisfaction of his wife. This means that his sexual drive must be oriented toward giving pleasure as well as toward getting pleasure. Hence a new demand for understanding, insight, self-discipline, and the combining of sex and love is placed upon the husband.

In the last analysis, the final appraisal of a man's success or failure as a husband is made by only one person, his wife. This appraisal rests primarily, but not entirely, on what kind of person he is and what her feelings about him are. It is at its core a personal appraisal and to a considerable degree strips the husband of cultural props and the protective coloration of overt conformity to cultural norms and relative success in meeting the criteria which reflect the institutional aspects of marriage. A man may be admirable in the eyes of his friends or even of his wife, have prestige in his occupation, supply his family with all that is necessary to maintain a more than adequate standard of living, be moral and law-abiding, be a good father; yet if his wife no longer loves him and they do not get along happily together, the assumption is made that he has failed as a husband. The converse may also be true.

This suggests that the expected role of husband or wife is defined only in part by society at large. It is also defined in part by the tastes, attitudes, hopes, expectations, assumptions, and biases of one other person, the marriage partner.

The Role of the Wife

A woman's choice of role is complicated today by the fact that she is caught between the pressures of three forces. On the one hand, there are the weights of tradition and her biological nature pushing her in the direction of homemaking and motherhood. On the other hand is the open door of opportunity in the world of gainful employment. Her choice is complicated by the fact that the four elements—marriage, homemaking, childbearing and childrearing, and employment—may be considered separable, so with one exception a woman may have any element or combination of elements with social approval. She may marry without becoming a homemaker. Control of conception makes it possible for her to marry but have no children, whether or not she becomes a homemaker. She may have a home of her own without marrying. Employment may be combined with the other three elements in a variety of ways. The only element she cannot have with complete social approval is motherhood without marriage, although a few unmarried women adopt children, and, in spite of a public opinion still largely unfavorable to nonmarital childbearing, some women keep the babies they bear out of wedlock. As a result of this separability of the four elements mentioned, women face a greater number of alternatives than formerly, and their choice is therefore more complex. In one respect, however, it is easier because the choice is made among more alternatives, with the result that there is less compulsion exerted by any one of them, whereas in earlier times there was more inclination to squeeze all women into the same mold. In those earlier days, though there were the same four elements involved, three of them—marriage, homemaking, and childbearing—were combined and accepted as a constellation, much as a man accepts the combination of marriage and breadwinning today, so that actually a woman's choice was limited to two alternatives. Most women chose to marry, and social expectations supported their singlemindedness. Relatively few married women were gainfully employed.

A wife not only has an economic function of her own, so to speak; she also has a socioeconomic role as the marital partner of a man with a particular occupation. For example, the differences in roles of the wife of a farmer as compared with the wife of a traveling salesman, the wife of a clergyman as compared with the wife of a businessman, the wife of a writer as compared with the wife of a physician, and the wife of a military man as compared with the wife of a banker are readily apparent. This matter of occupationally determined role requirement is coming more into prominence. Large corporations are giving it attention. Books written to meet the needs of wives attest to the slowly growing attention being given to it.

Whereas in earlier times the wife was expected to be able to produce many of the goods used by the family, her role has now shifted from that of producer to that of consumer. She is expected nowadays to be skilled in the art of purchasing. By economical and careful expenditure she "stretches" the purchasing power of income. The shift in role is not complete, however. Many wives make clothing or raise and preserve food products, and the traditional attitude toward "good home cooking" is still in our cultural climate.

In other ways, too, the wife's role is somewhat mixed. She has more independence, is given less direction and supervision, and has more freedom of choice than formerly. At the same time, through both law and public opinion, she is accorded more protection and in some circumstances may make demands upon her husband which a man very seldom makes upon a wife, such as suing him for divorce on the ground of nonsupport, making him responsible for her debts, or having the right to be awarded alimony.

While the wife is expected to fulfill a socioeconomic role equivalent in contribution if not in content to that of the wife of yesterday, she is also expected to be something not expected of the wife of the past, namely, an enthusiastic, responsive sexual companion who accepts her own femininity, her husband's masculinity, and the sexual aspect of their relationship with uninhibited pleasure rather than reluctant tolerance. The modern wife is expected not only to love her husband but also to like to love him. It is assumed that she will be a companion whether they are alone in the privacy of their home or at a social affair where the impression each makes is reflected upon the other. There are, of course, individual and class differences as to how fully such expectations are taken for granted. In the last analysis, the wife's role, too, as we said was true of the husband's, is in part, at least, a matter of his definition of her role and his appraisal of the degree of success or failure she exhibits in fulfilling it. She, too, may seem to meet all the cultural criteria and norms of a "good wife." But if her husband is disappointed in her and does not love her and they do not get along happily together, she is assumed to have failed as a wife.

GAINFULLY EMPLOYED MARRIED WOMEN

A phenomenon which simultaneously reflects the wife's changing role and contributes to it, and which is also affecting the role of the husband, is the rapid increase in married women's gainful employment in recent years.

The actual number of married women who are gainfully employed is increasing. Also, the proportion of married women among the employed is increasing. In 1900, 5.5 per cent of married women were gainfully employed, and 15 per cent of all employed women were married [Breckinridge, 1933]. In 1971, 41 per cent of married women were employed, and 63 per cent of employed women were married [U.S. Bureau of the Census, *Statistical Abstract,* 1972]. In the early years of this century very few women with children under eighteen years of age were employed. By 1940 the percentage was only 9, but by 1967 the percentage of such women had risen to 38 [U.S. Department of Labor, *1969 Handbook on Women Workers*]. Regardless, however, of the presence of children, married women are more likely than unmarried women to work part time [U.S. Department of Labor, 1970].

There has been an increase in the number and proportion of employed couples. In 1950, 22 per cent of all married couples were employed [U.S. Department of Labor, *1969 Handbook on Women Workers*]. By 1970, almost 40 per cent of all married couples were employed. Where the husband is under 25 years of age, almost half the wives are employed [*Statistical Bulletin,* October, 1970]. The percentage of wives in the labor force when the husband is not employed has always been higher than the percentage of those with employed husbands. By 1969, however, the difference between the percentages had become very slight. Women with employed husbands have been entering or remaining in the labor market more frequently than those with unemployed husbands. "It appears, then, that the trend is for wives to be in the labor force whether or not the husband is employed. Formerly, ten years ago, it appeared to make a difference, but at present, 1969, the husband's unemployment has little effect on the wife's labor force status" [Ferriss, 1971].

Problems Growing Out of Married Women's Gainful Employment

Arguments against the gainful employment of married women, as so often propounded in the recent past, sometimes with considerable emotional coloring, are today as outmoded as arguments against women's suffrage. The employment of married women is here to stay, and it behooves both sexes to learn to live with it. Widespread, though not universal, acceptance does not necessarily result in the elimination of all problems. There are no formulas for the solution of such problems.

In so far as a given family is concerned, however, it is not a question of whether married women should be employed. It is a question of whether a particular married woman, with her particular skills, personality, opportunities, interests, and tastes, with her particular husband and home situation, should be employed in a particular occupation. The effects of her employment on herself, her husband, her children, and her home will depend upon many factors, such as time, fatigue, type of work, and income, which no one but she and her husband can fully evaluate.

Children of employed mothers Although many women cease gainful employment, at least temporarily, when their children are young, many do not. Often, as mentioned earlier, the wife who is working to put her husband through school cannot afford to stop except, perhaps, for a very brief time after the birth of each child. The result is an unprecedented problem of providing daytime care for small children outside the home by persons other than parents. Opinions differ about whether such care is beneficial or harmful.

Not all the facts are known, but research indicates that it is not the mother's employment per se that is detrimental to children [Ferriss, 1971]. The critical considerations are the quality of person that she is, the quality of the relationship that she establishes with her children, the quality of care which the children receive, and whether or not the woman enjoys her work [Nye and Hoffman, 1963]. In a study of some 13,000 high school students, Moore and Holtzman found that students whose mothers were better educated and employed were aware of no more problems of adjustment than children of similarly educated, nonemployed mothers [Ramsey, Smith, and Moore, 1963]. Another consideration is whether the mother's employment affords her children an opportunity for cooperation and learning in the home or prematurely imposes upon them too heavy adult responsibilities. If we condemn wholesale the gainful employment of mothers, as some persons do, we indict unjustly those women whose circumstances give them no alternative to employment. Many widowed or divorced women, and women whose husbands do not earn enough to meet family needs, must be gainfully employed. Yet they do an excellent job of child rearing. The presence of the mother in the home does not guarantee the quality of her relationship with her family. As Iscoe says [Ramsey, Smith, and Moore, 1963], "the mere passage of time with a child does not constitute 'good motherhood.'" If the woman has a strong desire to be employed and feels that her children keep her from it, her relationship with her children may be adversely affected.

Breakdown of division of labor outside the home　This has not been the result exclusively of married women's employment but rather of the great influx of women in general into remunerative occupations, many of which had previously been monopolized by men. But married women have contributed abundantly to this influx. There has been infiltration from both sides; in recent years men have entered occupations previously assumed to be restricted to women, and women have entered occupations previously assumed to be restricted to men. Today one is hard put to find an occupation exclusively reserved for one sex. One may find segments of occupational areas, but to find an entire occupational area reserved for one sex is another matter.

As the division of labor has broken down, the old concept of "men's work" and "women's work" as distinct entities has begun to disappear. As men and women have found themselves in the same occupations, intersexual competition has increased. In earlier times, when occupational lines were clearly drawn, the sexes did not compete. Nowadays they seek the same jobs and at times accept different rates of pay for those jobs, thus sharpening the edge of competition.

Breakdown of division of labor within the home　The traditional clear-cut line of demarcation between "women's work" and "men's work" within the home has not disappeared, but it is gradually growing less clear. This has come about through many factors, one of which is employment of married women. The question, "How much should a husband be expected to participate in housework?" does not arise only because of wives' employment. But such employment sharpens the issue. It constitutes an additional push in overcoming the inertia of tradition and in increasing the momentum of social change.

In the present-day family, especially that in which the wife is employed, there is no accurate way of determining in advance and on the basis of tried and known traditional practice what portion of the total homemaking responsibility each spouse will accept. A problem arises when one spouse assumes that this can be done while the other spouse expects to have the housekeeping tasks apportioned on a functional or opportunistic basis rather than a traditional one.

The problem is not only one of the amount of work a given spouse does in the home. The problem is also one of attitude. For example, some wives complain that their husbands do not help enough with housekeeping and child care. Other wives, however, are not so much concerned with how much the husband does as they are with the reasons he gives for not doing more. An employed wife, for instance, can accomplish a great deal, even handling the two jobs of earning and housekeeping, if her husband is doing his best, granting time and skill limitations. On the other hand, if her husband does little because he rests his case on tradition and therefore resists doing "woman's work," the total task may prove too much for her. Conversely, the husband may face a similar problem of attitude in his wife's success or failure in her role as homemaker as he defines it. From his point of view it may be one thing for her to "let the house go" because of time and energy limitations involved in the twofold task of homemaking and employment. It may be quite another thing for her to neglect housework because of lack of interest or slovenly habits.

Comparative prestige In earlier days a woman's prestige depended upon her doing "woman's work." There was no problem for her in choosing that channel of activity which in her judgment would lead to greatest prestige. Today she may choose, and there has arisen the problem of the prestige accorded homemaking as compared with prestige accorded gainful employment. Many women choose the latter. Many other women accept the former reluctantly. Women often complain that men do not give enough prestige to woman's role as homemaker. That may be true. But many women make the same mistake they attribute to men in that they underrate their own importance as homemakers and accord homemaking too little prestige. Some women have no problem in this connection. They appreciate the importance of their homemaking role, and for prestige which comes from the "outside" they substitute conviction which comes from the "inside."

Americans, by and large, live in homes regardless of whether "home" is a penthouse apartment or a shack "on the other side of the tracks." In spite of all the reactions, protests, and name-calling—"homemaking is a pseudo-occupation," "the homemaker is a might-have-been," "homemaking is a form of slavery"—homemaking is still a major pursuit for women whether they are married or single, mothers or childless, employed or not employed. It is "a profession in disguise" [Decter, 1972]. People who insist that every individual has the right of freedom of choice in determining his or her life-style often assume, as in the case of sexual relations, that freedom of choice means choice of one alternative, in this case, employment. They seem to forget that freedom of choice may also mean choice of the other alternative, namely, homemaking. A woman should have freedom to choose either, without judgment or criticism and with equal prestige, recognition, and appreciation [see Lopata, 1971].

Pattern of family life There is no longer a standard pattern or class-determined pattern of family life in this country, as there used to be. Many factors have contributed to this change. One of them has been the increase in married women's employment outside the home. With variations in patterns of family living, any one of which may be "best" for a given couple, each couple must answer the question, "What pattern is best for us?" When people are given new alternatives from which to choose, some will find in their new freedom of choice new opportunities for enrichment of living that contributes to marital success. Others will find new opportunities for making errors in judgment which contribute to marital failure.

When the pattern of family life was imposed largely by society, there was little room for conflict. But nowadays, when it is determined to a greater extent by each couple, there is the possibility of one spouse's imposing a pattern on the other, with conflict frequently the result.

One of the prominent characteristics of American society is a striving in the direction of upward mobility, that is, a striving to better one's socioeconomic status, to move from one class level to that above it, to acquire at least the observable "outward" appurtenances, if not the unobservable "inner" philosophy, of the "next floor up." American society, unlike certain older societies, has been sufficiently fluid and uncongealed to permit such upward mobility to become one of our most commonly noted traits. At its best such striving may result in general cultural improvement. At its worst it may mean superficial "keeping up with the Joneses." One new tool that may be used to advance the process of upward mobility is the increased income derived from the wife's employment.

Consistency If married women's employment is one important factor in both the reflection and the causation of social and family change, there arises the problem of achieving a reasonable degree of consistency in expectations and demands which marital partners set up for one another. For example, can a husband expect his wife to finance his education, bear babies, keep house, be an enthusiastic sexual partner, and be an interested and stimulating companion at the same time? Can the wife expect the husband simultaneously to provide for her, agree to her freedom to have employment outside the home, participate in housekeeping, be a sexual partner, be a companion, be a father to her children, and accept traditional legal protection for her while she demands new rights? Perhaps so. We are only raising the question.

Some women, to be sure, are subject to the economic necessity of employment to support themselves, children, parents, or husbands who are incapacitated or to supplement their husbands' income. Other women whose husbands have adequate income are free to choose or not to choose gainful employment—but only so long as men do not have similar freedom. If men were given freedom of choice as to whether or not they would be breadwinners, women's freedom would be both modified and threatened [see Decter, 1972].

THE POSITION OF WOMEN IN MODERN AMERICA

Much water has passed under the bridge since 1863, when a man wrote the following in a memory book presented to a young woman: "The mission of woman—to light her home with smiles and to strew flowers along her husband's path," and since 1870, when Queen Victoria wrote to a Mr. Martin [Markun, 1930]:

> The Queen is most anxious to enlist everyone who can speak or write to join in checking this mad, wicked folly of "Woman's Rights," with all its attendant horrors, on which her poor feeble sex is bent, forgetting every sense of womanly feeling and propriety. Lady . . . ought to get a *good whipping*. It is a subject which makes the Queen so furious that she cannot contain herself. God created men and women different—then let them remain each in their own position.

That the queen was herself maintaining a status involving rights and privileges which her more humble sisters were in their lesser ways striving to attain and that she assumed that differences between men and women were all God-made and necessarily implied inferiority of status for the women does not alter the fact that she reflected the common attitude of the times and the fact that that attitude is now becoming passé.

The following appeared in the *Journal of the American Medical Association* on June 22, 1895: "Man has his place in the world, so has woman, and nature has drawn the line. . . . The modern false emancipation of woman . . . is a perversion of nature. . . . [The laws of nature] stand forever as a barrier to the attainment by women of that equality so much desired by the agitation of the present generation" [*JAMA*, June 22, 1970]. That such a statement appeared in a journal as prestigious as that of the American Medical Association less than a hundred years ago suggests how much progress has been made since that time.

It is not difficult to say that woman's social position has changed and still is changing. More and more women are gainfully employed both before and during marriage. As we have seen, this affects their relative position by giving them a type of independence that they did not have formerly. Technically, at least, a large proportion of the nation's wealth is "in the wife's name." Men are still expected to contribute to the support of their wives after the marriage tie is broken by divorce, but not to the same extent as formerly, for in many quarters there is a growing opposition to alimony.

Women have achieved suffrage. They have educational opportunities almost equal to those of men. As a group they have made intelligent use of those opportunities. Mothers have been somewhat emancipated from their children and are gradually being freed from bearing a greater number than they desire or can care for adequately. In earlier times, when less was known about, and there was not such widespread use of, contraceptives, to an appreciable degree the number of pregnancies a woman had depended upon her husband's interest in sexual intercourse and the exercise of his legal right to such intercourse, regardless of her interest. More recently contraceptives have permitted control of conception regardless of frequency of intercourse—but with the husband's cooperation or at least with his knowledge, owing to the difficulty of a wife's concealing from her husband the fact of her using a contraceptive even when his cooperation is not required. Now for the first time in history, with the development of oral contraceptives a wife can prevent conception without her husband's knowledge.

With the development of modern warfare women have lost some of the inviolability in war which they formerly had. Men are still the chief participators in warfare, both as fighters and as victims, but women are playing a more extensive role, especially as victims. The number of women in various branches of the military service is increasing, but women are not yet allowed to participate in combat. However, as war becomes more and more mechanized and less dependent upon individual strength, women's participation has been suggested in order to achieve equality of the sexes [Brown, Emerson, Falk, and Freedman, April, 1971].

Women's social influence is increasing. Women are making progress in the professions but have not yet achieved professional status equal to men's. They are also making progress in other occupations, but there is still a tendency for them to be given subsidiary jobs with lower salaries. Women still receive more social and legal protection than do men.

Both employed women and housewives are gaining an increased amount of leisure time, but one wonders whether they have as yet learned to use it to best advantage, though progress is being made.

For centuries, regardless of the proportion between the sexes, there has been an inclination for men to treat women as if they were a minority group, a subject class [see Millett, 1970; Hacker, 1951]. Jensen [1971] refers to women as the "majority minority." Women have been the victims of groundless generalizations; uncritical stereotypes; implications of inferiority; personal, social, political, and economic discrimination; legal and social restrictions; superstitious fear; occupational stratification; moral inconsistency; exploitation; and lack of understanding and appreciation in much the same way as minority peoples. So long as women "kept their place," men, in their idealistic moments, were willing to "put them on a pedestal" and gloss over their inferior status with a code of chivalry. The present trend is toward thinking of men and women as integral parts of the same group on a more nearly equal footing. Men's attitude toward women and treatment of them are changing. Today women are thought of as individuals more than they were formerly. There are still men who treat their wives as if those wives were minors under the guardianship of the husband, but the trend is toward equalitarian marriage.

Perhaps the most important change that has occurred—the one that in a way epitomizes the others—is increased freedom of choice. Women have more freedom of choice—in educational, social, and occupational matters; in choosing a husband; in getting married; in escaping an unhappy marriage; in bearing children—than they have ever had before. They are coming to play a larger part in determining their own destinies. But there is still a long way to go before the sexes have complete equality. This is the underlying reason for the women's liberation movement.

The Women's Liberation Movement

Early stirrings of the demand for women's rights and equality of the sexes began to appear in print about two hundred years ago. Momentum was gained during the nineteenth century as women became involved in the antislavery issue and later in the first part of the twentieth century as they campaigned for suffrage. Then the movement slowed somewhat. In recent years it has been revitalized by what some women's liberationists refer to as the "second wave."

The women's liberation movement, like other social movements, involves a variety of women (and some men) both as individuals and as groups. These groups have the same over-all objective: freedom and equality for women through the elimination of the "double standard" in the broadest sense of the term. But within this general context stated objectives vary. In some groups stated objectives are clear; in others they are confused. In some groups objectives are moderate; in other groups they are extreme. Some groups include women with balance and perspective and dedication to human betterment. Other groups contain women with limited perspective who overreact to their own situation and project their own attitudes and problems onto all women. A woman who devotes herself quietly but persistently to the improvement of women's status and opportunities through cooperation and understanding between the sexes is as much a liberationist as one who parades her protest with placards condemning men and the "system" or makes statements such as: ". . . All men should be killed. . . . Man has become an obsolete life form. . . . Until he gives up his existence, either voluntarily or by force, there will be no relief from suffering nor any moral progress on this planet" [Warrior, 1970].

The most commonly stated objectives of women's liberationists are complete freedom of self-determination and equality of the sexes, including sexual freedom equivalent to that of men. Equal pay for equal work is another, as is equal occupational opportunity. Feminists advocate the release of women from excessive pressures of homemaking and childbearing and child rearing with provision for day care for children when needed. Ready availability of both birth control information and contraceptives is widely sought. The elimination of male dominance and men's traditional power over women is also an objective. Men's holding women in low esteem, sometimes in contempt (referred to as *male chauvinism*), and discriminating against them are particularly galling to most women, and the eradication of contempt and discrimination is demanded.

It is not difficult for concerned persons of either sex to subscribe to objectives such as these. But there are other objectives which are open to question and some on which there is far from universal agreement. Mentioning these is not to be construed as questioning women's liberation *in toto* but only the assumptions and objectives of some liberationists, keeping in mind the variations among feminists indicated above.

Many liberationists, as well as other women and many men, have promoted, even demanded, legalized abortion on request as an adjunct to contraception and to establish the right of women to make unhampered judgments relative to their own bodies and the continuation or interruption of a pregnancy. Abortion is a major issue in present-day America. There is far from universal agreement on it, and the issue has yet to be solved to everyone's satisfaction. (Abortion will be discussed in Chapter 11.)

Some liberationists feel that the time is past for gradual reform and the only way women can improve their lot is to seize power, the power traditionally held and currently exercised by men. If such a thing were done, it would, no doubt, produce considerable change in the contemporary situation. But some say that such a change, even if it were feasible, would only substitute female power and chauvinism for male power and chauvinism. The tables would be turned, but nothing would be resolved.

Other not uncommon assumptions, reflected above and questioned by some liberationists, are that men are women's enemies and women must mobilize against them and that all women's problems and disadvantages are the fault of men and the "system"—none are the fault of women themselves [see Decter, 1972]. Some women lose sight of the fact that there are men concerned about women's status, freedom, and rights. A correlative assumption is that men have all the advantages and none of the disadvantages—that men have no problems. Perspective is lost when there is a failure to see that there are problems on both sides.

An assumption made by some liberationists but denied by others is that homemakers and mothers are domestic slaves. Here again, perspective seems to have been lost. If a woman makes a free choice to marry and freely chooses to become a homemaker and mother, and if she can terminate her marriage and change her status if she so desires, can she be termed a slave? It is true that some lower-class women reflect elements of bondage in their marital and maternal roles. On the other hand, many middle-class married women have leisure time, financial support, a comfortable standard of living, contraceptive control of childbearing, freedom of activity, and in many cases gainful employment. These women reflect anything but a state of domestic bondage. Many of them, of course, work hard and long; they have problems and pressures. They may have more children than they desire. They may even have chauvinistic husbands. But can they be termed slaves, who by definition have neither freedom nor rights?

The devaluing of marriage, homemaking, and motherhood by some liberationists is hardly conducive to greater contentment for the women who have chosen these roles and expect to remain in them while the wheels of social change slowly turn. Liberationists admit, sometimes grudgingly, that some women are satisfied to be homemakers. They enjoy their roles, and they like men. Some liberationists not only devalue marriage but would like to see it eliminated. No matter how one theoretically feels about marriage, no matter how many individuals may choose or suggest some alternative life-style, the elimination of marriage in the foreseeable future is highly unlikely.

Some liberationists advocate either the acceptance of lesbianism (female homosexuality) or its desirability or both. More than one women's liberation leader has let it be known that she is either lesbian or *bisexual* or *ambisexual* (that is, she participates in both homosexual and heterosexual relations). Acceptance of homosexuality by American society is changing. Attitudes are becoming more liberal. Homosexuals are becoming more outspoken and free in their behavior. Discrimination is waning. But some persons question making acceptance of homosexuality a direct objective of women's liberation rather than a separate issue more closely allied to human rights in general.

Like any social movement, the women's liberation movement has strengths and weaknesses. Undoubtedly it is making an impact on American culture, law, the status of women, and the relationships between the sexes. Certainly a phenomenon of such dimensions cannot be given adequate treatment in a few paragraphs. The reader desiring further information is referred to the special list of titles under Selected Readings at the end of this chapter.

The Relation of the Individual Woman to Status, Men, and Marriage

There are a number of things that the individual modern woman must do if she is to adjust to new and evolving life circumstances. She must in most instances prepare for gainful employment. In earlier days she passed directly from her parental home to that of her husband. What she learned about homemaking she learned chiefly from her mother. Now she usually prepares for at least temporary employment before marriage. In increasing numbers she is continuing to work after the wedding. If she does not marry, she has greater occupational freedom of choice than women have ever before had. If her husband dies, she usually must earn her own living.

She must have a knowledge of life and social affairs, for she has increased independence and freedom of choice and a new sense of self-reliance and direction. She takes a more extensive part in community life.

She must know something about science and other fields of knowledge. She must learn new techniques—for example, the techniques of consumption and the techniques of applying modern psychology to child rearing. She must learn to react with many kinds of people in circumstances calling for various feelings and types of involvement. She must learn to use a variety of sources of information. She must learn to participate in many kinds of groups [see Lopata, 1971].

She must understand herself, her resources, and her goals, for no longer does someone dictate her mode of living; traditional patterns are in a state of flux. The modern woman needs to learn how to avail herself of the new opportunities that have opened to her without at the same time overlooking the opportunities for, and losing the qualities prerequisite to, making a contribution in the noncompetitive areas, such as marriage and homemaking.

She must decide what she wants, what her objectives are to be. She cannot afford merely to drift. Nor can she expect to have everything in sight. Failure to decide leaves her confused, frustrated, restless, and discontented.

She must carefully study modern morals so that she does not confuse freedom with license.

She must understand men in a way different from formerly, for she is now on a different level with respect to them. She has more varied contacts with men and more freedom of choice in her associations. Men expect more from her and she from them. She is no longer an inferior, studying men in order to wheedle out of them the means to her own ends. She is a teammate in a new sense.

She must develop a more enlightened attitude toward sex, realizing that inhibitions that were considered appropriate in times past are all too frequently a barrier to successful adjustment now. She must substitute intelligently balanced attitudes for blind resistance, enthusiastic participation for uninterested tolerance in the sexual aspects of marriage. She must learn to accept wholeheartedly her own sexual classification and capacity and the masculinity and sexual interest of her husband.

If she marries, she must prepare for a new type of marriage relationship involving new attitudes of husband and wife toward each other, new expectations, new demands—but a relationship in which roles are no longer so clearly defined as formerly. Lack of clear-cut cultural definitions makes necessary greater insight, a higher degree of adaptability, and more carefully focused motivation if she is to contribute to the success of her marriage.

THE POSITION OF MEN IN MODERN AMERICA

In recent decades so much attention has been given to the question of the status of women that almost none has been given to that of the status of men. There are even some persons who assume that there can be no problem of men's position. Actually men, like women, can have a problem of definition of status, of determination of position, when and as social changes occur that upset traditional roles and expectations and make new definitions necessary. Helen Mayer Hacker [1957] writes of the "new burdens of masculinity." Bednarik [1970] discusses "the male in crisis."

One of the problems men face today is that there seems to be a widely accepted, clear-cut conception of what it means to be a "real he-man" in terms of the highly individualistic, frontier, sexually bisected society of the past, but there has not as yet been formulated a universally accepted concept of what it means to be a "real he-man" in the competitive, industrialized, urbanized, sexually blended society of the present. The individual man is expected to meet simultaneously both the traditional and the contemporary criteria of masculinity. How can a man satisfy his ego needs in this country today if there is lack of agreement on what a man is supposed to be and if he is expected to be at the same time more than one kind of person? For example, a man is expected to be simultaneously "red-blooded and two-fisted" on the one hand, gentlemanly and peace-seeking on the other. He is under one type of pressure to "get ahead," under another type of pressure to avoid giving too much weight to material success. He is supposed to feel sorrow and sympathy but not give way to crying. He is expected to cooperate with women as equals at the same time that tradition tells him that at times, especially in times of crisis, he must "take charge" and under no circumstances ever let a woman dominate him or "get the best" of him. And so it goes.

There cannot be such penetrating changes as those which have swept over the feminine world without correlative changes in the masculine world. The point is that the worlds of both sexes are in transition. There is no immediate prospect of a crystallization of these worlds into a static *status quo*. There is no way of knowing what the ultimate outcome will be. In the meantime there will remain an active issue concerning the position of men.

The Relation of the Individual Man to Status, Women, and Marriage

Factors irresistible as glaciers are at work to make a new woman out of the partially developed material passed on by tradition to the modern age. She is making increasingly better use of her resources. Her training is improving continually. Her social status is more nearly on a level with that of men. An assumption of woman's inferiority is as outmoded as a belief in evil spirits. Men's attitude toward women, though changing, tends to lag somewhat behind the modern scene; it is highly colored by tradition. If some men were to dress in a manner appropriate to their attitudes toward women, they would have to wear suits of armor.

Men need to face the facts and exhibit some of the objectivity and logical thinking for which they have a reputation. Men need to sweep their minds of cobwebs and look at women as they are, not as the voices of those long since dead have claimed that they are.

Men need to adjust to the unalterable fact that a new type of intersexual competition has arisen in a way previously unknown. They cannot afford to let the attitudes of their early male ancestors so color their thinking and so determine their course of action that they find themselves either in the position of a man standing on the shore trying to stop the tide by shouting at it or in the position of a player who seeks to win a game by haranguing his opponent or refusing to let him play.

Men need to introduce consistency into their treatment of women. A man who strikes a woman violates a code of chivalry and is branded a coward and a cad. But a man who uses a woman for selfish purposes, who exploits her sexually, is assumed to be merely "sowing his wild oats." Men need to realize that they cannot "eat their cake and have it too." They cannot expect to prepare themselves for marriage while they think of woman as fair prey for sexual exploitation. They cannot justify their criticism of women's sexual fears and inhibitions when men's sexual irresponsibility contributes to the establishment of those fears and inhibitions as a means of self-protection by women.

Men need also to change their attitude toward homemaking and to improve their preparation for participation in it. The day is past in which homemaking was solely a wife's responsibility, with the husband in the role of permanent guest who assumed he was head of the family because he supported it financially. As we have seen, the trend today is for the family to have no head or two heads, and homemaking is becoming a joint responsibility of husband and wife. This does not mean necessarily that they divide equally between them all aspects of housekeeping, family feeding, purchasing, and child rearing. It does mean that a man has a new role to play in the home and that he can no longer assume that domestic illiteracy is the only preparation he needs for it. It means also that a man recognize that homemaking represents a total job to be done. How the various aspects of it are apportioned between husband and wife may change as time goes on or even from day to day. But a problem arises when a man assumes that this apportionment can be arbitrarily determined in advance and permanently fixed solely on the basis of tradition.

A CONCLUDING OBSERVATION ON MALE AND FEMALE ROLES AND STATUS

There is confusion on the part of men and women both as to their own role and as to the role of the opposite sex. There is confusion as to definitions of masculinity and femininity. Generalizing broadly without research data to substantiate the generalization, we may speculate that to some degree this confusion leads men and women to arrive at the same point through diametrically opposite means.

With new opportunities for employment open to them and with attendant increased financial independence, occupational prestige, higher standard of living, and personal satisfaction, to some degree at least many married women reject woman's traditional role as full-time homemaker-mother and engage in out-of-home pursuits. On the other hand, in the absence of a clear-cut, universally accepted definition of masculinity consistent with present-day urban, industrial society, but still wanting to prove themselves "real he-men," contemporary males often shy away from new opportunities, such as participation in homemaking and child care, and fall back upon criteria of the past. They become overly absorbed in work, in itself an unquestioned criterion of manliness throughout history. Some spend much time in the development of physical strength even when such strength has no direct functional value in their particular type of life. Some take pride in sexual exploits. In either case, male or female, the result is often a reduction in the individual's personal involvement in family living—in the case of the male through overemphasis of the old, in the case of the female through overemphasis of the new. Working out a better balance in this connection is one of the unsolved problems of modern family life.

Legislation

We speak of American marriage as if it were something uniform throughout the country. Actually it would be more nearly accurate to speak of New York marriage, Missouri marriage, California marriage, and so on through the list, since the institution is defined by fifty-one sets of laws, including the District of Columbia's, and is not exactly the same under any two jurisdictions. This variety not only reflects a lack of standards but contributes to confusion and to the inclination to seek the most convenient legislation. If a couple want to marry and cannot conveniently do so in their own state because restrictions are irksome, they may go to another where the law is more lenient. In some states, for example, a couple must wait five days after applying for a license before the wedding may be performed; in others, three days; in others, not at all. Through a required waiting period a couple are given time to reconsider their decision to marry. In one county in Wisconsin it was found that in a nine-year period 235 couples applied for marriage licenses and did not return to claim them. "Those deflected from marriage by legal requirements seem to be poor risks for satisfactory marriage" [Shipman and Tien, 1965]. Such laws are often influenced by financial considerations. In 1961, for example, Iowa raised the minimum age for marriage and instituted a three-day waiting period. As a result many Minnesotans who formerly would have been married in Iowa were married in North Dakota, which had no waiting period. In 1962 marriages taking place in Iowa dropped almost one-fourth below the number for 1960 [*Statistical Bulletin*, May, 1963]. A similar situation exists relative to seeking lenient divorce legislation.

In many states there is too little checkup on the couple at the time they apply for a license. They may swear to false ages. In one study of applicants for marriage licenses it was found that in the case of 22.3 per cent of the persons involved there was some discrepancy between age stated on the application and age shown in the birth record [Christensen, Andrews, and Freiser, November, 1953]. The couple may give false addresses. Unless one of them later complains, there is no attempt to ascertain the truth. All but a few states require both applicants for a marriage license to present an affidavit or a medical certificate indicating freedom from venereal disease; but for the most part health requirements are limited to this type of infection.

In a considerable proportion of the states the law permits marriage at so early an age that the individual may not be mature, and preparation for marriage may be impossible. In some states a girl may marry before the age at which she may leave school, get a driver's license, vote, or sign a valid contract, or has reached puberty.

Marriage laws are an illustration of cultural lag. Modern social conditions are so different from those under which our marriage laws developed that new legislation is needed. But law tends to lag behind the need for change. Many marriage laws are not adapted to the present-day social scene, although progress is occurring.

Lack of Preparation for Marriage

Society does not demand or even expect preparation for marriage. Anyone may marry, provided that he seems to fulfill the meager requirements of the law. He may be scatterbrained, immature, and maladjusted. He may know practically nothing about marriage or its responsibilities. He may not be able to carry a normal economic load for a person in his class. He may make an obviously poor choice of partner. He may have preparation so slight that with an equivalent amount occupationally he would be unable to hold a job in a business office or to rise even to the lower limits of mediocrity in a profession. Yet society assumes toward marriage, even of the most poorly prepared, the attitude, "Whom God hath joined together let not man put asunder." Success in marriage is assumed to come "naturally." This attitude is reflected in the replies of some college students who were asked by the author whether success is something that has to be worked for, or whether it comes naturally to those who are in love. The latter answer was given by 118 out of a total of 1,151.

Preparation in the form of marriage education is gradually increasing in quality and extent and in the consciousness of certain portions of society. The process still has far to go before it can be said that America prepares its youth for marriage. Anyone who, in any sort of counseling capacity, has contact with young unmarried people or with married couples knows that among them can be found tragedy after tragedy, many of which would have been preventable through adequate preparation.

Obscurantism

Until recently there has been a veil of obscurantism cast about marriage and sex. This veil has now begun to lift. Substantial remnants of it are, however, to be observed on every hand. Even in these presumably enlightened times instances come to light in which a high school administration has the chapter on human reproduction literally cut out of a new biology textbook. In one recent case coming to the author's attention the administration even had the section on childbirth deleted from a syllabus on sex education. In one sense this obscurantism is part of society's lack of demand for preparation for marriage. In another sense it is more than simply a negative, a lack; it is a definite, positive impediment to preparation. Marriage is the only human endeavor in which ignorance is considered a virtue. In spite of all our supposed open discussion of sex and marriage, there is still an ample element of taboo. Sex is discussed more freely, for example, in casual conversation than it is in many schools. Innumerable families have no program of sex education, or sex education is as unplanned and uncontrolled as the development of Topsy, who just "growed." Recently there has been an "explosion" of books on various aspects of sex, but only a relatively small proportion of them have as their objective sound preparation for marriage.

In one study of 364 college students it was found that though 70.1 per cent felt that both parents should be responsible for the sex education of children, only 10.4 per cent indicated that both parents were actually the source of their information. When the sexes were considered separately, it was found that 17.9

per cent of the boys and 54.6 per cent of the girls mentioned the mother, while 20.5 per cent of the boys and 8.0 per cent of the girls mentioned the father as the source of sex information. In short, these students felt that the sex education of children should be planned and participated in by both parents, but they indicated that their own families were disappointing in this respect. Their school experience, too, had fallen short of their expectations; for though 50.8 per cent felt that the school should assume some responsibility with regard to sex education, only 25.0 per cent indicated that their schools had done so [Rockwood and Ford, 1945]. This study was made more than twenty-five years ago. Since then there has been some progress, but we have only begun to scratch the surface. In the year 1965 a study of 400 university students found that only 5 per cent of the males and only 14 per cent of the females had received what they considered to be adequate sex education from one or both parents. "An examination of questionnaire data in all the studies since . . . 1929 fails to reveal any appreciable improvement in the quality of parental sex education in spite of the current suppositions about increasing societal sophistication in this area" [Shipman, January, 1968].

When the 1,151 college students already mentioned were asked to check what they considered the best way to prepare for marriage, the replies were as follows:

Table 7.1

1. Remain ignorant of marriage	46
Because studying marriage is apt to destroy romance	14
Because there are things no girl should know before marriage	27
Because there is plenty of time after the wedding to learn what one needs to know	16
2. Make a thorough study of marriage relationships and problems	991
By taking a course in college	889
By reading good books on the subject	827
By discussing the subject with parents	715
By discussing the subject with teachers	426
By discussing the subject with friends of your own age	506
3. Miscellaneous replies volunteered by the students and not suggested in the inquiry form included:	
Discuss subject with a physician	23
Discuss subject with fiancé	25

The veil of obscurantism is reflected in these figures. Students whose replies fall into the first group are not numerous, but the number is significant. One could expect a larger proportion of the general population to express such an attitude when it is expressed by that number of college students. In the second group the number of students who want preparation for marriage but would turn for help to persons other than the instructor in a special college course indicates that some of these students feel they cannot get the information they need from parents or other teachers.

Anyone who is at all familiar with the behavior of young people knows that they discuss sex and other marriage-related topics. Then the question to be answered is this: Is it better for young people to discuss such topics with sound information or with poor information, under good auspices or under poor auspices, with competent guidance or without such guidance? Thoughtful persons dare give only one set of answers, and these spell education.

There is no "pillar of cloud by day or pillar of fire by night" to guide wanderers in the marital wilderness. The only adequate guides are intelligence, information, maturity, and emotional balance. When society realizes that to lift the veil of obscurantism on marriage does not mean to tear back the curtain that shields the intimacies of life from wanton public gaze but rather to substitute knowledge for ignorance, planning for drifting, effort for chance, idealism for superstition, and education for an agglomeration of misinformation, then preparation for marriage will be immeasurably advanced.

Wherever there is a need for remedy, there is a corresponding need for prevention. But remedy is often more dramatic than prevention and therefore receives more attention. The ambulance at the foot of the cliff may be more dramatic than the fence at the top, but in the "long pull" the latter may save more lives. With regard to failure in marriage and family life, the need for remedy is apparent and is approached through counseling, social casework, and similar avenues. In this area there is also a need for prevention, which may be approached in part at least through education. If we believe in education, and Americans do, we must believe that education can make a contribution to the improvement of marriage and family life.

Premarital Romance

There is an overemphasis on premarital romance and an underemphasis on marital success, as if the former guaranteed the latter. In movies, television, magazines, some books, many plays, and the public's attitude, the boy-meets-girl situation tends to take precedence over the situation of the happy marriage.

There is also in America a glorification of the youthful body. On billboards, in magazine advertisements, on television, in motion pictures—everywhere one turns—the youthful body is brought to his attention. From automobiles to citrus fruit, feminine beauty runs the entire gamut, associating more attention-getting qualities with supposedly less interesting events and objects.

Success in marriage depends upon something more than youthful beauty and the intensity of premarital romance. Putting the emphasis on beauty and premarital romance gives a false impression of the factors making for long-time success. In a subtle way and without either party's being aware of it, many a husband or wife, especially the latter, is in competition with the more or less standardized youthful beauty that is so widely publicized.

Overemphasis on Sex

One can hardly escape guessing that the current overemphasis on sex contributes to failure in marriage at the same time that freer discussion and a less puritanical approach to sex may contribute to success. There is not only overemphasis on sex in a quantitative sense but distorted emphasis in an interpretative sense. Sex is presented not primarily as something to be integrated with love into the value system of marriage, but rather as an end in itself, something to be used for self-gratification and status without regard for responsibility or love and with men and women the toys with which the game is played.

Low Standards of Success

The standards that society sets up for success in marriage are comparatively low and apply mostly to overt behavior. "A man's home is his castle," even if he detests living in it. A couple may have serious conflict and may have no affection for each other. There may be no understanding and no happiness in their relationship. But if they "put up a good front," they do not disturb other people, and neither complains to the court, as far as social standards are concerned their marriage passes muster. Society is also inclined to judge too largely in terms of stability: if a marriage lasts it must be good. One can be fairly sure that if a marriage does not last it is not successful. Many that do last are unsuccessful, too.

Lack of Serious Attitude

In many quarters there is a lack of serious attitude toward marriage. Many people are more familiar with the caricature of marriage than with real instances of happy, successful married life. There are many jokes about marriage and the people involved in it. It is a well-worn subject for television comedians. It is held up to ridicule. Unpalatable expressions, such as "getting hooked" and "putting one's head in the noose," lightly describe marriage in terms of its worst actualities rather than of its greatest possibilities.

Stereotypes

There are two ways to erect a house. One is the process of adding brick to brick and board to board at the site of building until the structure is completed. The other is to fasten together large sections of prefabricated materials constructed in advance to fit a prearranged plan and delivered ready for use at the site of building. In our working out of a point of view relative to life in the society in which we live, we use, figuratively speaking, a combination of these two methods. We do put together experience with experience, idea with idea, and fact with fact to contribute to the erection of a "structure" partly of our own making. We also build, in part, with large sections constructed by society and fitted, with few alterations, into the pattern of our thought. These large blocks of concept, attitude, and definition are stereotypes.

Stereotypes are seldom valid. They seldom even roughly fit the facts. They are ready and easy, but lazy, ways of arriving at judgments of other people and of various phases of social life. They standardize the thinking of the uncritical and color the thinking of many Americans. College professors are absentminded, disheveled, and impractical. Farmers are hayseedy. Redheads are hot-tempered. Fat persons are jolly and good-natured. Businessmen are interested only in profits and are insensitive to human welfare. Politicians are open to suspicion. Men are brave, strong, impersonal, and independent; women are easily frightened, weak, personal, and dependent. Our frequent and uncritical use of the term *typical* shows to what degree these stereotypes have come to be taken for granted.

There are similar stereotypes relative to home, marriage, family, husband, and wife. People are assumed to date, fall in love, marry, set up a home, bear and rear children, divide labor between husband and wife, and accept traditional roles, all according to stereotypes. When these stereotypes continue to affect our thinking at the same time that they have become less well adapted to modern conditions, when they define the shape of the hole into which both round and square pegs are expected to fit, when they play a part in determining the criteria by which success and failure in marriage are measured, when they become substitutes for insight, understanding, information, and a desire to plumb more deeply into the possibilities of marriage and family living, then they in turn also become factors which play a part in producing failure.

Tradition

The Second World War took the form of a conflict between armies and between governments. Basically, however, it was more than that. It was in part the armed phase of a conflict between two ideologies, between two ways of life: the totalitarian and the democratic. This conflict did not start with the war, and it was not resolved by the signing of peace treaties. It is still going on. It permeates many aspects of life. Some refer to it as a world revolution. Marriage and the family, too, are caught in the maelstrom. They are passing from a form roughly paralleling dictatorship and government by force to a democratic form of organization. The patriarchal family of the past no longer exists in traditional form. Yet some of the ideas and concepts with which present-day marriage is permeated have been carried over from the marriage of yesteryear. Individuals enter marriage with a generous soaking of tradition. Some of the traditional ways no longer operate so smoothly as they did. They are not fully adapted to modern conditions. On the other hand, certain phases of social life have not changed so rapidly as have others; there is a carry-over of traditional elements, with which some of the newer elements in marriage conflict. The problem is twofold. In either case, the result is conflict, transition, and confusion. Here again one may observe cultural lag.

Publicizing of Failure

Marital failure is played up in the press, and marital success is taken for granted. Failure is more spectacular, and apparently the public is more interested in it. Successful marriage is not news. When one sees headlines announcing the divorce of a well-known public figure, he feels as if he had learned something of importance. It is a subject to talk about. Just the thought of picking up a newspaper and reading headlines to the effect that millions of Americans are happily married seems ridiculous, so far have we taken success for granted and overstressed the significance of failure. Relatively little mention is made of marriages that endure. Of the 49 million married women in the United States in 1971, almost one-third had celebrated the twenty-fifth anniversary of their current marriage and 2.5 per cent had celebrated their fiftieth anniversary. Of the total, 34,000 had been married 65 or more years [U.S. Bureau of the Census, September, 1972].

DOOR OF ESCAPE—DIVORCE

The ready availability of divorce in this country gives American couples access to an unprecedented door of escape from marriages which they consider to be intolerable. The possibility of escape, however, does not create the desire to escape, though it may contribute to the ease with which a decision to escape is reached. On the other hand, the desire to escape does not necessarily open the door. But in any human endeavor the possibility of remedying errors or recovering from failure plays a part in determining the attitudes of the persons who engage in the endeavor. Our collective attitude toward divorce is one factor that colors our collective attitude toward marriage. The exact effect of divorce as a social phenomenon upon the failure of individual marriages cannot be measured with accuracy. Yet divorce as a social phenomenon is part of the cultural climate within which marriages occur. Hence divorce may be discussed as one of the factors in the social situation which have some bearing on marital adjustment. Divorce is in the news. There are many misconceptions and misplaced emphases. Many students come into contact with it through their own marital failure, in contemplating marriage to a divorced person, or through the marital affairs of relatives or friends.

Definition

Divorce is the legal severing of marriage ties which a court recognizes as having existed. The parties who were formerly married become ex-spouses. In divorce, a bona fide marriage is terminated. Divorce and annulment are different. In the latter the court declares a supposed marriage null and void; that is, the court officially recognizes that no marriage existed, though the couple or one of the two thought that it did. After annulment the couple are still single as they were before their "wedding," since they have never really been married. They are not "ex-spouses."

Rate

The divorce rate may be expressed in various ways, none of which are completely accurate. One of the commonest ways is the ratio of divorces to weddings in a given year. In 1971, there were 2,196,000 weddings and 768,000 divorces, a ratio of approximately 1 to 3 [U.S. Department of Health, Education, and Welfare, Aug. 30, 1972]. This is not equivalent to saying that one in three marriages ends in divorce, since the divorces granted in a given year represent marriages that, as a rule, occured before that year and since many marriages are terminated by death. But the cumulative effect through the years is bound to reflect such a ratio. Another way of expressing the divorce rate is the number of divorces per 1,000 population. In 1971, this rate was 3.7 [U.S. Department of Health, Education, and Welfare, Aug. 30, 1972]. Still another way is the number of divorces per 1,000 married women fifteen years of age or older. In 1969, this rate was 13.4 [U.S. Bureau of the Census, *Statistical Abstract*, 1972]. The latter two rates are shown in Figure 7.2.

Except for a temporary drop during the Depression, the divorce rate rose steadily until the time of the Second World War. In 1946, owing to the breakup of many "war marriages" and the effect of the war on other unstable marriages, the rate reached an all-time high. After that time the rate declined only to rise again in the 1960s. Unless factors contributing to the improvement of marriage and family life in American culture multiply, there is no reason to suppose that the rate will not continue to be high. Nevertheless, there is another way of looking at the divorce rate which presents a more optimistic picture. In any given year only about 1.5 per cent of existing marriages end in divorce.

Much is written about Nevada divorces. There is no gainsaying the fact that Nevada is a divorce mill. Its laws permit divorce after only a very brief period of residence. This makes divorce one of the state's chief industries. Since living there for six weeks and paying the attorneys' fees and other costs is expensive, Nevada has become a haven for divorce seekers of the upper economic level, although with the liberalization of grounds in other states this may be changing. Nevada flashes many a notorious and spectacular name through the channels of the news. As a result, the state has come to symbolize American divorce. But as a symbol it is not appropriate. Even with its large and well-publicized divorce business, only about 1 divorce in 60 is granted there [U.S. Bureau of the Census, *Statistical Abstract*, 1972]. On the other hand, of course, this is a large proportion of the total number of divorces when Nevada's population is taken into account. With just over 0.2 per cent of the population, Nevada grants almost 2.0 per cent of the divorces [U.S. Bureau of the Census, *Statistical Abstract*,

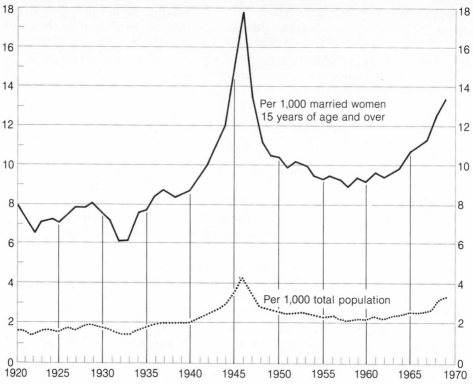

Figure 7.2 Divorce rates in the United States, 1920 to 1969. [*U.S. Department of Health, Education, and Welfare,* Monthly Vital Statistics Report, *vol. 20, no. 4, supplement 2, July 22, 1971.*]

1972]. In other words, the state grants almost ten times as many divorces as its population would suggest. Nevada has the highest divorce rate in the nation, almost six times as high as California, including Hollywood. Hollywood divorces often make the news, but Hollywood represents only a small, highly publicized segment of the population. There are couples living in Hollywood who have been married for many years.

A person is not permitted to have more than one spouse at a time, but he is permitted to have any number in succession, provided that the requirements of the law are met. MARRIAGE CHAMP SAYS SHE'S WIFE NUMBER FIFTEEN; SEVENTY-EIGHT AND MARRIED SIX TIMES, SHE WEDS EIGHTY, WHO HAS WEDDED SEVEN; BLONDE REVEALS TEN MARRIAGES; THESE SIX WOMEN HAVE HAD FORTY HUSBANDS; WIVES ARE HIS HOBBY—HAS HAD FOURTEEN—these are headlines of a type not infrequently encountered in newspapers and picture magazines. Ostensibly, our mores uphold monogamy. Marital records like these and others that are less pretentious reflect a loophole in the mores permitting what might be termed *serial,* or *progressive, polygamy.*

Divorce Rate and Extent of Failure

The divorce rate, high as it is, does not present an accurate picture of marriage failure, although as the divorce rate rises we may assume that its correlation with the failure rate increases. A marriage may be "broken" functionally as well as structurally. Many couples separate without divorce. Many separate before obtaining a divorce. Desertion is common. In 1967 the "separation ratio," that is, the number of men separated from their wives, was 20 per 1,000 married men. The "divorce ratio," that is, the number of men divorced from their wives, was 31 per 1,000 married men. In other words, among men with "disrupted marriages," 60 per cent were divorced, 40 per cent were separated [U.S. Bureau of the Census, Feb. 23, 1968]. Some couples continue to live together even after their marriages have become no more than the legal ashes of once flourishing relationships. In some cases a marriage broken by death would have been broken by divorce had the deceased lived longer. Thus, marital failure is more common than the divorce rate suggests. Since in each case of failure at least two persons are affected, the total number whose lives have been colored by unsuccessful marriage would be appalling if it could be ascertained. This is not cause for pessimism; it is, rather, an indication of the need for better preparation for marriage.

There is a common assumption that the increasing divorce rate actually indicates that more marriages are failing. This is not necessarily true. No one knows how many marriages are unsuccessful today as compared with years ago. Standards were different then. Expectations for husbands and wives were different. Roles were different. Another reason for the assumption that the marital situation is growing worse is that stability is considered a more reliable criterion of judgment than happiness and freedom. Stability is only easier to measure. Although instability may mean unhappiness, stability does not necessarily mean the opposite. In earlier days there was little for a couple to do about their unsuccessful marriage but grin and bear it. Public opinion frowned upon divorce, and there were few ways for the wife to support herself if she left her husband. The divorce rate today compared with that of earlier times proves only that more couples are escaping from marriages which to them have become intolerable. Modern social conditions have opened the door of escape, and more couples are passing through it. Divorce increases the visibility of failure.

When a careful observer compares a group of unsuccessful marriages in which there is no divorce with a group ending in divorce, he finds that all the elements characteristic of the latter are to be found in the former, with one exception, namely, the willingness to terminate the marriage in court. Some marriages seem to hold together in spite of elements contributing to failure because the couples are not willing to resort to escape. How, then, can anyone determine how much marital failure there is today as compared with, say, fifty years ago?

Divorce is a symptom or an effect of failure. It is not a cause. Couples resort to the courts only after their marriages have disintegrated. In some cases divorce is a secondary, rather than a primary, effect of maladjustment. For instance, a marriage is unsuccessful because the couple are incompatible. This incompatibility leads the husband to infidelity. The divorce is sought on the basis of adultery.

In considering marriage, we are inclined to do something that we avoid in connection with most other human endeavors. We make the broad assumption and postulate the universal expectation that all marriages should succeed. When some fail, we are surprised and conclude that the institution of marriage is disintegrating. It is in a state of transition but it is not, therefore, breaking down.

This assumption of success is desirable when the individual couple contemplate the future of their own marriage. They may enter it confident that it will be successful and will endure for life. In looking at all marriages taken as a group, however, the prognosis is variation rather than uniformity.

Most human endeavors and characteristics fall upon a normal curve of variability rather than upon a straight line or a fixed point. In college some students fail, others pass with honors, and the majority fall in between the extremes. In spite of the best preparation, individuals fail in their chosen occupations, and many never pass beyond mediocrity. Marriage is no exception to the general rule. Of the marriages contracted in any given year a certain proportion may be expected to fail, a large number will be relatively successful, and some will be outstanding. "One in three" may end in the divorce court, but we must not lose sight of the fact that "two in three" do not.

Is Divorce a Social Evil?

Divorce may be judged in terms of the ideal. Ideally, of course, it would be better if no marriage ever had to be terminated by divorce. On the other hand, divorce may be judged in terms of its alternatives. If no marriage, no matter what the degree of incompatibility, no matter how severe the personality damage to spouse and/or children, could be terminated by a legal route of escape, life for some persons could become unbearable indeed. Individuals would be victimized by the distorted personalities to which they were chained by law. Interpersonal relationships that ought to be conducive to emotional health and personal happiness would be forced to remain rooted in bitterness, conflict, and frustration. Some persons will contend that protection of spouse and children may be accomplished by means of legal separation without divorce. This is only partially true. Legal separation, plus court injunction in some cases, may keep individuals geographically apart, but this will not prevent a family from continuing to reflect the behavior and reputation of one of its members. Also, legal separation does not make possible a new attempt to establish the quality of family life that is approved even by those who disapprove of divorce.

Factors Affecting the Rate

As already implied, the factors affecting the divorce rate are not necessarily the same ones that contribute to marital failure, since divorce is merely the opening of the door of escape from failure. We have said that divorce is a symptom of failure in the individual marriage. The rate is also a symptom of social change. Much of this change has been in the direction of removing some of the outside props that used to keep marriages intact even when they were disintegrating on the inside. Modern marriage is like a tent the stakes of which have been pulled out one by one, each time making it more vulnerable to wind and storm. In earlier times marriages were held together in part by coercion from without. Now when they hold together it is largely through cohesion from within.

Some of the elements in the social situation that may contribute to the high divorce rate are: a higher standard of living, the higher status of women, new standards of marital success and new ideals of married life, a decline of religious authority, more widespread liberalism of thought, changed ideas of masculine supremacy, the breakdown of primary group control owing to increased urbanization, the greater ease with which divorce may be obtained, and the exploitation of divorce in the press. In addition to these there are the following elements:

The decline in the death rate Since the death rate has declined and the average span of life has lengthened, some marriages that might have been broken by death end in divorce. On the other hand, when a marriage ends in the death of one party, there is a not-uncommon assumption that that marriage was at least passably successful. In many cases, there would have been a divorce had the deceased spouse lived longer. When both death and divorce are considered, we find that there were actually more broken homes in earlier days in this country than there are today.

The kind of people this country is producing Generalizing broadly, Americans are comfort-loving. They are impatient with discomfort and inconvenience. They feel that whatever they do not like they have a right to change, either through established channels or by direct action. Americans are freedom-loving, and unhappy marriage may be interpreted as a form of restraint. "We have come . . . to regard the right of divorce as something like a civil liberty" [O'Neill, 1967]. In spite of their sensitivity to group pressure, Americans are individualistic, and personal welfare is often given precedence over the welfare of the group. Responsibility is often sidestepped for pleasure. A sense of duty is not conspicuous. There is an inclination to assume that what one is and does has its roots in early experience now beyond the individual's control and hence to relieve him, to some extent at least, from responsibility for his own behavior. Americans are generally sympathetic with the "underdog," give help to someone in dire need, lend support to a person or a group in time of unusual emergency or crisis. It is not too difficult to get such attitudes confused with self-concern when one is the "victim" of a marital situation assumed to be caused largely by the other spouse.

War The Second World War brought in its wake a high marriage rate, and many of these marriages were hasty, poorly founded unions. War breeds many ill-chosen marriages. Also, many marriages, like poorly built houses during an earthquake, collapsed, whereas they might have endured structurally had there been no war. Long separations during which husband and wife had different experiences, made new contacts, and lost interest in each other contributed to the breakup of many already existing marriages. With its necessary emphasis upon destruction and the insignificance of the individual, war changes the attitudes of some persons toward their responsibilities and toward the values by which they previously lived. In some cases, gaining one's own ends without considering others, or even through hurting them, weighs less heavily upon the conscience than in time of peace. The war also brought about great shifts in population and consequent increased breakdown of primary groups. High wages in war industries gave some persons the funds necessary to obtain divorces and gave others the quick money and, for them, unprecedentedly high income which often lead to loss of balance and perspective. War production provided many opportunities for wives who had not previously been employed to establish a new independence and escape the home.

Who Gets Divorces?

About seven out of ten divorces are granted to wives [U.S. Department of Health, Education, and Welfare, 1959]. A number of possible reasons may be given to explain why more wives than husbands are plaintiffs in divorce cases. (1) In some respects women have more at stake in marriage than do men. They are thus more inclined to feel the sting of failure. It may be that the other side of the coin of women's greater need to be chosen, as discussed earlier, is deeper hurt at rejection. (2) There is still enough chivalry in the relationships of the sexes so that, when a couple agree together to get a divorce, the husband assumes the blame and lets the wife bring suit. (3) More grounds are available to women in some states. For example, the ground of nonsupport is seldom used by husbands. (4) Courts on the whole are inclined to be more sympathetic with women than with men. (5) If the couple agree upon alimony, the court will more readily stipulate it if the wife is the plaintiff. (6) It may still be somewhat easier for a man to face public opinion. (7) Women have greater freedom in seeking divorce now than formerly and are using this freedom. (8) Men have more contact with the world outside the home and may have more frequent opportunity for infidelity. (9) It is easier for women to go away for a period, say, to Nevada, while men's occupational responsibilities are more likely to necessitate their remaining at home. (10) This is an era of traveling men, and men who spend much time away from home are more likely to be divorced than those whose occupations permit more home life.

Duration of Marriage with Relation to Divorce

In 1969, the median number of years that marriage endured before divorce was 6.9 [U.S. Department of Health, Education, and Welfare, July 22, 1971]. In 1950, it was 5.3 [U.S. Bureau of the Census, *Statistical Abstract*, 1972]. One divorce in

16 occurs during the first year of marriage [U.S. Department of Health, Education, and Welfare, December, 1970]. These figures show that couples do not rush into divorce as soon as, or with as little provocation as, is commonly assumed or as the exceptional spectacular case seems to indicate. It usually takes time for a couple to discover that their marriage is a failure. After that more time will pass before they bring themselves to the point where divorce is sought. In a study of 437 upper-middle-class Americans, Cuber and Harroff [1965] ". . . found practically no evidence of impulsive decisions to seek divorce. The overwhelming impression is the reverse: when divorce occurred in these people's lives, it typically came as an 'end of the rope' decision. . . ." Many couples wait until their children are grown, for about 1 divorce in 7 occurs after twenty years of marriage [U.S. Department of Health, Education, and Welfare, December, 1970].

Statistics of duration of marriage prior to divorce do not give an accurate picture of marital instability, however. Monahan [1962] refers to the "fragility of marriages." He points out that many couples separate much earlier than they get divorces. The real disruption of the marriage occurs at the time of separation; divorce only finalizes it. He points out also that duration of marriage to separation varies with region, time, social class, presence or absence of children, and frequency of marriage; that is, there is longer duration to separation in first marriages than in remarriages.

Divorce and Children

Approximately two-fifths of divorces are granted to childless couples [U.S. Department of Health, Education, and Welfare, July 22, 1971]. Does the presence of children contribute to the stability of marriage? Does marital stability increase as the number of children increases? Do couples whose marriages are stable tend to have more children? Statistical answers to these questions must be interpreted with caution, but they do indicate that the divorce rate for couples without children is higher than the rate for couples with children. Also, divorce rates tend to decline as the number of children increases. But the likelihood of divorce also declines with increasing age and with the duration of the marriage. Available data do not permit separating the effects of these three variables [U.S. Department of Health, Education, and Welfare, February, 1970]. "Occasionally, divorced couples have reported as many as 18 children" [U.S. Department of Health, Education, and Welfare, December, 1970].

The same factors that operate to make a couple avoid having children may contribute to the failure of their marriage and to their inclination to seek divorce. Furthermore, in many cases in which there are no children the divorce occurred rather early in the marriage, when there was insufficient time to have offspring. There is no way of determining whether such couples would have had children or not. In some cases there is no doubt that children are the reason for a couple's continuing to live together after their marriage has failed. In others, too, children serve as a very absorbing common interest, which binds the couple together and may counteract some of the factors operating to force them apart. There is no way of generalizing, and the statistics are inconclusive. We must beware the *post hoc, ergo propter hoc* (after this, therefore because of this) fallacy in thinking. It would be the height of the ridiculous to recommend that a couple have a child to prevent their failing marriage from ending in divorce, as if children were a specific for marital ills.

Grounds for Action

Grounds for divorce may be considered from two related points of view. They are the reasons alleged by a person seeking divorce on the basis of which he asserts that he has been injured and claims that a divorce should be granted. Grounds are also the categories of reasons for which the law permits divorce and the courts grant it. Grounds and causes are not necessarily the same, either for divorce in general or for the divorce of a specific couple. Usually what happens is something like this: A couple are incompatible. Their marriage is unsatisfactory. This leads one or both of them to commit some act—such as desertion, nonsupport, or adultery—which is a symptom of maladjustment but does fall within the categories of the law. On this basis one seeks divorce. Or, being incompatible, they may agree that they both want divorce. They then fit their situation into the most convenient legal category, often cruelty, so that the plea of one conforms to legal requirements and a divorce may be decreed. In many cases this amounts to a deliberate "trumping up" of grounds to satisfy the court. Hence statistics of divorce grounds do not present an accurate picture of conditions.

The word "give" is often used in connection with seeking a divorce—"His wife won't give him a divorce"—as if one spouse had the legal authority to grant a decree to the other spouse. Of course, neither party has such authority. What is meant in such a case is that one spouse wants a divorce but the other does not. The one who wants the divorce has no grounds upon which to get it. The one who does not want the divorce either has grounds but refuses to use them or refuses to trump up grounds which the other person will not contest.

Grounds vary from state to state. They have been worked out with more regard for institutional considerations, such as status, support, and rights, than for problems of personality adjustment. We consider love to be one of the major bases for marriage, if not the primary basis. Yet lack of love passes unrecognized as a basis for divorce. In historical studies, contemporary discussions, or critical analyses of divorce there is almost no mention of love. Its presence or absence is almost entirely disregarded in the rendering of court decisions.

Statistically the grounds are changing:

1 *As written in the laws of the several states:* The trend seems to be toward extending the number of grounds or toward eliminating all specific grounds in favor of one flexible one, as will be discussed later.
2 *As alleged in specific cases:* Desertion and adultery as grounds alleged have declined. Cruelty has increased. Just over half the divorces granted nowadays are granted on the specific ground of cruelty. If such grounds as "indignities," as defined, for example, in Missouri and Wyoming, were included as being

approximately synonymous with "cruelty" in many cases, the percentage would be increased. Only about 1 divorce in 4 is granted for desertion [Carter and Plateris, August, 1963], 1 in 85 for adultery. Such figures, however, vary considerably from state to state.

The definition of "cruelty" is constantly shifting and is difficult to ascertain with any degree of finality or assurance. Cruelty ranges from physical violence to the most ridiculous absurdities. Drummond [1934] cites cases in which divorce was granted on the ground of cruelty for the following reasons: because a wife would not speak for days at a time and, when she did open her mouth, it was only to consume the meals the husband prepared for the family and to complain about his cooking; because the husband required his wife to retire at nine o'clock; because the husband used Biblical language to insult his wife; because the husband failed to make his children stop playing the saxophone; because a wife claimed that a pet cat had deprived her of her husband's affection. A newspaper article states that a woman is seeking divorce on the ground of cruelty because her husband used her pet goldfish for bait. Another article quotes the judge as saying that there was ". . . a clear course of conduct on behalf of the wife dedicated to harassment, humiliation and the discomfort of the plaintiff," including ". . . placing a dead mouse in the plaintiff's lunch pail" [*The Austin American*, Feb. 26, 1968].

There is a not-uncommon assumption that construing "cruelty" to mean "mental cruelty" and hence to mean anything that a plaintiff alleges and a court will accept has occurred only in recent years as couples have sought ways to circumvent outmoded divorce laws. This may be true in the numbers of cases in which such redefinition is found. But per se it is not an innovation. Witness the following, published in 1889 [Convers]:

> Few venture to define "cruelty." In the decided cases we find certain actions held to constitute "legal cruelty" that strike one as being slight cause for any such far-reaching effect as an "absolute divorce." Very little reason exists when a divorce is granted because once a husband threw water over his wife and threatened more; because a woman contracted the itch, or other loathsome disease, from her husband; because a crosstempered man struck his wife once, kicked her over seven years later, and went for more than two years without speaking to her; because a man treated his wife coldly, was stingy towards her, neglected her in premature labor, and roughly unbraided her for the noise she made when suffering pain.
>
> Such are some of the instances in which there was bodily injury. "Cruel and inhuman treatment to endanger the life of his wife" is the language of the Iowa statutes, which leads one to expect that there the very highest degree of cruelty only would be allowed as cause; but the court interprets the language thus: "If austerity of temper, petulance of manner, rudeness of language, a want of civil attention, occasional sallies of passion, do threaten bodily harm, they amount to legal cruelty."
>
> Tried to kick her once but failed, used abusive epithets, and finally refused to speak for months, this is "cruelty!" Here and there one may still find an effort to confine "cruelty" to bodily harm, but generally it extends to mental suffering. Here the greater part of the decisions point to the pain inflicted by false charges of unchastity. In a Kentucky case the man was rough, "with a vulgar and profane

mannerism, had but little attraction for a melancholy and sensitive wife. She knew, however, the man before she married him. They were own cousins. After the marriage she entertained the belief that marriage of cousin with cousin was prohibited by the divine law, and this fact, connected with her bad health and the want of sympathy on the part of her husband, aided greatly, no doubt, in the destruction of her peace and happiness. . . . The husband often spoke uncivilly to her, used the most profane and vulgar language in her presence, neglected her in many instances," but, for all that, made "persistent efforts to bring about a reconciliation;" but all in vain, it was "extreme cruelty."

"Marry in haste and repent at leisure" is well-illustrated by the family history shown in a Kansas case, where most of the acquaintance and courtship was by letter! He was cross to her; said she had a "hellish or a devilish tongue;" several times said before her that he "did not believe Bessie (her child) was his child;" sent her, when away, a valentine with an ugly woman feeding a child from a bottle, getting an employee of the post-office to write on the margin, "I like children of my own," and to address it; and on her return refused to receive her; being guilty thus of "extreme cruelty." Or again, for a wife to write and send anonymous letters charging her husband with criminal intimacy with his clerk's wife was such "extreme cruelty" as to gain the husband his divorce.

A husband in a room alone with his wife by indirection charged her with incest and advertised her in the local papers as having deserted him; and this too was "extreme cruelty." "A reasonable apprehension of injury is sufficient" to cause cruelty is so commonly held as to need no references.

To quote a learned judge, "Everybody knows that there may be a refinement of cruelty practiced on the part of one of the parties towards the other, unconnected with gross and abusive language or epithets, or with anything personally violent or threatening, which may render the marriage state absolutely intolerable, and the discharge of the duties of married life an impossibility." Under this nearly anything can be cruelty.

The statistical change in cruelty as an alleged ground for divorce may show one or more of several things: (1) That courts are becoming more lenient in granting divorce. (2) That divorce is being granted on less serious grounds. (3) That the true causes of marital failure are being recognized and their seriousness acknowledged. If this is true, it means that fewer couples are having to perjure themselves in order to obtain release. (4) That *cruelty* may be more readily established and proved than other grounds. The term is more flexible and permits broader interpretation by the court than, say, *adultery* or *nonsupport*. There is evidence to indicate that most divorces are obtained on those grounds that are the least unpleasant to allege under the law [Carter and Plateris, August, 1963] according to the "principle of least stigma." (5) That we are taking a more intelligent attitude toward divorce. (6) That courts and the general public are becoming more willing to have divorces granted for incompatibility, though in only four states, Alaska, Oklahoma, Nevada, and New Mexico, is it specified as such among the grounds for divorce defined by statute. In California, "irreconcilable differences" is specified as a ground. In Texas, "on the petition of either party to a marriage, a divorce may be decreed without regard to fault if the marriage has become insupportable because of discord or conflict of personalities that destroys the legitimate ends of the marriage relationship and prevents any reasonable expectation of reconciliation" [Texas Family Code, 1970]. In a few states, courts have considerable discretion in granting divorces for grounds not specifically provided by statute. In the state of Washington, for example, a court may grant a divorce for any ground it considers sufficient, if it is satisfied that the couple can no longer live together. In general, we still make couples lie about incompatibility, disguise it, and squeeze it into the most convenient category of the law. (7) That more is expected of marriage today, that standards of success are rising. When expectations are not achieved, escape is permitted. The standards of success are becoming more personal and less institutional.

EFFECTS OF DIVORCE

Effects of Divorce upon the Couple

For some individuals divorce is jumping from the frying pan into the fire. It does not solve their problem. There is a difference between "solution" and "escape." After the decree and the removal of the immediately aggravating circumstances, the divorcé often feels that he loved his spouse more than he realized, that the situation was not so bad after all, that the divorce was too hasty, and that the decree is regrettable. There are, too, of course, persons from whom divorces are obtained against their will. They may have committed some offense which gives the other person ground for divorce, or they may be disinclined to use a defense, yet they may not want a divorce. For such persons a divorce may be profoundly disruptive.

The divorced person faces several problems. He must settle the conflict and rebellion within himself. He must repair wounded pride. He must readjust his habits. Often he does not realize until he is called upon to change them how much a part of his life many habits have come to be. He must reorganize his social relationships and friendships. He must grow accustomed to a new relationship with his children, whether he is separated from them or has them with him without the other parent. He must reorient his sexual life. If the person left alone by divorce is a woman, she must usually arrange for support.

Marriage, even a marriage that is not particularly satisfactory, has a way of becoming part of an individual, part of his life, part of his personality. He develops behavior patterns having his marriage at the core. He cannot readily erase the memories of courtship days and the early years of marriage. The image of the spouse-that-used-to-be plagues him. In the idealization lent by time and distance he may forget the unpleasant aspects of his marriage and magnify those that were pleasant. At best, the divorced individual must go through a period of readjustment. In few cases is it easy. In some instances divorce does solve problems or afford effective escape from those that are insoluble. In other instances the problems are too deep-set to be solved by court decree. The individual, though altering the type of problem he confronts, does not decrease the intensity of the problem situation.

Effects of Divorce upon Children

It is often impossible to separate the effects of divorce, as such, from the effects of the failing home situation because divorce is preceded by marital failure. The child may not be aware of this, however, and sometimes the divorce brings to an unexpected end a relationship that he had never questioned. This happens even with persons of college age, who in many cases are taken aback when parents announce their intention of getting a divorce.

The child of divorced parents is in a position somewhat akin to that of the middle horse in a three-horse team, which is pulled now in one direction, now in another, now in both at once, as it attempts to accommodate itself to the movements of the other two horses. The child is torn between conflicting loyalties. He tries to cooperate with and to understand two persons who are at odds and do not understand each other. If he lives with each of them at different times, he is pulled first one way, then another. In neither home is he prepared for living in the other. He may be inclined to lean more toward one parent, and this leads to disappointment. He lives in a society where home and parents are taken for granted. He has, therefore, to face the attitude of his contemporaries, some of whom may chide him for his equivocal family status. There may be a carry-over of the attitude that divorce is a disgrace, and the child must defend himself against this. He may fear adverse public opinion or loss of prestige. In short, he is likely to develop a feeling of insecurity, and this feeling may lead him to compensatory behavior, which makes for more or less maladjustment. This is not always true. Some children of divorced parents are very well adjusted. There is much to be said for a child's living in harmony and security with one parent rather than in an atmosphere of conflict and insecurity with two.

SUGGESTED REMEDIES

Before it is possible to talk intelligently about remedies for the situation in which marriage and divorce are seen to be, the objectives must be made clear. Is the objective to decrease divorce or to increase marital success? The latter would lead to the former, but the former would not produce the latter. If the aim is merely to reduce the number of divorces, this could be accomplished by making divorce more difficult through legal impediments. That would be to treat symptoms rather than the disease. More stringent divorce laws would not make marriages more successful; they would only prevent escape.

Legalizing divorce by mutual consent has often been suggested, and there is something to be said for it. At present, a couple may marry by mutual consent, but they may not unmarry on this basis, although permitting divorce on the ground of incompatibility or irreconcilable differences or legalizing no-fault divorce as in Texas approaches divorce by mutual consent. By and large, at present, if one spouse wants a divorce and brings suit against the other on some ground defined by law, the divorce is usually granted. If both parties want a divorce and agree that one will allege certain grounds and that the other will make no defense, their agreement may be interpreted as collusion. If the collusion is discovered, the court may dismiss the suit. The couple's mutual desire to get a divorce or property agreements made on the possibility that a divorce may be obtained usually do not in themselves constitute collusion, if the divorce action is initiated in the usual manner and on acceptable grounds. For example, a husband who committed adultery might be fully as desirous of having a divorce as the wife who sued him for it; but the fact that they both wanted it would not be collusion. In no case, however, can the couple obtain a divorce merely because they both want it.

In most states, when one spouse sues the other for divorce, it is possible for the defendant to initiate a countercharge to the effect that the plaintiff has also been guilty of an offense that constitutes a ground for divorce. This is termed *recrimination.* Sometimes in such cases the divorce is granted to neither party. This means, in essence, that if one party has committed an offense, a divorce may be granted, but that if both parties have offended and the situation is roughly twice as bad, neither can obtain a divorce. There are exceptions to this condition, however. The statutes of Nevada, for example, include the theory of *comparative rectitude.* If, in an action for divorce in that state, it appears that both parties have committed offenses that constitute grounds for divorce, the court may grant a decree to the party it deems less at fault.

By and large, in order to obtain a divorce under our present system, one party must prove injury by the other, and it must be injury of a type defined by the law of a particular state. A divorce suit savors of adversary litigation. If the couple themselves recognize that they have both been injured, they cannot get a divorce unless they conceal their understanding and perjure themselves in court to "prove" that one was innocent and the other guilty. This means that in actual practice we already have divorce by mutual consent, but it has not been legalized.

In discussing divorce by mutual consent there is a tendency to begin with the present system and set it up as a norm. This makes necessary the justification of change. One could just as well, perhaps even better, start with divorce by mutual consent and insist that the proponents of the *status quo* justify divorce granted on the plea of only one spouse when the other may or may not want it. We do not force people to marry, but we do force them to remain married or to become unmarried against their will. Perhaps neither system is entirely desirable to the complete exclusion of the other. What is needed is not divorce either as we have it at present or by mutual consent, but divorce when a marriage has ceased to function for either the couple or society—when it is necessary—whether one or both parties desire it. This implies laws adapted to present needs and interpreted by courts having insight into marital problems. It implies the elimination of an attitude and a system through which modern marriage is squeezed into outmoded forms.

Those who believe that divorce by mutual consent would jeopardize marriage and produce an unprecedented increase in the divorce rate have only to look to the countries where such divorce is legalized. Their rates are lower than ours [United Nations, 1962].

In lieu of more stringent divorce laws some persons have suggested stricter marriage laws. The latter would no doubt prove the more effective. There is also needed more thorough enforcement, both of new laws and of the ones already on the statute books. More thorough premarital medical examinations, more careful investigation of applicants for licenses, more adequate age qualifications, and other similar stipulations would no doubt play a part in preventing ill-advised marriages.

Uniform laws have also been suggested. Certainly even the proponents of variety for the sake of experimentation must admit that variety need not extend from one extreme to another. There can be an approach to uniformity without identity. The greatest danger in making marriage and divorce laws uniform in all states is that uniform laws would represent compromises. As it is, some states are more progressive than others. Compromise would mean the loss of some of the progress secured in the more advanced states. There is no hope of achieving uniformity through Federal legislation, since the Constitution does not give the Federal government authority to regulate marriage and divorce. All marriage and divorce laws are state laws. To get a Federal law the Constitution would have to be amended; and the possibility of obtaining passage of such an amendment is so remote that, at present at least, it is not worth considering.

In the last analysis, the most effective remedy for the situation in which marriage and divorce now stand is education—the gradual, slow, tedious education of a public, part of which is inert and apathetic and not even aware of the need for preparing people for marriage or for departing from timeworn and threadbare tradition. It is hoped that, coupled with education, counseling facilities will continue to increase and improve. The advancement of marriage depends also upon the raising of the general cultural level and improving the emotional, social, and intellectual adjustment of the individual, for, as mentioned earlier, marriage can be no better than the people in it.

SELECTED READINGS

Albert, Ethel M.: "The Roles of Women: Question of Values," in Seymour M. Farber and Roger H. L. Wilson (eds.): *The Potential of Woman*, McGraw-Hill Book Company, New York, 1963, pp. 105–115. (Paperback.) Similarities and differences between the sexes; sex roles; "who is qualified to make an objective investigation of women?"

Brenton, Myron: *The American Male*, Fawcett Publications, Inc., Greenwich, Conn., 1967. (Paperback.) Recently there have been numerous books on women but few on men. "The fundamental purpose of this book is . . . to encourage men to be men." Discusses the problems of masculine identity, men's involvement in the family, the relationship of men to women, "myths" about sex differences, and men and the sexual revolution.

Goode, William J. (ed.): *The Contemporary American Family*, Quadrangle Books, Inc., Chicago, 1971. (Paperback.) Nature, functions, and problems of the family;

how the family is changing and may change in the future. Also includes material on the women's liberation movement.

Hacker, Helen Mayer: "Women as a Minority Group," *Social Forces*, vol. 30, no. 1, pp. 60–69, October, 1951. Also in Hamida Bosmajian and Haig Bosmajian (eds.): *This Great Argument: The Rights of Women*, Addison-Wesley Publishing Company, Inc., Reading, Mass., 1972, pp. 127–145. (Paperback.) Excerpts in Nona Glazer-Malbin and Helen Yougelson Waehrer (eds.): *Woman in a Man-made World*, Rand McNally & Company, Chicago, 1972, pp. 39–44. (Paperback.) Men's treatment of women as if they were a minority group; women who want to be men.

————: "The New Burdens of Masculinity," *Marriage and Family Living*, vol. 19, no. 3, pp. 227–233, August, 1957. Discusses some of the problems and conflicts of men as their roles have changed in American society.

Skolnick, Arlene S., and Jerome H. Skolnick (eds.): *Family in Transition*, Little, Brown and Company, Boston, 1971. (Paperback.) A book of readings "addressed mainly to those who hold conventional assumptions about the necessity of the nuclear family, the inherent nature of male and female sex-role differences, and the unchangeability of human nature." Discusses women's liberation and the "abortion revolution."

THE WOMEN'S LIBERATION MOVEMENT

Andreas, Carol: *Sex and Caste in America*, Prentice-Hall, Inc., Englewood Cliffs, N.J., 1971. (Paperback.) "For those who feel either overwhelmed or impressed by the rapid growth of the movement for the liberation of women, those who would like to know where it is coming from and where it is going, this book will offer some clarity. . . ."

Bird, Caroline, with Sara Welles Briller: *Born Female: The High Cost of Keeping Women Down*, rev. ed., Pocket Books, a division of Simon & Schuster, Inc., New York, 1971. (Paperback.) Discusses discrimination against women, women as an oppressed and underprivileged group, and the women's liberation movement.

Cudlipp, Edythe: *Understanding Women's Liberation*, Coronet Publications, Inc., New York, 1971. (Paperback.) Discusses the development of the women's liberation movement and some of the persons and groups involved and also reasons for which the author believes it has failed women and is not yet a "real movement."

Decter, Midge: *The New Chastity and Other Arguments against Women's Liberation*, Coward, McCann & Geoghegan, Inc., New York, 1972. A critical analysis of women's liberation, its shortcomings and weaknesses, and the "impassioned, not always accurate, rhetoric of its prophetesses." The author contends that women's real difficulties are not with the denial of freedom but with unprecedented freedom that gives them a wide range of choices from which the movement is advocating retreat.

Firestone, Shulamith: *The Dialectic of Sex: The Case for Feminist Revolution*, William Morrow & Company, Inc., New York, 1970. (Paperback.) The author accepts the biological inequality of the sexes but says that to survive in our time traditional sex roles must be politically broken down.

Friedan, Betty: *The Feminine Mystique*, W. W. Norton & Company, Inc., New York, 1963. (Paperback.) One of the leaders of women's liberation discusses the modern woman's confusion and conflict of roles.

Greer, Germaine: *The Female Eunuch*, McGraw-Hill Book Company, New York, 1971. (Paperback.) Author's objective is to advocate the emancipation of women rather than to promote any organization. Women are "the most oppressed class" for whom "slaves is not too melodramatic a description." "If women are to effect a significant amelioration in their condition . . . they must refuse to marry." "Women have very little idea of how much men hate them."

Hobbs, Lisa: *Love and Liberation: Up Front with the Feminists*, McGraw-Hill Book Company, New York, 1970. Author is critical of many common assumptions as well as some assumptions of feminists. Believes in importance of love and "warns that the feminist movement runs the risk of being bogged down in hatred." Says the sexes are complementary and believes marriage will endure because it is needed.

Komisar, Lucy: *The New Feminism*, Warner Paperback Library, New York, 1972. (Paperback.) An introduction to the women's liberation movement for the younger woman "who wants to know where she stands."

Millett, Kate: *Sexual Politics*, Doubleday & Company, Inc., Garden City, N. Y., 1970. (Paperback.) A critical analysis of the "sexual revolution" (using the term in a broader sense than just sexual freedom), especially the effect of the patriarchal system on the relationships of the sexes.

Making Marriage Meaningful

In this chapter we shall discuss some of the processes, types of behavior, and personality traits which play a part in making marriage succeed or fail. Or, since success and failure are not distinct entities but rather aspects of a continuum, perhaps it would be more nearly accurate to say that we shall discuss some of those factors the combined effect of which determines the level of adjustment in marriage. We cannot hope to discuss all such factors. There are many which are beyond the scope of this book. Therefore, we shall discuss those about which the reader may, if he will, do something either through self-examination on a conscious level, or through putting them into effect in his marital behavior, or through avoiding them. This is not equivalent to giving the reader an oversimplified "do-it-yourself" manual, "Happy Marriage in Three Easy Lessons." The reader is addressed as a person concerned about preparation for his own marriage and therefore presumably motivated to do whatever he can to contribute to its success. Any discussion such as that which follows is unavoidably generalized, suggesting that in working out an individual marriage there is ample room for ingenuity, imagination, and the infusion of the reflections of many facets of individual personalities. The cultural framework within which marriages occur exerts some pressure toward similarity of structure. But within that structure a couple have almost limitless flexibility of interrelationship and function. In the following discussion, then, we shall consider some of the factors within marriage that need to be understood in order to further the individual's contribution to such interrelationships and functions.

eight

CONFLICT IS NORMAL

Some conflict in marriage is normal and to be expected. Two personalities could not live in such intimate union without it unless both of them were completely apathetic, accepting the relationship with bovine placidity. Men and women being as they are, each with peculiar aims yet each having to take account of the existence of the other, there is a pull away from, as well as an attraction toward, each other. Sumner and Keller [1927] term the association of the sexes *antagonistic cooperation.* There is much to be said for such a description. Conflict is not always overtly manifest; it may be covert. It does not always mean quarreling. Nor does it necessarily mean failure. A couple need not give up their marriage as lost the first time there is conflict, tension, or a difference between them. A husband

and wife need not agree upon everything or even like each other's every trait. It is not only disagreement but the manner in which it is expressed that causes difficulty. It is important, however, to agree upon basic goals, at least to reach a workable compromise concerning them.

AN UNDERSTANDING OF PERSONALITY AND BEHAVIOR

Personality may be thought of as the sum total of the individual—his habits, behavior, thought patterns, emotional responses, moods, attitudes, reactions to people and situations, hopes, fears, aspirations, and countless other things that make him an individual, a person. To say that an individual *is* a personality is more nearly accurate than to say that he *has* a personality. To say that an individual has "personality" is to refer to something relatively limited, that is, certain desirable traits, such as cheerfulness, enthusiasm, vivaciousness, forcefulness, and so on. These traits, however, are only part of his total personality. Personality includes character. Character is composed of those parts of personality that have to do with value judgments, that is, with judgments of right and wrong, and good and evil. Personality is not quantitative. No one has any more or less than anyone else. Personalities may vary as to type or quality but not as to amount.

Strictly speaking, personality is not inborn. In a sense, however, some of its ingredients are. An individual's body structure, the way he is "put together," the way he functions, his temperament, and his aptitudes constitute the equipment with which the newborn child meets and begins to adjust to his environment. His personality becomes a product of the interaction between his equipment and his environment.

Part of the individual's environment is other people. His reactions to other people and theirs to him play a part in molding his personality. The reactions of others begin even before the individual is born. His parents, for example, may want a boy rather than a girl, or vice versa. They begin to think of the unborn child accordingly. They may choose a name for him. The individual's mother, and perhaps even his father and siblings, notice his growth and prenatal movements. So the stage is set for his personality development even before his birth.

A personality may be compared to an iceberg only a small portion of which is visible above the surface of the water. This small portion, however, and the much larger portion hidden from sight below the surface are integral parts of the same mass. An individual's observable, overt behavior represents only a relatively small proportion of his total personality. The rest is there, nonetheless, some portions permanently hidden from view or appearing above the surface only now and then as the waves of circumstance cause the berg to rise and fall in the experiences of life.

Most of us exhibit traits and types of behavior that are not readily changed through our own efforts. What is true of ourselves is also true of our wives, husbands, or fiancés. They, too, are not readily changed. On the other hand, there are traits that may be altered through effort and analysis. Fuller understanding of human reactions may contribute significantly to the improvement of mutual adjustment. If we understand why a person is as he is, that very understanding tends to make our relations with him more agreeable, even though we cannot change him. We may not be able to alter his behavior; but we may alter our interpretation of his behavior, and that in itself is significant. Fuller knowledge also enables us to play a more effective role in directing our own development. Although one may not be able to change all his undesirable traits, he may through knowledge and understanding make the most of his limitations and prevent making undesirable traits worse, more obvious, or more obtrusive.

All Behavior Has a Cause or Causes

Perhaps, to be more nearly accurate, we should say that all behavior has antecedents or is the outgrowth of contributing factors. To think in terms of causes as such often leads to oversimplification and mechanism. At any rate, the behavior which an individual exhibits always has roots. These may arise in relatively recent circumstances or may extend to remote childhood. They may go back to important experiences or to relatively insignificant incidents. Physiological processes also are not without their effect. The individual is the product of his inborn characteristics plus his experience. This concept, however, should not be oversimplified. Experience is not to be thought of only in terms of large segments, such as crises, shocks, family life, college career. It may also be considered in terms of a continuum of change in environment, moods, physiology, contacts, ideas, emotions, and events, extending through more than 85,000 seconds per day and through every day of life. None of this experience is lost.

These two views of experience may be compared to one's contemplation of the human body. The body may be regarded in terms of arms, legs, stomach, other vital organs and apparently unitary parts, with their functions or dysfunctions and injuries considered as single experiences. On the other hand, the body may be thought of in terms of microscopic cells, which in aggregates form organs whose functions and changes may be interpreted as the product of minute influences and infinitesimal physiological processes. Just as the body's functions are the sum total of metabolic changes in untold millions of cells, so the individual's behavior and personality are the end product of innumerable experiences, some great, some small; some remembered, most forgotten.

Since we live in only the instantaneous present, the roots of behavior must of necessity be in the past, except in so far as current physiological processes may affect behavior. An individual may change his attitude toward the past or may through present and future experience alter its products; but he cannot change the past itself. It leaves so indelible an impression upon him that he can change only through building up new patterns of behavior. He cannot change merely by saying so or by having someone else tell him to do so. His experiences may lead him to make a decision involving change, so he seems to alter his conduct by voluntary act of will. Actually, however, he alters his conduct because of his experience. Remote past experience forms a matrix in which more immediate experience serves as the precipitating cause of his present behavior or future changes; but he is still the product of his biography.

When confronted with a new situation, an individual reacts effectively or ineffectively, depending upon how and to what degree the new is related to the old and bound up with experience. The past may have laid upon him a hand so heavy that he cannot accept or assimilate the new—for example, the parent who is opposed to the freedom that is taken for granted by his children. In such a case, the new is resisted because the old has become crystallized, so to speak, and the individual has no interest in assimilating the new. In other instances he may be interested in solving a new problem but be unable to do so because there has been nothing in his experience to which the problem may be related or because he relates the new to aspects of the old which enable him to reach only an inadequate solution. In a specific instance, a woman trained as a nurse and having considerable hospital experience before marriage is having difficulty in adjusting to the marital situation because she treats her husband as if he were a patient. The firm tones and positive directions effective in caring for the cantankerous sick are resented by the husband, who expects mutual give-and-take and resists her efforts to direct him. There is no doubt of the wife's devotion and good intentions; but she is meeting the marital situation ineffectively because she interprets the new only in terms of the old.

Conditioning

In understanding the roots of behavior one fruitful concept is that of *conditioning*. Conditioning accounts for most of our fears, tastes, and attitudes. Fears of animals, of high places, of enclosed places, of men, women, sex, or marriage develop in this manner. Food tastes are largely the result of conditioning, and in this conditioning custom plays a significant role. Some foods are palatable, others are not so, because of conditioning. The same food may be accepted under one name but may seem disgusting under another.

An individual may become conditioned through a single experience that leaves an indelible impression or through the repetition of a lesser stimulus, a "dripping faucet" type of experience. One serious accident may make a person fear driving an automobile. One case of overeating may make a child lose his appetite for a given food. A child's learning not to touch things that do not belong to him comes as the result of repeated "no, no's" or slight punishment, but his learning not to touch a hot stove may be the result of one experience.

Complexes

It is in this way that complexes are built up. A *complex* is a group or series of connected reactions, set off, so to speak, by a single stimulus, which may have little direct connection with the total response and which produces a response often out of proportion to the intensity of the stimulus. The whole complex may take on the emotional tone of one of the elements in it. Usually the emotional tone is marked.

One explanation for the intensity of the response in such situations is that the individual reacts as if he were reacting to a total situation, whereas he is reacting to only a part of it. If, for example, a complicated situation were represented by *ABC*, these three letters representing the stimuli that act upon him in that situation, and if his total response is represented by *XYZ*, the recurrence of part of the situation, say *A*, may be sufficient to produce *XYZ*. This may happen even when *A* occurs in a setting different from the original one and in combination with other elements, for example, *AEF*.

Everyone has complexes, some good, some not. Let us suppose that the reader receives a letter from his fiancée. Actually, the letter is nothing more than ink on paper, and his reading is merely the interpretation of symbols. But the letter arouses a chain of responses, a complex, the emotional tone of which is out of proportion to the intensity of the stimulus when the latter is thought of as paper and ink. In a way, the letter is a substitute for the fiancée, and the response to the letter is similar to the response to the actual presence of the fiancée, though less intense than that would be. Consider the attitude of some persons in this country toward women's smoking cigars. The sight or the mere thought of a woman with a cigar sets off a complex of ideas, attitudes, and opinions involving not only smoking but often immorality, the "double standard," sin, and religion. The emotional tone of the response is out of proportion to the stimulus.

In almost any group one may readily start a heated discussion by mentioning race, politics, or religion. People often have complexes related to these subjects. Money is another frequent focal point for complexes. So is sex.

If through experience an individual has developed a complex of inferiority, his complex may be brought into play by the slightest stimulus. Someone says something that he interprets as disparaging, or someone looks at him or does something equally insignificant. His response is out of proportion to the intensity of the stimulus. The term *inferiority complex* is much abused, much overworked, and often used very loosely, but it is useful in making clear how a cluster of responses may form around one original response and assume an intense emotional tone.

Not every feeling of inferiority or insecurity indicates an inferiority complex, however. An individual might feel inferior, for example, if he were forced into competition with a person who was obviously superior to him. He might feel insecure in a situation where there was obvious risk. In such cases the feeling of inferiority or insecurity springs directly from an objective appraisal of the factors in the immediate situation and is commensurate with them. His approach to the situation is a direct effort either to prevent unfavorable consequences or to remove causes. When an individual has an inferiority complex, on the other hand, he reacts to an immediate situation as if it were a past situation. He does this because a pattern of response that developed as a result of the past has been carried over, so to speak, in such a way that it may be evoked by situations that have little or no relationship to the original one, and the response is not commensurate with the actual situation. He may even respond as if he were inferior when he is not. Such an individual may attempt to compensate for his assumed inferiority in a way that is directed at neither the inferiority, as such, nor the causes of it. Sometimes his compensation takes the form of a nonverbal excuse, for example, a psychosomatic illness.

If one person is aware of another person's complexes, he may go a long way toward making their mutual relationship more harmonious by setting off the desirable complexes and avoiding the stimuli that set off the others. For example, if a woman has built up a complex of a pleasant, romantic type that may be touched off by flowers, the way is open for her husband to increase their mutual happiness by a very simple means. If, on the other hand, she has built up a complex involving money, sex, or some other aspect of marriage the arousing of which produces tension, aggravation, or fear, the setting off of such a complex may, when possible, be avoided.

Complexes are altered or removed through experience and reconditioning. They cannot be removed by argument or demand. No one can pull his complexes out by the roots and remove them from his personality by act of will alone. Most human beings live more by their habits and emotions than by their intellectual processes. Consequently, logic, reason, and scientific arguments are frequently ineffective in influencing behavior.

Negative Adaptation

One aspect of conditioning, in the broad sense, is *negative adaptation*. A stimulus may lose its original effectiveness and fail to evoke any response. A student may become accustomed to noise which at first prevented concentration upon studies. He may even come to "need" the noise which at first disturbed him. For example, when he was a freshman, he could not study when his roommate turned on the radio. Now that he is a senior, the first thing he does when he sits down to study is turn on the radio. Personal peculiarities which at first were irritating may gradually come to be overlooked. A girl who dislikes housework when it is done in her parental home may overcome this dislike when she does it in her own home. In such cases the response is lost because the stimulus is followed by other stimuli and the first one loses its effectiveness in producing a given simple response. Negative adaptation is one part of personality adjustment. In connection with some aspects of getting along with people, it is something that may be cultivated.

Mores and Folkways

One important factor in the conditioning process is custom or, more technically, the *mores* and *folkways*, which are the accepted customs of the group, the former being considered the more essential and unchangeable. Mores and folkways vary from group to group. They put colored glasses upon each individual reared under their influence, determining in appreciable measure his tastes, attitudes, and point of view. Personality is in part socially determined. Each individual develops in a cultural climate, much of which he takes for granted and accepts without question. The mores and folkways determine to considerable degree our attitudes toward morals, monogamy, etiquette, property, religion, and numerous other things which are part and parcel of our particular culture and way of life. Since the mores and folkways vary from group to group, area to area, and time to time, in associating with other people one may well take into consideration those that have played a part in conditioning their behavior.

In a sense, we may think of American culture as being made up in part of elements common to all Americans and in part of numerous subcultures which are different and at times bring their adherents into conflict. It is for this reason that certain types of mixed marriage are difficult. We may think of masculine and feminine subcultures. These, too, are taken for granted. It is partly for this reason that the sexes behave differently, are sometimes in conflict, often do not understand each other, and frequently have a problem of communication, as discussed later.

Other Aspects of Behavior

Without going into detail we may mention some other considerations relative to behavior that have a bearing on marital adjustment.

Behavior is affected by physiological processes. Fatigue, hunger, illness, moods, worry, and the menstrual cycle all leave their mark. Individuals differ in the degree to which their behavior shows the effects of such items and in the degree to which they voluntarily control them.

People are inclined to become angry or irritated when they are thwarted. Such irritation may be reduced either by decreasing the irritant or by increasing resistance to it.

Each individual seeks to maintain what he considers a satisfactory position for himself in his own estimation and in the eyes of others. If he does not maintain this position through actual achievements, in self-defense he may attempt to maintain it through some means, such as rationalization, projection of blame, aggression, or alcoholic escape, or he may try to protect himself from the expectation of maintaining it through some means, such as hypochondria, withdrawal, or psychosomatic illness.

Observable "surface" phenomena often represent only the symptoms rather than the cause of an individual's behavior. On the other hand, "surface" phenomena are not necessarily a reflection of an individual's underlying attitudes. An expression of anger, for example, may be only an instance of habitual response on the part of a person with a quick temper. It does not necessarily indicate a lack of love. How "surface" phenomena are to be evaluated can be determined only on the basis of insight into a given personality.

An individual cannot be expected to change his behavior unless the situation is provided in which change can occur.

People are often most easily offended by those closest to them in affection and esteem. The more a personal relationship is idealized, the smaller is the pinprick necessary to deflate it.

If you agree with a person on little things, you may more effectively disagree with him over more important matters. If you regularly disagree with someone over little things, you have already lost part of the battle when it comes to a more important issue because the latter is merely another in a series of items upon which to disagree.

No one is entirely an introvert or extrovert. But different persons may lean to one side or the other of the introvert-extrovert fence. In so doing, they exhibit both different behavior and different needs. One type of individual cannot suddenly be made into the other, no matter how much a spouse may desire such a change.

Whenever possible, it is better to be positive rather than negative—the word "positive" being used in the sense of constructive and complimentary, not in the sense of dogmatic and overconfident, and "negative" in the sense of censorious and depreciatory, not in the sense of a negative reply to a question. An ounce of appreciation, it is said, is worth a pound of criticism. Reward is more effective than punishment. Praise is more efficacious than blame. Noting an individual's successes is preferable to noting his failures. The old saying, "If you can't say something good about a person, don't say anything," may be trite, but it has values as well as limitations. One need not be a Pollyanna; but certainly many unfavorable remarks result in no gain and are better left unsaid. They may be made about inconsequentials, but the remarks themselves are not inconsequential.

Criticism, censure, and blame have their place; but they are to be used with discretion. It is only the relatively rare person who can accept criticism impersonally and objectively without resentment, defense, or balking. This is due in part to the double-barreled nature of criticism; an individual reacts to both the fact of criticism and the content of criticism. Constructive criticism is more effective than destructive criticism. When one must use the latter, he usually finds it more readily accepted if he prefaces it with something favorable. Suppose, for example, you have two things to tell a person, one favorable, the other unfavorable. If you begin with the latter, a barrier is immediately erected between the two of you. By the time you have reached the favorable comment the resentment, hurt feelings, and defenses of the other person have already become part of the situation. If, however, you begin with the favorable comment, the way is paved for the unfavorable one, and the criticism is put into a new perspective. The other person feels that you are on his side instead of against him and is more likely to accept the criticism with grace.

To make criticism effective, the other person's goals and motivations must be taken into account. If the criticism seems like a means of helping him achieve his goals, instead of a means by which his desires are thwarted, he will more readily act upon it.

Nagging is so much more likely to be an expression of feeling on the part of the nagger than an insightful attempt to influence the motivations and behavior of the person nagged that it seldom accomplishes what it is presumably intended to achieve. Instead, it may make the other individual more determined to do or not to do what he is nagged about. It may make him fight back, or, if not, he may seek other outlets for his emotions. It may make his emotions accumulate, only to explode eventually. It may make him seek escape from the nagging situation. It may lead him to immunize himself to everything the spouse says, to give up in desperation, or to be completely defeated. It may make him hypersensitive to whatever the spouse says because there is a carry-over of reaction from one instance of nagging to the next. Separate instances of nagging are not entirely discrete phenomena such as are indicated by *A, B, C, D* in Figure 8.1A, with the couple settling back to the zero line of emotion after the nagging is over. Rather, instances of nagging are like *W, X, Y, Z* in Figure 8.1B. After each instance of nagging both the nagger and the recipient of the nagging carry over a mood, sustain a hypersensitivity, so that there is a residue of emotion giving the next instance of nagging a head start. After the separate instances of nagging, the couple do not return to the zero line of emotion. Each instance sensitizes them further in preparation for the next. The recipient, then, tends to think of the nagging almost as a continuous process.

None of these responses can produce better human relationships or more satisfactory marriage. One cannot change the "inside" of a person by continual hammering upon the "outside." Nagging also reveals the points at which the nagger is vulnerable. It calls attention to the items concerning which he may readily be hurt or irritated.

People more readily accept criticism directed at what they do or say than criticism directed at them as persons. Criticism which amounts to classification is especially likely to be resisted. For example, "What you did was careless" is directed toward an act; "Only a careless person would do what you did" is directed toward a person and amounts to classification "You spoiled the party by your behavior" is criticism; "You always spoil parties by your behavior" approaches classification. The use of supercharged words, such as "stupid," "lazy," and "selfish," may seem to the person criticized like classification. For example, an individual might react more strongly against being told that he made a stupid mistake than to being told that he made an unfortunate mistake.

Some persons do improve through criticism. Others respond more readily to encouragement. Criticism makes them self-conscious. They then have difficulty in improving, especially if their efforts are witnessed by the person who did the criticizing, and even more especially if that person depreciates their efforts at improvement with further criticism or reminds them of the former criticism as the reason for their efforts.

Suggestions are most effective when given at the so-called "psychological

Figure 8.1A

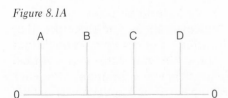

Figure 8.1B

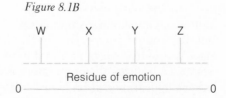

moment," even if that moment has to be waited for or created. It is useless to expect a person to give his full attention and consideration to a suggestion if he is absorbed in something else. He will listen more closely if he himself has asked for the suggestion, and in many cases he may be brought to this point.

Advice is a type of suggestion. Usually advice that is given when not sought is worse than useless. There is no more fruitless activity than the wholesale distribution of advice as if it were advertising handbills. One of the most pointless types of advice is that prefaced by the phrase "If I were you." Obviously I am not you and therefore cannot look at a situation through your eyes. There is no validity in assuming that what I think would be good for me in your situation would also be good for you. Advice, too, is only advice. It is to be taken or not taken as the other person sees fit. It is not command. The adviser has performed his function when he has given the advice. He is under no obligation to insist upon its acceptance and need not feel personally affronted if it is not acted upon.

OTHER FACTORS

Perspective

If you hold a penny very near one eye and shut the other, you can blot out a roomful of people or the whole panorama of nature. This happens, not because the penny is more important than the people or the landscape, but because something near your eye blinds you to more important objects farther away. You lack perspective. If you toss the penny away from you, it becomes an insignificant speck in your field of vision.

In marriage, perspective may be absent. Something close may blind one to something more important. One element in a situation may be fixed upon and magnified to the detriment of the whole.

If an individual fails to see the whole marital situation with its parts in their proper relationships; if he fails to discriminate between essentials and nonessentials, between the temporary and the permanent, between those things that do and those that do not bear a relationship to the more important elements in the marriage, between those which can damage the marriage and those which are only irritating; if he cannot see the forest for the trees, he lacks perspective. As time goes on, many couples grow to realize that what upset them at first actually did not affect their marriage. Looking back in retrospect they see that their relationship has been unimpaired. If at first they had discriminated between things of lesser and things of greater significance, their initial concern would have been unnecessary.

In the early days of marriage, adjustments have to be made to relatively minor circumstances; some couples fail to anticipate these, and therefore, they get them out of perspective and find them disturbing. For example, a couple may have a problem sleeping in a double bed or using the same bathroom, with her cosmetics and his shaving materials in evidence. They may be annoyed by each other's appearance at breakfast, with him still unshaved and her still wearing her hair-styling equipment. One may be disturbed by the other's snoring.

Loss of perspective is apparent in those cases in which a couple get to the point where anything that happens in the marriage in a way represents the entire marriage, and conflict over a relatively inconsequential incident can be almost as bitter as if the whole marriage were threatened. In one case, for example, the wife went to the refrigerator to get a drink of cold water. On a shelf she found a can of fruit opened but uncovered. She called her husband and said, "Why do you leave a can of fruit in the refrigerator like this?" He retorted, "Why should I cover it when I'm soon going to eat it?" An argument ensued. Out of the argument grew an evening-long quarrel which the couple considered serious enough to discuss with a counselor the next day.

It is a common opinion that "little things" often make for failure in marriage. The term *little things* may be defined only from a specific point of view. They may be "little" to a casual observer, but not to the couple themselves. Much depends upon the relative significance assigned to them, upon perspective. When perspective is lacking, "little things" may damage a marriage. Deriving the suggestion from a hunting situation, someone has said, "If you spend all your time swatting mosquitoes, you will never shoot your deer." Some couples give so much attention to "tremendous trifles" that they miss the essential meaning of marriage.

One "tremendous trifle" which illustrates this point and about which there are many jokes, perhaps because it actually is a problem in many a marriage, is toothpaste. Individuals who leave the cap off or squeeze the tube in the middle are often a source of irritation to those who put the cap back on or squeeze the tube from the end and assume that their way is naturally the only right way, failing to see that their perfectionism and criticism may be a source of annoyance for the individual whose approach to toothpaste is less meticulous and more casual. Some couples start each day with conflict over toothpaste, sacrificing the good spirit that might otherwise begin another day of their marriage to a "tremendous trifle." One student reported that her parents had had such conflict over toothpaste during their entire marriage. Her mother was a "middle-squeezer" and her father was an "end-squeezer." On their twentieth wedding anniversary they discussed the problem and each bought the other a tube of toothpaste, thus ending two decades of conflict by a very simple means that might have been thought of years before.

This matter of "tremendous trifles" is two-sided, however. It is true that "if you spend all your time swatting mosquitoes, you will never shoot your deer." On the other hand, life would be unbearable if one lived in a swarm of mosquitoes. It is partly a question of whose perspective is involved. It is granted that "I" should have perspective on the little things that "you" do. But if "you" permit an accumulation of little things which annoy "me" because "you" do not have perspective on "me" and the marriage, if your self-concern outweighs your other-concern, you cannot expect "me" to live in oblivious complacency in the swarm of mosquitoes "you" produce.

Accuracy is sometimes gotten out of perspective. Under certain circumstances accuracy is important. But it is not equally important under all circumstances, as some couples seem to assume. Some husbands and wives constantly correct one another, even in the presence of other persons, in a way that amounts practically to nagging. The least inaccuracy calls forth a correction, although it may have no bearing on the point of a story or the interpretation of a report of personal events.

Overemphasis upon sex in marriage is a symptom of distorted perspective. Sex is not all of marriage, any more than the room in the penny experiment is all copper. The more unsuccessful their sexual adjustment is, the more prominent sex is likely to be in a couple's thinking.

If an individual fails to see himself in relation to the total situation and to his spouse—if, for example, personal desire, selfish whims, and hurt feelings are given precedence over the success of the marriage—he lacks perspective. If the marriage is more important than part of it, what difference does it make who takes the initiative in patching up a quarrel during which perspective has been momentarily lost? In this latter statement, however, the implication is that after the patching up of the quarrel the couple's relationship will be a happy one and the marriage successful. It is conceivable, too, that the relationship as it is or as it would have to be reestablished would not be more valuable than the feelings of one of the parties if the latter were seriously affected. When we suggest that it makes no difference who takes the initiative in patching up a quarrel, we are referring to the ups and downs of normal marriage rather than to the steady trends of alienation which, in some cases, have already led the couple to the brink of disaster.

Failure to think of successful marriage as a goal worth striving for is a symptom of lack of perspective. Unawareness that success requires effort, understanding, and idealism and is not incidental and automatic is a symptom. Unwillingness to go more than halfway to achieve success is another.

Working out a successful marriage may be compared to writing a theme. If the theme does not seem perfect after the first attempt, the writer does not tear it up and start anew with an entirely new subject and then repeat this process again and again until a perfect finished product is achieved without revision. Rather, he chooses a topic, works and reworks it, changes words here and there, rewrites sentences and paragraphs, injects new ideas and deletes irrelevant ones until the final product is what he wants it to be and is as well done as his capacities permit.

If successful marriage is a goal worth striving for, it may be set up as a definite objective. Instead of following the path of least resistance, the couple may work toward that objective. Suppose that you are going on an automobile trip. Someone asks you where you are going and you say, "I don't know; I'll tell you when I get there." You step into your car and drive down every well-paved road merely because it is well paved. You may arrive somewhere; you may not. That would not be your plan. First, you would decide upon a destination. Next you would work out an itinerary. Then you would take the roads leading to your destination, even though some of them were rough, the driving was sometimes hard, and you had to make some detours. You would not turn back at the first detour or stretch of poor pavement. It is sensible to lay out the best possible itinerary, but that is not the same as following the path of least resistance.

Generalizing on too few instances is an indication of lack of perspective. When an individual makes *once* become *always* or *never,* he shows that he does not see the whole for the part. "You never remember a thing I tell you," says the irate wife whose husband has forgotten a single instruction. "You're always spending too much money," says the husband whose wife's latest shopping venture has been expensive. The person who concludes that the inevitable little mistakes of the first years of marriage represent permanent maladjustments lacks perspective.

A philosophy of life enabling a couple to meet a crisis is a factor contributing to successful adjustment; its absence is a factor contributing to failure. A mature person knows that sooner or later in everyone's life crises come. Friends and relatives die. Illness occurs. Children are born. Disappointments of one sort or another impose themselves upon existence. The inability to make the best of an unchangeable situation or to tolerate a situation until there is time or opportunity for change may lead to poor adjustment. At times people are called upon to learn to live with insoluble problems. Someone has said, "It takes internal props to withstand external pressure." Someone else has said, "Not all the water in the seven seas can sink a ship unless that water gets inside." A philosophy of life to meet a crisis supplies those internal props and acts as the agency for keeping the water from getting inside.

In a sense, such a philosophy of life is a type of perspective—the whole of life is seen, rather than only some of its parts. When we think in terms such as these, we may think of religion as a type of perspective. So are idealism and a sense of humor. These three things—religion, idealism, and a sense of humor— do as much as any other three factors to enable the individual to see himself in the total life situation and to see the relationships between the whole and the parts.

Focal Points

If there is tension in a marital situation, anything may become a focal point for conflict. The focal point for conflict may be relatively unimportant and may not be the true cause or even closely connected with it. As with an individual, so with a couple, the obvious cause of behavior is not always the real one. Conflict in marriage is very obtrusive to the couple who experience it. If it becomes serious and permeating enough to produce failure, that failure, impending or actual, is extremely important to both husband and wife. Failure in marriage is a "big" thing. Therefore, the couple, oversimplifying, reason that it must have a "big" cause, and they seek for one. Among the most obvious, most tangible, possible "big" causes are such things as children, sex, money, in-laws, religion, and use of leisure time. Sometimes one of these is the true cause of conflict. At other times it is only the hook on which the conflict is hung; and the true causes are numerous subtle influences less obvious and hence less readily analyzed. Failure is usually the result of numerous contributing factors rather than the result of a single, simple cause, no matter how important this one cause may seem. Figuratively speaking, marriages that fail seldom "go on the rocks," as is commonly said. They are more likely to be wrecked on piles of sand—the combined and cumulative effect of numerous contributing factors, no one of which alone would be sufficient to produce failure.

Depending upon personalities and circumstances, the same things that serve to bind some couples closer together serve to wedge others apart. Children, property, money, religion, sex, and numerous other factors may serve either as adhesive or as repellent, depending upon the way the couple react to them. None of these factors can produce conflict unless the couple have attitudes and personality traits that permit conflict to arise. Some marriages succeed while containing elements that contribute to the failure of others. Maladjustment is largely a subjective process, a result of whole personalities reacting to a total situation. The situation alone cannot produce maladjustment.

The *post hoc, ergo propter hoc* (after this, therefore because of this) fallacy in thinking is often found in the analysis of marriage adjustment. In such analysis it is important to be sure that cause and effect are in the proper order. A couple have open conflict over money. Money seems to be the cause of their disharmony. But what personality traits have led them to have conflict over money? Its use may be effect as well as cause. Honeymoon experiences are frequently said to be the cause of a wife's poor sexual adjustment. Sometimes they are. In other cases, however, personality traits that made possible the reactions exhibited in the early days of marriage also play a part in producing the maladjustment. The honeymoon experiences are results as well as causes. Conflict over one thing may itself become a factor in developing reactions which, in turn, make for other conflict. In this way a chain of cause and effect springs up. If this chain is not broken at some point and the situation is not reversed or stabilized, the couple grow farther and farther apart. This process is termed *alienation* [Waller, 1951].

Focal points may also be considered in a positive sense. A couple may further their marital adjustment by centering their marriage on meaningful points of interest. This does not imply permanent crystallization. It implies only the employment of a kind of emotional centripetal force that draws them together. For example, a child or their home may be a focal point. So may participation in a common activity such as a hobby. A regular ritual of some sort, such as a traditional manner of celebrating a special occasion, for example, a holiday or birthday, may serve periodically to bring attitudes, memories, aspirations to a focus. A couple with imagination and ingenuity may set up such focal points most meaningful to themselves.

Use of Money

The use of money may serve as a binding factor for a couple, affording common interests and establishing common goals. It may also be a focal point for, or a cause of, conflict. One couple may find happiness on an income identical in amount with that of another couple who are suing for divorce because of it.

Amount of income and its relation to happiness are also relative to expectations. If both husband and wife are accustomed to a modest standard of living, or if they are committed to an occupational field in which monetary returns are typically low, they may never hope for a large income. If, however, their expectations run higher than their possible income, the amount of the latter may be a thorn in their flesh.

A man's salary check is made payable to himself. For this reason, some men assume that they alone earn that salary. If the wife cares for the home, children, and husband; is skilled in consumption; makes social contacts that assist the husband in his profession or broaden family experience; is a companion who enriches his life, stirs his ambitions, aids him in his work, gives him something to work for, they earn the income jointly. This is implied in the concept of community property as recognized in the Federal law which permits a couple to make a joint income tax return, using only the husband's income as a base but thereby reducing the total tax to be paid.

So far as marital happiness is concerned, the actual method of handling income is not so important as the means by which the couple arrive at the employment of that method. If the method is agreeable to both partners, almost any method can be made to work successfully. If, on the other hand, the method represents an imposition upon one partner by the other, through either insistence or irresponsibility, and it is therefore reluctantly tolerated rather than willingly accepted, any method can give rise to conflict.

There is no standard budget, no distribution of income that will automatically fit every couple's needs. Published materials help, but they alone cannot solve a couple's problem. To expect them to do so would be the same as to expect every man to wear the same size mail-order suit.

A budget need not be considered absolutely inflexible. As unpredictable needs or opportunities arise, it may be adjusted to them. Furthermore, the couple must expect to make mistakes. The budget is a tool, a means to an end. It is not an end in itself and should not become master rather than servant. It need not be so much in evidence at all times that it becomes a source of irritation, thus defeating its own purpose. It can become a bone of contention, a cause of friction, a source of conflict. But so can a hand-to-mouth handling of income.

Both husband and wife are consumers, and modern economic conditions are putting an ever-increasing responsibility upon the consumer. This is especially true of the wife, since ordinarily most of the family purchasing falls to her. A woman may well ask herself this question, "Would I marry a man only as well prepared to earn money as I am to spend it?" One of the modern wife's chief functions has become her role as specialist in consumption. By careful buying to lower expenses, she may raise the relative family income. As we said in another connection, some of the wife's traditional functions have been taken away from her. What can she substitute in their stead? Knowledge of consumption is one answer to this pertinent question. There are many aids at her disposal. She may make a distinct contribution to family life by taking advantage of them.

Use of Leisure Time

Leisure time may be defined as time that is free from economic pursuits, including homemaking. It is time in which the individual has greater freedom of choice as to how it shall be employed. Modern social conditions have increased the amount available to both sexes. They have also created new opportunities and new problems.

Young couples frequently are not aware of the importance of the use of leisure or of the fact that its use may constitute a problem in marriage. An opinion often expressed by students is that, if a person has leisure, he will know what to do with it and there is no use talking about it. Experience proves that many do not know what to do with leisure time. They pass time instead of using it. They spend it instead of investing it. The expression "kill time" is indicative of a not uncommon attitude. The use of time is important in marriage because it is usually in their nonworking hours that husband and wife are most closely associated. Their leisure-time pursuits contribute, for good or ill, to the development of their relationship. Those pursuits may become focal points in either a positive or a negative sense. They may serve as common interests or as points of departure for conflict. They may increase tension or dissipate it. They may preserve romance or allow it to atrophy. It is not essential that all these pursuits should represent common interests. In marriage it is important that there be individual interests as well as those held by both partners.

A husband's schedule is often more rigid than a wife's because of the difference in occupational pressure, unless, of course, she too is employed. The wife may budget her time so that she and her husband will have leisure together. If she does the unpostponables first, she can readily adjust her schedule so that leisure-time pursuits may be included. If, on the other hand, she has an inclination to do postponables first, she may find that there are things she must do when her husband is free.

One is tempted to be almost dogmatic concerning the married woman's use of leisure and to say that no woman can be as good a wife by devoting her entire life to housework and the demands of her family as she can be if she devotes an ample portion of her time to other pursuits. Everything she does to contribute to the development of her personality and the enrichment of her life makes an indirect contribution to the life of her home and family provided that it is not so time consuming that home and family are neglected. The same is true of the husband. The couple's task is not only to maintain a dwelling. It is also to create a set of attitudes and relationships. The woman who claims to feel guilty when she takes time from her household duties for recreation does not conceive of homemaking in its broadest terms. It would be more appropriate for her to feel guilty when she allows household duties to prevent her from participating in recreational activities.

One source of conflict in marriage is boredom. When two people are bored, they may magnify little things in their relationship because their perspective is distorted. Little things occurring in a setting of interesting activities and imaginative, enthusiastic approaches to life are more likely to remain little things. But the same little things occurring in a setting where there is little to contrast them with or draw attention from them may loom out of proportion to their importance. Also, open conflict over them may break the monotony. It is difficult to understand how intelligent, educated people with all their faculties can be bored in present-day America, where all about them are opportunities for interesting pursuits. Yet the fact remains that some of them are bored, and their marriages often suffer because of their boredom. One place where a start can be made in making life and marriage more interesting is in the imaginative, creative use of leisure time.

Motivation

One of the most important factors in making marriage succeed is motivation, commitment, the will to succeed. This suggests setting up marriage as a goal toward which the couple will strive, taking care that other goals, perhaps worthy in themselves, such as occupational ambition or child rearing, do not divert the couple's efforts from achieving success in the marriage itself and lead them to relegate marriage to a position subordinate to that of their other objectives.

Such commitment involves work, not in the sense of employment, but rather in the sense of the expenditure of time and effort for marital success. Such effort entails ego surrender, that is, considering the success of the relationship as being more important than the feelings of the persons in it, self-discipline in channeling one's own behavior, and the application of patience and perseverance to problem solving. It entails ingenuity in providing new experience in marriage so that there is no "letdown." This does not imply that there must be as much romanticizing in marriage as there is before the wedding. But it does imply that marriage does not inevitably have to involve a loss of enthusiasm and adventure.

The demands of family living make some routine in marriage necessary. But routine may be servant, not master. It may be a means to an end rather than an end in itself. Many educated, intelligent women become what might be called "kitchen-minded." In this state they are mentally and emotionally saturated with housework, and their outlook is bounded by the walls of their dwellings. Everything is submerged in and by housekeeping and the immediate demands of the family. This does not imply that slovenliness is a virtue and is more desirable than system. System implies efficiency; routine implies deadening repetition. Figuratively speaking, romance need not be sacrificed to getting the dishes done.

Men may suffer from the masculine equivalent of "kitchen-mindedness." They become choked by ticker tapes, buried under piles of sales tickets, covered with grease, or deafened by the sound of gears. They "keep their eye on the ball" with such concentration and single-mindedness that they lose sight of other things.

Some husbands and wives grow to take each other for granted. Each one becomes a sort of habit to the other. "Marriage," said Balzac, "must continually vanquish a monster that devours everything: the monster of habit." Habit may destroy spontaneity. It may make husband and wife as unstimulating and as predictable as a perpetual-motion machine. Constant rubbing in one spot may wear the garments of romance so thin that the original cloth is no longer seen because of the patches.

Why should two complex personalities lack variety in their relationship?

Monogamy and monotony are not synonymous. Seeking variety in the sense of discovering new facets of the other spouses's personality, looking for new things that can be done together or old ones that may be revived, makes for sustained interest and prevents the marriage from falling into a rut of habit. It is possible to have variety in a marriage relationship, rather than a variety of partners where there is only a partially complete relationship with each one.

Habit is not an unadulterated evil, however. Many of its aspects may enrich a marriage. For example, habits of courtesy make any relationship smoother. It is puzzling to know why so many people seem to assume that a wedding ceremony creates the privilege of being rude, that it is a signal for discontinuing toward husband or wife the courtesies that are exhibited toward less meaningful persons.

Acceptance

As we have seen, the wedding ceremony indicates on the part of each party in marriage an acceptance of the other person as that person is. This does not preclude expectation of growth. It does raise a serious question about the advisability of attempted reform. To accept another person as that person is does not mean that there is never any conflict or irritation in marriage. It does mean that conflict and irritation are kept in perspective. Ideally, this acceptance should be complete and unqualified.

In day-by-day living, however, with more or less ordinary personalities, there may be limits to acceptance. The threshold of intolerance is lower in some persons, higher in others. For example, what if there is found a considerable discrepancy between role expected and role played? A man expects his wife to be highly domestic and maternal but finds himself married to a woman who rejects the wife-mother role in favor of employment. A woman expects her husband to be an interested, attentive, affectionate companion but marries a man who is "all business" and is no more romantic than the proverbial "bump on a log." How far can a person be expected to go in accepting such things as impotence, frigidity, infidelity, mental illness, homosexuality, brutality, or what is defined as immorality?

Some couples, even with a problem less serious than any of those mentioned, find themselves at what seems like a crossroads in their marriage; they reach a low point two or three years after the wedding. It appears to them that their marriage has deteriorated to the point where they have almost given up. Yet they still cling to the marriage in the hope that something can be made of it. Their problem is basically a discrepancy between what their marriage is and what they hoped it would be. If they go on as they have been going, the marriage may terminate in failure. On the other hand, they may, if they will, take a new inventory. They may reevaluate the marriage and each other in terms of actual present assets and liabilities rather than in terms of their dreams at the time of the wedding. Often, at this point, if they can accept one another and the marriage as each is, they can work out a good marriage, even though it may not coincide exactly with their earlier, perhaps less realistic, expectations.

This process of reevaluation plus new acceptance, combined with more realistic expectations based on greater insight into what each spouse is and what each has to contribute to the marriage, is not infrequently called for in a young marriage. This is especially true if the couple knew each other only a relatively brief period and therefore not too well before the wedding. They married with romantic enthusiasm at a high pitch and a great deal of momentum generated by physical appeal. They are carried along for a while but ultimately reach the point where their marriage, if it is to endure, must be put on a more realistic footing. Like opening a Christmas gift in fancy wrapping, they need to strip the unreality from their expectations and look inside to see what they actually have to work with. Klemer [1965] refers to unrealistic expectations as a major cause of what he terms "marriage disease."

RECOGNITION OF INDIVIDUAL PRIVATE WORLDS

Each individual lives in a private world of which he is the center and which is partly his own creation. True, we all live on the same planet, but the earth is not our world. One's own world is one not of sensation alone but also of meaning. Sensations are the raw materials out of which experience is constructed. They are not isolated. Each new one fits into a complex pattern formed of all the individual's experience up to date. Meaning depends not upon sensation but upon interpretation, which in turn rests upon all experience. In a sense, then, the world is a unique "illusion" to each person. Each individual is a unique "illusion" to every other individual. It is for this reason that two persons may react so differently to a third person—for example, parents' reaction to a child, a husband's and wife's reaction to the mother of one of them, the reader's reaction to a possible marriage partner as compared with his parents' reaction to that person.

At best, it is possible for one person to penetrate another's world to only a slight degree. Certainly no one but the individual himself can live in it. In a sense, we are all hermits—each partly isolated from other people. This is because only a fraction of one's experience is communicable. Communication depends upon language and other symbols. Of necessity, these are generalizations. Words are definitions determined by common agreement and based upon the assumption that, given a set of circumstances, all human beings will react the same. Therefore, words can express only that part of an individual's experience which he has in common with other people. The same is true of other symbols.

When two persons "see" the "same" color—that is, when the same light rays enter the eyes of both individuals—they may use the same word to express what they "see," for example, "red." There is no way of proving that their total experience is the same. If language is analyzed far enough, eventually it is reduced to words which are indefinable and depend for their intelligibility upon the assumption that all persons have identical experience. When A says to B, "The color I see is red," A is in one sense communicating his experience. In another sense, A is stimulating B to recall his own. Let the reader imagine how he would explain "red" to a man born blind, and he will understand how one person can communicate with another only in so far as there are common elements in their experience. How can one fully communicate what he experiences in looking at a sunset, listening to a symphony, or being in love? After experience has been described and communicated as nearly completely as behavior and all known symbols permit, after it has been subjected to as nearly complete scientific analysis as is possible at present (and probably for some time to come), there is still an incommunicable, indescribable, unanalyzable residue, which is the individual's own and is unique.

Living in a private world gives each individual a unique *frame of reference* that makes all experience relative. Imagine that your stature was decreased by 24 inches. Your world would be altered because your frame of reference would change. Other people would appear in a new light. Doorways, automobiles, houses, and store windows would all seem larger. It would take longer to walk to places. From all objects light would come to your eyes from a different angle. In a crowd you would have a new perspective. You would find yourself better adapted to some sports, less well adapted to others. In some occupations you might be at a disadvantage; in others you might have an advantage over taller persons.

All this would be true as a result of a simple change in stature. One may understand, then, how each individual has a unique frame of reference, how each one's experience causes him to look at life through different eyes, and how all experience is relative. No two persons have an identical total experience. No two have identical personalities. Hence, no two have the same frame of reference. Moreover, each person sees both himself and others. He cannot see himself as others see him or see others as they see themselves. Each individual, therefore, is part of the worlds of others in a way different from being part of his own world.

To individual differences add sex differences. The world seems different to a woman from what it seems to a man. Occupations, clothes, other people, children, reproduction, homes, and sex—all appear in a different light, depending upon whether the frame of reference is masculine or feminine. It is impossible for one sex to look at life entirely through the other's eyes. Many of the experiences of one are completely foreign to the other, and there is no known method of communication. Take, for example, motherhood. There is no way for a woman fully to explain to a man what it is like to be pregnant or to give birth to a baby. Because of the difference in social pressures and role expectations under which the sexes live and which are ingrained in them from birth onward, it is sometimes difficult for a man to explain to a woman his attitude toward his job. There is no way for a man to look at either women or other men through a woman's eyes, no way for a woman to look at either men or other women through a man's eyes. There is no way for one sex to know what the other experiences when in love. Under the most favorable circumstances in the best marriages, where there is as nearly complete understanding between husband and wife as is humanly possible, there is still an unbridgeable gulf of sex difference.

This unbridgeable gulf is accentuated by the fact that the sexes are not only different, but complementary. We may assume that the greater the difference between two individuals, the greater the difficulty of their communicating. When to difference we add "polarity," each sex being oriented in part toward the other sex and, therefore, as different as possible in some ways, we can appreciate the fact that communication between the sexes is often incomplete. This does not imply that the sexes cannot communicate. It implies only that their communication rests upon special understanding of each other, not only as two individuals but as male and female.

Communication

Communication is important in marriage. Yet, as suggested above, it is necessarily incomplete. But an awareness of this inevitable incompleteness is itself a contribution to marital adjustment. Unawareness of such unavoidable incompleteness may create an impasse.

One often hears it said that when a couple have a marital problem, they should talk it over. So far as it goes and to the extent to which this implies getting the problem out into the open instead of "bottling it up," this is good. But because of the inevitable incompleteness of communication, discussion is not an automatic solution to all problems. There can be discussion without communication.

When a couple seek counseling help on a marriage problem, each spouse is wont to assume that he or she is stating and dealing with the facts. To a degree this may be true. But actually neither the husband, nor the wife, nor the counselor deals with facts alone. Each spouse gives the counselor not a factual analysis but rather an interpretation of the marital situation. The counselor, then, works partly with facts and partly with such interpretations. It is for this reason, among others, that it is so important, if at all possible, for both spouses to visit a counselor if their marriage is in difficulty, no matter how much one as compared with the other may seem to be at fault.

Because of the incompleteness of communication and their living in private worlds, understanding between husband and wife is also incomplete. It is important to understand that they cannot always understand. When a couple who are motivated to make their marriage succeed reach the end of communication and therefore of understanding, they are called upon to commit an act of faith, an acceptance of difference based on trust, confidence, and love.

How may communication in marriage be improved? There is no formula, no shortcut, no "quick and easy way." But a few suggestions may be made.

Both the individual who has something to say and the individual who is expected to listen must be motivated to try to improve their mutual communication. Communication is not a one-sided process. There is a difference between talking and communicating.

There is also a difference between listening and hearing. Oversimplifying, *hearing* connotes merely the perception of sound. *Listening* connotes attention to sound in an effort to derive meaning. Granted functioning auditory apparatus, an individual may have sound thrust upon him so that he cannot avoid hearing it. Or he may "close his mind to it" so that the sound is not perceived. If he is listening, he will "open his mind to it" through attention, interest, and concern. A couple are having an angry quarrel. They are shouting at each other. They cannot avoid hearing the sound. Neither pays attention to what the other loudly says, and the exchange goes on as if each were reciting a monologue. Another couple discuss a topic of mutual concern. They are eager to reach an understanding. Each lets the other know that what is being said is being "received" and considered. The first couple are talking. The second couple are communicating.

The content of communication may be resisted because of the tone of voice or attitude of the speaker; it is not only what is said but the manner in which it is said to which a listener reacts.

Listening is an active, rather than a passive, art. One person can facilitate another's speaking or make it more difficult by the way he listens. If attention is diverted or haphazard, if the listener does something like read the paper or drum on the table with his fingers, the speaker's problem is increased. Conversely, the speaker cannot expect full attention if he addresses the listener under circumstances such that the latter cannot give complete attention; for example, a husband talks to his wife as she puts dinner on the table or bathes the baby, and she talks to him when he is sleepy or tense from business worries.

Luce [1970] points out that people "walk to different drumbeats." There is individuality in tempo and rhythm. "Individual variation in time structure appears to be quite as pronounced as is variation in athletic talent, height, and temperament." One's ability to think, to discriminate, to solve problems, and to do tasks and one's feelings, alertness, and sensitivity all change within the twenty-four-hour cycle. "We are different persons at 10 A.M. than at 10 P.M." If husband and wife seek to improve their mutual communication, attention needs to be given to the point in each individual's time structure at which communication is attempted.

There are what may be termed *selective attention* and *selective inattention*. The listener hears what he wants to hear or "tunes out" what he does not want to hear. Selective inattention may occur when a worried husband hears nothing of what a wife says except a reference to the money she spent in shopping, or a tired wife "tunes out" all of a husband's report of his day at work except his mention of his business partner's going on a week-end trip with his family. Selective inattention, as suggested earlier, is also one of the reasons for the ineffectiveness of nagging.

Not even commonly used words necessarily have the same meaning for both persons. Hence it becomes important for each person to seek to learn the other's vocabulary, not only the colloquialisms and special words used but also the shades of meaning and emotional tones of words. For some persons certain words are emotionally supercharged in the sense of being especially unacceptable because they are reacted to against a backdrop of highly individualized personal experience and point of view.

A speaker ordinarily assumes that the meaning of a word he uses will evoke the same meaning for the listener. But, because of his experience, the listener may interpret the word differently or give it no meaning at all. Use of a word does not by itself create understanding of it. Communication may be improved by ascertaining the meaning of words, especially key words. This may seem too obvious to mention. Yet people continue to talk without knowing whether the person listening knows what they are talking about. Harper [May, 1958], a marriage counselor of long experience, says, "One of the most common sources of communication difficulty in a marriage relationship is that situation where one spouse *assumes* he knows what the other means. . . ."

Looking at this problem another way, we may say that a word fits more or less well or not at all into a listener's frame of reference. If it fits reasonably well, speaker and listener communicate. If it does not fit, no communication occurs. Speaker and listener may have frames of reference sufficiently similar in some respects to permit the word to fit even though their total frames of reference are different. In Figure 8.2, the shaded circle represents a given word, as used by speaker *A*. The word fits into the frame of reference of listener *B*, but not into the frame of reference of listener *C*. Hence *A* can communicate with *B* but not with *C*.

Men and women often use the same vocabulary with somewhat different meaning or connotation because of the masculine and feminine subcultures from which interpretations emerge. Consider, for example, the overtones of meaning of the following words when used by one sex as compared with the other: "cry," "fight," "mother," "wedding," "corsage."

As indicated in an earlier chapter, women are more likely than men to read a personal reference into something said, and men are more likely to make statements intended to have no such reference. If communication is to be improved, both sexes must understand the possibility of having this difference become a factor in a discussion, even though the difference is not universal.

Communication is furthered to the degree that each person is aware of complexes, special sensitivities, fears, values, biases, and points of resistance of the other person so that no unnecessary barriers to communication are introduced. Communication is also furthered to the degree that each individual is confident that he will be understood and accepted, not judged and rejected.

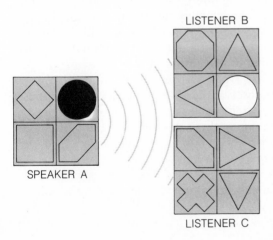

Figure 8.2 Diagrammatic representation of the relationship of a word to frames of reference.

Hence, he is free to divulge his thoughts and feelings, his worries and concerns, his failures and mistakes. Masters and Johnson [1970] mention learning to communicate and "exchange vulnerabilities."

Insight into the other person's handling of facts and ideas facilitates communication. Does he use facts with accuracy or with distortion and exaggeration? Does he welcome new facts to increase his understanding, or does he resist new facts? The placard which reads, "Don't bother me with facts; my mind's made up" is intended to be humorous, but it is descriptive of a large proportion of the population, especially regarding the nonmaterial aspects of life and human relations. An understanding of the topic under discussion also facilitates communication. Two people can hardly communicate effectively unless they are talking about the same thing.

Fear

Various sorts of fear may play a part in marital adjustment. Fear of submerging one's own personality in that of the spouse, of loss of liberty, of one's own abilities or, rather, of their lack or inadequacy may elicit reactions that are unfavorable to success.

Fear of losing the affection and fidelity of the other person is common. This is *jealousy*. Jealousy is a fear reaction. There are two shades of meaning for the term. If an individual has an intense desire to preserve something meaningful to him and would defend it against any attempt to destroy it but in fighting for it is confident that he will win, he may be said to be jealous. If, on the other hand, he seeks to preserve something meaningful to him but fears that he will lose and be unable to retain it, he may be said to be jealous in the ordinary sense of the term. Grold [May, 1972] refers to jealousy as "the rage at being dispensed with or betrayed." The first type of jealousy may be illustrated by a couple's efforts to preserve their home against the insidious attack of some relative who would destroy their happiness if he could. The second type is that exhibited by the husband who sees another man manifesting interest in his wife and fears that he will be unable to retain her affection and fidelity against the onslaught of a seemingly more attractive person. The husband may not analyze his fear to this extent; but it is present, nevertheless. His reaction may be anger or hate, as far as he is aware of it; but at bottom it is due to insecurity.

Jealousy may be divided into two types upon another basis, namely, (1) justifiable jealousy, that based upon observation of the behavior of the spouse; and (2) unjustifiable jealousy, that based not upon fact but only upon the insecurity, inferiority feeling, or suspicion of the jealous person. In the first type, the wife may know that her husband is interested in another woman and may feel helpless to hold him. In the second type, the husband has exhibited no suspicious behavior; but because the wife feels insecure, she becomes jealous when he no more than talks with a woman business associate or converses with the woman who sits next to him at a dinner.

For several reasons jealousy is self-defeating. (1) Love and fidelity cannot be forced through suspicion and surveillance. The only love worth having is that which is given freely and voluntarily. (2) The other person resents the lack of trust. (3) Even when justifiable, jealousy is not addressed to the true causes of the infidelity. Therefore, effort which might be directed to the solution of the problem is dissipated without gain. (4) A jealous person is likely to be hard to live with and, therefore, is likely to become unattractive. This may make the spouse lose interest and do exactly what it was feared he would do, thus furthering the end the jealousy was intended to prevent. (5) Jealousy tends to be a symptom of immaturity and is often part of an immature pattern of behavior that is not conducive to happy marriage. (6) Jealousy often involves projection of blame. The jealous person does not say, "I am jealous because I am fearful and insecure." He says, "I am jealous because of what you are doing."

It is not the fact of jealousy alone, but also its expression, that affects a marriage. Expression of it entails criticism, suspicion, questioning, nagging, demands for explanation, displays of temper, moodiness, loss of respect, attempted domination, restriction of freedom, or any of a number of other irritating and irksome attributes and experiences. Sometimes the jealous spouse refuses to believe the truth. The more the other person tries to explain that there is no cause for jealousy, the more jealous the first one becomes, insisting that the explanation is only an attempt to "cover up." Thus the couple sink deeper and deeper into the quicksand of alienation.

Jealousy, however, may have one mitigating quality that compensates in a minor way for its unpleasantness and may make the bitter pill easier to swallow. The fact that an individual manifests it may be an indication that he does not wish to lose the other person, that he wants to preserve their relationship. This thought is worth the consideration of anyone who has a jealous spouse.

Domination

The results of actual or attempted domination are relative and depend upon the personalities involved. By and large, however, domination is unhealthful. Some marriages become what might be termed "battles for prestige." The question to which the couple seek the answer is not "How may we work best together?" but "Who will give in?" [Knopf, 1932]. An individual who makes marriage a power struggle because he insists upon exercising masculine authority or she has a personality need to dominate is seeking to get his or her own way rather than to contribute to the success of the marriage.

Alfred Adler [1937] speaks of a "household run by water power." He refers to a home ruled by a wife's tears. An individual may resort to "illness" in order to dominate a spouse. A wife may become a stickler for etiquette or may use punctuality as a weapon. She may overstress her own weakness and so much admire what her husband does that he becomes burdened with expectations of further success. If the husband does not succeed, the wife blames others for having hindered him. This binds the pair more closely together and gives the wife more power over the husband. Some women marry men who are physically disabled; behind their pretense of pity and sympathy is the wish to dominate.

One not uncommon type of attempted domination is a demand for gratitude. "If it were not for me, you wouldn't be where you are today"; "I've put up with a lot for you"; "Think what you were before I married you." When gratitude is voluntary and spontaneous, it is good for both concerned. When it is demanded, it is likely to become resentment. It throws new light upon the thing done and upon the person who makes the demand.

When the demand for gratitude takes the form of supposed martyrdom, playing up sacrifices and flaunting them in the face of the other person, it becomes especially insidious. "A sacrifice labeled as such is like a gift with the price tag deliberately left on; it is more of an insult than a compliment" [Wile and Winn, 1929].

Overdependence

Marriage is for mature persons; the overdependent, parasitic, clinging-vine type of individual does not fall into that category. Considerable dependence of one spouse on the other is natural and desirable. When it reaches the point of evasion of responsibility, failure to make a contribution to the success of the marriage, or inability to carry out one's half of the bargain, it is detrimental.

Overdependence may also be a symptom of immaturity in that it may result partly from narcissism, that is, self-love. A wife, for example, may identify herself with her husband and by inference praise her wise choice of spouse by continually calling attention to his virtues. She subordinates herself to him, bowing, scraping, yes-yesing, taking his slightest wish as a command. To the husband this may become tiresome. If he actually believes that he is all that she seems to think he is, this type of behavior may affect his personality.

What sometimes passes for overdependence may actually be domination. By submission and yielding, by manifesting an apparent need for help and guidance, by expecting another to make one's decisions and assume one's responsibilities, one person may in part control the other's behavior.

"Homeopathic Remedies"

Years ago there was a school of medical thought one of the tenets of which was this: To cure a disease there should be administered a drug which in a healthy person would produce symptoms similar to those of the illness. For example, to cure a fever, the physician would administer a drug that would raise the patient's temperature. This was homeopathic medicine, "homeopathic" being derived from two Greek words meaning "like" and "suffering."

In medical practice homeopathic remedies are outmoded. In marriage they should be, but unfortunately they are not. Such remedies in marriage take the form of retaliation in kind. An attempt is made to remedy a maladjustment by deliberately doing what the other person has done, when that proved annoying, instead of seeking and remedying the real cause of the maladjustment. There is a duplication of the undesirable behavior of the spouse. A wife is hurt by something the husband does. To remedy the injury and prevent his doing it again, she intentionally hurts him. A wife is sarcastic; the husband responds with sarcasm. Criticism is countered with criticism. One attempts to dilute his own offense or error by pointing out that the other does the same thing or something equally bad. A husband is extravagant. To cure him of his weakness for spending money and to show him the difficulties caused by an extravagant spouse, the wife becomes extravagant. This is supposed to balance the budget and also to change the husband's behavior. "Homeopathic remedies" balance neither the financial nor the marital ledger. Two minuses do not make a plus, nor two wrongs a right. Such behavior not only does not alleviate the condition toward which it is directed but has a tendency to multiply irritations, since the number of offensive stimuli as well as the sensitivity of both persons is increased. Each one reacts to the other's action plus the other's attitude.

Tension

Tension may be defined as a physiological, emotional, or mental state tending to give rise to activity. The activity is not necessarily directed toward removing the cause of the tension. The tension tends to spread from one area of life to others, to be cumulative and to explode with a slight stimulus which may have little or no relation to the cause of the tension. For example, a man has been harried all day by complaining, cantankerous clients. His emotions have been frequently aroused, and fatigue has gradually increased. For professional reasons he has had to maintain an appearance of patience, good nature, and self-control. At the end of the day he goes home. One of the children does some trivial thing to disturb him, and he explodes in a fit of anger. The gun is loaded, and the child pulls the trigger. The explosion is not directed toward removing the cause of the tension, and the stimulus has little relation to the cause.

Some couples are skilled at reading the signs of each other's tension. Others are not. It would not be unthinkable to utilize special signals as a means of letting each other know that unusual tension exists and of appealing to the other for patience and consideration. In *Who's Boss?*—one of the films in the Marriage for Moderns Series—as such a signal the wife wears her apron astern and the husband enters the house twirling his hat on his finger. Such signals may seem silly and juvenile, but they are not so silly and juvenile as a pointless quarrel growing out of tension and precipitated by something inconsequential. Also, the use of such simple signals indicates that each spouse is aware of his own tension and hypersensitivity; this is the first step toward an effective handling of the situation.

Tension may be dissipated so that the cumulative effect is prevented and relief is afforded. Every married couple and every individual needs what might be termed *tension relievers*. Often a little ingenuity, like a little oil, is all that is needed to smooth troubled water or prevent friction from wearing down a relationship. A couple may develop techniques for letting off steam as it accumulates, instead of waiting until it blows up their marriage. It is difficult to say just what these tension relievers may be for a given couple because each case is individual. Each couple may through observation, experiment, and the exercise of imagination determine them and put them into effect.

Sometimes, in spite of all efforts at prevention, tension gives rise to quarreling. It is somewhat risky either to recommend or deliberately to plan upon quarreling as a means of reducing tension. Only a rare couple are equipped to handle it in that way. There is no way of guaranteeing that both persons will react to it in the same manner. There is too great a possibility of its producing more tension than it was intended to relieve. When and if, however, a couple do quarrel, there are several things which they might try to keep in mind. We might term these "rules" for quarreling. (1) Unless cumulative experience suggests the contrary, each may assume that what the other says and does during the quarrel is the product of the tension involved and is not a true reflection of that individual's personality. (2) Each may assume that whatever judgments he makes during the quarrel are invalid. The judgments upon which action are based are better formed at a time when the individual is relatively calm and has regained his perspective. (3) Both may try to keep the quarrel within bounds. It need not be allowed to spread to aspects of their relationship, their situation, or their personalities that had nothing to do with its origin. The couple need not shift from attacking the problem to attacking each other. (4) A quarrel may be kept private. It need not be allowed to occur in the presence of others, especially children. (5) A quarrel may further a couple's adjustment if, instead of letting it generate ill will and insecurity, the couple forget it when it is over, let bygones be bygones, carry no grudges, and take a step forward in the clarified atmosphere following the storm. (6) Since the marriage is more important than the feelings of either party and in most cases much more important than the difference which precipitated the quarrel, it is important that each be willing to go more than halfway to effect a reconciliation. Sometimes the first step in this direction is easier for the person less at fault because his pride is not so great an obstacle to an apology. (7) The sooner after the quarrel the couple return to the pattern of affection and conversation which characterizes their marriage, the easier it will be; the longer they delay such a return, the more difficult it is likely to be.

In spite of the fact that we pride ourselves on living in a scientific age, most of us do not approach life scientifically. Actually we live in an age in which science is given a great deal of attention and in which science and scientists contribute to a technology that is widely enjoyed. But the "average person's" world view and his attitude toward, and interrelationships with, other people are highly colored by assumptions, impressions, tradition, folklore, emotions, and wishful thinking. These are fertile soil in which to germinate tension, argument, and quarreling because they are more likely to befog the need for facts than to lead to an elucidation of them. When two people argue, each one is convinced that he is defending truth. If each could see that he is more likely merely to be supporting an unsubstantiated point of view, less tension would be generated.

It is almost a self-evident, universally accepted truth that there are in-laws who are selfish, scheming, shortsighted, prying, interfering, demanding, or malicious. There are those who have not kept pace with the development of their children and fail to realize that the latter have grown up and become independent. There are others who are unselfish, generous, farsighted, and considerate. Some of them grow to be closer to the child-in-law than his own parents have been. Some in-laws make a real contribution to the success of a marriage and help a couple over rough spots in their adjustment. More is said about the first type, and there is a tendency to generalize upon them.

Whenever there is an in-law problem, the young couple as well as their parents are in the midst of it. No person can have in-laws without being an in-law. Not all the friction is precipitated by the older generation. So much has been said about in-laws, so many jokes have been made about mothers-in-law, that they have acquired a regrettable reputation. As a result, young couples often enter marriage on the defensive, with a chip on the shoulder, so to speak, almost daring their in-laws to knock it off. If ever inadvertently or intentionally it is knocked off, the trouble begins.

When a man and woman fall in love and marry, usually each respects the intelligence of the other. If each has been accustomed to thinking that his parents were agreeable people, there is a possibility that he is right. The other partner may, then, make that assumption until the facts prove otherwise.

If there is a bona fide in-law problem, the young couple need first of all to be certain of their perspective. The success of their marriage is to be put above everything else, even above attachment to parents. Husband and wife come first. Otherwise the individual exhibits immaturity, unless the spouse is unbearable and the marriage has hopelessly failed. The situation calls for all the tact, diplomacy, and consideration the couple can command, but it calls for firmness and intelligence, as well.

Understanding the problem faced by the couple's in-laws may help to facilitate adjustment. A family is an in-group; it exhibits cohesion. Even when the members are in conflict with each other, there is an inclination to stand united against external pressure and against members of the out-group. A child-in-law is a member of the out-group. It takes time and requires some readjustment fully to accept him as a member of the in-group. He is considered an outsider, and there are some things that one does not do with an outsider. One does not tell him family secrets. One does not express affection for him without reserve. One does not appear in his presence in a state of dishabille.

The in-law problem is not dissimilar to that of a nation in assimilating immigrants. A nation, too, is an in-group. When an immigrant seeks citizenship, there is a responsibility on both sides. The nation has a responsibility for helping the immigrant understand its ways, its language, its laws, and its people. The immigrant, on the other hand, is expected to make some effort to acquire such understanding and to adapt himself to the nation's pattern of life. If the nation is suspicious of him, thwarts him, or sees nothing good in what he brings to it, or if the immigrant resists the nation's ways, criticizes its pattern of life, or refuses to learn its language, the process of assimilation is blocked. Similarly, when a young in-law enters a family, if the family refuses to help him become assimilated, resists his overtures of good will, or rejects him as a person, or if the young in-law sees nothing good in the family's way of life, criticizes it, tries to remake it, or is antagonistic to family members, again assimilation is blocked and the in-law problem is accentuated.

Parents acquire their natural child when it has no opinions to express, no prejudices, resentments, habits, tastes, or ideas of its own. The child is gradually assimilated into the family and molded by the parents to fit their pattern of life. The child-in-law is precipitated into the family, sometimes unexpectedly, sometimes against the family's will, and always with ideas, tastes, habits, and personality already developed.

Parents may resent the transfer of a child's affection from themselves to another person. There may be a conflict in roles, that is, in the expectations set up by parents and spouse. The parents think of the husband or wife as their child and expect a continuation of the child role, the parent-child relationship. The spouse thinks of the person not as child but as adult, with a specific status and responsibility.

A child is accustomed to having his parents interfere with his doings, ask questions about his plans, speak freely concerning his ideas. He accepts this from them and they in turn accept similar behavior from him. Not so with in-laws, each of whom considers the other a member of the out-group. Furthermore, older in-laws and younger ones have been reared in different eras. Their points of view may differ, and there has been neither time nor opportunity to have the corners worn smooth by constant rubbing of difference against difference, as is the case of parents and children. The mutual assimilation and adjustment of in-laws is not always easy. Anything that can serve to further the process is worth trying. What hinders the process is worth avoiding.

Principle of Least Interest

This principle was stated, ungrammatically for emphasis, by the late Willard Waller [1951], following a lead from E. A. Ross. Waller applied the principle to the courtship process, but it is also applicable to the marital relationship. According to this principle, when two persons are emotionally involved in a relationship, the conditions of the association will be dictated by and the relationship will be controlled by the person who has the lesser interest in it. The less involved individual can afford to make the greater demands because he has less at stake. The more involved individual is impelled to make more concessions because the discontinuance of the relationship would be more serious for him.

A similar and related but not identical principle is this: If a husband and wife have a pronounced difference in their degree of insight into the marital relationship and in their awareness of each other's needs and of the nature of marriage, that person with the greater insight and awareness often has to make the greater adjustment in order to assure the continuance of the relationship [Waller, 1951]. This may seem at first glance to be unfair. But looking at it realistically, there may be no alternative.

If a relationship is dominated by the person with less interest in it and/or less insight into it, it is clear that in cases where the demands are excessive they may contribute to failure. In other cases, where the more interested, more insightful person can manage the relationship satisfactorily or can make the required adjustments, there can be success. In any case, however, there is likely to be loss of mutuality.

Law of Diminishing Returns

The law of diminishing returns is ordinarily mentioned in the field of economics. Freely interpreted, it may be applied to marriage. Strictly speaking, what we are discussing may be more nearly like the law of marginal utility. But to the noneconomist "diminishing returns" suggests something that "marginal utility" does not.

In economics this law suggests that as a series of units of a given economic good are acquired or consumed, each successive item in the series, though similar to the one preceding it, is less attractive or less valuable to the collector or consumer. For example, if a man is acquiring real estate, the tenth piece will be less important to him than the first or second piece, and the hundredth piece would be less important still. A similar thing would be true of cars, money in the bank, or clothes. Suppose the reader is very hungry when he sits down to dinner. His first helping is consumed with great relish. The second helping is not eaten quite so enthusiastically as the first. The third, fourth, fifth, and so on, decrease in attractiveness until, if he were put under pressure to eat more and still more, he would eventually be repulsed by the food rather than attracted by it. Yet each helping of food is approximately like the one before it.

The law of diminishing returns is applicable to a number of aspects of marriage. Perhaps its most important application is in connection with the couple's sexual experience. When sex is combined with love and integrated into a growing, expanding marital relationship, the sexual element itself is enriched. True, the couple may note a decrease in frequency of intercourse as time goes on, but this does not necessarily imply a decrease in interest, responsiveness, or meaning.

On the other hand, when sex is divorced from love, it is more likely to be subject to the law of diminishing returns. It is at least partly for this reason that couples who marry on the basis of physical appeal which they confuse with love often reach the point where the marriage seems to die, to reach a dead level. Actually some such couples scarcely know each other. They do not have the necessary requisites to build a marriage. Some of them do not even have enough in common to quarrel. Such cases not infrequently come to a counselor's attention. When the law of diminishing returns has left its imprint on their sexual relationship, the couple no longer have anything left.

Outside Help

Outside assistance may become an important factor in success in marriage because in some cases a couple exhaust their own resources and, though they have a will to succeed, do not know the next steps to take. In many cases of this kind outside help may give them the suggestion, impetus, or reorientation needed. When home remedies fail in marriage, it is good sense to turn to an expert, just as one would in case of an injury or a disease. It is better to do that than to let a marriage atrophy or die in agony.

Friends may, in rare cases, be of assistance. Usually they lack the knowledge required and have too biased a point of view toward the couple. A physician or a clergyman may be of assistance if he is well informed and has some insight into psychological problems and marital adjustment, and if he sees more than the physiological or moral aspects, as the case may be.

In many communities there are professional marriage counselors or counseling agencies where for a nominal fee one may get as nearly expert help as is possible at the present stage of knowledge. A marriage need not be on the brink of failure before a couple visit one of these agencies. For some couples they are educational centers rather than clinics to treat maladjustment. The couple may go for budget help, advice in child rearing, information on contraception, suggestions as to the use of leisure time, or any of a host of similar matters, having as the objective the enrichment of marriage and family life rather than the bare necessity of salvaging them.

One cannot, however, expect a complex adjustment problem to be solved in cliché fashion by a paragraph in a newspaper column or a snap judgment on a radio or television program. The newspaper advice column has a place. It is, in fact, the only agency available to large numbers of people who are confused and need assistance. It must also be admitted that the writers of newspaper columns recognized the need for preparation for marriage and for aid to those already married before that need was recognized by many educators and members of other professions, some of whom are not yet aware of it. Whenever possible, in cases where counseling is wanted, it is better to turn to a competent professional counselor who can give the case careful, thorough, individual attention.*

Choice of counselor must be made cautiously. There are persons who set themselves up as counselors but who are unqualified or even outright unscrupulous. Quacks and charlatans may often be recognized by one or more of the following: (1) They make extravagant claims. (2) They make much of asserting that they are able to handle a great variety of problems. (3) They advertise. (4) They stress fees; their fees are high. (5) They demand payment in advance for service not yet rendered. (6) They display diplomas or certificates from unheard-of schools. (7) They profess to have unusual degrees, for example, Doctor of Psychology. (8) When asked about their training and experience, they are vague

*The American Association of Marriage and Family Counselors will provide the names and addresses of qualified counselors in various parts of the country. Executive director: Dr. C. Ray Fowler, 225 Yale Avenue, Claremont, California 91711; (714) 621-4749.

MARRIAGE IN PROCESS

and evasive. (9) They make snap diagnoses. (10) They put pressure on the client to return for further counseling.

SELECTED READINGS

Bernard, Jessie: *The Sex Game*, Prentice-Hall, Inc., Englewood Cliffs, N.J., 1968. "Beginning with the premise that men and women are essentially different, emotionally as well as biologically," the author "concerns herself with communication between the sexes on all levels. . . . The result is a clear demonstration of how men and women will react differently under the same conditions, how they easily misinterpret each other's words and actions."

Bird, Joseph, and Lois Bird: *Marriage Is for Grownups: A Mature Approach to Problems in Marriage*, Image Books, Doubleday & Company, Inc., Garden City, N.Y., 1971. (Paperback.) A husband-wife team of marriage counselors discusses some of the problem areas in marriage including communication, sex, use of alcohol, infidelity, and in-laws.

Harper, Robert A.: "Communication Problems in Marriage and Marriage Counseling," *Marriage and Family Living*, vol. 20, no. 2, pp. 107–112, May, 1958. A marriage counselor explains how he helps couples improve their communication.

Mace, David R.: *Getting Ready for Marriage*, Abingdon Press, Nashville, Tenn., 1972. Author is optimistic about marriage. Discusses what each person brings to marriage, goals and plans, "how to live with sex," and how to locate a marriage counselor. Author is one of the pioneers and an outstanding world leader in the development of marriage counseling.

Troelstrup, Arch W.: *The Consumer in American Society: Personal and Family Finance*, 4th ed., McGraw-Hill Book Company, New York, 1970. Discussion of various aspects of money management and purchasing.

Sex in Marriage

Were there no sex, there would obviously be no marriage. Therefore, a sexual element is to be expected in marriage. It is this element that makes marriage different from other enduring human relationships. Sex is by no means the whole of marriage, but it is basically important. At times it is underemphasized; at other times it is overemphasized. Satisfactory adjustment sexually and in other ways (if they may be separated for purposes of discussion) go hand in hand, reacting one upon the other. Where there is failure, it may be cause or effect, depending upon circumstances. If the couple's adjustment in general is unsatisfactory, there may be a sexual element at the root of the difficulty. On the other hand, unsatisfactory sexual adjustment may be the result of nonsexual factors. Success in either increases the probability of success in the other, but neither guarantees the other [see Clark and Wallin, September, 1965]. More women in very happy marriages reach orgasm most of the time, but some women in very unhappy marriages also reach orgasm most of the time [Gebhard, 1970]. Often sexual maladjustment is blamed for marital failure when it may be only one among several causes or the result of the factors that are working together to make the marriage fail. Under such circumstances sex may become a focal point, the hook on which the couple hang their marital wraps, so to speak.

Sexual adjustment and personality adjustment are aspects of a single process. There is not one problem of adjusting personalities in marriage and another separate one of sex. Sex in marriage is not a simple physical act, distinct in itself. It is one component of a complex whole, ramifying through other elements, which in their turn ramify through it, a thread of changing hue inextricably woven into the warp and woof of life.

nine

THE NATURE OF SEX

As has been said before, the physical aspects of sex are important, but sexual experience is more than physical. Sex in marriage contains emotional, ideal, other-than-physical elements which in a way are more important than the physical elements as such. In sexual union there is not only the contact of bodily organs but also the contact of personalities. ". . . Sexual response represents interaction between people. . . . Sex removed from the positive influence of the total personality can become boring, unstimulating, and possibly immaterial" [Masters and Johnson, 1970].

Just as it is incorrect to think of sex as only physical, it is also incorrect to think of it as only psychic or emotional. The physical element can be neither avoided nor denied. It is the matrix out of which the psychic elements grow and is simultaneously one of their most potent means of expression. Allan Fromme [1966] refers to sexual intercourse as "bodily conversation." It is a form of communication, just as a kiss or a handshake is a form of communication. There is no reason for assuming that the "purpose" of sex in human beings is only or primarily reproduction. Reproduction is often a result of sexual intercourse, and for many married couples it may be a motivation. But the sexual relationship between husband and wife goes beyond procreation. It is creative as well as procreative.

In lower animals the function of the sex act is reproduction. Animal mating is a transitory, fleeting experience often limited to one or more brief periods during the year. In humans, sexual experience is not limited either to the act itself or to a specific time. It is part of an extensive process of growth and discovery. In its broadest sense it is one of the most fruitful sources for some of the deepest, richest satisfactions known. Assuming that sex is for reproduction alone is like assuming that, since we depend upon eyesight to move about and to make a living, seeing is for practical purposes only, and there should be created no beauty beyond the line, form, and color necessary for self-maintenance. It relegates man to the level of the lower animal and denies him the ability to take the raw materials of nature and out of them fashion a work of art.

We may think of the sexual urge as "instinctive," that is, as the product of inborn behavior patterns. We cannot, however, leave sexual adjustment in marriage to "instinct" because the biological urge is overlaid with tradition, habits, and attitudes all of which make it more complex than the mating instinct of lower animals and, at the same time, more subject to inhibition, repression, and distortion. Instead of the sexual act's being a simple, automatic, biological reaction for which no training is necessary and which training could not improve, in its most highly developed form in man it becomes a complex type of behavior which depends not only upon physical desire and its satisfaction but also upon ideas, ideals, the influence of custom, past experience, and the attitude of husband and wife toward each other. It is as different from the mating of lower animals as the building of a home is different from the construction of a nest, as the composition of a symphony is different from the warbling of a bird.

AN UNDERSTANDING ATTITUDE TOWARD REACTIONS

Mutuality

In Chapter 1 the conclusion was drawn that, owing partly to biology and partly to experience, men and women are different but complementary. It may, therefore, be assumed that they both derive satisfaction from a complementary relationship. The most nearly complete complementary relationship is sexual intercourse. We cannot say that male and female derive identical satisfaction from such intercourse, because their experiences are not comparable. The male's is "outside" his body; the female's is "inside" her body. His is one of penetration; hers is one of containment. We can say, however, that the experiences of the sexes in sexual intercourse are equally intense and satisfactory. But the complementarity of such intercourse is not fully realized if it is on a physical basis only without overtones of less tangible but equally real qualities.

Stating that sexual union is the most nearly complete complementary relationship for a man and a woman and that it contains great possibilities for satisfaction for each is obviously equivalent to saying that sexual experience is not masculine only, as is sometimes assumed. It is a shared experience and a sharing process. It is mutual. Women have natural sexual desire, just as men do, although it may take a somewhat different form and be aroused by different stimuli. When a woman does not experience such desire, there are two probable explanations. (1) It has been trained out of her. It has been so overlaid with inhibitions and/or fears that it cannot find expression. She has built up, or has had built up for her, a wall about herself so effectively corralling natural impulses that they have ceased to demand exercise. (2) There has been nothing in her experience up to date to arouse her desire. She is, as we say, "unawakened." Some women remain so until their experiences with loving husbands bring to the fore an urge that they were not aware could exist. There are women who have a sexual urge but do not recognize it as such. Some refuse to admit what they feel. But there are relatively few women who for some underlying physiological cause are completely devoid of sexual interest. Unfortunately our cultural tradition has all too frequently taught that women should be neuter, that sex is not "ladylike," and that sexual union is a masculine prerogative for masculine satisfaction to which a woman is bound to submit. There could be nothing further from the truth.

This is not equivalent to saying that all women have an equally ardent interest in sexual experience or an equal responsiveness to sexual stimuli. The sexual urge, like all things natural, falls on the normal curve of variability. Some women, like some men, are more passionate; some are less so. There is the possibility for all gradations from greatest to least. At best, it is difficult to say that a woman who seems sexually cold is therefore unable to respond, even though we think in terms of inhibitions rather than physiology. All that may safely be said is that under a given set of circumstances she seems unresponsive. Under other circumstances she might be different. Furthermore, sexual unresponsiveness is the result of multiple causation. There is no one thing, no one condition, that will invariably produce it.

Let us go back for a moment to a point mentioned above. Young women are sometimes worried about their sexual adequacy. In their reading or in discussions they have learned that women experience a sexual urge, just as men do. These women have never experienced anything that they identified as sexual desire. Often they are not averse to a controlled amount of affection and fondling on the part of men, and they like to date. But they have come to feel that they are "undersexed" or that they will be unable to respond to a husband in the way they vaguely realize that women can.

A woman of nineteen, for example, lets men kiss her but has no inclination to be more intimate. She likes to date and associate with men but prefers to go out with many different ones rather than to limit herself to one. Her women friends have told her how men arouse them. Both men and women tell her she is undersexed. She has heard that a woman may experience sexual desire, but she herself has never been conscious of any such urge. As a result, she has worried about her condition until she has almost reached the conclusion that she is abnormal and unfit for marriage. Her attitude toward sex is somewhat naive, perhaps, but on the whole it is healthy and there do not seem to be any special fears, inhibitions, or aversions. Nevertheless, she cannot imagine herself as ever being intimate, even with a husband whom she might love. Her failure so to picture herself is due to her inability to anticipate anything which is entirely foreign to her experience and for which she has no conscious desire.

There is nothing the matter with such a woman. She is neither abnormal nor undersexed. She is unawakened. Up to date, there has been nothing in her experience to cause her to react in a way that she can identify as sexual or to feel a desire of a specifically sexual nature. She finds pleasure in being with men and in having them kiss her. This is a broad, generalized type of sexual experience, but she does not think of it as such. There are many women like her. They are just as normal as the women who have more readily identifiable sexual desire or response. They need not worry about their condition. The probability is that after they fall in love and marry they will eventually find themselves as responsive as any, allowing, of course, for individual variations. When they marry, however, such women need not insist upon maintaining their former attitude. They may permit themselves to move on to new experiences. In one case a woman who had been unawakened before marriage found herself very responsive with her husband. Yet for two years after the wedding she cried each time intercourse and orgasm occurred because early in life she had been taught that only "bad" women were passionate, and she continued to have feelings of guilt.

To say that the unawakened woman will probably be responsive in marriage is not the same as saying that the woman with strong inhibitions and feelings of repugnance, to whom sex is something to be repressed or suppressed, and who is conscious of reacting against it, will become equally responsive. Such a woman may try to rethink the whole subject, may examine her past to learn if possible why she feels as she does, and may talk the matter over with some informed and understanding counselor who may help her reach a new attitude. She may change her attitude, too, when she begins to think of sex specifically in terms of a relationship with a husband whom she loves, rather than thinking of it in a more or less general and abstract way.

Girls exhibit interest in boys and curiosity about sex just as boys show interest in girls and are curious about anatomical differences, intercourse and reproduction. Sex seems natural to a child until distortions of the educative process make it appear otherwise. It is a strange side light upon our culture that some natural processes are accepted as they are with no implication of good or bad, while others equally natural are highly colored with moral or aesthetic condemnation.

Attempting to shut sex out of one's life does not raise one to a higher plane of existence, as some people suppose. It only relegates one to a more incomplete and more arid existence. In the last analysis, sex cannot be shut out. Whether it finds natural expression or not, no matter where it is put, from one extreme of manifestation to the other, it will play a part in affecting the individual's life. If it is repressed or avoided, it is still not without its effect. One may as well try to rule our metabolism.

Woman's Reaction

Generalizing, even though a woman is not inhibited and has not attempted to shut sex out of her life, her sexual arousal tends to be less spontaneous than is the case with a man and depends to great extent upon her husband, his expression of affection, his own desire, and his insight, understanding, and skill as her lover. A man may be compared to starting a fire with dry tinder and dry wood. The materials may be carelessly thrown together, and one match is enough to make them leap into flame. Arousing a woman may be compared to starting a fire in the rain. The materials have to be put together carefully. The match has to be shielded after it is struck. The new flame must be protected, perhaps fanned, until the heat generated is sufficient to overcome the dampness. Only then will it burn untended, and even then it may easily be extinguished. This is not true of all women. As we have said, there are variations among them as to the strength of their impulses. This is more likely to be true early in a marriage than later and is certainly true in the case of the unawakened woman discussed above. Before marriage, a man may be more conscious of sexual desire, and his interest tends to be more specific. Later, if the couple's adjustment is successful, the wife may be as clearly aware of her urges as the husband is of his. In some cases the wife is more passionate than the husband and desires more frequent intercourse than he does.

Until they have had satisfactory sexual experience, women as a rule do not have a problem of control comparable to men's. Hence, they have a somewhat different situation to cope with before marriage. Freedman [1967], a psychologist who has done research on college and university students and has taught at the university level for many years, says, "I have been impressed in the course of my research by the capacity of young women to carry on very well without any physical sexual activity whatsoever—including masturbation."

Because sex is feminine as well as masculine, women as well as men can reach a climax in sexual intercourse. In men there is a dual reaction, namely, orgasm, which is a neuromuscular response, and ejaculation, which is the discharge of seminal fluid containing the sperm cells. Actually the two reactions typically occur so nearly simultaneously that they are thought of as one. In women there is nothing equivalent to ejaculation. There are lubricating secretions, but they do not involve special sensations, as does ejaculation. A woman may be aware of the moisture but she does not feel the process of secretion as a man feels ejaculation. Women can, however, achieve orgasm. This has no relationship to the production of egg cells, which are secreted at the rate of, roughly, one per month, irrespective of intercourse. Nor is there any established relationship between orgasm and conception, as is frequently assumed; conception can occur with or without orgasm. In women orgasm is sometimes referred to as a "nervous explosion," an "explosive physiological entity" [Masters and Johnson, 1966], during which accumulated tension is released, and there are muscular contractions and relaxations and sensations of touch. This all proves very pleasurable and satisfying both physically and emotionally. To describe what a man or woman actually feels when experiencing orgasm or orgasm plus ejaculation, as the case may be, is impossible. The important thing is that the reader realize that orgasm in women can occur, not that a detailed analysis of it be given [for analysis in detail, see Masters and Johnson, 1966].

The intensity of this reaction in sexual intercourse varies from individual to individual and from time to time in the same individual, and there may be a difference between husband and wife. It is not necessary that all persons react equally intensely. As long as the experience is agreeable to both husband and wife and both find pleasure in it, it may be considered relatively adequate.

Some women never achieve orgasm. This does not prove that they are unhappy in their marriages. Nor does it indicate an absence of love. A husband and wife may love each other, but their sex adjustment may be incomplete. Nor does absence of orgasm or infrequent orgasm indicate that a wife does not enjoy sexual intercourse with her husband. Research reveals that a considerable proportion of wives report that they enjoy intercourse yet seldom or never reach orgasm [Wallin and Clark, 1963; McGuire and Steinhilber, October, 1970; Raboch, 1970].

A woman can find a peculiarly feminine satisfaction in intercourse when her husband reaches a climax, and this fact makes her "feel like a woman." She may also experience another peculiarly feminine satisfaction, namely, being held—that is, cuddled—as an end in itself, as part of foreplay before intercourse, and after intercourse during the "afterglow" [Hollender, October, 1971; Golden, May, 1971]. Here is something having no true parallel in men but something to be understood by men.

Some women never achieve any satisfaction in their sexual life. Such women not only miss the pleasure that their relationship with their husbands might produce but often must endure what to them is uninteresting or repugnant. They may be psychologically virgin, though not so anatomically. They tolerate sex; they do not really experience it. Others become physically and emotionally aroused but fail to reach orgasm. Instead of their finding pleasure and release, their experience ends in nervous tension, restlessness, disappointment, or irritation.

No woman need conclude that occasional failure will be harmful. Either type of woman—the one who is indifferent, inhibited, repressed, unresponsive, or the one who is responsive but whose experience tends habitually to be incomplete, unsatisfying, and productive of tension rather than relief of tension—may often be assisted in making a more adequate adjustment if she, and her husband, will consult a marriage counselor. Although a woman of the first type may have no interest in improving her own adjustment, she should for the sake of her husband at least make the effort. If sexual union is the most nearly complete complementary experience possible for a husband and wife, it is obvious that it cannot be full and rich if the wife's participation is fragmentary.

Rights and Duties

Sexual intercourse is sometimes considered a masculine right and feminine duty. This attitude was more common in the past, but it has not yet disappeared. It is still reflected in the laws of some states, where a man may demand that his wife submit to intercourse and may divorce her if she refuses. It is also reflected in laws which give the wife the right of annulment or divorce if the husband is impotent and, therefore, cannot perform the sexual act. This duty-right attitude is cold, one-sided, and unchallenging as compared with the attitude that sex is a mutual experience, entailing mutual satisfaction and the expression of affection, trust, and desire by both parties rather than the imposition of rights and the unwilling performance of duty.

In a sense, a right is established at the wedding, but only in the sociological and legal sense. It is better to think of the situation as presenting opportunities for both persons rather than to think of it as a trap for the woman or a bargain by which she agrees to submit to masculine demands in return for which she gains status and security. Any man who enters marriage with the intention of demanding his rights shows plainly the shallowness of his attitude toward his wife. He is more than old-fashioned; he is medieval.

Success and Failure

As already explained, the achievement of the deepest, most lasting satisfaction in sexual intercourse is not "natural" in the sense of being "instinctive." It is an art. An art requires time, patience, thoughtfulness, perseverence, and understanding for its fullest development. Interest and urge are "instinctive," but human beings have worked out means of expression that are more than automatic and that transcend the "natural." Sex has been raised to the plane of creative achievement.

Since this is true, a couple need not be discouraged if success is limited or absent at first. Few couples reach the greatest possible success immediately. The sexual relationship of husband and wife is not merely a series of isolated, unrelated incidents. It is a growing relationship which becomes deeper and richer as time goes on. There is no reason to assume that the achievement of the first success is the end and goal and that there is nothing to look forward to. As they grow older, the couple may grow closer to each other in this as well as in other ways.

They need not be disappointed if they never reach perfection in their sexual life. Human beings never reach perfection in anything; at best, they merely approach it. They may strive for it but never actually expect to attain it. If the couple are successful a good proportion of the time, that is about all that can be expected. If in rare instances a couple approach more closely to the perfect ideal, so much the better. Most couples, even though very happily married, fall short. This is not the equivalent of being content with mediocrity, but there is a danger in setting an impossible, unattainable goal, as, for example, the expectation of the wife's having orgasm every time intercourse occurs or the couple's having simultaneous orgasm every time intercourse occurs.

Even in those cases in which a couple's sexual experience does grow richer, the zest and tumultuousness of the early years of marriage may gradually change from pounding breakers to the more deeply flowing currents of later married life. No loss accrues in such a transition; there is only change. There may be gain. If, for example, as time passes a couple find that intercourse becomes less frequent, that does not necessarily indicate that there is less interest or that their relationship is not successful. It implies only that after the first dash from the starting line they are finding their stride and that intercourse in the more specific sense is becoming part of a greatly broadened shared experience.

In developing a new skill or new art, the novice makes many errors. In learning to walk, skate, play tennis, swim, drive a golf ball, or bid a bridge hand we perpetrate so many mistakes that after mastering the necessary technique we look back in embarrassed retrospect on the immensity of our previous ignorance and the incredibility of our original awkwardness. We do not let our mistakes defeat us; nor do we stop with them. We overcome them. We correct them. A newly married couple are novices confronted with the problem of learning a new art and acquiring a new skill. They are almost certain to make mistakes at first. They may feel that their ignorance is stupendous and their clumsiness colossal. They need not leap to conclusions and defeat themselves. They may learn by their mistakes. With patience, understanding, intelligence, self-analysis, an ample amount of love, and a liberal sprinkling of a sense of humor, errors may be corrected. To give up in defeat because sexual adjustment is not complete at the very beginning and because there are mistakes is just as unnecessary and foolish as it would be to lie prone for the rest of one's life because one fell down the first time one tried to walk. Each successful act of intercourse plays a part in conditioning both husband and wife so that success in the future becomes easier. Hence, care, patience, perspective, and a will to succeed pay large dividends.

In almost all cases in which there are difficulties that prevent adequate sexual adjustment, those difficulties are matters of attitude and habit rather than of anatomy. In discussing frigidity, McGuire and Steinhilber [1964, 1970] mention the "small segment . . . due to organic disorders." There are relatively few cases of structural defects that prevent sexual harmony, and most of these may be discovered in a premarital medical examination and remedied by medical treatment. A couple who have unusual handicaps or hindrances need not conclude that these are irremediable until every resource, including professional counseling, has been drawn upon.

The majority of couples have no difficulties at all, except perhaps the normal readjustments involved in making any transition such as that from single life to marriage. These require only time, patience, and intelligence. We do not mean to imply that a couple direct their attention toward nothing but possible difficulties. Quite the opposite is true. Nevertheless, if there are difficulties, these may be faced frankly and objectively.

In working out a satisfactory sexual adjustment, husband and wife may help each other considerably. Each may help the other understand reactions and attitudes. The wife may explain to the husband what pleases and what displeases her. Reticence or secrecy based upon false modesty, conceit, or ignorance is one of the most effective obstacles to success.

What a Wife Needs to Understand

When she enters marriage and begins a new phase of her emotional life, there are several things that a woman needs to understand. First of all, she needs to realize that hers is not the only problem. Her husband has one, too. It is that of helping her to the best start. She may help him as much as she can. She needs also to realize that she has married a man, not a neuter organism. He is a masculine being with strong masculine impulses. He probably has good intentions, but he may have little finesse and may possibly lack understanding of her, her reactions, or the sexual relationship [see Golden, May, 1971]. Whatever generalizations he has gathered from books, discussions, friends, or counselors need to be applied and adapted to specific individual circumstances. He may observe his wife's reactions and contemplate her attitudes. He could not have read about her in a book. She may therefore give him time to learn. She cannot expect too much at first. Together they may work out an adjustment. One beauty of the experience is that it is worked out together and that it cannot be taken cut and dried from a textbook or marriage manual. What they finally evolve is, therefore, uniquely their own. Some men know more than others, but the wife may at least give her husband the benefit of the doubt. It is not at all unknown for what would otherwise have developed into a satisfactory adjustment to be nipped in the bud because the wife was too ready to draw unwarranted conclusions.

The wife needs also to be aware of the fact that some men have a tendency to become angry, irritated, or impulsive when they have been aroused sexually only to be thwarted, especially if the frustration is the result of what seems to the man to be an arbitrary and unreasonable denial on the part of the wife. We are not suggesting that the wife always be submissive, but only that she be prepared to understand.

A wife needs to understand, too, that, though a man's sexual experience may appear to be largely of a physical nature, it also includes a considerable degree of ego involvement. A man derives some pleasure from sexual intercourse whether or not his wife is responsive. But his experience is intensified if she responds because he knows he has contributed to her pleasure. If, over a long period, she is unresponsive and he grows to feel that he is imposing himself on his wife, especially if she lets him know that she feels it is an imposition, he may eventually come to avoid intercourse or even become impotent and be unable to perform the sexual act. Assuming that a husband has any sensitivity at all, he wants to feel enthusiastically accepted by his wife both as a man and as her sexual partner. If she rejects him as the latter, she can defeat him. "The susceptibility of the human male to the power of suggestion with reference to his sexual prowess is almost unbelievable" [Masters and Johnson, 1970].

A situation that gives rise to fear is not necessarily inherently fearful. An experience that produces a feeling of aversion is not always inherently repugnant. For example, one person attempts to ride horseback, is thrown, picks himself up, tries again, and eventually learns both to enjoy it and to do it well. Another person tries to ride, is thrown, and thereafter is afraid not only of riding but also of being near horses. One girl, aged ten, is frightened by a man's approaches and for the remainder of her life is fearful of sex and afraid of men. Another girl, a victim of rape, has a healthy, optimistic attitude toward sex, falls in love enthusiastically, and has a happy marriage. If a wife who has inhibitions and fears associated with sex can come to see that it was not sex alone but rather her reaction to some situation involving sex that made her as she is, she may more readily change her attitude toward her relationship with her husband. It will also help if she can understand that her husband does not represent the situation that gave rise to her attitudes. Rather, he represents a new situation the elements of which are referred to in the same terminology but with new meaning. If a wife's attitudes prevent her from finding sexual experience satisfactory or, in other cases, prevent her from being glad that she does find it satisfactory, she may direct her resentment toward her own attitudes or their source rather than toward her husband.

Occasionally it happens that, because of what she has read or heard or because of her own interest, the wife expects to have her first sexual intercourse almost immediately after the wedding, only to find that her husband seems to lack interest. She may be not only interested but eager to consummate their relationship, to enter a new adventure together, and to express her love for her husband. His attitude disappoints her, hurts her pride, and worries her, for she wonders why he feels as he does. Fortunately, there are few cases of this sort. It is more common for the man to be more interested than the woman. If, however, a bride does find herself in such a predicament, she need not leap to conclusions before she has ascertained the real cause.

There are a number of possible explanations for the husband's apparent attitude. He may actually lack interest; his natural sexual drive may be weak or lacking. Such men are rare, however. The husband may fear sex or consider it disgusting, unclean, or sinful. Such men, too, are rare, much rarer than women who have similar attitudes. He may think that sexual intercourse is for reproduction only and avoid it because he does not feel ready to assume the responsibility of a family [see Masters and Johnson, 1970]. Any of these first three attitudes an observant girl could probably detect before marriage. He may be afraid of his own ability to measure up to what is expected of him as a husband. He wants their relationship to be as nearly perfect as possible, and he underestimates his own adequacy. Such a man needs encouragement and trust. Criticism or hysterics will not help him. Because of the strain of a large wedding and its accompaniments, he may be fatigued. He may be shy, nervous, or embarrassed. He may be showing consideration for his wife. He knows she is tired. He feels that it is better that they become accustomed to being together at first and that their new relationship be approached gradually. This is always a possibility. The safest assumption for the wife to make is that this represents her husband's attitude unless and until she has reason to believe otherwise. Although it usually does, there is no good reason for assuming that a couple's first sexual union must occur on their wedding night, just because that is traditional. There may be sound reasons for postponing it. The tradition developed in a period when sexual intercourse was considered a masculine prerogative to which a passive and uninterested wife was forced by custom to submit.

What a Husband Needs to Understand

Just as there are various things that the wife needs to realize, so there are several of which the husband needs to become aware. He needs to understand that he has married a woman, a feminine being who will react as a woman and not as a man. She may have had no premarital sexual experience. Even if she had such experience, this does not guarantee that she will be responsive, passionate, interested in intercourse, and devoid of inhibition and fear. A man may have premarital intercourse and still not learn what he needs to know regarding a wife and their relationship in marriage. In some cases the wife scarcely knows what to expect in marriage. She may be ignorant of some of the most elementary facts. There are educated women who are ignorant of masculine anatomy and do not fully understand the anatomy and functions of their own bodily organs. Many women do not know how men react. Many are unaware that sex is a feminine as well as a masculine experience and that women as well as men may derive satisfaction from it. If the wife has gathered any general knowledge from reading or discussion, she, too, needs to apply this to the individual situation. She may have good intentions and be anxious to do the right thing and to please her husband, but she may not understand fully what is involved. She too needs to be given time to learn.

If the wife is a woman who before marriage was conscious of no desire that she identified as sexual, that desire will not be created by the wedding. Some men act as if the ceremony were all that is necessary to change an unawakened woman into a passionate wife. They fail to understand that this transformation depends upon the husband, not upon the ceremony.

A husband needs to realize further that his wife is more inclined than he to have inhibitions and fears centering on sex and its expression. Sometimes her fear is vague. At other times it is more specific, and sexual intercourse recalls a fear situation that occurred early in her life, in the recalling of which she again experiences emotions similar to those that she felt at the time.

It is easy for a woman to let her attitude toward sexual union be influenced by her attitude toward menstruation. If she has painful periods, she may let this fact color her attitude toward sex in general. After puberty a girl is more likely to associate her genital organs with pain and with a process of which she is half ashamed and which she seeks to conceal, while a boy is more inclined to associate his with pleasurable sensation. Menstruation and sexual union, though somewhat related anatomically, are two distinct processes.

A woman may, as we have already suggested, fear pregnancy or childbirth and let this color her attitude toward intercourse. Such a fear may be ameliorated by securing advice on the control of conception from an informed physician and following that advice carefully. Dependence upon hearsay, advice of friends, advertisements, or incomplete knowledge is to be avoided. Reliable control of conception may not remove a wife's fear of childbirth because that fear probably has its roots deep in her past. But it will remove the necessity for letting the fear affect the couple's relationship, and the woman may so consider it. She may believe that sex is for reproduction only and wish to avoid it unless she feels ready to have a baby. She may fear the pain of her first sexual intercourse. Women frequently hear exaggerated accounts of the pain suffered by a bride on her wedding night, or they listen to old wives' tales of one sort or another. As a result, they come to develop an unnecessary and ill-founded fear. We shall consider the matter of pain later.

In order to make this discussion of inhibitions and fears more concrete, let us cite a few cases of college women in whom one or more of these attitudes may be found. The first is a woman of nineteen. Her parents are separated and, though she sees her father occasionally, she feels that she does not really know him. Her home life is not too pleasant. Her mother is very conservative and has never told the daughter anything about sex. Recently, a sister married several months after becoming pregnant. The mother's attitude toward marriage is unhealthy, and she has talked against it to the daughter. The woman has a genitourinary disease of long standing that has necessitated frequent, painful treatment. She has concluded that if sexual union involves any pain similar to that which she suffers in these treatments, she wants to avoid it. For a long time she thought little of sex, but now she has fallen in love and wants to make her marriage successful. She is aware of the importance of sex in marriage and does not want to marry until her point of view has changed; for, because of the above influences, she has developed an attitude that is a mixture of indifference and disgust. She cannot understand why or how a couple could bring themselves to have intercourse. At the same time, she is not averse to having her fiancé show affection for her.

Another woman comes for a conference because she is worried about something that she heard in a discussion with other students. Her parents are very strict, and her mother has taught her that men are bestial. In the discussion she discovered that several women have a similar opinion and so fear marriage. She herself is afraid. All her life she has wished that she were a boy and regretted that her freedom was restricted. She likes to date and says that she hopes some day to marry. At the same time, she says she does not like men. Menstruation is very painful for her. She has such a dread of the pain of childbirth that she herself is aware of the need for changing her attitude. She has gathered considerable misinformation about the pain of first sexual union and wonders whether a woman can be happy in marriage if she takes no interest in sex.

A woman of eighteen feels that she is in love with a man who seems to fit her ideal. She says that as far back as she can remember she has had a fear of sex. Until she was about seventeen she had no clear idea as to what sexual intercourse is. At that time she acquired some incomplete information from a woman of her own age. Previously, she had known that babies sometimes resulted from sexual union, but she did not know why or how. She was fairly sure that kissing would not produce pregnancy but had a vague idea about a woman's becoming pregnant if a man came too close to her. She has never felt any specific sexual desire and cannot imagine having sexual intercourse with a husband. She feels that sex is for reproduction only, and she is, therefore, opposed to the use of contraceptives. She has heard something about the pain at first intercourse but does not understand any reason for it. She has developed a fear of sex in marriage because she does not know what to expect and because she has heard exaggerated tales.

Attitudes such as these may make marital adjustment difficult, especially if in the early days of marriage something occurs that the woman does not understand and that seems to bring her fears to a focus. But attitudes are acquired, and they may be changed. Back of each one there is an underlying cause, some experience or educative process out of which the attitude grew. Discovering the underlying factors and looking at them from the vantage point of greater maturity and fuller information usually lead to dispelling what otherwise might become a cloud hanging over a marriage. This is especially true if the woman herself realizes the need for change and takes the initiative in talking with someone who can help her.

If the woman marries before change occurs, the husband is presented with a challenge to all the patience and understanding of which he is capable. If he handles the situation correctly, he may play an important role in assisting the wife to change her point of view and to move to a less inhibited, less fear-ridden level of existence. If, however, he bungles his opportunity, he may set deeper the fears that impede their adjustment.

In addition to the attitudes mentioned above, many women, and some men, have inhibitions in connection with the exposure of their own bodies or feel embarrassed at witnessing that of others. Some women, about to be married, express more uneasiness at the prospect of seeing the husband unclothed than at the prospect of being seen unclothed themselves. These inhibitions, too, are the result of conditioning, of training, and the latter is highly colored both by the need for self-protection and by convention. Convention still prohibits complete exposure of the body under many conditions. But marriage alters circumstances. What is prohibited among the unmarried is not only acceptable but expected between husband and wife. There is no conventional restriction on their bodily exposure. If one or the other carries into the marriage relationship inhibitions having their origin in the premarital standard, that person is doing something fundamentally not different from insisting upon swimming fully clothed because a bathing suit is not appropriate apparel for a shopping trip or a formal reception.

If a husband understands that his bride may be more concerned over the bodily exposure of both persons than he can appreciate, he will approach such exposure with tact, patience, and consideration. If he becomes impatient and blurts out something like, "What are you acting like that for; we're married, aren't we?" he may set deeper the inhibitions he ought to help her to remove. If a bride understands not only that her husband is likely to take bodily exposure for granted but also that he is "visual-minded" and that his is not the wanton gaze of "men" but rather the observation of the man whose love for her and idealization of her make her attractive in his sight, the man into whose care she placed her happiness at the time of the wedding, she may anticipate bodily exposure with more insight and less apprehension.

SOME PROBLEMS IN ADJUSTMENT

Fear of Pain

A couple's first sexual intercourse sometimes involves pain for the woman. The pain may be accompanied by slight bleeding. This is due partly to the fact that the opening of her genital tract, or more specifically the external aperture of the vagina, is partially closed by a membrane called the *hymen*, sometimes referred to as the "maidenhead." If the lining of the vagina is dry because of a paucity of lubricating secretions which accompany responsiveness, this fact may contribute to the woman's discomfort. During the first act of intercourse the hymen is stretched and, in infrequent cases, torn slightly so that a few drops of blood escape. Women often hear exaggerated accounts of this process or those based upon rare instances in which a husband was brutal or based upon the experiences of an exceptional woman whose attitudes or anatomy made sexual union inordinately difficult. There is also a residue of an attitude toward first sexual intercourse that originated in an earlier period in history when sex was considered a masculine prerogative and a feminine duty, when there was no idea of mutuality, when it was not unknown for a man to be unnecessarily rough and hasty in order to "prove" that his wife was virgin. As a result, some women come to fear their first sexual intercourse. In a study of 1,000 marriages that were still unconsummated (that is, the couple had not yet had sexual intercourse) after periods of one to twenty-one years, Blazer [May, 1964] found that in one-fifth of the sample the reason given for the nonconsummation was fear of pain in initial intercourse.

It cannot be emphasized too strongly that such a fear is unnecessary. Granting that the husband is something better than a savage, the pain, if there is any at all, will be slight and of brief duration. In many cases there is no pain whatever. If there is any, the woman needs to realize that it is the pain of transition, of growth, of moving from one stage of existence to a more mature one. It is natural pain. It might be compared to the pain of cutting teeth—not that it feels like teething, but there are similarities as to naturalness and significance. No one would deliberately enter adult life with his milk teeth or with no teeth at all because the cutting of permanent ones is a painful process (usually more painful than the stretching of the hymen). Neither does a woman need to allow herself to become conditioned against sexual experience or let her first experience precipitate fears and inhibitions just because there may be temporary discomfort. The bleeding, if there is any at all, will be insignificant.

The process of stretching the hymen is similar, in some ways, to that of putting on new kid gloves. If the gloves are carefully worked onto the fingers the first few times they are worn, they gradually stretch until they accommodate themselves to the wearer's hand. The same gloves forced on hastily and roughly will tear instead of stretching.

In rare instances a wife's fear reacts upon the muscles of her genital organs, causing them to contract so vigorously that the very pain she is afraid of is increased. She then finds herself in a vicious circle: the more she fears the experience, the greater is the pain; and the greater the pain, the more she fears it. If she can be brought to accept the experience without resistance, the cause of discomfort will be removed. In other rare instances some anatomical defect prevents intercourse. In either case, or we might say in any case in which there seems to be unusual difficulty, in which the pain is experienced more than once or twice or in which the bleeding persists, a physician should be consulted. Practically all such difficulties can be remedied. Even in these unusual and extreme instances there is no cause for alarm. Above all, the wife need not let the temporary discomfort color her attitude toward the whole future of her marriage. She may be careful here, as in regard to menstrual pain, not to confuse normal elements with abnormal ones.

There is a considerable variation among females as to the extent, toughness, and elasticity of the hymen. Allowing for overgeneralization and oversimplification, the diagrams in Figure 9.1 depict five possible conditions of the virginal hymen. In life, since the tissues are soft, the labia [see Figure 10.4] touch or almost touch (except as they may separate during tumescence, as mentioned below), and the vagina is a collapsed tube like a toy balloon with no air in it. Sometimes the vagina is referred to as a "potential cavity." Obviously, if it can stretch to accommodate the passage of a baby in childbirth, it can stretch enough to accommodate the erect penis in intercourse. In some women the hymen is so slight as to be almost nonexistent (Figure 9.1a). In a sense, such women are born the anatomical equivalent of nonvirgin. In most women there is an irregular opening amply large for menstrual discharge, but not large enough for intercourse without the hymen's being stretched (b). In a diagram, of course, only the shape and size of the opening can be depicted. There is no way of indicating the thickness or elasticity of the hymen. In some cases there are two or more openings (c), and in some a number of small openings (d), permitting menstrual discharge, but not large enough for intercourse. In a rare case, there is no opening; the hymen forms a "drum-head" closure (e). In such a case, a woman may menstruate for some time and the menstrual discharge is dammed up behind the imperforate hymen. Eventually the discharge becomes dehydrated and forms a tarry mass which causes discomfort and makes necessary an incision to create an opening.

Assuming tumescence and/or the use of lubricating jelly, as mentioned

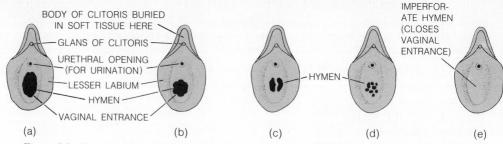

Figure 9.1 Diagrammatic representation of five conditions of the virginal hymen. The dark areas represent openings into the vagina.

below, in first intercourse a woman with hymen (a) would have no problem. A woman with hymen (b) would have the problem of stretching, as discussed above. If the hymen is unusually tough and inelastic or the opening is unusually small, first intercourse for such a woman is facilitated by premarital medical assistance. A woman with hymen (c) or (d) would have pain and bleeding at first intercourse. The possibility of a woman's having hymen (c) or (d) is one of the strongest arguments for a premarital pelvic examination. If a woman has successfully used menstrual tampons, she has evidence that she does not have hymen (c) or (d). Hymen (e) would present a woman with a serious problem in her first intercourse. But a woman with such a hymen is likely to seek medical aid before marriage.

The hymen has been known to return to a seemingly virginal state after having been stretched in sexual intercourse. In some cases the hymen is stretched by accident, by masturbation, by sports activities, by the use of the tampon type of menstrual protection, during a medical examination, or manually or mechanically at a physician's suggestion. Consequently, the condition of the hymen is no certain, never-failing indication of the virginity or nonvirginity of a woman presumably virgin at the time of marriage. A husband who hastily concludes that his bride has had previous intercourse because she has neither pain nor bleeding as a result of their first sexual intercourse betrays his ignorance of anatomical variations and reflects an outmoded attitude. So does a responsive woman who fears, or the husband of such a woman who concludes, that if she exhibits responsiveness the first time they have intercourse, it seems to indicate that she has had previous sexual experience and is not virgin.

When a woman is sexually aroused, her labia become tumescent, that is, somewhat swollen because of the increased blood supply, and this tumescence causes them to move apart and turn outward slightly so that the entrance to the vagina is enlarged and made more "funnel-shaped." Accompanying this tumescence there is a transudation, a "sweating," of fluid from the wall of the vagina, lubricating both the vagina and the labia [Masters and Johnson, 1966]. Both tumescence and lubrication facilitate the penetration of the vagina by the erect penis. As mentioned earlier, a woman may feel the presence of this lubricating fluid as moisture, but she does not feel the process of its transudation as a man feels the process of ejaculation. In the absence of tumescence and lubrication, penetration of the vagina by the erect penis may be uncomfortable or painful. A solution to this problem may be found in the use of a vaginal jelly which melts at body temperature and is a substitute for natural lubrication. Such lubricating jelly may be purchased at drug stores without a prescription.

Premarital Medical Examination

Partly because of the possibility of discomfort experienced by some women in their first sexual intercourse and partly because of the relatively remote possibility of there being some unusual anatomical condition, some women prefer to have the hymen stretched by a physician or according to his directions before marriage. An examination of this membrane and the physician's recommendation as to what should be done about it may be made part of the premarital medical examination, part of which is a pelvic, including a vaginal, examination. We may go further and say that this is one of the chief purposes of that examination. If the physician concludes that it is advisable, the membrane may be stretched mechanically or manually or, in some cases, cut. The pain associated with the latter process is so slight that only a local anesthetic is necessary. If this is done, the process becomes associated with the impersonal atmosphere of the physician's office rather than with the husband and the honeymoon. Some women prefer this; others do not. If it is done by a physician or according to his directions, however, informing the fiancé will prevent the possibility of his concluding that his bride is not virgin.

Since the chief function of the premarital medical examination is preparative rather than prohibitive, it is recommended that both man and woman have the examination. They may go to the same physician at different times or to different physicians. In either case, they should try to choose one who understands human sexuality. He should be aware of the new developments in this field and be interested in this type of examination. He should also be willing to take time to talk with the couple and answer their questions. If the couple go to different physicians, they do well to visit specialists, the man going to a urologist, the woman to a gynecologist or obstetrician. A woman who contemplates such an examination with embarrassment may realize that to the doctor she is a patient, not an eligible woman. His attitude is strictly impersonal. It is unlikely that she will present him with anything new or anything he has not observed many times before. She may also simplify her problem by choosing a woman physician.

Several hundred years ago, when the practice of midwifery in Europe was taken over by men, these first obstetricians were known as "male midwives." At that time there was so high a premium upon feminine modesty, especially in the upper class, that women insisted that during delivery they be completely draped in sheets and the obstetrician deliver the baby only by his sense of touch without ever seeing any part of the woman's genital anatomy [Findley, 1933]. Nowadays a woman who insisted upon such a procedure during delivery would not be able to find an obstetrician to accede to her wishes, and she would be considered eccentric, to say the least. It is taken for granted that an obstetrician will examine a woman's anatomy both before and during delivery. There is need for similar acceptance and objectivity relative to the premarital pelvic examination. Unfortunately, however, there are some women whose attitude still reflects the false modesty of the distant past—to their own detriment.

Even if a woman does find it difficult to have a premarital pelvic examination, she may well ask herself this question: "Which is better, to have such an examination in spite of hesitation and embarrassment, or possibly, at the time of first intercourse on her honeymoon, to confront an anatomical problem which neither she nor her husband is equipped to solve?"

Scheduling the examination far enough in advance of the wedding will make it possible to carry out the physician's recommendations without excessive haste, to read what he suggests, and to return to him for further discussion. If they choose their physician carefully, a couple may feel free to ask him about anything that they do not understand in connection with sex and reproduction. There will probably be a number of points growing out of the examination or their reading that will not be fully clear or on which they desire further information. No matter what they may have read or gathered from other sources, it is often advisable for them to talk through with the physician the matter of sexual adjustment. They should not consider the matter closed until they have had answered all the questions that they feel the need for asking. In most cases one of these will pertain to control of conception, and on this the physician may make recommendations. Such discussion may also facilitate their own communication relative to sex later.

The Husband's Responsibility

Premarital examination and even stretching of the hymen by the physician do not relieve the husband of his responsibility in initiating his wife into the sexual aspect of marriage or the woman of the responsibility for cooperation and the development of an enlightened attitude. If the husband considers her initiation as a chore to be hurried through in order more quickly to make possible the unimpeded satisfaction of his own desires, he not only shows his ignorance of marriage, sex, and feminine reactions but also exhibits toward his wife an attitude of exploitation that is inconsistent with mutuality and sharing. By the exercise of gentleness and patience, by the sacrifice of his own immediate pleasure if necessary, the husband may carefully lay a foundation for a satisfactory relationship for the future. If he is blinded by the surging impulses of the moment, he may for temporary gain pay the price of lifelong failure and incompleteness. Roughness, haste, selfishness, and thoughtlessness in the early days of sexual adjustment may produce severe psychological trauma, leaving permanent scars upon a marriage and an unbridgeable gulf in the husband-wife relationship. Referring to honeymoon husbands, Golden [May, 1971] says, "They usually probe, push, and are quickly satisfied, leaving the female with mixed feelings about this sexual act. This is often a rude awakening during the honeymoon which may set in motion a train of emotional traumas which extend throughout married life." With their attitude toward sex and their ignorance of a woman's reactions and of what successful adjustment in marriage requires, some men are in the position of a person who is employed for a job but fails to inquire what the job involves. With pick and shovel on his shoulder, he reports for work, thinking of the contractive power of his biceps, only to find that he is to do watchmaking and that the requirements are patience, finesse, delicacy of operation, and lightness of touch. Other men are like an individual who is presented with a fine violin. He assumes that the only matter to be considered is the fact of possession and that possessing the instrument is all that is necessary to prepare him to play it. Hence, whatever he does to it ought to produce music as long as he enjoys doing it. Fortunately, not all men—not even most—are like this. It is mentioned not to frighten the female reader but to make the male reader sharply aware of his role and responsibility.

There is no reason for a young husband to hurry to demonstrate his potency. No doubt his wife will eventually appreciate masculine vigor, but she expects it to be mingled with a generous admixture of love, understanding, and consideration. Neither *masculinity* nor *virility* implies riding roughshod over a finely balanced and delicate relationship.

In the last analysis, a man has no reason to take pride in his virility. That is a gift of nature, which he has had no part in creating. He may, however, take pride in his ability to give his wife sexual satisfaction. That is an achievement of which he may well be proud because it is an art of his own making.

As the demonstration of masculine virility is nothing for a husband to be proud of, so unnatural reserve and false modesty are nothing to which a wife may turn as a source of pride. It is no more womanly to be inhibited and emotionally undeveloped than it is manly to be bestial and inconsiderate.

Differences Between Men and Women

Since men and women are different physically, one might expect to find a difference in their sexual behavior. In men the sexual impulse may be brought to a sharp focus within a short time and is somewhat localized in the genital organs. In women it tends to be more diffused and generalized and involves the entire body. The genital organs are involved, of course, but not nearly so exclusively as in the male.

The vagina is not so sensitive to either pain or sexual stimulation as is commonly assumed. However, there is an area in the vagina which is sensitive to stimulation, especially that produced by pressure. The muscles (especially the pubococcygeus muscle) surrounding the vagina are sensitive to stimuli [Kegel, October, 1952]. The labia at the entrance to the vagina are sensitive. There is universal agreement neither as to the role played by the vagina in orgasm nor as to whether the vagina or the clitoris [see Figure 10.4] is the primary seat of orgasm. On the average the clitoris is about the size of a small bean. It is buried in soft tissue just above and forward of the entrance to the vagina. Many women are unaware of its presence as an organ, although they may be aware of its location as an area of stimulation and response in sexual intercourse or masturbation. The clitoris is stimulated by bodily contact and movement during intercourse. It may also be stimulated by manual or other rubbing of the area of its location by either the woman or her husband. But direct manual stimulation of the glans of the clitoris is likely to prove uncomfortable [Masters and Johnson, 1966]. Occasionally a woman who has a clitoris that is larger than average becomes aware of its presence when it responds to stimulation. Structurally the clitoris is like a rudimentary penis. It is to the penis of the male what the rudimentary breast of the male is to the developed breast of the female. The rudimentary breast and the clitoris in the male and female, respectively, constitute a clear-cut instance of overlap, or blending, of sexual characteristics due to common embryological development, as discussed in an earlier chapter. In structure the clitoris is homologous to (that is, derived from the same source and similar to, but not identical with) the penis. It has a glans, a spongelike interior, a similar nerve and blood supply. Unlike the penis, however, it has no passage through it and therefore has no function in either secretion or excretion.

In response to sexual stimulation the clitoris becomes tumescent, that is, enlarged, because of an increased blood supply in the "spongy" internal tissue. There is no universal agreement as to whether this tumescence is true erection, as in the case of the penis. There has been a widespread assumption to the effect that there is true clitoral erection. Research by Masters and Johnson [Winokur, 1963], however, casts doubt on this assumption and suggests that the clitoris responds to sexual stimulation "in specific vasocongestive patterns, just as do the vaginal barrel, labia, breasts, etc.," but that it is a fallacy to define this as erection. What appears to be erection of the nipples of the breasts in response to stimulation or as a result of temperature change is due to the contraction of smooth muscle fibers and is not true erection [Haagensen, 1956]. Research indicates that the clitoris is slower to respond than the penis [Winokur, 1963]. The specific terminology to be applied to the reaction of the clitoris is not so important for our purpose as the fact that the clitoris does respond to sexual stimulation in a way not dissimilar to that of the penis and that the clitoris is one major seat of sexual response in the female. Kistner [1964] refers to it as the "nerve center" for intercourse. While orgasm may be brought about by stimulating the clitoris after the surgical removal of the vagina if a woman has been conditioned to sexual stimulation and response, the opposite is also true, namely, that, after conditioning, a woman may have orgasm following removal of the clitoris [Masters and Johnson, 1970, 1966; Jones, Jr., and Scott, 1971].

There is currently a "debate" on whether there is a difference between clitoral orgasm and vaginal orgasm relative to area of stimulation, location of response, and intensity of response. Some say that there is a difference and that the difference is important. Others say there is no difference and the "debate" centers on a false issue.

Statements such as the following are not uncommon: Many women state that "attainment of orgasm during intravaginal intercourse is usually more deeply satisfying than that reached solely through clitoral or other stimulation" [Harper and Stokes, 1971]. "Women's vaginal orgasm is pure fiction" [Ejlersen, 1969]. ". . . The old idea that the clitoris is entirely the site of erotic sensation in the woman must be modified" [Jones, Jr., and Scott, 1971]. "If the vaginal orgasm is widely believed to be a myth it is because it *is* a myth for all but a few women" [Hobbs, 1970]. Millett [1970] says, "While there is no 'vaginal orgasm' per se, there is of course, orgasm in vaginal coitus (and probably one of a different experiential character than that produced by exclusively clitoral stimulation) just as on any occasion when the clitoris is stimulated." Koedt [1971], says ". . . A false distinction is made between the vaginal and the clitoral orgasm." She goes on to say that while there are many areas of sexual arousal, there is only one area of orgasmic response, namely, the clitoris. "All orgasms are extensions of sensation from this area. . . . They are all clitoral orgasms. . . . Vaginal orgasm . . . does not exist."

Women reading such conflicting statements may be confused or even become concerned that their own sexual response is abnormal. Or a husband reading such statements may approach his wife in a way that prevents orgasm instead of promoting it. For example, if he reads that orgasm is clitoral, he may attempt to stimulate the glans of his wife's clitoris directly, a procedure which can produce discomfort, even pain [Masters and Johnson, 1966, 1970], as mentioned above.

During masturbation and during the foreplay preceding intercourse there is likely to be considerable clitoral stimulation. During intercourse there is considerable vaginal stimulation. A woman is already on the way to response psychologically before she voluntarily begins the act of masturbation. This fact undoubtedly contributes to the intensity of her response. During intercourse a woman may or may not be partly aroused before foreplay or intercourse. Intercourse may occur without her complete arousal. Hence her response may be less intense. On the other hand, during intercourse the relationship with her male partner is part of the total situation, and her response is not exclusively physical. Whatever fantasies she may have during masturbation are not equivalent to the relationship with an actual partner during intercourse. Also, during masturbation the woman herself regulates the stimulation, while stimulation in intercourse is regulated largely, but not entirely, by the male partner [see Gebhard, 1970].

Perhaps the point of view most likely to lead to understanding is one that considers a woman a totality rather than a cluster of somewhat disconnected parts and that thinks of her as responding as a total person rather than only in some particular part of her body. "Are clitoral and vaginal orgasms truly separate anatomic entities? From a biologic point of view, the answer to this question is an unequivocal No. . . . From an anatomic point of view, there is absolutely no difference in the responses of the pelvic viscera to effective stimulation. . . . Clitoral and vaginal orgasms are not separate biologic entities" [Masters and Johnson, 1966]. Sherfey [1972] says that "it is a physical impossibility to separate the clitoral from the vaginal orgasm" and that "one must think and talk in terms of a clitorally produced or a vaginally produced orgasm (or both, or a breast-produced, a thought-produced, or a whatever-produced orgasm). Physiologically all orgasms are the same" [see also McGuire and Steinhilber, October, 1970; Fisher, 1973].

After interviews with more than 250 women concerning their sexual experience, McDermott [1970] says that in her opinion the distinction between clitoral and vaginal orgasm "is relevant only to medical science at present." She believes that "once a woman has discovered the best means of realizing sexual satisfaction, has conveyed this to her partner and is happy with the result, she should turn a deaf ear to all the various theories." She goes on to say that, if a woman is worried because she does not seem to have vaginal orgasms, she should "forget it and enjoy what she has got. . . . When some women say that they cannot have a vaginal orgasm, what they really mean is that they cannot have an orgasm through intercourse but only through manual or oral stimulation."

A woman's experience of orgasm is not only visceral; it is emotional, and it is subjective. Measurement and comparison of biologic responses are not the "whole story." On the other hand, there is no way accurately to measure and compare subjective experiences. For a particular woman, then, the issue of clitoral versus vaginal orgasm becomes as pointless and unanswerable as the dilemma "Which came first—the chicken or the egg?" Her total satisfaction in the sexual relationship is the crucial issue, whether it be via one type of orgasm or another or a combination, via orgasm without distinction as to type, or even via no orgasm at all. Furthermore, there is no reason to assume that orgasm is the same for all women or the same for any particular woman at different times.

For a woman sexual intercourse is more likely to be part of a larger experience in which ideal elements play an important role. This is not to say that a man's experience is limited to the physical, for his, too, may be more comprehensive. But in his reactions the physical is more clear-cut and specific. In men sexual desire is aroused by both internal and external stimuli, whereas in women it is more subject to external influences, though internal ones play a part. Both sexes respond to such stimuli as sight of each other, expressions of affection, and physical contact. Both have memory and imagination. Such factors affect a man more readily and more quickly than they affect a woman. In addition, a man is subject to an internal stimulus, namely, the accumulation of seminal fluid in the seminal vesicles [Mahan and Broderick, 1969; Guyton, 1971]. If one could divide the sex drive into segments, one might say that an important part of it in a man is the desire for relief from this accumulation of fluid. There is nothing in a woman's experience quite analogous to this. She may be subject to nervous or muscular tension, but no more so than a man. Because this urge for release is foreign to a woman's experience, it is impossible for her fully to understand how a man feels when he has been sexually aroused. As a couple's sexual experience together develops, however, the wife becomes increasingly responsive to external stimuli and more consciously sensitive to internal ones.

Because external stimuli play so large a part in her reactions, her dependence upon her husband is little short of complete. On the other hand, a man derives some pleasure from the emission of the seminal fluid under almost all circumstances. His sexual experience is far from complete unless it, too, has in it the other-than-physical elements; but because of the explicit nature of his physical response, he may easily be betrayed into concluding that sexual experience is entirely physical and exclusively masculine. Furthermore, because of this accumulation of fluid, the ease with which it is evacuated, and the pleasure derived from that process, a man is less dependent upon his wife for physical satisfaction than she is upon him. As a result, unless he is enlightened, he is likely to be dominated by his own desire, forgetting her and her dependence upon him. Masters and Johnson [1970] mention that, because of "the fact of women's physical necessity for an effectively functioning male sexual partner," the female is in a "relatively untenable position from the point of view of equality of sexual response."

By and large, women are slower than men to reach orgasm and also slower to "subside" afterward. Sometimes this latter period is referred to as the "afterglow." The metaphor is taken from a sunset—the sun has gone down but the sky is still red. A man's reactions are more likely to be very quick and to end more or less abruptly. Shortly after orgasm he may be subject to almost overwhelming sleepiness. If he yields to this sleepiness, from her point of view deserting his wife when she wants attention, an expression of love, and affection beyond the momentary culmination of orgasm, ecstasy may be followed by devastating disappointment [see Goldman and Milman, 1969]. When this happens repeatedly, some women conclude that they are being "used" because the man seems interested only in his own satisfaction. In some cases masculine ignorance in this connection is scarcely less than appalling. In one case, the young wife was very responsive. Intercourse had been particularly satisfactory, and she was "basking" in the "afterglow"—an experience for which there is no descriptive vocabulary but about which women sometimes say, "There's nothing quite like it." The husband's thoughts were elsewhere, and without warning he said, "Do you know what? I'd like to buy a motorcycle." He did not understand why his wife turned away from him and began to cry. "What did I do wrong?" he asked the counselor the next day.

Allowing for diagrammatic oversimplification, Figure 9.2 represents the reactions of the two sexes in intercourse, assuming a reasonably responsive couple, in love, with no unusual inhibitions. The line 0-0 represents zero interest in sex. *W* is the wife's relationship to this line—above the line of zero interest but below the point of husband's interest *H*. *X* represents the wife's orgasm, and *WX* the foreplay which leads to it. *Y* represents the husband's orgasm-ejaculation, and *HY* the stimulation which leads to it, suggesting also the self-discipline which he must exercise after he is aroused if he is to help his wife reach orgasm. *XZ* is the

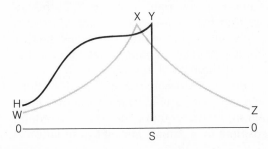

Figure 9.2 Diagrammatic representation of reactions in sexual intercourse.

"afterglow." *YS* is the husband's abrupt subsidence after orgasm-ejaculation, and *S* is the point at which he may experience sleepiness. Ideally, the climaxes would be simultaneous, but such an ideal is probably achieved by only a small proportion of couples and only part of the time. For a couple to expect simultaneous climax each time intercourse occurs is unrealistic. The diagram represents the second most desirable situation—the wife's orgasm occurs first. The third most desirable would be for the husband's to occur first, in which case he would need to continue to stimulate the wife either by continued intercourse, if he can sustain his erection, or by manual means so that her orgasm would follow (assuming that it is to occur, but as we have seen, it is not absolutely essential that it occur each time intercourse takes place). In some cases the wife resorts to masturbation.

Typically, a woman needs preparation for intercourse—some women more, some less. This preparation continues as foreplay leading to orgasm. Such preparation, such foreplay, is not a mechanical thing. It is an outgrowth of frequent expression of affection and trust intensified periodically as a direct preface to a culmination in intercourse. In this process, especially in its final stages, there need be no barrier, physical or otherwise, between husband and wife. No parts of the body need be considered subject to taboo so far as tactile contact is concerned. Any act or expression that furthers the process is acceptable and desirable, provided that (1) it does not cause pain or disgust to either party; (2) it does not indicate or produce a fixation at a low level of adjustment; (3) it does not make either person feel guilty; (4) it does not become a regular substitute for normal sexual intercourse; (5) it is safe. An occasional case is reported in which a wife was stimulated sexually by her husband's blowing air into her vagina to inflate it. Aronson and Nelson [July, 1967] mention seven such cases. Air under pressure has been known to enter the blood stream of the uterus, causing an air embolism which proved fatal. Such an embolism is more likely to occur if the woman is pregnant, has just recently had a baby, is menstruating, or has just stopped menstruating [Aronson, December, 1969; Freeman, July, 1970; Herzig, April, 1972; Mace, June, 1972]. Long, rough, dirty fingernails can be a special hazard, since the membranes of the labia, vagina, or clitoral area may be scratched during manual stimulation of the female by the male.

Even the generalizations listed above (except, of course, the last one) cannot be assumed to be universally applicable. There may be couples to whom they do not apply. In mentioning their sexual behavior couples often say something to this effect: "We do thus and so. Is this right? Is it good?" In the last analysis whatever the husband and wife do together—*anything*—provided it is mutually agreed upon and not imposed by one upon the other, provided that it is safe, and provided that it does not become a problem to other people, is right and good. There are no rules, no standards but their standards.

No matter what one may think about sex before marriage, there is nothing more moral or more "right" than sexual intercourse in marraige. A man is more inclined than a woman to be amenable to, and tolerant of, this sexual freedom, especially at first. Many a woman needs time to acclimate herself to a situation in which all the bars are down, even though the other person is the man she loves. Beginning in early childhood a female is, of necessity, taught to protect herself from males. It is unfortunate when she fails to see that such protection is a temporary expedient and she comes to assume that it is woman's natural state and she must protect herself from even her husband.

Preparation

In preparing his wife for sexual intercouse, much depends upon a husband's skill as a lover, his so-called and much-written-about *technique*. The term does not imply merely maneuvers and manipulations. It implies a thorough understanding of everything necessary to make his wife's, and consequently his own, experience the fullest possible. Often the word "technique" is used in a too narrow sense. Frequently it is assumed that some mechanical process is all that is needed or that such a process supersedes and replaces love, affection, trust, and other similar qualities. In one case, both husband and wife were frustrated to the point of complete impasse. He had been trying to stimulate her to orgasm by the use of a small, soft paintbrush. The more he tried, the farther from orgasm she seemed to be, and the more desperate they both became. The use of a hand-held electric vibrator to stimulate the wife is sometimes recommended. There are women who respond to such stimulation, especially in masturbation, but it would be difficult to imagine anything better designed to cool the ardor of many a wife, who expects intercourse to be part of a highly personalized relationship rather than a depersonalized manipulation. Some current books, even best sellers, recommend practices so bizarre that the reader may well doubt the author's seriousness in suggesting them and may certainly doubt the author's understanding of the sexual relationship, especially women's participation in it. If one were to take some books on this subject at their apparent face value, one might assume that, overnight, any man could become a great lover and sweep any woman, whether she loved him or not, to supreme and incomparable heights of ecstasy by the mastery of some sleight of hand. Nothing could be more misleading. Technique is important but not all-important. When a couple's relationship is successful, technique is only one of the factors to which credit is due. When it is unsuccessful, only part of the blame may be put upon this aspect. If a sexual problem has its roots in attitudes and emotions, it cannot be solved by manipulating anatomy. The sexual act—to be complete—must involve meaning as well as sensation. Meaning has a permanence about it that sensation lacks, and meaning cannot be produced by technique.

Much—too much—is sometimes made of the so-called "positions in intercourse" or "coital postures." Some writers list, describe, divide, subdivide, classify, diagram, or present photographs of dozens, even hundreds, of positions. A recent book [Harkell, 1969] presents 197 such photographs. Some poses more nearly resemble postures of acrobatics rather than expressions of love. Some (as do pictures in some other books) suggest activities that would appeal more to males than to females. Another book [Kokken, 1967] presents 426 pictures of such postures; all depict the male and female separately, none showing them together, and all are photographs of artists' mannequins. A newly wed couple relying on such books would have to take a research assistant on their honeymoon to help them make choices from such extensive catalogues. To many young persons contemplating marriage, this cataloguing makes intercourse seem like an engineering problem, whereas it should be a spontaneous expression of love, affection, and desire with the emphasis on abandonment and oneness, not on posture. To many women diagrams of postures make intercourse seem animal-like, and they react negatively to them. It must be admitted that a variety of positions in intercourse is possible. A particular couple may discover which ones are best for them through experimentation.

The twin cities of Niagara Falls, New York, and Ontario, Canada, attract some 35,000 honeymoon couples annually. Dr. Boris A. Golden, who has practiced in this area for twenty-three years, interviewed twenty-one other physicians who had been in practice an average of fifteen years. Collectively these physicians have been called upon to help a multitude of young couples with sexual problems. Golden writes [May, 1971], "Male sexual interests may confuse the female. To an inhibited bride the suggestion of a strip-tease, black negligee, high heels, or any other evidence of her husband's voyeuristic pleasures may provoke panic. Various unusual positions of intercourse may suggest perversion of the worst sort."

A list of positions for kissing could be worked out similar to that for intercourse. But we assume that persons in love will discover ways to embrace without making a choice from a catalogue of postures—and as a matter of fact they do.

It is true that much may be gained from reading and discussion, and some of the prerequisites for sexual harmony are readily learned. There is, however, no standard technique, no universal formula. Individual differences, attitudes, background, fears, relative intelligence, depth of affection, irritating circumstances, personality traits, understanding of anatomy, and similar items need to be taken into account. A couple need to work out what to them is an acceptable relationship, not only on the basis of stock information and injunction but also by exploration, experimentation, variation, ingenuity, and discovery. This latter process is in itself one means toward successful adjustment. Love-play in marriage should be spontaneous and contain subtleties. For a husband always to make a direct sexual approach to his wife not only shows that he does not understand her reactions but is likely to make her avoid him because at the time he is more fully prepared for sexual intercourse than she. He may also defeat his purpose if he gives her the impression that every time he expresses affection for her in any way he expects intercourse inevitably to follow or if after intercourse there is a period during which he seems uninterested and unaffectionate. She should not be made to feel that intercourse is a price that she must pay for love or that it constitutes a prelude to apathy.

In preparatory play and in intercourse a woman does not, as is sometimes supposed, have an entirely passive role. As her inhibitions fade, she may follow her impulses when she becomes aware of them. In the early days of marriage she needs most of all to abandon herself to her husband and to lose herself in this new experience with him. For some women that is more readily said than done because all their lives they have been taught not to abandon themselves, and to make a complete about-face is not easy.

A woman derives pleasure from yielding to the man she loves, a pleasure as remote from masculine experience and understanding as ejaculation is remote from a woman's comprehension. Responsive women often experience a foretaste of such yielding in their reactions to men's expressions of affection before marriage. In trying to describe this experience, for which there is no special vocabulary, a woman may say, "When he kisses me, I get butterflies in my stomach," or "When he kisses me, my knees turn to water." These are yielding, receptive, or accepting responses. A man does not get "butterflies in his stomach" or have his "knees turn to water." He becomes more like a coiled spring. Responsive women have a great asset in their capacity and readiness to respond and in their derivation of pleasure from it. They should be glad for it, not ashamed of it. That same responsiveness, however, becomes a liability when it is not understood, when it is uncontrolled and unselective, or when it is unaccompanied by good judgment.

Above all, a woman need not worry about technique, especially at first. As time goes on she will discover how she may most effectively participate. If she focuses her attention upon details, women's reactions being diffused as they are, she puts the emphasis exactly where it does not belong. What we are saying, however, applies to specific sexual union. In the matter of responding to her husband's love-making a wife may and usually does resort to all the subtleties that she employed in courtship. There is no reason, biological, psychological, ethical, or otherwise, why a wife should not take an active part in a couple's love-play, even taking the initiative in stimulating her husband.

Sexual adjustment in marriage is not unusually difficult of achievement. Neither does it come automatically, without intelligence, effort, or understanding. Further to allay the fears of those who may feel that such achievement is beyond the realm of possibility and quite beyond their resources, we may generalize to this extent. Except in those relatively rare instances in which unusual physical defects or uncommonly strong inhibitions or fears make successful sexual adjustment abnormally difficult, any healthy, intelligent couple who are in love and are otherwise happily married may work out a satisfactory sexual adjustment if they persevere and approach the problem sensibly, even though at first there may seem to be obstacles in their path. Some couples have no problems at all; satisfactory sexual experience comes to them as easily and naturally as their mutual love. Others have minor problems, readily solved. Relatively few, even extreme cases, are entirely hopeless [Friedman, 1962].

Other Considerations

Several miscellaneous considerations bearing upon sexual adjustment may be mentioned briefly.

1 Both husband and wife need some knowledge of the anatomy and physiological reactions of both self and the other person. In the study of 1,000 unconsummated marriages already referred to [Blazer, May, 1964], the two main reasons given for the nonconsummation in 5 per cent of the cases were ignorance regarding the exact location of the sex organs and the avoidance of an attempt at intercourse to prevent embarrassment and mistakes. Stokes lists as the third most frequent reason, among his patients, for wives remaining virgin "plain ignorance on the part of one or both partners about how to proceed . . ." [Harper and Stokes, 1971]. Although "it seems inconceivable that such lack of knowledge of sexuality should exist," Dubin [May 8, 1972] mentions two couples who "didn't know that they never actually had intercourse." There are no statistics to show how common such ignorance is in the general population. In reports such as these there is no way of knowing how many individuals stated ignorance as a reason for avoiding intercourse when the true reason was to be found in the personalities of the couple. Nevertheless, that such ignorance should be found at all in these presumably enlightened times is interesting. It is reflected in the queries of college students who ask such questions as the following, reported verbatim: "What is circumcision?" "Can a girl become pregnant without having intercourse?" "Can a girl become pregnant without reaching a climax?" "When does a woman achieve orgasm—before or during the act of sexual intercourse?" "Is it possible to become pregnant as a result of mouth-genital contact if the semen is swallowed?" "In intercourse, how far does the penien [sic] penetrate the vagina, or does it; what happens?" "Does the pill regulate you so you can use the rhythm system or does it actually prevent pregnancy?" "What is orgasm in the male and female?" "Is intercourse possible after a hysterectomy?" "What is a douche?" "What is oral intercourse; is it kissing or otherwise? (P.S. I have to know before the weekend.)" "Where is the hymen?" "During childbirth where does the baby come out of the mother's body?" "Do boys menstruate?" "Does the hymen completely close the entrance to the vagina until it is broken?" "Can masturbation make a boy's hips broad like a girl's?" Included in the knowledge needed is the fact that in response to sexual stimulation internal secretions lubricate the vagina. To the degree to which the wife accepts sexual intercourse this process is facilitated. As mentioned earlier, it may be supplemented by the use of a lubricating jelly.

2 In their sexual life there need be no mechanical regularity as to time, place, or frequency. Spontaneity furthers responsiveness; mechanism destroys it. Usually sexual intercourse should be mutually desired before it is consummated, allowing for the difference in degree of preparation needed by husband and wife and taking into account the fact that accumulation of seminal fluid creates a problem for the husband but not for the wife. If she understands this latter point, sexual intercourse may be considered mutually desirable, even though the wife is not sufficiently aroused to reach orgasm.

Young persons often wonder about the danger of too frequent intercourse. There is no such danger as long as the experience is mutually desirable and as long as it is followed by a sense of well-being, relaxation, and oneness rather than a sense of regret, repugnance, guilt, or excessive fatigue. A woman may repeat intercourse over and again, and some women report a series of orgasms. Because of the ejaculation of the seminal fluid, Nature puts a brake on the male. He may be able to repeat ejaculation several times within a brief period, but the possibilities are far from limitless and well below the frequencies sometimes reported by males whose imagination and self-aggrandizement surpass their secretory capacity.

3   In the female, the urethra (the tube that leads from the bladder to the exterior) is relatively short and its opening is near the opening of the vagina (see Figure 10.4). Typically, there is a variety of organisms found in this area. Hence, it is not uncommon for bacteria to be forced through the urethra into the bladder during intercourse. When this occurs, cystitis (infection of the bladder) may result. Cystitis may occur in any woman. But women with little or no sexual experience seem to be especially susceptible, probably because they have not had time to develop an immunity. The term *honeymoon cystitis* is used to refer to the condition in newly married women. Some women become panicked at the onset of symptoms, such as pain, a burning sensation, and a feeling of urgency in urination. Some fear they have a venereal disease. Honeymoon cystitis is not a condition calling for panic, but it is a condition calling for immediate medical attention for accurate differential diagnosis and treatment [Linton, August, 1971; Golden, May, 1971].

4   An attitude of leisure is important. Haste, like mechanism, can be defeating. A couple should not consider intercourse something to be hurried through because there are other things waiting to be done. Nor should either party be put under pressure to achieve. "The male partner must be careful not to inject any personal demand for sexual performance into his female partner's pattern of response. The husband must not set goals for his wife. He must not try to force responsivity. . . . Sexual response can neither be programmed nor made to happen" [Masters and Johnson, 1970].

5   Physical cleanliness will bear reference, since sexual contact is so intimate.

6   A young couple should be able to have privacy when they want it. Inquisitive neighbors, obtrusive relatives, a feeling of general uneasiness because of the possibility of intrusion or because of thin-walled apartments—all make adjustment difficult. If privacy is not possible, it is in some cases advisable to change residence. It is better to have an inferior residence, if necessary, than an inferior relationship.

7   Fatigue often hinders adjustment. It cannot always be avoided in daily life, but the relation between fatigue and sexual adjustment may be understood and kept in mind. Johnson and Masters [1964] consider fatigue and preoccupation to be major deterrents to sexual responsiveness.

8   The probability is that, because of the aesthetic element involved and the woman's disinclination to do so, few couples have intercourse during the wife's menstrual period. But intercourse at that time is not dangerous [Martin and Long, June, 1969], as was formerly thought.

9 Whether intercourse is advisable or inadvisable during all or part of a woman's pregnancy is a decision to be made by her obstetrician on the basis of his knowledge of her particular condition. Medical opinions differ about the advisability of such intercourse. Speert and Guttmacher [1956] say: "Coitus in moderation is safe. . . . There is no foundation for the age-old belief that coitus at the time of the first missed periods is conducive to abortion. . . . In late pregnancy coitus sometimes results in premature rupture of the membranes and consequent onset of premature labor. . . . Intrauterine infection is also a potential hazard of this accident." Data derived from a study of 200 pregnant women suggest that orgasm, but not intercourse per se, may be a factor in initiating premature labor [Goodlin, Keller, and Raffin, December, 1971]. Greenhill [1965a] believes we should ". . . urge deemphasizing abstinence during the final weeks of pregnancy," since intercourse at this time seems to be of little obstetrical significance if the woman is comfortable while it occurs. Donald [1964] says that "ideally speaking" there should be abstinence between the eighth and fourteenth weeks and during the last four weeks. Hyams [April, 1972] says, "While there is no proof that coitus in the second or third trimester induces premature labor, it is undoubtedly safest to abstain from intercourse in the last four weeks of gestation." Mann and Cunningham [October, 1972] say that "in the average, normally progressing pregnancy there is no reason to interdict intercourse." Gorbach [1972] makes this statement: "If sexual intercourse in pregnancy caused miscarriages, the human race probably would have petered out many millions of years ago." In the light of such divergence of opinion, the wisest course of action for a couple is to discuss the matter with their obstetrician and follow his suggestions, since he will make those suggestions on the basis of his knowledge of a particular woman and her pregnancy. Except for the hypothetical possibility of inducing premature labor, there is no evidence that intercourse endangers the fetus.

Periodicity

Many women manifest *periodicity of sexual desire*. Both sexes exhibit variations in intensity of interest and desire, not only from individual to individual but in the same person at different times. These latter variations depend upon fatigue, other interests and concerns, bodily functions, proximity of husband and wife, and frequency and recency of intercourse. Superimposed upon this irregular series of changes in the individual, there is in many women a more nearly regular cyclical or rhythmic change, which bears a relation to the menstrual cycle. One might say that the man is like a lake; he exhibits waves or calm. The woman is like an ocean; in addition to waves and calm she exhibits tides. Some women are conscious of no such periodicity. Others experience a heightened desire just before menstruation, just after menstruation, before and after, midway between periods, or at some other time relative to the menstrual cycle. In some the periodicity is regular and recurs each month; in others it is irregular. Whether this variation in interest is physiologically, psychologically, or otherwise conditioned is irrelevant here. If it exists, it is important in marriage.

A summary of the studies of seventeen investigators indicates that they all report periodicity before menstruation, after menstruation, or in midcycle, or a combination of two or three of these times in various numbers of women [Cavanagh, February, 1969]. Ascertaining the exact number of women who are conscious of this cyclical change in their sexual interests is not so important as recognizing that a considerable proportion of women do experience it. A given husband is confronted with the problem of understanding one wife, not with a problem in statistics.

There are only two means by which a husband may understand his wife in this particular regard: observation and information. He may observe her carefully to see whether there is any variation in her attitudes and responses during the menstrual cycle. Ordinarily no one can furnish him with information about his wife, however, except the wife herself. She may help her husband by carefully noting her inclinations, and she need not hesitate to let her feelings become known to him. Both husband and wife may learn how to detect and recognize each other's needs and desires, as well as feel free to make their own desires known. This need not always be done by direct statement. There are other more indirect and subtle means known to anyone who is less than completely naive in the matter of making love.

This discussion of periodicity of desire is not meant to imply that sexual intercourse is possible or advisable only at those relatively infrequent intervals when a woman experiences a heightened sexual interest. It does imply that at various times a different approach is necessary and there may be various degrees of responsiveness. There may, too, be times not only when a woman is less interested but when intercourse may be distasteful to her. At such times a husband cannot expect his wife to respond.

It is interesting to note in passing that, in women who are aware of the periodicity of sexual desire, heightened interest does not always coincide with that phase of the menstrual cycle when the ovum is released and conception is possible. This may be another bit of evidence to add weight to the argument of those who maintain that the function of sex is not primarily reproduction. In lower animals reproduction is the function of sexual union, and among mammals periods of seeking or accepting copulation on the part of the female coincide with release of the ovum, and thus with the possibility of conception.

Premenstrual Syndrome

For some women there is a brief period during the menstrual cycle, usually just prior to the onset of menstruation but sometimes earlier and at times persisting for a day or two after menstruation begins, when they exhibit one or more of a cluster of symptoms. These symptoms together are termed the *premenstrual syndrome*, sometimes referred to as *premenstrual tension*, although tension is only one of the possible symptoms. Fluhmann [1956] says that though estimates of the number of women who exhibit the premenstrual syndrome vary, a reasonable estimate would be 60 per cent; Israel [1967] estimates about two-thirds. Sutherland and Stewart [June, 1965] found 39 per cent in a study of 150 women. In discussing the premenstrual syndrome, writers [Gill, January, 1943; Novak, 1944; Hoffman, 1944; Hamblen, 1945; Lamb, Ulett, Masters, and Robinson, May, 1953; Kroger and Freed, 1956; Bowes, 1956; Fluhmann, 1956; Kessel and Coppen, July, 1963; Dalton, 1964; Lloyd, 1964e; Janowsky and Gorney, July-August, 1966; Greenhill, 1961, 1966; Israel, 1967; Paschkis, Rakoff, Cantarow, and Rupp, 1967; Ivey and Bardwick, May-June, 1968; Novak, Jones, and Jones, Jr., 1970] mention headache, anxiety, inability to concentrate, depression, emotional outbursts, crying spells, hypersensitivity, unexplainable fears, imperative ideas, insomnia, contrariness, exaggeration of trifles, loss of inhibitions, cruelty, and a host of other symptoms among which is "going on food binges," which Melody [April, 1961] found in 80 per cent of 200 women studied. In a sense, such symptoms are uncontrollable by the woman herself. At least the feelings are uncontrollable; their expression may be controlled to some degree. Certainly a woman need not take undue advantage of the situation because she gets the impression that statistics justify any type of behavior and that she is the victim of something beyond her control.

Evidence suggests that there is a relationship between menstruation and premenstrual symptoms and accident proneness. In one study, 52 per cent of a group of women involved in accidents had their accidents during menstruation or the four days immediately prior to it [Dalton, November, 1960]. In another study, it was found that 62 per cent of the violent crimes committed by women were perpetrated in the premenstrual phase of the menstrual cycle [Morton, Additon, Addison, Hunt, and Sullivan, June, 1953]. The premenstrual syndrome and dysmenorrhea (painful menstruation) seldom occur in the same woman. Women show no tendency to commit crimes while suffering dysmenorrhea as they do during the premenstrual syndrome [Dalton, 1964]. It has been found that during menstruation and the premenstrual phase of the menstrual cycle women exhibit a decline in level of academic work, make lower scores on intelligence tests, become more strict disciplinarians if they have positions of authority, become less alert in creative work, are more likely to be absent from work or to quit their jobs because of some irritation, and exhibit a higher rate of suicide and attempted suicide [Dalton, 1964; Mandell and Mandell, May, 1967].

None of the above implies that, because they experience cyclical changes, women are unfit to participate in decision making in the home, in occupations, or in public affairs; that they are unfit to engage in certain professions or to hold public office; or that women are inferior to men [see Barnes, February, 1971]. Women's cyclical nature is not something to be "pooh-poohed" by either men or those women who make the same mistakes some men do in letting emotion and bias obscure facts. Women's cyclical nature is something to be understood by both sexes.

A husband may observe his wife to determine whether or not she exhibits premenstrual symptoms and, if so, when they occur, what they are, and whether they are regular and thus predictable. Otherwise, if she has such symptoms, he will be baffled by her behavior. If he learns to predict her behavior, he can avoid "triggering" certain symptoms, can accept others, and can consider some days each month as "off the record" because, although psychological factors may play a part [Shader and Ohly, April, 1970], her behavior on those days is mainly the result of upset body chemistry. If a husband is not aware of this, he may wonder why the loving wife of yesterday, for whom he cares so much and who expressed her affection so warmly, has seemed to make an about-face and, without apparent provocation, cut him to the quick today. Tomorrow her mood will probably have passed. She may wonder why she felt as she did and be sorry for it; but at the time she may have enjoyed her cruelty. No husband should reach any conclusion concerning his wife's attitude toward him until he has carefully ascertained the relation of that attitude to her menstrual cycle. No wife should conclude that her attitude toward her husband during such a period of depression or irritability is permanent or represents her "true self." A woman's "true self" is what she is over a period of about twenty-eight days, not what she is at a given moment. Generalizing somewhat, we may say that during a large part of a woman's life, namely, from the menarche to the completion of the menopause, her body, unlike that of a man, is at any given time in some phase of a cycle.

During the period immediately preceding menstruation many apparently normal women have an increase in body weight varying from about 2 to occasionally as much as 15 to 25 pounds. [Lloyd, 1964e; Southam and Gonzoga, January 1, 1965; Reeves, Garvin, and McElin, April 1, 1971]. This increase in weight is manifested in generalized swelling, in swelling of the hands and feet, in puffiness of the face and eyelids. Some women complain of feeling bloated. They are aware of a noticeable increase in girth, and their clothes feel tight. This swelling is due to water retention in the body tissues, not in the bladder, which, in turn, is thought by some investigators [Dalton, 1964] to be due to retention of sodium. Some doubt this [Kistner, 1964], suggesting that the cause is unknown. Such retention of water is considered by some to be at least one of the factors contributing to the premenstrual syndrome, but there is not universal agreement on this point [Bruce and Russell, August 11, 1962]. Symptoms such as water retention and its resultant weight gain may be relieved by limiting fluid intake, eating a salt-free diet, and taking a diuretic, that is, a drug which causes an increase in urination [Fluhmann, 1956; Bowes, 1956]. But there is disagreement as to whether this relieves other symptoms [Page, Villee, and Villee, 1972]. Treatment should, of course, be prescribed by a physician.

Adjustment

We have been setting a comparatively high standard and discussing the better type of adjustment. Suppose that a person marries an individual who does not do all that we have suggested. Either husband or wife may or may not be able to attain a high degree of success. If the individual who is not well adjusted is aware of this fact, he may see a counselor, acquire further information, or analyze himself in so far as his knowledge permits. In most instances there is little to be gained by talking the problem through with friends or other laymen. The probability is that they know no more than the individual himself and are prone to generalize from one case, which is usually their own. Above all, neither one of the spouses needs to conclude that the situation is hopeless and that immediate separation or divorce is the solution.

If it is the wife who is incompletely adjusted and the husband realizes this but she does not, he may adopt any of several courses: (1) try new methods of approach or allow more time for foreplay; (2) talk the problem over with her to see whether he is doing something that displeases her; (3) suggest that she seek counseling help; (4) compromise, if it seems impossible for the wife's adjustment to become fully successful, as sometimes success comes after years of marriage— a couple should not give up easily, especially if the wife is eager to succeed or if their relationship is partly or occasionally complete; (5) examine time, place, and circumstances to determine whether there are obstacles to success to be found in the environment; (6) suggest that there be a medical examination to determine whether there are physical defects; (7) talk the problem over with a competent counselor. If, after all these resources have been drawn upon, the adjustment seems incomplete, the couple may continue to do the best they can.

If it is the husband's role that is faulty, the following suggestions may be of use to the wife. (1) She may help him to learn more about their relationship, if he is the type of man willing to learn and is amenable to suggestion. She may explain her own reactions to him. At the same time she must remember that very few men exactly fit a textbook pattern; some men express themselves in one way, some in another. (2) If the husband seems hasty and a bit rough and sexual intercourse seems rather frequent, the wife may rest assured that in all except rare cases time will, at least in part, remedy these conditions. (3) She may consult a competent counselor about her specific problem. Generalizations are not adequate. This is especially important if the husband lacks interest or is impotent. (4) Reading may help if the couple are open-minded and willing to learn and choose their books carefully. In recent years a flood of books on sex has become available, and many articles on various aspects of the subject may be found in popular magazines. Some of these materials are helpful. Many, however, as indicated earlier, are poor, inaccurate, misleading, focused on unusual practices, less than helpful, and in some cases even disturbing, especially to women. (5) In the earlier part of marriage, the one solution for many a problem is time to learn.

The best preparation for successful sexual adjustment in marriage is the development of a healthy, balanced attitude, free of unnecessary and unfounded inhibitions and fears, together with the acquisition of sound, reliable information. No matter how much the couple have read or may pride themselves upon knowing, it is still often advisable for them to talk through the matter of sexual adjustment with a competent counselor so that they may think in terms of specifics rather than in terms of generalities. There is no single book that can be guaranteed to give them all the information that they need. In many ways every couple's adjustment is unique.

SELECTED READINGS

Belliveau, Fred, and Lin Richter: *Understanding Human Sexual Inadequacy*, Bantam Books, Inc., New York, 1970. (Paperback.) A nontechnical discussion of the research findings presented in Masters and Johnson's *Human Sexual Inadequacy*. Also includes personality sketches of Masters and Johnson, tells how their work started, and how it was first received.

Bird, Lois: *How to Be a Happily Married Mistress*, Doubleday & Company, Inc., Garden City, N.Y., 1970. The author is happy to be a woman and wants wives to be sexual companions rather than "just housewives." "This is a book on the fun of loving a husband. . . ." Hence the use of the word "mistress" in the title. Makes suggestions on understanding a husband, improving communication, and how a wife may contribute to the couple's sexual relationship.

Hastings, Donald W.: *A Doctor Speaks on Sexual Expression in Marriage*, Little, Brown and Company, Boston, 1966. Discusses the honeymoon, sexual intercourse, impotence, frigidity, masturbation, menopause, sexual development, and children's curiosity about sex.

Lehrman, Nat: *Masters and Johnson Explained*, Playboy Press, Chicago, 1970. (Paperback.) Analysis in nontechnical language of both of the Masters and Johnson reports. Includes reports of interviews with Masters and Johnson.

McCary, James Leslie: *Human Sexuality*, 2d ed., D. Van Nostrand Company, Inc., New York, 1973. A discussion of many aspects of human sexuality including sexual disorders, variant behavior, aphrodesiacs, myths, and fallacies.

———: *Sexual Myths and Fallacies*, Van Nostrand Reinhold Company, New York, 1971. Myths and fallacies concerning sexual behavior.

Mace, David R.: *Sexual Difficulties in Marriage*, Fortress Press, Philadelphia, 1972. (Paperback.) Addressed to readers who have sexual difficulties in marriage. Discusses role of sex in marriage, sexual problems, what can be done about them, and how professional counseling may help.

Seaman, Barbara: *Free and Female*, Coward, McCann & Geoghegan, Inc., New York, 1972. "The first book to report on women's sexual needs and capacities from a feminist point of view. . . . Gives the facts, untainted by male prejudice." Discusses clitoral versus vaginal orgasm, what women like in men, women's criticisms of men's sexual techniques, malpractice among gynecologists, venereal disease, a criticism of the pill, and children of liberated women.

Stone, Hannah M., and Abraham Stone: *A Marriage Manual*, rev. by Gloria Stone Aitkin and Aquiles J. Sobrero, Simon & Schuster, Inc., New York, 1970. Written by a husband and wife, both physicians, in question-and-answer form as if a couple were talking with their doctor. Discusses various aspects of sex and reproduction.

With the present-day American emphasis upon the individual, we are often inclined to think of persons as independent, somewhat isolated units who live in groups by choice and may accept or reject the influence of those groups at will. Actually people do not live this way. Each individual lives as a member of each of a network of clusters. Only within limits may he choose which clusters. Only within very much narrower limits may he choose whether he will be affiliated with clusters at all. For example, he may choose the occupational group with which he will affiliate himself. He may decide to be a member of this or that religious organization. He may live in the country or in the city. In his adult life he could even live on an island of which he was the only inhabitant. But with respect to some of the groups that are most influential in molding his personality—for example, his sex group and his family—he ordinarily has no freedom of choice at all. The family, not the individual, is the nuclear unit of society. Parents as well as children are members of nuclear families, but parental membership comes through decision to marry and through biological processes that are at least partially under their voluntary control. As a couple move from marriage to family living, both sides of this coin become apparent. Hence it is appropriate that we consider the process by which children are produced, how their production may be controlled and planned, and what happens to human interrelationships as a result of these processes.

The following chapter on pregnancy and childbirth precedes the discussion of contraception, since the process of reproduction must be understood before the topics of conception control and abortion can be made clear.

part 4

FROM MARRIAGE TO THE FAMILY

I've never felt better about myself.

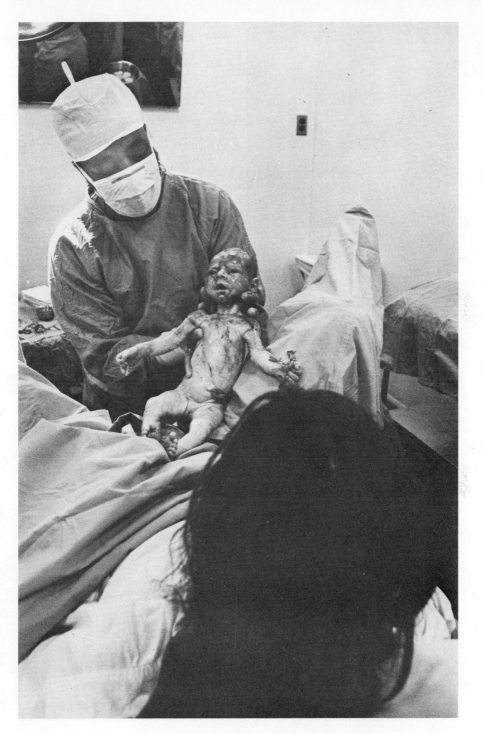

Six seconds old.

Jason gets hungry about every three hours now.

It feels good to sit and let Khari fall asleep on my lap.

*Raising these two sure has its
ups and downs.*

Harold helps me a lot with Ari.

We all share a discovery.

Nito and I are very close.

Connie needs my attention, too.

Leroy would never finish his dinner if I didn't coax him into it.

At her age Leoni is interested in every-thing.

I take the kids to the park whenever I can.

I like our home.

Pregnancy and Childbirth

If one were asked to choose that thing in the universe which had greatest relative potentiality, he could advance reasonable arguments for choosing the fertilized human egg (*zygote*)—that almost microscopic bit of protoplasm that constitutes the beginning of the new human individual and is smaller than the period at the end of this sentence. Here is a potential that dwarfs the awesome release of nuclear energy, that makes the explosion of a super-nova seem like pointless force, that renders all the radiation of the sun in a measure subordinate to itself, as means is subordinate to end. For perhaps a billion years Nature has been working to perfect the organism that arises from that fertilized egg and the determiners of hereditary traits which that egg contains—determiners passed to it in unbroken succession from countless generations of ancestors and to be passed on to countless generations of descendants.

Contained within the zygote are also the regulators of a pattern of growth that is complex beyond comprehension. Two hundred billion times the egg multiplies itself between fertilization and birth, trillions of times between fertilization and adulthood, by a process involving not only increase in numbers but also specialization of form and function and a continuous series of interrelated changes, a chain reaction, extending from fertilization to death. It is a pattern that produces multiplicity and diversity but also unity, as the multicelled body behaves as an entity and says, "This is I."

Start with an almost microscopic zygote. "Add" nothing but food, water, salts, oxygen, and other nonliving materials. Give it a few years in a favorable environment, and we find it falling in love, establishing enduring relationships, creating beauty, contemplating values, seeking truth, and asking, "Who am I? Where did I come from? Why am I here? Where am I going?" All the art, literature, government, science, ethics, philosophy, and religion that we know spring from that zygote. All the reachings and searchings that characterize the human mind are, in a sense, contained within it. For the first nine months it lives and grows in complete darkness, continuously submerged in water, and, during the latter part of the period, upside down a good part of the time. This it can never do again. From the moment of fertilization it is a separate organism, living within its mother, to be sure, but never part of its mother. In a sense, the zygote controls the mother's body more than it is controlled by her body. It is her body that

ten

changes to adapt itself to the zygote, while the zygote takes advantage of the adaptations. When we take into account the difference in size, it is not surprising that the means by which the zygote communicates to the mother's body that fertilization has taken place is not completely understood. This is an oversimplification of the situation to dramatize the relationship. When at last the baby emerges from the mother's body, ordinarily by forces that she neither voluntarily initiates nor can willfully control, it is already a highly complex and well-developed individual, endowed with a unique ability to learn and a unique capacity to grow. This is the "miracle" of human reproduction.

It is around this "miracle" of reproduction that a couple may build their perspective relative to having children. Cost, inconvenience, and obstetrical detail need not blind them to the essential process and its meaning. It is as participant in this "miracle" that a woman, especially, may find profound fulfillment. Since reproduction ordinarily (an exception would be artificial insemination, discussed later) requires the participation of both husband and wife and literally a part of each is necessary for fertilization to occur, one may readily see what an exhilarating, fascinating, and satisfying experience having a child may be for a happily married pair.

DETERMINERS OF HEREDITY

Chromosomes and Genes

The nucleus of each cell in the body contains *chromosomes*, on which are located *genes*. The genes are complex molecules and are the determiners of hereditary traits. For each such trait exhibited by the organism, with some exceptions, there are two genes or sets of genes, one received from either parent. In the *somatic* (*body*) *cells* there are forty-six chromosomes (twenty-three pairs), while in the *gametes* (sex cells—*ova* and *spermatozoa*) there are only twenty-three chromosomes, one member of each pair. Thus in order to recreate the twenty-three pairs found in each body cell, two gametes must unite.

Cells increase in number through a process of division (*mitosis*); that is, each cell divides to form two cells, these two to form four, and so on. Each chromosome is longitudinally double [King, 1962]. When the cell divides, each chromosome splits lengthwise and each half goes to a new cell, where it duplicates itself. Thus each new cell has the same chromosomal content, the same genetic constitution, as the original cell. This process is shown schematically in Figure 10.1, where the number of chromosomes is kept to one pair to make the illustration simpler.

After division each "half-chromosome" develops into a whole one, which has the same relative genetic content (genes) as the half. Each new cell is, therefore, like the original cell as far as chromosomal content is concerned. Since all body cells have a common origin in a single cell, all have the same chromosomal content.

In the formation of the gametes, however, the chromosomes, instead of splitting into halves, act as units. One whole chromosome of each pair goes to one new cell. The other whole chromosome goes to the other new cell. The number of chromosomes in each new cell is reduced to half, and the process is termed *meiosis,* or *reduction division.* When two cells unite in fertilization, the original number of chromosomes is restored. This process is shown schematically in Figure 10.2.

For each hereditary trait exhibited by the organism there are, with some exceptions as mentioned above, at least one pair of genes. Since chromosomes act as units in the formation of the gametes, only one of the genes for a given trait is carried by a gamete. The chromosomes may be "shuffled" and "dealt" to the gametes as playing cards are shuffled and dealt to players. The statistical probability of two gametes having identical genetic content may be compared to the probability of a player's receiving two identical hands after two separate shufflings and deals, assuming that on each deal he received half of the fifty-two cards. His chance would be expressed in figures of astronomical magnitude. Since this same enormous number of possible combinations of genes is found in the gametes of each parent and the number of gametes also is colossal, one may readily see why, even with the billions of people in the world, there are no two exactly alike. (One-egg twins have the same genetic constitution and in this sense are alike.) It has been estimated that the odds against two identical individuals (other than one-egg twins) being born are 1 followed by more than 9,000 zeros. Such a number does not even have a name.

The Gametes

An *ovum* (plural, *ova*), or female gamete, commonly called *egg*, is globular and is about 1/200 inch in diameter. It is just visible to the naked eye. All the ova needed

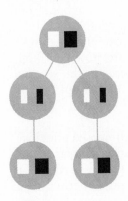

Figure 10.1 Schematic representation of mitotic cell division.

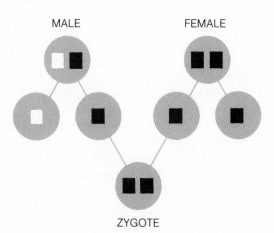

Figure 10.2 Schematic representation of reduction division and fertilization.

to produce the population of the world—more than 3 billion—could be contained within the shell of a hen's egg [Hartman, 1962]. At that, ova are the largest cells in the body and are 60,000 times the volume of sperms. A clump of 60,000 sperms would be just visible to the naked eye [Hartman, 1962]. In an egg such as a hen's, the ovum itself constitutes only an infinitesimal fraction of the whole; the rest is food material for the developing embryo. There is no correlation between the size of the ovum and body size. The ova of rabbits, whales, dogs, gorillas, pigs, and cows, for example, all have approximately the same dimensions.

Sperms (*spermatozoa*), or male gametes, are minute and are shaped, roughly, like tadpoles. There is an oval head approximately 1/5,000 inch long, a middle piece, and a comparatively long tail, making the total length about 1/500 inch. The more than 3 billion sperms needed to produce the population of the world could be accommodated in a container about the size of an aspirin tablet.

Ova are nonmotile; that is, they cannot move by their own power. Sperms, however, propel themselves by lashing their tails in much the same way as a tadpole swims. Relative to their size, they get about fairly well, moving approximately 1/7 inch per minute. Since each sperm is about 1/500 inch long, this means that it swims 500 times its length in 7 minutes. A human being walking at an average pace covers about 500 times his height, or approximately 1/2 mile, in 7 minutes. Relative to their size, sperms swim about as fast as we walk.

ORGANS AND PROCESSES IN REPRODUCTION

The Production of Sperms

Sperms form in minute tubes within the *testes* (*testicles*), which are two oval-shaped organs suspended in the *scrotum*. [See Figure 10.3 for a diagrammatic representation of male genital anatomy.] These tubes are coiled and would total several hundred feet in length if straightened out. Among the tubes lie the *interstitial cells* that produce the male hormone, *testosterone*, which plays a part in masculinization. The temperature within the scrotum is 2.5 to 4.5°F lower than body temperature [Albert, 1961]. Were it the same, sperm formation could not take place. While the sperms are still immature, they pass, by ciliary action, from the tubules in each testis into the corresponding *epididymis* (a tightly coiled tube about twenty feet long) [Hartman, 1962]. Here, and to some extent in the lower portion of each *vas deferens* (plural, *vasa deferentia*), they are stored [Bishop, 1961; Oliven, 1965; Odell and Moyer, 1971]. They are not stored in the *seminal vesicles*, as was formerly supposed [Wershub, 1962]. During their sojourn in the epididymis, [Bishop, 1961], the sperms acquire the capacity for motility and are capable of movement but remain in a quiescent state.

The *seminal fluid* (*semen*) is a whitish, viscous mixture composed principally of the secretions of the *prostate gland* and the seminal vesicles [Anderson and Speroff, March, 1971; Odell and Moyer, 1971]. At least the vesicular portion of it is stored in the seminal vesicles [Lowsley, Hinman, Smith, and Gutierrez, 1942; Mitsuya, Asai, Suyama, Ushida, and Hosoe, January, 1960; Price and Williams-

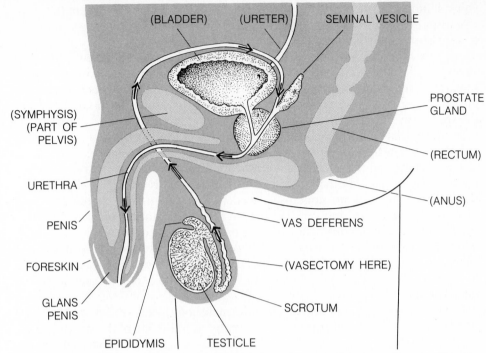

Figure 10.3 Male genital organs. Names in parentheses do not indicate genital organs. Note the arrows showing the path of sperms.

Ashman, 1961; Oliven, 1965]. During sexual excitation the "spongy" interior of the penis becomes engorged with blood, causing the organ to increase in both size and rigidity and enabling it to enter the vagina. During ejaculation, the sperms are moved up through the vasa deferentia by *peristalsis* (waves of muscular contraction) or by a contraction-shortening process in the vasa deferentia and enter the *urethra*. At this point, through a delicately timed mechanism, they are mixed with the seminal fluid which is being ejaculated. At this time the sperms become active [Oliven, 1965; Odell and Moyer, 1971] owing to the acid-neutralizing effect of the prostatic secretion [Guyton, 1971].

Seminal fluid is ejaculated during sexual intercourse. It may also be discharged during masturbation and periodically is discharged spontaneously during sleep, as mentioned in an earlier chapter.

Sperms are produced in prodigious numbers. It has been estimated that during his lifetime an average human male produces about a trillion sperms [Hartman, 1962]. Such an estimate is of necessity a broad and only loosely accurate generalization. But it does serve to dramatize the number of sperms. Counting at the rate of five per second and continuously with no break at all, it would take more than 5,000 years to count the sperms produced by one man. In a single ejaculation of seminal fluid (about a teaspoonful) there may be hundreds of millions of sperms. Yet, compressed together, they would occupy a space equivalent in size only to the head of a pin. In a single ejaculation, then, there are often more than enough sperms, if every one were used, to produce a population larger than that of the United States.

Once discharged, the sperms move in all directions and diffuse through the vagina. Ordinarily some pass into the uterus, but by what specific means this is brought about is not yet fully known. Various explanations have been suggested, but all rest upon hypotheses that are as yet unproved. It has been said both that the sperms swim against currents and that they are carried along by currents. If there were some subtle attraction exerted by the ovum, sperms would not enter the uterus when there was no ovum to be fertilized; yet this is known to occur. It has been suggested that electrical charges orient the sperms toward the cervix. It has also been suggested that some of the seminal fluid is ejaculated directly into the uterus. There is no conclusive evidence to prove that there is suction produced by the opening and closing of the cervix during orgasm, as some suggest, though later contractions of the muscular walls of the uterus and tubes may play a part. In fact, conception can take place as a result of rape or in cases in which no orgasm occurs. It is hypothetically possible that some sperms may be forced into the uterus through the movements of the genital organs in sexual intercourse.

How long sperms live after leaving the male body is still unproved. Assuming that there are no unusual conditions, estimates as to the life of the sperms within the female genital tract vary. The period during which they remain effective is relatively brief, probably not more than twenty-four to forty-eight hours.

The Production of Ova

Ova are produced in the *ovaries,* two oval-shaped organs 1 to 2 inches long siutated on either side of the *uterus.* [See Figure 10.4 for a diagrammatic representation of female genital anatomy.] Formation of ova occurs only in prenatal life. Before birth most of them degenerate and the total number is very much reduced. It has been estimated that there are about a half million immature ova in the ovaries of a newborn female infant. By puberty this number has been greatly reduced. Fewer than 400 are ovulated during a typical woman's reproductive life. There is no evidence that new ova are formed after birth as is sometimes assumed [Baker, August, 1964; Arrata and Iffy, October, 1971].

Ordinarily, ova mature and are released from the ovary one at a time in response to hormones produced by the pituitary gland. The *follicle-stimulating hormone* (*FSH*) causes the formation of the *Graafian follicle,* a blisterlike prominence about 3/4 inch in diameter which is filled with fluid and eventually bulges out the surface tissue of the ovary. The follicle secrets a hormone (*estrogen*) which brings about preliminary changes in the uterus in the process of that organ's preparation for the reception of a zygote. At length, in response to FSH plus the *luteinizing hormone* (*LH*), also produced by the pituitary gland, the follicle bursts and the ovum is discharged. This release of the ovum is termed *ovulation,* and on the average occurs once in twenty-eight days.

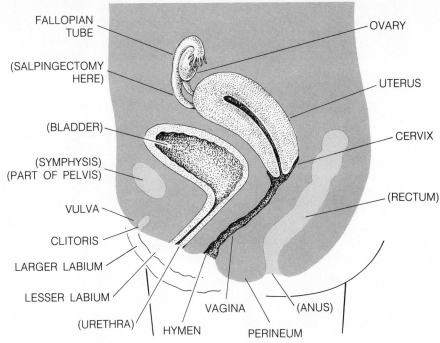

Figure 10.4   Female genital organs. Names in parentheses do not indicate genital organs.

After ovulation, the lining cells of the Graafian follicle undergo change and form the *corpus luteum* (yellow body), which secretes another hormone (*progesterone*) which, together with the estrogen, carries still further the preparation of the uterus for pregnancy. If pregnancy occurs, the progesterone and estrogen secreted by the corpus luteum hold the uterus in a condition favorable to sustaining it until this function can be taken over by a hormone secreted by the placenta. Eventually the corpus luteum degenerates, leaving a small scar on the surface of the ovary. This also occurs in the menstrual cycle, which will be discussed later.

After the ovum leaves the ovary, its life is subject to as much conjecture as is the life of sperms. Probably its effective life, the period during which it may be fertilized, is not more than a few hours, the probable maximum being twenty-four. The ends of the tubes in close conjunction with, but not directly connected to, the ovaries divide into fringelike projections (*fimbriae*) which, at the time of ovulation, are activated to come into even closer contact than usual with the ovary. There is also evidence to suggest that the muscles in the wall of the tube may contract and relax, developing suction similar to that in a bellows, and that by this suction the ovum is drawn into the tube [Engle, 1952]. Both the fimbriae and the interior surface of the tubes are lined with tiny hairlike protuberances (*cilia*) which have the capacity to move with a whiplike motion. They move more vigorously toward the uterus than toward the ovaries on the return stroke. Thus a

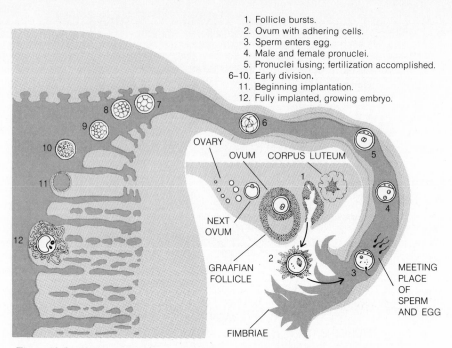

1. Follicle bursts.
2. Ovum with adhering cells.
3. Sperm enters egg.
4. Male and female pronuclei.
5. Pronuclei fusing; fertilization accomplished.
6–10. Early division.
11. Beginning implantation.
12. Fully implanted, growing embryo.

OVARY

OVUM   CORPUS LUTEUM

NEXT
OVUM

GRAAFIAN
FOLLICLE

FIMBRIAE

MEETING
PLACE
OF
SPERM
AND EGG

Figure 10.5   The journey of the ovum (enlarged) from ovulation to implantation.

current is set up. The ovum, which has been released from the ovary, is drawn into the tube near which it has been released and starts its migration toward the uterus. The passage through the tube has a diameter only about as large as a broom straw, but that is ample for the movement of the egg. [See Figure 10.5.]

The ovum is moved along also by tubal peristalsis, that is, waves of muscular contraction in the tube [Greenhill, 1960; Kistner, 1964]. One may envisage the process of tubal peristalsis by imagining a marble in a rubber hose. By pressing the walls of the hose with one's fingers at the back of the marble and sliding the fingers along, one may move the marble. The entire journey from ovary to uterus requires a period of about six to seven days. Unless it has been fertilized, the effective life of the ovum will have ceased before it has reached its destination.

Fertilization

Fertilization is the union of sperm and ovum. It ordinarily takes place in one of the fallopian tubes. Sperms are usually deposited in the vagina near the relatively small entrance to the uterus (external *os* in the *cervix*, that is, the small end of the uterus). They immediately begin to swim in all directions in the vagina. Some pass into the uterus and into the tubes, but, as mentioned earlier, by what specific means this is brought about is not fully known. In one deposit of seminal fluid, even though it may contain several hundred million sperms, many will never enter the uterus. Of those that do, many will enter the wrong tube. Many are likely to be defective, to die shortly after being deposited, or for some other reason to make little or no progress in the direction of the ovum. Only relatively few will actually reach the egg. It has been estimated that, of the millions of sperms deposited in the vagina, fewer than 100 will reach the site of fertilization, a reduction of 99.99 per cent [Odell and Moyer, 1971]. Hence, typically, a large number of sperms must be deposited for fertilization to occur. It used to be assumed that, since the ovum as released from the ovary is surrounded by cumulus cells from the follicle (that is, cells from the lining of the follicle which cling to it), a large number of sperms had to reach the ovum and produce sufficient enzyme to digest away enough cells so that one sperm could reach the ovum proper. Now the pendulum has swung in the opposite direction, to the view that a single sperm carries enough enzyme to make a path for itself in reaching the ovum [Blandau, 1961].

When a sperm meets the ovum, its head penetrates the latter's outer wall, and its nucleus fuses with the nucleus of the egg, reestablishing the twenty-three pairs of chromosomes. After one sperm has penetrated the ovum, ordinarily other sperms are prevented from doing so. Since the life span of both the sperms and the ovum is relatively brief, it is obvious that, for fertilization to occur, the sperms must be deposited very near the time of ovulation. At the time of fertilization the new individual's sex and hereditary traits are determined. After fertilization the zygote continues its journey through the tube to the uterus, in the wall of which it implants itself. *Implantation* is also referred to as *nidation*.

Conception occurs through *insemination* (entrance of sperms into the female genital tract). Insemination may be by natural means or by artificial (mechanical) methods in those instances in which natural means fail or there is need for special control. Artificial insemination will be discussed later.

Parthenogenesis This is the process by which an ovum develops without fertilization. It is known to occur naturally among some lower animals and has been brought about experimentally with some such animals. There is no authenticated instance of human parthenogenesis [Ashley, 1962]. How, then, may reports of "parthenogenesis" be explained? For example, a newspaper headline reads, "VIRGIN BIRTH" REPORTED "CONFIRMED" IN ENGLAND.

Parthenogenesis might be erroneously presumed in a case of pregnancy following incomplete intercourse and due to sperms in the preejaculate, a secretion preceding ejaculation. There is also another possibility of erroneous assumption. If conditions of moisture, temperature, acidity-alkalinity, location of the ovum in the tube, and number and vigor of sperms were unusually favorable, sperms contained in seminal fluid deposited at the external entrance to the vagina (for example, in "heavy petting" which was just short of intercourse) might swim past an intact hymen, through the vagina and uterus, and into the tube. Or sperms might be propelled past the hymen and into the vagina by the force of ejaculation. Under such circumstances fertilization could occur in a woman still technically virgin because the penis had never penetrated the vagina in sexual intercourse and the hymen, therefore, remained unaltered [Friedman, 1962;

Greenhill, 1965a; Oliven, 1965; Masters and Johnson, 1966; Neubardt, 1967; Stone and Stone, 1970; Kistner, 1969a; Sjövall, 1970; Glass and Kase, 1970]. In one case reported to the author by the attending obstetrician (Dr. Georgia Legett), a woman having an intact hymen with two small openings (as in Figure 9.1c), neither large enough for intercourse to have occurred, had to have the hymen cut before she could be delivered of a full-term baby. Occasionally a case is reported in which a physician is convinced, but, of course, cannot prove, not only that the above occurred but also that the sperms passed through the fabric of underclothing. Such a case is reported by Golden [May, 1971]. The woman was on her honeymoon when pregnancy was diagnosed. On examination the hymen was found to be thick and intact with a very small opening. She admitted to having done some "heavy petting" before marriage but insisted that she had never removed her panties. She had felt moisture at times but did not understand where it came from. In fact, though a college graduate, she admitted that she did not even understand sexual intercourse. This case was "substantiated by surgical photographs."

Development of the Fetus

After fertilization, the zygote continues its migration through the tube to the uterus, a journey requiring six to seven days, as mentioned earlier. By the time it reaches the uterus, it has already divided into some 200 cells [Odell and Moyer, 1971]. When it reaches the uterus, it remains free for a period. Then, after several days, it embeds itself in the wall of the uterus, which, through hormone action, has been prepared for its arrival. This process of implantation is accomplished through corrosive action, the zygote dissolving the tissues of the uterine wall and burying itself. In this process the zygote literally digests some of its mother's tissue as food.

As the cells of the zygote continue to multiply, some become specialized to form the *placenta,* the roots, so to speak, through which the fetus receives its food and oxygen. These will be described later. Other cells form the *umbilical cord,* the *amnion,* and the *fetus* proper. Many students have difficulty in visualizing this process because they think of the placenta and the cord (also the amnion) as being part of the mother. Fetus, cord, and placenta make up one unit (see Figure 10.9, p. 362). They develop from the zygote in much the same manner as the leaves and branches, trunk and roots of a plant develop from a seed, though, strictly speaking, there are important differences between a zygote and a seed.

Let us carry further the comparison of the zygote to a seed, a comparison which must be made with caution. The most favorable place for a seed to grow is in a specially prepared garden plot. But a seed can grow, at least for a while, anywhere that its roots can find nutriment—the lawn next to the garden plot, a crack in a walk, or a pile of debris. Similarly, the most favorable place for the zygote to grow is in the uterus. But it can grow, at least for a while, anywhere that its "roots" can find food, water, and oxygen. The most common nonuterine location of growth is in one of the fallopian tubes. A tubal pregnancy is one form of *ectopic* pregnancy. Other forms are rare but do occur. In some cases, for example, the ovum is fertilized before it reaches the tube [Berlind, July, 1960], even before it leaves the ovary in occasional instances [Kistner, 1964; Greenhill, 1965a], or a tubal pregnancy ruptures but the embryo does not die and continues to develop outside the uterus in the abdominal cavity. In such cases, the placenta may be attached to the ovary, the outside of the uterus, ligaments, or other abdominal organs. "Abdominal" pregnancies rarely continue to full term, but instances have been known. In these, of course, the child must be delivered by Caesarean section. The purpose of this discussion is not to emphasize ectopic pregnancy. But often the unusual highlights the usual, and these infrequent cases of extrauterine pregnancy highlight the fact that fetus, placenta, and cord constitute a unit and are all "baby."

Prenatal development extends through approximately nine calendar months. During this period the following changes occur. Figures and stages mentioned represent averages. Allowance must be made for variation in individual cases. [See Figure 10.6 for early stages of development.]

End of first month By the end of the first month the embryo is about 1/4 inch long. It weighs only a small fraction of an ounce. Many organs have begun to form, but the embryo does not look human. At this early stage, only an expert could distinguish a human embryo from that of a lower animal. Blood has begun to form. What will develop into the heart has already begun to pulsate.

End of second month The embryo is now about 1¼ inches long. It now weighs about 1/14 ounce. The organs have continued their development, and some have assumed their permanent functions. Budlike projections that will form the limbs are noticeable, but fingers and toes are not yet completely formed. The tail has shrunk and will soon disappear, except for a few bones at the lower end of the spine (*coccyx*), which are embedded in other tissue. The face begins to look more

Figure 10.6 Early development of embryo and fetus.

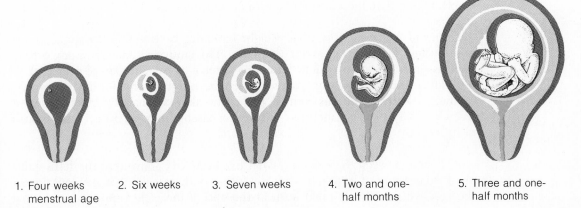

1. Four weeks menstrual age

2. Six weeks

3. Seven weeks

4. Two and one-half months

5. Three and one-half months

nearly human. The embryo may move slightly, but this movement is not detectable by the mother or her obstetrician. Genital organs have appeared and, if the embryo is aborted and carefully examined, the sex may be ascertained. After the second month the new individual is termed a *fetus* rather than an embryo.

End of third month   The fetus now weighs about an ounce and is approximately 3 inches long. Arms, legs, hands, fingers, toes, and ears are formed. Nails have begun to form. The fetus appears definitely human, but the head is very large in proportion to the rest of the body. Teeth have begun to develop in sockets in the jawbones. Vocal cords are formed.

End of fourth month   The weight is now 5 to 6 ounces, and the length is 6 to 8 inches. This latter represents about one-third the height at birth. The head is still disproportionately large. The heartbeat is audible through a stethoscope. Limb movements may sometimes be felt by the mother. The body of the fetus is covered with a downlike coat (*lanugo*), which in most cases disappears during the eighth or ninth month. Eyebrows and eyelashes have appeared. The skin is somewhat transparent. The skin ridges, which in later life will make fingerprints possible, have already formed.

End of fifth month   The fetus now weighs about 1 pound and is 10 to 12 inches long. Nails are well formed. Head hair has appeared. A mixture of fatty secretion and dead skin cells forms a cheesy covering (*vernix caseosa*) on the surface of the body. Fetal movements may be clearly felt by the mother. If born at this time, the fetus will survive only a few moments at best.

End of sixth month   The weight is about 2 pounds and the length about 14 inches. The child may live for a few hours if born at this time but has only an extremely slight chance of survival.

End of seventh month   The weight has increased to about 3 pounds and the length to about 16 inches. A child born at this time has a fair chance of survival.

Eighth and ninth months   The weight increases by this time to about 7 or 8 pounds and the length to about 20 inches. The lanugo disappears. Body organs have assumed their permanent functions in most cases. The skin of white babies is reddish and the eyes are bluish in color, but their final tone cannot be predicted. Fatty tissue has formed under the skin, so that the fetus looks less wrinkled than in earlier months. The vernix caseosa may persist even until birth at full term.

It may be seen by reviewing what has been said above that the fetus gains about 80 per cent of its weight after the fifth month and about 50 per cent during the last two months. A child born at the end of the eighth month has a good chance of survival, much better than at the end of the seventh month, in spite of the common belief to the contrary. In fact the closer to full term (nine months) the birth occurs, the better are the chances of the child's living.

During a good part of prenatal life the fetus goes through processes similar to those through which it will go after birth. It moves its limbs. It swallows amniotic fluid, about 1 pint per day near term [Pritchard, March, 1965], which is then absorbed through the walls of the digestive tract much as food and water will be later. It takes shallow "breaths," drawing small amounts of amniotic fluid into the lungs. It excretes small amounts of urine. It has alternate periods of activity and rest and may even wake and sleep as it does after birth. It responds to sounds [Ferreira, 1969] and to pressure, for example, on the mother's abdomen. A remarkable photograph by Lennart Nilsson [Tanner and Taylor, 1965; *Life*, Apr. 30, 1965] even shows a 4½-month fetus apparently sucking its thumb.

Duration of Pregnancy

Pregnancy usually lasts 266 to 270 days (about forty weeks, nine calendar months). Conception cannot occur unless there is an ovum to be fertilized. Thus conception usually occurs somewhere in the middle of the menstrual cycle. This point will be discussed more fully later. It is impossible to ascertain the exact date of fertilization, even though the exact date of fruitful insemination is known, since time is required for the sperm to reach the egg. A variation of a few days in the length of pregnancy is neither unusual nor abnormal. It is, therefore, impossible to forecast the exact date of the child's birth.

A physician who promises delivery on a predetermined date because he plans to go on his vacation or because the couple want the child born on a holiday, or for some similar reason, is either misleading the couple or planning to resort to induced labor. The latter is not considered by some physicians to be the best obstetrical practice when there is no acceptable medical indication for it [Greenhill, 1965a, 1966; Taylor, August, 1969; Hatch, Feb. 15, 1969]. "We are still a long way from 'elective delivery'" [Donald, 1964].

The nine-month period is considered full term. Delivery of the child after seven months of prenatal development (that is, during the eighth or ninth month) is considered premature. Ordinarily any child born before term or weighing less than 5½ pounds is considered premature. Earlier delivery is termed *abortion*. The term *miscarriage* is commonly applied to spontaneous abortion.

Not uncommonly there are reports of unusually long pregnancies. A pregnancy can continue for a relatively brief period beyond the typical 266 to 270 days. But this overtime period cannot ordinarily be extended for very long, because the placenta begins to degenerate [Greenhill, 1961]. Reports of unusually long pregnancies are subject to errors of calculation. For example, a woman has a baby eleven months after her last menstrual period. She assumes an eleven-month pregnancy. Actually she had a normal nine-month pregnancy preceded by two months of amenorrhea.

Fetal Protection and Food and Oxygen Supply

As the fetus grows, the uterus enlarges to accommodate it, growing and expanding from a small, pear-shaped organ about 3 inches long and weighing about 2 ounces to an oval organ about 15 inches long and weighing about 2 pounds. Fitting snugly against the inside surface there develop several membranes. The one that will concern us is the *amnion*, which, like the placenta and umbilical cord, arises from the zygote and is thus part of the fetus rather than part of the mother. What is left of the amnion after delivery is expelled with the placenta and cord as afterbirth. Inside the amnion are 1 to 4 pints of amniotic fluid. In this fluid the fetus is suspended. At first it floats about, anchored by the placenta and cord. As it increases in size it fits more snugly inside the uterus [see Figure 10.7].

Earlier in this chapter it was stated that when the zygote implants itself in the wall of the uterus, it continues to divide, and some of the cells form "roots," so to speak. These "roots" multiply, eventually forming the placenta, a disk-shaped organ which when fully developed is 7 to 9 inches in diameter, is about 1 inch thick in the middle, and weighs about 1 pound. Strictly speaking there is a maternal as well as a fetal portion to the placenta, namely, the changed tissue of the uterus at the site of attachment (*decidua basalis*). But for our purpose we shall consider the placenta only as being part of the fetus. On the side in contact with the uterine wall, the placenta is covered with thousands of rootlike projections (*villi*), which branch out in all directions and ramify through the tissue of the uterus [see Figure 10.8]. The area of a smooth disk 9 inches in diameter is approximately 64 square inches. The branching and rebranching of the villi increase the area of the uterine side of the placenta to some 70 square feet, about four times the skin area of an adult [Schumann, 1936]—a fact that is important

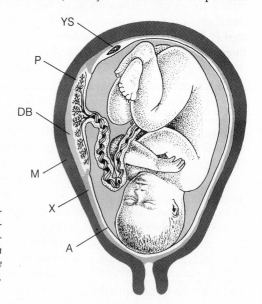

Figure 10.7 Full-term fetus in uterus. Abbreviations: YS, yolk sac; P, placenta; DB, decidua basalis (the portion of the endometrium—that is, the lining of the uterus—to which the placenta is attached); X, decidua vera (the remaining portion of the endometrium); M, muscular wall of the uterus; A, amnion.

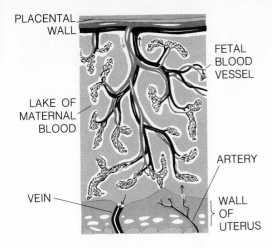

PLACENTAL WALL

FETAL BLOOD VESSEL

LAKE OF MATERNAL BLOOD

ARTERY

VEIN

WALL OF UTERUS

Figure 10.8 Highly magnified, diagrammatic representation of placental villi.

when we consider that this means 70 square feet of absorption surface for food, water, and oxygen.

The villi are loops of blood vessels. These converge to form several large vessels (two arteries and one vein), which extend through the umbilical cord to the fetus. The cord is about 2 feet long and ½ inch in diameter. It is twisted into a spiral by the uneven growth of the blood vessels and the movements of the fetus.

There is no direct connection between the blood stream of the mother and that of the fetus. The fetus manufactures all its own blood; it gets none from its mother. Its circulatory system is a "closed circuit." The villi protrude into the *lacunae* ("lakes" of blood in the wall of the uterus). All food material that reaches the fetus must pass through the membranes of the villi. The process may be compared to the absorption of water through the roots of a plant in an ivy bowl [see Figure 10.9]. Waste products pass in the opposite direction and enter the mother's blood stream through the membranes of the villi. The actual process of food's passing through the membranes is not difficult to understand when one stops to realize that all food passing into his own blood stream must be in solution and pass through the membranes of his intestinal tract and his own blood vessels, since there is no direct, open-ended connection between blood vessels and intestines. Oxygen is absorbed from the mother's blood just as food is. One writer [Barron, 1960] refers to the placenta as the "fetal lung." Thus the fetus can live without breathing.

The fetus lives in a controlled environment, and relatively little that occurs in the outside world seriously affects it. Temperature is controlled by the mother's body temperature. Food and water are filtered through the membranes of the villi. The amniotic fluid distributes pressure evenly over the body of the fetus and, in so doing, acts as a shock absorber and renders the fetus virtually "weightless." The fluid also acts as lubrication between the fetus and the membranes of the uterus, assuring the fetus unimpeded motility [Ostergard, April, 1970]. Most disease germs are filtered out by the membranes of the villi. Only relatively few bacteria can pass from mother to child, and these not in every case. The

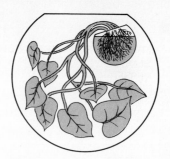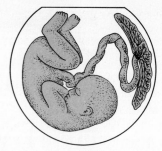

Figure 10.9 Fetus, cord, and placenta compared to a plant. [Adapted from a sculptured birth series by Dickinson and Belskie in "Birth Atlas," Maternity Center Association, New York.]

organisms producing syphilis and tuberculosis do sometimes penetrate the defenses.

Viruses can pass from mother to fetus through the placenta. In a study of 1,915 cases of mumps, measles, polio, and other viral disease, Kaye and Reaney [May, 1962] found abnormalities in the babies in 86 cases (4.5 per cent) and abortion in 115 cases (6 per cent). In a study of 94 cases of mumps, Hyatt [May, 1961] found that 15 per cent of the babies were aborted or stillborn and that 16 per cent had congenital defects. The virus causing smallpox can affect the fetus [Villee, 1960]. The fetus is much more vulnerable to such diseases during the first trimester (three months) of pregnancy. After that the disease is unlikely to cause damage unless, of course, it precipitates spontaneous abortion or premature delivery.

In recent years *rubella* ("German measles"), a viral infection, has come into prominence as a cause of fetal abnormalities. If the mother has rubella during the first trimester of pregnancy, there is a chance that her baby will be affected. If she has it during the first two months, the chance is greatly increased. If she has it after the third month, the chance is markedly decreased. The most common consequences of rubella are fetal death, deafness, cataracts, heart conditions, and mental deficiency caused by damage to the central nervous system [Mayes, 1963]. Because of shortcomings in the method of investigating this problem, earlier reports suggested that the chances that the child would be defective were about nine in ten. As a result, many physicians advised therapeutic abortion. Now it appears that a woman's chances of bearing a normal baby are about nine in ten. In other words, generalizing broadly and keeping in mind the increased risk if rubella is contracted during the first two months of pregnancy, the situation is the reverse of what it was originally assumed to be. As a result, some physicians are now reluctant to recommend therapeutic abortion, unless there is good reason to assume that the fetus has been affected.

A vaccine for the prevention of rubella became commercially available early in 1969. Since that time millions of people have been vaccinated, especially children between the age of one year and puberty. Women of childbearing age may safely be given the vaccine, but it is very important to avoid administering it shortly before or during pregnancy, since the vaccine may be hazardous to the fetus [Meyer and Parkman, Jan. 25, 1971; Chin, Ebbin, Wilson, and Linnette, Jan. 25, 1971; Maeck and Phillips, Feb. 15, 1972]. "The main hope for the future lies in the active immunisation of non-immune adolescent girls with the rubella vaccine" [Smithells, 1971].

In rare cases fetuses have been affected when the mother was vaccinated for smallpox during pregnancy [Bourke and Whitty, June 13, 1964], especially if the woman was previously unvaccinated [Moloshok, September, 1966]. There is evidence to indicate that a female fetus may be masculinized by hormones administered to the mother during pregnancy [Greenhill, 1960]. Too much anesthesia during childbirth may cause the reactions of the fetus to be depressed to the point where breathing is affected. Narcotic drugs may pass through the placenta to the fetus. A large proportion of the babies of female narcotic addicts are born addicted and experience withdrawal symptoms; their birth weight is low and their death rate high [Stone, Salerno, Green, and Zelson, Mar. 1, 1971; Zelson, Rubio, and Wasserman, August, 1971]. Thalidomide, a synthetic drug used as a sedative, tranquilizer, and sleeping medication, caused several thousand cases of severe malformation (*phocomelia*, a condition in which arms and/or legs are malformed or absent) before it was discovered to be the causative agent and was subjected to control [Greenhill, 1962a; Taussig, June 30, 1962].

There is a growing body of evidence to the effect that babies of mothers who smoke during pregnancy have a lower birth weight and a higher rate of prematurity and are therefore at greater risk than the babies of nonsmoking mothers [Savel and Roth, September, 1962; Gillespie, September, 1964; Donnelly, September, 1964; McDonald and Lanford, October, 1965; Peterson, Morese, and Kaltreider, December, 1965; Illsley, 1967; Underwood, Kesler, O'Lane, and Callagan, January, 1967; Murphy and Mulcahy, Sept. 1, 1971; Comstock, Shah, Meyer, and Abbey, Sept. 1, 1971; Ochsner, November, 1971; Surgeon General, 1972, 1971; Butler, Goldstein, and Ross, Apr. 15, 1972].

In spite of reports such as these and others like them, the evidence is not universally accepted. In one study, the babies of women who never smoked, those born during the period that the mothers smoked, those born before the mothers started to smoke, and those born after the mothers quit smoking were compared. The conclusion reached was that the higher incidence of low-birth-weight babies was due not to the smoking but to the smoker [Yerushalmy, Jan. 15, 1972]. In the light of such reports, the need for further research is obvious, and the importance of the individual woman's checking with her obstetrician and following his suggestions is clear.

Alcoholic beverages, when used in moderation, appear to have no effect on the fetus [Speert and Guttmacher, 1956]. Alcohol used to excess, however, may have a depressant effect unfavorable to the fetus's normal functioning after birth.

If the maternal blood does not afford the fetus the food materials he requires, parasite that he is, he will "eat" his mother. Not that he literally ingests her, but he will draw upon her tissues for his own growth. However, it is not true, as some persons believe, that a woman must lose "a tooth for every child" [Hytten and Thomson, 1970]. The fetus does not take calcium from the mother's teeth. Besides, the woman may regulate her diet so that the child is supplied with the food, salts, calcium, and other substances that he needs.

There is a relationship between the quality of a woman's diet and the health of her baby. The relationship between the amount of food she eats and the size of her baby is not so clear, although there is evidence that there is a positive association between the mother's weight gain and the baby's birth weight. There is also a positive association between the mother's prepregnancy height and weight and the baby's size. According to the Committee on Maternal Health, Food and Nutrition Board [1970], "taller, heavier mothers have larger babies than smaller, lighter mothers." If a woman overeats because she believes she must "eat for two," the excess is likely to be stored as fat in her own body rather than simply transferred to the baby. On the other hand, she cannot keep the weight of the baby down, presumably to make delivery easier, merely by reducing the quantity of food consumed—unless she reduces it to the point of starvation [Bourne and Williams, 1953; Comm. Matern. Health Food Nutr. Bd., 1970]. Generalizing, we may say that the size of the baby is determined by heredity (structure of mother), duration of pregnancy, possibly to some extent by the mother's food intake [Page, Villee, and Villee, 1972], and perhaps by the development of the placenta, although this last item is being increasingly questioned. There may be other factors involved, such as the biochemistry and circulation of the mother's blood, and the effects of these on infant size are beginning to be suspected.

One may readily understand why a woman gains weight during pregnancy. There is a tendency for fat to be deposited. The breasts enlarge, preparatory to supplying the baby with food. Her blood volume increases by 20 to 40 per cent, adding about 2 to 3 pounds, and there is some retention of water in body tissues [Ferreira, 1969; Hytten and Thomson, 1970]. The fully developed placenta weighs 1 to 2 pounds, the enlarged uterus about 2, the amniotic fluid 1 to 4, and the child itself, when it has reached full term, 7 to 8.

Maternal Impressions

Can the baby be affected by what the mother does, sees, or thinks during pregnancy? There is a common belief that it can. The following "instances" of maternal impressions are typical. As is common during pregnancy, a woman developed a craving for a particular food, in this case, cherries. At the market she found that cherries were unavailable, because out of season, and therefore she could not buy any. When the baby was born it had a growth "just like a cherry" on its upper lip. A woman was chopping wood, holding a small ax in her right hand. The ax slipped and cut her left hand. She grasped her left hand with her right one to stop the bleeding. When her baby was born it had no fingers on its left hand.

What happens in cases of "observed" maternal impressions and birthmarks is probably this: A child is born with some particular trait. The mother wonders about the trait and seeks for an explanation. During her nine-month pregnancy she is almost certain to have had some experience into which she can read what she thinks should be there. Then by turning the situation around she has an "explanation" of the trait. If the child has no birthmark, no explanation is required, and so the woman's experiences during pregnancy are not recalled.

There are some investigators, however, who interpret research data as indicating that a woman's emotional state during pregnancy can affect the development of the fetus and its behavior after birth [Ferreira, 1969]. Other investigators are not convinced. At best it is difficult to separate the effect of the woman's experiences from the effect of hereditary factors and immediately postnatal factors; that is, a woman with a given physiological and psychological makeup has both the experiences and the baby.

Sex Determination

The sex of the fetus is determined by the combination of chromosomes in the zygote. Other factors may play a role in some cases, as discussed in an earlier chapter, in causing the individual to shift from one side of the sexual fence to the other or to fall into an equivocal position somewhere between maleness and femaleness. Nevertheless, at the moment of fertilization the pattern is usually set.

With regard to the chromosomes of sex determination, all ova are alike; they all bear an X chromosome. Sperms bear either an X or a Y chromosome. When in the process of fertilization an XX combination is produced, the individual develops into a female. An XY combination produces a male. On the X and Y chromosomes there are genes other than those determining sex. The Y chromosome, however, is smaller than the X and contains fewer of these than the corresponding X chromosome. Therefore, in the male certain traits are the result of the action of one gene alone, while in the female these traits are the result of two genes acting together. Hence, some traits tend to be sex-linked and occur much more frequently in males than in females.

Sex determination in the genetic sense is not the same as ascertaining the sex of the fetus. Guttmacher [1933] mentions a number of supposed "tests" used for this purpose. According to these "tests," if the baby kicks on the mother's right side, it will be a boy; if it kicks on her left side, it will be a girl. A boy is "carried high"; a girl is "carried low." Loss of hair by the mother indicates a girl; more profuse hair growth, a boy. A boy is more active than a girl. If the mother develops a preference for sweet foods, the baby will be a girl; a preference for sour foods indicates a boy. Boys are believed to cause more nausea. As Guttmacher points out, all such "tests" are without foundation in fact.

It is interesting to note how such "tests" reflect traditional attitudes toward the sexes, as do standards of behavior as mentioned in Chapter 1. A male baby presumably kicks on the right side and is carried high (superior status), is more active and causes the mother to have more nausea and a taste for sour foods (aggressive and troublesome). A female baby, on the other hand, presumably kicks on the left side and is carried low (inferior status), is less active and causes the mother to have less nausea and a taste for sweet foods (submissive and agreeable).

Until recently there was no accurate means of ascertaining the sex of the fetus in the uterus. The difference between male and female heartbeat is not reliable, since there is so much overlapping. This is true also of fetal size. If the fetus is aborted after the first six or so weeks of pregnancy, sex may be ascertained, but such a fetus, of course, dies. Before the end of six weeks of pregnancy the cells that will form the gonads (testes or ovaries) are undifferentiated, and the genital organs exhibit the same development in both sexes; hence the sex of the fetus cannot be ascertained by examining these organs.

It is now known that in the somatic cells of the female there is usually a dark mass (*sex chromatin* or *Barr body*) that is usually not present in the cells of the male. The presence or absence of this mass may be established through microscopic examination by the end of the second week of embryonic life. But, of course, no such examination could be made at this early stage unless the fetus were aborted. During prenatal development, fetal skin cells flake off and remain in the amniotic fluid. By midpregnancy such cells may be examined by withdrawing a small quantity of amniotic fluid from the uterus by means of a hypodermic needlelike instrument which is introduced into the uterus through the abdominal wall. This procedure is termed *amniocentesis*. It is relatively safe, but not completely without risk, and is not always successful [Hutchinson, 1967; Papp, Gardo, Herpay, and Arvay, September, 1970]. Another method of ascertaining the sex of the fetus, also dependent upon amniocentesis, is the examination of cells taken from the amniotic fluid, stained, and examined microscopically under ultraviolet light. Y chromosomes appear fluorescent; X chromosomes do not [Cervenka, Gorlin, and Bendel, June, 1971; Khudr and Benirschke, Aug. 15, 1971; Valenti, Lin, Baum, Massobrio, and Carbonara, Apr. 1, 1972]. There are sometimes medical reasons for which it is important to ascertain the sex of the fetus. The procedure is out of proportion to what is learned just to satisfy parental curiosity, and the end would hardly justify the means.

Means for controlling the sex of the child are as fantastic as some of the "tests." GIRL IS BORN IN ACID TEST TO FIX SEX, reads a newspaper headline. The article goes on to say that the use of an acid douche will ensure the birth of a girl; an alkaline douche, the birth of a boy. A theory expounded in some quarters holds that, if the wife is "dominant," the child will be a girl; if the husband is "dominant," the child will be a boy. Another theory states it a bit differently, holding that the sex of the child is dependent upon the degree of masculinity and femininity in both persons. Such theories have no basis in fact. At the present stage of scientific knowledge there is no practical means by which the sex of the child may be controlled.

SIGNS OF PREGNANCY

When a woman has reason to believe that she may be pregnant, she wants to know the facts as soon as possible so that she may plan accordingly. There are several types of symptoms that may aid in diagnosing her condition. These are termed *presumptive* and *positive* signs. Disregarding for the moment the conditions that make tests for pregnancy possible, the relationship between mother and baby may be dramatized by pointing out that the presumptive signs of pregnancy are exhibited by the mother, while positive signs are exhibited by the fetus.

There are cases of "false pregnancy" (*pseudocyesis*) in which hormonal factors or emotional factors, such as a great desire for a baby or a deep fear of having one [McDonald, March-April, 1968], cause a woman to exhibit signs of pregnancy when she is not pregnant at all [Greenhill, 1965a; Israel, 1967]. Such signs may include menstrual disturbances, abdominal enlargement, breast changes, softening of the cervix, nausea, weight gain, and "movements of the fetus" as "felt" by the woman [Brown and Barglow, March, 1971]. In one case symptoms of pregnancy appeared after the woman had had a hysterectomy (surgical removal of the uterus) [Greaves, Green, and West, 1960]. In an even more unusual case, a thirty-three-year-old male with developing schizophrenia and messianic yearnings was convinced that he was pregnant and showed signs of pregnancy, namely, distention of the abdomen, morning nausea, and "felt" movements of the fetus. Examination uncovered no physiological illness or pathological condition. His symptoms disappeared after psychiatric treatment [Knight, March, 1971]. Husbands sometimes exhibit symptoms of pregnancy, such as morning nausea, when their wives are pregnant but ordinarily do not believe themselves pregnant as in the case mentioned above [Trethowan, November, 1972].

If a woman can exhibit signs of pregnancy when she is not pregnant, can the reverse also be true: Can she be pregnant and not know it? Of course, no woman can know that she is pregnant immediately after the pregnancy begins. Apparently some women go to term and are not aware that they are pregnant until labor starts. At least there are reports of and by such women. In such cases, of course, the only evidence of the woman's unawareness is her own statement. If, however, a woman were subject to long periods of amenorrhea, if she were very obese so that abdominal enlargement would not show or would appear to be "more of the same," if for neurotic reasons she would "shut out" the signs of pregnancy, if she were unusually imperceptive, or if some other similar condition existed, she could be pregnant and not know it. Cases do come to one's attention through newspaper reports or personal experience. For example, in one case coming to the author's attention, after the birth of her baby, a university co-ed and her husband both insisted that they had not known that she was pregnant. She visited the university health center because of abdominal cramps and was astounded and disbelieving when the physician informed her that she was in labor. On the way to her room in the hospital she remonstrated with the nurse, saying, "This is ridiculous." But she soon had about six pounds of proof that the physician's diagnosis was correct.

Presumptive Signs

Temporary cessation of menstruation   This is one of the first signs noticeable, but it is not reliable, since factors other than pregnancy (for example, illness, tumors, nervous shock, experience highly colored with emotion, change of climate, even going to college) may interrupt the menstrual cycle. Worry about possible pregnancy may cause menstruation to be delayed or cause a period or two to be missed. Some women are so irregular that an occasional rather long delay is not unusual.

If for some reason implantation is delayed or the ovary continues to function or some other unusual condition occurs, a woman may have what appears to be menstruation after fertilization takes place [Arrata and Iffy, October, 1971]. When this occurs, the flow is usually scanty. In some instances, bleeding due to other factors is mistaken for menstruation.

Morning sickness   About half of pregnant women have some degree of nausea in the morning. In many of these the symptoms are mild. In only a few are the symptoms severe [Greenhill, 1965a]. Morning sickness may be relieved by medication and usually disappears by the end of the third month. Some cases are due to physiological changes, but there is reason to believe that others are the result of suggestion or emotional disturbance. If a woman has heard that illness accompanies pregnancy, she may expect it and have her expectations fulfilled through the machinations of her mind. If she fears or resists pregnancy, that too may contribute to her illness.

Increased frequency of urination   This is due to congestion in certain blood vessels.

Increased vaginal secretion   This is especially noticeable in women who have previously had considerable vaginal discharge.

Changes in the breasts   Slight pain, a sense of fullness, increased size of nipples, increased pigmentation around the nipples, secretion of a fluid termed *colostrum*, increased size of breasts, prickling or tingling sensations, increased blood supply so that blood vessels may be seen under the skin—these are all symptoms accompanying pregnancy but are not positive proof that conception has occurred.

Changes in the vaginal lining   The lining becomes congested and bluish in color.

Enlargement of the abdomen   This occurs rather late for diagnosis in ordinary cases and may be due to some factor other than pregnancy, for example, a tumor.

Softening of the cervix   In the nonpregnant state, the cervix is firm.

Changes in the form, size, and position of the uterus   As pregnancy progresses, the uterus becomes larger, less pear-shaped and more nearly globular, and at first tends to slope forward more than ordinarily.

Intermittent uterine contractions   At about the end of the second month the uterus begins to contract at irregular intervals (Braxton Hicks contractions).

These contractions may be detected by the obstetrician but are not felt by the mother. Since no dilation of the cervix accompanies these contractions, they do not constitute true labor.

Ballottement, or repercussion The fetus is at first too small, and late in pregnancy too large, for this sign to be used, but between the sixteenth and the thirty-second week the physician may, during an examination of the woman, push the fetus gently and feel it rebound against the wall of the uterus [Greenhill, 1965a].

Basal body temperature The basal body temperature is the body temperature of an individual upon waking in the morning. It tends to be maintained at a relatively high level during pregnancy. A level of 98.8 to 99.9°F, maintained for more than sixteen days, is highly suggestive of pregnancy. Diagnosis of pregnancy based on body temperature is accurate in 97 per cent of cases [Greenhill, 1965a]. In order to use this method, records of temperatures must be kept both before and after conception, and other possible causes of elevated temperature must be ruled out.

Breast temperature In one study [Birnbaum, March, 1966] it was found that as early as one week after the first missed menstrual period there is a measurable rise in the temperature of the breast.

Positive Signs

The positive signs of pregnancy are certain evidence of its occurrence, since these signs can be produced by no factors other than a fetus.

Movement of the fetus in the uterus This movement is noticeable for the first time usually during the fourth or the fifth month, that is, about halfway through the pregnancy. The fetal movements are often vigorous and may be distinctly felt by the mother. In advanced pregnancy they may be seen or felt by an observer.

Fetal heartbeat This is audible to the physician by means of a stethoscope, usually at about the fourth month. By means of an ultrasonic instrument the heartbeat of the fetus can be detected as early as the twelfth week, sometimes even the tenth week, after the last menstrual period. [Johnson, Stegall, Lein, and Rushmer, September, 1965]. The fetal rate varies from 120 to 160 beats per minute, which is about twice the mother's rate under normal conditions. Thus the two beats may be distinguished.

The shape of the fetus This may be felt through the abdominal wall.

The appearance of the fetus in an X-ray photograph This method of diagnosis is possible only late in pregnancy after other signs have appeared. Therefore, it is usually unnecessary. X-ray studies are sometimes made before delivery, however, to determine the size of the fetal head relative to the opening in the mother's pelvis or to assist in the diagnosis of multiple pregnancy. Such studies should supplement, not replace, careful clinical observation. Exposure to X rays for photographic purposes is not to be confused with exposure for therapy or the careless exposure of technicians.

TESTS FOR PREGNANCY

The positive signs are observable only when pregnancy is well advanced. The presumptive signs are not conclusive, and few of these are observable during the very early stages of pregnancy. The importance of some means of diagnosing pregnancy shortly after it begins is apparent. This means has been provided by pregnancy tests.

The placenta produces several hormones, one of which is termed *human chorionic gonadotropin* and is referred to as HCG. Through the processes of metabolism and excretion, HCG passes into the urine of the pregnant woman where it is detectable by about the tenth day after ovulation. Since HCG is produced by the placenta, it is found only during pregnancy. Also, since it is produced by the placenta rather than the fetus, its presence indicates only live placental tissue, not a live fetus [Hon, 1961]. Placental tissue may live after the death of the fetus, but the death of the fetus follows promptly upon the death of the placenta. In some cases a test may be positive after childbirth or abortion, since enough HCG remains in the woman's blood to pass into the urine.

The biologic tests for pregnancy, in which urine from a presumably pregnant woman is introduced into test animals (in female rabbits, mice, or rats HCG causes ovulatory changes in the ovaries; in frogs or toads HCG causes the release of eggs in females and sperms in males), have a high degree of accuracy but the disadvantage of having to keep the animals on hand. Biologic tests are being replaced by immunologic (chemical) tests that have the advantages of giving results both early in pregnancy and soon after the test is made and of being easy to administer even in the physician's office. One test, utilizing latex particles coated with HCG and requiring only one drop of urine, can be used as early as ten to fourteen days following the first missed menstrual period, can be completed in only three minutes, and is reported to have a reasonably high degree of accuracy [Yahia and Taymor, January, 1964; Jacobson and Davis, February, 1965]. In another test, previously preserved red blood cells and an antibody in a special disposable container are mixed with one drop of urine and one drop of water. The mixture is allowed to settle for forty-five minutes. This test requires minimum equipment and is 96 per cent accurate [Lav, Jan. 1, 1971]. In another test, serum instead of urine is used. In still another, a hormone is administered orally or hypodermically. Since the dosage is limited, a condition of hormone withdrawal is produced. If the woman has vaginal bleeding following this procedure, she is assumed not to be pregnant. If she has no vaginal bleeding, she is assumed to be pregnant.

The perfect test for pregnancy has not yet been devised. All known tests involve a margin of error. Some are contraindicated in a few cases. If a test is administered very early in a presumed pregnancy and is negative, it should be repeated later. At the present stage of knowledge, accuracy of diagnosis is increased by supplementing a test with a vaginal examination. Even then there is a margin of possible error.

CHILDBIRTH

Some two weeks before the onset of labor, the fetus shifts its position so that it is lower in the pelvis and has started to enter the birth canal. This process is termed *lightening.* Sometimes women refer to it as "settling" or "dropping." In some cases, at about this time there are nonprogressive contractions of the uterus continuing for perhaps a few hours and termed *false labor.* When the fetus has reached full term, that is, when it has reached its full prenatal development, complicated factors not fully understood cause the uterus to contract, and labor begins. Recent research suggests that the fetus itself may be at least one factor in initiating and sustaining labor through the release of substances causing uterine contractions [Chard, Hudson, Edwards, and Boyd, Dec. 10, 1971; Turnbull and Anderson, 1971]. During pregnancy the uterine muscle cells increase, not only in number but also in size, to prepare the organ for its role in expelling the fetus. As the uterus contracts from the top downward, pushing the child against the cervix, the cervix dilates until it is practically effaced for the time. Changes in the uterus and the progress of the child during labor are shown in Figures 10.10 to 10.17.

Labor may be divided into three stages: first stage—from the beginning of contraction (not of dilation, since in many cases dilation is under way before labor starts) to the complete dilation of the cervix; second stage—from this point to the birth of the child; third stage—from the birth of the child to the expulsion of the afterbirth and the final contraction of the uterus. At the beginning of the first stage the pains accompanying contraction are slight and rather far apart (twenty minutes or more). As labor progresses, they occur closer together in an increasingly rapid rhythm. As contraction proceeds, one side of the amniotic sac ("bag of waters") is forced by pressure to protrude through the opening in the cervix. At length the sac bursts and some of the amniotic fluid is discharged. In some cases this discharge is the announcement of the onset of labor. If the membrane ruptures prematurely (*dry birth*), the cervix may be dilated too rapidly. In some cases the onset of labor is announced by a somewhat bloody vaginal discharge, the "show," caused by the loosening of the mucous plug which is normally found in the cervix; but such discharge may occur before or after the onset of labor and is, therefore, not a reliable indication of its onset.

The average (mean) duration of labor in American women is about twelve hours for first babies and about eight hours for subsequent deliveries [Greenhill, 1965a]. Such figures must be interpreted with caution, however. The average (mean) is derived by including all labors, those that are longer than average as well as those that are shorter. It may, therefore, be misleading. The modal duration of labor—that is, the length that occurs most frequently—is about half the mean.

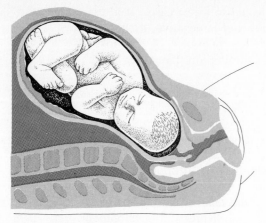

Figure 10.10 Fetus at term before beginning of labor.

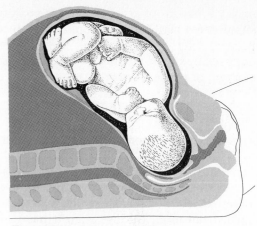

Figure 10.11 Labor: cervix dilating.

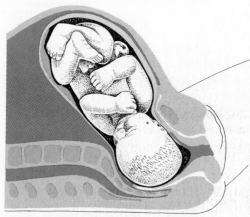

Figure 10.12 Labor: cervix completely dilated. Note the amniotic sac.

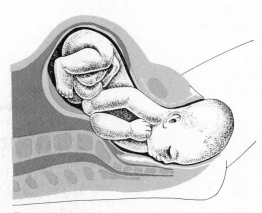

Figure 10.13 Labor: head begins to appear. Note the rotation of the head.

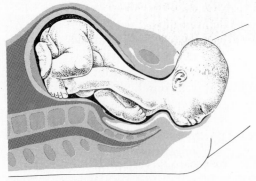

Figure 10.14 Labor: head turns upward.

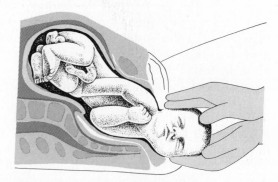

Figure 10.15 Labor: birth of shoulders.

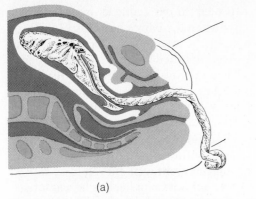
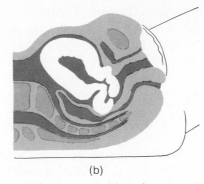

(a)   (b)

Figure 10.16   Labor: uterus after birth of the baby. (a) Placenta almost separated from the uterus; (b) uterus after expulsion of the placenta.

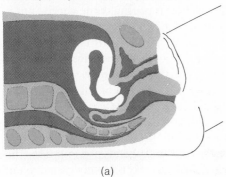
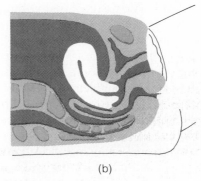

(a)   (b)

Figure 10.17   Uterus after delivery: (a) fifth day after delivery; (b) fourteenth day after delivery.

Women who have never borne a child are sometimes disturbed by descriptions such as that above because they do not visualize the situation accurately. They imagine themselves lying on the delivery table with their knees drawn up and their feet in supports throughout labor. Such an imaginary picture is inaccurate. Ordinarily when a woman goes to the hospital for delivery, labor is already well advanced, a good part of it having occurred at home. The woman is put to bed in a labor room where her husband may visit her and where she will remain until it is almost time for the baby to be born. Then she is taken to the delivery room where she will be for a relatively brief time, in some cases only a few minutes.

During the early part of the first stage of labor the pain is relatively mild. It increases in intensity as labor progresses and the contractions of the uterus become stronger and closer together (every two to three minutes). The pain becomes more severe during the second stage of labor, which lasts an hour or so for first babies and about twenty minutes for subsequent ones [Greenhill, 1965a], though there is, of course, considerable variation among women. Put differently, a woman in a normal delivery with her first child can be expected to pass through the second stage in no more than twenty to thirty pains, and in some cases less than twenty. The number may be expected to be reduced in subsequent deliveries. The pain of labor reaches its crest when the baby's head passes through the muscular ring at the external opening of the vagina and emerges from the mother's body. This passage is usually accomplished in one strong expulsive movement, and the process lasts only a few moments. The pain of the third stage of labor is usually not severe, and the mother may experience only a drawing sensation. Ordinarily this stage is relatively brief, usually lasting just a few minutes.

As labor progresses from first through second stage, the child moves slowly through the birth canal, pushed along by the contractions of the uterus. Progress is not continuous, however. When the uterus contracts, the child is moved forward. When it relaxes, the child slips back, but not so far back as he was moved forward. Progress is made, therefore, by alternate forward and backward movements in increasingly rapid rhythm, until at the very end it is predominantly forward. The tissue of that portion of the uterus that is normally the cervix, but is now more or less indistinguishable from the rest of the organ except for the opening, moves past the child's head. In about 95 per cent of cases the baby enters the birth canal head first. In the other 5 per cent he enters feet first, buttocks first (breech presentation), or in some other manner. One of the problems in such deliveries is that the umbilical cord, instead of passing from the child's abdomen past the feet to the placenta, passes between the child's head and the wall of the birth canal. Hence it may be subjected to so much pressure that the circulation of blood through the cord ceases and the child's oxygen supply is cut off. In some instances in which there is not a head presentation the obstetrician may turn the child in the uterus. This process is termed *version* and may be done by external manipulations, as one would turn a baby under a blanket, or by the doctor's working through the vagina, grasping the baby with one hand while assisting externally with the other.

The child's head is almost as broad as its shoulders. Owing to the relatively large proportion of cartilage and small proportion of bone in its skeleton, its body is somewhat flexible. The head is more rigid than most parts, but even the head yields somewhat to pressure. At times a child's head is pressed out of shape during the birth process (*molding*). This is often a matter of concern to young couples who have just had their first baby. They conclude that it is abnormal, not knowing that Nature takes care of this situation and that, unless there has been some complication, the head will soon reshape itself.

The child's head must pass through the opening in the mother's pelvis, and the fit is close. For this reason it is most important for the mother to have the obstetrician measure her pelvis as soon as she becomes pregnant, if he has not done so before. When he knows what to expect, he may prepare for it. Any opening through which the head will pass will accommodate the rest of the body. Hence, after the head is born the rest is relatively easy, and the body is rapidly expelled.

There is evidence to show that during pregnancy, especially in young women, owing to a softening of the cartilage, there is a degree of relaxation in the pubic joint (the place at which the pelvic bones meet in the fore part of the body) and that this relaxation permits a slight increase in the gap between the bones. This process prepares the pelvis for childbirth. Opinions differ, however, as to the extent to which this condition influences the course of labor. The probability is that in most cases the influence upon labor is relatively minor. We can be sure that the pelvic bones do not open in the manner of a double door to permit the baby to pass through without resistance.

In addition to the resistance afforded by the snug fit of the birth canal, during childbirth the child's head meets three points of resistance, namely, the cervix, the mother's pelvis, and the muscles surrounding the external opening of the vagina. If these muscles are unyielding and if in pressing against them the child's head is subjected to too great pressure for too long, the blood supply to the brain may be reduced to the point of damage to brain tissue due to oxygen deprivation. There may also be damage to the mother. The obstetrician may facilitate the child's progress and relieve the pressure on its head by one or both of two procedures. He may use obstetrical forceps [see Figure 10.18], whose function is as much to protect the child's head as to facilitate its movement through the muscular ring. The other procedure involves an incision in the muscle tissue surrounding the entrance to the vagina. Such an incision is made under anesthesia and is termed an *episiotomy*. Its function is to increase the size of the vaginal opening and permit the ready passage of the child through it. It is safe and constitutes a small price in maternal discomfort for the welfare of the baby.

In recent years the vacuum extractor (sometimes referred to as *ventouse*) has been given publicity as a possible alternative to the obstetrical forceps in some cases, since it does not provide as much traction as the forceps, while under certain circumstances having an advantage over the forceps. This device consists of a suction cup which fits onto the crown of the baby's head. By this means the obstetrician may assist the baby's passage through the birth canal. The vacuum extractor has been used more widely in Europe than in this country. There is a good deal of difference of opinion among American obstetricians as to its value and safety. In some cases, it has been used with success. In others, babies have been injured, as they have been with forceps or by their mother's resistant tissues [Thompson, May, 1962; Donald, 1964; Greenhill, 1965a; Malmström and Jansson, December, 1965; Chalmers, 1971, 1963].

In extreme cases, when the passage of the baby through the mother's bony pelvic opening is impossible or would entail too great risk, or when the uterus does not contract properly and is ineffective, Caesarean section may be used. A Caesarean section is an abdominal operation in which the uterus is opened surgically and the child is removed from the mother without passing through the

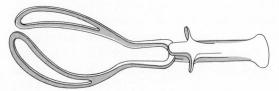

Figure 10.18 Obstetrical forceps.

375

birth canal. Ordinarily, by measuring the baby's head by means of X ray or ultrasound [Willocks, McDonald, Duggan, and Day, February, 1964], the obstetrician can predict whether such an operation will be necessary, and plans may be made accordingly. Sometimes, however, he elects to let the mother go through trial labor to see whether she can be delivered normally. If she cannot, a Caesarean section is then performed. Childbirth is a natural process. Caesarean section is not, and it involves risk, as any major operation does. In skilled hands the outcome is usually favorable, especially when the operation is planned, and it is also usually fraught with less risk than an extraordinarily difficult delivery. Caesarean section is not, however, as some persons suppose, a simple means of avoiding normal delivery. Caesarean section also involves risk to the baby. Babies born by means of Caesarean section have a higher mortality rate than babies born by the natural vaginal route. A woman may have several Caesarean sections without any unfavorable consequences. "We are no longer afraid to perform four and more cesarean sections on a patient. . . . Today we encounter women who have had six and more cesarean sections, apparently without any harm" [Greenhill, 1964]. One report mentions a woman who had thirteen Caesarean sections over an eighteen-year period, resulting in thirteen healthy babies [*Ob. Gyn. News*, Oct. 15, 1967]. Some physicians used to recommend that, if a woman had two living children delivered by Caesarean section, she be sterilized during her third such operation. But ". . . the clinical evidence no longer supports such a practice" [Piver and Johnston, November, 1969], attitudes on this matter are changing, and today fewer physicians are inclined to make such a recommendation. Certainly it should not be made routinely.

Normally the child cries as soon as it is born; in some cases, as soon as the head is born. In rare cases the child cries while it is still in the uterus. This cry fills the lungs with air. If the child does not cry spontaneously, oxygen is introduced into its respiratory tract. This method usually resuscitates the infant. Violent manipulations, such as swinging by the feet, immersion into hot and cold water alternately, and pulling on the tongue, belong to a past era and have no place in modern obstetrics.

Immediately after it is born, the baby is identified. This is accomplished by placing something around its neck with identification on it, taping something to its back, recording its palm prints, recording its footprints (which are easier to obtain with a newborn infant than are palm prints), or a combination of methods. Recently a new method of identification has been developed [Fields, Falls, Warren, and Zimberoff, July, 1960]. It was found that each baby's ears are unique in form and that the ears of different babies can be distinguished from one another. The method involves photographing the baby's ear protruding through a hole in a card on which are recorded the mother's fingerprint and other pertinent data so that complete identification is available on one photographic print.

After the baby emerges from the mother's body, the umbilical cord is bound or clamped near the baby's abdomen. This is not done until the cord has stopped pulsating, however, showing that circulation of blood through the placenta has ceased. If it is done too soon, more blood than the baby can afford to lose may still be in the placenta and cord. The cord is then severed. The mother feels no pain when this is done because the cord is part of the baby. The baby feels no pain because there are no nerves in the cord. The stub of cord attached to the child's body eventually drops off, leaving a small scar, the navel or umbilicus. To prevent infection that might cause blindness, an antiseptic substance is put into the infant's eyes.

It is interesting to note in how many ways Nature prepares the child for the birth process. His body is flexible. He is temporarily immune to many common diseases. He can live longer than an adult without breathing. He requires no food for a day or two. He is relatively insensitive to pain. He cannot recall the experience.

Shortly after the birth of the child the contractions of the uterus separate the placenta from the uterine wall, and the placenta, with what is left of the cord and amnion, is expelled. This is the afterbirth. It has served its purpose and is now waste material, though the placenta is carefully examined to make sure that no portion of tissue has remained in the uterus to serve as the seat of infection or to cause hemorrhage. When the afterbirth has been expelled, hormones cause the uterus to contract, squeezing the ends of the blood vessels together and preventing bleeding.

From this point on for about six weeks, the mother goes through a period of recuperation, during which the genital organs gradually assume approximately their original size and shape. Recovery is usually rapid and proceeds without mishap if the woman follows the physician's instructions. If she does so, there is no reason why she should have a permanently protruding abdomen, have permanently enlarged breasts, or become permanently overweight.

Relief of Pain

A competent obstetrician will do what he can do with safety to make a woman comfortable during labor and delivery, but he cannot safely guarantee the complete absence of pain. At the present stage of knowledge there is no drug, combination of drugs, or nonchemical technique that can eliminate all the pain of labor with complete safety in all cases [Flowers, Jr., 1967; Flowers, 1970]. Excessive anesthesia may damage the child. "In his response to drugs, the newborn infant is qualitatively and quantitatively different from the mother. . . . The newborn shows marked susceptibility to the depressant effects of drugs used in labor" [Flowers, 1970]. Therefore no woman should make impossible demands of her obstetrician, and no obstetrician should make promises that he cannot safely fulfill.

Generalizing, there are three types of drugs used for obstetrical pain relief: *anesthetics*, which produce other insensibilities, even unconsciousness, as well as insensitivity to pain; *analgesics*, which produce insensitivity to pain without affecting other sensibilities; and *amnesic agents*, which produce forgetfulness. Generalizing again, these drugs are administered in the following ways [Flowers, Jr., 1967]:

1 Hypodermic injection.
2 Paracervical block, in which an injection is made into the tissue on either side of the cervix.
3 Pudendal block, in which injections are made to block the nerves supplying the lower part of the vagina and the surrounding area.
4 Inhalation of a gaseous substance.
5 Spinal anesthesia, in which the anesthetic drug is introduced into the space between the spinal cord and the bony structure of the spinal column. *Saddle block* is one type of spinal anesthesia.
6 Continuous conduction anesthesia, in which a flexible needle or a small plastic tube is introduced into the space within the bony structure of the lower part of the spinal column and taped into position, permitting the introduction of the anesthetic solution a little at a time. This procedure makes possible a degree of control of the quantity of drug introduced that is not possible with spinal anesthesia. Female students who have never borne a child often have difficulty in visualizing this process and may be somewhat taken aback at the idea of having such equipment taped to the lower part of the back. Women who have had continuous conduction anesthesia do not find this a problem. The reader must remember that we are discussing pain relief, not pain production.
7 General anesthesia.

Exactly what drugs are to be used and how they are to be administered is a decision that must be made by the obstetrician and/or anesthesiologist in each case. Generalization is impossible. The decision will depend upon the woman's preference, the physician's preference and special skills, the woman's condition and reaction to certain drugs, the hospital staff and equipment available, and other similar considerations. All known methods of pain relief have advantages and disadvantages. None is perfect.

Much has been written in recent years, some of it prematurely and some irresponsibly, about anesthesia in obstetrics. Popular writers have often given the impression that the day is at hand when all women will be spared all the pain of labor by a simple, universally applicable, absolutely safe technique. Unfortunately, such is not the case. Varieties of spinal and continuous conduction anesthesia have been given special publicity because of their dramatic effects. When continuous conduction anesthesia is successful, it is very good. However, it cannot be used in all cases. Some women cannot tolerate the drugs employed. Its administration requires special skill. It can be administered safely only in an adequately staffed and equipped hospital; it is not to be used casually. The patient must have a trained person in constant attendance. Some women complain of headaches after having had spinal anesthesia. There is an element of risk involved but much less risk than there was a few years ago. In obstetrical anesthesia and analgesia encouraging steps forward have been taken, but the final answer has not yet been found. This is, however, no reason for a woman to fear childbirth; as we shall see, for a woman in good health having a baby is one of the safest things she can do. Her answer to the questions about anesthesia is to choose a competent obstetrician.

"Natural childbirth" implies labor and delivery without anesthesia or analgesia or with a minimum of either, as advocated by Dr. Grantley Dick-Read and others. There are women who prefer this method, and some report that the birth of the baby was an exhilarating experience. The advocates of "natural childbirth" have performed a service in calling attention to the importance of physiological preparation through exercise, relaxation, and improvement of general health and to psychological preparation through increased understanding, acceptance, and elimination of tension and fear. But "natural childbirth" is neither universally applicable nor universally desired. It is an "intellectual approach" to childbirth ". . . which should be encouraged but not necessarily recommended" [Flowers, Jr., 1967]. We must beware thinking of any method as *the* method and must think in terms of what is best for a particular woman under particular circumstances. Otherwise, what might be a helpful addition to the art and science of obstetrics becomes a cult that may do more harm than good.

Hypnosis has been used successfully to relieve the pain of childbirth in some cases. It has certain advantages, especially where the woman cannot tolerate anesthetic drugs. On the other hand, not all women can be hypnotized with equal success. Even for those who can be hypnotized, a period of preparation is necessary. Hypnosis should be employed only by qualified individuals who have had proper training in its use. Such training must involve more than mere proficiency in hypnotic techniques. There must also be sufficient knowledge of psychiatry and of symptoms of mental illness to enable the hypnotist to recognize those cases in which hypnosis would be dangerous. "Only the combination of an adequately trained physician and a well-adjusted patient eliminate the potential hazards of hypnosis" [Flowers, Jr., 1967]. In obstetrics, then, hypnosis, though a helpful tool in some cases, has limited usefulness [Eastman, February, 1962]. It is ". . . a technique which will never find wide acceptance among the majority of obstetricians" [Flowers, Jr., 1967].

An interesting apparatus for the relief of pain during the first stage of labor is the decompression device [Greenhill, 1959, 1962b; Heyns, 1963]. This device consists of a dome-shaped decompression chamber constructed of plastic and steel and fitted over the woman's abdomen. Air is then drawn from the chamber, reducing the inside pressure to about one-fifth the external atmospheric pressure. This exerts a sucking force on the abdomen, causing it to bulge out. During contractions the uterus rises forward, and the abdominal wall becomes taut. If the uterus collides with the abdominal wall, pain is increased. The decompression device prevents or minimizes the collision, permitting the uterus to rise forward unopposed by the taut abdominal wall. In this way less uterine energy is expended, and both fatigue and pain are reduced. The decompression device has been used with some success, but results have not been consistent enough to justify its use as a routine measure to replace other methods of pain relief [Greenhill, 1963; Donald, 1964; Shulman and Birnbaum, June 1, 1966].

Even in cases in which no anesthetic or analgesic is employed and the birth occurs with none of the benefits of modern medical science, the pain of childbirth is soon forgotten. It is difficult to remember any pain. A woman may remember her reactions to the pain, but to recall the actual experience of pain is quite another matter. In the fascinating experience of seeing the newborn offspring, nursing it, caring for it, and planning for its future, the mother quickly forgets the inconvenience of pregnancy and the pain of labor. Many women plan for a second child before leaving the hospital with the first one.

The pain of childbirth should not be approached in the light of old wives' tales or in the light of an individual woman who happened to have difficult labor or did not want to have a baby. It should be approached in the light of modern science and put into correct perspective. Pain may be the most immediately obvious aspect of childbirth while the process is going on, but it is not the most important aspect. Furthermore, pain and risk are not necessarily correlated. The more the woman dissociates them in her thinking, the more readily she can accept the pain.

Childbirth without fear is possible for every woman who is willing to face the facts intelligently, maturely, and squarely for the very simple reason that there is no longer anything to fear. Many of the unfavorable attitudes that some women hold toward childbirth have their roots in the past, when having a baby was a "descent into the valley of the shadow." But those days are gone forever. If she is in good health at the time she becomes pregnant, if she has adequate prenatal care, and if she is attended by a competent obstetrician, having a baby is now one of the safest things a woman can do. Childbirth without risk has been all but completely achieved.

When we include all the women who have babies in and out of hospitals, all those who have inadequate as well as those who have adequate prenatal care, all those who have poor care at delivery as well as those who have skilled care, all those who have an illness or defect during pregnancy, all those who have miscarriages or induced abortions as well as those who carry their babies to term, and those of all ages and all races, we find that in 1971 the maternal mortality rate (deaths due to complications of pregnancy and childbirth per 100,000 live births) was 20.5. This rate is equivalent to one maternal death for every 4,875 live births [U.S. Department of Health, Education and Welfare, Aug. 30, 1972]. In 1940, the rate was 376.0; in 1950, it was 83.3 [U.S. Bureau of the Census, *Statistical Abstract,* 1972]. From 1967 through 1968 the maternal death rate for white women was 18.4. The rate was 13.0 at ages under 20 (as compared with 35.3 for nonwhite women in the same age group), 10.1 at ages 20 to 24, 13.5 at ages 25 to 29 [*Statistical Bulletin,* June, 1972]. Taken as a group, nonwhite women have a maternal mortality rate about four times as high as white women [*Statistical Bulletin,* June, 1972]. Since the Second World War the rates for all women of all races have shown about the same relative decline, but the numerical disparity still persists [*Statistical Bulletin,* December, 1968].

This reduction in maternal mortality rate is one of the more dramatic but less publicized advances in modern medicine. At the time the reader was born, the rate was several times what it is today. In the decades immediately before that, when the rate was only beginning to decline, the reader's mother may have acquired attitudes which, in some cases, she passed on to her child.

Obstetrical practice is continually improving. Medical students and nurses are receiving better training. Refresher courses for physicians are growing in popularity. Hospital facilities are being improved and extended. One hospital (Memorial Hospital in Long Beach, California) reports only two maternal deaths in over 50,000 deliveries. One of these was a woman who had been advised not to become pregnant because of kidney disease. The other was a woman who developed complications after leaving the hospital [*Ob. Gyn. News*, Sept. 1, 1967].

More and more agencies, both private and public, are directing their attention to better prenatal care and better care both during and after delivery. More people are being educated in the hygiene of pregnancy and are being taught both what to expect in pregnancy and what to seek in the way of care. Premarital examinations are increasing in both frequency and quality. Use of X ray and ultrasound makes possible the detection of conditions that may give rise to difficulty in labor. Improved methods of diagnosis, immunization, and treatment make it possible to prevent more of the complications that arise during pregnancy as a result of diseases present before pregnancy began. More is being learned about antibiotics and other drugs. Anesthesia, analgesia, and methods of treating hemorrhage are being improved. All this plus the experience of some communities leads to the prediction that the maternal mortality rate can be still further reduced.

The female reader will probably begin her childbearing in her late teens or early twenties, a favorable time. Like 95 per cent of the women who become mothers, she will be attended by a physician, perhaps by a specialist in obstetrics. Like more than 98 per cent of mothers, her child will be delivered in a hospital. She will have adequate prenatal and postnatal care. She will know enough about pregnancy and childbirth to follow her physician's instructions and to be cooperative. In short, in the light of what was said above, she will have childbirth almost without risk. She may, therefore, have childbirth completely without fear.

Perhaps by reading between the lines of a few letters written by women still in the hospital after the birth of their babies we may gain insight into the relative values of joy and pain. These letters express not exceptional but typical attitudes. The women who wrote them give no indication of thinking of their recent experience as a forbidding "descent into the valley of the shadow." The reason there are not more such documents is that few women write them, not that only a few women feel this way. The women who wrote these did not know at the time that they would be read by anyone except the friends to whom they were addressed. Hence there was no reason for being anything except straightforward and sincere. There is no evidence of polishing the facts for publication. Personal details are omitted from these restatements; the rest is in the women's own words. Mrs. A writes:

At last the great "Johnny" has arrived. Can you believe it? "He" is a lovely girl—nicer and sweeter than any other in the nursery. She is just too precious for words. I am so proud of her and you should see my husband: he just beams all over. It's just as if he had a halo around his head. I love him so very much. Just wait until you fall in love and see what sensations and thrills really are. He and the baby are all my life now. I can hardly wait to get out to take care of them.

The hospital is lovely. I just lie here and push a button and my every wish is gratified. The nurses are wonderful and are so sweet and patient.

The baby weighed seven pounds, eleven and three-quarter ounces. She is still slightly pink but is toning down a bit. She is strong enough to hold her little head up and pushes away with her hands when they bring her to nurse. She honestly chews so hard I am sore; but that little mouth is so sweet I just love to have her touch me.

I guess I had a rather hard time with labor but my husband was with me until the last forty minutes. They would give me ether and then my husband would say, "Can you see me?" and I would answer, "Yes." Then the doctor would say, "Can you see *me*?" and I would say, "No." I can't remember that at all but they told me about it afterward. When I came to, I couldn't realize that it was all over and I had a daughter.

Mrs. *B* writes:

First I must apologize for staying away from the nice dinner you prepared for us Sunday. I really intended to come but I had other very important business on Sunday.

Now I can get down to business and *rave*! That boy is simply marvelous and I can see a new life for ———— [the husband] and me. It's even more wonderful than I thought it would be and you know I've been thrilled for nine months.

The baby looks like ———— [husband]—has black hair, big feet and big hands—and is the sweetest baby in town. I'm so happy I have to cry a little every once in a while. It still seems too good to be true. I only hope that someday you will celebrate a blessed event. It's worth all the pain and all the sacrifice; it's wonderful. And Dr. ———— is a great man and a great doctor. I almost felt like kissing him.

I am still on my back and writing is rather difficult. . . .

Mrs. *C* writes:

Your letter came this morning. Gee, but I'm happy. Now don't let me start raving over my boy. Did I ever say I wanted a girl?

Now I'll tell you about him this once and God forbid that I become one of those raving mothers. He's fat enough to be cute. His little cheeks hang over a bit. His blond hair is a bit mouse-colored but is going to curl. His hands and feet are exactly like ————'s [husband's]; his ears and nose are mine; and the rest of him seems to be all his own. His nails were so long at first that he scratched his face; but now he has had a manicure and only slaps his mother because she does not have enough to satisfy his appetite. Today I hope to accomplish that.

For the first two days I was a bit worried about his IQ. They say a newborn baby knows only one thing and that is how to nurse. Well, he didn't even know that or at least he didn't give a care; but last night he learned his lesson and now the rest is up to me.

Miss ———— is the old maid superintendent of the hospital. When I was starting into labor, she dropped in to see me. I asked her to tell me the proper technique for

FROM MARRIAGE TO THE FAMILY

reacting to the pains in order to get maximum results. She just laughed and said, "Now that's a question to ask an old maid." I said, "I mean, theoretically." She did tell me very clearly just how one was supposed to do it. I followed it as nearly as I could and I know it hastened things.

The doctor was certainly pleased with the outcome. I think he was a bit worried. He wouldn't give me enough dope to deaden a flea. Afterwards he said, "I knew you'd forgive me in the end." Just think—twenty-four hours after I saw you I was back in my room on an "ether jag" with an eight-pound baby in the nursery.

When you have your baby—wherever you go and whomever you have to deliver you—have confidence in your doctor. Forget every worry; that's half the battle. I may be insane but if that man said, "If I cut off your left ear, your eyesight will never dim," I'd believe him and say, "O.K., go ahead."

Here it is 10:20 and I have not finished the letter I started at the crack of dawn. There is certainly not a dull moment here.

Mrs. D writes:

A week ago today I gave birth to a darling baby boy. I'm so thrilled about him that you'd think I was the first one ever to have a baby. I'm writing you about it now because I want to tell you how thankful I am for the discussions we had in class and for the opportunity of reading those letters from women who had just had babies. [Mrs. D is referring to the three letters above.] They made things so much easier for me mentally. I kept thinking of how they felt about it when untactful people would say to me, "You'll find out that it's not easy, etc., etc." One mother had the grace to say, "Oh, the pain—that's the first thing you forget." And that is what you can tell the girls that I say, too.

I'll admit that the first day I wondered whether I could ever have any playmates for my son (I'd like four, in all); but in another twenty-four hours I couldn't remember how terrible the pain was. Anyway, what's a half hour or so of pain when you get a lifetime of happiness for it? I don't think a child would want a woman for his mother if she couldn't stand that much for him. My son's daddy is in the Air Corps in Europe. It wasn't as nice having him gone at this time but at least he didn't have to pace the floor while he waited for me.

Mrs. E writes:

Before I became pregnant, my knowledge of the actual birth of a baby consisted of a few old wives' tales and bits of information from friends. After I was sure of my pregnancy, I became much more aware of the actual truth about childbirth. I realize that the more you know about something, the less you fear it, and believe that it is very important for a woman who is going to have a baby to know as much as possible about it.

My experience during labor and childbirth was a happy and somewhat humorous one. My labor began with the show of blood. As soon as I noticed it, I called my doctor and was told that labor would soon follow. Then I called my husband out of his Saturday morning class. He raced home as quickly as possible, and, like most expectant fathers, he was very excited. At this time my pains were not very severe. I was anxious but not afraid because I knew what to expect.

Sunday morning I felt fine and decided to go to church. I passed up Sunday School because I didn't feel like sitting through two services. The contractions continued during the service and were a little more painful. After church, we ate out since I didn't feel like cooking. We spent the afternoon timing the contractions and taking a long walk around the campus. By eight o'clock Sunday evening, after the pains had occurred at three-minute intervals for two hours, my husband called the doctor who agreed to meet us at the hospital.

My clothes for the hospital had been packed for two weeks, so we went directly to the hospital. By one A.M. Monday the pains were much more severe and labor progressed slowly and continued throughout the night. Monday morning I sat up, combed my hair, and fixed my face between contractions. I don't remember anything after that, but my precious son was born at 11:14 A.M. that Monday morning.

Mrs. *F* writes:

Our third little girl was born last Saturday night at 7:10 P.M. She weighed 6 lb. 5 oz. and looks just like her daddy. She is bald on top with a fringe of red fuzz, very much like Jiggs in the funny paper. Jennifer is another Read method baby—this time completely successful. I had her without anesthetic or sedative of any sort. I came to the hospital Friday night about 10 P.M., after my water broke, and then did nothing until Saturday afternoon about 2:30 P.M. Then my labor began. I called my husband and he came and stayed with me in my room during the first part. I relaxed easily with the pains and about 5:30 I went back to the labor ward. I relaxed well until the very end of the first stage when the pains became too strong to relax with. During the last few first stage pains, which were very sharp, I took a deep breath and held it till it passed. With the first second stage "pain" all pain ceased entirely and a new feeling began, a good "bearing down" feeling which was entirely painless. I was rushed to the delivery room after I announced that the second stage had begun and the baby was coming fast. The doctor asked me not to bear down while he rushed into his gloves, and I was surprised to find that I could control when the contractions would come. When he was ready I bore down good and the baby was born. I immediately popped up on an elbow and saw him lift her up. She made a few noises and was laid across my tummy and I watched while the cord was tied and cut. She was then carried to a table to be wrapped in a blanket and I was asked to lie back down and push once more. I popped up again to see the afterbirth and about that time the baby gave a good loud yell. The nurse brought her over for me to see once more before they took her to the nursery.

By that time I was cleaned up and ready to leave, so the doctor gave me a hand to sit up and I slipped off the table and walked out in the hall. I didn't feel at all weak and wanted to walk to my room; but my bed was already at the delivery room door so I climbed up and got a ride to my room. My husband was waiting there and as I rolled through the door I said, "Hi, honey. I'm hungry." Then I told him we had another daughter. While he went to round up some crackers for me to eat, I used the telephone by my bed to call some of my friends and tell them we had a girl. They were all amazed to hear me. I felt wonderful and got up several times during the night. I've been up and around ever since. I don't feel at all as if I'd had a baby and I am the happiest person in the world. The Read method worked so beautifully all the way that there was no need for fuss. There was nothing about any of it that I couldn't bear perfectly well and I was totally fascinated by every minute of it. I could have a dozen more just like it—but this is the end.

Lactation

For a brief period after the birth of the child the mother's breasts secrete colostrum, a substance that may have food value for the child and acts as a mild laxative but is not true milk. Colostrum is usually supplemented with water given by bottle. True milk appears in two to five days. Breast feeding is on the decline in this country [Eastman, June, 1963]. Pediatricians are not as insistent upon it as they used to be. This is due in part to increased knowledge of infant nutrition and in part to improvement in prepared formulas. But breast feeding has by no means lost all of its proponents. Many pediatricians recommend it. Some psychologists, psychiatrists, anthropologists, and similar specialists feel that the method of infant feeding is influential in the psychosocial development of both mother and child. Montagu [Eastman, June, 1963], an anthropologist, in discussing breast feeding, mentions the "psychophysiological benefits" conferred upon mother and child by their "continuing symbiotic relationship" and calls breast feeding "very important for their further development." Some women derive a special satisfaction from breast feeding. Others do not. Some feel guilty when they cannot or do not nurse their babies. Such a feeling of guilt is unnecessary and inappropriate. It stems from attitudes of the past rather than from present-day knowledge of child rearing. Some mothers are reluctant to nurse their babies because they fear permanent breast enlargement and impairment of appearance. If a woman follows her physician's instructions, such a fear is groundless.

Contrary to common assumption, it is possible for a woman to become pregnant while nursing. Menstruation may start, or conception may occur without the reinstitution of the menses. In a study of 2,197 women it was found that among those who nursed their babies three or more months, menstruation had begun by the end of the third month in 26 per cent. Among those who nursed their babies six or more months, menstruation had begun by the end of the sixth month in 60 per cent. Among women who did not breast-feed their babies at all, menstruation had begun by the end of the third month in 90 per cent and by the end of the sixth month in "virtually all" [Salber, Feinleib, and MacMahon, November, 1966]. In a study of 2,885 patients of Johns Hopkins Hospital it was found that one-fourth of the white women and one-third of the black women became pregnant within twelve months after delivery; 36 per cent of the whites and 47 per cent of the blacks were still nursing their babies when conception occurred [Guttmacher, 1937].

Multiple Births

Twins occur about once in 100 live births. Three or more babies in one birth tend to occur as follows: If twins occur once in n births, triplets will occur once in n^2 births, quadruplets once in n^3 births, and quintuplets once in n^4 births (the Hellin-Zeleny hypothesis). In recent years in this country there have been two authenticated sets of quintuplets which survived beyond infancy. Only five other such cases are known elsewhere in the world [*Statistical Bulletin*, April, 1972].

Sextuplets and septuplets have occurred rarely, but they have lived in only one case, a set of sextuplets born to a woman who had been given Pergonal, a fertility drug. Five of the six babies lived [Lachelin, Brant, Swyer, Little, and Reynolds, Mar. 25, 1972]. In 1967, the only authenticated set of octuplets (four boys, four girls) was born to a twenty-one-year-old woman in Mexico City. The babies were about two months premature and died shortly after birth [*Time*, Mar. 17, 1967]. A television news report on June 12, 1971 mentioned a woman in Sydney, Australia, who "had been administered a fertility drug" and bore nine babies all of which died [also *J.A.M.A.*, Aug. 9, 1971]. The twinning rate varies with the age of the mother. It is lowest in the teens, then the rate rises up to ages from 35 to 39, after which it declines [*Statistical Bulletin,* April, 1972].

Twins are of two types: one-egg (monovular, monozygotic, so-called "identical") twins, and two-egg (binovular, dizygotic, so-called "fraternal") twins. About one-third of all twins are of the former type. One-egg twins are produced when the zygote has developed into a cluster of cells which breaks apart. Such twins are, in a sense, parts of the same individual. They have the same genetic constitution, are thus always of the same sex, and resemble each other very closely; but, being subject to prenatal and postnatal environmental influences, they are not so nearly identical in appearance and behavior that they cannot be distinguished by persons who know them well. Sometimes they are "identical" in the sense of being alike. At other times they are "mirror images" of each other; for example, one twin's right hand is like the other's left hand. Whether they are "identical" or "mirror image" depends upon factors involved in the twinning process, such as the time and plane of splitting in the cluster of cells. According to one point of view, the later the splitting occurs, the more different mirror-image twins are likely to be [Scheinfeld, 1967]. According to another point of view, mirror imaging is unrelated to such splitting and occurs no more frequently than would be expected by chance [Bulmer, 1970].

When the splitting is incomplete, conjoined twins, commonly referred to as "Siamese," result. Such twins are rare. In many cases they die before or soon after birth. If they live, they may or may not be separable through surgery, depending upon where and how they are joined and what organs they have in common. Most one-egg twins have one common placenta with two amnions and two cords [Hertig, 1960]. A minority have two placentas, which may or may not be fused. Very rarely one-egg twins are found in the same amniotic sac [Timmons and de Alvarez, Aug. 1, 1963; Goplerud, February, 1964] [see Figure 10.19].

Two-egg twins are produced when two ova are released at one time and fertilized by two sperms. They are not produced by having two sperms fertilize one ovum, as is sometimes assumed. Two-egg twins may be of the same or of different sex. They have different genetic constitutions and are no more closely related than any two children having the same parents. They have two placentas, but these sometimes fuse, making classification difficult and at times leading to error. Two-egg twins have two amnions and two cords.

The individual children in a multiple birth are usually smaller than the child in a single birth, but their combined weight is often greater than that of a single

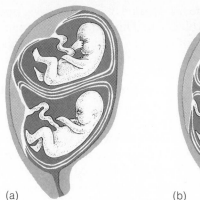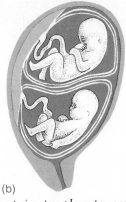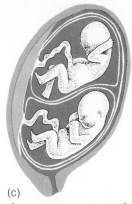

(a)   (b)   (c)

Figure 10.19   Twinning. (a) Two-egg twins: two placentas; each fetus with two sacs, amnion inside and chorion outside; sex may be different; fraternal twins. (b) Two-egg twins: two placentas have merged; each fetus has both membranes, amnion and chorion; sex may be different. (c) One-egg twins: one placenta; each fetus with inner sac (amnion); single outer membrane (chorion) envelops both; same sex; identical twins. [Adapted from sculptured birth series by Dickinson and Belskie in "Birth Atlas," Maternity Center Association, New York.]

child. The smaller size of the individuals is due in part to the fact that in the majority of cases multiple births occur prematurely.

There is evidence to indicate that two-egg twinning is hereditary in the female (as it would have to be since this type of twinning involves the release of two ova), but the evidence is inconclusive relative to one-egg twinning. Not only daughters but also other female relatives—such as sisters—of women who have borne two-egg twins have a greater-than-average chance of bearing two-egg twins. Women who are themselves twins also are more likely to have twins. Furthermore, once a woman has borne twins, her chances of having twins in subsequent pregnancies are increased beyond the average rate [Scheinfeld, 1967; Bulmer, 1970]. In 1961 a thirty-seven-year-old woman bore her seventh set of twins. In 1944 a Canadian woman bore her sixth set of all-surviving twins in eight years of marriage. In 1954 a woman was reported as having three sets of twins, one set of triplets, and seven singletons. In 1958 a woman gave birth to her third consecutive set of twins in twenty-seven months [Scheinfeld, 1967]. A woman known to the author had two sets of twins, one of triplets, and three singletons. These are, of course, extreme cases, but they support the assumption that a woman who has once borne twins is likely to do so again. Let the female reader note, however, that what is said above is expressed in terms of greater-than-average chance. There is no certainty involved in the individual case, and other factors, such as the age of the mother, play a part. The evidence does not suggest that "twinning skips generations" as is commonly believed. Multiple births still remain the exception rather than the rule, as indicated earlier.

It is ordinarily assumed that the sperms which fertilize the two ova in the production of two-egg twins are deposited during the same act of insemination. Could such twins be produced by sperms from different acts of insemination, provided the inseminations occurred during the brief period in which the two ova released at one time of ovulation were fertilizable? This process is termed *superfecundation,* and the answer to the question is in the affirmative. Two-egg twins can even have different fathers if a woman has sexual intercourse with two men within a brief time span [Bulmer, 1970], or if, as we shall discuss later, a mixture of the seminal fluid of the husband and that of a donor is used in artificial insemination.

An unusual case was taken to court in Baltimore in 1960 [Eastman, February, 1961]. The man in question admitted intercourse with a woman who had borne twins but disclaimed paternity. Blood tests indicated that he could have been the father of one twin but not of the other. The woman claimed that she had had intercourse with no other man during the period in which the twins must have been conceived. The judge ruled that her statement was insufficient and that she must have been withholding evidence. Since the man could not have been the father of one twin, the final verdict was "not guilty," and he was ruled to be the father of neither twin.

Ordinarily twins are born with a relatively brief time interval between them. How are reports of unusually long intervals to be interpreted—for example, a report of two babies born to the same mother 56 days apart [Eastman, February, 1961] and another of two babies 65 days apart [Drucker, Finkel, and Savel, October, 1960]? Are such babies twins in the ordinary sense? Do they represent separate pregnancies in a double uterus [Bulmer, 1970]? Or do they represent another type of multiple pregnancy, termed *superfetation*? In superfetation one pregnancy is started and then, after a time interval sufficient to permit another ovulation, a second pregnancy is started by means of fertilization effected by a sperm from a later insemination. Until the first is terminated, the two pregnancies progress concurrently. Superfetation has been produced experimentally in lower animals [Greenhill, 1959]. It is highly doubtful that it ever occurs in humans, and it has never been authenticated beyond all question [Bulmer, 1970]. Cases are reported, however, in which the data indicate a high degree of possibility [Fontana and Monif, April, 1970].

The characteristics of the various forms of multiple births are summarized in Table 10.1.

CHOOSING AN OBSTETRICIAN

The importance of adequate prenatal care for the prospective mother cannot be overemphasized. Her health, both present and future, and her baby's well-being hinge in large measure upon her care during pregnancy. There are many useful books and pamphlets on this subject, and the reader is urged to refer to them. The woman's best protection, however, is a competent obstetrician.

The obstetrician should not be chosen only for his ability to diagnose and treat disease. Pregnancy is not a disease. He should be chosen primarily for his ability to handle cases of pregnancy. What is significant is the number of successful deliveries he has to his credit, not the number of operations or the

Table 10.1.   Forms of multiple births

TYPE OF BIRTH	OVULATIONS	NUMBER OF OVA	INSEMINATIONS	NUMBER OF SPERMS
Identical twins	1	1	1	1
Fraternal twins	1	2	1	2
Superfecundation	1	2	2	2
Superfetation	2	2	2	2

number of occasions on which he has let women reach the brink of disaster only to save them in the nick of time.

Preferably he (or she) should be a physician equipped to handle the pregnancy from the first visit to the care of the mother after she leaves the hospital. He need not be able singlehandedly to meet all emergencies; that is too much to ask of any physician. But it is essential that he be able to recognize and detect emergencies and be willing to call in a consultant if necessary. Some obstetricians work closely with a pediatrician, especially when a particular problem, such as that caused by the Rh factor, is anticipated.

The obstetrician's personality is important, since his contact with the prospective mother is so intimate. She should not be forced to have a physician whom she dislikes and with whom she cannot get along. His training is important. So is the extent of his experience. Does he have enough obstetric cases to gain experience? Does he let himself become so busy that he must resort to time-saving techniques, such as induction of labor or use of forceps, unnecessarily and for his own convenience rather than for the patient's good? Is he so busy that he delegates so much to nurses that the peculiar relationship between obstetrician and mother is rendered unsatisfactory? "The obstetrician who depends upon the obstetrical nurse to follow his patients in labor and who wishes to be called only when delivery is imminent is not practicing obstetrics in the best sense of the term; he is a doctor who delivers babies. . . . No analgesia can take the place of considerate and conscientious care by the obstetrician . . ." [Crampton, May, 1961]. Does he keep abreast of new developments? Is obstetrics his special interest, or is it only incidental in a general practice? Will he, indeed may he, take his patients to a reputable hospital? All these considerations are important.

A problem not infrequently faced by young couples is that of choosing an obstetrician soon after having settled in a new community, before sufficient time has elapsed for them to become thoroughly acquainted. In such cases, information may be gathered from friends or from persons at the husband's place of employment. The local hospital may yield some data. The couple may write to their physician in their home town and ask him to recommend someone. Learning to which obstetrician the wives of other obstetricians go for their own deliveries may be helpful.

Before the couple put their case in the obstetrician's hands, they may talk it over with him. Let them remember that they are employing him, not he them. They have a right to know what his techniques are, how many visits he will recommend before delivery, what care he will continue after delivery, to what hospital he takes his patients, what his attitude is toward induced labor, what he does concerning relief from pain, and what the total cost will be.

Once the obstetrician is chosen, he should be told everything relevant to the case. No detail, no matter how insignificant it may seem to the couple, should be withheld. Questions should be freely asked. Any obstetrician worth his salt would rather have the couple ask innumerable questions than let a clue remain hidden which, if revealed, might prevent complications.

Once the obstetrician is chosen, too, his instructions should be followed faithfully, explicitly, and thoroughly. The couple should never let other people's advice supersede the doctor's instructions. If they do not like the way he handles their case, they may change obstetricians. But as long as they accept a particular physician's services, they should cooperate to the utmost and have complete confidence. Such confidence is a *sine qua non* of good obstetrical procedure. Both physician and patient may play a part in establishing the rapport demanded by the nature of their relationship.

PREGNANCY AND THE COUPLE'S ADJUSTMENT

We are accustomed to saying that such and such a woman is pregnant. In one sense that is correct; in another it is not. It would be more nearly accurate to say that there is pregnancy in the family. Pregnancy is in many ways a social condition. It certainly involves both husband and wife; it also involves their relatives, the mores of the society, and the laws of the state.

Having a baby is a joint enterprise from the very beginning. The father's physiological role may not be so prominent as the mother's, but he has indispensable psychological and economic functions. The husband suffering the throes of becoming a parent is made the butt of many a joke. Much humorous discussion and literature are directed toward the "care and treatment" of expectant fathers. The father's situation is anything but a joke. A child needs two parents, and the father has a responsibility. There are many things that he may do to make the wife's nine months of pregnancy more enjoyable. He may assist with the housework or employ someone to do it. He may make certain that he and his wife do interesting things in their leisure time. He may prepare for the baby's coming by making things for the nursery. He may understand what is occurring so that he may help his wife follow the doctor's instructions and will know what to do in case an emergency arises. Together he and his wife may attend prenatal classes in infant care, which are becoming increasingly available in many communities. The wife is likely to be more than ordinarily dependent upon him, and he can do much to color her attitude, favorably or unfavorably, toward both the present and future pregnancies. Some pregnant women develop temporary personality traits that make them somewhat difficult to live with. It is important that the husband understand this fact and adjust himself accordingly.

Not the least of the father's functions is economic. Babies cost money. When the total cost of a child is taken into consideration, reckoning from early pregnancy through infancy, childhood, adolescence, to young adulthood, and including all expenses borne by parents from the initial doctor's fee to college education, the picture is breathtaking. Each time a couple have a child, the financial responsibility they assume is roughly equivalent to that involved in purchasing a new home on their socioeconomic level.

A question that often arises in connection with the prospective father is whether he should be in the delivery room (as distinguished from the labor room) when his baby is born. Some hospitals and obstetricians will permit him to be present; others will not. In one study, a questionnaire was sent to the chiefs of obstetrics in 342 hospitals, each having at least 1,000 deliveries annually. Of the 267 replies, 81 per cent reported that husbands were not allowed in the delivery room. Of the remaining 19 per cent, half restricted attendance to medical-personnel husbands, and the other half (only about 10 per cent of the total) allowed unrestricted attendance [Allan, January, 1966]. Much depends upon the attitude of the wife. If his presence would reassure her, he may be useful. If his presence would cause her to worry, he would be less than useless. Some men want to witness the birth; others do not. Some feel that witnessing it makes the child seem more their own, since they are more nearly participators. "We have never had cause to regret the presence of a husband at his wife's delivery. Often, husbands lend much help in encouraging the vigorous physical efforts necessary for spontaneous birth," says one obstetrician [Margolis, 1970].

There are arguments aginst the husband's being present at the delivery. He may get in the way of doctor or nurses. Typically the delivery room is not equipped to accommodate observers. He may become emotionally upset and conclude that the doctor is not doing all he can. He may have little or no background for interpreting what he sees and hence may misinterpret it. If he presumes to give the doctor suggestions or asks too many questions, he becomes a nuisance. He carries germs. Through long strain he may faint. Doctor and nurses have more important duties than reviving an unconscious father. Medically speaking, he is usually of little or no help. One obstetrician's opinion is that "most patients do better with professional personnel than with the family in the labor suite" [Benson, 1971].

Unless her obstetrician advises to the contrary, a woman may with some exceptions pursue her regular activities, including housework, during pregnancy. There are many sports in which she may engage, though she may not usually ride horseback, dive, or do similar things that are more or less violent in character. Sexual intercourse may be engaged in unless there are special considerations for which the obstetrician advises against it. In a healthy pregnancy, in which there is no abnormal condition of fetus, uterus, or placenta, the fetus is not readily dislodged, and spontaneous abortion is not brought about by the ordinary activities of life.

If the woman is employed, however, adjustments in her work may be indicated, depending upon the nature of her occupation. In discussing women in industry, McCall and Trace [December, 1960] point out that pregnancy often reduces a woman's work efficiency. It may play a part in shortening her span of concentration. As the uterus enlarges, the woman becomes more vulnerable to accident. Chronic fatigue is to be avoided. Among women in industry, spontaneous abortion occurs at about the same rate as in the general population unless working conditions involve noxious materials. But among the infants of such women, the mortality rate is almost twice as high as among the offspring of housewives if the women stop work before the end of the twenty-eighth week of pregnancy and almost three times as high if they work beyond that time. McCall and Trace [December, 1960] suggest that minimum standards should provide that women not work for six weeks before, and two months after, delivery. Here again the woman's obstetrician should make the final judgment.

Another question that is sometimes raised concerns the extent of the father's participation in infant care. Many modern fathers participate with enthusiasm. Others feel that infant care is the mother's responsibility. Still others, never having had experience with infants, are afraid of their own child. They feel awkward in holding it and fear that they will hurt it. The question of the father's participation in infant care is not one only of the contribution he can make to such care. It is also one of the contribution that such care can make to him. What will he miss if he does not participate? There is evidence to suggest that the human mother has no "maternal instinct" in the strict sense of the term but that through handling, fondling, caring for, and nursing the baby she very quickly learns to love it. Of course, this process is greatly facilitated if the woman wants a baby very much and eagerly anticipates having it. Also, in every culture there is a pattern of expectation which colors the rearing of girls and orients them in the direction of motherhood. Certainly there is no paternal instinct. The father, too, learns to love the child through anticipation, caring for it, and fondling it. Furthermore, the day-to-day development of an infant is a fascinating process. As the baby's world expands and he becomes aware of more and more of his environment, many a modern father wants to be part of that world from the beginning with a strong affectional bond between himself and the child already established. He does not want to wait and then be introduced into the child's world later merely because infant care is time- and energy-consuming.

SELECTED READINGS

Boston Children's Medical Center: *Pregnancy, Birth and the Newborn Baby*, Delacorte Press, Dell Publishing Co., Inc. New York, 1972. A nontechnical guide to pregnancy, birth, and the first six weeks of the baby's life. Discusses the psychological as well as the physiological aspects of childbearing; complications of pregnancy and childbirth; natural childbirth; care of the newborn.

Gaddis, Vincent, and Margaret Gaddis: *The Curious World of Twins*, Hawthorn Books, Inc., New York, 1972. (Paperback.) Multiple births; fertility drugs; life stories of twins, triplets, and other multiples; conjoined twins. Nontechnical. Many photographs.

Ingelman-Sundberg, Axel, and Claes Wirsén, with photographs by Lennart Nilsson, Britt Wirsén, and Claes Wirsén: *A Child Is Born*, translated by Annabelle

MacMillan, Dell Publishing Co., Inc., New York, 1966. (Paperback.) Discusses prenatal development. Contains remarkable color photographs.

Liley, H. M. I., and Beth Day: *Modern Motherhood*, Random House, Inc., New York, 1966. Discusses the unborn and the newborn and pregnancy and childbirth, not only from the point of view of the woman but also from the "point of view" of the fetus; the development of the fetus and the young child as an individual; prenatal and postnatal care and hygiene. Includes an appendix of "practicalities" relating to diet, layette, etc. The author is a pediatrician and mother of five children.

Scheinfeld, Amram: *Twins and Supertwins*, J. B. Lippincott Company, Philadelphia, 1967. Discusses the "inside view of the fascinating lives of the multiple-born"; the special characteristics, problems, and relationships of twins; suggestions for the parents of twins. "Supertwins" are triplets, etc. Includes case histories.

Weber, Laura E.: *Between Us Women*, Doubleday & Company, Inc., Garden City, N.Y., 1962. Written by a woman physician for women. The objective is to answer women's questions about prenatal care, pregnancy, childbirth, and postnatal care.

Conception Control and Abortion

Most couples want children and, under favorable circumstances, have them. Hence, conception control does not necessarily imply that a couple will remain voluntarily childless. Conception control implies only that a couple have the number of children that they want when they want them, when they are ready for them, at sufficiently long intervals to permit the wife to maintain good health and to give birth to healthy babies. It also implies a number consistent with the control of population growth. In short, conception control implies parenthood by choice rather than parenthood by chance.

There is not unanimous opinion about the exact meaning of conception and pregnancy relative to fertilization and implantation (nidation). In some quarters fertilization and conception are assumed to be synonymous, and pregnancy is assumed to begin when either occurs. This is the traditional point of view and probably that of the majority of the general public. In other quarters fertilization and conception are assumed to be different, while conception and pregnancy are assumed to be synonymous; conception (pregnancy) begins, not at fertilization, but at nidation (when the zygote implants itself in the wall of the uterus). According to the first point of view, conception control implies any means of preventing fertilization; and the destruction of the zygote, even before implantation, is considered to be induced abortion. According to the second point of view, conception control includes not only the prevention of fertilization but also the prevention of implantation; and induced abortion would be limited to any means employed to destroy the zygote (or embryo or fetus) after implantation.

Since there is this divergence of opinion, we shall include in the following discussion of conception control mechanical and chemical contraceptives which either prevent fertilization or prevent implantation. We shall also include the "safe period" and sterilization. We shall discuss induced abortion in the usual sense of the term as implying a process which interrupts pregnancy after nidation, recognizing that while this is a means of birth control, it is not a means of conception control.

REQUIREMENTS FOR MEANS OF CONCEPTION CONTROL

Whatever may be the means of conception control that a couple employ, it is essential that the chosen means fulfill the following requirements: (1) It should be

eleven

395

relatively effective, that is, as effective as modern medical science can make it. No method is entirely foolproof. The methods most commonly recommended by informed physicians and reliable clinics, when used with intelligence and care, are nearly enough 100 per cent reliable to make possible the removal of fear of unwanted pregnancy. (2) It should be relatively easy to use, simple, and readily understood. (3) It should be readily available and relatively inexpensive. (4) It should be aesthetically acceptable to both parties and distasteful to neither. (5) It should permit satisfactory sexual intercourse. (6) It should be relatively safe. (7) It should be temporary, in the sense that its use may be terminated at will, unless for some special reason the couple desire sterilization.

Calderone [1964] states three "contraceptive axioms": "1. *Any* method . . . is more effective than *no* method. 2. The most effective method is the one the couple will use with the greatest consistency. 3. Acceptability is the most critical factor in the effectiveness of a contraceptive method."

Conception control should be adapted to the individual couple by a competent, well-informed physician upon the basis of his knowledge of the couple's anatomy and needs. It should not be used upon the recommendation of friends, drugstore clerks, advertisements, or oversimplified publications.

UNDERSTANDING CONCEPTION CONTROL

In order to understand how conception control functions, we must understand how ova and sperms are produced and how fertilization takes place, as already discussed. We must also understand the nature of the menstrual cycle.

Menstrual Cycle

Let us assume that ovulation occurs but that fertilization does not follow. As we have seen, the Graafian follicle secretes a hormone (*estrogen*) which causes certain changes in the uterus. After the ovum has been discharged from the follicle, the cells of the latter undergo change, forming the corpus luteum (yellow body). The corpus luteum secretes another hormone (*progesterone*) which, together with the estrogen, causes further changes in the uterus and prepares this organ for the reception of the zygote. One of the changes is that which occurs in the blood vessels in such a way that small "lakes" of blood (*lacunae*) are formed within the wall of the uterus. This process of preparation requires about two weeks. If fertilization does not occur, after about ten days [Wallach, June, 1967] the corpus luteum degenerates and ceases to function [see Figure 11.1]. The hormones (estrogen and progesterone) which it secreted and which sustained the uterus in its receptive, prepregnant state are withdrawn. This causes the lining of the uterus (*endometrium*) to break down and loosen itself from the uterine wall. The lining and some of the blood from the lacunae and blood vessels are discharged. This is menstruation. Getting rid of the preparations for pregnancy requires several days, and then the cycle begins over again. Thus we see that it is not ovulation that causes menstruation. Menstruation is caused by the with-

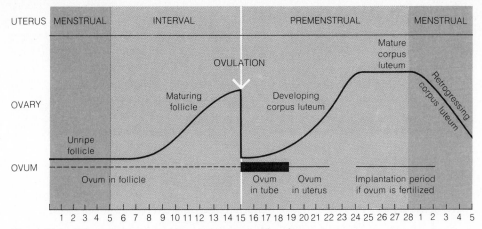

| UTERUS | MENSTRUAL | INTERVAL | | PREMENSTRUAL | | MENSTRUAL |

Figure 11.1 Schematic representation of the menstrual cycle.

drawal of the hormones (estrogen and progesterone) secreted by the corpus luteum, which in the event of fertilization would continue to be produced for a while until the placenta began to secrete a hormone with a similar function.

In some cases a type of menstruation occurs without there having been ovulation and the formation of a corpus luteum. Such menstruation is termed *anovulatory* and is the result of estrogen withdrawal, the Graafian follicle forming and being absorbed without bursting to release the ovum. The difference between the two types of menstruation is shown in summary form in Table 11.1.

The length of the menstrual cycle varies in different women. Often for some time after puberty the cycle is irregular. Then, as the girl matures, a rhythm is established. When women are considered as a group, the length of this rhythm falls on the normal curve of variability. Twenty-eight days, the ordinarily assumed cycle, is the one that falls near the middle of the curve. In one study it was found that about 10 per cent of the women had cycles ranging in length from 6 to 23 days; about 10 per cent, ranging from 35 to 409 days; the great majority (about 80 per cent), ranging from 24 to 34 days [Greenhill, 1957].

In the individual woman the length of the cycle may vary from time to time for various reasons. Most women are regularly irregular, if we may so express it for emphasis. Hartman [1936] cites a study showing that only 0.7 per cent of cases were "absolutely regular"; 10 per cent varied from 1 to 3 days; 30 per cent, from 4 to 7 days; 44 per cent, up to 10 days; 56 per cent, 11 or more days. Hartman later [1962] refers to a "regular" cycle as one varying no more than 6 days and states that about 75 per cent of women have such cycles; the other 25 per cent have cycles even more irregular. One early investigator, Fraenkel [Hartman, 1962], made a statement which has now become classic relative to the study of the menstrual cycle: "The only regular feature of the menstrual cycle is its lack of regularity." Another investigator, Holt [Hartman, 1962], has said, "Not the slightest evidence pointing toward perfect regularity has so far produced even a single exceptional individual." He goes on to say that if such a perfectly regular

Table 11.1. Steps in the menstrual cycle

Ovum matures.
Follicle forms.
Follicle secretes estrogen.
Estrogen changes uterus.

OVULATORY	ANOVULATORY
Follicle bursts (ovulation).	Follicle does not burst (no ovulation).
Corpus luteum forms.	Follicle absorbed.
Corpus luteum secretes progesterone and estrogen.	Estrogen withdrawn.
Progesterone and estrogen change uterus.	Menstruation.
Corpus luteum degenerates.	
Progesterone and estrogen withdrawn.	
Menstruation.	

individual is ever found, "she will constitute a true medical curiosity." Still another investigator [Beer, June, 1970] has said, ". . . Complete temporal regularity of menstruation throughout the life span in any individual is a myth. . . ." Pincus [1965] refers to "a completely normal woman" as "primarily a statistic."

When we think only in terms of time sequence, we see that ovulation and menstruation alternate (assuming ovulatory cycles). But when we think in terms of cause and effect, we must think of menstruation as following ovulation, not of ovulation as following menstruation. Yet, in seeking to predict the time of ovulation, a woman may erroneously think of menstruation-ovulation, since she knows the dates of her last menstrual period but not the date of ovulation. This error is made easier to commit by the fact that in numbering the days of the menstrual cycle, the day on which menstruation begins is considered the first day of the cycle as well as the first day of the period.

Ordinarily menstruation begins about two weeks after ovulation, no matter how long the cycle. In other words, the preovulatory phase of the cycle (the period between menstruation and ovulation) is much more variable than the postovulatory, or premenstrual, phase of the cycle (the period between ovulation and menstruation). Here again, however, there is both wide variation among women and variation in the cycles of any given woman. The two-week period mentioned above represents a generalization based upon averages. Hartman [1962] cites studies based on different methods of ascertaining the date of ovulation which indicate that ovulation may occur on any day of the menstrual cycle from the fourth onward and which suggest that the preovulatory phase may vary from a few days to several months and the postovulatory phase from less than a week to almost a month. Young [1961a] points to evidence suggesting that ovulation may even occur during menstruation. Fluhmann [1956] states that, in twenty-eight- to thirty-day cycles, ovulation may occur at any time from the seventh to the twenty-first day.

Various attempts have been made to pinpoint the time of ovulation. Among them are measurement of the hormones in women's blood or urine, microscopic study of the corpus luteum, study of changes in cells from the vagina, examination of uterine tissue and activity, correlation of artificial insemination and

FROM MARRIAGE TO THE FAMILY

conception, studies of the pregnancies of the wives of military personnel home on short leaves, records of pain which may possibly be associated with ovulation, studies of intermenstrual bleeding, and the correlation of ovulation and basal body temperature.

Some women experience pain in the region of the ovaries at about that time of the menstrual cycle when ovulation might be expected to occur. Some of these women claim that the pain alternates from side to side in alternate months. Such pain is referred to as intermenstrual pain, or *mittelschmerz.* Since the opening of the follicle to release the ovum requires only a few moments, intermenstrual pain can hardly be produced only by the actual momentary bursting of the follicle. But data do suggest that it is associated with the over-all process of ovulation [Hartman, 1962]. It may be caused by a slight hemorrhage following ovulation [Lloyd, 1964e].

Some women experience intermenstrual bleeding—that is, vaginal bleeding— at about the time ovulation might be presumed to occur. Such bleeding, sometimes called "midmonth stain," leads some women to the erroneous conclusion that they menstruate twice a month. It is caused by the fact that there is an increased blood supply in the woman's ovaries and uterus at the time that the follicle ripens. This blood supply produces congestion in the wall of the uterus, resulting in the leakage of a small amount of blood into the uterus through the lining of that organ, but without any break in that lining.

There is a correlation between ovulation and a woman's basal body temperature (BBT). BBT is the temperature taken immediately upon waking in the morning, before the woman gets out of bed or has anything to eat or drink. As soon as she begins to move about, her temperature rises slightly. The temperature must be taken by a special or clinical thermometer and read to within tenths of a degree. Differences between the lowest and highest temperature in a given menstrual cycle must be at least 0.4°F to be considered significant [Hartman, 1962].

Presumably the estrogen secreted by the growing follicle is a temperature depressant and causes the woman's BBT to fall as ovulation is approached. Her BBT reaches its lowest point at about the time of ovulation. Then the progesterone secreted by the corpus luteum causes the BBT to rise. This is termed the *thermal shift.* The BBT remains at the higher level until about the time of menstruation [Hartman, 1962]. If pregnancy occurs, the BBT remains at a relatively high level [see Figure 11.2].

BBT records are difficult to interpret because they are not so clear and regular as an oversimplified explanation seems to suggest. There is much variation among women and in a given woman during a series of cycles. BBT and ovulation do not always coincide [Greenhill, 1954; Farris, 1956]. Conception has been recorded in a case where intercourse occurred ten days prior to the thermal shift and in other cases where isolated intercourse took place more than forty-eight hours before the shift [Garcia, June, 1967]. There are many factors, other than those involved in the menstrual cycle, which can cause a change in body temperature.

As intimated in an earlier chapter, menstruation is a natural, normal

(a)

(b)

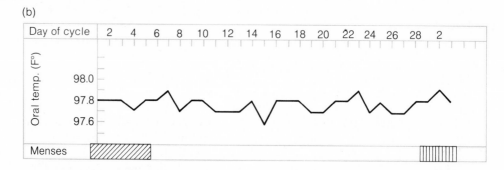

(c)

Figure 11.2 Typical oral basal body temperature curves in (a) a normal cycle, (b) an anovulatory cycle, and (c) early pregnancy. [From Ernest W. Page, Claude A. Villee, and Dorothy B. Villee, Human Reproduction, W. B. Saunders Company, Philadelphia, 1972; used with permission of author and publisher.]

function and ordinarily is not exceedingly painful, though it may be accompanied by a brief period of depression, fatigue, or irritability. Painful menstruation (*dysmenorrhea*) is a consequence of some dysfunction, some maladjustment, which is to be clearly distinguished from the function itself. Dysmenorrhea may be the result of hypersensitivity of the lining of the uterus, too tightly closed cervix, unusual flexion of the uterus backward or forward, atrophy of the uterus, tumors, inflammation of organs adjacent to the uterus, infection, congestion due to constant standing, disorders of the endocrine glands, allergies, constipation, and other similar contributing factors. It may also be due to subtle psychological factors, for example, resistance to the fact of being a woman. Many cases of dysmenorrhea may be relieved by adequate medical treatment. A woman subject to painful periods should see her physician. She should not depend upon patent medicines purchased on the recommendation of advertisements or clerks in drugstores.

Menstruation is not only natural and normal but, if we may personify Nature for a moment, is given special attention as a somewhat exceptional phenomenon. It is limited to human beings and some of the primates. In all other instances, bleeding is an indication of trouble. Menstrual bleeding is an indication of good health. In other instances, the blood clots to stop the bleeding. Menstrual blood does not clot in the usual way, thus permitting the bleeding to continue. Occasional small clots are within normal limits. Actually, menstrual blood does clot but the clots tend to liquefy before the blood leaves the uterus [Novak, Jones, and Jones, Jr., 1970].

METHODS OF CONTRACEPTION

The "Safe Period" or "Rhythm"

In constructing a diagram, Figure 11.3, to represent the fertile period and the infertile, or "safe," period in a woman's menstrual cycle, broad generalization and oversimplification are unavoidable. In this figure, m indicates the menstrual period (as distinguished from menstrual cycle), about five days. The menstrual period begins about fourteen days after ovulation, o. The ovum is thought to be fertilizable for a maximum of twenty-four hours. But even though the day of ovulation might be ascertained, the moment of this occurrence cannot be pinpointed. There may also be variation in the effective life of ova. Also, chronologically the difference between, say, one day and two days may be just a couple of minutes—11:59 P.M. to 12:01 A.M.—and we are discussing "safe period." Hence two days have been allowed as the period during which the ovum might possibly be fertilized. This two-day period is designated as oy. Sperms deposited in the woman's genital tract are thought to have an effective life of twenty-four to forty-eight hours. Here again an extra day has been allowed for possible variation. Sperms deposited during the three-day period xo may live long enough to fertilize an ovum released at o. Sperms deposited during the two-day period oy would be present at the same time the ovum is present. The period xy, then, represents the fertile period, and the period yx represents the "safe period," since there is no ovum to be fertilized during this period.

Theoretically, then, every woman has a "safe period." The problem is to know when it occurs. There are so many variables involved that determination is impossible with completely constant accuracy and in all women.

The "safe period," which depends upon avoidance of intercourse just before and just after ovulation, would be further negated if ovulation ever occurred at an unusual time during the menstrual cycle as a result of intercourse. Such

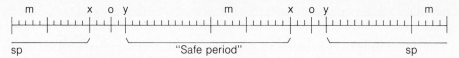

Figure 11.3   Phases of the menstrual cycle to show the "safe period." Abbreviations: m, *the menstrual period (5 days); from first day of menstrual period to last day before next period, 28 days;* o, *ovulation;* xo, *period during which sperms deposited might live long enough to fertilize ovum released at* o; oy, *period during which fertilizable ovum is possible;* xy, *fertile period;* y, *point after which no fertilizable ovum is present;* yx, *"safe period."*

ovulation is termed *reflex ovulation* or *coitus-induced ovulation.* It is known to occur in subhuman mammals. It has not been proved in humans, but there is evidence that leads some investigators to consider it a possibility [Clark and Zarrow, Apr. 1, 1971].

Means of ascertaining the time of ovulation have been discussed. At the present stage of knowledge, all such means have limitations. Furthermore, they are more useful in indicating that ovulation has occurred than in predicting when it will occur and are, therefore, more helpful to couples who want to determine the fertile period in order to have a child than to those who want to determine the infertile period in order to avoid having one. For these two types of couples failure has different consequences. The former may simply try again to carry out their plan. But the latter are called upon to abandon one plan and adopt another. What is needed to make the "safe period" safe is an accurate means of predicting the time of ovulation.

The menstrual cycle, including the time of ovulation [Rock, 1970], may vary from month to month in a given woman. Even though she may keep a record for several months and may seem to be regular, there is no way for her to know that she will be regular in the future. The irregularity of women as a group has already been discussed.

No one knows precisely how long sperms and egg live and remain effective. Surely there is no way of determining this for a given woman each time there is a possibility of her becoming pregnant.

It is impossible to ascertain precisely how long it takes sperms to make their way to the ovum, since this may vary from time to time and depends in part upon anatomy and conditions within the female genital tract, such as the mucous plug in the cervix, and the vitality of the sperms. The "safe period" is useless during the interval between delivery of a baby and the reestablishment of menstruation. This interval may be of several months' duration.

Theoretically every woman has a "safe period," but practically, because of the variables involved, the "safe period" is not entirely safe. A significantly higher failure rate is reported by couples who employ the "safe period" than by couples who employ the most effective methods of contraception [Freedman, Whelpton, and Campbell, 1959; Hartman, 1962]. We cannot, however, dismiss it arbitrarily. Further research may make dependence upon it more reliable. For couples whose religious convictions forbid the use of chemical or mechanical contraceptives, the "safe period" is the next best thing. If they choose to rely upon it, they need to keep careful records of the woman's menstrual periods and discuss the problem with an informed counselor, rather than depend upon oversimplified printed tables or guidebooks.

In addition to the uncertainty of the method, there is another argument against relying upon the "safe period" to prevent conception. Relying upon the "safe period" means that the couple's sexual life is regulated by the probability and avoidance of conception—that is, by the calendar—rather than by their mutual love and desire. If a couple are especially anxious to prevent pregnancy, they may allow more than five days for the fertile period. Couples have been known to allow fifteen days. This results in what might be termed *semi-continence*.

Incomplete Intercourse

Coitus interruptus is one form of incomplete intercourse. It is sometimes referred to as *withdrawal*. In coitus interruptus the penis is withdrawn from the vagina just before ejaculation, and the seminal fluid is discharged outside the woman's body. This is an ancient and widely known method of conception control. It is the type mentioned in the Old Testament (Gen. 38:8–10). It is unreliable because it requires precise timing and a very high degree of self-control on the part of the male. When the point of orgasm-ejaculation is reached, muscular contractions occur that are not subject to voluntary control. Masters and Johnson [1970] refer to "ejaculatory inevitability." Also, before the ejaculation of the seminal fluid, there is a discharge of a small amount of glandular secretion (the *preejaculate*) of which the man is unaware and the function of which is apparently lubrication and/or acid neutralization. The preejaculate may also contain sperms [Oliven, 1965; Masters and Johnson, 1966; Sjövall, 1970]. Ordinarily the number of sperms in the preejaculate is not large enough to effect fertilization, but fertilization by this means is possible. Coitus interruptus is likely to be less satisfactory to both sexes than is complete intercourse.

Coitus Reservatus is another form of incomplete intercourse, in which ejaculation is intentionally suppressed so that the point of "ejaculatory inevitability" is not reached. The exact mechanism of such suppression is difficult to explain. Perhaps a parallel familiar to both sexes is the intentional "holding back" of urination under stress. Coitus reservatus entails the same shortcomings as coitus interruptus.

Mechanical Contraceptives

Many couples use a combination of both mechanical and chemical contraceptives to ensure greater effectiveness.

Diaphragm   This is a shallow, cuplike device made of soft rubber with a springy outer edge. It fits snugly against the wall of the vagina and covers the cervix. When used with a jelly or cream which is put into the diaphragm and around the edge before the device is inserted into the vagina and which both seals the contact between diaphragm and vaginal wall and also is spermicidal (kills sperms), the diaphragm forms a relatively effective barrier to sperms' entering the uterus. It causes no side effects. It is made in a variety of sizes and must, therefore, be fitted by a physician. Once fitted, however, the diaphragm may be inserted by the woman sometime before intercourse (using her fingers or a plastic inserter) [see Figure 11.4]. After intercourse it should be left in place for several hours—perhaps until the next morning—and then removed for cleansing and drying.

Cervical cap This device is smaller than the diaphragm and fits directly over the cervix. It is made of plastic or rubber, the former having certain advantages. It is used in conjunction with a jelly or cream and must be fitted by a physician.

Condom This is a thin, rubber sheath which fits over the erect penis. At ejaculation, the seminal fluid is retained in the condom and does not enter the vagina. The condom may be used with a lubricating vaginal jelly. It may also be used with a spermicidal jelly.

The condom is a readily available and widely used means of contraception. Some men do not like it because it reduces sensation. If the device has even a microscopic hole in it, sperms may get into the vagina. Hence, it is sometimes recommended that before it is used the condom be tested by slight inflation. Some investigators, however, feel that such testing is unnecessary and inadvisable. Tietze [1970a] says, ". . . 'Pinholes' are probably not a common cause of contraceptive failure because the amount of semen escaping through a small hole would in most cases not be sufficient to permit conception." He goes on to say that with standards of manufacture and quality control as high as they are, testing by the user may do more harm than good through careless handling. "Modern methods of manufacture and testing have obviated the need for individual re-testing before use; indeed, attempts to inflate by blowing may merely

Figure 11.4 The diaphragm and its use: (a) the diaphragm; (b) application of spermicidal jelly; (c) compressing the diaphragm before manual insertion; (d) plastic introducer; (e) checking for correct insertion.

(a)   (b)

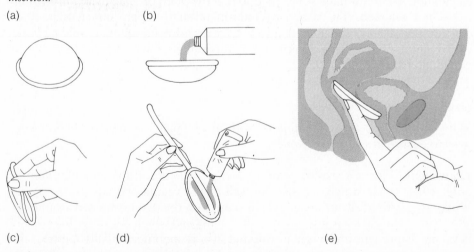

(c)   (d)   (e)

result in damage to the article through contact with a jagged finger-nail" [Peel and Potts, 1969].

The above statements cannot give the user a final answer to the question of testing, since it is he who must decide what chance he is willing to take. The Food and Drug Administration (FDA) does what it can to detect faulty products and remove them from the market. In "FDA Papers" [for example, July-August, September, and November, 1971, and July-August, 1972] there are reports of shipments of condoms ordered destroyed because they contained holes. But the FDA cannot be expected to examine all the millions of condoms used daily in this country.

A condom of poor quality or one used without adequate vaginal lubrication may break. In one case coming to the author's attention an unmarried couple were so fearful of pregnancy that the man wore two condoms, only to have the friction between them cause both of them to break. If a man loses erection quickly after ejaculation, a condom may slip off the penis or seminal fluid may escape from the open end. If the device is put on after intercourse has been started, there may be ejaculation or secretion of the preejaculate before the condom is in place [Neubardt, 1967]. The condom, then, like other contraceptive devices, has a failure rate. If the condom—made especially for contraceptive use—has a failure rate, it is highly unlikely that plastic film (such as Saran Wrap), used by some men, is more effective and highly likely that it is much less effective.

Intrauterine contraceptive device (IUD or IUCD) The IUD is a device, usually plastic but sometimes metal, which is placed in the uterus by means of a special inserter which stretches the IUD so that it will pass through the cervix. IUDs are often inserted during menstruation or shortly after termination of pregnancy because at such times there is certainty that the woman is not pregnant. Also, during menstruation she is bleeding, and the cervix is open. Hence, the IUD causes little, if any, additional discomfort. After insertion the device assumes its original shape or adapts itself to the inside contour of the uterus. The insertion must be done by medical personnel; it cannot be done by the woman herself as with the diaphragm. Once inserted, the device may be left in place indefinitely, providing there are no side effects necessitating its removal. It does not interfere with menstruation or ovulation or, usually, with sexual intercourse. IUDs are made in various shapes and sizes, not all equally effective. Commonly used forms are shown in Figure 11.5. Other forms are being developed and tested. Which device is to be chosen depends upon a particular woman's condition and tolerance, her physician's preference, and whether she previously has been pregnant, as discussed later.

How the IUD prevents conception is not fully understood. According to one theory, by increasing tubal peristalsis it hastens passage of the ovum through the fallopian tube so that the egg is not sufficiently prepared or "capacitated" for fertilization [Willson, February, 1965], but other investigators say this has not been demonstrated [Davis and Lesinski, September, 1970]. There is no evidence that the device causes the zygote to be expelled from the uterus, as is sometimes

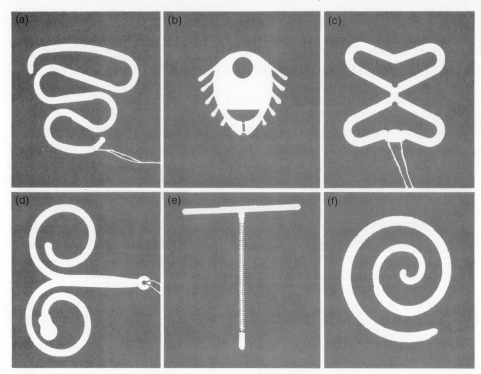

Figure 11.5   Common forms of IUDs. Top row, left to right: Lippes loop, Dalkon shield, Birnberg bow. Bottom row, left to right: double coil, Tatum T, Margulies spiral.

believed [Davis, Sept. 1, 1972]. Another theory, for which evidence is accumulating, suggests that since the IUD is a foreign body, it produces a biochemical response in the endometrium (lining of the uterus). This response includes an increase in the number of cells that are naturally present and that play a part in reducing the number of sperms in their passage through the female genital tract. The result is destruction of sperms before they can reach the ovum for fertilization or, if sperms do reach the ovum, destruction of the zygote after fertilization, and thus no implantation occurs [Moyer and Mishell, Sept. 1, 1971; Tatum, Apr. 1, 1972; Davis, Sept. 1, 1972, 1971].

Probably more than size and shape, there are at least two other factors that play a part in determining the effectiveness of IUDs. One is the extent of contact between the device and the inside surface area of the uterus: the greater the extent of contact, the greater the degree of effectiveness [Davis and Lesinski, September, 1970; Davis, Sept. 1, 1972, 1971]. Another factor is the chemical composition of the device. For example, it has been found that very fine copper wire wound around the stem of the Tatum T device increases its effectiveness [Davis and Lesinski, September, 1970; Zipper, Tatum, Medel, Pastene, and Rivera, Mar. 1, 1971; Davis, Sept. 1, 1972, 1971]. This and the addition of various chemicals to plastic devices are being further tested.

Some women expel the IUD, often during menstruation and sometimes without being aware that expulsion has occurred. For this reason some of the devices have "tails" which are left protruding from the cervix when the device is inserted. The woman or her physician may feel the "tail" with a finger and thus be sure that the device is still in place. It is difficult to generalize with accuracy on the rate of expulsion because rates vary for different devices and statistics in studies of expulsion vary. But, to make a broad generalization, we may say that the IUD is expelled by 2 to 20 per cent of women who use it. Southam [September, 1964] refers to expulsion as "one of the most troublesome problems," and Margulies [October, 1964], the inventor of the spiral, refers to it as the "major unresolved problem."

The IUD has a high success rate, but failures do occur. In some cases, women become pregnant with the device in place. But the story of a baby born grasping its mother's IUD in its little hand is fiction, not fact. In other cases, the cause of failure is the woman's unawareness that the device has been expelled. Again, generalization is difficult for the reasons mentioned above. Failures are reported for all forms of IUDs. To assume a failure rate of 2 to 10 per cent would be a generalization not out of keeping with the facts that are presently known [Margulies, 1962; Lippes, 1962; Southam, September, 1964; Tietze and Lewit, October, 1964; Willson, February, 1965; Lehfeldt, Kulka, and Liebman, November, 1965; Hall, 1967, Jan. 1, 1966; Tietze, 1967, June, 1966; McCammon, January, 1967; Loraine and Bell, 1968; Peel and Potts, 1969; Davis, 1971]. With the use of "second-generation" IUDs both the failure rate and the expulsion rate are declining [Davis, Sept. 1, 1972].

In a few cases IUDs have been found in the body cavity outside the uterus. One possible explanation of this phenomenon is that the device worked its way through the wall of the uterus. A more probable explanation is that at the time of insertion, the inserter perforated the wall of the uterus, and the IUD was placed in the body cavity [Willson, 1967; Davis, 1971]. The plastic material of which most IUDs are made is relatively inert chemically. Hence, usually, but not always, an IUD in the body cavity is "clinically silent" [Davis, June, 1966]; that is, it causes no symptoms. Perforations occur with an over-all frequency of perhaps 1 in 1,000 insertions [Davis, June, 1966] and with a frequency of perhaps 1 in 5,000 when the insertions occur ten or more weeks after termination of pregnancy [Davis, 1971]. Serious consequences are rare, and fatal infection occurs in perhaps 1 case in 500,000 [Scott, March, 1968; Davis, 1971].

In some women the IUD causes side effects other than those mentioned. Pain, bleeding, inflammation, ectopic pregnancy, or increased blood loss during menstruation sometimes occur and in some cases result in the removal of the device for medical reasons. The IUD can be inserted in women who have never been pregnant "provided the device is compatible with the smaller size range of uterine cavities and has good retention qualities" [Davis, 1971]. However, women who have never been pregnant have a higher incidence of side effects, and for this reason some physicians do not fit them with IUDs [Hall, 1970]. There is no evidence that the IUD causes cancer or infertility [Davis, Sept. 1, 1972].

Other mechanical blocks Jellies, creams, or suppositories which melt at body temperature and diffuse through the vagina are sometimes used as barriers to sperms. Foaming substances may be introduced into the vagina for a similar reason. A sponge placed in the vagina at the entrance to the cervix is sometimes used, often in conjunction with a jelly or cream. None of these barriers is so effective as those mentioned above.

Chemical Contraceptives

Spermicides Creams, jellies, foaming tablets, aerosol foam, and suppositories have a spermicidal (sperm-killing) function as well as that of providing or improving a mechanical barrier to sperms, as mentioned above. Used alone, however, they are not so effective as combination methods.

Douching is primarily a means of removing sperms from the vagina rather than a means of killing them. But spermicidal solutions are sometimes used. Some women douche with solutions of dangerous poisonous or corrosive chemicals. If a woman feels that she must douche, she may use just warm water, which is as effective as a strong chemical solution in killing sperms, unless, of course, her physician recommends something else. At best, douching is not very effective as a contraceptive measure because sperms may enter the uterus before the douching can be accomplished. Douching has one of the highest failure rates of all contraceptive methods. If douching in general has a high failure rate, it is very likely that douching with a bottle of Coca-Cola, as done by some women, has an even higher failure rate. It is also dangerous in that it might possibly cause a gas embolism.

Douching is unnecessary for cleanliness. Internal areas need no cleansing. External areas may be cleansed with soap and water. Douching washes away "protective levels of residual acidity in the vagina" and makes that organ more vulnerable to infection. It is not necessary after intercourse. ". . . External washing with soap and water is all that is necessary to maintain security from postejaculatory drainage and to avoid any suggestion of postcoital odor" [Masters and Johnson, 1970]. Of course, if a physician recommends douching for a particular condition, a woman should follow his directions.

Oral contraceptives, pills Ovulation occurs as the result of the combined action of two hormones (FSH, follicle-stimulating hormone, and LH, luteinizing hormone) produced by the pituitary gland in response to signals from the hypothalamus, a part of the brain. Estrogen, produced by the follicle, and estrogen and progesterone, produced by the corpus luteum, bring about changes in the uterus in preparation for pregnancy. If pregnancy does not occur, the corpus luteum degenerates, estrogen and progesterone are withdrawn, and menstruation takes place. If pregnancy does occur, the corpus luteum continues to secrete estrogen and progesterone until the placenta produces a hormone with a similar function. This placental hormone thus sustains the pregnancy and, through hormonal influence on the pituitary gland, inhibits the secretion of FSH and LH and prevents ovulation during the pregnancy.

There are several types of contraceptive pills. The type which is probably the most widely used contains a combination of synthetic estrogen and synthetic progesterone (progestin). Counting the first day of menstruation as day one, a woman takes the first of twenty pills on day five, whether or not she has stopped menstruating. She takes one pill each day for twenty days. Within a few days after taking the twentieth pill she will begin to menstruate. Then on day five she begins another series of twenty pills. Since they are a combination of estrogen and progesterone, the pills act in two ways: They bring about changes in the uterus, and then, after the twentieth pill has been taken, the equivalent of estrogen-progesterone withdrawal occurs, as in the natural menstrual cycle, and menstruation begins. While the twenty pills are being taken, a condition equivalent to the secretion of hormones by the corpus luteum during pregnancy is established, and ovulation is inhibited. In a sense then, the pills set up a "pseudopregnancy," (not to be confused with false pregnancy or pseudocyesis). The regimen and action of this type of pill are shown diagrammatically in Figure 11.6. As mentioned earlier, a physician may prescribe the pill for a woman soon to be married so that her menstrual cycle becomes regularized. This enables her to set her wedding date at a time when she is not menstruating, and ovulation is inhibited so that she is assured of contraceptive protection on her honeymoon.

Another type of contraceptive pill is that which adapts the regimen to the calendar—"three weeks on, one week off." The woman starts each series of pills on the same day of the week. A modification of this regimen, designed to prevent forgetfulness, involves the woman's taking a pill every day—twenty-one pills containing hormones followed by seven placebos (pills containing inactive ingredients) of a different color [DiSaia, Davis, and Taber, January, 1968].

Another type of pill is sequential. Starting on day five of the menstrual cycle, the woman takes fifteen or sixteen pills (depending on the brand) containing only estrogen. Then for five or six days she takes pills containing a combination of estrogen and progesterone. Opinions differ about the relative merits of combination and sequential pills, but the weight of the evidence suggests that the combination pills are more effective [Drill, 1966; Goldzieher and Rice-Wray, 1966; Maas, 1966; Edgren, 1969; Tietze, 1970; Feldman and Lippes, August, 1971].

It is generally assumed that the estrogen-progesterone pills act to inhibit ovulation as previously explained. But there may be other factors at work. One possibility is that the mucous secretion of the cervix is reduced in quantity, and its viscosity is increased, thus tending to prevent penetration of it by sperms [Peel and Potts, 1969; Garcia, 1970; Beacham and Beacham, 1972].

Contraceptive pills containing only progesterone are being tested. They seem to produce fewer side effects than the estrogen-progesterone pills, but they also have a higher failure rate [Mears, Vessey, Andolšek, and Oven, June 21, 1969; Eckstein, Whitby, Fotherby, Butler, Mukherjee, Burnett, Richards, and Whitehead, July 22, 1972]. Because of the small dosage involved, these pills are sometimes referred to as mini-pills. The mechanics of their action is not fully known, but research continues.

Whichever type of pill is used, it is very important that the recommended regimen be adhered to meticulously. A pill should be taken at the same time each

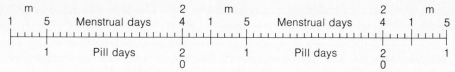

Figure 11.6 An adaptation of Figure 11.3 to show the operation of the contraceptive pill. The menstrual period is indicated by m; menstrual day five is pill day one no matter how long the menstrual period; menstrual day twenty-four is pill day twenty. Note that there is no ovulation.

day. Otherwise what appears to be calendar regularity may amount practically to missing a pill. For example, if a woman took a pill at breakfast time at 7:00 A.M. yesterday and does not take her next one until bedtime at 11:00 P.M. today, she has taken a pill "each day" but with an interval of forty hours, almost two days. For each pill missed, the possibility of ovulation, and hence the risk of pregnancy, increases [Pincus, 1965]. If a pill is missed, it should be taken within the next twenty-four hours, and then the next pill should be taken at the regular time [Drill, 1966]. As an extra safeguard a woman who misses one or more pills may use some other method of contraception in addition to the pills until her next period. When used correctly, the combination pills constitute practically a 100 per cent effective contraceptive. "The oral contraceptive tablets are the most effective means known for the control of fertility for family planning purposes" [Drill, 1966]. Pregnancies do occur in women "taking" pills, but the indications are that such pregnancies are due to human failure rather than to method failure.

Effective as they are, however, contraceptive pills are not perfect. Some women cannot (or at least should not) take them. For example, pills are contraindicated (that is, conditions in the woman make the use of the pills inadvisable) for women who have undiagnosed vaginal bleeding, a history of circulatory disease, malignant tumors (cancers) of the breast or genital tract, fibroid (benign) tumors of the uterus, or liver disease. Some women with kidney disease, asthma, epilepsy, or migraine may use them, but only with caution and under a physician's careful supervision. Occasional cases have been reported in which pills used early in pregnancy—before the woman was aware of her condition—were thought to cause masculinization of a female fetus, but such cases are doubtful and, if they occur at all, are rare. Nonetheless, pregnancy should be ruled out before a woman starts using pills. Since the pills may inhibit lactation and thus reduce the secretion of milk, they are contraindicated for nursing mothers [Drill, 1966]. In one study [Gambrell, July, 1970] it was found that twice as many women who started taking oral contraceptives immediately after childbirth, as compared with women who did not take them, stopped breast feeding by the end of six weeks because of decreased milk secretion.

It is because of considerations such as those mentioned above that it is so important for a woman to have a medical examination, including a vaginal examination and a "Pap smear," before beginning to use the pills. A "Pap smear," so called because it was introduced by Dr. George N. Papanicolaou, involves a technique for the diagnosis of cancer through the microscopic examination of cells taken from the cervix. Indiscriminate use of pills by unmarried women for contraceptive protection in premarital intercourse and pills procured in some manner other than through responsible medical channels, by prescription (for example, from pharmacist friends or other women), and without medical examination and supervision and a Pap smear is contraindicated. How could such women know whether it was safe for them to take the pills? How could they know which pills were best for them? In light of the attitudes toward sex and oral contraceptives that have developed in the past few years there is no excuse for a woman who wants to use the pill in premarital intercourse to do so without competent medical advice. Unfortunately, some physicians are indiscriminate in prescribing the pill, merely granting a woman's request for it without medical precautions. This, too, is contraindicated. On the other hand, some physicians refuse to prescribe the pill for unmarried women because of their own attitudes toward premarital intercourse. It is not the physician's role to judge how a woman will use the pill; he should judge only whether she can use it safely. In addition to a medical examination before she begins using pills, a woman should have a periodic checkup while she is using them. Oral contraceptives are composed of powerful ingredients. A woman takes the pill to avoid pregnancy. It would be only sensible for her to do everything necessary to prevent any possible unfavorable side effects.

Oral contraceptives do cause side effects in some women. Among these side effects are nausea, dizziness, fatigue, nervousness, depression, irritability, headache, intermenstrual bleeding (break-through bleeding or spotting), breast soreness, weight gain, and melasma. The last condition is a "blotchiness" or brownish patches on the skin, particularly on the face and forehead. Melasma is similar to chloasma, the so-called "mask of pregnancy" [Kistner, 1969a; Garcia, 1970]. Most women who develop melasma consider it a minor nuisance. Said one of Kistner's [1969a] patients, "I'd rather be blotchy than pregnant." Ordinarily side effects, if they occur at all, are mild and temporary; but they need to be evaluated by a physician. Hence the importance of periodic checkups. Occasionally side effects are so severe or of such long duration that a woman has to shift to another type of oral contraceptive or discontinue the use of pills altogether.

Available data neither establish nor refute a causal relationship between oral contraceptives and cancer of the breast or genital organs [Drill, 1966; Goldzieher and Rice-Wray, 1966; Peel and Potts, 1969; Kistner, 1969a; Garcia, 1970; Vessey, Doll, and Sutton, Sept. 23, 1972]. In fact, the opposite has been suggested, namely, that oral contraceptives may inhibit cancer [Ayre, Reyner, Fagundes, and LeGuerrier, October, 1969]. But this conclusion, too, is neither established nor refuted. It is known, however, that oral contraceptives will cause a more rapid growth of already-existing fibroid (nonmalignant) tumors. Hence, as a precautionary measure, pills are contraindicated in cases of detectable existing malignancies. Cancer-causing substances have a long latency period. They may be present in the human body for years before their effects become apparent. It may, therefore, be a long time before any evidence of a relationship between oral contraceptives and cancer is known. The fact that the pill has been available for contraception since 1959 and is now used by millions of women throughout the world with as yet no conclusive evidence linking it to the cause of cancer will no doubt lead to its continued acceptance.

Research data do not suggest either an increase or a decrease in fertility following the discontinuation of oral contraception. There is no rebound effect of hyperfertility, as is sometimes assumed. Nor is there any unfavorable effect on subsequent babies [Wallach, September, 1968; Peterson, September, 1969; Mears, 1968; Garcia, 1970; Robinson, Feb. 1, 1971].

The effect of oral contraceptives on the female libido (sex drive) is uncertain, and, in fact, there may be none. Some women report an increase, others a decrease, and still others no change in sex drive [Goldzieher and Rice-Wray, 1966; Bakker and Dightman, September, 1966; Garcia, September, 1968; Loraine and Bell, 1968].

It is sometimes difficult to distinguish between physiological causes and psychological causes of the side effects of oral contraceptives. Since they are powerful chemical agents to which women react differently, they undoubtedly produce side effects in some women. But there is also evidence that in some women side effects are produced by the knowledge—or by the assumption—that they are taking the pill [Kroger, 1968; Lidz, September-October, 1969]. In one study of 398 women, some were given placebos (pills containing inactive ingredients) while the others were given oral contraceptives, and the incidence of nervousness, depression, and weight gain was similar in the two groups [Goldzieher, Moses, Averkin, Scheel, and Taber, Dec. 15, 1971]. In another study 167 women whose fertility had been proved by pregnancy and who were interested in becoming pregnant again were given a daily placebo tablet but were told that they were taking oral contraceptives. The women reported a great variety of side effects including decreased libido, increased libido, headache, abdominal pain, dizziness, dysmenorrhea, nervousness, nausea, sleeplessness, increased appetite, decreased appetite, weight gain, and "cured" dysmenorrhea, as if they had actually been taking oral contraceptives [Aznar-Ramos, 1969].

Oral contraceptives and thromboembolic disease   Reports of some side effects of oral contraceptives are based on women's subjective judgment relative to their own symptoms. For example, who but the woman herself knows whether her sex drive has increased or decreased or how much pain she experiences? Reports of other side effects are based on medical diagnosis, for example, coagulation of blood and growth of benign tumors. Among the latter type of side effects, namely, those based on medical diagnosis in which a woman's subjective judgment plays no part, one of the most serious is thromboembolic disease (thrombophlebitis). (Even here, however, there is the possibility of bias, carelessness, the influence of the physician's subjective judgment, or error in diagnosis.) A thrombus is a blood clot that is stationary. An embolus is a blood clot that moves from its site of origin. In the type of thrombophlebitis of concern in connection with oral contraceptives, a blood clot (or clots) forms in a deep vein (or veins) of the leg. Such a clot may move, for example, to a lung, thus producing a pulmonary embolism.

Does the pill cause thrombophlebitis? In recent years this question has instigated research; motivated journalists and scientific writers to produce a deluge of books and articles of varying merit; polarized many medical personnel into pro or con camps; led the Food and Drug Administration to appoint special committees and publish their reports; caused the American Medical Association to publish a pamphlet to be distributed to patients by physicians whenever oral contraceptives are prescribed; involved hearings by members of the U.S. Senate; caused some women to discontinue the pill because of fear; caused other women to disregard unfavorable evidence and continue using the pill on the assumption that, if there is a risk, it is less threatening than the risk of pregnancy; and, in general, caused confusion and ferment in both professional and lay minds.

What are the research data, and how may they be evaluated? Since the issue has not yet been resolved to everybody's satisfaction, perhaps the best we can do is to present data, analyses, and comments on both "sides." Whatever conclusion the reader may reach after reading this material is not the final answer for any particular woman. Her answer comes when she discusses oral contraception with her physician in the light of his knowledge of her specific condition, and on this basis he makes a recommendation, and she makes a choice. If a preliminary examination were sought by every woman considering the use of the pills and insisted upon by every physician prescribing them, many cases of undesirable side effects would be prevented.

In 1967 the Medical Research Council of Great Britain reported that "there can be no reasonable doubt that some types of thromboembolic disorder are associated with the use of oral contraceptives. . . . We conclude . . . that the oral contraceptives are themselves a factor in the production of the disease." The report stated further that "the attributable risk of death from these diseases may . . . be of the order of 3 per 100,000 users per year." This is the report that triggered the furor regarding the safety of oral contraceptives; that has been so frequently quoted—sometimes out of perspective; and that led some women to discontinue using the pill.

The original research was extended, and further reports were published. In one [Inman and Vessey, Apr. 27, 1968] a "strong association" between oral contraceptives and pulmonary embolism was emphasized. Others [Vessey and Doll, June 14, 1969; April 27, 1968] stated that cases of thromboembolic disease sufficiently severe to require hospitalization occurred almost ten times more frequently in users of oral contraceptives than in nonusers. Studies made in the United States are reported as being consistent with the British studies [Markush and Seigel, March, 1969; Seigel and Markush, July, 1969] but not always with identical differences in risk between users of the pill and nonusers [Sartwell, Masi, Arthes, Greene, and Smith, November, 1969].

Some investigators, however, do not accept the above findings, because of the research methodology involved [Nanni, Sept. 12, 1970; Preston, Dec. 1, 1971], and present later studies which reach different conclusions. It is pointed out that although medications similar to the oral contraceptive have been used for years in the treatment of menstrual disorders and in amounts far in excess of the amounts in the pill, thromboembolic disease is rarely reported [Drill and Calhoun, Sept. 30, 1968; Charles, 1968]. Drill [Jan. 31, 1972] summarizes a number of studies using different methodology and based on results reported for over 80,000 women who received oral contraceptives for a total of more than 1 million cycles. He concludes that there was no increase in the incidence of thromboembolic disease when oral contraceptives were employed. He points out that the British studies showed only an association, not a cause-effect relationship, between oral contraceptives and thromboembolic disease. British investigators also admit this possibility [Inman and Vessey, Apr. 27, 1968; Vessey and Weatherall, July 13, 1968]. This is an important point. Statistically, items may be found to vary concommitantly—that is, in the same direction at the same time—without being in a cause-effect relation. For example, in one study it was found that the incidence of heart disease varied with number of bathrooms in the home, years of schooling, and church attendance [J.A.M.A., Nov. 30, 1970]. Obviously there must have been factors involved that did not come to light in the study. Andrews [July, 1971] points out that since studies show an increase in thromboembolic disease in males as well as females, there must be factors other than oral contraceptives involved. One of these factors may be smoking. In one study [Kay, Smith, and Richards, 1969] it was found that there were more heavy smokers among users of oral contraceptives than among nonusers. The investigators who made this study conclude that "no observed morbid change can be unreservedly attributed to the use of oral contraceptives if the possible influence of associated smoking habits has not been excluded."

That the relationship between oral contraceptives and thromboembolic disease has not been clarified to everyone's satisfaction is shown by the comments of other investigators. "There have been at least five unsuccessful attempts by well-qualified medical groups to evaluate statistically the association between thromboembolic disorder and use of oral contraceptives. . . . In each instance the verdict was equivocal: the association could be neither established nor disproved on the basis of available data" [Tietze, September, 1968]. ". . . The results are inconclusive" [Charles, 1968]. Efforts have "repeatedly failed to show a significant correlation . . ." [Kistner, 1969a]. "From the data that is known, there is no scientific evidence to suggest any contraindication to the use of the oral contraceptives in the healthy female" [Garcia, September, 1968].

In short, the risk of developing thromboembolic disease from using oral contraceptives has not been finally established. Nor has it been disproved. If there is such a risk, it is relatively small, and the risk of dying from pulmonary embolism resulting from thromboembolic disease is small indeed. A woman's choice is not between risk and no risk; her choice is between various degrees and types of risk. If a woman uses no contraceptive or a contraceptive with a failure rate higher than that of the pills, she runs the risk of pregnancy, and with pregnancy goes the risk of developing conditions—including thromboembolic disease—which may prove serious, even fatal. The "risk of thromboembolic disease is much greater in pregnant women than in subjects receiving oral contraceptives" [Loraine and Bell, 1968]. There are many life activities which involve risk but which are accepted because the risk/benefit ratio is considered favorable. All modes of travel involve risk. Smoking has been shown to be a cause of lung cancer, yet millions of Americans continue to smoke. In fact, "for normal healthy women the danger of oral contraception has been calculated to be less than that of smoking one cigarette a day" [MacDonald, 1971a]. Such comparisons of risk must, of course, be interpreted with caution.

It is interesting—and somewhat puzzling—to note that while, on the one hand, there is much expressed concern about the possible death rate from thromboembolic disease caused by oral contraceptives, on the other hand there is also much vehement support for the liberalizing of abortion laws. Abortion even under the best circumstances involves risk, and deaths are reported.

When health and life are in question, wisdom lies in caution. Therefore, a woman may assume that although it has not been finally established, there is probably a slight risk involved in using oral contraceptives. This probable risk must be weighed against other risks and also the objectives she hopes to achieve—the ratio of risk to benefit. There are factors coming to light which qualify the possible risk. There is some evidence that women with type O blood have a lower incidence of thromboembolic disease than women with other blood types [Tindall, 1971]. There is evidence that low-dosage pills play a part in eliminating side effects. Also, with so many brands of oral contraceptives available, there are pills with different proportions of estrogen and progesterone, and, at her physician's suggestion, a woman may change from one type of pill to another which she tolerates better. There is some evidence of a correlation between the estrogen content of the pill and the incidence of thromboembolic disease [Inman, Vessey, Westerholm, and Engelund, Apr. 25, 1970].

Suggesting that a woman assume that there is a slight risk involved in using oral contraceptives is an indirect way of emphasizing again the importance of a preliminary examination before starting to take the pill, follow-up examinations while the pill is being taken, and giving attention to and reporting to the physician any warning symptoms so that more serious symptoms may be prevented. A writer in the *British Medical Journal* warns that "while there is no cause for panic about the possible consequences of widespread use of the present types of oral contraceptives, neither is there room for complacency" [B.M.J., Apr. 27, 1968]. In "What you should know about 'the pill,'" the pamphlet prepared by the American Medical Association [1970], appears the following: "Oral contraceptives, when taken as directed, are drugs of extraordinary effectiveness. As with other medicine, side effects are possible. The most serious side effect is abnormal blood clotting. The fact is that serious problems are relatively rare, and the majority of women who would like to use the pill can do so safely and effectively."

Not all the side effects of oral contraceptives are unfavorable. In some women the pill relieves symptoms of the premenstrual syndrome [Barber, Graber, and O'Rourke, 1969], reduces the discomfort of dysmenorrhea, and/or shortens the menstrual period and decreases the quantity of menstrual discharge [Pincus, 1965]. But available evidence does not support the assumption that oral contraceptives postpone the onset of the menopause [Goldfarb, 1964; Böving, 1965; Goldzieher and Rice-Wray, 1966]. Some persons have expressed fear that women who take the pill may bear children in their fifties or later. Such fears are without foundation in fact.

One of the most important questions regarding oral contraceptives concerns their long-term effects, since the pill affects the pituitary gland (via the hypothalamus). A direct effect on the ovaries cannot be ruled out but at the present stage of knowledge is highly theoretical [Wallach, September, 1968]. As developments in medicine go, oral contraceptives are relatively new, and their use is the subject of much research. They are widely used. Some women have used them for years. Most of the ill effects have been minor and temporary. The outlook is hopeful. But the facts are not yet all known because there has not yet been sufficient time for long-term effects to become manifest.

Even assuming, however, that as the years go on, cases of unfavorable long-term effects are observed, this fact will have to be evaluated in the light of the widespread beneficial effects the pills have had for countless women, just as the unfavorable side effects now known, even including the possibility of thrombophlebitis, are evaluated in terms of benefits. This is done with all types of medical procedures. Any medication, even one widely used and considered an "old standby," produces ill effects in a few persons who are especially sensitive to it or take it in excessive dosage. For example, aspirin produces mild side effects in many persons and severe side effects in some. Some individuals cannot tolerate penicillin. And so it goes. The disadvantage to a few must be weighed against the advantage to the many, and acceptance of oral contraceptives is no exception.

Objections are sometimes raised to comparing oral contraceptives to medication for disease, because pregnancy is not a disease and therefore does not present the same type of urgency. But in the mind of the woman who wants to prevent conception, pregnancy is equivalent to a disease, involving discomfort, inconvenience, and risk, just as disease does. If a woman has an unwanted pregnancy, she may even go to the extreme of having an abortion to remedy it. Hence, she looks upon oral contraceptives as drugs to prevent a threatening condition.

In addition to medical considerations in connection with oral contraceptives, there are sociomarital considerations that are being given increasing thought. Oral contraceptives force both the husband and wife to confront his or her own sexuality and that of the other person. The wife is called upon to understand and accept a new-found sexual freedom and to live with a sexual relationship in which "built-in" risk of pregnancy as a rationalization for sexual restraint has been removed. The husband is called upon to "measure up" to new demands on the part of the wife or what he may fear will be new demands, a situation to which he may react unfavorably. But Kistner [1969a] says, "In my opinion, the pill poses a problem for only a minority of husbands and even then it exposes only those problems that were latent in the marriage."

Oral contraceptives, to a greater degree than any other contraceptive known, present the possibility of the wife's controlling conception without her husband's being aware that she is doing so. We can only speculate on what the ultimate reverberations of this fact may be, for example, in a marriage in which the wife approves of contraception but the husband does not or in a situation in which the husband wants a child but the wife does not.

As oral contraceptives become increasingly available to unmarried women, a new vulnerability for men will be created. In cases of premarital intercourse, for example, in which the woman assures the man that there is no risk of pregnancy because she is taking the pill, he will have only her word that she is not only using the pill but meticulously following the proper regimen for its use. If she is not using the pill or is not following the proper regimen and as a result she becomes pregnant, the man has a new reason for rationalizing irresponsibility—"You said you were taking the pill, so it's your problem. Don't expect any help from me." Such a situation also gives a man a new reason for disclaiming paternity. As we said earlier and as studies have shown, it is unrealistic to assume that all unmarried women who have intercourse will use the pill responsibly. Widespread use of the pill could give women a degree of sexual freedom equivalent to that of men, but such freedom would have to be based on actual use, not only on availability. What the ultimate result will be remains to be seen.

Other Forms of Contraception

Research continues on other forms of contraception. One approach involves the prevention of sperm formation. Contraceptive pills will prevent sperm formation, but their feminizing effect and their depressing action on the male's sex drive rule them out as antifertility drugs in men [Garcia-Bunuel, June, 1966]. A drug which has no feminizing effect and which can induce infertility in the male for periods up to 140 days per injection is being studied [Garcia-Bunuel, June, 1966]. Substances acting directly on the testes provide another possible method of preventing sperm formation. Two of these have been found to be effective when given orally in small doses to rats but not when given to rabbits. Whether their effect on human males will be like the effect on rats or on rabbits is not yet known [Garcia-Bunuel, June, 1966]. Attempts have been made to immunize males in such a way as to prevent sperm formation, but so far these attempts have been without success [Garcia, September, 1968]. There have also been attempts to immunize women against sperms but, again, without success [Garcia-Bunuel, June, 1966]. However, immunological techniques do hold promise [Meyer, 1967]. A drug which may prevent pregnancy by rendering the cervical mucus hostile to sperms has been reported [Connell, May 21, 1966]. A once-a-month pill for women has been tried with some success [Maqueo-Topete, Berman, Soberon, and Calderon, November-December, 1969; Lotvin and Berman, June, 1970]. A once-a-month injection for women and the implanting of a hormone under the skin so that it is slowly absorbed have been tried experimentally with some success, but these methods are not yet sufficiently developed for general use [Jungck, 1967; Garcia, September, 1968]. A contraceptive injection that has effects lasting for three months after it is given to women is being studied [Zartman, May 21, 1966; Seymour and Powell, October, 1970]. An injection to be given once every six months is being tested, but preliminary data on its effectiveness are not very encouraging [Tyler, Levin, Elliot, and Dolman, June, 1970].

A pill that may be taken by the woman at any time during the six days following intercourse, the so-called "morning-after" pill, has been developed and shows promise [Morris and van Wagenen, May 21, 1966]. Such a pill was administered to 1,000 women of childbearing age within seventy-two hours after intercourse. In 715 cases the intercourse had occurred at or within three days of midcycle, usually the woman's most fertile time. There were no pregnancies [Kuchera, October, 1972, Oct. 25, 1971]. This pill prevents implantation of the zygote.

The IVD (intravaginal device—not to be confused with the IUD, intrauterine device) is an innovation which offers promise and is being studied further [Mishell, Lumkin, and Stone, Aug. 1, 1972]. It consists of a plastic ring which contains a progesterone-like hormone. The ring is inserted into the vagina. The hormone is slowly absorbed and inhibits ovulation. After the initial fitting by a physician, the woman herself inserts the device on the fifth day of her menstrual cycle and removes it three weeks later. Shortly after removal she will menstruate as a result of hormone withdrawal.

All these approaches to contraception are still experimental. None, as yet, replaces the methods explained earlier.

Sterilization

Sterilization, although not a form of contraception, is a means of conception control. It may be voluntary or involuntary. There are numerous ways by which it may occur: for example, overexposure to X ray; castration; removal of the ovaries (ovariectomy or oophorectomy); cryptorchidism (undescended testes); and disease, such as mumps, gonorrhea, or tuberculosis. The methods commonly employed in effecting voluntary sterilization are *vasectomy* in the male and *salpingectomy* (tubal ligation) in the female. These operations are usually, but not always, successful. Hence, voluntary sterilization, like other forms of conception control, has a failure rate—low, to be sure, but nonetheless real. Because of its high success rate, however, voluntary sterilization is becoming increasingly common in this country. The latest authoritative estimates suggest that more than 3 million living Americans, probably two-thirds of them men, have obtained voluntary sterilization. There is estimated to have been a total (male and female) of about 1 million voluntary sterilizations in 1970, and the annual number is rising [Higgins, 1972].

Vasectomy involves tying and cutting or cutting and electrically cauterizing (fulgurating) the vasa deferentia, the tubes through which the sperms pass from the epididymes. The vasa deferentia are near the surface of the scrotum. They are readily accessible to the physician through a small, superficial incision. This incision is made under local anesthesia and the tube on either side is tied and cut or cut and cauterized. This provides a barrier, a "roadblock," to the passage of sperms. The sperms, which continue to be produced in the testes and are prevented by the "roadblock" from passing through the tubes, are absorbed by the body. Since the interstitial cells which secrete the masculinizing hormone in the testes remain undisturbed, vasectomy produces no change in the man's physique, secretion and discharge of seminal fluid, sexual drive, or capacity to have intercourse. The only change is the absence of sperms in the seminal fluid, but it takes a while, sometimes several weeks, for this to be accomplished, since there may be sperms beyond the vasa deferentia at the time of the operation. The absence of sperms can be ascertained by semen analysis. Since vasectomy does not affect masculinity, vasectomy and castration are radically different and are not to be confused.

Hypothetically, vasectomy may be reversed by rejoining the cut ends of the tubes and assuring that the internal passageway is unobstructed. The method for attempting this is to put a nylon thread or some other chemically inert substance in each tube when the ends are sewn together, leave it there until the tubal tissue heals around it, and then to remove it. (One is reminded of the way some women pierce their earlobes for the insertion of earrings.) But reversal of the vasectomy cannot be accomplished in all cases, partly because of the difficulty of reestablishing the passageway through the tube and partly, perhaps, because after vasectomy a man may produce antibodies against his own sperms [J.A.M.A., June 12, 1971].

Salpingectomy (tubal ligation) involves tying and cutting or cutting and electrically cauterizing the fallopian tubes or using metal clips to close them [Haskins, October, 1972]. The tubes are accessible to the physician through an incision in the abdominal wall or an incision in the posterior wall of the vagina [Smith and Symmonds, September, 1971]. In recent years a new technique (laparoscopy) has been used. While the patient is under anesthesia, a tubular instrument is introduced through the abdominal wall into the abdominal cavity. Through this instrument others are inserted, and in this way the physician can cut each fallopian tube and electrically cauterize the open ends. This technique shows promise. It has proved as successful as other methods. The woman may leave the hospital the day of the operation or the following morning. There is a reduction in the size of the scar. "Not only is the cosmetic factor important here, but there is a psychologic factor that appears to be important in some cases, since there is no visible scar to remind the patient of her sterility" [Barton, 1972].

Salpingectomy provides a barrier, a "roadblock," to the passage of the ovum and sperms through the tube and prevents them from meeting. Since the ovaries remain undisturbed, it produces no change in the woman's physique, sexual interest, or sexual capacity. In fact, her interest in sexual intercourse may be increased if it was previously colored by fear of unwanted pregnancy. Ova prevented from passing through the tube are absorbed. As in the case of vasectomy, hypothetically salpingectomy may be reversed. But reversal is not readily accomplished, would involve a second operation, and would be less likely to be requested than in the case of vasectomy because so large a proportion of sterilizing operations on either partner are sought because of some condition in the wife or her pregnancies which makes conception inadvisable and which is not likely to change after the salpingectomy. On the other hand, a man might request reversal of vasectomy in a second marriage. It is for this reason that some physicians recommend salpingectomy rather than vasectomy.

In spite of the fact that salpingectomy is a more complicated procedure than vasectomy, in some cases in which a couple seek sterilization the husband insists that his wife rather than he have the necessary operation. He confuses sterility with lack of masculinity or mistakenly assumes that if he has a vasectomy, his sexual capacity will be altered.

Ignorance of the effects of sterilization is found even among educated persons. A questionnaire regarding attitudes toward sterilization submitted at Cornell University drew 1,059 respondents, 75 per cent of whom were male. They represented the physical and biological sciences, the humanities, and the social sciences. There were 294 faculty members, 174 graduate students, 264 upper-classmen, and 327 freshmen. Almost half (49 per cent) of the respondents expressed ignorance or uncertainty about whether vasectomy would prevent ejaculation, and 37 per cent were certain, or thought it probable, that salpingectomy would interfere with the menstrual cycle [Eisner, Van Tienhoven, and Rosenblatt, Jan. 23, 1970].

Summary: The Effectiveness of Conception Control

In summarizing and in generalizing on the effectiveness of means of conception control, it is important to remember that pregnancy rates are the result of both method failure and human failure. It is also important to keep in mind that no one method is best for all couples or necessarily best for a given couple at all times. Research data vary, and we can only generalize broadly. We might divide methods of conception control into categories [Pincus, 1965; Drill, 1966], not including abstention from intercourse, which is guaranteed to be 100 per cent effective except in relatively rare instances in which seminal fluid is deposited at the entrance to the vagina, as discussed earlier. These are only categories of relative effectiveness, disregarding side effects. Hence they are not categories of desirability.

1 Most effective: sterilization, oral contraceptives. The pill is virtually 100 per cent effective when used properly. The over-all failure rate is very low (lower for the combination pills than for the sequential pills). In evaluating the pill we must keep in mind that there is a difference between effectiveness of *use* (the failure rate of pills when used—"virtually 100 per cent effective") and effectiveness of the *method* (the failure rate of pills as a means of contraception in a given population). The fact that some women cannot use the pill is, in a sense, an aspect of method failure.
2 Low failure rate: IUDs, diaphragms, condoms. These devices have the lowest failure rate except for oral contraceptives and sterilization. Some investigators would put IUDs into the first category.
3 Considerable failure rate: jellies, foams, suppositories used alone.
4 Highest failure rate: "safe period" (rhythm), douche, incomplete intercourse.

In short, the perfect means of conception control has not yet been developed. There are contraceptives other than the pill with a high rate of effectiveness. If a woman cannot use the pill, she and/or her husband may use a form of conception control which cannot guarantee prevention of pregnancy but can give reasonable assurance of such prevention, or they may seek voluntary sterilization, an alternative being sought by increasing numbers of Americans, as suggested earlier.

Infertility

There is confusion with regard to the terminology employed to describe childlessness. Some persons use "fecundity" to indicate the capacity to have children, "subfecundity" thus meaning reduced capacity, and "fertility" to indicate actually having children, "infertility" thus meaning childlessness. Others employ the terms with the definitions reversed: "fertility" is used to refer to the capacity to have children, with "relative infertility" meaning reduced capacity, and "fecundity" used to indicate children born. In either case, "sterility" indicates zero capacity, hence no children. We shall use "fertility" and "infertility" as meaning capacity and "childlessness" as meaning the absence of children. Childlessness may be voluntary or involuntary.

The proportion of couples involuntarily childless is variously estimated by different investigators. Probably the proportion is at least 10 per cent. Their childlessness is due to some condition in the husband, in the wife, or in both. Ordinarily it is the result of several factors operating in conjunction.

Involuntary childlessness is commonly referred to as "sterility." Actually, only part of the cases are due to this cause, if the term is used in the strict sense. It is better to speak of relative fertility and relative infertility. The population is not divided into two distinct groups one of which is fertile and can produce offspring and the other of which is sterile and cannot do so. The ability to produce offspring falls on the normal curve of variability, as do all human traits, and consequently ranges from very high fertility on the one hand to absolute sterility on the other.

Relative infertility may be temporary or permanent, remediable or irremediable. Many couples experience a brief period during which conception does not occur even though no contraceptive measures have been taken, for the time elapsing between the wedding and the birth of the first child is commonly longer than nine months.

Among the factors contributing to infertility are chance, age, general health, certain infectious diseases, tumors, overexposure to X ray or radium, removal of the genital organs, relatively low fertility in both spouses, genetic incompatibility (a condition in which the genes contain lethal, that is, death-producing, factors which kill the zygote), excessive acidity in the female genital tract, hormone deficiency, infantile genital organs, abnormal position of the uterus, too tightly closed cervix, obstruction in the cervix, closed fallopian tubes, or too few or defective sperms. When there are fewer than 20 million sperms per cubic centimeter of seminal fluid, relative infertility may result. A lower sperm count does not render conception impossible but does make it less likely. Cases have been found in which pregnancy occurred when the husband's sperm count was between 1 million and 10 million. A similar thing may be said if a man produces a high percentage of defective sperms.

Another factor contributing to infertility in women is anovulatory menstrual cycles. As we have seen, a kind of menstruation can occur without ovulation. Some women have more such cycles than do others. There is evidence to suggest that the average fertile woman ovulates normally only about 85 per cent of the time, and a healthy woman may have three or four anovulatory cycles per year [Young, 1961a]. It would be safe to assume, then, that some women have an even higher incidence of anovulatory cycles. Some women do not menstruate at all.

Clomiphene, a drug commercially called "Clomid," has been found to induce ovulation in nonovulating women in some cases, when used in conjunction with certain hormones. Pregnancies have occurred following such induced ovulation. Compared with pregnancies in general, an increased proportion of such pregnancies terminate in spontaneous abortion or in multiple births [Kistner, 1966; Goldfarb, June, 1967; Loraine and Bell, 1968]. In one study of 160 pregnancies it was found that there was a 10.8 per cent spontaneous abortion rate and a 12.3 per cent multiple pregnancy rate (compared with about 1 per cent for pregnancies in general). There were 18 pairs of twins, 1 set of triplets, and 1 set of quadruplets [Goldfarb, Morales, Rakoff, and Protos, March, 1968]. In another series of 300 clomiphene-related pregnancies, there were 22 pairs of twins, 2 sets of triplets, and 1 set of quadruplets [Kistner, December, 1965]. Clomiphene has also been found effective in increasing the production of sperms and in improving their quality [Palti, December, 1970]. Another drug, menotropins, commercially called "Pergonal," is a purified preparation of gonadotropins extracted from the urine of postmenopausal women. It contains primarily follicle-stimulating hormone (FSH) and some luteinizing hormone (LH). When administered for nine to twelve days and followed by the administration of human chorionic gonadotropin (HCG), it effects ovulation in certain cases of infertility in women. As with Clomid, an increased proportion of pregnancies following the administration of Pergonal terminate in spontaneous abortion or in multiple births. Multiple births have accounted for 20 per cent of all Pergonal-related births. Three-fourths of these multiple births were twins; one-fourth produced three or more babies [Cutter Laboratories]. In one series of 43 pregnancies, there were 20 singletons, 14 sets of twins, and 9 sets of triplets. In another series of 14 pregnancies, 6 resulted in multiple births and included 1 set of quadruplets [Shearman, 1969]. In a series of 1,450 pregnancies, 129 were multiple: 113 sets of twins, 8 sets of triplets, 6 sets of quadruplets, and 2 sets of quintuplets [Shearman, 1969].

Clomid and Pergonal are both useful in the treatment of infertility. But their use is limited to only certain types of cases and both drugs sometimes produce side effects in addition to excessive ovulation.

During the menopause, a woman's fertility decreases. When the menopause is complete, she is infertile. During the menopause, a woman may have anovulatory menstrual cycles. On the other hand, she may possibly continue to ovulate occasionally without the follicle and corpus luteum producing enough hormones to bring about menstruation when they are withdrawn. Some women cease menstruating rather abruptly at the onset of the menopause. In others the menstrual discharge gradually diminishes in quantity. In still others the menstrual periods become farther and farther apart until they cease altogether. Because of this last possibility, which might mislead a woman into concluding that the menopause was complete when it was not, and the possibility that a woman may continue to ovulate without menstruating, and thus conclude that the menopause was complete, some women dispense with conception control and have unexpected pregnancies late in life—sometimes twenty or more years after the birth of the last previous child.

If a woman has her ovaries removed (ovariectomy, oophorectomy) for medical reasons, she will have the equivalent of abrupt, immediate menopause. Her physician may give her hormone therapy to assist her body in making the necessary transition. A woman does not necessarily lose her sex drive and responsiveness when her ovaries are removed. Her sex drive and responsiveness may be maintained by hormones secreted by the adrenal glands, especially if she has been conditioned to a pattern of satisfactory sexual response [Winokur, 1963; Lloyd, 1964c; Oliven, 1965; Kane, Lipton, and Ewing, 1969]. In popular parlance, surgical removal of the uterus, tubes, and ovaries is referred to as a "complete hysterectomy." Strictly speaking, however, "hysterectomy" refers to the removal of only the uterus.

In males one cause of infertility is *cryptorchidism*. The testes develop within the body cavity. During the seventh and eighth prenatal month they descend into the scrotum, where the temperature is low enough to permit the formation of sperms, as explained earlier. If the testes do not descend normally by the time puberty is completed and nothing is done medically or surgically to effect their descent, the male may be sterilized by his own body heat. Also, a high percentage of undescended testes are abnormal; that is, they are undescended because they are abnormal, not abnormal because they are undescended [Scott, February, 1961].

It is estimated that one-third of infertile marriages are due primarily to the husband, one-third to the wife, and one-third to impaired fertility in both [Lloyd, 1964d]. The exact proportion is not so important as the fact that husbands are much more frequently at "fault" than some of them have known or have been willing to admit.

Through careful diagnosis by a medical specialist the contributing factors in infertility may in many instances be discovered. Once these factors are discovered, remedy is possible in a large percentage of cases. The first step for the couple who want a baby and have been unsuccessful in having one is to visit a specialist, explain their situation and marital history, and follow his advice. If they are serious about wanting a child, he will suggest that they submit to a series of examinations and tests. The process may be long and perhaps expensive, depending upon the readiness with which causal factors are discovered and corrected. Complete cooperation of the couple—both of them—is essential.

With the ego that tradition has built up in men and with their customary confusion of masculinity and fertility, some husbands are offended when it is suggested that they may be at fault. Some even object to examination and testing. Such behavior is absurdly juvenile, for there is no necessary relationship between masculinity and fertility, and a man cannot increase his fertility by refusing to measure it.

Some physicians suggest that the husband be tested first. The tests for him are easier of administration than those for the wife. If there are found in him factors that may contribute toward the couple's infertility, the physician may begin to remedy these and thus possibly save the couple much time and expense. The tests for the wife are more extensive and require more time. To start with her might involve a long and expensive procedure, only to find at last that the husband was responsible anyway.

There is a not uncommonly held theory to the effect that some cases of relative infertility are "cured" by adoption. The assumption is that the infertility is caused by a combination of delicately balanced factors. "Much infertility is due to mild deviation from normal physiology . . ." [Grant, November, 1969]. As the couple try unsuccessfully to have a child, the tension which increases tips the balance in the direction of infertility. Then, at long last, they adopt a child. This turns their attention away from their infertility and concern. Thus tension is reduced, and the balance is tipped in the direction of fertility. Soon after adopting a child, the wife becomes pregnant. In one study made some years ago [Perkins, 1936], it was found that in 273 cases of adoption, 200 of the adoptive mothers who had never been pregnant before had a child within an average of thirty-nine months after the adoption and within ten years after the wedding. But does this prove that fertility was increased by the adoption? Or would they have become pregnant anyway in a period that long? Undoubtedly some women become pregnant soon after adopting a child. But recent evidence does not support the view that there is a cause-and-effect relationship between adoption and conception, at least not in most cases. There may be exceptions. The percentage of previously childless women who become pregnant after adoption is not greatly different from the percentage of such women whose infertility is ended spontaneously without adoption [Greenhill, 1961, 1962b; Weinstein, June, 1962; Aronson and Glienke, September-October, 1963; Rock, Tietze, and McLaughlin, May-June, 1965]. Over a third of women who are administered fertility tests also become pregnant—without ever knowing why they were infertile [Grant, November, 1969].

ARTIFICIAL INSEMINATION

Artificial insemination is the process of transferring seminal fluid from the male to the female by mechanical means rather than by sexual intercourse. The seminal fluid is ejaculated during masturbation or incomplete intercourse into a glass container. This fact has given rise to the term *test-tube baby*. The fluid is then redeposited in the vagina at the entrance to the cervix, or sometimes directly into the uterus, by means of a syringelike device. It is done at the request of the couple in cases in which the husband has low fertility, in which there is some anatomical condition making natural insemination difficult, or in which there is some eugenic consideration, such as the husband's carrying an undesirable hereditary trait, or for some similar reason. There is no way of ascertaining with accuracy how frequently it occurs, since physicians' records are not made public. One "guess" is 20,000 times per year [Finegold, 1964].

Artificial insemination is of two types. In one type the woman's husband provides the seminal fluid. This type is referred to as *AIH* (artificial insemination—husband). This type might be used, for example, if some anatomical condition made natural insemination unusually difficult, or the woman had to maintain an unusual posture so that the seminal fluid could remain at the cervix long enough for sperms to enter the uterus, or the husband's sperm count was low and, by combining the sperms from several samples of seminal fluid, a higher concentration of sperms was achieved. In the other type an anonymous donor, to whom the couple are also anonymous, is chosen by the physician and provides the seminal fluid for remuneration. This type is referred to as *AID* (artificial insemination—donor). Sometimes AID is called "semiadoption," since the physician who performs it is, in effect, placing an adopted child in the couple's home [Novak, Jones, and Jones, Jr., 1970]. Some physicians mix a small quantity of the husband's seminal fluid with that of the donor. Then, if the woman conceives, there is no way of proving which man is the father of the child. Such a procedure, it is claimed, facilitates the husband's acceptance of the child and eliminates legal problems that might arise relative to the child's being the husband's heir. Other physicians feel that AID should be performed only with carefully chosen, mature couples and that with such couples subterfuge is unnecessary. In cases of AID, legal complications may be avoided by the husband's adoption of the child. But adoption involves court procedure and a degree of publicity which many couples want to avoid. Hence, they simply keep the fact of artificial insemination secret and present the child to relatives and friends as their natural offspring. Courts have ruled that a child born to a married couple is legally the husband's if the couple have regular intercourse and if the husband accepts the child as his own [Karow, Gentry, and Payne, 1969].

Artificial insemination has been common practice in animal breeding for some time. It facilitates control of such breeding and eliminates the necessity of transporting large and often valuable breeding stock. It also enables a given male to sire more offspring than he could sire by means of natural insemination. In recent years animal seminal fluid has been quick-frozen and shipped to owners of females, who then thaw it, dilute it, and use it in artificial insemination.

In such quick-freezing of seminal fluid, liquid nitrogen, or some similar substance, is used to lower the temperature rapidly to about 350 degrees (Fahrenheit) below zero. In natural freezing, as for example in cold weather, or in the type of freezing that occurs in a home refrigerator, water inside cells crystallizes and the cells are killed. In quick-freezing, the intracellular water vitrifies (that is, instead of crystallizing, it becomes like glass, a "solid liquid"), and cellular processes cease, but the cells are not killed [Herman, 1960].

Frozen human sperms have been used in artificial insemination and normal children have resulted [Sherman, September-October, 1964; Freund and Wiederman, 1966; Behrman and Sawada, July-August, 1966; Bunge, September, 1970; Ersek, June 5, 1972]. The first such baby was born in 1953 and at latest report, some nineteen years later, was in good health. Since 1953 some 300 healthy babies have been conceived in this manner [Ersek, June 5, 1972]. The longest recorded time that frozen human sperms were stored and were used successfully in artificial insemination is about ten years [Ersek, June 5, 1972].

The freezing of sperms makes it possible to maintain sperm banks (sometimes called "cryobanking"), just as there are blood banks and organ banks, and several such depositories are already in operation. This permits a further extension of methods employed to assist childless couples. For a fee, a man may have his seminal fluid frozen and stored to be used if he changes his mind about fathering additional children after sterilization by vasectomy; if he is widowed or divorced and remarries; if he is in an occupation, such as working with radioactive material, that might endanger his fertility; or if he marries a woman much younger than himself who might want more children during his old age or even after his death.

Many persons, especially women, resist the idea of sperm banks. Such banks provide an extension of artificial insemination, not a substitute for natural fruitful insemination where it is possible. Only yesterday the idea of blood banks and organ banks was resisted, and although they have not yet been universally accepted, all such depositories represent a beneficial adjunct to modern medicine.

ABORTION

Abortion is usually defined by state law as the expulsion of the fetus (or embryo or zygote) from a woman's body before it is viable, that is, before it can survive outside her body. It is defined by the medical profession as expulsion of the fetus (or embryo or zygote) before the end of the twentieth prenatal week [Stedman's Medical Dictionary, 22d ed., 1972]. Abortions are of four types, as follows.

Types of Abortion

Spontaneous This type of abortion occurs because of some condition in the woman and/or fetus (or embryo or zygote)—in other words, in the pregnancy—and without deliberate interference. Spontaneous abortion is commonly termed *miscarriage.*

There are many factors that may play a part in causing spontaneous abortion. One of them is a defective fetus. Thus, such an abortion is not always an unmixed tragedy. In one study, 48 per cent of spontaneously aborted fetuses were found to be abnormal. In another study, 46 per cent were abnormal. In still another, it was found that 80 per cent of the fetuses aborted at the end of the first month were defective, and half of those aborted in the second month were defective. In the third and fourth months, only about 12 per cent were abnormal [Greenhill, 1944]. In another study [Brotherton and Craft, April, 1972], 60 per cent of the fetuses were abnormal. In one study of spontaneous abortion, chromosome complications were found in almost one-fourth of the cases [Carr, September, 1965]. Broadly speaking, about one-third of the fetuses in spontaneous abortions are defective [Greenhill, 1948]. Greenhill [1945] estimates that there are at least five times as many deformed fetuses among those aborted as there are deformed babies among those born at full term. The proportion may be even higher than this, since by no means all aborted fetuses are subjected to examination.

Potter [November, 1962] concludes from her studies that there are "probably well over a million spontaneous abortions" each year in this country, that "most of them result from abnormal development of the embryo or villi," and that, if those that occur so early that the woman is unaware or uncertain that she was pregnant are included, the number would be "in the neighborhood of four to five million." Some occur so early that the woman is not even aware that she has been pregnant and assumes that she has had an unusual menstrual period. Such very early abortions are sometimes referred to as *silent abortions*.

Illegal An illegal abortion is brought about through deliberate interference with the pregnancy and in violation of state law. It is impossible to determine accurately the relative proportions of spontaneous and illegal abortions, because in order to evade the law many illegal abortions are reported as having been spontaneous.

There are a variety of physiological consequences of illegal abortion. Because of the use of antibiotics and chemotherapy, fatal infections are not so common as they used to be. Improved means of controlling hemorrhage have reduced but not eliminated death from this cause. However, in a study of deaths from illegal abortions in New York City [Helpern, October-December, 1959], it was found that "what one encounters most . . . is the case in which there is immediate or rapid death as the result of the method utilized, usually by crude, ignorant, nonmedical persons." In this study it was also found that there "were more deaths from crudely performed criminal abortion, some with very severe injury, among single women, who in desperation are more apt to expose themselves to the crude abortionist than are the married" [Deep and Jacobson, February, 1965]. The New York City Department of Health has noted that, in 1962, more than half of all the deaths recorded as "maternal deaths" were the result of illegal abortions [Kistner, February, 1965]. In Philadelphia the proportion is reported as 50 per cent, and "this fact apparently holds true in other areas of the country" [Schwarz, 1968]. In addition to the women who die as a result of criminal abortion, there is an unascertainable number who become ill or sterilized, or who have menstrual disturbances or complications in future pregnancies.

The physiological risk is great in illegal abortion chiefly because of the type of person who performs the operation and the conditions under which he works.

He knows that he is violating the law and medical ethics. He knows, also, however, that in most instances he is protected, since the woman wishes to keep the abortion secret. The criminal abortionist feels no responsibility for the health of the woman because his reputation depends not upon his skill and success as a surgeon but upon his willingness to violate the law. He is interested in dollars rather than patients and may be unable to make a legitimate living. He may not even be a physician. For example, in one case coming to this writer's attention the abortionist was a laundress. In another, in which the woman died, the abortionist was a pharmacist. The abortionist cannot take the woman to a reputable hospital. Hence, the operation is performed in an inferior hospital, in a hospital controlled by the abortionist or his associates, in his office, or in his residence. To protect himself, not the patient, he may work without the assistance of a nurse. For the same reason he may not permit the patient to know his identity or have anyone accompany her. His instruments are often not carefully sterilized. (Said one co-ed in defense of her choice of abortionist, "His instruments *looked* clean.") His techniques are frequently crude and unskilled. Since his practice is illegal and undercover, he is not subject to control by the American Medical Association and feels no responsibility for maintaining the high standards of that organization. After the operation, the woman usually goes directly back to her place of residence, since the abortionist supplies no convalescent care.

Partly because of the manner in which abortionists function and partly because state laws, though defining abortion as a punishable offense, often almost protect abortionists by making their apprehension difficult—for example, by requiring that they be caught in the act—few abortionists are convicted.

Therapeutic This is a legal abortion induced by a physician in a case in which continuation of the pregnancy would endanger the life or jeopardize the health (physical or mental) of the woman or in which serious fetal deformity is suspected. Actually, with modern antibiotics and chemotherapy there are relatively few cases in which therapeutic abortion is indicated literally to save the life of the woman [Friedman, 1965b]. Therapeutic abortions for medical reasons have become less common [Niswander, 1967], but for nonmedical reasons more common in recent years [Niswander, Klein, and Randall, July, 1966]. Today, therapeutic abortions are performed for psychiatric, eugenic (fetus may be defective), humanitarian (cases of rape), or socioeconomic reasons. In the light of the U.S. Supreme Court decision discussed below, such reasons, or at least some of them, may be expected to continue, especially relative to abortion in the last three months of pregnancy. Thus, even if abortion on request during the first six months of pregnancy becomes widely accepted, the concept of therapeutic abortion will not become passé.

Abortion on request This is legalized abortion for no reason other than the woman's desire to terminate the pregnancy. This amounts to legalizing abortions which heretofore have been camouflaged and rationalized as therapeutic or have been performed surreptitiously and illegally. Whether abortion *should* be controlled by law is one question. Whether it *can* be is another. Experience has shown that abortion cannot be legally controlled, and the only feasible and realistic alternative is to put the responsibility for decision where it belongs, namely, upon the woman and her physician. Human behavior can never be completely controlled by law. One may argue that if this be true, why have laws prohibiting anything, for example, theft, murder, or careless driving? In a democracy laws are enforceable to the degree to which they are supported by the mores, by public opinion. American society learned this during the days of Prohibition. Even though laws cannot prevent all infractions, they can provide penalties for infractions and thus reflect the societal mores. But laws can be applied only when infractions are discoverable. A large proportion of the illegal abortions that occur not only are not, but cannot be, detected and proved. There is far from universal support for antiabortion laws, and penalties for infractions of such laws have proved to be infeasible.

Sometimes abortion on request is referred to as "voluntary abortion," "elective abortion," or "abortion on demand." The latter term can be taken to imply that the physician has no choice in the matter, whereas "abortion on request" implies freedom of choice by both woman and physician. Advocates of abortion on demand sometimes forget that the physician may have scruples against it or may refuse to perform the operation because of the risk involved in a particular case. We take for granted that in any type of case a physician will make a judgment relative to medical risk and that he is under no obligation to become a party to a risk he deems too great. In abortion on request the final decision is made by the woman and her physician with no legal restrictions except those relating to safety, the age of the fetus, and the qualifications of the abortionist. The term "voluntary abortion" does not specifically distinguish between "voluntary" and "request." A woman has a therapeutic abortion voluntarily in the sense that she agrees to it; it is not forced upon her, except perhaps in some rare or hypothetical case in which a woman's condition prevents her giving consent, so that her husband or her physician makes the decision. "Request" implies that there is nothing to which a woman agrees; she simply wants the abortion. In a similar way, the term "legal abortion," as sometimes used to include both therapeutic abortion and abortion on request, makes no distinction between the differences in motivation in the two types. A woman may not want an abortion but may feel it is necessary.

In advocating abortion on request some persons suggest that denying a woman such an abortion results in "compulsory pregnancy." In one sense this is true. In another sense it is not. "Compulsory pregnancy" is misleading and must be interpreted with caution. Otherwise a false impression is given. Women are not compelled to become pregnant. In fact, a woman could not be compelled to become pregnant, even though all the preliminaries to pregnancy were set in operation or although she might have these preliminaries forced upon her, as in a case of rape. The initiation of pregnancy is a process subject to negative, but not to positive, control. It may be prevented, but it cannot be compelled. Unwanted pregnancy is usually the result of human failure in the misuse or nonuse of contraceptives or of method failure, more often the former. Even the continuation of pregnancy cannot be considered "compulsory." Only its termination can be prohibited. Unless this distinction is made, attention is diverted from the real issue, and the impression is given that women themselves have no responsibility in becoming pregnant and that pregnancy is imposed upon them by that anonymous, amorphous "other" to which problems are so often attributed.

Among the first states to pass liberalized abortion legislation were Alaska, Hawaii, Washington, and New York. In the first three of these, the only legal restrictions are that the abortion must be performed by a licensed physician, in an accredited hospital, and before the fetus has reached a specified age, and that the woman must have resided in the state for a specified time. The New York law went into effect on July 1, 1970. It removed all restrictions except that the abortion must be performed by a "duly licensed physician," with the consent of the woman, and within twenty-four weeks after conception. After twenty-four weeks of pregnancy, abortion could be performed only to save the woman's life.

Early in 1973, in a 7-to-2 decision, the U.S. Supreme Court [*Roe v. Wade*, no. 70-18] declared restrictive abortion laws unconstitutional because they represent an invasion of a woman's privacy, to which she has a constitutional right, determined by Court interpretation, since "the Constitution does not explicitly mention any right of privacy." The Court stated that a decision regarding abortion during the first three months of pregnancy rests with the woman and her physician [see also *Doe v. Bolton,* no. 70-40], because during this period abortion is relatively safe for the woman. During the second three months of pregnancy state law may regulate conditions and procedures pertaining to the woman's safety, for example, the qualifications of the physician performing the abortion and the medical facility in which the abortion occurs. Thus, during the second three months of pregnancy the state may begin to intrude on the woman's privacy.

The Court held that at some time during the last three months of pregnancy the fetus becomes viable, that is, able to live outside the woman's body. At this point the state's interest in "potential life" outweighs the woman's individual rights and the state may prohibit abortion except when necessary to protect the health or preserve the life of the woman. The Court refers to the fetus as "potential life" in the later months of pregnancy but not in the earlier months. In the later months the state may also prohibit abortion because "the risk to the woman increases as her pregnancy continues."

This Court decision, in effect, established abortion on request, at least during the first six months of pregnancy, on a nationwide basis. But, said Justice Harry A. Blackmun in writing the majority decision, ". . . some argue that the woman's right is absolute and that she is entitled to terminate her pregnancy at whatever time, in whatever way, and for whatever reason she alone chooses. With this we do not agree. . . . We conclude that the right of personal privacy includes the abortion decision but that this right is not unqualified and must be considered against important state interests and regulation" [*Roe v. Wade*, no. 70-18]. The shift from the present situation to the more liberal one now permitted will, of course, take time. It will not occur without opposition, as the experience with New York's liberalized law has shown.

It is important to understand and to keep in mind that neither liberalized legislation nor the Court decision is a recommendation that a woman have an abortion; rather, either establishes only that she be able to decide legally whether she will have an abortion, as she has decided illegally in the past. A parallel is found in the repeal of Prohibition. Repeal was not a recommendation that people drink; it permitted them only to decide legally whether and how much they will drink.

As it is already considered in some quarters, abortion will probably come to be looked upon as an adjunct of contraception, something that a woman can fall back upon when contraception fails or is not used. Such a situation will not meet with the approval of everyone, just as the repeal of Prohibition did not meet with the approval of everyone.

Passing laws or making judicial decisions and solving problems are related but distinct processes, and neither of the former guarantees the latter. Making abortion on request legal does not automatically resolve all issues. There are a number of issues that will remain "live" for some time to come, perhaps indefinitely. We can only raise these issues as food for thought; we cannot resolve them. Their resolution must emerge from the thinking of each individual as she or he considers facts and weighs values. Justice Blackmun recognized this [*Roe v. Wade*, no. 70-18]:

> We forthwith acknowledge our awareness of the sensitive and emotional nature of the abortion controversy, of the vigorous opposing points of view, even among physicians, and the deep and seemingly absolute convictions that the subject inspires. One's philosophy, one's experiences, one's exposure to the raw edges of human existence, one's religious training, one's attitudes toward life and family and their values, and the moral standards one establishes and seeks to observe, are all likely to influence and to color one's thinking and conclusions about abortion. . . . Our task, of course, is to resolve the issue by constitutional measurement free of emotion and predilection.

There is a common assumption that legalizing abortion on request will eliminate all the problems heretofore associated with illegal abortions. Unfortunately, such is not the case—at least at the present stage of medical knowledge and experience. As medical personnel gain more experience in using improved methods and as hospital facilities are better adapted to abortion procedures, risks and complications will undoubtedly decrease. But to expect all risk to be eliminated is as unrealistic as to expect completely risk-free surgery, and the risks of abortion must be weighed against the risk involved in pregnancy and childbirth.

When New York's law went into effect, there was a flood of requests for legal abortions. One "round-number" estimate of abortions performed during the first year under the new law is 115,000 to 200,000 [Schaefer, March, 1971; Ingraham and Longood, March, 1971; Rovinsky, September, 1971; Kahn, Bourne, and Tyler, Jr., December, 1971; Weisman, Jan. 1, 1972]. It is estimated that perhaps one-third of these abortions were performed on women from outside New York State. The New York City Department of Health [October, 1972] estimates that, during the first two years, 402,059 abortions were performed in New York City (174,059 during the first year, 228,000 during the second). There were 6,000 repeaters. During the first year, out-of-city residents accounted for 61.7 per cent of these abortions, during the second year 66.5 per cent. During the two years 205,287 (51 per cent) of the abortions performed in New York City were performed on women from out of state. These women came from every state and the District of Columbia, and 7,732 came from other countries [New York City Department of Health, October, 1972].

During the first year of liberalized abortion in New York, complications were not uncommon. Since many women were aborted in physicians' offices or other nonhospital facilities and there was no possible follow-up on out-of-state women in many cases, accurate figures on total abortion deaths are not available. Estimates suggest a death rate of 8 per 100,000 for abortions performed in hospitals and 38 per 100,000 for others [Ingraham and Longood, March, 1971; Rovinsky, September, 1971; Stone, Gordon, and Rovinsky, Nov. 1, 1971]. Among the causes of death were the facts that some physicians were inexperienced in the use of new techniques, that some abortions were performed relatively late in pregnancy, and that some women from outside the state returned home while they still needed medical supervision, and similar factors [Rovinsky, September, 1971; Kahn, Bourne, and Tyler, Jr., December, 1971]. In New York City there were eight deaths following legal abortion in each of the two years, including three during the first trimester in the first year, one during the first trimester in the second year. The death rate for the first year was 4.6 per 100,000 abortions, for the second year 3.5 per 100,000 abortions. In each year there was "one reported death that occurred outside the City following legal abortions performed in the City," but "some such cases may have been missed." The study mentions underreporting [New York City Department of Health, October, 1972].

As mentioned earlier, further experience with abortion on request will undoubtedly lower the risk of death still further. According to the report of the New York City Department of Health [October, 1972], "the most important conclusion that can be drawn from the two-year data is that abortion can be provided safely on a large scale." But "safely" is a relative term. "Contrary to prior publicity, abortion is *not* as safe as the proverbial tooth extraction" [Rovinsky, September, 1971]. "With added time and the development of greater expertise, hopefully techniques and procedures will evolve which will minimize risks even further. In the meantime the public must not be beguiled by speakers and writers (mostly nonmedical) who discuss 'over-restrictive' standards and promote the concept that abortions are simple, easy, and innocuous. Such people are doing the women a grave disservice" [Pakter, Harris, and Nelson, March, 1971]. The risk involved in abortion, like the risk involved in the use of oral contraceptives, must be weighed against other considerations.

In spite of the ready availability of legal abortion, indications are that illegal abortions are still being performed in New York. The exact number, of course, is unknown [Schaefer, March, 1971]. It may be assumed that the death and complication rates for illegal abortions are higher than those for legal abortions. Apparently, no country that has liberalized its abortion laws has completely eliminated illegal abortion [Schaefer, March, 1971]. Among the reasons for this are that unmarried women may be afraid to have their parents learn about the pregnancy; married women want to remain anonymous; women may become panicky when they face delays in hospital bookings, especially if they have delayed the abortion decision until late in pregnancy; and women may not be able to afford the cost. There is reason to assume, however, that the number of illegal abortions decreases after abortion is legalized.

The Nature of the Fetus

One of the unresolved, and perhaps unresolvable, issues relative to abortion is the nature of the fetus (or embryo or zygote). What is it? Is it merely tissue, a mass of cells? Is it a human being, a human life, a human organism, a human person, or a human individual? When does human life begin—at fertilization; at implantation; at a given point in prenatal development; at quickening (that is, when the woman feels fetal movements); when the fetus becomes viable; or at birth? Purely scientific answers to these questions are not possible. They are not subject to proof. Empirical data cannot provide the answers. The answers depend upon value judgments, and, as implied earlier, these value judgments are subjective and individual and involve emotional, ethical, moral, philosophical, religious, biological, psychological, and sociological considerations. The Supreme Court did not attempt to define the nature of the fetus. "We need not resolve the difficult question of when life begins. When those trained in the respective disciplines of medicine, philosophy, and theology are unable to arrive at a consensus, the judiciary, at this point in the development of man's knowledge, is not in a position to speculate as to the answer" [*Roe v. Wade*, no. 70-18]. It stated further, "The Constitution does not define 'person' in so many words." Its use of the word "person" is such that it has application only postnatally and does not indicate "with any assurance, that it has any possible pre-natal application. . . . The word 'person' as used in the Fourteenth Amendment, does not include the unborn" [*Roe v. Wade*, no. 70-18]. Therefore, the fetus's right to life is not guaranteed by the Fourteenth Amendment.

Some maintain that from the moment of fertilization the fetus is a human being, and its destruction is equivalent to murder. "There can be little doubt that the fetus is in fact an entity and thus has legal rights to enjoy protection of his potentialities" [Friedman, 1965b]. In other words, the fetus is human because it has human potentialities. But others turn this argument around and maintain that the fetus is not actually a human being but is only potentially a human being. They say that the destruction of a fetus is no more the destruction of a human being than the destruction of a seed is the destruction of a tree, the eating of an egg is the eating of a chicken, or the burning of blueprints is the burning of a house. The weakness in this reasoning, however, is that a woman does not know during the earliest stage of pregnancy that a zygote is present. It takes time to diagnose pregnancy and more time to decide on an abortion. Then it may take a while to schedule the operation. By this time the seed may be a seedling, though not a tree; the egg may be a chick, though not a chicken; and the house may be under construction, though not complete.

Opponents of abortion maintain that pregnancy is not comparative; that is, a woman is either pregnant or not pregnant; she cannot be more pregnant or less pregnant at any time during pregnancy. Therefore she is pregnant with a human being whether this be the first minute after fertilization or the last minute before birth.

The zygote receives the genetic code at fertilization. It is maintained that "a being with a human genetic code is man. . . . All the zygote/fetus needs to be one of us is time" [Noonan, 1970]. Some say the fetus is human because it has human parents. Others say the fetus becomes human as it develops human attributes, yet there is no point in prenatal development at which a clear-cut line of distinction can be drawn, on one side of which the fetus would be considered human and on the other side of which not human.

It is interesting to note that the Supreme Court decision refers to the "pregnant mother" and mentions "saving the life of the mother," and "preservation of the life or health of the mother" [*Roe v. Wade*, no. 70-18]. A "mother" is ordinarily assumed to be a female who has borne (or has adopted or has a commonly understood relationship to) offspring. A human "mother" is assumed to imply human offspring. Did the Court unwittingly and by implication define the nature of the fetus after stating that it would not attempt to do so?

It is sometimes maintained that the fetus is not human until it is viable or until it is born. This argument raises the knotty problem of time. Is the fetus human in the later months of pregnancy but not in the earlier months? In the first six months of the New York law, twenty-six fetuses were born alive during legal abortions. Most lived for only a few minutes, but one survived and was placed for adoption. There apparently had been a miscalculation of the beginning of the pregnancy; this fetus was at least twenty-eight weeks old. In each of the other cases in which the fetus was born alive, the abortion was performed to save the life of the woman [Pakter, Harris, and Nelson, March, 1971; Stone, Gordon, and Rovinsky, Nov. 1, 1971]. As long as the law specifies a time limit for abortion that is relative to length of fetal life, errors will occur that result in abortion of fetuses older than the legal limit, as in the case just mentioned.

Drawing the line of permissibility for abortion at viability contributes to confusion. Viability cannot be ascertained prenatally in a given case. It does not occur at a given moment or at a specific point in fetal development or on a given calendar date. Viability can be generalized upon, but in an individual case it can be ascertained only by trial: If the aborted fetus lives, it is viable; if it does not live, it is obviously not viable. There is also the possibility that improved medical procedures might increase the likelihood of fetal survival and thus extend viability earlier into fetal life. Drawing the line for abortion at viability also introduces an incongruity. If abortion of a viable fetus is prohibited and abortion of a nonviable fetus is permitted, it amounts to prohibiting the abortion of a fetus that might survive outside the woman's body while permitting the abortion of a fetus for which the abortion removes all chance of survival.

O'Donnell [1970] says, "Since we do not know when the products of human conception are human, then the destruction of them at any period implies a willingness to destroy them even if they are human." If there be any validity in such a statement, how is the line to be drawn between abortion and infanticide?

There are certain inconsistencies which add to the confusion. On the one hand, abortion on request is supported, in part, because of the assumption that the fetus is not human. On the other hand, there is a growing science of fetology, and efforts are being made medically to save fetal life, for example, through intrauterine transfusion and even transfusion of the fetus temporarily removed from the uterus, as if the fetus were human and deserved the professional attention usually accorded humans. A case occurred in which the court ordered an intrauterine transfusion in spite of the fact that the parents' religious conviction led them to refuse consent. In the conflict between the fetus's right to life and the parents' religious freedom, the court decided in favor of the fetus [Noonan, 1970]. "All states . . . now allow recovery for prenatal injuries, sometimes those occurring as early as the first month of pregnancy" [Granfield, 1970]. "The law now recognizes the concept that an unborn child is a legal entity and injury to him is equivalent to injury to any other person. The same standard of care which a physician owes to any other patient is owed to him as long as the physician knows or should know of his existence" [Holder, Dec. 14, 1970]. Once a child is born alive, legal action in its name may be brought against anyone who caused him injury before birth. In short, the law regarding injuries before birth implies that the fetus has human rights. A law permitting abortion on request implies that the fetus has no rights.

There is no simple, capsule solution to the problem of the nature of the fetus. Every individual who arrives at a definition of the fetus in his own thinking and every woman who has an abortion—thinkingly or by implication—makes a cluster of value judgments concerning human life. He or she either must admit that abortion at any fetal age destroys a human life or must maintain that no human life is destroyed by abortion at any fetal stage or must draw a line at some arbitrary point in fetal development on one side of which the fetus is considered human, and on the other side it is nonhuman. For thoughtful persons, the drawing of such a line presents a difficult problem. It is one thing to theorize about this issue and arrive at a point of view regarding abortion in general. It is another thing for a woman to resolve the issue in her own thinking, especially if she is pregnant. One might guess that in many cases, if a woman wants a baby, she is inclined to think of the fetus as a human being from the time of conception or at least from the time of the diagnosis of pregnancy. She plans for its coming, feels herself fulfilled as a woman, is excited by indications of the baby's development such as the first felt movements, speculates on a name for it; if an abortion is medically indicated, she obtains one through necessity and with regret. If a woman does not want a baby, she may think of the fetus as nonhuman, as tissue, as a mass of cells, or as something imposed upon her that she rejects. These rationalizations may make it possible for her to decide upon an abortion.

Actually, many women are not sufficiently conversant with embryological development to have a clear understanding of what the fetus is or even of what it looks like at various stages of growth. Referring to second-trimester abortions, that is, abortions performed during the second three months of pregnancy, Neubardt and Schulman [1972] report that after an abortion, women have said that they would not have agreed to the abortion if they had known that they carried a "formed fetus." About 25 per cent of Neubardt's and Schulman's patients decide not to have an abortion when they learn that a "formed fetus" will be aborted. These two physicians also say, "Our professional staff has found that aborting a fetus beyond 19 or 20 weeks of gestation is distasteful. Thus we will not abort after this period except on medical indications."

The Rights of the Woman

Advocates of abortion say that a woman has a right to decide what happens to her own body and therefore has a right to have an abortion without any legal restrictions. The fact that the fetus (or embryo or zygote) is a separate biological entity and is never part of the woman's body is said to be only a technicality, because it affects her body. No conclusion regarding the rights of the woman can be reached without some definition of the fetus. Also, life cannot have absolute value; its value must be relative to circumstances. For example, killing in self-defense is practically universally approved, because it means the destruction of one life for the preservation of another. Life is valued not in terms of absolutes but in terms of alternatives. It is relatively easy to approve of abortion if the fetus is a threat to the woman's life or health. The alternatives are clear: well-being of the woman versus well-being of the fetus. But what about a woman's desire to rid herself of a fetus which is no real threat to her physical or psychological well-being but only to her comfort and convenience? She simply wants to terminate the pregnancy. This is the issue. It cannot be resolved to everybody's satisfaction, and, ultimately, its resolution depends upon value judgments, whether these judgments are made by lawmakers, medical personnel, lay persons in general, or pregnant women in particular. There are points of confusion to be thought through relative to the rights of the woman, just as there are points of confusion relative to the nature of the fetus.

If a woman has the right to decide what happens to her body, does she also have the right to refuse her husband sexual intercourse over a long period of time, even though the acceptance of intercourse was implied when she married? If a wife feels she has the right so to deny her husband intercourse and he divorces her for this reason (as he may in some states), what has happened to her right? She cannot have the right to refuse intercourse and the right to remain married simultaneously. Does a woman not relinquish rights as well as gain rights when she marries?

If a woman decides to have intercourse without contraception, has she not made a decision regarding what may happen to her body, and should she not assume responsibility for the consequences of that intercourse?

Is abortion only a question of whether a woman has a right to decide what happens to her own body, or is it also a question of when? For example, if it is assumed that she has a right to have an abortion during the third prenatal month, does she have an equal right in, say, the eighth or ninth month? Would she have the right to terminate the pregnancy in the eighth month and let the fetus die because she did not want to continue the pregnancy? Would she have the right to ask the obstetrician to dismember the fetus in the ninth month and remove it from her body a part at a time so that she would not have to go through labor and childbirth? If your answer to the last question is negative, you have, by implication, established a point in prenatal life at which the fetus becomes human, defined the woman's right to decide what happens to her body as relative rather than absolute, and imputed the right to life to the fetus. If your answer is affirmative, you have, by implication, established birth as the time at which the fetus becomes human, defined the woman's right to decide what happens to her body as absolute, and deprived the fetus of the right to life. The probability is that most people would strongly disapprove of the procedure mentioned and find even the suggestion of it abhorrent (and, of course, no obstetrician would agree to such a procedure), thus indicating that the issues are neither as clear nor as simple as generalized statements seem to imply.

Some arguments which favor abortion on request contend that unwanted children have more problems and maladjustments than wanted children; that, in view of the population explosion, there are enough children without increasing their numbers with those that are unwanted; and that unwanted children are more likely than wanted children to be abused and neglected. Granting the validity of such arguments, there still remains the fact that an unwanted child has at least a chance in life; a dead child has no chance. How is a line to be drawn relative to time? For example, one study reported that "the great bulk of neonaticides [killings of children on the day of birth] are committed simply because the child is not wanted" [Resnick, April, 1970]. In this country there is no legal distinction between the murder of adults and the murder of newborn infants [Resnick, April, 1970]. But there is now a distinction between the killing of the newborn and the killing of the unborn. Persons who say this is a specious argument are by implication defining the nature of the fetus in terms of time, development, and location relative to the woman's body.

These points are mentioned to show how much more complicated the issue of abortion on request is than is suggested by the commonly heard argument—dissociated from other considerations—that a woman has a right to decide what happens to her own body. To expect to exercise such a right without reference to anybody or anything else except her own desire and without thinking through the issue is naive. Rather than rationalizing away of the nature of the fetus, or assuming that the fetus is a thing without value, the issue needs to be faced for what it is: the rights of the woman versus the rights of the fetus.

The rights of the fetus must be weighed, not only against the rights of the woman and perhaps those of the man, but also against the ultimate consequences of overpopulation, including not only the deaths of babies but also of people of all ages through famine, disease, war, and crime, as well as the tragedies of increased numbers of seriously handicapped and genetically disadvantaged people. Usually, when a woman requests an abortion, her first concern is her own condition and desire, not a world problem. But perspective need not be limited to the individual woman. If, on the other hand, the rights of the fetus are to be weighed against the consequences of overpopulation, the responsibility of both man and woman for conception control also should be weighed against these consequences. And whatever the definition of the nature of the fetus, to assume that it, rather than the couple who conceived it, is the key to the solution of the population problem may be considered a projection of blame and a sidestepping of responsibility.

The Rights of the Man

One consideration which needs to be given thought is the rights of the man with whom the woman had the intercourse that initiated the pregnancy. In the voluminous publications regarding abortion on request relatively little is said about the rights of the man. He is not mentioned in the Supreme Court decision, except in a footnote which reads, "Neither . . . do we discuss the father's rights, if any exist in the constitutional context, in the abortion decision. . . . We are aware that some statutes recognize the father under certain circumstances" [*Roe v. Wade,* no. 70-18]. Seldom is the requirement of his consent to an abortion specified in the law [Holtzman, March, 1971]. Not only is his consent not required, but a physician may perform an abortion over his objections. If the male is not the woman's husband, the omission of his consent may be understandable. But what if he is her husband? Should he have a voice in the matter? Should he have a legal right to insist that she have an abortion if she does not want one? Should he have a legal right to insist that she not have an abortion if she does want it? Should his consent be required by law?

Who is responsible for the fetus? If a woman has a child which her husband does not want, he still has a legal responsibility for the child's support. By what logic can it be assumed that a woman should not be required to have an unwanted child but a man can be so required? If the consequences of being an unwanted child are as described earlier, the man as well as the woman contributes to these consequences. Assuming that he is available, a woman cannot place a child for adoption without her husband's consent. She may use contraceptives without his consent and even without his knowledge. Physicians usually require the consent of both parties to the sterilization of either of them. Is there a parallel between any of these situations and abortion?

Suppose a man wants a child as an heir and his wife wants an abortion; does he have any rights? Suppose he opposes abortion on religious grounds, for example, if he is Catholic and his wife is Protestant; does he have any rights? Suppose an unmarried woman threatens a paternity suit, and the man wants her to have an abortion; does he have any rights? Suppose the woman wants the child, but the man is married to someone else and does not want his wife to know about the pregnancy or feels that he could not afford to contribute to the child's support; does he have any rights? In some states property acquired during a marriage is considered community property to which both husband and wife have claims. Is a fetus like community property in that it was acquired by joint effort during a marriage? "The legal question . . . of a husband's proprietary rights to wife and/or fetus are unresolved, and are generating much heat but little light in academic legal circles" [Rovinsky, September, 1971]. Here is another unresolved issue, mentioned to indicate how much more complex the matter of abortion on request is than is often assumed. Of course, it might be said that a decision regarding abortion is like any other family decision, such as the purchase or sale of a house, and should be reached by mutual agreement of husband and wife—that it cannot, indeed should not, be considered a matter to be regulated by law. The difficulty of enforcing restrictive abortion laws may indicate some public support of this viewpoint.

Even a consideration of the male's rights is not the "whole story." What about his responsibility? He has a responsibility for the child if the woman does not have an abortion. Does he also have a responsibility for participating in the decision regarding abortion? Increasingly, the prevention of conception is being left to the woman. If, in addition, the male forfeits or is deprived of any responsibility for the outcome of pregnancy, will his responsibility for sex and for the woman as a person eventually erode away? Since taking responsibility for another person is at least as indicative of manliness as the ability to impregnate, will man unknowlingly be deprived of the very thing he seeks [see Kennedy, 1972]?

Other Effects of Liberalized Abortion

As abortion laws become liberalized, will abortions become more numerous, and will there be a shift from illegal to legal abortion? As yet the answers are not known. But there is evidence to suggest that as legal abortion becomes more readily available, there is a decrease in illegal abortion and a concurrent decrease in deaths from such abortions. Legalizing abortion will also affect both the birth rate and the illegitimacy rate.

There is no universal agreement on the possible harmful psychological effects of abortion. Studies seem to indicate that such consequences are uncommon and, when they occur, are not serious [Walter, September, 1970; Pasnau, August, 1972]. These studies seem to show that, in general, women who have abortions accept them. Perhaps this is to be expected, since they make a free choice in most cases. The abortion situation is a selective one. Some advocates of abortion emphasize the absence of psychiatric symptoms among women who have had abortions, but not all possible psychological consequences can be measured by such symptoms. It is difficult to ascertain whether women feel guilt, because an investigator has only the woman's word and her subjective reactions to judge by.

It is sometimes thought that liberalized abortion laws result in a more casual attitude toward contraception. It is also sometimes assumed that less educated women will be more casual because they do not understand contraception or how to get contraceptives and that more educated women know about contraceptives and will use them more readily and consistently. In one study of 297 women who had abortions on request in New York, almost 54 per cent had some college education and another 29 per cent graduated from high school, while most of the others were still in school. Yet 48 per cent admitted that they were not using a contraceptive when they became pregnant [Murray, March, 1971]. In another study of 250 women who had abortion on request in New York the great majority had at least some high school or college education and about 9 per cent were college graduates, yet almost 60 per cent reported that they knew about contraceptives but had not used them when they became pregnant [Osofsky, Osofsky, Rajan, and Fox, March, 1971]. There is an irony suggested here. Advocates of premarital sexual freedom assume that, with effective contraceptives so readily available, no woman needs to become pregnant against her will. On the other hand, advocates of abortion on request assume that many women do become pregnant against their will.

Methods of Inducing Abortion

It is sometimes assumed that safe abortion may be brought about by self-administered abortifacient drugs. Such is not the case. "There is no safe, reliable drug available at this time which will cause termination of pregnancy in human beings" [Nathanson, August, 1970]. This statement applies to self-administered abortifacient drugs; prostaglandins will be discussed later. Many of the drugs used are not only ineffective, but also dangerous. Some may cause injury or death. The use of abortifacient pastes is to be condemned and has been known to be fatal [Greenhill, 1972]. There is reason to believe that, ordinarily, a pregnant woman will not abort as a result of using drugs unless the fetus is dead, or the pregnancy is unhealthy, and a condition exists that makes abortion easy or imminent, or the dosage is great enough to be definitely dangerous to her well-being.

Sometimes women attempt self-induced abortions by introducing sharp objects into the uterus or by douching with poisonous or caustic solutions. Needless to say, such procedures are extremely dangerous. Of all the douching solutions used in attempts to induce abortions, "perhaps the most common, as well as the most lethal, are soap solutions" [Schwarz, 1968]. A soapsuds douche may result in an air embolism (air in the circulatory system) or in kidney failure due to the chemical in the soap [Deep and Jacobson, February, 1965; Hibbard, November, 1969], either of which may prove fatal.

Women sometimes resort to violent procedures such as rolling downhill or driving over rough roads in an attempt to bring about an abortion. Such procedures are scarcely to be recommended. Often, in spite of the violence no abortion is produced. The woman finds that a healthy pregnancy is difficult to dislodge.

Medical methods employed to induce abortion are as follows. They are not of equal merit in all circumstances. Which one will be employed for a particular woman is something to be decided by her physician on the basis of her condition, the duration of her pregnancy, the hospital facilities available, and similar considerations. None is without risk [Manabe, October, 1972].

Dilation and curettage This method, referred to as "D & C," involves a physician's dilating (stretching) the cervix and scraping away the contents of the uterus (fetus, placenta, and amniotic sac) with a sharp instrument (curette). The operation is done under anesthesia. It is used for abortion through the twelfth week of pregnancy.

Vacuum aspiration This operation involves removal of the contents of the uterus by suction. It is used for abortion through the twelfth week of pregnancy. Vacuum aspiration is a relatively new procedure. It has several advantages over D & C; for example, it can be done with or without cervical dilation, it takes less time than D & C, and it causes less bleeding. Because of the size of the instruments a vacuum aspiration can be performed with no anesthesia or with local or general anesthesia. It can be done on an outpatient basis requiring no hospital stay. Reports suggest that this method is relatively safe and produces few complications [Strausz and Schulman, August, 1971; Goldsmith and Margolis, June 15, 1971; Loung, Buckle, and Anderson, Nov. 20, 1971; Ingraham and Longood, March, 1971; Nathanson, March, 1971].

Saline injection (amnioinfusion) This technique, sometimes referred to as "salting out," is used only after sixteen weeks of pregnancy. It involves the insertion of a hypodermic-needlelike instrument through the abdominal wall— under local anesthesia—and into the amniotic sac. A small amount of amniotic fluid is withdrawn and replaced with a 20 per cent salt solution. Within about forty-eight to seventy-two hours the woman will usually go into labor and deliver fetus and placenta. This, of course, should occur in a hospital. Usually a woman may leave the hospital within a few hours after the expulsion of the contents of the uterus. Complications are few, but this method cannot be used in all cases [Mackenzie, Roufa, and Tovell, March, 1971; Ingraham and Longood, March, 1971; Ballard and Ballard, Nov. 1, 1972].

Use of prostaglandins Prostaglandins are complex chemicals produced by the human body. The first prostaglandin was discovered almost fifty years ago. It was misnamed, because it was believed to be produced by the prostate gland. Since that time, a number of prostaglandins have been identified, and they have been found in menstrual fluid, the endometrium, amniotic fluid, the umbilical cord, blood during labor, placental blood vessels, the thyroid gland, the lungs, and other tissues in both male and female [Moghissi, 1972]. The richest source is seminal fluid; thirteen separate prostaglandins are found in it alone [Moghissi, 1972]. These prostaglandins are thought to be produced by the seminal vesicles [Anderson and Speroff, March, 1971; Moghissi, 1972; Karim, 1972].

Prostaglandins are known to stimulate smooth muscle to contract. Therefore, they have been used recently in experiments to bring about contractions of the uterus. Several investigators have used prostaglandins to bring about labor at term [Karim, 1972]. They have also been used to induce abortion but have the disadvantage of side effects [Horton, 1972; Moghissi, 1972]. Because of these side effects when administered intravenously, some investigators feel the method has "limited clinical usefulness" [Csaop, Sauvage, and Wiest, Dec. 15, 1971; Gillett, Kinch, Wolfe, and Pace-Asciak, Feb. 1, 1972] and "offers little advantage over classical means of inducing abortions" [Cantor, Jewelewicz, Warren, Dyrenfurth, Patner, and Vande Wiele, July 1, 1972]. Some investigators [Karim, 1972; Kirshen, Naftolin, and Ryan, June 1, 1972] feel that the use of prostaglandins for abortion does not compare favorably with suction in the first three months but does compare favorably with other methods during the second three months.

The use of prostaglandins is not the same as the use of the abortifacient drugs mentioned earlier. Research continues on various prostaglandins and different methods of administration. They hold some promise as a means of inducing abortion, especially in the early months of pregnancy [Moghissi, 1972]. Whether this promise is fulfilled depends upon the results of further research.

In one study [Horton, 1972], investigators administered a prostaglandin to women a few days following their first missed menstrual period. Bleeding started 2 to 3 hours later. It is reported that "a number of women in Sweden unable or unwilling to use conventional methods now rely exclusively on prostaglandins for contraceptive purposes" [Horton, 1972]. Whether this is contraception or abortion is a matter of definition.

Hysterotomy This method (not to be confused with hysterectomy, the removal of the uterus) involves a surgical opening of the uterus through abdominal incision, as in Caesarean section. It is used when other methods cannot be employed, or when a woman wants to combine a sterilizing operation (salpingectomy) with the abortive operation.

The Future of Abortion

In the last analysis, as the U.S. Supreme Court has indicated, whether a woman has an abortion is not a matter to be regulated by law, but a decision to be made by herself and her physician. Liberalized legislation should not lead us to consider abortion lightly or casually. As suggested earlier, liberalizing laws and making judicial declarations are not equivalent to recommending that women have abortions but are only means by which women may be allowed legally to decide whether they will have abortions. All reasonable help should be provided so that women can understand what abortion involves and understand the importance of having an abortion as early as possible. It is important that women be educated in techniques of contraception and where and how to procure contraceptives and also that they be motivated to use contraception so that they may more fully take responsibility for their own sexual behavior.

RH FACTOR

The Rh factor is a substance found in the blood. It derives its name from the fact that it was discovered during the course of experiments to learn what happened when the blood of one species was introduced into another. One type of animal used in the experiments was the Rhesus monkey. An individual in whose blood the Rh factor is present is designated as Rh-positive. One from whose blood it is absent is designated as Rh-negative. Actually, there are several Rh factors. But we shall generalize and discuss them as if there were only one and say that about 85 per cent of the white population is Rh-positive. Nonwhite races appear to be almost entirely Rh-positive. There are also other types of mother-fetus blood incompatibility, but Rh incompatibility has received a good deal of publicity in recent years.

Whether an individual is Rh-positive or Rh-negative is determined by heredity. Rh-positive is dominant; Rh-negative is recessive. This means that an individual's blood will be Rh-positive if he receives two positive genes from his parents (homozygous) or if he receives one positive gene and one negative gene (heterozygous). At the present stage of knowledge, there are no tests to distinguish with certainty between the two types of Rh-positive, though there are tests that make it possible to "guess" the more probable type of the husband [Queenan, 1967] and helpful evidence may sometimes be obtained from an analysis of an individual's family tree. Actually, there are more than one pair of genes involved, but again we shall generalize. In order to have Rh-negative blood, the individual must receive two negative genes. As we saw in an earlier chapter, when sperms or ova are formed, the pairs of chromosomes, and hence pairs of genes, separate. Therefore, the combinations shown in Table 11.2 are possible, letting a plus sign (+) indicate a positive gene and a minus sign (−) indicate a negative gene. The proportions given apply to large numbers of families. A particular couple of the type indicated in situation 6, for example, might, by chance, have all negative children.

The instance in which the Rh factor ordinarily can cause a problem is that indicated in situations 4 and 7 in Table 11.2; that is, the mother is Rh-negative, and the father and child are Rh-positive. Generalizing, such a situation occurs in only about 10 per cent of pregnancies, and sensitization of the mother occurs in only about 5 per cent of these, or in about one pregnancy in two hundred. In other words, the incidence of sensitization among Rh-negative women is about 5 per cent [Charles and Friedman, 1969; Clarke and McConnell, 1972]. Many Rh-negative women who are married to homozygous (two genes for Rh-positive, as in situations 1, 2, and 4 in Table 11.2) Rh-positive husbands have several children without any of them being affected [Dacie, 1967]. However, if a woman gives birth to one baby that is affected, subsequent babies are likely to be affected [Davidsohn, 1965].

Although it is generally true that there is no direct connection between mother and fetus, that the placental "roots" (villi) are part of a closed fetal circulatory system and merely extend into, but do not connect with, the mother's blood stream, "the placenta is rarely, if ever, a completely tight seal" [Cohen,

Table 11.2. Possible Rh-positive–Rh negative combinations

	FATHER	MOTHER	OFFSPRING
1.	++(positive)	++(positive)	all++(all positive)
2.	++(positive)	+−(positive)	$1/2$++;$1/2$+−(all positive)
3.	+−(positive)	++(positive)	$1/2$++;$1/2$+−(all positive)
4.	++(positive)	−−(negative)	all+−(all positive)
5.	−−(negative)	++(positive)	all+−(all positive)
6.	+−(positive)	+−(positive)	$1/4$++;$1/2$+−;$1/4$−−($3/4$ positive;$1/4$ negative)
7.	+−(positive)	−−(negative)	$1/2$+−;$1/2$−−($1/2$ positive;$1/2$ negative)
8.	−−(negative)	+−(positive)	$1/2$+−;$1/2$−−($1/2$ positive;$1/2$ negative)
9.	−−(negative)	−−(negative)	all−−(all negative)

Zuelzer, Gustafson, and Evans, May, 1964]. It is now established that fetal blood cells do "cross the placental barrier" and pass in minute quantities into the maternal circulation, at least in a considerable proportion of cases [Clayton, Feldhaus, and Whitacre, June, 1964; Turchetti, Palagi, and Lattanzi, November, 1965; Clayton, Feldhaus, Phythyon, and Whitacre, August, 1966; McLarey and Fish, July 15, 1966]. Fetal blood cells may also pass into the maternal circulation during the third stage of labor (when the placenta is separated from the uterine wall), during abortion, during amniocentesis, or during Caesarean section [Roberts, 1957; Zipursky, Pollack, Chown, and Israels, 1963; Clark and Jacobs, May, 1964; Dacie, 1967; Goldman and Eckerling, September, 1972]. The amount of blood passing from fetus to mother need not be very great to produce an effect. In some cases 0.1 cubic centimeter of Rh-positive blood is sufficient [Queenan, 1967]. In situations 4 and 7 in Table 11.2, the Rh factor can cause a problem only if such passage occurs.

When an individual is vaccinated for smallpox, a small amount of vaccine, a foreign substance, is introduced into his blood stream. His body reacts to this foreign substance and produces chemicals termed *antibodies*. The antibodies remain in the individual's blood stream for some time. If the organisms that cause smallpox find their way into his blood stream, the antibodies destroy them. Hence, he is immunized against the disease.

When an Rh-negative mother has an Rh-positive fetus and fetal blood cells pass into the maternal circulation, the mother's body may react to the Rh-positive blood of the child as to a foreign substance and produce antibodies. It is as if the mother were vaccinated against the blood of her baby. The result is a type of sensitization termed *isoimmunization*. When the antibodies from the mother pass back through the placenta into the blood of the fetus, having been formed to protect the mother from the fetus's Rh-positive blood, they damage red cells in that blood. Because of this damage, the condition in the child is termed *hemolytic* (blood-damaging) *disease of the newborn*. Since the part of the fetal blood damaged is the red cells and the condition causes the fetus to produce immature red cells (erythroblasts) at a rapid rate, the disease is also termed *erythroblastosis fetalis*.

Even when the mother is Rh-negative and the fetus is Rh-positive and there is the passage of fetal blood cells into the maternal circulation and the mother's body reacts to the baby's blood, she is not likely to produce enough antibodies in one pregnancy to affect the child. Or it may be that since it takes some time for antibodies to be produced, the first baby is born before it can be affected [Clarke and McConnell, 1972]. The above statement must be qualified, however. It is the number of pregnancies, not the number of live-born children, that must be considered. For example, if a woman has two spontaneous abortions or stillbirths before she bears a live baby, so far as the Rh problem is concerned she would count three pregnancies. If an Rh-negative woman had a transfusion of Rh-positive blood, antibodies would be produced that would give her a "head start" on her first pregnancy. Since the Rh factor was discovered in the early 1940s, there are women of childbearing age who may have had such a transfusion. In the absence of such transfusion the incidence of isoimmunization in a first pregnancy is very low, but it is not unknown [Queenan, 1967]. In some cases this may possibly be due to the fact that the woman received an initial stimulus in antibody formation from her own mother's Rh-positive blood cells before birth [Taylor, August, 1967].

The antibodies produced by the mother damage the fetus's red blood cells. As a result of this damage, a chemical (*bilirubin*) is released and accumulates in the fetus's blood. This chemical is a pigment, and its presence produces a yellowish skin discoloration (jaundice). Since the red cells carry oxygen, damage to them reduces the oxygen-carrying capacity of the fetal blood. Hence the child may exhibit symptoms of anemia. The combined effect of the anemia and the chemical (bilirubin) may cause brain damage with resultant mental retardation or cerebral palsy. It may even cause death. Since the red cells are formed in the liver of the fetus, this organ may enlarge in an effort to produce cells more rapidly than they are damaged [Allen and Diamond, 1957]. At the other extreme, the child's symptoms may be very mild and involve no more than a discoloration of the milk teeth which disappears when these teeth are replaced by permanent ones.

The Rh factor is something to be understood and taken into account when the blood types of the parents are such that a problem may arise. This factor is, however, not as fearsome as was first thought. The publicity accompanying its discovery set into motion a fear that has not yet been allayed. Part of the reason that the Rh factor need not be feared as much as was originally thought is the fact that methods of detecting the problem by measuring the concentration of antibodies in the mother and by determining the condition of the fetus through the examination of amniotic fluid obtained by means of amniocentesis have been developed [Liley, 1964; Queenan, 1967]. Methods of treating the affected baby have also been developed. One method is an exchange transfusion by which the baby's Rh-positive blood is partially, or almost entirely, replaced with Rh-negative blood [Wu and Oh, 1969]. Such a transfusion is typically done through the umbilical vein which is left readily available when the umbilical cord is cut [Howell and Flowers, December, 1964]. A more recently developed method, used for the first time by A. W. Liley in 1963, involves introducing a long needle, guided by X ray or by means of a fluoroscope with closed-circuit-television image intensification [Work, Jaffe, Campbell, and Whitehouse, March, 1966], through the abdominal wall of the mother, through the wall of the uterus, and into the abdominal cavity of the fetus. Then a fine plastic tube is introduced through the needle, and the latter is withdrawn. Through the plastic tube Rh-negative blood is transfused into the abdominal cavity of the fetus. From there it is absorbed via the baby's lymphatic system [Queenan, 1967]. Intrauterine transfusion is ingenious and dramatic and has saved babies' lives. But it is not without risk. It is "by no means the ideal answer to the treatment of Rh disease" [Friesen and Bowman, 1967]. It is ". . . not recommended as a routine" [Bowes, Drose and Bruns, Nov. 15, 1965]. Its use is indicated only in extreme cases.

If the use of Rh-negative blood in such cases is puzzling, several things might be kept in mind. The first problem is to give the baby blood that will function in the presence of the antibodies which passed to him from his mother. Since the antibodies are designed to damage Rh-positive blood cells, the baby is given Rh-negative blood. He will not react to this blood by the production of antibodies, since it is the Rh-negative individual who reacts to Rh-positive blood, not vice versa. Furthermore, the transfused Rh-negative blood will not produce antibodies in reaction with the baby's Rh-positive blood, since the antibodies are not formed in or by blood but in the spleen, liver, bone marrow, and/or lymph nodes [Carpenter, 1956]. The baby, Rh-positive by heredity, will continue to form Rh-positive blood which will gradually replace the Rh-negative blood with which he was transfused.

Several new approaches to the treatment of the baby give promise of reducing the need for exchange transfusions by increasing the baby's ability to excrete bilirubin. One method is the medication of the mother with phenobarbital for several weeks before delivery [Halpin, Jones, Bishop, and Lerner, July, 1972]. Another is to subject the newborn infant to fluorescent light. Still another is early feeding of the newborn infant (within the first twelve hours after birth) which tends to decrease the absorption of bilirubin in the intestinal tract [Lucey, 1971].

Sometimes, when it is likely that the child will be erythroblastotic, the obstetrician induces labor so that the baby is born early. This does not prevent erythroblastosis, but it does prevent some stillbirths [Scott, 1963; Allen and Diamond, 1957].

If the situation discussed above is reversed, that is, if the mother is Rh-positive, the fetus is Rh-negative, and there is the passage of maternal blood cells into the fetal circulation, why is the mother not affected by antibodies produced by the fetus? There are several reasons. First, an immature organism usually has a lower capacity to produce antibodies than does a more mature one [Carpenter, 1956]. Second, the difference in body size, and hence in quantity of blood (with resultant dilution), would make a difference. Third, there is no possibility of an accumulation of antibodies in the fetus through successive pregnancies.

Since in so many cases Rh-positive fetal blood cells enter the maternal circulation late in pregnancy or during labor and delivery, a method has been devised for preventing isoimmunization in women who have not yet become sensitized. If Rh-positive fetal blood cells do pass into the Rh-negative maternal circulation, the woman's body reacts to them and forms antibodies, as explained previously. But this antibody formation takes some time. Therefore, within seventy-two hours after delivery (or abortion or Caesarean section) the nonsensitized woman is injected (intramuscularly) with a special anti-Rh–gamma-globulin preparation, commercially called "RhoGAM" or "Gamulin Rh," procured from the blood plasma of Rh-negative women who have developed a high concentration of antibodies or from male volunteers who have been stimulated to produce antibodies [Friedman, 1969]. Just how this preparation functions is not fully known. It may destroy Rh-positive fetal blood cells as antibodies formed in an Rh-negative woman's body during pregnancy damage the blood cells of an Rh-positive fetus. Hence, the woman does not produce antibodies against fetal blood, and isoimmunization is prevented [Freda, 1966; Hamilton, December, 1967; Queenan, 1967]. Or it may be that the preparation suppresses the mother's antibody response to the Rh-positive fetal cells [Clarke, June, 1971]. Apparently the antibodies introduced in the anti-Rh–gamma-globulin injection gradually disappear from the woman's blood so that there are none left to pass into the blood of a fetus in a subsequent pregnancy.

ADOPTION

There were 175,000 child adoptions in this country in 1970, more than half by nonrelatives. Of the total, 69,000 were placed by social agencies [U.S. Bureau of the Census, *Statistical Abstract*, 1972]. Adoption is no longer considered an act of charity through which a homeless child is given maintenance. It is deemed a privilege for the adoptive parents as well as for the child. The future welfare of all concerned is taken into consideration. Not only is the child chosen; the adoptive home and parents also are chosen. Actually, in recent years the concept of "adoptability" has changed. Formerly the emphasis was upon finding a child for a family. Now the emphasis is upon finding a family for a child [Boehm, 1965]. The staffs in the better agencies insist upon meeting the prospective adoptive parents, investigating their social and economic position, and sending a special investigator to see the home and talk with friends. In this way adults and child are "fitted" to each other. Race, religion, intelligence, nationality, education, and cultural background of natural and of adoptive parents are matched in so far as this is possible. So carefully is this done in some cases that the child actually looks like the new parents and could easily pass as their own offspring. Many couples desire this similarity. On the other hand, as the world situation has changed owing to war and other catastrophes, an increasing number of couples are adopting children of other races and nationalities. Some couples combine sterilization with this sort of adoption as their contribution to zero population growth, seeking to care for children already born rather than adding new ones to an already overpopulated world.

Usually the agency collects all available facts pertaining to the child's background. These are kept on file. Some agencies reveal as much as the adoptive parents wish to know. Others hold that the less the new parents know the better off both the child and they will be, since knowing the child's background may lead them to "read into" his behavior something that is there only in their own imagination. In general, trusting the staff of a reliable agency is a better safeguard than knowing the necessarily incomplete data on the child's origin. The identity of natural parents is usually not revealed to adoptive parents, and vice versa. Hence there is very little chance of the former's appearing at an inopportune time to upset the child's adjustment. When the baby is left with the agency, all claim to it is relinquished.

No defective child is offered for adoption without the prospective adoptive parents' being apprised of the defects. They are not obliged to accept the baby if they do not want it. In the better agencies all children remain in a temporary home for observation, medical attention, and testing for at least a brief period before being placed.

When the child is taken by the prospective adoptive parents, it is on probation, so to speak, for a time. If during this period before the final papers have been signed it develops any defects not observable in infancy, it may be returned to the agency. Few babies are returned, since many defects may be observed very early in life and there is but slight chance of others developing. A couple who adopt a child run very slight risk of receiving one who is defective—certainly no more risk than in having one of their own, and probably less. When they adopt a baby, they can at least see what they are getting.

Experience proves that adopted children love and are loved as much as natural ones. The biological parents, if anything is known about them, are strangers; if nothing is known of them, they are merely words and a source of mild curiosity.

In the rearing of the child, his adoption should be made a natural part of his life, something that he takes for granted. He should be told of it as soon as he is able to understand. He should not, however, be reminded of it in a disparaging way. No gratitude should be demanded, and his shortcomings should never be blamed on the fact of adoption. Some adoptive parents speak of their "adopted child" or "chosen child." In this way the child grows up with the idea of adoption accepted casually. Cases are known in which a child has boasted to his playmates, "I was chosen because my parents loved me, but yours had to take you." In one case in which a couple had adopted several children, two of them were overheard discussing a new friend, who was the natural child of her parents. "Let's not tell her that we're adopted," they agreed, "it might make her feel bad."

SELECTED READINGS

Calderone, Mary Steichen (ed.): *Manual of Family Planning and Contraceptive Practice*, 2d ed., The Williams & Wilkins Company, Baltimore, 1970. Compilation of materials prepared by some sixty persons relative to contraceptive methods, effectiveness, legal aspects, research, and sterilization and organizations involved in family planning.

Finegold, Wilfred J.: *Artificial Insemination*, Charles C Thomas, Publisher, Spring-field, Ill., 1964. Nontechnical discussion of medical, legal, emotional, and religious aspects. Includes case histories and anecdotes.

Gillette, Paul J.: *Vasectomy: The Male Sterilization Operation*, Paperback Library, New York, 1972. (Paperback.) What the operation is and its effects and legal aspects, what religious leaders say about it, and what men who have had it say about it. Includes a list of vasectomy clinics and a list of organizations and agencies that assist financially.

Kasirsky, Gilbert: *Vasectomy, Manhood, and Sex*, Springer Publishing Company, Inc., New York, 1972. Answers to commonly asked questions; frozen sperm banks; techniques; reversibility; clinics where vasectomy is available. One chapter on vasectomy from a woman's point of view was written by the author's wife.

Kistner, Robert W.: *The Pill: Facts and Fallacies about Today's Oral Contraceptives*, Delacorte Press, Dell Publishing Co., Inc., New York, 1969. Nontechnical discussion of contraceptive pills, how they work, side effects, effectiveness, other forms of contraception, attitude of the Catholic Church. Author is a gynecologist of many years' experience who has done research on oral contraceptives.

Lader, Lawrence (ed.): *Foolproof Birth Control: Male and Female Sterilization*, Beacon Press, Boston, 1972. Discusses voluntary sterilization for both sexes; newer techniques; frozen sperm banks; medical insurance for voluntary steriliza-tion; effects on marital adjustment; how to select a physician or clinic. Includes list of clinics.

Mace, David R.: *Abortion: The Agonizing Decision*, Abingdon Press, Nashville, Tenn., 1972. (Paperback.) Written for the pregnant woman who wants information to help her reach a decision regarding abortion in accordance with her value system.

Wood, H. Curtis, with William S. Rubin: *Sex without Babies*, Lancer Books, Inc., New York, 1971. (Paperback.) The author is a former president of the Association for Voluntary Sterilization. Discusses sterilization for both sexes; laws; costs; medical attitudes; contraceptive methods and abortion techniques.

Wylie, Evan McLeod: *The New Birth Control*, Grosset & Dunlap, Inc., New York, 1972. Nontechnical discussion of tubal ligation and vasectomy, voluntary ster-ilization and health insurance, sperm banks, doctors, hospitals, and the Church. Includes list of vasectomy clinics and clinics and hospitals where female sterilization is performed by laparoscopy and culdoscopy. Also contains a list of sperm banks.

Child Rearing and Family Living

FUNCTIONS OF THE FAMILY

The family has several functions:

1 It is the basic, nuclear unit in society. Statistically, society is composed of individuals. These individuals, however, are not entirely separate one from another. They occur and function as members of clusters of individuals. Some of these clusters are biologically produced and cohesive. Some are culturally produced and cohesive. The family is an outgrowth of both types of factors. The family is characterized by mutual aid and protection. It is an agency for the preservation and transmission of the cultural heritage of the group. In some cultures "family" suggests a structure different from that found in this country, but the central function is the same.

2 The family is a socially approved means for the production, nurture, rearing, and socialization of children. In our culture it is also a means of identifying children.

3 The family develops parents. As the family is a means of socializing children, so it is also a means of maturing and stabilizing parents. There are as great opportunities for personal growth in having children as there are in being children. In this "age of the child" there is some inclination to overlook the fact that parenthood as an end in itself is as important as parenthood as a means of child production and rearing. Parents are not merely adults who devote a part of their lives to the rearing of children who, in their turn, will devote their lives to the rearing of children, ad infinitum. Social theorizers who speculate on the comparative values of child rearing in the family versus child rearing by the state often base their arguments only on the welfare of the child. They do not think of parents and forget what might happen to them under some untraditional scheme.

twelve

In fulfilling these functions the present-day American family is confronted by new conditions and new demands. With increased urbanization there has been extensive proliferation of the number and types of groups, or aggregates, with which an individual may be affiliated. Some of these compete with the family for his time, interest, support, and loyalty. Individuals are drawn away from the family in a great variety of directions. Generalizing broadly, in earlier times there were more demands on the individual for the good of the family. Now there are more demands on the family, not only for the good of the individual, but also for the welfare of the many nonfamily clusters of which the individual is a member.

The present-day American family is "losing" its members, not only because of the centrifugal force mentioned above but also because of the increasing fragmentation of the extended family with a corresponding decrease in the centripetal force which previously bound the family together. In earlier days an extended group of "blood" relatives, including even remote cousins, thought of themselves as "family" in a way less commonly found today. In those earlier times a greater variety of relatives often shared the same dwelling or were closely associated residentially. Grandmothers, maiden aunts, and similar persons often played a part in the family economy, helped with the housework, cared for children, and contributed to their own support through useful service. The rapid rise of the baby-sitter and the difficulty many couples have in finding responsible sitters show how far from this earlier arrangement we have moved. In earlier days, when a son married, he and his wife often settled near his parents, perhaps on a portion of their land. Many homes were occupied by the same family generation after generation, giving children a type of "roots" that present-day apartments, small dwellings, and mobility no longer afford.

In earlier days, an individual was often appraised in part on the basis of his family membership. The reputation of his family was projected onto him in a way that is now seldom found. Nowadays, especially in large metropolitan communities, there is so much acquaintance among individuals who know little or nothing about each other's families that such family-based evaluation is rarely possible. Family status is not "inherited" in the way it used to be.

In earlier times, children, like older persons, had a place in the family economy, doing chores and in larger numbers than today leaving school relatively early in order to earn. Now children tend to be "mouths to be fed" rather than "hands to work." In this sense the aged are becoming more like children. They, too, are becoming "mouths to be fed" rather than "hands to work." Society in general and the family in particular have only begun to solve this growing problem.

One of the functions of the family is the transmission of the cultural heritage of the group from one generation to the next. But in rapidly changing times and amid the complexities and crosscurrents of present-day American society, what cultural patterns and values are to be transmitted? In the rearing of children, how insistent should parents be in adhering to the attitudes and standards of yesterday, how adaptive and permissive in accepting the shifting norms of today or anticipating the emerging patterns of tomorrow?

Contributing to this problem is the rapid evolution of new pressures being brought to bear on the processes of attitude formation and behavior-pattern determination. In earlier times such pressures grew largely and more or less directly out of the life of the family and the community in which the family lived, with the addition, of course, of some ideas derived from reading, the mingling of people, immigration, travel, and social theorizing. The new and highly influential factor today is the introduction of mass media of communication that were hitherto unknown. Media such as movies, radio, and television in a sense make each family a miniature "melting pot" for the ideas, norms, and cultural patterns of the entire world, not just of the community in which the family is situated. But these media also intrude into the family pressures, suggestions, subtle germinal ideas, and behavior patterns which do not come from the life of the community in which the family lives but in many instances are artificial, synthetic, false, and at best presented for profit by a few individuals who are remote from the family and unconcerned about it. It is not surprising that parents wonder about child rearing and that some families fall short in performing their functions.

One function of the family which has come into prominence, but not into existence, in recent years is its contribution to the mental health of its members. The family more than any other single agency lays the foundation for mental health or illness, for good or poor adjustment to life. Therefore, in the discussion of child rearing which follows, considerable attention will be given to the role of the family in meeting children's needs.

CHILD REARING

For several decades there has been so much said and written about the problems of child rearing, with much profit to be sure, that many parents have come to feel worried and harried. They are badgered by this theory or that. The pendulum of "the right way to do it" swings first one way then the other. Harassed parents try to keep pace with the swing or feel guilty when they fail to do so. Some have conflict with their own parents or parents-in-law because of differences in attitude and method that arise from generation to generation. "Pick up the child when it cries." "Don't pick up the child when it cries." "Show the child affection." "Don't show the child affection." Should there be scheduled feeding or demand feeding? Or shall we call the latter "self-regulatory feeding"? So it goes. Some modern young parents accept, rear, and enjoy their children with a natural but responsible casualness that would make the "patternizers" of the recent past throw up their hands in horror.

The rearing of children may be approached with greater confidence and relaxation and with less apprehension and tension if several points are recognized:

1   There is no single method of child rearing that is *the* way. Various methods are effective with different parents, different children, under different circumstances. Method should be individualized. There is no over-all or catchall method that applies equally well to all cases. One may readily note in observing children one knows that there may or may not be a complete correlation between quality of personality and the method of rearing which contributed to it. This generalization applies, of course, within reasonable limits and to more or less deliberately chosen methods of child rearing, not to every influence or condition under which children grow. Even when the latter

is included, however, the correlation between quality of personality and the life conditions from which the personality emerged is far from complete.

2 No child is reared without some problems. The path of parent-child relationships is never perfectly smooth. It is never possible to predict in advance, and therefore to prepare for, every circumstance that will arise. Parents are called upon to do the best they can in a dynamic relationship involving ever-changing circumstances within which there is interaction between growing organisms each of which is in many ways unique. Much as the parents may know about children and family living through study or experience, part of the time they must "play by ear." Study and experience are useful assets, but they are not guarantees of flawless child rearing.

Any problem that parents have with a particular child is in all probability not unique. It is almost certain to have been faced and solved—or lived with—by other parents. Sometimes an erroneous assumption of uniqueness leads parents to be unnecessarily pessimistic about a given problem.

The definition of a "problem" is ordinarily formulated by the person who has it rather than the person who is it. Parents speak of "problem children." But children refer to "problem parents." We may safely guess that there are as many of the latter as there are of the former. It depends from which side the issue is raised.

3 Usually to become seriously maladjusted a child must be subjected to a chronologically extended and circumstantially extensive distorted pattern of development. Serious maladjustment in children is not ordinarily produced by occasional, isolated parental mistakes that occur within a healthy pattern of parent-child relationships.

4 Someone has defined a child as "potential with a push." A personality has an "internal push" toward normal development, just as the body has a built-in "mechanism" which directs its changes toward physical health. One aspect of child rearing is to stay out of the way of the child's natural maturation. This does not imply letting the child "run wild." It implies only that personality develops by an "unfolding" as well as by an educative process.

5 Parents alone cannot provide everything a child needs for his development. A child is reared by a multiplicity of agencies. The older he becomes, the greater the number of these becomes. To some extent parents can control the selection of such agencies or modify their influence on the child. But the parents' possibilities in this regard are not limitless. This by no means implies lack of parental effort or concern. It does imply understanding and acceptance of the inevitable and the importance of providing a child early with a foundation of experience, learning, and security upon which he may evaluate such extraparental influences.

One is tempted to make a broad generalization. Under dissection its shortcomings are readily discernible. But as a point-of-departure principle for those approaching parenthood it may prove tranquilizing. The generalization is this: If parents love a child and let him know that he is loved, if they provide him with opportunities to grow as an individual and as a member of society and stay out of the way of his natural development, if they keep the door of communication open at all times for all topics, then they may make some mistakes in child rearing without seriously damaging the child, and the child will be prepared to meet and evaluate the extraparental influences with which he comes into contact.

Children's Needs

With the above in mind let us turn our attention to some of the needs of children. Whether these are biologically or culturally determined will not be our concern. They are discussed because in the last analysis successful child rearing is the process of successfully meeting children's needs with reference to the needs of others and within the cultural framework of a given society.

In many respects the needs of children and the needs of adults are similar, at least in so far as verbal description of them is concerned. Hence in reading the following discussion of children's needs the reader may ask himself, "Which are also needs of adults? How can such needs be met in marriage? What contribution can one spouse make toward meeting the needs of the other?"

Some needs are universal. Others are individual. If a child's needs are not met in helpful, constructive ways, he may resort to damaging, destructive ways of meeting them.

Security If an infant is held and then suddenly deprived of support, he becomes terrified. This is one of man's few "instinctive" reactions. It suggests that the need for security is present in human beings from the very beginning of life. "Insecurity" is used as a catchall explanation of numerous personality traits and types of behavior, especially when not all the factors in a given situation can readily be diagnosed. The concept has considerable usefulness and validity, nonetheless. Throughout his life the individual does those things which, according to his particular frame of reference, will produce security or avoid insecurity.

A child is not born with a feeling of security; he acquires such a feeling through experience. He learns it first from his parents through their manner of treatment of him. A young child's world is almost completely filled with the processes of functioning physiologically, growing, and learning. Because his experiences are limited and the cumulative total is small, each separate experience constitutes a relatively larger part of the whole, so to speak, than is true with an adult. For example, eating is an insignificant part of an adult's total life activity, whereas it is a very significant part of a young child's. Similar experiences are not in the same proportion in child life as in adult life. Furthermore, both needs and behavior are more elemental in a child than in an adult. As a result, some things which adults take for granted are more fascinating, more poignant, and more meaningful to a young child and are, therefore, more likely to be a source of learning for the child than for the adult. In the light of this it may readily be seen that such things as feeding, fondling, cuddling, and holding a child, which an adult often mistakenly assumes are more or less incidental, may lay the groundwork for the child's feeling of security. Such experiences leave an indelible, though usually not recalled, impression on the child. Such a simple procedure as a mother's holding her baby snugly in her arms, or a father's holding the baby in his even stronger arms, is one of the roots of a child's feeling of security. It is no accident that hymns and other religious utterances sometimes refer to the "arms of God" in an attempt to present a figurative description of the type of security which an individual may derive from religious faith.

A child may also develop a feeling of security through being trusted, being accepted, being recognized for achievement, and sharing in family activities and secrets, and in similar ways. Some of these will be discussed in the paragraphs which follow.

In order to have a feeling of security a child must be helped to develop it. It must emerge from activities which the parents initiate but through which the child responds to the parents and through which his response grows. It cannot be provided "secondhand." It cannot come through activities which the parents initiate but which the child resists or which deprive him of the opportunity to grow. For example, parental overprotection, which is presumably designed to make the child secure, at least in the physical sense of the term, actually ultimately gives him a feeling of insecurity. The reason for this is that, when the parents are overprotective, the child is deprived of an opportunity to learn and the parents rather than the child meet a present-life situation. Hence the child is not equipped to get along without the parents. Ultimately this eventuates in insecurity.

New experience In order to grow, and some would say in order to be happy, an individual needs new experience. In a way new experience and security may be at odds with each other. The individual grows and matures as he learns to feel secure in new experiences and new situations. It goes without saying that for some persons new experience adds zest to living. Others are content with a more nearly changeless *status quo.* One problem parents face in this age of passive recreation and the common question, "Where do we go?" rather than, "What do we do?" especially in large cities, is that of how to provide a child with growth-producing new experience within limits of reasonable safety and control.

Self-preservation "Self-preservation," we say, "is the first law of life." In human beings it involves more than physical self-preservation. As we saw in an earlier connection, self-preservation includes also preservation of the "self," the "I," which makes every person different from every other. Each person has a private world, a world partly of his own making, which he seeks to preserve and protect but which he himself may alter as his interpretations of experience change. If life as he finds it is too complex for him, he may manufacture an unreal "world" which, from his point of view, is a more satisfactory explanation of his experiences than is the world of reality.

Love The individual has a need to love and to be loved. In early years the individual's love in both the giving and the receiving is self-centered. As he matures his love more and more reflects concern for the "other than self." A child learns to love through being loved. But this does not happen through his always being the center of attention and the recipient of love. He must also learn concern for others, for without such concern he cannot learn to love. All of us know of cases in which children have become so accustomed to receiving love without learning to give it that they remain self-centered persons all their lives.

Children of both sexes seek and need affection from parents of both sexes. In our culture the major breakdown in this four-way giving and receiving of affection is often to be found in the relationship of father and son, especially after the latter has ceased to be a small child. The traditional standard of manliness in this country discourages kissing as an expression of affection between two post-pubertal males. Some fathers are so sensitive to this prohibition that they are reluctant to kiss even very young sons.

But there are ways other than kissing through which father and son may show affection for one another. A paternal arm across a boy's shoulders, a slap on the back, or a son's hand upon his father's arm may express deep and warm affection. Some fathers and sons find a partial solution to the problem of expressing affection in acceptable masculine ways through what might be termed a playful or nonthreatening negative rather than a direct, positive approach, for example, a punch in the chest, wrestling, and "horseplay." Some have worked out a special vocabulary of terms that are ordinarily used in a highly derogatory sense, but when used upon each other, with a special meaning known to father and son, these same words become terms of endearment. There are also, however, some fathers and sons who have retained kissing as an expression of affection even into the sons' adulthood. Their kissing may occur only on special occasions and it is typically not mouth-to-mouth kissing. It is more likely to occur in private than in public. But the important point is that in some cases it does occur.

Belonging   The individual needs to identify himself with others and have a sense of belonging to a group. The first and most natural group to which he belongs is the family. When this sense of belonging is undermined, the child naturally feels insecure. He may turn to persons other than the family to satisfy his needs. Unwanted children often exhibit such behavior. It is important, in disciplining a child, to be certain that the child is given the impression that it is his act and not himself that is rejected by the parent.

As the child matures, he forms affiliations with groups other than the family. This is especially apparent in the teens, when the pressure of the peer group becomes almost irresistible. At this stage of development the child is often inclined to give more weight to the judgments of his contemporaries than to those of his parents. This may not be carried to such an extreme that parents' judgments are given no weight at all. But if parents do not understand this phase of their child's development, they may accentuate the very process they deplore. The young adolescent is under tremendous pressure to conform to the ways of the peer group. If parents do not make some concessions in this process, they may "lose" the child completely. Perhaps the wisest plan is to make concessions on less important things and "hold the line" on a few essentials. In so doing, parents may well try to distinguish between those things the child wants to do which may be damaging or dangerous and those which are merely different from the way the parents think they should be done.

An individual can best achieve a sense of belonging when he accepts some responsibility for the group to which he belongs. In present-day urban and suburban living, with its breakdown of primary groups and the consequent dispersal of loyalties, this is not always easy to arrange in the family. It may be achieved, however, by such means as participation in household tasks, sharing family recreation and pleasures, and, within the limits of the individual's ability to understand, sharing in family problems and troubles. In some cases parents deprive a child of an opportunity to share in the total life of his family by shielding him from the unpleasant aspects of family living.

Communication   Man is a communicating mammal, and the individual's life is inextricably interwoven with the lives of others through communication. One aspect of belonging is communication. As mentioned earlier, the fact that each person lives in a private world makes communication incomplete, but there is no way to solve this problem completely. A problem that parents can solve is that which arises when they themselves arbitrarily thwart a child's communication because of their own lack of interest in what the child wants to communicate or because they feel that the content of the communication is inappropriate, as, for example, when a child is rebuffed for asking a question regarding reproduction. Once the door of communication is closed, the latch and hinges soon become rusty, and in many cases it becomes difficult if not impossible to reopen it.

Keeping the door of communication open, however, is not always accomplished without problems. One father complained that his children had learned that he disciplined them for their misdeeds less severely or not at all when they told the truth. He felt that at times they "worked" him. But in weighing the pros and cons, he concluded that keeping the door of communication open, retaining good rapport with his children, and in this way having greater opportunity to help them think through their behavior and develop self-discipline, was more important than his disciplining them in every instance, even if they did "work" him on occasion.

Sense of achievement   Typically human beings have a desire for recognition. In children recognition and a sense of achievement are closely related. Mature individuals may more readily separate them. If a child does not get the recognition he needs under desirable auspices, he may seek it under undesirable auspices.

Because of this combination of needs—namely, for achievement and for recognition—the typical individual likes to feel useful. Sometimes helping a child to feel useful increases rather than decreases the work of the parent, for example, when a little girl wants to help her mother bake a cake. But it is worth an investment of time and effort, for in feeling useful the child not only satisfies a need per se but also strengthens his ties with the family group.

Reaching out Man is the only organism that reaches out beyond his immediate experience. He does this in numerous ways, two of which are creative imagination and religious faith. As an individual matures, his reaching out should mature. Yet many persons' religious faith stops developing at a childish level. This is due in part to the fact that one factor in the extension and maturing of faith is the process of probing the unknown with penetrating questions. If parents assume, as some do, that questioning and faith, doubting and believing, are antagonistic rather than complementary, a child's fluid reaching out may be thwarted by crystallized dogmatism and fear. When a child questions what parents assume to be established truth, the parents may well be assured that, if it is truth, the child, like themselves, will come to accept it; if it is not truth after all, he has the right to discover this. Truth can be challenged but it cannot be threatened. The more vigorously it is attacked, the more firmly it becomes established.

Children's creative imagination is sometimes not so carefully channeled as that of adults; and the children themselves cannot always distinguish between the imagined and the real. This leads some parents to confuse the child's imaginings with dishonesty. They punish him for the latter and eventually cripple the former.

In American culture conformity is considered a virtue. In some cases in which recognition and prestige are given to outstanding individuals, it is quantitative difference rather than qualitative difference that is recognized. The outstanding individual is "like everyone else, only more so." For example, the high school valedictorian, the beauty queen, the best of this or that is often basically a conformist; the individual may exhibit no true originality, no true creativity.

Parents are not free of pressure toward conformity where their children are concerned. Psychological tests, personality rating scales, tables of one sort or another, norms for children of a given age, the grade level system in schools, and so on, though useful, subtly suggest conformity. Hence parents sometimes sacrifice a child's individuality by molding him so that he will conform instead of releasing him to be creative. This does not imply letting him become so out of step with his peers that he fits nowhere into the social scheme or letting his personality become maladjusted. It does imply helping him develop the creativity inherent in every normal personality.

When we compare the number of young children who have insatiable curiosity, who make works of art which, though crude, are creative, who play-act, who make up stories about imaginary characters, who sing songs they have composed, beat out a rhythm, or dance spontaneously, with the number of adults who are creative in similar ways, we realize that somewhere between childhood and adulthood conformity has overshadowed creativity and originality.

Growth and development We said earlier in this chapter that personality develops by an "unfolding" as well as by an educative process. This implies that the individual goes through stages of development. Within broad limits these stages are similar for all persons. Not all individuals, however, pass through the same stage or reach the same point at the same age. Each individual has his own "built-in" pattern and rate of growth.

Generalizing somewhat, each stage of growth is typified by certain forms of behavior. For example, most children creep before they walk. Many suck their thumbs in their early years. Sometimes behavior at a given stage seems to the parents to represent retrogression, or backsliding, as compared with a previous stage. For example, some children develop reasonably satisfactory table manners in their early years but revert to infantile eating habits temporarily at about the onset of adolescence, much to the despair of their parents. It would help parents to realize that, unless there are special factors at work to produce something in the nature of a fixation in the child, stage-typical behavior is ordinarily not habit-forming. This means that stage-typical behavior is something into which the child grows but out of which he also grows. Take for example, thumb-sucking. Parents torture their children with foul-tasting drugs, mechanical devices, threats and punishment, and torture themselves with concern and anxiety to stop this practice. Unless, as is true in some cases, the child is pressing his thumb against his palate in such a way that he pushes his front teeth forward, the practice is harmless. Almost all children grow out of it. Being stage-typical behavior, it is usually not habit-forming.

One reason that parents often persist, even in the face of continual failure, in trying to alter stage-typical behavior through instruction, nagging, threat, punishment, and a free exuding of their own tension and anxiety is that they fear that whatever a child is permitted to do in his early years he is likely to continue to do throughout his life. If the child runs out of the house unclothed, they fear that he will become a nudist. If a little boy wears his sister's clothes while play-acting, the parents wonder whether he will become a transvestite. If a child leaves toys lying around, the parents fear that he will be careless about leaving his clothes strewn around after he is married. They fail to realize that it is not so much leaving things around at an early age and because of a brief interest span that makes an adult careless but rather the fact that someone, either through constant haranguing or through picking up after the child, teaches him that he has no responsibility in this regard, that somebody will assume his responsibility for him.

The direction of a child's development is determined in part by factors within himself. Part of his development, however, is determined by the pattern and framework of life into which he grows. This framework is provided in part by the family. In other words, in a given respect the child may not at first conform to the family pattern. Since, however, the direction of his growth is not predetermined, he may grow in one direction as readily as in another. The family pattern, then, is the framework within which he will grow. For example, a little child has no appreciation of courtesy. He is born uncivilized, and the process of civilization takes time. If the family provides him with a pattern of habitual courtesy, he is likely to become courteous. If on the other hand the family provides him with a pattern of habitual lack of attention to courtesy, he is likely to become discourteous. In order to accomplish the former, the family must continue to provide the pattern of courtesy even while the child is too immature to be expected to exhibit the courtesy of an adult.

If parents do not exhibit consistency in establishing the pattern into which they expect the child to grow, it is not surprising when the child disappoints them. For example, many parents see no need to be courteous to a little child. Yet they are irritated when their child is discourteous to them. Some parents see nothing wrong with telling a child untruths. Some thoughtlessly embarrass a child in front of his companions. Some are impatient when a child wants to talk with them and they tell him they do not have time to talk. Then when the child is reluctant to leave his play when his parents want to talk with him, they consider him disobedient. Sometimes parents punish a child when he honestly reports some misdemeanor. Then they wonder why the child becomes dishonest. Some betray a child's confidence, then wonder why he ceases to confide in them. Some assure the child that he is trusted, then spy on him.

Inconsistency is also apparent in those instances in which parents disagree on the handling of a child. The child soon learns to "play" one parent against the other or to seek the approval of the parent who is more lax in giving permissions or in meting out punishment.

A child's learning is the result of three processes, namely, experience, maturation, and instruction. Parents sometimes fail to distinguish between the last two processes, with the result that they expect a child to learn through instruction before through maturation he has reached a point where this is possible for him. Instruction is to no avail until learning readiness has been achieved through growth. For example, a child aged one could not be taught to read no matter how good his instruction. If instruction is started too early—that is, before readiness has been established—it will be ineffective. If instruction is continued after readiness is established, the child may learn quickly; but he would have learned by about the same time if instruction had been delayed until readiness was established. In fact, the child will learn some things without instruction merely through his own maturation.

This failure to distinguish between maturation and instruction, especially verbal instruction, may be made clear, perhaps, by means of a parable. A certain man planted a seed. He was very eager to have the seed grow into a plant that would bear fruit. Every day he addressed first the seedling, then the plant, saying, "I want you to bear fruit. Please do so." At last, one day, the plant did bear fruit. The man said, "See, I told you I could teach the plant to bear fruit." All the people said, "What a wonderful teacher he is. He has taught the plant to bear fruit." This is not meant to imply that there is no place for verbal instruction in child rearing. But there is often too much dependence upon verbal instruction and too little insight into the process of maturation. Sometimes, as in the parable above, the former is given credit more appropriately due the latter. Also, when there is too great dependence upon words, a child may immunize himself to verbal exhortation so that words intended to eventuate in learning result only in an increased resistance to verbal injunction. His parents then may as well "save their breath."

Being an individual No two children are identical, not even "identical" twins. Each child is unique. Each has his own rate and pattern of growth, allowing for broad similarities at different stages of development, as mentioned above. Each has his own temperament. Each has his own abilities and aptitudes. Yet these facts do not keep some parents from trying to make children alike, or from seeking to make a child into a replica of a parent, or from attempting to squeeze a square peg into a round hole. Wise parents set their expectations for a child according to the child's ability to achieve, not according to the achievements of other children or according to some arbitrary and unreasonable parent-imposed standard. For example, among the college educated there is often such a premium put upon academic achievement in children that a child who is a "muscle learner" rather than a verbal learner is looked down upon and may be forced to attempt success in a field for which he has no aptitude. A boy who might do very well as a mechanic is forced through parental pressure to work for a university degree, with the result that the child becomes an unhappy, maladjusted failure who is subtly rejected by his parents.

A similar problem is found in the situation in which parents expect a child to enter a given occupation because of family tradition or parental leanings or to serve as a vicarious success for a parent who was prevented by ability or circumstance from entering the occupation of his choice. College and university counselors meet many of this type of student—a kind of living human sacrifice to thwarted parental ambitions.

Consider both the parental attempt to squeeze the square peg into the round hole and the effect of the parents' effort to keep their son immature in the following statement by a university senior, aged twenty-three, who was on scholastic probation. Said he, "I want to go into teaching. But my father is a physician, and his father was a physician. My parents insist that I go into medicine. I'm not interested in medicine, and I'm having trouble in my science and math courses. Mamma says that if I don't make my grades, she won't let me use the car."

If a child is to be an individual, he cannot be expected to agree with his parents on everything. He has a right to make his own judgments, within, of course, limits of ability and safety, as mentioned earlier.

If each child is to be considered an individual, no child should be penalized for something he cannot possibly control. Sometimes, for example, a child is discriminated against because he is the eldest child in the family, because he is less attractive in appearance than other children in the family, because, as indicated above, he lacks some ability that is prized by his parents, or because of his sexual classification. For example, the parents discipline their son severely, but they are more lenient with their daughter. One of the most devastating experiences for a child is to be a second-class citizen in his own family because his parents consider another child their favorite.

A child is a child. He is not a small adult. Therefore, he should not be expected to act like an adult; or perhaps we should say the child should not be expected to act as an adult is expected to act. For example, a child may be intelligent; but this fact does not necessarily make him reasonable under given circumstances. He cannot be expected suddenly to change his behavior merely because someone older than he tells him to change it. He does not have, indeed cannot have, the foresight of an adult. A child is naturally somewhat selfish. He must gradually learn to be generous. He cannot be expected suddenly to exhibit adult altruism.

Independence   A child, like a ship, is to be launched. Some parents are like the proverbial man who carefully built a boat in his garage only to find that the boat was too large to pass through the garage door and hence never reached the water. Launching a child into adult independence is a prolonged, carefully planned process. It necessitates as much development on the part of the parent as on the part of the child. Many a parent who is a "good" parent for an infant remains the parent of an infant psychologically even when the offspring has grown to adulthood. The result is actual or attempted "apron strings." When the time comes that a child can get along without his parents because he is an independent young adult, the parents may well take pride in their achievement. Many parents, however, make the day of the child's independence a day of sorrow.

Facing reality   In so far as it may be safe to do so, a child may be allowed to learn from his own experiences rather than from instruction. He needs to learn to face and, if possible, to accept the consequences of his acts. For example, he will learn more about the use of money by being allowed to spend his money unwisely and thus being deprived of something he wants than he will learn through verbal instruction.

Children are sometimes allowed to evade reality in such a way that the child is started on the road to emotional maladjustment. For instance, a child is permitted to rationalize, alibi, and shirk responsibility to such an extent that he grows to assume that this is the way life is to be lived.

Discipline   Children need discipline. It is one method of learning. It can give a child a sense of security when it defines his limitations, that is, the framework within which he may operate. Many a parent has had the experience of having a child "push" him to the point of exasperation. Then the parent "blows up," the air is cleared, the child is given a definition of his area of operation, of his limitations, and peace and harmony are restored. Discipline can also give a child a sense of security when it helps him to get past previous misbehavior and to get rid of a sense of guilt growing out of it.

To fulfill its function, discipline need not always be negative; it may also be positive. In fact, whenever possible it should be positive. Teaching a child to save or to cooperate in household tasks is as much part of discipline as is punishment. One of the common errors in child rearing, as in other areas of life where one person seeks to modify the behavior of another, is the assumption that the elimination of small faults results in the production of large virtues. A series of "don'ts" may be necessary on occasion; but it does not necessarily follow that in place of the behavior modified by the "don'ts" will be put behavior that is positive and constructive.

In order to accomplish its purpose and to be appreciated by a child, punishment must be fair and not too harsh. It should also be appropriate to the misdeed. Sometimes parents make a child dislike what is fundamentally a good thing because they use that good thing as punishment. For example, one of the greatest satisfactions in life is that which comes from work. Work, providing that it is honest and useful, deserves to be respected. If, however, parents impose work on a child as a means of punishment, it is not surprising that the child may grow to dislike it. This is especially true of certain household chores.

Nagging is ineffective as discipline for several reasons. It permits the child to evade the consequences of his behavior with only a tongue-lashing as punishment, and to the tongue-lashing he may readily immunize himself. Nagging exposes the vulnerable spots of the nagger. It provides the child with an effective weapon for penalizing the parent. Nagging "tells" the child what is annoying to the parent. If, then, the child wants to annoy the parent, he knows how to do it.

To spank or not to spank—that is the perennial question in any discussion of discipline. On the one hand are those who deplore any suggestion of corporal punishment or penalizing physical contact between parent and child. On the other hand are those who consider spanking a form of communication. Arguments are presented on either side.

Evidence [Sears, Maccoby, and Levin, 1957] indicates that spanking often does not accomplish what it is intended to accomplish. Its good effects, if any, are likely to be temporary; its harmful effects may be permanent. It is not a substitute for true discipline because it involves learning through fear rather than through trust. It is negative rather than positive. Not all children respond to spanking in the same way. Some are humiliated and embittered by it and become resentful. The parent-child relationship may break down.

Earlier in this chapter the importance of consistency in child rearing was stressed. What about the matter of consistency when parents teach a child that striking his playmates is not the most desirable way of getting along with them and that under no circumstances is he ever to strike his parents; yet the parents strike the child?

Spanking is more likely to be a means of relieving parental feelings than an effective means of training a child. In some families it is a last resort, implying that it occurs when a parent is "at the end of his rope" because of tension, fatigue, or frustration. Spanking is often a reflection of ignorance; the parent knows no better form of discipline. It may be an expression of rejection of child by parent or an outgrowth of aggression. In some families spanking is the principal means of discipline used, and in such cases it is especially harmful.

What was said above is not meant to imply that a child's personality will be permanently warped if his parents spank him occasionally. Parents, being human, have their "weak moments." In the complexities of family living they are not always free of fatigue and tension and do not always govern their every act by carefully considered theory. A happily married couple may have a bitter quarrel, knowing that in so doing they fall short of their own ideal of marriage. They regret what has happened and try to avoid it in the future. In like manner a parent may have an occasional similar experience with a child. It is important that the parent realize that he has resorted to a procedure that falls short of the ideal and might better be avoided and that he has solved nothing. To assume that spanking is the best form of punishment is like assuming that quarreling is the best way to achieve adjustment in marriage.

Acceptance Overlapping several of the items already indicated but deserving separate mention is the need for acceptance. Each individual wants to be accepted for what he is, if possible as he conceives himself to be. Such acceptance is found in probably its purest form in the family where a child is loved by his parents without comparison with other children and without regard to whether or not he deserves to be loved. Lack of such unqualified acceptance, as for example in the case of a mentally retarded child, creates one of the most critical problems of childhood.

There is another aspect of acceptance, namely, acceptance of oneself. This implies learning to live with one's limitations. It also implies acceptance of one's sexual classification and its attendant role. An individual cannot, of course, accept his own sexual classification unless he can simultaneously accept the classification of the opposite sex. In learning to accept his sexual classification the individual develops a concept of his sexual role. Somehow, too, he must learn to fit his sexual impulses into the societal pattern. This suggests the need for education for sexuality.

EDUCATION FOR SEXUALITY

Nature and Objectives

Because of the traditionally narrow definition of "sex education," a new term, "education for sexuality," is coming into use. Education for sexuality is the process of teaching an individual to understand and accept himself as a whole person and as such to relate himself to other people in a healthy, constructive, and meaningful manner. In a two-sexed world this includes the individual's understanding and accepting his own sexual classification and behavior plus his understanding and accepting the sexual classification and behavior of members of the opposite sex. It includes his learning to fit his sexuality into a satisfactory societal pattern. One of the central objectives of child rearing is the achievement of a balance between socialization and conformity to the societal structure, on the one hand, and individual freedom, growth, and realization of innate potential, on the other. Nowhere is the need for such a balance more apparent than in connection with education for sexuality.

In order to achieve the above, the individual needs factual information, to be sure. But he needs much more than factual information, especially that minimum regarding genital anatomy and physiology commonly referred to as "the facts of life." The individual needs to understand sex not as a limited facet of life that is somehow regrettably superimposed upon more desirable aspects of living, as sex is often represented. He needs, rather, to understand sex as a way of life. In order to do this, in addition to acquiring sound factual information he must develop healthy attitudes, carefully weigh values, thoughtfully impute meaning to sexual behavior, and establish creative interpersonal relationships. Whatever values he accepts relative to sex need to be consistent with the value system upon which his individual life is being built and with the value structure of the society within which he lives.

Time to begin   "When should I start to give my child sex education?" is a question often asked by parents. Actually, there is no time to "start," just as there is not a specific time to start to teach a child to be honest or to be a good citizen. We assume that the teaching of honesty and citizenship will be an integral part of the child's learning from birth onward. So it should be with education for sexuality.

If we may stretch a point for emphasis, we may say that education for sexuality begins before birth—not in the sense of verbal communication with the fetus, but in the sense of education for sexuality's having its roots in the attitudes of the parents toward the process by which the child was conceived.

Communication versus telling   Some parents assume that they can avoid giving a child education for sexuality by telling him nothing about sex. They assume that lack of verbal instruction means lack of communication. The opposite is true. When the parents give the child no verbal instruction, they communicate to him that sex is a topic so mysterious, so unpalatable, and so difficult to discuss—for them—that he had better seek information elsewhere.

Parental behavior in the home is also a means of communication whether or not anything is said about sex. The child soon learns through observation that there are differences between the sexes both as to anatomy and as to role. He cannot help but observe whether his parents are affectionate with each other, whether they accept their roles with enthusiasm or resistance, and a host of similar items. Such observations constitute part of education for sexuality.

Parents who do not give a child verbal instruction might well wonder about such questions as these: Will ignorance protect a child from misinformation, shock, perhaps even tragedy? What is a child to think if his parents give him the impression that sex is "bad" and then his mother becomes pregnant and the child knows that the parents have engaged in a process they feel is unfit to be discussed?

Bodily Exposure

A young child takes his anatomy for granted, at least until he is taught otherwise. Sooner or later he discovers his genital organs. This discovery is part of his exploration of his world. To a little child everything he encounters is new and interesting. Things and experiences no longer interesting to adults are fascinating to the young child because the entire world is new to him, and he explores it with all the equipment Nature provides him for sensing and perceiving. In so far as it is possible to do so, he uses all his senses in his observations. He touches the soft fur of a rabbit with exuberant delight. He listens to the ticking of a watch with rapt attention. His horror-stricken, germ-conscious parents find him putting anything movable into his mouth. His curiosity is insatiable. He performs simple experiments, such as holding the family cat by the tail, to see what will happen.

In the course of such a process of observation and experimentation the child discovers his genital organs. He then proceeds to learn more about them, how they are constructed, what sensations he has when he handles them. He soon learns that there are two types of people in the world, male and female, and his interest and curiosity extend to the differences between them. So he proceeds to satisfy his curiosity. Since all normal children have this curiosity as to how the sexes are constructed, it is not unusual for two children of opposite sex to make their observations simultaneously. To them such a thing is as natural as tasting a new food.

Let us imagine two children, a boy and a girl, four years of age. They are playmates. They are curious about the differences in their genital organs. In a corner of the garage they set about satisfying their curiosity. By happenstance the mother of the little girl enters the garage to get something out of storage at just the moment that the two children are observing each other's genital organs. The mother becomes very wrought up. She sends the little boy home with an excited stream of invective following him like a swarm of angry bees. She hurries her daughter into the house. The little girl cannot avoid getting the impression that something terrible has occurred, that her mother is deeply disturbed, that she herself has committed an act which, at least in her mother's judgment, classifies her as "bad." There are girls who reach marriageable age still bearing the scars of such an experience.

How much better it would have been if the little girl's mother had treated the situation as natural and inoffensive. Perhaps the children need some help in understanding what is acceptable behavior in our society, what is "family" and what is not. But they are not to be condemned, frightened, and punished for adult fears and inhibitions projected onto the natural behavior of childhood. They are not to be traumatized through shock into acquiring a sense of guilt that is felt first only by the parent.

In connection with the question of bodily exposure on the part of family members within the home, opinions differ widely. There are parents who believe that every effort should be made to protect all family members, especially parents, from even the casual gaze of others. Such parents dress behind closed doors, bathe behind carefully inculcated "no trespassing" warnings, and become upset at accidental exposure. On the other hand there are parents who treat bodily exposure within the home as natural and to be taken for granted by family members. They draw a distinction, however, between observation of genital anatomy and observation of sexual behavior. When all the pros and cons are considered, and assuming that the parents do not make a cult of nudity, it seems clear that the more nearly natural bodily exposure within the home is taken to be, the healthier the child's attitude toward such exposure will be. When parents are overly meticulous in preventing children from observing the parents' bodies, the children's curiosity is increased, or at least certainly not decreased, and is more likely to lead to attempts to satisfy it outside the home under auspices unknown to parents and in situations permitting no questions to be asked.

Bodily exposure in the home can be just as "forced" as artificial barriers can be. There are times when any individual, child or adult, seeks privacy. Such privacy is to be respected by all family members. But an occasional demand for privacy is not the same as an over-all fear of bodily exposure.

One problem giving concern to many women, even some of those who are relatively uninhibited in the matter of bodily exposure within the home, is that of whether a child, especially a boy, should be permitted to see the mother unclothed when she is wearing external menstrual protection. Menstruation is as natural as any other bodily function. In these presumably modern times there is no need to read into it the connotations of mystery, shame, and uncleanliness that were associated with the process in the past. Sooner or later the child will learn about menstruation. If the mother is sufficiently objective about it to permit him to do so, he can understand and accept it without emotion or undue curiosity even at an early age.

Children's Questions

There is widespread agreement to the effect that a child's questions concerning sex and reproduction should be answered, not evaded. In no way, either by act or implication, should the child be made to feel that an honest question about something which is natural to him is inappropriate or "bad." One reason for which some parents avoid a child's questions, with a show of emotion on the part of the parent, is that the parent, not the child, is embarrassed to discuss the subject. To cover up this embarrassment the parent repulses the child with an assertion that that sort of question should not be asked.

Before a parent can answer a child's question intelligently, he must ascertain what the child has asked. The real question may not be readily apparent in the verbal statement of it. This is illustrated in the well-worn story about the child who rushed up to his mother and said, "Mother, where did I come from?" The mother thought, "This is it," and launched into a long, previously prepared dissertation on reproduction. The child tried to interrupt, but the mother would not permit him to do so. When the mother finally finished, feeling that at last she had done successfully what she had long anticipated with apprehension, the child exclaimed, "But Mother, that's not what I meant. Billy down the street says he came from Chicago, and I wanted to know where I came from."

In answering a child's question, the parent must consider the child's readiness to understand. A preschool child is not prepared to understand an explanation that would be more appropriate for a medical student. The child needs to be told only as much as he can absorb at the time. One is reminded of the little girl who said, "I don't like to ask Mother questions like that because she always tells me too much." If the parents keep the door of communication open, the child will return to the same question over and over again as he grows older. Each time he can be given further detail. No matter how many times the child repeats the same question, the question should be answered.

There are some persons who feel that a child's questions concerning sex or reproduction should be answered immediately upon being asked. In general this is a satisfactory working principle. But in the complexity of family living it is not always possible to meet ideal standards, and parents should not feel guilty or inadequate, as some do, when they fall short, especially if the over-all parent-child relationship is healthy. For instance, if we may exaggerate to make a point, a father need not feel guilty if he does not stop carving the Thanksgiving turkey and let the guests wait to be served just so he can answer the questions of a child who has chosen this inopportune moment to ask why babies have fathers. He can tell the child that he will discuss the question later. Then he keeps his word and does discuss it later.

Vocabulary

There are different schools of thought regarding what vocabulary is best in teaching children about sex and reproduction. At one extreme are the advocates of technical, scientific, medical terminology. Every anatomical part, every physiological process is to be called by the correct technical term. At the other extreme are the adherents of the "do-do, da-da" point of view. Everything is to be described in the most evasive type of "baby talk" so that camouflage of the natural is as nearly complete as human ingenuity in manufacturing new vocabulary will permit. Sometimes this process is carried to such an extreme that communication is limited to parent and child because no one else knows the meaning of the terms the two of them have concocted.

Neither of these extremes is entirely consistent with ordinary day-to-day living in our culture. Adults do not refer to every anatomical part and every physiological process by its correct technical term at all times regardless of circumstance. Neither do they use only substitute vocabulary. Common parlance represents a compromise, a combination of technical and substitute vocabulary. Some of the latter is conventionalized.

The fundamental problem is one of communication, of imparting information, of imputing correct meaning, of facing rather than evading facts. There is also the correlative problem of avoiding giving the child a false impression. One of the commonest instances of such a false impression is using an unpalatable term to mean menstruation.

Accepting One's Sexual Classification

If, as suggested earlier, one of the objectives of education for sexuality is to help a child to accept his sexual classification, parents must find a way to teach girls to accept with understanding such natural female functions as menstruation and childbirth. Yet many a girl is not helped toward such acceptance either because her parents engender a negative attitude in her or because they do nothing to engender a positive one. Since children learn by observation and "contagion" as well as by verbal instruction, many a girl "picks up" a negative attitude during her observation of her parents' treatment of each other or through chance remarks made by one parent or the other and not intended as instruction for the girl. For example, the child is affectionate. She seeks warmth, security, and attention from other people. She seldom or never sees her father kiss her mother. Without reasoning it out, she begins to feel that, if that is what a woman can expect from a man, she regrets that she is female. She hears her mother make a remark about menstruation or hears her complain because she is pregnant again. Mother and daughter are doing dishes while the husband-father reads the paper. Mother complains about the lack of cooperation on the part of the man, but, instead of particularizing her complaint so that it is directed to a certain act on the part of a given man, she generalizes and says something to the effect that women have to do chores while men can relax. Translated, this is equivalent to telling the daughter that it is better to be a man than to be a woman.

The acceptance of one's sexual classification is not a problem limited to girls. Boys more readily, perhaps, accept their maleness than girls accept their femaleness. But some parents thoughtlessly allow such acceptance to become an assumption of prerogative. In their effort to make a son a "real man" they permit the development of the idea that to be manly means to exploit girls, to sow "wild oats," to have premarital sexual exploits, sometimes with complete disregard of the fact that someone else's daughter may have to reap the "wild oats" their son sows. Instead of emphasizing respect for girls and deemphasizing the "wild oats" approach to manliness, they lightly approve the latter on the ground that "boys will be boys" and thereby unwittingly detract from the former. In the last analysis what constitutes manliness differs with time, place, circumstance, and cultural demands. There is a wide gulf of difference between being an aboriginal, primordial male who gives free rein to natural impulses and a modern, civilized man who lives by a standard of values.

Masturbation

The day is past when masturbation was referred to as "self-abuse," just as the day is gone when nocturnal emissions were termed "pollutions." Masturbation is such a widespread phenomenon of childhood that attitudes toward it should be evaluated with this fact in mind. Studies show that in young males masturbation is reported as being just short of universal, and an appreciable majority of young females are reported as at some time engaging in the practice.

In the natural inclination to explore both their environment and their bodies most children sooner or later discover that their genital organs are endowed with special sensitivity and that in the stimulation of these organs pleasurable sensation can be produced. If the child does not become acquainted with this fact through his own curiosity, he is likely to learn it from other children.

Contrary to common assumption, there is no evidence to prove that masturbation per se is physically harmful. Masturbation, as such, which involves only sexual self-stimulation, should be carefully distinguished from the dangerous practice of a girl's inserting some object into her vagina either in an attempt at masturbation or merely through curiosity. Among objects removed from girls' vaginas have been hairpins, safety pins, crayons, paper clips, beads, sand, stones, marbles, shells, nuts, corks, vaginal tampons, toilet tissue, parts of toys, coins, and even a plastic pencil [Schneider and Geary, December, 1971]. Anyone would agree that such insertion of sharp, unclean objects is dangerous; and physicians are not infrequently called upon to remove such objects, sometimes after injury has caused infection or hemorrhage.

Masturbation may become psychologically damaging to the degree to which the child is led to develop a sense of guilt associated with it. Such a sense of guilt is instilled by parents or others who appraise the practice in terms of sin or immorality.

Parents have been known to try to prevent a child, especially a son, from masturbating by threatening the child with consequences that the parents know will not follow but which place upon the child an unbearable burden of fear and guilt. For example, one mother told her young son that, if he persisted in masturbating, his genital organs would fall off. Another told her son that masturbation would make him insane. Such untruths can do a child incalculable harm.

"What should I do if I discover that my child masturbates?" is a common questions asked by parents. There are a number of things such parents might do.

1 Relax. The child will do himself no harm.
2 Do not make an issue of it. Do not "read into" it something which is not there. Do not connect in the child's mind the act of masturbation with parental emotional upset, threat, and condemnation.
3 Recognize that childhood masturbation tends to fall into the category of stage-typical behavior, which does not ordinarily eventuate in permanent habits over which the individual has no control. Most persons either stop masturbation when they grow older, especially after marriage, or modify its frequency and practice it through choice subject to voluntary control. They control it; it does not control them. It does not dominate their lives, as parents often fear it will.
4 Sometimes masturbation is a symptom of a problem which does call for parental attention. For example, if a child masturbates excessively because he is bored and lonely and has learned that masturbation is something he can do with pleasure and by himself, the provision of companionship and interesting activities may meet a need for him and make the masturbation less "neces-sary" to him.
5 Do not drive the practice "under cover" by threat of punishment. If a child is inclined to masturbate, he will find a time and place to do it. If his parents

threaten him for doing it in one place about which they know, he will find another that is less likely to be discovered by them.

6 Do not expect a child to discontinue a pleasurable practice by an act of will, a level of determination and self-discipline that would do credit to an adult.

7 Keep the door of communication open. There is no reason why a child should not be able to discuss his masturbation with his parents just as he would discuss any other type of behavior. Such discussion should be permitted, not forced. That is, the child rather than the parents should take the initiative, though the parents might suggest the possibility of discussion. Children in some families do take such initiative because the parents have set up no barrier between themselves and their child. A child who voluntarily discusses masturbation with his parents pays them a profound compliment. They should not "let him down." A child could hardly be expected to take the initiative in discussing with his parents something which he knows in advance they condemn and will condemn him for doing.

Education for Sexuality Is Unavoidable

As suggested earlier in this chapter, education for sexuality is unavoidable. Parents cannot avoid giving a child education for sexuality by avoiding verbal instruction relative to sex. A child learns through other channels besides that of verbal instruction. There is a difference between instruction and communication. Parents' choice is not between education for sexuality and no education for sexuality. Their choice is between good education and poor education. No matter what they do or do not do, say or do not say, the child receives his first, and sometimes his most indelible, education for sexuality from them.

FAMILY DEVELOPMENT

The family is a dynamic institution. It changes in slow, evolutionlike fashion as part of over-all cultural change. Each family, too, is dynamic. It changes as the number, ages, needs, and behavior of family members change and as the family as a group adapts itself to fluid circumstances. No matter where the family is found, in whatever area, class, or culture, at whatever period in history, certain broad similarities are to be observed in the stages through which it passes, just as there are broad similarities in the stages through which individuals pass in their development from infancy to old age. This universal similarity among families has given rise to the concept of the *family life cycle.* The stages of this cycle overlap but are nonetheless distinguishable, much as the stages in the development of an individual overlap but are distinguishable; for example, infancy, childhood, adolescence, adulthood, middle age, and so on, may be thought of as stages of development, even though each merges imperceptibly into the next and there is no clear-cut line of demarcation between them. In order for a family to move successfully through the several stages of the family life cycle, it must complete the *developmental tasks* at each stage. A developmental task, in the life of an individual or a family, is a task which arises at a given period of life, the successful completion of which leads to happiness and to success with later tasks, while the failure to complete it leads to unhappiness, social disapproval, and difficulty with later tasks [Havighurst, 1953].

Duvall [1971] discusses the several stages of the family cycle with the developmental tasks to be completed at each stage. The following is a very much condensed résumé of that discussion.

1 *The beginning family: establishment phase.* This stage starts with the wedding and continues until the first pregnancy. The developmental tasks of this stage include the establishment of a home and a pattern of living together as a couple and as members of an extended family and community.

2 *The beginning family: expectant phase.* This stage starts with the awareness of pregnancy and continues until the birth of the first child. The tasks of this stage include the reorganization of the home, the budget, the couple's various interpersonal relationships, and their philosophy of life to prepare for the arrival of the baby.

3 *The childbearing family.* This stage begins with the birth of the first child and continues until this child is thirty months old. Developmental tasks include adapting living arrangements to the needs of a young child. (Some refer to this process as "child-proofing" the home.) They also include meeting new expenses, reworking patterns of husband-wife responsibility, establishing new systems of communication and new interpersonal relationships with each other and with relatives, and fitting into the community as a young family.

4 *The family with preschool children.* This stage involves the couple's learning to rear their children at the same time that they continue to develop as a couple, meeting new costs and new responsibilities.

5 *The family with school-age children.* This stage involves such developmental tasks as helping children to grow, providing for each family member's needs, learning to cooperate together as a family, and relating the family to a community.

6 *The family with teen-agers.* In this stage the needs of all members put new demands upon the family. Sometimes needs conflict. New patterns of money usage and communication must be worked out. Family responsibilities may be shared in a new way. The husband and wife, as well as each child, have need for continued development as persons. The parents also are called upon to develop a point of view consistent with teen-age values and activities.

7 *The family as a launching center.* This stage marks the beginning of family contraction. During this stage the children are prepared for leaving home to become independent and to establish new families. The parents must prepare themselves for this and for a renewal of their relationships as a couple.

8 *The family in the middle years.* In this stage the couple are called upon to readjust their living conditions, to adapt themselves to the "empty nest," to develop new, or pursue already established, interests and friendships. During this stage many couples draw closer together.

9 *The aging family.* This stage involves making satisfactory living arrangements,

learning to live on retirement income, maintaining meaningful contacts with friends, children, and grandchildren, providing for illness, developing a philosophy that will enable the individual to face bereavement, and finding new meanings and reaffirming old meanings in life.

Our purpose in mentioning this succession of stages in the family life cycle with the developmental tasks of each stage has been to emphasize the importance of looking ahead. To make family life successful, parents as well as children must develop and mature. A "good" parent is actually a series of "good" parents, each having different responsibilities and performing different functions at various levels of development. Preparation for marriage means more than preparation for a wedding and for the first part of marriage. It means preparation for a way of life that in the great majority of cases characterizes a couple for as long as they both live.

SELECTED READINGS

Arnstein, Helen S.: *Your Growing Child and Sex*, The Bobbs-Merrill Company, Inc., Indianapolis, 1967. "A parent's guide to the sexual development, education, attitudes, and behavior of the child from infancy through adolescence." Describes general behavior patterns and attitudes at different stages and contains suggestions on how to deal with them.

Child Study Association of America, Inc.: *What to Tell Your Child about Sex*, rev. ed., Meredith Press, Meredith Publishing Company, Des Moines, 1968. Information for parents; answers to questions.

del Solar, Charlotte: *Parents' Answer Book: What Your Child Ought to Know about Sex*, Grosset & Dunlap, Inc., New York, 1971. Produced by the Parent and Child Institute. Includes discussion of sex education and model answers to 100 questions which a parent can translate into language suitable for a given child.

Gruenberg, Sidonie Matsner (ed.): *The New Encyclopedia of Child Care and Guidance*, Doubleday & Company, Inc., Garden City, N.Y., 1968. Covers a variety of topics and answers many questions.

Johnson, Eric W.: *Love and Sex in Plain Language*, J. B. Lippincott Company, Philadelphia, 1967. "Modern parents who believe they can best help their children by telling them the whole truth about sex will be the audience for this book." Discusses love and sex, sexual intercourse, contraception, prenatal development and childbirth, and adolescent sex problems and presents "a constructive perspective on love and sex to which boys and girls may look forward."

Salk, Lee, and Rita Kramer: *How to Raise a Human Being: A Parents' Guide to Emotional Health from Infancy through Adolescence*, Random House, Inc., New York, 1969. A guide for understanding the changing needs of children during critical periods of their maturation.

Schwartz, Alvin: *A Parent's Guide to Children's Play and Recreation*, Crowell-Collier Publishing Co., New York, 1963. A discussion of toys, games, etc.; use of trips in children's education; how to introduce a child to good music, etc.

References

Abbott, Walter M.: *The Documents of Vatican II,* The American Press, New York, 1966.

Ackerman, Nathan W.: *The Psychodynamics of Family Life,* Basic Books, Inc., Publishers, New York, 1958.

Albert, A.: "The Mammalian Testis," in William C. Young (ed.), *Sex and Internal Secretions,* 3d ed., The Williams & Wilkins Company, Baltimore, 1961, chap. 5.

Albrecht, Ruth E., and E. Wilbur Bock: *Encounter: Love, Marriage, and Family,* Holbrook Press, Inc., Boston, 1972.

Allan, Malcolm S.: "Husband-attended Deliveries," *Obstetrics and Gynecology,* vol. 27, no. 1, pp. 146–148, January, 1966.

Allen, Fred H., Jr., and Louis K. Diamond: *Erythroblastosis Fetalis,* Little, Brown and Company, Boston, 1957.

American Medical Association: *What you should known about "the pill"* (pamphlet), Chicago, 1970.

American Social Health Association: *Today's VD Control Problem,* New York, 1971.

Anderson, Gerald G., and Leon Speroff: "Prostaglandins and Abortion," in George Schaefer (ed.), "Legal Abortions in New York State: Medical, Legal, Nursing, Social Aspects (July 1–December 31, 1970)," *Clinical Obstetrics and Gynecology,* vol. 14, no. 1, pp. 1–324, March, 1971, pp. 245–257.

Andrews, William C.: "Oral Contraception: A Review of Reported Physiological and Pathological Effects," *Obstetrical and Gynecological Survey,* vol. 26, no. 7, pp. 477–499, July, 1971.

Aronson, Howard G., and Carl F. Glienke: "A Study of the Incidence of Pregnancy following Adoption," *Fertility and Sterility,* vol. 14, no. 5, pp. 547–553,

September-October, 1963; abstracted in *Obstetrical and Gynecological Survey,* vol. 19, no. 1, pp. 158–159, February, 1964.

Aronson, Marvin E.: "Fatal Air Embolism Caused by Bizarre Sexual Behavior during Pregnancy," *Medical Aspects of Human Sexuality,* vol. 3, no. 12, pp. 33–39, December, 1969.

―――― and Philip K. Nelson: "Fatal Air Embolism in Pregnancy Resulting from an Unusual Sex Act," *Obstetrics and Gynecology,* vol. 30, no. 1, pp. 127–130, July, 1967.

Arrata, W. S. M., and L. Iffy: "Normal and Delayed Ovulation in the Human," *Obstetrical and Gynecological Survey,* vol. 26, no. 10, pp. 675–689, October, 1971.

Ashley, David J. B.: *Human Intersex,* The Williams & Wilkins Company, Baltimore, 1962.

The Austin American, Feb. 26, 1968.

Ayre, J. Ernest, Franklin C. Reyner, Wilma B. Fagundes, and J. Maurice LeGuerrier: "Oral Progestins and Regression of Carcinoma In Situ and Cervical Dysplasia: Cytologic Evaluation," *Obstetrics and Gynecology,* vol. 34, no. 4, pp. 545–560, October, 1969.

Aznar-Ramos, Ramón: "Side Effects Utilizing Placebo," in Edward T. Tyler (ed.), *Progress in Conception Control 1969,* J. B. Lippincott Company, Philadelphia, 1969, pp. 54–60.

Baker, T. G.: "A Quantitative Cytological Study of Germ Cells in Human Ovaries," *Proc. Soc. Roy. Med.,* vol. 56, p. 417, 1963; abstracted in *Obstetrical and Gynecological Survey,* vol. 19, no. 4, pp. 700–701, August, 1964.

Bakker, Cornelis B., and Cameron R. Dightman: "Side Effects of Oral Contraceptives," *Obstetrics and*

Gynecology, vol. 28, no. 3, pp. 373–379, September, 1966.

Ballard, Charles A., and Francis E. Ballard: "Four Years' Experience with Mid-trimester Abortion by Amnioinfusion," *American Journal of Obstetrics and Gynecology*, vol. 114, no. 5, pp. 575–581, Nov. 1, 1972.

Banner, Edward A. (ed.): "Rh Factor," *Clinical Obstetrics and Gynecology*, vol. 7, no. 4, pp. 901–1055, December, 1964.

Barber, Hugh R. K., Edward A. Graber, and James J. O'Rourke: *Are the Pills Safe?* Charles C Thomas, Publisher, Springfield, Ill., 1969.

Bardwick, Judith M.: "Psychological Conflict and the Reproductive System," in Judith M. Bardwick, Elizabeth Douvan, Matina S. Horner, and David Gutmann, *Feminine Personality and Conflict*, Brooks/Cole Publishing Company, Belmont, Calif., 1970.

———: *Psychology of Women*, Harper & Row, Publishers, Incorporated, New York, 1971.

———, Elizabeth Douvan, Matina S. Horner, and David Gutmann: *Feminine Personality and Conflict*, Brooks/Cole Publishing Company, Belmont, Calif., 1970.

Barnes, Allan C.: "The Opening of the Second Front," *Obstetrics and Gynecology*, vol. 37, no. 2, pp. 320–322, February, 1971.

Barron, Donald H.: "The Placenta as Fetal Lung," in Claude A. Villee (ed.), *The Placenta and Fetal Membranes*, The Williams & Wilkins Company, Baltimore, 1960, chap. 4.

Barton, John J.: "Laparoscopy in Gynecologic Practice," in Ralph M. Wynn (ed.), *Obstetrics and Gynecology Annual 1972*, Appleton Century Crofts, New York, 1972, pp. 351–372.

Bauman, K. E.: "Selected Aspects of the Contraceptive Practices of Unmarried University Students," *American Journal of Obstetrics and Gynecology*, vol. 108, no. 2, pp. 203–209, 1970. Also in *Medical Aspects of Human Sexuality*, vol. 5, no. 8, pp. 76–89, August, 1971.

Beach, Frank A. (ed.): *Sex and Behavior*, John Wiley & Sons, Inc., New York, 1965.

Beacham, Daniel Winston, and Woodard Davis Beacham: *Synopsis of Gynecology*, 8th ed., The C. V. Mosby Company, St. Louis, 1972.

Bednarik, Karl: *The Male in Crisis*, translated by Helen Sebba, Alfred A. Knopf, Inc., New York, 1970.

Beer, Alan E.: "Differential Diagnosis and Clinical Analysis of Dysfunctional Uterine Bleeding," in Edward S. Wallach (ed.), "Dysfunctional Uterine Bleeding," *Clinical Obstetrics and Gynecology*, vol. 13, no. 2, pp. 361–488, June, 1970, pp. 434–450.

Behrman, S. J., and Yoshiaki Sawada: "Heterologous and Homologous Inseminations with Human Semen Frozen and Stored in a Liquid-Nitrogen Refrigerator," *Fertility and Sterility*, vol. 17, pp. 457–466, July–August, 1966.

Bell, Robert R.: *Premarital Sex in a Changing Society*, Prentice-Hall, Inc., Englewood Cliffs, N.J., 1966.

——— and Jay B. Chaskes: "Premarital Sexual Experience among Coeds, 1958 and 1968," *Journal of Marriage and the Family*, vol. 32, no. 1, pp. 81–84, February, 1970.

Benjamin, Harry: *The Transsexual Phenomenon*, Julian Press, Inc., New York, 1966.

Benson, Ralph C.: *Handbook of Obstetrics and Gynecology*, 4th ed., Lange Medical Publications, Los Altos, Calif., 1971.

Berlind, Melvyn: "The Contralateral Corpus Luteum: An Important Factor in Ectopic Pregnancy," *Obstetrics and Gynecology*, vol. 16, no. 1, pp. 51–52, July, 1960.

Bernard, Jessie: "The Fourth Revolution," in Ruth E. Albrecht and E. Wilbur Bock (eds), *Encounter: Love, Marriage, and Family*, Holbrook Press, Inc., Boston, 1972a.

———: *The Future of Marriage*, World Publishing Company, New York, 1972b.

———: *Remarriage*, Harper & Row, Publishers, Incorporated, New York, 1956.

Birnbaum, Stanley J.: "Breast Temperature as a Test for Pregnancy," *Obstetrics and Gynecology*, vol. 27, no. 3, pp. 378–380, March, 1966.

Bishop, David W.: "Biology of Spermatozoa," in William C. Young (ed.), *Sex and Internal Secretions*, 3d ed., The Williams & Wilkins Company, Baltimore, 1961, chap. 13.

Bishop, Edward H. (ed.): "Prematurity," *Clinical Obstetrics and Gynecology*, vol. 7, no. 3, pp. 641–748, September, 1964.

Blaine, Graham B.: "Sex on the Campus," in Henry

Anatole Grunewald, *Sex in America*, Bantam Books, Inc., New York, 1964, pp. 18–28.

Blandau, Richard J.: "Biology of Eggs and Implantation," in William C. Young (ed.), *Sex and Internal Secretions*, 3d ed., The Williams & Wilkins Company, Baltimore, 1961, chap. 14.

Blazer, John A.: "Married Virgins: A Study of Unconsummated Marriages," *Journal of Marriage and the Family*, vol. 26, no. 2, pp. 213–214, May, 1964.

Boehm, Bernice R.: "Adoption," in Harry L. Lurie (ed.), *Encyclopedia of Social Work*, 15th issue, National Association of Social Workers, New York, 1965, pp. 63–68.

Boggs, Thomas R.: "Mortality and Morbidity from Hemolytic Disease of the Newborn," in Edward A. Banner (ed.), "Rh Factor," *Clinical Obstetrics and Gynecology*, vol. 7, no. 4, pp. 901–1055, December, 1964, pp. 933–944.

Bosmajian, Hamida, and Haig Bosmajian (eds.): *This Great Argument: The Rights of Women*, Addison-Wesley Publishing Company, Inc., Reading, Mass., 1972.

Bourke, Geoffrey J., and Richard J. Whitty: "Smallpox Vaccination in Pregnancy: A Prospective Study," *British Medical Journal*, vol. 1, pp. 1544–1546, June 13, 1964.

Bourne, Aleck W., and Leslie H. Williams: *Recent Advances in Obstetrics and Gynecology*, McGraw-Hill Book Company, New York, 1953.

Böving, Bent G.: "Anatomy of Reproduction," in J. P. Greenhill, *Obstetrics*, 13th ed., W. B. Saunders Company, Philadelphia, 1965, chap. 1.

Bowes, Kenneth (ed.): *Modern Trends in Obstetrics and Gynecology*, Paul B. Hoeber, Inc., New York, 1956.

Bowes, Watson A., Jr., Vera E. Drose, and Paul D. Bruns: "Amniocentesis and Intrauterine Fetal Transfusion in Erythroblastosis," *American Journal of Obstetrics and Gynecology*, vol. 93, no. 6, pp. 822–841, Nov. 15, 1965.

Brasch, R.: *How Did It Begin?* David McKay Company, Inc., New York, 1965.

Breckinridge, Sophonisba: "The Activities of Women outside the Home," in *Report of the President's Research Committee on Social Trends*, McGraw-Hill Book Company, New York, 1933, pp. 709–750.

Bremer, Johan: *Asexualization*, The Macmillan Company, New York, 1959.

British Medical Journal, vol. 2, no. 5599, pp. 187–188, Apr. 27, 1968.

Broderick, Carl B. (ed.): *A Decade of Family Research and Action*, National Council on Family Relations, Minneapolis, 1971.

Broderick, Carlfred B., and Jessie Bernard (eds.): *The Individual, Sex, and Society*, The Johns Hopkins Press, Baltimore, 1969.

Bromley, Dorothy Dunbar, and Florence Haxton Britten: *Youth and Sex*, Harper & Row, Publishers, Incorporated, New York, 1938.

Brotherton, Janet, and I. L. Craft: "A Clinical and Pathologic Study of 91 Cases of Spontaneous Abortion," *Fertility and Sterility*, vol. 23, no. 4, pp. 289–294, April, 1972.

Brown, Barbara A., Thomas I. Emerson, Gail Falk, and Ann E. Freedman: "The Equal Rights Amendment: A Constitutional Basis for Equal Rights for Women," *The Yale Law Journal*, vol. 80, no. 5, pp. 872–985, April, 1971.

Brown, Edward, and Peter Barglow: "Pseudocyesis: A Paradigm for Psychophysiologic Reactions," *Archives of General Psychiatry*, vol. 24, no. 3, pp. 221–229, March, 1971.

Brown, William J.: "The National VD Problem," *Medical Aspects of Human Sexuality*, vol. 6, no. 2, pp. 152–178, February, 1972.

Bruce, Joan, and G. F. M. Russell: "Premenstrual Tension: A Study of Weight Changes and Balances of Water, Sodium, and Potassium," *The Lancet*, vol. 2, pp. 267–271, Aug. 11, 1962.

Bulmer, M. G.: *The Biology of Twinning in Man*, Oxford University Press, New York, 1970.

Bunge, R. G.: "Some Observations on the Male Ejaculate," *Fertility and Sterility*, vol. 21, no. 9, pp. 639–644, September, 1970.

Burgess, Ernest W., and Paul Wallin: *Engagement and Marriage*, J. B. Lippincott Company, Philadelphia, 1953.

Butler, N. R., H. Goldstein, and E. M. Ross: "Cigarette Smoking in Pregnancy: Its Influence on Birth Weight and Perinatal Mortality," *British Medical Journal*, vol. 2, no. 5806, pp. 127–130, Apr. 15, 1972.

Buxton, C. Lee (ed.): "Medical Practice and Population Control," *Clinical Obstetrics and Gynecology*, vol. 7, no. 3, pp. 749–875, September, 1964.

Calderone, Mary Steichen (ed.): *Abortion in the United States*, Paul B. Hoeber, Inc., New York, 1958.

————: "Family Planning: Its Role in Human Cost Accounting," *Pennsylvania Medical Journal*, vol. 66, no. 10, pp. 31–34, October, 1963.

———— (ed.): *Manual of Contraceptive Practice*, The Williams & Wilkins Company, Baltimore, 1964.

———— (ed.): *Manual of Family Planning and Contraceptive Practice*, 2d ed., The Williams & Wilkins Company, Baltimore, 1970.

Cantor, B., R. Jewelewicz, M. Warren, I. Dyrenfurth, A. Patner, and R. L. Vande Wiele: "Hormonal Changes during Induction of Midtrimester Abortion by Prostaglandin $F_2\alpha$," *American Journal of Obstetrics and Gynecology*, vol. 113, no. 5, pp. 607–615, July 1, 1972.

Carpenter, Philip: *Immunology and Serology*, W. B. Saunders Company, Philadelphia, 1956.

Carr, David H.: "Chromosome Studies in Spontaneous Abortions," *Obstetrics and Gynecology*, vol. 26, no. 3, pp. 308–326, September, 1965.

Carrington, Elsie R. (ed.): "Teratology," *Clinical Obstetrics and Gynecology*, vol. 9, no. 3, pp. 593–706, September, 1966.

Carter, Hugh, and Paul C. Glick: *Marriage and Divorce: A Social and Economic Study*, Harvard University Press, Cambridge, Mass., 1970.

———— and Alexander Plateris: "Trends in Divorce and Family Disruption," *Indicators*, U.S. Department of Health, Education, and Welfare, Washington, August, 1963.

Cavanagh, John R.: *The Popes, the Pill, and the People*, The Bruce Publishing Company, Milwaukee, 1965.

————: "Rhythm of Sexual Desire in Women," *Medical Aspects of Human Sexuality*, vol. 3, no. 2, pp. 29–39, February, 1969.

Cawood, C. David: "Petting and Prostatic Engorgement," *Medical Aspects of Human Sexuality*, vol. 5, no. 2, pp. 204–218, February, 1971.

Cervenka, Jaroslav, Robert J. Gorlin, and Richard P. Bendel: "Prenatal Sex Determination," *Obstetrics and Gynecology*, vol. 37, no. 6, pp. 912–915, June, 1971.

Chalmers, J. A.: "The Vacuum Extractor," in R. J. Keller (ed.), *Modern Trends in Obstetrics*, Butterworth, Inc., Washington, 1963, chap. 8.

————: *The Ventouse*, Lloyd-Luke (Medical Books) Ltd., England, 1971.

Chard, T., C. N. Hudson, C. R. W. Edwards, and N. R. H. Boyd: "Release of Oxytocin and Vasopressin by the Human Foetus during Labour," *Nature*, vol. 234, no. 5328, pp. 352–353, Dec. 10, 1971.

Charles, Allan G., and Emanuel A. Friedman: *Rh Isoimmunization and Erythroblastosis Fetalis*, Appleton Century Crofts, New York, 1969.

Charles, David (ed.): *Progress in Conception Control 1967*, J. B. Lippincott Company, Philadelphia, 1967.

————: "Thromboembolic Phenomena in Relation to Oral Contraception," in Dean L. Mears (ed.), *Progress in Conception Control 1968*, J. B. Lippincott Company, Philadelphia, 1968, pp. 25–40.

Charny, Charles W., Ramon Suarez, and Nader Sadoughi: "Castration in the Male," *Medical Aspects of Human Sexuality*, vol. 4, no. 5, pp. 80–83, May, 1970.

Chin, James, Allan J. Ebbin, Miriam G. Wilson, and Edwin H. Linnette: "Avoidance of Rubella Immunization of Women During or Shortly Before Pregnancy," *Journal of the American Medical Association*, vol. 215, no. 4, pp. 632–634, Jan. 25, 1971.

Christensen, Harold T.: "Child Spacing Analysis via Record Linkage: New Data Plus a Summing Up of Earlier Reports," *Marriage and Family Living*, vol. 25, no. 3, pp. 272–280, August, 1963.

————: "Studies in Child Spacing: I—Premarital Pregnancy as Measured by the Spacing of the First Birth from Marriage," *American Sociological Review*, vol. 18, no. 1, pp. 53–59, February, 1953.

————, Robert Andrews, and Sophie Freiser: "Falsification of Age at Marriage," *Marriage and Family Living*, vol. 15, no. 4, pp. 301–304, November, 1953.

———— and Christina F. Gregg: "Changing Sex Norms in America and Scandinavia," *Journal of Marriage and the Family*, vol. 32, no. 4, pp. 616–627, November, 1970.

———— and Hanna H. Meissner: "Studies in Child Spacing: III—Premarital Pregnancy as a Factor in Divorce," *American Sociological Review*, vol. 18, no. 6, pp. 641–644, December, 1953.

Clark, Alexander L., and Paul Wallin: "Women's

Sexual Responsiveness and the Duration and Quality of Their Marriages," *American Journal of Sociology,* vol. 71, no. 2, pp. 187–196, September, 1965.

Clark, J. H., and M. X. Zarrow: "Influence of Copulation on Time of Ovulation in Women," *American Journal of Obstetrics and Gynecology,* vol. 109, no. 7, pp. 1083–1085, Apr. 1, 1971.

Clark, Thomas L., and Warren M. Jacobs: "Isoimmunization of the Rh-negative Mother during the Third Stage of Labor," *Obstetrics and Gynecology,* vol. 23, no. 5, pp. 764–767, May, 1964.

Clarke, C. A.: "The Mechanism of Action of Rh-Immune Globulin," in John T. Queenan (ed.), "The Rh Problem," *Clinical Obstetrics and Gynecology,* vol. 14, no. 2, pp. 491–646, June, 1971, pp. 611–624.

Clarke, Cyril A., and Richard B. McConnell: *Prevention of Rh-Hemolytic Disease,* Charles C Thomas, Publisher, Springfield, Ill., 1972.

Clayton, Everett M., Jr., William Feldhaus, James M. Phythyon, and Frank E. Whitacre: "Transplacental Passage of Fetal Erythrocytes during Pregnancy," *Obstetrics and Gynecology,* vol. 28, no. 2, pp. 194–197, August, 1966.

———, ———, and Frank E. Whitacre: "Fetal Erythrocytes in the Maternal Circulation of Pregnant Women," *Obstetrics and Gynecology,* vol. 23, no. 6, pp. 915–919, June, 1964.

Cleckley, Hervey: *The Mask of Sanity,* 4th ed., The C. V. Mosby Company, St. Louis, 1964.

Clemens, Alphonse H.: *Design for Successful Living,* 2d ed., Prentice-Hall, Inc., Englewood Cliffs, N.J., 1964.

———: *Marriage and the Family: An Integrated Approach for Catholics,* Prentice-Hall, Inc., Englewood Cliffs, N.J., 1957.

Cohen, Flossie, Wolf W. Zuelzer, David Gustafson, and Margaret M. Evans: "Mechanisms of Isoimmunization I: The Transplacental Passage of Fetal Erythrocytes in Homospecific Pregnancies," *Blood,* vol. 23, no. 5, pp. 621–646, May, 1964.

Committee on Maternal Health, Food and Nutrition Board, National Research Council: *Maternal Nutrition and the Course of Pregnancy,* National Academy of Sciences, Washington, 1970.

Comstock, G. W., F. K. Shah, M. B. Meyer, and H. Abbey: "Low Birth Weight and Neonatal Mortality Rate Related to Maternal Smoking and Socioeconomic Status," *American Journal of Obstetrics and Gynecology,* vol. 111, no. 1, pp. 53–59, Sept. 1, 1971.

Connell, Elizabeth: *Science News,* May 21, 1966.

Convers, D.: *Marriage and Divorce in the United States,* J. B. Lippincott Company, Philadelphia, 1889.

Coser, Ruth Laub (ed.): *The Family: Its Structure and Functions,* St. Martin's Press, Inc., New York, 1964.

Crampton, C. B.: "Uncomplicated Obstetrics: A Revaluation," *Connecticut Medicine,* vol. 25, no. 5, pp. 279–283, May, 1961.

Crist, Takey: "Contraceptive Practices among College Women," *Medical Aspects of Human Sexuality,* vol. 5, no. 11, pp. 168–176, November, 1971.

Csapo, A. I., J. P. Sauvage, and W. G. Wiest: "The Efficacy and Acceptability of Intravenously Administered Prostaglandin $F_2\alpha$ as an Abortifacient," *American Journal of Obstetrics and Gynecology,* vol. 111, no. 8, pp. 1059–1063, Dec. 15, 1971.

Cuber, John F.: "May-September Marriages," *Sexual Behavior,* vol. 1, no. 2, pp. 9–17, May, 1971.

——— and Peggy B. Harroff: *The Significant Americans,* Appleton Century Crofts, New York, 1965.

Cutright, Phillips: "Out-of-wedlock Teenage Births," *Ob-Gyn Observer,* April, 1972.

Cutter Laboratories, Inc., *Treatment of Female Infertility with Pergonal (Menotropins),* Berkeley, Calif.

Dacie, J. V.: *The Haemolytic Anaemias, Part IV,* 2d ed., Grune & Stratton, Inc., New York, 1967.

Dalton, Katharina: "Menstruation and Accidents," *British Medical Journal,* vol. 2, no. 5210, pp. 1425–1426, Nov. 12, 1960.

———: *The Premenstrual Syndrome,* William Heinemann Ltd., London, 1964.

Davidsohn, Israel: "Fetal Erythroblastosis and the Rh and Other Blood Factors," in J. P. Greenhill, *Obstetrics,* 13th ed., W. B. Saunders Company, Philadelphia, 1965, pp. 779–793.

Davis, Hugh J.: "Intrauterine Contraceptive Devices: Present Status and Future Prospects," *American Journal of Obstetrics and Gynecology,* vol. 114, no. 1, pp. 134–151, Sept. 1, 1972.

———: *Intrauterine Devices for Contraception: The IUD,* The Williams & Wilkins Company, Baltimore, 1971.

———: "Status of Intrauterine Devices in Clinical Practice," *Current Medical Digest*, vol. 33, no. 6, pp. 873–879, June, 1966.

——— and John Lesinski: "Mechanism of Action of Intrauterine Contraceptives in Women," *Obstetrics and Gynecology*, vol. 36, no. 3, pp. 350–358, September, 1970.

Davis, Katherine B.: *Factors in the Sex Life of Twenty-two Hundred Women*, Harper & Row, Publishers, Incorporated, New York, 1929.

Decter, Midge: *The New Chastity and Other Arguments against Women's Liberation*, Coward, McCann & Geoghegan, Inc., New York, 1972.

Deep, Anthony A., and Ivan Jacobson: "Soap-induced Abortion," *Obstetrics and Gynecology*, vol. 25, no. 2, pp. 241–244, February, 1965.

Dewhurst, Christopher J., and Ronald R. Gordon: *The Intersexual Disorders*, Baillière, Tindall & Cassell, Ltd., London, 1969.

Diamond, M.: "A Critical Evaluation of Ontogeny of Human Behavior," *Quarterly Review of Biology*, vol. 40, pp. 147ff, 1965; quoted in Elizabeth Bing and Esselyn Rudikoff, "Divergent Ways of Parental Coping with Hermaphroditic Children," *Medical Aspects of Human Sexuality*, vol. 4, no. 12, pp. 73–88, December, 1970.

Dickinson, Robert Latou, and Lura Beam: *The Single Woman*, The Williams & Wilkins Company, Baltimore, 1934.

DiSaia, Philip J., Clarence D. Davis, and Ben Z. Taber: "Continuous Tablet Therapy for Oral Contraception," *Obstetrics and Gynecology*, vol. 31, no. 1, pp. 119–124, January, 1968.

Donald, Ian: *Practical Obstetric Problems*, 3d ed., Year Book Medical Publishers, Inc., Chicago, 1964.

Donnelly, James F., Jr.: "Etiology of Prematurity," in Edward H. Bishop (ed.), "Prematurity," *Clinical Obstetrics and Gynecology*, vol. 7, no. 3, pp. 641–748, September, 1964, pp. 647–657.

Drill, Victor A.: *Oral Contraceptives*, McGraw-Hill Book Company, New York, 1966.

———: "Oral Contraceptives and Thromboembolic Disease, I. Prospective and Retrospective Studies," *Journal of the American Medical Association*, vol. 219, no. 5, pp. 583–592, Jan. 31, 1972.

——— and David W. Calhoun: "Oral Contraceptives and Thromboembolic Disease," *Journal of the American Medical Association*, vol. 206, no. 1, pp. 77–84, Sept. 30, 1968.

Drucker, Paul, Jerrold Finkel, and Lewis E. Savel: "Sixty-five Day Interval between the Births of Twins," *American Journal of Obstetrics and Gynecology*, vol. 80, no. 4, pp. 761–763, October, 1960.

Drummond, Isabel: *Getting a Divorce*, Alfred A. Knopf, Inc., New York, 1934.

Dubin, Lawrence: "Various Sexual Problems Blamed for Male Infertility," *Journal of the American Medical Association*, vol. 220, no. 6, pp. 780–781, May 8, 1972.

Dublin, Louis I.: *Factbook on Man*, The Macmillan Company, New York, 1965.

Duffy, Benedict J., Jr., and Sister M. Jean Wallace: *Biological and Medical Aspects of Contraception*, University of Notre Dame Press, Notre Dame, Ind., 1969.

Duvall, Evelyn Millis: *Family Development*, 4th ed., J. B. Lippincott Company, Philadelphia, 1971.

Eastman, Nicholson J. (ed): editor's comments, *Obstetrical and Gynecological Survey*, vol. 16, no. 1, February, 1961; vol. 17, no. 1, February, 1962; vol. 18, no. 3, June, 1963; vol. 19, no. 6, December, 1964.

Eastman, William F.: "First Intercourse," *Sexual Behavior*, vol. 2, no. 3, pp. 22–27, March, 1972.

Eckstein, P., Margaret Whitby, K. Fotherby, Christine Butler, T. K. Mukherjee, J. B. C. Burnett, D. J. Richards, and T. P. Whitehead: "Clinical and Laboratory Findings in a Trial of Norgestrel, a Low-dose Progestogen-only Contraceptive," *British Medical Journal*, vol. 3, no. 5820, pp. 195–200, July 22, 1972.

Edgren, Richard A.: "The Biology of Steroidal Contraceptives," in Daniel Lednicer (ed.), *Contraception: The Chemical Control of Fertility*, Marcel Dekker, Inc., New York, 1969, pp. 23–68.

Ehrlich, Shirley Stendig: "The Psychological Impact of New Parenthood," in Boston Children's Medical Center, *Pregnancy, Birth and the Newborn Baby*, Delacorte Press, Dell Publishing Co., Inc., New York, 1972, pp. 223–229.

Ehrmann, Winston: *Premarital Dating Behavior*, Holt, Rinehart and Winston, Inc., New York, 1959.

Eichler, Lillian: *The Customs of Mankind*, Doubleday & Company, Inc., Garden City, N.Y., 1925.

Eisner, Thomas, Ari Van Tienhoven, and Frank Rosenblatt: "Population Control, Sterilization, and

Ignorance," *Science*, vol. 167, no. 3917, p. 337, Jan. 23, 1970.

Ejlersen, Mette: *Sexual Liberation*, translated by Marianne Kold Madsen, Award House, Universal Publishing & Distributing Corporation, New York, 1969.

Elias, James E.: "Teenage Sexual Patterns: An Examination of the Risk-Taking Behavior of Youth," *Social Health Papers #5*, pp. 10–14, American Social Health Association, New York, 1969.

Engle, Earl T. (ed.): *Studies on Testis and Ovary, Eggs and Sperm*, Charles C Thomas, Publisher, Springfield, Ill., 1952.

Enovid Bulletin no. 7, October, 1961, G. D. Searle & Company, Chicago.

Ersek, Robert A.: "Frozen Sperm Banks," *Journal of the American Medical Association*, vol. 220, no. 10, p. 1365, June 5, 1972.

Exner, Max Joseph: *Problems and Principles of Sex Education: A Study of 948 College Men*, Association Press, New York, 1915.

Farris, Edmond J.: *Human Ovulation and Fertility*, J. B. Lippincott Company, Philadelphia, 1956.

Federal Security Agency: *Vital Statistics of the United States*, part 1, 1949.

Feldman, Joseph G., and Jack Lippes: "A Four-year Comparison between the Ultilization and Use-Effectiveness of Sequential and Combined Oral Contraceptives," *Contraception*, vol. 3, p. 93, 1971; abstracted in *Obstetrical & Gynecological Survey*, vol. 28, no. 8, pp. 594–595, August, 1971.

Ferreira, Antonio J.: *Prenatal Environment*, Charles C Thomas, Publisher, Springfield, Ill., 1969.

Ferriss, Abbott L.: *Indicators of Trends in the Status of American Women*, Russell Sage Foundation, New York, 1971.

Fields, Charles, Hugh C. Falls, Charles P. Warren, and Manuel Zimberoff: "Ear of Newborn as Identification Constant," *Obstetrics and Gynecology*, vol. 16, no. 1, pp. 98–102, July, 1960.

Findley, Palmer: *The Story of Childbirth*, Doubleday & Company, Inc., Garden City, N. Y., 1933.

Finegold, Wilfred J.: *Artificial Insemination*, Charles C Thomas, Publisher, Springfield, Ill., 1964.

Finger, F. W.: "Sex Beliefs and Practices among Male College Students," *Journal of Abnormal and Social Psychology*, vol. 42, pp. 57–67, 1947.

Fisher, Seymour: *The Female Orgasm*, Basic Books, Inc., Publishers, New York, 1973.

Fiumara, Nicholas J.: "Ineffectiveness of Condoms in Preventing Veneral Disease," *Medical Aspects of Human Sexuality*, vol. 6, no. 10, pp. 146–150, October, 1972.

Fletcher, Joseph F.: *Situation Ethics: The New Morality*, The Westminster Press, Philadelphia, 1966.

Flowers, Charles E.: "Systemic Medication," in Sol M. Shnider (ed.), *Obstetrical Anesthesia*, The Williams & Wilkins Company, Baltimore, 1970, pp. 60–70.

—— and Sol M. Shnider: "Effects of Labor, Delivery and Drugs on the Fetus and Newborn," in Sol M. Shnider (ed.), *Obstetrical Anesthesia*, The Williams & Wilkins Company, Baltimore, 1970, pp. 37–48.

Flowers, Charles E., Jr.: *Obstetric Analgesia and Anesthesia*, Paul B. Hoeber, Inc., New York, 1967.

Fluhmann, C. Frederic: *The Management of Menstrual Disorders*, W. B. Saunders Company, Philadelphia, 1956.

Fontana, John, and Gilles R. G. Monif: "Superfetation," *Obstetrics and Gynecology*, vol. 35, no. 4, pp. 585–588, April, 1970.

Food and Drug Administration: *Papers*, vol. 5, no. 6, July-August, 1971; vol. 5, no. 7, September, 1971; vol. 5, no. 9, November, 1971; vol. 6, no. 6, July-August, 1972.

Foy, Felician A. (ed.): *1973 Catholic Almanac*, Our Sunday Visitor, Inc., Huntington, Ind., 1972.

——: *1967 National Catholic Almanac*, Doubleday & Company, Inc., Garden City, N.Y., 1967.

——: *1968 National Catholic Almanac*, Doubleday & Company, Inc., Garden City, N.Y., 1968.

Freda, Vincent J.: "Prevention of Isoimmunization to the Rh Factor in Obstetrics," in J. P. Greenhill (ed.), *The Year Book of Obstetrics and Gynecology* (1966–67 Year Book Series), Year Book Medical Publishers, Inc., Chicago, 1966, pp. 275–289.

Freedman, Mervin B.: *The College Experience*, Jossey-Bass, Inc., Publishers, San Francisco, 1967. Chap. 7, "The Sexual Behavior of American College Women: An Empirical Study and an Historical Survey," is also found in Ailon Shiloh (ed.), *Studies in Human Sexual Behavior: The American Scene*,

Charles C Thomas, Publisher, Springfield, Ill., 1970, chap. 13.

Freedman, Ronald, Pascal K. Whelpton, and Arthur A. Campbell: *Family Planning, Sterility, and Population Growth*, McGraw-Hill Book Company, New York, 1959.

Freeman, Roger K.: "Pneumoperitoneum from Oral-genital Insufflation," *Obstetrics and Gynecology*, vol. 36, no. 1, pp. 162–164, July, 1970.

Fremantle, Anne (ed.): *The Papal Encyclicals*, New American Library of World Literature, Inc., New York, 1956.

Freund, M., and J. Wiederman: "Factors Affecting the Dilution, Freezing and Storage of Human Semen," *Journal of Reproduction and Fertility*, vol. 11, no. 1, 1966; abstracted in *Obstetrical and Gynecological Survey*, vol. 21, no. 4, pp. 655–656, August, 1966.

Friedman, Emanuel A.: "Analgesia," in J. P. Greenhill, *Obstetrics*, 13th ed., W. B. Saunders Company, Philadelphia, 1965a, pp. 378–385.

———: "Prevention of Rh Isoimmunization," in Allan G. Charles and Emanuel A. Friedman (eds.), *Rh Isoimmunization and Erythroblastosis Fetalis*, Appleton Century Crofts, New York, 1969, pp. 203–218.

———: "Therapeutic Abortion," in J. P. Greenhill, *Obstetrics*, 13th ed., W. B. Saunders Company, Philadelphia, 1965b. chap. 36.

Friedman, Leonard J.: *Virgin Wives*, Tavistock Publications, Ltd., London, 1962.

Friesan, Rhinehart F., and John M. Bowman: "Fetal Transfusion in Utero in Rh Disease," in Stewart L. Marcus and Cyril C. Marcus (eds.), *Advances in Obstetrics and Gynecology*, vol. 1, The Williams & Wilkins Company, Baltimore, 1967, chap. 17.

Fromme, Allan: *The Ability to Love*, Farrar, Straus & Giroux, Inc., New York, 1965.

Fujita, Byron N., Nathaniel N. Wagner, and Ronald J. Pion: "Contraceptive Use among Single College Students," *American Journal of Obstetrics and Gynecology*, vol. 109, no. 5, pp. 787–793, Mar. 1, 1971.

Gagnon, John H., and William Simon (eds.): *The Sexual Scene*, Trans-Action Books, Aldine Publishing Company, Chicago, 1970.

Galton, Lawrence: "VD: Out of Control?" *Sexual Behavior*, vol. 2, no. 1, pp. 17–24, January, 1972.

Gambrell, Richard D.: "Immediate Postpartum Oral Contraception," *Obstetrics and Gynecology*, vol. 36, no. 1, pp, 101–106, July, 1970.

Garai, Josef E., and Amram Scheinfeld: "Sex Differences in Mental and Behavioral Traits," *Genetic Psychology Monographs*, vol. 77, 2d half, pp. 169–299, May, 1968.

Garcia, Celso-Ramon: "Clinical Aspects of Oral Hormonal Contraception," in Mary Steichen Calderone (ed.), *Manual of Family Planning and Contraceptive Practice*, 2d ed., The Williams & Wilkins Company, Baltimore, 1970, pp. 283–330.

———: "Detection and Diagnosis of Ovulation," in Luigi Mastroianni, Jr. (ed.), "Ovulation," *Clinical Obstetrics and Gynecology*, vol. 10, no. 2, pp. 343–430, June, 1967, pp. 380–389.

——— (ed.): "Oral Contraception," *Clinical Obstetrics and Gynecology*, vol. 11, no. 3, pp. 623–752, September, 1968.

———: "Tubal Ligation: Reversibility Should Guide the Operative Approach," *Ob-Gyn Observer*, vol. 11, no. 4, p. 2, June, 1972.

——— and Gregory Pincus: "Clinical Considerations of Hormonal Control of Human Fertility," in C. Lee Buxton (ed.), "Medical Practice and Population Control," *Clinical Obstetrics and Gynecology*, vol. 7, no. 3, pp. 749–875, September, 1964, pp. 844–856.

Garcia-Bunuel, Rafael: "New and Experimental Methods of Fertility Control," *Current Medical Digest*, vol. 33, no. 6, pp. 889–899, June, 1966.

Gebhard, Paul H.: "Factors in Marital Orgasm," in Ailon Shiloh (ed.): *Studies in Human Sexual Behavior: The American Scene*, Charles C Thomas, Publisher, Springfield, Ill., 1970a, chap. 23.

———: "Female Sexuality," in Paul H. Gebhard, Jan Raboch, and Hans Giese: *The Sexuality of Women*, translated by Colin Bearne, Stein and Day Incorporated, New York, 1970b, pp. 10–43.

———, Wardell B. Pomeroy, Clyde E. Martin, and Cornelia V. Christenson: *Pregnancy, Birth and Abortion*, Paul B. Hoeber, Inc., New York, 1958.

———, Jan Raboch, and Hans Giese: *The Sexuality of Women*, translated by Colin Bearne, Stein and Day Incorporated, New York, 1970c.

Giese, Hans: "The Sexuality of Women," in Paul H. Gebhard, Jan Raboch, and Hans Giese, *The Sexuality of Women*, translated by Colin Bearne, Stein and Day Incorporated, New York, 1970, pp. 97–136.

Gilbert Youth Research: "How Wild Are College Students?" *Pageant*, vol. 7, pp. 10–21, 1951.

Gill, Merton M.: "Functional Disturbances of Menstruation," *Bulletin of the Menninger Clinic*, vol. 7, no. 1, pp. 6–14, January, 1943.

Gillespie, Luke: "Smoking and Low Birth Weight," in Edward H. Bishop (ed.), "Prematurity," *Clinical Obstetrics and Gynecology*, vol. 7, no. 3, pp. 641–748, September, 1964, pp. 658–665.

Gillett, P. G., R. A. H. Kinch, L. S. Wolfe, and C. Pace-Asciak: "Therapeutic Abortion with the Use of Prostaglandin $F_2\alpha$," *American Journal of Obstetrics and Gynecology*, vol. 112, no. 3, pp. 330–338, Feb. 1, 1972.

Glass, Robert H., and Nathan G. Kase: *Woman's Choice*, Basic Books, Inc., Publishers, New York, 1970.

Golden, Boris A.: "Honeymoon Sexual Problems," *Medical Aspects of Human Sexuality*, vol. 5, no. 5, pp. 139–152, May, 1971.

Goldfarb, Alvin F.: *Advances in the Treatment of Menstrual Dysfunction*, Lea & Febiger, Philadelphia, 1964.

———: "Clomiphene Citrate: Its Effect in Some Ovulatory Defects," in Luigi Mastroianni, Jr. (ed.), "Ovulation," *Clinical Obstetrics and Gynecology*, vol. 10, no. 2, pp. 343–417, June, 1967, pp. 390–400.

———, Antonio Morales, Abraham E. Rakoff, and Peter Protos: "Critical Review of 160 Clomiphene-related Pregnancies," *Obstetrics and Gynecology*, vol. 31, no. 3, pp. 342–345, March, 1968.

Goldman, George D., and Donald S. Milman (eds.): *Modern Woman: Her Psychology and Sexuality*, Charles C Thomas, Publisher, Springfield, Ill., 1969.

Goldman, Jack A., and Benjamin Eckerling: "Prevention of Rh Isoimmunization after Abortion with Anti-Rh₀(D)-Immunoglobin," *Obstetrics and Gynecology*, vol. 40, no. 3, pp. 366–370, September, 1972.

Goldsmith, Sadja, and Alan J. Margolis: "Aspiration Abortion without Cervical Dilation," *American Journal of Obstetrics and Gynecology*, vol. 110, no. 4, pp. 580–582, June 15, 1971.

Goldzieher, Joseph W., Louis E. Moses, Eugene Averkin, Cora Scheel, and Ben Z. Taber: "Nervousness and Depression Attributed to Oral Contraceptives: A Double-blind Placebo-controlled Study,"

American Journal of Obstetrics and Gynecology, vol. 111, no. 8, pp. 1013–1020, Dec. 15, 1971.

——— and Edris Rice-Wray: *Oral Contraception: Mechanism and Management*, Charles C Thomas, Publisher, Springfield, Ill., 1966.

Good, Frederick L., and Otis F. Kelly: *Marriage, Morals, and Medical Ethics*, P. J. Kenedy & Sons., New York, 1951.

Goode, William J.: *World Revolution and Family Patterns*, The Free Press, New York, 1963.

Goodlin, Robert C., David W. Keller, and Margaret Raffin: "Orgasm during Late Pregnancy," *Obstetrics and Gynecology*, vol. 38, no. 6, pp. 916–920, December, 1971.

Goplerud, Clifford P.: "Monoamniotic Twins with Double Survival," *Obstetrics and Gynecology*, vol. 23, no. 2, pp. 289–290, February, 1964.

Gorbach, Arthur: "A Healthy Pregnancy," in The Boston Children's Medical Center, *Pregnancy, Birth and the Newborn Baby*, Delacorte Press, Dell Publishing Co., Inc., New York, 1972, pp. 73–93.

Gordon, Albert I.: *Intermarriage*, Beacon Press, Boston, 1964.

Gordon, Michael, and M. Charles Bernstein: "Mate Choice and Domestic Life in the Nineteenth-Century Marriage Manual," *Journal of Marriage and the Family*, vol. 32, no. 4, pp. 665–674, November, 1970.

Granfield, David: *The Abortion Decision*, rev. ed., Image Books, Doubleday & Company, Inc., Garden City, N.Y., 1971.

———: "A Catholic Lawyer's View," in Robert E. Hall (ed.), *Abortion in a Changing World: I*, Columbia University Press, New York, 1970, pp. 149–156.

Grant, Alan: "Spontaneous Cure Rate of Various Infertility Factors or Post Hoc and Propter Hoc," *Australian & New Zealand Journal of Obstetrics and Gynaecology*, vol. 9, pp. 224–227, November, 1969.

Graves, Lester R., Jr., and J. T. Francisco: "Medicolegal Aspects of Rape," *Medical Aspects of Human Sexuality*, vol. 4, no. 4, pp. 109–120, April, 1970.

Gray, Madeline: *The Normal Woman*, Charles Scribner's Sons, New York, 1967.

Greaves, Donald C., Phillip E. Green, and Louis Jolyon West: "Psychodynamic and Psychophysiological Aspects of Pseudocyesis," *Psychosomatic Medicine*, vol. 22, no. 1, pp. 24–31, 1960.

Green, Richard, and John Money (eds.): *Transsexualism and Sex Reassignment*, The Johns Hopkins Press, Baltimore, 1969.

Greenblatt, Robert B.: "Menstrual Physiology," in Alvin F. Goldfarb (ed.), *Advances in the Treatment of Menstrual Dysfunction*, Lea & Febiger, Philadelphia, 1964, pp. 13–25.

——— (ed.): *Ovulation*, J. B. Lippincott Company, Philadelphia, 1966.

Greenhill, J. P.: *Analgesia and Anesthesia in Obstetrics*, 2d ed., Charles C Thomas, Publisher, Springfield, Ill., 1962a.

———: *Obstetrics*, 13th ed., W. B. Saunders Company, Philadelphia, 1965a.

———: *Obstetrics in General Practice*, 3d ed., Year Book Medical Publishers, Inc., Chicago, 1945; 4th ed., 1948.

——— (ed.): *The 1943 Year Book of Obstetrics and Gynecology*, Year Book Medical Publishers, Inc., Chicago, 1944.

——— (ed.): *The Year Book of Obstetrics and Gynecology, 1954–55*, Year Book Medical Publishers, Inc., Chicago, 1954; *1957–58* (1957); *1959–60* (1959); *1960–61* (1960); *1961–62* (1961); *1962–63* (1962b); *1963–64* (1963); *1964–65* (1964); *1965–66* (1965b); *1966–67* (1966); *1972* (1972).

Grold, L. James: "Patterns of Jealousy," *Medical Aspects of Human Sexuality*, vol. 6, no. 5, pp. 118–126, May, 1972.

———: "Swinging: Sexual Freedom or Neurotic Escapism?" *American Journal of Psychiatry*, vol. 127, no. 4, pp. 521–523, October, 1970.

Group for the Advancement of Psychiatry: *The Right of Abortion: A Psychiatric View*, Charles Scibner's Sons, New York, 1970.

Guttmacher, Alan Frank: *Into This Universe*, The Viking Press, Inc., New York, 1937.

———: *Life in the Making*, Garden City Books, New York, 1933.

———, Robert E. Hall, Christopher Tietze, and Harriet Pilpel: "Legal Abortion," *Medical Aspects of Human Sexuality*, vol. 5, no. 8, pp. 50–75, August, 1971.

Guyton, Arthur C.: *Textbook of Medical Physiology*, 4th ed., W. B. Saunders Company, Philadelphia, 1971.

Haagensen, C. D.: *Diseases of the Breast*, W. B. Saunders Company, Philadelphia, 1956.

Hack, M., M. Brish, M. Serr, V. Insler, and B. Lunenfeld: "Outcome of Pregnancy after Induced Ovulation," *Journal of the American Medical Association*, vol. 211, no. 5, pp. 791–797, Feb. 2, 1970.

Hacker, Helen Mayer: "The New Burdens of Masculinity," *Marriage and Family Living*, vol. 19, no. 3, pp. 227–233, August, 1957.

———: "Women as a Minority Group," *Social Forces*, vol. 30, no. 1, pp. 60–69, October, 1951. Also in Hamida Bosmajian and Haig Bosmajian (eds.), *This Great Argument: The Rights of Women*, Addison-Wesley Publishing Company, Inc., Reading, Mass., 1972, pp. 127–145. Excerpts in Nona Glazer-Malbin and Helen Youngelson Waehrer (eds), *Woman in a Man-made World*, Rand McNally & Company, Chicago, 1972, pp. 39–44.

Hall, Robert E.: "A Comparative Evaluation of Intrauterine Contraceptive Devices," *American Journal of Obstetriccs and Gynecology*, vol. 94, no. 1, pp. 65–77, Jan. 1, 1966.

———: "The Future of Therapeutic Abortions in the United States," in Gerald B. Holzman (ed.), "Implementation of Legal Abortion: A National Problem," *Clinical Obstetrics and Gynecology*, vol. 14, no. 4, pp. 1109–1338, December, 1971, pp. 1149–1153.

———: "Intrauterine Devices: Clinical Aspects," in Mary Steichen Calderone, *Manual of Family Planning and Contraceptive Practice*, 2d ed., The Williams & Wilkins Company, Baltimore, 1970.

———: "A Three Year Study of the Lippes Loop," *Bulletin of the Sloane Hospital for Women*, vol. 13, no. 1, pp. 1–5, spring, 1967.

Halpin, Thomas F., Albert R. Jones, H. Lee Bishop, and Saul Lerner: "Prophylaxis of Neonatal Hyperbilirubinemia with Phenobarbital," *Obstetrics and Gynecology*, vol. 40, no. 1, pp. 85–90, July, 1972.

Hamblen, E. C.: *Endocrinology of Women*, Charles C Thomas, Publisher, Springfield, Ill., 1945.

Hamblin, Robert L., and Robert O. Blood, Jr.: "Pre-marital Experience and the Wife's Sexual Adjustment," *Social Problems*, vol. 4, no. 2, pp. 122–130, October, 1956.

Hamilton, Eugene G.: "Prevention of Rh Isoimmunization by Injection of Anti-D Antibody," *Ob-*

stetrics and Gynecology, vol. 30, no. 6, pp. 812–815, December, 1967.

Hamilton, G. V.: *A Research in Marriage*, Albert & Charles Boni, Inc., New York, 1929.

Hampson, Joan G.: "The Case Management of Somatic Sexual Disorders in Children: Psychologic Considerations," in Charles W. Lloyd (ed.), *Human Reproduction and Sexual Behavior*, Lea & Febiger, Philadelphia, 1964, chap. 13.

Hampson, John L.: "Determinants of Psychosexual Orientation," in Frank A. Beach (ed.), *Sex and Behavior*, John Wiley & Sons, Inc., New York, 1965, pp. 108–132.

——: "Deviant Sexual Behavior; Homosexuality; Transvestism," in Charles W. Lloyd (ed.), *Human Reproduction and Sexual Behavior*, Lea & Febiger, Philadelphia, 1964, chap. 28.

Häring, Bernard: *Marriage in the Modern World*, translated by Geoffrey Stevens, The Newman Press, Westminster, Md., 1966.

Harkell, Robert L.: *The Picture Book of Sexual Love*, Cybertype Corp., New York, 1969.

Harper, Fowler V.: "Sex and the Law," in Charles W. Lloyd (ed.), *Human Reproduction and Sexual Behavior*, Lea & Febiger, Philadelphia, 1964, chap. 25.

Harper, Robert A.: "Communication Problems in Marriage and Marriage Counseling," *Marriage and Family Living*, vol. 20, no. 2, pp. 107–112, May, 1958.

—— and Walter Stokes: *45 Levels to Sexual Understanding and Enjoyment*, Prentice-Hall, Inc., Englewood Cliffs, N.J., 1971.

Hartman, Carl G.: *Science and the Safe Period*, The Williams & Wilkins Company, Baltimore, 1962.

——: *Time of Ovulation in Women*, The Williams & Wilkins Company, Baltimore, 1936.

Haskins, Arthur L.: "Oviduct Sterilization with Tantalum Clips," *American Journal of Obstetrics and Gynecology*, vol. 114, no. 3, pp. 370–377, October, 1972.

Hatch, Merton C.: "Maternal Deaths Associated with Induction of Labor," *New York Journal of Medicine*, vol. 69, no. 4, pp. 599–602, Feb. 15, 1969.

Havighurst, Robert J.: *Human Development and Education*, Longmans, Green & Company, Ltd., London, 1953.

Helpern, Milton: "The Problem of Criminal Abortion," *Quarterly Review of Surgery, Obstetrics and Gynecology*, vol. 16, no. 4, pp. 231–234, October-December, 1959.

Herman, H. A.: "Frozen Semen," in Enos J. Perry (ed.), *The Artificial Insemination of Farm Animals*, 3d ed., Rutgers University Press, New Brunswick, N.J., 1960, chap. 18.

Hernton, Calvin C.: *Sex and Racism in America*, Doubleday & Company, Inc., Garden City, N.Y., 1965.

Hertig, Arthur Y.: "Pathological Aspects," in Claude A. Villee (ed.), *The Placenta and Fetal Membranes*, The Williams & Wilkins Company, Baltimore, 1960, chap. 8.

Herzig, Norman: "Air Embolism Caused by Oral-genital Acts," *Medical Aspects of Human Sexuality*, vol. 6, no. 4, pp. 84–85, April, 1972.

Heyns, O. S.: "Theory and Application of Abdominal Decompression," in R. J. Kellar (ed.), *Modern Trends in Obstetrics*, Butterworth, Inc., Washington, 1963, chap. 9.

Hibbard, Lester T.: "Abortion, Gas Embolus, and Sudden Death," *California Medicine*, vol. 110, p. 305, 1969; abstracted in *Obstetrical and Gynecological Survey*, vol. 24, no. 11, pp. 1368–1370, November, 1969.

Higgins, Donald H., Director, Public Relations, Association for Voluntary Sterilization, Inc., New York, personal communication, 1972.

Hobbs, Lisa: *Love and Liberation*, McGraw-Hill Book Company, New York, 1970.

Hoffman, Jacob: *Female Endocrinology*, W. B. Saunders Company, Philadelphia, 1944.

Hohman, Leslie B., and Bertram Schaffner: "The Sex Lives of Unmarried Women," *American Journal of Sociology*, vol. 52, no. 6, pp. 501–507, May, 1947.

Holder, Angela Roddy: "Prenatal Injuries," *Journal of the American Medical Association*, vol. 214, no. 11, pp. 2105–2106, Dec. 14, 1970.

Hollender, Marc H.: "Women's Wish to Be Held: Sexual and Nonsexual Aspects," *Medical Aspects of Human Sexuality*, vol. 5, no. 10, pp. 12–26, October, 1971.

Holtzman, Lester: "Medical-legal Considerations of Abortion in New York State under the New Abortion Law," in George Schaefer (ed.), "Legal Abortions in

New York State: Medical, Legal, Nursing, Social Aspects (July 1-December 31, 1970)," *Clinical Obstetrics and Gynecology*, vol. 14, no. 1, pp. 1–324, March, 1971, pp. 36–47.

Holzman, Gerald B. (ed.): "Implementation of Legal Abortion: A National Problem," *Clinical Obstetrics and Gynecology*, vol. 14, no. 4, pp. 1109–1338, December, 1971.

Hon, Edward H.: *A Manual of Pregnancy Testing*, J. & A. Churchill, Ltd., London, 1961.

Horton, E. W.: *Prostaglandins*, Springer-Verlag, OHG, Berlin, Heidelberg, 1972.

Howell, Doris A., and Charles E. Flowers: "Recent Advances in the Treatment of Hemolytic Disease of the Newborn," in Edward A. Banner (ed.), "Rh Factor," *Clinical Obstetrics and Gynecology*, vol. 7, no. 4, pp. 901–1055, December, 1964, pp. 945–956.

Huffman, John W. (ed.): "Gynecology of Adolescence," *Clinical Obstetrics and Gynecology*, vol. 14, no. 4, pp. 961–1108, December, 1971.

Hutchinson, Donald L.: "Amniotic Fluid," in Stewart L. Marcus and Cyril C. Marcus (eds.), *Advances in Obstetrics and Gynecology*, vol. 1, The Williams & Wilkins Company, Baltimore, 1967, chap. 8.

Hyams, Leonard L.: "Coital Induction of Labor," *Medical Aspects of Human Sexuality*, vol. 6, no. 4, p. 90, April, 1972.

Hyatt, Herman W., Sr.: "Relationship of Maternal Mumps to Congenital Defects and Fetal Deaths, and to Maternal Morbidity and Mortality," *American Practitioner*, vol. 12, no. 5, pp. 359–363, May, 1961.

Hytten, F. E., and A. M. Thomson: "Maternal Physiological Adjustments," in Committee on Maternal Nutrition, Food and Nutrition Board, National Research Council, *Maternal Nutrition and the Course of Pregnancy*, National Academy of Sciences, Washington, 1970, pp. 41–73.

Illsley, Raymond: "The Sociological Study of Reproduction and Its Outcome," in Stephen A. Richardson and Alan F. Guttmacher (eds), *Childbearing: Its Social and Psychological Aspects*, The Williams & Wilkins Company, Baltimore, 1967, pp. 75–141.

Ingraham, Hollis S., and Robert J. Longood: "Abortion in New York State since July, 1970," in George Schaefer (ed.), "Legal Abortions in New York State: Medical, Legal, Nursing, Social Aspects (July 1-December 31, 1970)," *Clinical Obstetrics and Gyne-cology*, vol. 14, no. 1, pp. 1–324, March, 1971, pp. 5–24.

Inman, W. H. W., and M. P. Vessey: "Investigation of Deaths from Pulmonary, Coronary, and Cerebral Thrombosis and Embolism in Women of Childbearing Age," *British Medical Journal*, vol. 2, no. 5599, pp. 193–199, Apr. 27, 1968.

———, ———, Barbro Westerholm, and A. Engelund: "Thromboembolic Disease and the Steroidal Content of Oral Contraceptives: A Report to the Committee on the Safety of Drugs," *British Medical Journal*, vol. 2, no. 5703, pp. 203–209, Apr. 25, 1970.

Israel, S. Leon: *Diagnosis and Treatment of Menstrual Disorders and Sterility*, 5th ed., Harper & Row, Publishers, Incorporated, New York, 1967.

Ivey, Melville E., and Judith M. Bardwick: "Patterns of Affective Fluctuation in the Menstrual Cycle," *Psychosomatic Medicine*, vol. 30, no. 3, pp. 336–345, May-June, 1968.

Jacobson, Benjamin D., and Merle B. Davis: "A Simple and Rapid Immunologic Test for Pregnancy, Based on Agglutination-Inhibition," *Obstetrics and Gynecology*, vol. 25, no. 2, pp. 192–196, February, 1965.

Janowsky, David S., and Roderic Gorney: "The Curse, I: Vicissitudes & Variations in Female Fertility Cycle," *Psychosomatics*, vol. 7, pp. 242–246, July-August, 1966.

Jensen, Oliver: *The Revolt of American Women*, rev. ed., Harcourt Brace Jovanovich, Inc., New York, 1971.

Johnson, Virginia, and William H. Masters: "Sexual Incompatibility: Diagnosis and Treatment," in Charles W. Lloyd (ed.), *Human Reproduction and Sexual Behavior*, Lea & Febiger, Philadelphia, 1964, chap. 26.

Johnson, Wayne L., H. Fred Stegall, John N. Lein, and Robert F. Rushmer: "Detection of Fetal Life in Early Pregnancy with an Ultrasonic Doppler Flowmeter," *Obstetrics and Gynecology*, vol. 26, no. 3, pp. 305–307, September, 1965.

Jolly, Hugh: *Sexual Precocity*, Charles C Thomas, Publisher, Springfield, Ill., 1955.

Jones, Howard W., Jr., and William Wallace Scott: *Hermaphroditism, Genital Anomalies and Related Endocrine Disorders*, 2d ed., The Williams & Wilkins Company, Baltimore, 1971.

Josselyn, Irene M.: "Sexual Identity Crises in the

Life Cycle," in Georgene H. Seward and Robert C. Williamson (eds.), *Sex Roles in Changing Society*, Random House, Inc., New York, 1970.

Journal of the American Medical Association, vol. 212, no. 7, p. 1137, May 18, 1970; vol. 212, no. 12, p. 2029, June 22, 1970; vol. 214, no. 9, p. 1636, Nov. 30, 1970; vol. 217, no. 6, pp. 757–759, Aug. 9, 1971; vol. 220, no. 11, pp. 1419–1420, June 12, 1971.

Jungck, E. C.: "Once-a-Month Injection, Pill, or Pellet?" in David Charles (ed.), *Progress in Conception Control 1967*, J. B. Lippincott Company, Philadelphia, 1967, chap. 8.

Kaats, Gilbert R., and Keith E. Davis: "The Dynamics of Sexual Behavior of College Students," *Journal of Marriage and the Family*, vol. 32, no. 3, pp. 390–399, August, 1970.

Kahn, James B., Judith P. Bourne, and Carl W. Tyler, Jr.: "The Impact of Recent Changes in Therapeutic Abortion Laws," in Gerald B. Holzman (ed.), "Implementation of Legal Abortion: A National Problem," *Clinical Obstetrics and Gynecology*, vol. 14, no. 4, pp. 1109–1338, December, 1971, pp. 1130–1148.

Kane, Francis J., Morris A. Lipton, and John A. Ewing: "Hormonal Influences in Female Sexual Response," *Archives of General Psychiatry*, vol. 20, no. 2, pp. 202–209, 1969.

Kanin, Eugene J.: "Premarital Sex Adjustments, Social Class, and Associated Behaviors," *Marriage and Family Living*, vol. 22, no. 3, pp. 258–262, August, 1960.

——: "Sex Aggression by College Men," *Medical Aspects of Human Sexuality*, vol. 4, no. 9, pp. 25–40, September, 1970.

—— and David H. Howard: "Postmarital Consequences of Premarital Sex Adjustments," *American Sociological Review*, vol. 23, no. 5, pp. 556–562, October, 1958.

Karim, S. M. M. (ed.): *The Prostaglandins: Progress in Research*, Wiley-Interscience, John Wiley & Sons, Inc., New York, 1972a.

Karim, Sultan M. M.: "Prostaglandins and Human Reproduction: Physiological Roles and Clinical Uses of Prostaglandins in Relation to Human Reproduction," in S. M. M. Karim (ed.), *The Prostaglandins: Progress in Research*, Wiley-Interscience, John Wiley & Sons, Inc., New York, 1972b, pp. 71–164.

Karow, William G., William C. Gentry, and Sheldon Payne: "Artificial Insemination: Indications and Ra-

tionale," *Lying-in (Chicago)*, vol. 2, pp. 34–38, January, 1969, abstracted in J. P. Greenhill (ed.), *The Year Book of Obstetrics and Gynecology 1969*, Year Book Medical Publishers, Inc., Chicago, 1969, pp. 410–411.

Katz, Joseph: "Four Years of Growth, Conflict, and Compliance," in Joseph Katz, Harold A. Korn, Ving Ellis, Peter Madison, Susan Singer, Marjorie M. Lozoff, Max M. Levin, and Nevitt Sanford, *No Time for Youth*, Jossey-Bass, Inc., Publishers, San Francisco, 1968a, pp. 3–73.

——, Harold A. Korn, Ving Ellis, Peter Madison, Susan Singer, Marjorie M. Lozoff, Max M. Levin, and Nevitt Sanford: *No Time for Youth*, Jossey-Bass, Inc., Publishers, San Francisco, 1968b.

Kay, Clifford R., Alwyn Smith, and Bernard Richards: "Smoking Habits of Oral Contraceptive Users," *The Lancet*, vol. 2, no. 7632, pp. 1228–1229, 1969.

Kaye, Bernard M., and Burnell V. Reaney: "Viral Diseases in Pregnancy: Prevention and Fetal Effects," *Obstetrics and Gynecology*, vol. 19, no. 5, pp. 618–621, May, 1962.

Keefer, Chester S. (ed.): *Human Ovulation*, Little, Brown and Company, Boston, 1965.

Kegel, Arnold H.: "Sexual Functions of the Pubococcygeus Muscle," *The Western Journal of Surgery, Obstetrics and Gynecology*, vol. 60, no. 10, pp. 521–524, October, 1952.

Kellar, R. J. (ed.): *Modern Trends in Obstetrics*, Butterworth, Inc., Washington, 1963.

Kennedy, Eugene C.: *The New Sexuality: Myths, Fables, and Hang-ups*, Doubleday & Company, Inc., Garden City, N.Y., 1972.

Kephart, William M.: *The Family, Society, and the Individual*, 3d ed., Houghton Mifflin Company, Boston, 1972.

Kessel, Neil, and Alec Coppen: "The Prevalence of Common Menstrual Symptoms," *The Lancet*, vol. 2, no. 7298, pp. 61–64, July 13, 1963.

Khudr, Gabriel, and Kurt Benirschke: "Fluorescence of the Y Chromosome: A Rapid Test to Determine Fetal Sex," *American Journal of Obstetrics and Gynecology*, vol. 110, no. 8, pp. 1091–1095, Aug. 15, 1971.

Kilgo, Reese Danley: "Can Group Marriage Work?" *Sexual Behavior*, vol. 2, no. 3, pp. 8–14, March, 1972.

King, Robert C.: *Genetics*, Oxford University Press, New York, 1962.

Kinsey, Alfred C., Wardell B. Pomeroy, and Clyde E. Martin: *Sexual Behavior in the Human Male*, W. B. Saunders Company, Philadelphia, 1948.

———, ———, ———, and Paul H. Gebhard: *Sexual Behavior in the Human Female*, W. B. Saunders Company, Philadelphia, 1953.

Kirkendall, Lester A.: *Premarital Intercourse and Interpersonal Relationships*, Julian Press, Inc., New York, 1961.

Kirshen, Edward J., Frederick Naftolin, and Kenneth J. Ryan: "Intravenous Prostaglandin $F_2\alpha$ for Therapeutic Abortion," *American Journal of Obstetrics and Gynecology*, vol. 113, no. 3, pp. 340–344, June 1, 1972.

Kistner, Robert W.: *Gynecology Principles and Practice*, Year Book Medical Publishers, Inc., Chicago, 1964.

———: "Induction of Ovulation with Clomiphene Citrate (Clomid)," *Obstetrical and Gynecological Survey*, vol. 20, no. 6, pp. 873–900, December, 1965.

———: "Medical Indications for Contraception: Changing Viewpoints," *Obstetrics and Gynecology*, vol. 25, no. 2, pp. 285–288, February, 1965.

———: *The Pill: Facts and Fallacies about Today's Oral Contraceptives*, Delacorte Press, Dell Publishing Co., Inc., New York, 1969a.

———: "The Use of Clomiphene Citrate, Human Gonadotropin, and Human Menopausal Gonadotropin for Induction of Ovulation in the Human Female," in *Advances in Gynecological Endocrinology, Proceedings of the Symposium*, Charleston, South Carolina, 1965, Excerpta Medica Foundation, New York, 1966, pp. 12–23.

———: *The Use of Progestins in Obstetrics and Gynecology*, Year Book Medical Publishers, Inc., Chicago, 1969b.

Klemer, Richard H. (ed.): *Counseling in Marital and Sexual Problems*, The Williams & Wilkins Company, Baltimore, 1965.

———: *Marriage and Family Relationships*, Harper & Row, Publishers, Incorporated, New York, 1970.

———: "What Has Happened to Marriages?" in Richard H. Klemer (ed.), *Counseling in Marital and Sexual Problems*, The Williams & Wilkins Company, Baltimore, 1965, chap. 2.

Knight, James A.: "Sexual Implications of Money," *Medical Aspects of Human Sexuality*, vol. 3, no. 6, pp. 29–35, June, 1969.

———: "Unusual Case: False Pregnancy in a Male," *Medical Aspects of Human Sexuality*, vol. 5, no. 3, pp. 58–71, March, 1971.

Knopf, Olga: *The Art of Being a Woman*, Doubleday & Company, Inc., Garden City, N.Y., 1932.

Koedt, Anne: "The Myth of Vaginal Orgasm," in Leslie B. Tanner (ed.), *Voices from Women's Liberation*, New American Library, Inc., New York, 1971, pp. 158–166.

Kokken, Sha: *A Happier Sex Life*, translated by Robert Y. Tatsuoka, Ikeda Publishing Company, Ltd., Tokyo, 1964; U.S. edition by Sherbourne Press, Los Angeles, 1967.

Kretchmer, Norman, and Dwain H. Walcher (eds.): *Environmental Influences on Genetic Expression: Biological and Behavioral Aspects of Sexual Differentiation*, (Fogarty International Center Proceedings, no. 2) National Institutes of Health, Bethesda, Md., 1969.

Kroger, W. S.: "Psychophysiologic Aspects of Oral Contraception," in Dean L. Moyer (ed.), *Progress in Conception Control 1968*, J. B. Lippincott Company, Philadelphia, 1968, chap. 8.

Kroger, William S., and S. Charles Freed: *Psychosomatic Gynecology*, The Free Press of Glencoe, Inc., Chicago, 1956.

Kuchera, Lucile Kirtland: "Postcoital Contraception with Diethylstilbestrol," *Journal of the American Medical Association*, vol. 218, no. 4, pp. 562–563, Oct. 25, 1971.

———: "Stilbestrol as a 'Morning-after' Pill," *Medical Aspects of Human Sexuality*, vol. 6, no. 10, pp. 169–177, October, 1972.

Lachelin, Gillian C. L., H. A. Brant, G. I. M. Swyer, V. Little, and E. O. R. Reynolds: "Sextuplet Pregnancy," *British Medical Journal*, vol. 1, no. 5803, pp. 787–790, Mar. 25, 1972.

Lal, Gobind Behari: "Complementarity of the Sexes," in Harry Benjamin, *The Transsexual Phenomenon*, Julian Press, Inc., New York, 1966, pp. 167–171.

Lamb, Wanda M., George A. Ulett, William H. Masters, and Donald W. Robinson: "Premenstrual Tension: EEG, Hormonal and Psychiatric Evaluation," *American Journal of Psychiatry*, vol. 109, pp. 840–848, May, 1953.

Landis, Carney et al.: *Sex in Development*, Paul B. Hoeber, Inc., New York, 1940.

Landis, Judson T., and Mary G. Landis: *Building a Successful Marriage*, 4th ed., Prentice-Hall, Inc., Englewood Cliffs, N.J., 1963.

Lav, H. Lorrin: "A New Simple Immunassay for Human Chorionic Gonadotropin," *American Journal of Obstetrics and Gynecology*, vol. 109, no. 1, pp. 29–31, Jan. 1, 1971.

Leach, William H.: *The Cokesbury Marriage Manual*, rev. ed., Abingdon Press, Nashville, Tenn., 1961.

Lednicer, Daniel (ed.): *Contraception: The Chemical Control of Fertility*, Marcel Dekker, Inc., New York, 1969.

Lehfeldt, Hans: "Psychology of Contraceptive Failure," *Medical Aspects of Human Sexuality*, vol. 5, no. 5, pp. 68–77, May, 1971.

——, Ernest W. Kulka, and H. George Liebmann: "Comparative Study of Intrauterine Contraceptive Devices," *Obstetrics and Gynecology*, vol. 26, no. 5, pp. 679–688, November, 1965.

Levin, Max, Albert Ellis, Judith Bardwick, Richard C. Robertiello, Leah C. Schaefer, and Mary Boulton: "Is There Any Difference between 'Vaginal' and 'Clitoral' Orgasm?" *Sexual Behavior*, vol. 2, no. 3, pp. 41–45, March, 1972.

Leyburn, James G.: *Frontier Folkways*, Yale University Press, New Haven, Conn., 1935.

Lidz, Ruth W.: "Emotional Factors in the Success of Contraception," *Fertility & Sterility*, vol. 20, no. 5, pp. 761–771, September-October, 1969.

Life, vol. 58, no. 17, p. 68, Apr. 30, 1965.

Liley, A. W.: "Amniocentesis and Amniography in Hemolytic Disease," in J. P. Greenhill (ed.), *The 1964–65 Year Book of Obstetrics and Gynecology*, Year Book Medical Publishers, Inc., Chicago, 1964, pp. 256–265.

Linton, Eugene B.: "Honeymoon Cystitis," *Medical Aspects of Human Sexuality*, vol. 5, no. 8, pp. 111–116, August, 1971.

Lippes, Jack: "A Study of Intra-uterine Contraception: Development of a Plastic Loop," in Christopher Tietze and Sarah Lewit (eds.), *Intra-uterine Contraceptive Devices*, International Congress Series no. 54, Excerpta Medica Foundation, New York, 1962, pp. 69–75.

Liu, William T. (ed.): *Family and Fertility*, University of Notre Dame Press, Notre Dame, Ind., 1967.

Lloyd, Charles W.: "Control of Fertility," in Charles W. Lloyd (ed.), *Human Reproduction and Sexual Behavior*, Lea & Febiger, Philadelphia, 1964a, chap. 22.

——: "Gonadal Failure in the Adult Male," in Charles W. Lloyd (ed.), *Human Reproduction and Sexual Behavior*, Lea & Febiger, Philadelphia, 1964b, chap. 20.

—— (ed.): *Human Reproduction and Sexual Behavior*, Lea & Febiger, Philadelphia, 1964c.

——: "Infertility," in Charles W. Lloyd (ed.), *Human Reproduction and Sexual Behavior*, Lea & Febiger, Philadelphia, 1964d, chap. 21.

——: "Problems Associated with the Menstrual Cycle," in Charles W. Lloyd (ed.), *Human Reproduction and Sexual Behavior*, Lea & Febiger, Philadelphia, 1964e, chap. 15.

—— and James H. Leathem: "Fertilization, Implantation and Pregnancy," in Charles W. Lloyd (ed.), *Human Reproduction and Sexual Behavior*, Lea & Febiger, Philadelphia, 1964, chap. 7.

—— and ——: "Reproductive Cycles, Oogenesis, Ovulation and Conception," in Charles W. Lloyd (ed.), *Human Reproduction and Sexual Behavior*, Lea & Febiger, Philadelphia, 1964, chap. 6.

Locke, Harvey J.: *Predicting Adjustment in Marriage*, Holt, Rinehart and Winston, Inc., New York, 1951.

Lopata, Helena Znaniecki: *Occupation: Housewife*, Oxford University Press, New York, 1971.

Loraine, John A., and E. Trevor Bell: *Fertility and Contraception in the Human Female*, E. & S. Livingstone, Ltd., Edinburgh and London, 1968.

Lotvin, Boris Rubio, and Edel Berman: "Once-a-Month Oral Contraceptive; Quinestrol and Quingestanol," *Obstetrics and Gynecology*, vol. 35, no. 6, pp. 933–936, June, 1970.

Loung, K. C., A. E. R. Buckle, and Mary M. Anderson: "Results in 1,000 Cases of Therapeutic Abortion Managed by Vacuum Aspiration," *British Medical Journal*, vol. 4, no. 5785, pp. 477–479, Nov. 20, 1971.

Lowrie, Samuel H.: "Early Marriage: Premarital Pregnancy and Associated Factors," *Journal of Marriage and the Family*, vol. 27, no. 1, pp. 48–56, February, 1965.

Lowsley, Oswald Swinney, Frank Hinman, Donald R. Smith, and Robert Gutierrez: *The Sexual Glands of the Male*, Oxford University Press, New York, 1942.

Luce, Gay Gaer: *Biological Rhythms in Psychiatry and Medicine*, National Institute of Mental Health, Washington, 1970.

Lucey, Jerold F.: "Changing Concepts Regarding Exchange Transfusions and Neonatal Jaundice," in John T. Queenan (ed.), "The Rh Problem," *Clinical Obstetrics and Gynecology*, vol. 14, no. 2, pp. 491–646, June, 1971, pp. 586–596.

Lurie, Harry L. (ed.): *Encyclopedia of Social Work*, 15th issue, National Association of Social Workers, New York, 1965.

Maas, J. M.: "The Use of Sequential Therapy in Contraception," in Robert Greenblatt (ed.), *Ovulation*, J. B. Lippincott Company, Philadelphia, 1966, pp. 206–215.

McCall, Milton L., and Robert J. Trace: "Effects of Pregnancy on Women in Industry," *Pennsylvania Medical Journal*, vol. 63, no. 12, pp. 1773–1778, December, 1960.

McCammon, Robert E.: "The Birnberg Bow as an Intrauterine Contraceptive Device," *Obstetrics and Gynecology*, vol. 29, no. 1, pp. 67–70, January, 1967.

McCance, C., and D. J. Hall: "Sexual Behavior and Contraceptive Practice of Unmarried Female Undergraduates at Aberdeen University," *British Medical Journal*, vol. 2, no. 5815, pp. 694–700, June 17, 1972.

McDermott, Sandra: *Female Sexuality: Its Nature and Conflicts*, Simon & Schuster, Inc., New York, 1970.

McDonald, Robert L.: "The Role of Emotional Factors in Obstetric Complications: A Review," *Psychosomatic Medicine*, vol. 30, no. 2, pp. 222–237, March-April, 1968.

——— and Cecil F. Lanford: "Effects of Smoking on Selected Clinical Obstetric Factors," *Obstetrics and Gynecology*, vol. 26, no. 4, pp. 470–475, October, 1965.

MacDonald, Ronald R.: "Clinical Pharmacology of Progestogens," in Ronald R. MacDonald (ed.), *Scientific Basis of Obstetrics and Gynaecology*, J. and A. Churchill, London, 1971a.

———: *Scientific Basis of Obstetrics and Gynaecology*, J. and A. Churchill, London, 1971b.

Mace, David R.: "Acceptable Sexual Variety in Marriage," *Medical Aspects of Human Sexuality*, vol. 6, no. 6, pp. 153–157, June, 1972.

———: *Sexual Difficulties in Marriage*, Fortress Press, Philadelphia, 1972.

McGuire, Terence F., and Richard M. Steinhilber: "Frigidity, the Primary Female Sexual Dysfunction," *Medical Aspects of Human Sexuality*, vol. 4, no. 10, pp. 108–123, October, 1970.

——— and ———: "Sexual Frigidity," *Mayo Clinic Proceedings*, vol. 39, no. 6, pp. 416–426, June, 1964.

Mackenzie, John M., Arnold Roufa, and Harold M. M. Tovell: "Midtrimester Abortion: Clinical Experience with Amniocentesis and Hypertonic Installation in 400 Patients," in George Schaefer (ed.), "Legal Abortions in New York State: Medical, Legal, Nursing, Social Aspects (July 1-December 31, 1970), *Clinical Obstetrics and Gynecology*, vol. 14, no. 1, pp. 1–324, March, 1971, pp. 107–123.

McLarey, Don C., and Stewart A. Fish: "Fetal Erythrocytes in the Maternal Circulation," *American Journal of Obstetrics and Gynecology*, vol. 95, no. 6, pp. 824–830, July 15, 1966.

Maeck, John Van S., and Charles A. Phillips: "Rubella Vaccine Program: Its Implications in Obstetric Practice," *American Journal of Obstetrics and Gynecology*, vol. 112, no. 4, pp. 513–518, Feb. 15, 1972.

Mahan, Charles S., and Carlfred B. Broderick: *Human Reproduction*, in Carlfred B. Broderick and Jessie Bernard (eds.), *The Individual, Sex and Society*, The Johns Hopkins Press, Baltimore, 1969.

Malmström, Tage, and Inge Jansson: "Use of the Vacuum Extractor," in George J. L. Wulff (ed.), "Forceps Delivery," *Clinical Obstetrics and Gynecology*, vol. 8, no. 4, pp. 811–918, December, 1965, pp. 893–913.

Manabe, Yukio: "Interruption of Pregnancy at Midterm by Intrauterine Application of Solutions," *Obstetrical and Gynecological Survey*, vol. 27, no. 10, pp. 701–710, October, 1972.

Mandell, Arnold J., and Mary P. Mandell: "Suicide and the Menstrual Cycle," *Journal of the American Medical Association*, vol. 200, no. 9, pp. 792–793, May 29, 1967.

Mann, Edward C., and Gary Cunningham: "Coital Cautions in Pregnancy," *Medical Aspects of Human Sexuality*, vol. 6, no. 10, pp. 14–25, October, 1972.

Maqueo-Topete, Manuel, Edel Berman, Javier Soberon, and Juan Jose Calderon: "Pill-a-Month Contraceptive," *Fertility and Sterility*, vol. 20, no. 6, pp. 884–891, November-December, 1969.

Marcus, Stewart L., and Cyril C. Marcus (eds.): *Advances in Obstetrics and Gynecology*, vol. 1, The Williams & Wilkins Company, Baltimore, 1967.

Margolis, Alan J.: "Preparation of the Obstetrical Patient," in Sol M. Shnider (ed.), *Obstetrical Anesthesia*, The Williams & Wilkins Company, Baltimore, 1970, pp. 51–56.

Margulies, Lazar C.: "Intrauterine Contraception: A New Approach," *Obstetrics and Gynecology*, vol. 24, no. 4, pp. 515–520, October, 1964.

————: "Permanent Reversible Contraception with an Intra-uterine Plastic Spiral (Permaspiral)," in Christopher Tietze and Sarah Lewit (eds.), *Intra-uterine Contraceptive Devices*, International Congress Series no. 54, Excerpta Medica Foundation, New York, 1962, pp. 61–68.

Markun, Leo: *Mrs. Grundy*, Appleton Century Crofts, Inc., New York, 1930.

Markush, Robert E., and Daniel G. Seigel: "Oral Contraceptives and Mortality Trends from Thromboembolism in the United States," *American Journal of Public Health*, vol. 59, no. 3, pp. 418–434, March, 1969.

Marmor, Judd: "Sex for Nonsexual Reasons," *Medical Aspects of Human Sexuality*, vol. 3, no. 6, pp. 8–21, June, 1969.

Martin, Chester B., Jr., and Eugene M. Long, Jr.: "Sex during the Menstrual Period," *Medical Aspects of Human Sexuality*, vol. 3, no. 6, pp. 37–49, June, 1969.

The Mass on the Day of Marriage, according to the text in the *Collectio Rituum 1964* by the National Catholic Welfare Conference, revised in accordance with the directive of May 4, 1967, Sacred Congregation of Rites, Leaflet Missal Company, St. Paul, Minn., 1968.

Masters, William H.: "The Sexual Response Cycle of the Human Female: I. Gross Anatomic Considerations," *The Western Journal of Surgery, Obstetrics and Gynecology*, vol. 68, no. 1, pp. 57–72, January-February, 1960.

————: "The Sexual Response Cycle in the Human Female: Vaginal Lubrication," *Annals of the New York Academy of Sciences*, vol. 83, art. 2, pp. 301–317, Nov. 18, 1959.

———— and Virginia E. Johnson: "Anatomy and Physiology," in Charles W. Lloyd (ed.), *Human Reproduction and Sexual Behavior*, Lea & Febiger, Philadelphia, 1964, part II, chap. 25.

———— and ————: "The Human Female: Anatomy and Sexual Response," *Minnesota Medicine*, vol. 43, pp. 31–36, January-December, 1960.

———— and ————: *Human Sexual Inadequacy*, Little, Brown and Company, Boston, 1970.

———— and ————: *Human Sexual Response*, Little, Brown and Company, Boston, 1966.

———— and ————: "The Sexual Response Cycles of the Human Male and Female: Comparative Anatomy and Physiology," in Frank A. Beach (ed.), *Sexual Behavior*, John Wiley & Sons, Inc., New York, 1965.

Mastroianni, Luigi, Jr. (ed.): "Ovulation," *Clinical Obstetrics and Gynecology*, vol. 10, no. 2, pp. 343–430, June, 1967.

Mayes, Bruce: "The Effect of Rubella on the Fetus," in R. J. Kellar (ed.), *Modern Trends in Obstetrics*, Butterworth, Inc., Washington, 1963, chap. 11.

Mead, Margaret: "Marriage In Two Steps," in Herbert A. Otto (ed.), *The Family in Search of a Future*, Appleton Century Crofts, New York, 1970, chap. 7. Reprinted from *Redbook Magazine*, July, 1966.

Mears, Eleanor: *International Journal of Fertility*, vol. 13, pp. 340–345, October-December, 1968; abstracted in J. P. Greenhill (ed.), *The Year Book of Obstetrics and Gynecology 1969*, Year Book Medical Publishers, Inc., Chicago, 1969, pp. 404–405.

————, M. P. Vessey, Lidija Andolšek, and Antonija Oven: "Preliminary Evaluation of Four Oral Contraceptives Containing only Progestogens," *British Medical Journal*, vol. 2, no. 5659, pp. 730–734, June 21, 1969.

Medical Research Council: "Risk of Thromboembolic Disease in Women Taking Oral Contraceptives," a preliminary communication by a subcommittee, *British Medical Journal*, vol. 2, no. 5548, pp. 355–359, May 6, 1967.

Melody, George F.: "Behavioral Implications of Premenstrual Tension," *Obstetrics and Gynecology*, vol. 17, no. 4, pp. 439–441, April, 1961.

Merit Publishing Company: *National Survey of High School High Achievers*, Northfield, Ill., 1970, 1971.

Meyer, Henry M., Jr., and Paul D. Parkman: "Rubella Vaccination: A Review of Practical Experience," *Journal of the American Medical Association*, vol. 215, no. 4, pp. 613–619, Jan. 25, 1971.

Meyer, Robert: "The Male Pill?" in David Charles (ed.), *Progress in Conception Control 1967*, J. B. Lippincott Company, Philadelphia, 1967, chap. 10.

Millett, Kate: *Sexual Politics*, Doubleday & Company, Inc., Garden City, N.Y., 1970.

Mills, C. Wright: "Methodological Considerations of the Sociology of Knowledge," *American Journal of Sociology*, vol. 46, no. 3, pp. 316–330, November, 1940.

Mishell, Daniel R., Mary Lumkin, and Sergio Stone: "Inhibition of Ovulation with Cyclic Use of Progestogen-impregnated Intravaginal Devices," *American Journal of Obstetrics and Gynecology*, vol. 113, no. 7, pp. 927–932, Aug. 1, 1972.

Mitsuya, Hideo, Jun Asai, Keiji Suyama, Takao Ushida, and Kenzo Hosoe: "Application of X-ray Cinematography in Urology: I. Mechanism of Ejaculation," *Journal of Urology*, vol. 83, no. 1, pp. 86–92, January, 1960.

Moghissi, Kamran S.: "Prostaglandins in Reproduction," in Ralph M. Wynn (ed.), *Obstetrics and Gynecology Annual 1972*, Appleton Century Crofts, New York, 1972.

Moloshok, Ralph E.: "Fetal Risk Associated with Maternal Systemic Injections," in Elsie R. Carrington (ed.), "Teratology," *Clinical Obstetrics and Gynecology*, vol. 9, no. 3, pp. 593–706, September, 1966, pp. 608–622.

Monahan, Thomas P.: "When Married Couples Part: Statistical Trends and Relationships in Divorce," *American Sociological Review*, vol. 27, no. 5, pp. 625–633, October, 1962.

Money, John: "Factors in the Genesis of Homosexuality," in George Winokur (ed.), *Determinants of Human Sexual Behavior*, Charles C Thomas, Publisher, Springfield, Ill., 1963, chap. 2.

—— (ed.): *Sex Research: New Developments*, Holt, Rinehart and Winston, Inc., New York, 1965.

——: "Sexually Dimorphic Behavior, Normal and Abnormal," in Norman Kretchmer and Dwain H. Walcher (eds.), *Environmental Influences on Genetic Expression: Biological and Behavioral Aspects of Sexual Differentiation* (Fogarty International Center Proceedings, no. 2), National Institutes of Health, Bethesda, Md., 1969, pp. 201–212.

—— and Anke A. Ehrhardt: *Man & Woman Boy &*

Girl, The Johns Hopkins University Press, Baltimore, 1972.

Montagu, M. F. Ashley: *Adolescent Sterility*, Charles C Thomas, Publisher, Springfield, Ill., 1946.

Morris, John McL., and Gertrude van Wagenen: *Science News*, May 21, 1966.

Morton, J. H., H. Additon, R. G. Addison, L. Hunt, and J. J. Sullivan: "A Clinical Study of Premenstrual Tension," *American Journal of Obstetrics and Gynecology*, vol. 65, no. 6, pp. 1182–1191, June, 1953.

Moyer, Dean L. (ed.): *Progress in Conception Control 1968*, J. B. Lippincott Company, Philadelphia, 1968.

—— and Daniel R. Mishell: "Reactions of Human Endometrium to the Intrauterine Foreign Body," *American Journal of Obstetrics and Gynecology*, vol. 111, no. 1, pp. 66–80, Sept. 1, 1971.

Munro, Alistair: "Human Sexual Behavior," in Ronald R. MacDonald (ed.), *Scientific Basis of Obstetrics and Gynaecology*, J. and A. Churchill, London, 1971.

Murdock, George Peter: *Social Structure*, The Macmillan Company, New York, 1960.

Murphy, John F., and Risteard Mulcahy: "The Effect of Age, Parity, and Cigarette Smoking on Baby Weight," *American Journal of Obstetrics and Gynecology*, vol. 111, no. 1, pp. 22–25, Sept. 1, 1971.

Murray, R. Richard: "Abortion in an Upstate Community Hospital," in George Schaefer (ed.), "Legal Abortions in New York State: Medical, Legal, Nursing, Social Aspects (July 1-December 31, 1970)," *Clinical Obstetrics and Gynecology*, vol. 14, no. 1, pp. 1–324, March, 1971, pp. 141–148.

Nanni, Luis F.: "Thromboembolic Disease and the Pill," *British Medical Journal*, vol. 2, no. 5723, p. 644, Sept. 12, 1970.

Nathanson, Bernard N.: "Drugs for the Production of Abortion: A Review," *Obstetrical and Gynecological Survey*, vol. 25, no. 8, pp. 727–731, August, 1970.

——: "Suction Curettage for Early Abortion: Experience with 645 Cases," in George Schaefer (ed.), "Legal Abortions in New York State: Medical, Legal, Nursing, Social Aspects (July 1-December 31, 1970)," *Clinical Obstetrics and Gynecology*, vol. 14, no. 1, pp. 1–324, March, 1971, pp. 99–106.

—— and George Lawrence: "Should Abortion Be Available on Request?" *Sexual Behavior*, vol. 1, no. 7, pp. 64–71, October, 1971.

Neubardt, Selig: *A Concept of Contraception*, Trident Press, a division of Simon & Schuster, Inc., New York, 1967.

—— and Harold Schulman: *Techniques of Abortion*, Little, Brown and Company, Boston, 1972.

Neumann, Hans H., and Janet M. Baecker: "Treatment of Gonorrhea: Penicillin or Tetracyclines?" *Journal of the American Medical Association*, vol. 219, no. 4, pp. 471–474, Jan. 24, 1972.

A New Catechism, Herder and Herder, Inc., New York, 1967.

New York City Department of Health: *New York City Abortion Report: The First Two Years*, October, 1972.

New York Times Magazine, Nov. 21, 1965, sect. 6, p. 33.

Niswander, Kenneth R.: "Medical Abortion Practices in the United States," in David T. Smith (ed.), *Abortion and the Law*, The Press of Case Western Reserve University, Cleveland, 1967, pp. 37–59.

——, Morton Klein, and Clyde L. Randall: "Therapeutic Abortion: Indications and Techniques," *Obstetrics and Gynecology*, vol. 28, no. 1, pp. 124–129, July, 1966.

Noonan, John T., Jr.: *Contraception*, The Belknap Press, Harvard University Press, Cambridge, Mass., 1966.

—— (ed.): *The Morality of Abortion: Legal and Historical Perspectives*, Harvard University Press, Cambridge, Mass., 1970.

Novak, Edmund R., Georgeanna Seegar Jones, and Howard W. Jones, Jr.: *Novak's Textbook of Gynecology*, 8th ed., The Williams & Wilkins Company, Baltimore, 1970.

Novak, Emil: *Textbook of Gynecology*, The Williams & Wilkins Company, Baltimore, 1944.

Nye, F. Ivan and Lois W. Hoffman (eds.): *The Employed Mother in America*, Rand McNally & Company, Chicago, 1963.

Ob. Gyn. News, vol. 2, no. 19, p. 38, Oct. 15, 1967; vol. 2, no. 16, p. 27, Sept. 1, 1967.

Ochsner, Alton: "Influence of Smoking on Sexuality and Pregnancy," *Medical Aspects of Human Sexuality*, vol. 5, no. 11, pp. 78–92, November, 1971.

Odell, William D., and Dean L. Moyer: *Physiology of Reproduction*, The C. V. Mosby Company, St. Louis, 1971.

O'Donnell, Thomas J.: "A Traditional Catholic's View," in Robert E. Hall (ed.), *Abortion in a Changing World*, Columbia University Press, New York, 1970, pp. 34–38, 51.

Oettinger, Katherine Brownell: "Illegitimacy Problems: A 1962 Priority," in *Proceedings of the Conference on Unwed Mothers*, The Social Hygiene Society of D.C. and Mt. Vernon Place Methodist Church, Washington, 1962, pp. B-1–B-8.

Oliven, John F.: *Sexual Hygiene and Pathology*, 2d ed., J. B. Lippincott Company, Philadelphia, 1965.

O'Neill, William L.: *Divorce in the Progressive Era*, Yale University Press, New Haven, Conn., 1967.

Osofsky, Joy D., Howard J. Osofsky, Renga Rajan, and Michael R. Fox: "Psychologic Effects of Legal Abortion," in George Schaefer (ed.), "Legal Abortions in New York State: Medical, Legal, Nursing, Social Aspects (July 1–December 31, 1970)," *Clinical Obstetrics and Gynecology*, vol. 14, no. 1, pp. 1–324, March, 1971, pp. 215–234.

Ostergard, Donald R.: "The Physiology and Clinical Importance of Amniotic Fluid. A Review," *Obstetrical and Gynecological Survey*, vol. 25, no. 4, pp. 297–319, April, 1970.

Otto, Herbert A. (ed.): *The Family in Search of a Future*, Appleton Century Crofts, New York, 1970.

—— (ed.): *The New Sexuality*, Science and Behavior Books, Inc., Palo Alto, Calif., 1971.

Packard, Vance: *The Sexual Wilderness*, David McKay Company, Inc., New York, 1968.

Page, Ernest W., Claude A. Villee, and Dorothy B. Villee: *Human Reproduction: The Core Content of Obstetrics, Gynecology and Perinatal Medicine*, W. B. Saunders Company, Philadelphia, 1972.

Pakter, Jean, David Harris, and Frieda Nelson: "Surveillance of the Abortion Program in New York City: Preliminary Report," in George Schaefer (ed.), "Legal Abortions in New York State: Medical, Legal, Nursing, Social Aspects (July 1–December 31, 1970)," *Clinical Obstetrics and Gynecology*, vol. 14, no. 1, pp. 1–324, March, 1971, pp. 267–299.

Palti, Z.: "Clomiphene Therapy in Defective Spermatogenesis," *Fertility & Sterility*, vol. 21, no. 12, pp. 838–843, December, 1970.

Pannor, Reuben, Fred Massarik, and Byron Evans: *The Unmarried Father*, Springer Publishing Co., Inc., New York, 1971.

Papp, Z., S. Gardo, G. Herpay, and A. Arvay: "Prenatal Sex Determination by Amniocentesis,"

Obstetrics and Gynecology, vol. 36, no. 3, pp. 429–432, September, 1970.

Paschkis, Karl E., Abraham E. Rakoff, Abraham Cantarow, and Joseph J. Rupp: *Clinical Endocrinology*, 3d ed., Paul B. Hoeber, Inc., New York, 1967.

Pasnau, Robert O.: "Psychiatric Complications of Therapeutic Abortion," *Obstetrics and Gynecology*, vol. 40, no. 2, pp. 252–256, August, 1972.

Patterns of Disease, Parke, Davis and Company, Detroit, September, 1964.

Pavela, Todd H.: "An Exploratory Study of Negro-White Intermarriage in Indiana," *Journal of Marriage and the Family*, vol. 26, no. 2, pp. 209–211, May, 1964.

Peck, N. W., and F. L. Wells: "Further Studies in Psycho-sexuality of College Graduate Men," *Mental Hygiene*, vol. 9, no. 3, pp. 502–520, July, 1925.

———— and ————: "On the Psycho-sexuality of College Graduate Men," *Mental Hygiene*, vol. 7, no. 4, pp. 697–714, October, 1923.

Peel, John, and Malcolm Potts: *A Textbook of Contraceptive Practice*, Cambridge University Press, London, 1969.

Peretti, Peter O.: "Premarital Sexual Behavior between Females and Males of Two Middle-sized Midwestern Cities," *Journal of Sex Research*, vol. 5, no. 3, pp. 218–225, August, 1969.

Perkins, H. F.: "Adoption and Fertility," *Eugenical News*, vol. 21, pp. 95–101, 1936.

Perry, Enos J. (ed.): *The Artificial Insemination of Farm Animals*, 3d rev. ed., Rutgers University Press, New Brunswick, N.J., 1960.

Peterson, K. M.: *Early Sex Information and Its Influence on Later Sex Concepts*, unpublished M.A. thesis, Library of the University of Colorado, 1938. Mentioned in Winston Erhmann: *Premarital Dating Behavior*, Holt, Rinehart and Winston, Inc., New York, 1959.

Peterson, William F.: "Pregnancy Following Oral Contraceptive Therapy," *Obstetrics and Gynecology*, vol. 34, no. 3, pp. 363–367, September, 1969.

————, Kenneth N. Morese, and D. Frank Kaltreider: "Smoking and Prematurity," *Obstetrics and Gynecology*, vol. 26, no. 6, pp. 775–779, December, 1965.

Pillay, A. P., and Albert Ellis: "Sex, Society and the Individual," *The International Journal of Sexology*, Bombay, India, 1953.

Pincus, Gregory: *The Control of Fertility*, Academic Press, Inc., New York, 1965.

Piver, M. Steven, and Robert A. Johnston, Sr.,: "The Safety of Multiple Cesarean Sections," *Obstetrics and Gynecology*, vol. 34, no. 5, pp. 690–693, November, 1969.

Polk, Barbara Bovee, and Robert B. Stein: "Is the Grass Greener on the Other Side?" in Constantina Safilios-Rothschild (ed.), *Toward a Sociology of Women*, Xerox College Publishing, Xerox Education Group, Waltham, Mass., 1972.

Pope Paul VI: "An Apostolic Letter Issued 'Motu Proprio' Determining Norms of Mixed Marriages, March 31, 1970," National Conference of Catholic Bishops, Washington, 1970.

————: *Humanae vitae*, July 29, 1968.

Pope Pius XII: *Moral Questions Affecting Married Life: the Apostolate of the Midwife* (pamphlet), Paulist Press, New York, 1951.

Porterfield, Austin L., and H. Ellison Salley: "Current Folkways of Sexual Behavior," *American Journal of Sociology*, vol. 52, no. 3, pp. 209–216, November, 1946.

Potter, A. L.: "Cesareans Galore," *Rhode Island Medical Journal*, vol. 52, no. 2, pp. 106–116, February, 1967.

Potter, Edith L.: "Defective Babies Who Die before Birth," *Clinical Pediatrics*, vol. 1, no. 2, pp. 73–74, November, 1962.

President's Commission on the Status of Women: *American Women* (report), Washington, 1963.

Preston, S. N.: "The Oral Contraceptive Controversy," *American Journal of Obstetrics and Gynecology*, vol. 111, no. 7, pp. 994–1007, Dec. 1, 1971.

Price, Dorothy, and H. Guy Williams-Ashman: "The Accessory Reproductive Glands of Mammals," in William C. Young (ed.), *Sex and Internal Secretions*, The Williams & Wilkins Company, Baltimore, 1961, chap. 6.

Pritchard, Jack A.,: "Deglutition by Normal and Anencephalic Fetuses," *Obstetrics and Gynecology*, vol. 25, no. 3, pp. 289–297, March, 1965.

Quay, Paul M.: *Contraception and Married Love*

(pamphlet), The Family Life Bureau, National Catholic Welfare Conference, Washington, 1961.

Queenan, John T.: *Modern Management of the Rh Problem*, Paul B. Hoeber, Inc., New York, 1967.

—— (ed.): "The Rh Problem," *Clinical Obstetrics and Gynecology*, vol. 14, no. 2, pp. 491–646, June, 1971.

Raboch, Jan: "Studies in the Sexuality of Women," in Paul H. Gebhard, Jan Raboch, and Hans Giese: *The Sexuality of Women*, translated by Colin Bearne, Stein and Day, Incorporated, New York, 1970, pp. 48–94.

Ramsey, Glenn V., Bert Kruger Smith, and Bernice Milburn Moore: *Women View Their Working World*, The Hogg Foundation for Mental Health, University of Texas, Austin, 1963.

Reeves, Billy D., James E. Garvin, and Thomas W. McElin: "Premenstrual Tension: Symptoms and Weight Changes Related to Potassium Therapy," *American Journal of Obstetrics and Gynecology*, vol. 109, no. 7, pp. 1036–1041, Apr. 1, 1971.

Reevy, William Robert: *Marital Prediction Scores of College Women Relative to Behavior and Attitudes*, unpublished Ph.D. dissertation, Pennsylvania State University Library, 1954. Mentioned in Winston Erhmann: *Premarital Dating Behavior*, Holt, Rinehart and Winston, Inc., New York, 1959.

Reiss, Ira L.: *The Family System in America*, Holt, Rinehart and Winston, Inc., New York, 1971.

——: "How and Why America's Sexual Standards Are Changing," in John H. Gagnon and William Simon (eds.), *The Sexual Scene*, Trans-Action Books, Aldine Publishing Company, Chicago, 1970a, pp. 43–57. Also in Ailon Shiloh (ed.), *Studies in Human Sexual Behavior: The American Scene*, Charles C Thomas, Publisher, Springfield, Ill., 1970b, pp. 200–209.

——: "Premarital Sexual Standards," in Carlfred B. Broderick and Jessie Bernard (eds.), *The Individual, Sex, and Society*, The Johns Hopkins Press, Baltimore, 1969, pp. 109–118.

——: *Premarital Sexual Standards in America*, The Free Press of Glencoe, Inc., New York, 1960.

—— (ed.): *"The Sexual Renaissance in America,"* *Journal of Social Issues*, vol. 22, no. 2, pp. 1–137, April, 1966a.

——: "The Sexual Renaissance: A Summary and Analysis," *Journal of Social Issues*, vol. 22, no. 2, pp. 123–137, April, 1966b.

——: *The Social Context of Premarital Sexual Permissiveness*, Holt, Rinehart and Winston, Inc., New York, 1967.

Resnick, Phillip J.: "Murder of the Newborn: A Psychiatric Review of Neonaticide," *American Journal of Psychiatry*, vol. 126, no. 10, pp. 1414–1420, April, 1970.

Richardson, Stephen A., and Alan F. Guttmacher (eds.): *Childbearing: Its Social and Psychological Aspects*, The Williams & Wilkins Company, Baltimore, 1967.

Riemer, Svend: "Married Students Are Good Students," *Marriage and Family Living*, vol. 9, no. 1, pp. 11–12. February, 1947.

Riley, Gardner M.: *Gynecologic Endocrinology*, Paul B. Hoeber, Inc., New York, 1959.

Roberts, G. Fulton: *Comparative Aspects of Haemolytic Disease of the Newborn*, William Heinemann, Ltd., London, 1957.

Roberts, Ron E.: *The New Communes*, Prentice-Hall, Inc., Englewood Cliffs, N.J., 1971.

Robinson, Ira E., Karl King, and Jack O. Balswick: "The Premarital Sexual Revolution among College Females," *The Family Coordinator*, vol. 21, no. 2, pp. 189–194, April, 1972.

Robinson, S. C.: "Pregnancy Outcome Following Oral Contraceptives," *American Journal of Obstetrics and Gynecology*, vol. 109, no. 3, pp. 354–358, Feb. 1, 1971.

Rock, John: "Calendar Rhythm: General Considerations," in Mary Steichen Calderone (ed.), *Manual of Family Planning and Contraceptive Practice*, 2d ed., The Williams & Wilkins Company, Baltimore, 1970, pp. 376–381.

——, Christopher Tietze, and Helen B. McLaughlin: "Effect of Adoption on Fertility," *Fertility and Sterility*, vol. 16, no. 3, pp. 305–312, May-June, 1965.

Rockwood, Lemo D., and Mary E. N. Ford: *Youth, Marriage, and Parenthood*, John Wiley & Sons, Inc., New York, 1945.

Ross, Robert T.: "Measures of the Sex Behavior of College Males Compared with Kinsey's Results," *Journal of Abnormal & Social Psychology*, vol. 45, pp. 753–755, 1950.

Routtenberg, Lilly S., and Ruth R. Seldin: *The*

Jewish Wedding Book, Schocken Books, New York, 1968.

Rovinsky, Joseph J.: "Abortion in New York City: Preliminary Experience with a Permissive Abortion Statute," *Obstetrics and Gynecology*, vol. 38, no. 3, pp. 333–342, September, 1971.

———: "Clinical Effectiveness of a Contraceptive Cream," *Obstetrics and Gynecology*, vol. 23, no. 1, pp. 125–131, January, 1964.

Roy, Rustum, and Della Roy: *Honest Sex*, New American Library, Inc., New York, 1969.

Rudolph, Andrew H.: "Control of Gonorrhea: Guidelines for Antibiotic Treatment," *Journal of the American Medical Association*, vol. 220, no. 12, pp. 1587–1589, June 19, 1972.

Salber, E. J., M. Feinleib, and B. MacMahon: "The Duration of Postpartum Amenorrhea," *American Journal of Epidemiology*, vol. 82, no. 2, pp. 347–358, November, 1966.

Samenfink, J. Anthony, and Robert L. Milliken: "Marital Status and Academic Success: A Reconsideration," *Marriage and Family Living*, vol. 23, no. 3, pp. 226–227, August, 1961.

Sandberg, Eugene C., and Ralph I. Jacobs: "Psychology of the Misuse and Rejection of Contraception," *Medical Aspects of Human Sexuality*, vol. 6, no. 6, pp. 34–70, June, 1972. Also in *American Journal of Obstetrics and Gynecology*, vol. 110, no. 2, pp. 227–242, May 15, 1971.

Sartwell, Philip E., Alfonse T. Masi, Federico G. Arthes, Gerald R. Greene, and Helen E. Smith: "Thromboembolism and Oral Contraceptives: An Epidemiologic Case-control Study," *American Journal of Epidemiology*, vol. 90, no. 5, pp. 365–380, November, 1969.

Savel, Lewis E., and Edward Roth: "Effects of Smoking in Pregnancy: A Continuing Retrospective Study," *Obstetrics and Gynecology*, vol. 20, no. 3, pp. 313–319, September, 1962.

Saxton, Lloyd: *The Individual, Marriage, and Family*, 2d ed., Wadsworth Publishing Company, Inc., Belmont, Calif., 1972.

Schaefer, George (ed.): "Legal Abortions in New York State: Medical, Legal, Nursing, Social Aspects (July 1–December 31, 1970)," vol. 14, no. 1, pp. 1–324, March, 1971.

Scheinfeld, Amram: *Twins and Supertwins*, J. B. Lippincott Company, Philadelphia, 1967.

Schneider, George T., and William L. Geary: "Vaginitis in Adolescent Girls," in John W. Huffman (ed.), "Gynecology of Adolescence," *Clinical Obstetrics and Gynecology*, vol. 14, no. 4, pp. 961–1108, December, 1971, pp. 1057–1076.

Schroder, Ralph: "Academic Achievement of the Male College Student," *Marriage and Family Living*, vol. 25, no. 4, pp. 420–423, November, 1963.

Schroeter, Arnold L., and James B. Lucas: "Gonorrhea: Diagnosis and Treatment," *Obstetrics and Gynecology*, vol. 39, no. 2, pp. 274–285, February, 1972.

Schumann, Edward A.: *A Textbook of Obstetrics*, W. B. Saunders Company, Philadelphia, 1936.

Schwarz, Richard H.: *Septic Abortion*, J. B. Lippincott Company, Philadelphia, 1968.

Science News, vol. 89, no. 21, p. 392, May 21, 1966.

Scott, James S.: "Developments in Haemolytic Disease of the Foetus and Newborn," in R. J. Kellar (ed.), *Modern Trends in Obstetrics*, Butterworth, Inc., Washington, 1963, chap. 5.

Scott, L. Stuart: "Unilateral Cryptorchidism: Subsequent Effects on Fertility," *Journal of Reproduction and Fertility*, vol. 2, pp. 54–60, February, 1961.

Scott, Roger D.: "Critical Illnesses and Deaths Associated with Intrauterine Devices," *Obstetrics and Gynecology*, vol. 31, no. 3, pp. 322–327, March, 1968.

Sears, Robert R.: "Development of Gender Role," in Frank A. Beach (ed.), *Sex and Behavior*, John Wiley & Sons, Inc., New York, 1965.

———, Eleanor E. Maccoby, and Harry Levin: *Patterns in Child Rearing*, Harper & Row, Publishers, Incorporated, New York, 1957.

Segal, S. J., A. L. Southam, and K. D. Shafer (eds.): "Intra-uterine Contraception," Proceedings of the Second International Conference, October, 1964. International Congress Series, no. 86., Excerpta Medica Foundation, New York, 1964.

Seigel, Daniel G., and Robert E. Markush: "Oral Contraceptives and Relative Risk of Death from Venous and Pulmonary Thromboembolism in the United States," *American Journal of Epidemiology*, vol. 90, no. 1, pp. 11–16, July, 1969.

Seward, Georgene H., and Robert C. Williamson (eds.): *Sex Roles in Changing Society*, Random House, Inc., New York, 1970.

Seymour, R. J., and L. C. Powell: "Depomedroxyprogesterone Acetate as a Contraceptive,"

Obstetrics and Gynecology, vol. 36, no. 4, pp. 589–596, October, 1970.

Shader, Richard I., and Jane I. Ohly: "Premenstrual Tension, Femininity, and Sexual Drive," *Medical Aspects of Human Sexuality*, vol. 4, no. 4, pp. 42–49, April, 1970.

Shearman, Rodney P.: *Induction of Ovulation*, Charles C Thomas, Publisher, Springfield, Ill., 1969.

Sherfey, Mary Jane: *The Nature and Evolution of Female Sexuality*, Random House, Inc., New York, 1972.

Sherman, J. K.: "Research on Frozen Human Semen: Past, Present and Future," *Fertility and Sterility*, vol. 15, no. 5, pp. 485–499, September-October, 1964.

Sherman, Julia A.: *On the Psychology of Women*, Charles C Thomas, Publisher, Springfield, Ill,, 1971.

Shiloh, Ailon (ed.): *Studies in Human Sexual Behavior: The American Scene*, Charles C Thomas, Publisher, Springfield, Ill., 1970.

Shipman, Gordon: "The Psychodynamics of Sex Education," *The Family Coordinator*, vol. 17, no. 1, pp. 3–12, January, 1968.

——— and H. Yuan Tien: "Nonmarriage and the Waiting Period," *Journal of Marriage and the Family*, vol. 27, no. 2, pp. 277–280, May, 1965.

Shnider, Sol M. (ed.): *Obstetrical Anesthesia*, The Williams & Wilkins Company, Baltimore, 1970.

Shulman, Howard, and Stanley J. Birnbaum: "Evaluation of Abdominal Decompression during the First Stage of Labor," *American Journal of Obstetrics and Gynecology*, vol. 95, no. 3, pp. 421–425, June 1, 1966.

Simon, Paul, and Jeanne Simon: *Protestant-Catholic Marriages Can Succeed*, Association Press, New York, 1967.

Sjövall, Elisabet: "Coitus Interruptus," in Mary Steichen Calderone (ed.), *Manual of Family Planning and Contraceptive Practice*, 2d ed., The Williams & Wilkins Company, Baltimore, 1970, pp. 433–437.

Sloane, R. Bruce (ed.): *Abortion: Changing Views and Practice*, Grune & Stratton, Inc., New York, 1971.

Smith, Reginald A., and Richard E. Symmonds: "Vaginal Salpingectomy (Fimbrectomy) for Sterilization," *Obstetrics and Gynecology*, vol. 38, no. 3, pp. 400–402, September, 1971.

Smithells, R. W.: "The Prevention and Prediction of Congenital Abnormalities," in Ronald R. MacDonald (ed.), *Scientific Basis of Obstetrics and Gynaecology*, J. and A. Churchill, London, 1971, chap. 10.

Southam, A. L., and F. P. Gonzoga: "Systemic Changes during the Menstrual Cycle," *American Journal of Obstetrics and Gynecology*, vol. 91, no. 1, pp. 142–165, Jan. 1, 1965.

Southam, Anna L.: "Intrauterine Devices," in C. Lee Buxton (ed.), "Medical Practice and Population Control," *Clinical Obstetrics and Gynecology*, vol. 7, no. 3, pp. 749–875, September, 1964, pp. 814–828.

Speert, Harold, and Alan F. Guttmacher: *Obstetrical Practice*, Landsberger Medical Books, New York, 1956.

Stambler, Sookie (ed.): *Women's Liberation: Blueprint for the Future*, Charter Communications, Inc., New York, 1970.

Statistical Bulletin, vol. 44, May, 1963; vol. 48, July, 1967; vol. 48, September, 1967; vol. 49, December, 1968; vol. 51, January, 1970; vol. 51, June, 1970; vol. 51, October, 1970; vol. 52, July, 1971; vol. 52, December, 1971; vol. 53, April, 1972; vol. 53, June, 1972, Metropolitan Life Insurance Company, New York.

Stoller, Robert J.: *Sex and Gender*, Science House, Inc., New York, 1968.

Stone, Hannah M., and Abraham Stone: *A Marriage Manual*, rev. by Gloria Stone Aitken and Aquiles J. Sobrero, Simon & Schuster, Inc., New York, 1968.

Stone, L. Joseph, and Joseph Church: *Childhood and Adolescence*, Random House, Inc., New York, 1957.

Stone, Martin L., Myron Gordon, and Joseph Rovinsky: "III The Impact of a Liberalized Abortion Law on the Medical Schools," *American Journal of Obstetrics and Gynecology*, vol. 111, no. 5, pp. 728–735, Nov. 1, 1971.

———, Louis J. Solerno, Marvin Green, and Carl Zelson: "Narcotic Addiction in Pregnancy," *American Journal of Obstetrics and Gynecology*, vol. 109, no. 5, pp. 716–723, Mar. 1, 1971.

Strausz, Ivan K., and Harold Schulman: "500 Outpatient Abortions Performed under Local Anesthesia," *Obstetrics and Gynecology*, vol. 38, no. 2, pp. 199–205, August, 1971.

Sullenger, Thomas Earl: *Neglected Areas in Family Living*, The Christopher Publishing House, Boston, 1960.

Sumner, William Graham, and Albert Galloway Keller: *The Science of Society*, Yale University Press, New Haven, Conn., 1927.

Surgeon General: "Smoking and Pregnancy," from "The Health Consequences of Smoking, 1971," U.S. Department of Health, Education, and Welfare, Washington.

————: "The Health Consequences of Smoking," *A Report of the Surgeon General, 1972*, U.S. Department of Health, Education, and Welfare, Washington.

Sutherland, Hamish, and Iain Stewart: "A Critical Analysis of the Premenstrual Syndrome," *The Lancet*, vol. 1, pp. 1180–1183, June 5, 1965.

Tanner, James M., and Gordon Rattray Taylor: *Growth*, Time-Life Books, a division of Time, Inc., New York, 1965.

Tanner, Leslie B. (ed.): *Voices from Women's Liberation*, New American Library, Inc., New York, 1971.

Tatum, Howard J.: "Intrauterine Contraception," *American Journal of Obstetrics and Gynecology*, vol. 112, no. 7, pp. 1000–1023, Apr. 1, 1972.

Taussig, Helen B.: "A Study of the German Outbreak of Phocomelia," *Journal of the American Medical Association*, vol. 180, no. 13, pp. 1106–1114, June 30, 1962.

Taylor, E. Stewart: editor's comments, *Obstetrical and Gynecological Survey*, vol. 22, no. 4, p. 610, August, 1967; vol. 23, no. 1, p. 92, January, 1968; vol. 24, no. 8, p. 1092, August, 1969.

Terman, Lewis: *Psychological Factors in Marital Happiness*, McGraw-Hill Book Company, New York, 1938.

Texas Family Code, 1970.

Thomas, John L.: *Marriage and Rhythm*, The Newman Press, Westminster, Md., 1957.

Thompson, Spencer G. (ed.): *Pediatric Currents in General Practice*, vol. 11, no. 5, May, 1962, Ross Laboratories, Columbus, Ohio.

Tietze, Christopher: "The Condom," in Mary Steichen Calderone (ed.), *Manual of Family Planning and Contraceptive Practice*, 2d ed., The Williams & Wilkins Company, Baltimore, 1970a, pp. 424–428.

————: "Effectiveness and Acceptability of Intrauterine Contraceptive Devices," *American Journal of Public Health*, vol. 55, p. 1874, 1965; abstracted in *Obstetrical and Gynecological Survey*, vol. 21, no. 3, pp. 483–486, June, 1966.

————: "Intra-uterine Contraception," in Stewart L. Marcus and Cyril C. Marcus (eds.), *Advances in Obstetrics and Gynecology*, vol. 1, The Williams & Wilkins Company, Baltimore, 1967, chap. 35.

————: "Intra-uterine Contraceptive Rings: History and Statistical Appraisal," in Christopher Tietze and Sarah Lewit (eds.), "Intra-uterine Contraceptive Devices," *Proceedings of the Conference, April 30-May 1, 1962, International Congress Series No. 54*, Excerpta Medica Foundation, New York, pp. 9–20.

————: "Probability of Pregnancy Resulting from Single Unprotected Coitus," *Fertility & Sterility*, vol. 11, no. 5, pp. 485–488, 1960.

————: "Relative Effectiveness," in Mary Steichen Calderone (ed.), *Manual of Family Planning and Contraceptive Practice*, 2d ed., The Williams & Wilkins Company, Baltimore, 1970b, pp. 268–275.

————: "Statistical Assessment of Adverse Experiences Associated with the Use of Oral Contraceptives," in Celso-Ramon Garcia (ed.): "Oral Contraceptives," *Clinical Obstetrics and Gynecology*, vol. 11, no. 3, pp. 623–752, September, 1968, pp. 698–715.

———— and Sarah Lewit: "Intra-uterine Contraception: Effectiveness and Acceptability," in S. J. Segal, A. L. Southam, and K. D. Shafer (eds.), "Intrauterine Contraception," *Proceedings of the Second International Conference, October, 1964, International Congress Series No. 86*, Excerpta Medica Foundation, New York, pp. 98–110.

———— and ———— (eds.): "Intra-uterine Contraceptive Devices," *Proceedings of the Conference, April 30–May 1, 1962, International Congress Series No. 54*, Excerpta Medica Foundation, New York.

Time, Mar. 17, 1967, p. 67; Aug. 31, 1970, pp. 15–23; Dec. 14, 1970, p. 50; Dec. 28, 1970, pp. 22, 34–39; Mar. 20, 1972 (special issue).

Timmons, J. Daniel, and Russell R. de Alvarez: "Monoamniotic Twin Pregnancy," *American Journal of Obstetrics and Gynecology*, vol. 86, no. 7, pp. 875–881, Aug. 1, 1963.

Tindall, V. R.: "Aetiology and Pathology of Pulmonary Embolism," in Ronald R. MacDonald (ed.), *Scientific Basis of Obstetrics and Gynaecology*, J. and A. Churchill, London, 1971.

Tobin, T. E.: *When Is Rhythm Allowed?* Lignorian

Pamphlets, Redemptionist Fathers, Lignori, Mo., 1962.

Toffler, Alvin: *Future Shock*, Random House, Inc., New York, 1970.

Trethowan, W. H.: "Pregnancy Symptoms in Men," *Sexual Behavior*, vol. 2, no. 11, pp. 23–27, November, 1972.

Trythall, Sylvester W.: "The Premarital Law," *Journal of the American Medical Association*, vol. 187, no. 12, pp. 900–903, Mar. 21, 1964.

Turchetti, G., R. Palagi, and E. Lattanzi: "Anemia in the New Born Due to Transplacental Fetal Hemorrhage," *Obstetrics and Gynecology*, vol. 26, no. 5, pp. 698–701, November, 1965.

Turnbull, A. C., and Anne B. M. Anderson: "Uterine Function in Human Pregnancy and Labour," in Ronald R. MacDonald (ed.), *Scientific Basis of Obstetrics and Gynaecology*, J. and A. Churchill, London, 1971, chap. 3.

Tyler, Edward T. (ed.): *Progress in Conception Control 1969*, J. B. Lippincott Company, Philadelphia, 1969.

———, Marvin Levin, Julia Elliot, and Helen Dolman: "Present Status of Injectable Contraceptives: Results of 7 Years Study," *Fertility & Sterility*, vol. 21, no. 6, pp. 469–481, June, 1970.

Underwood, Paul B., Kelvin F. Kesler, John M. O'Lane, and Dwight A. Callagan: "Prenatal Smoking Empirically Related to Pregnancy Outcome," *Obstetrics and Gynecology*, vol. 29, no. 1, pp. 1–8, January, 1967.

United Nations: *Demographic Yearbook 1961*, New York, 1962.

U.S. Bureau of the Census: *Population Characteristics*, Current Population Reports, ser. P-20, no. 352, Nov. 18, 1966; ser. P-20, no. 159, Jan. 25, 1967; ser. P-20, no. 170, Feb. 23, 1968; ser. P-20, no. 204, July 13, 1970; ser. P-20, no. 222, June 28, 1971; ser. P-20, no. 223, Oct. 7, 1971; ser. P-20, no. 233, February, 1972; ser. P-20, no. 234, March, 1972; ser. P-20, no. 236, June, 1972; ser. P-20, no. 239, September, 1972; ser. P-20, no. 241, October, 1972; ser. P-20, no. 242, November, 1972; ser. P-23, no. 36, Apr. 16, 1971; ser. P-25, no. 441, Mar. 19, 1970; ser. P-25, no. 476, February, 1972.

———: *Statistical Abstract of the United States, 1972*, 1972.

U.S. Department of Health, Education, and Welfare: *Facts of Life and Death*, 1970.

———: *Infant, Fetal, and Maternal Mortality, United States, 1963*, National Center for Health Statistics, ser. 20, no. 3, September, 1966.

———: *Monthly Vital Statistics Report*, vol. 18, no. 12, supplement, Mar. 27, 1970; vol. 19, no. 13, "Annual Summary for the United States, 1970," Sept. 21, 1971; vol. 20, no. 13, "Annual Summary for the United States, 1971," Aug. 30, 1972; vol. 20, no. 4, supplement, July 22, 1971; vol. 20, no. 4, supplement 2, July 22, 1971; vol. 21, no. 4, supplement 2, July 25, 1972.

———: "Projections of the Population of the United States by Age, Sex and Color to 1990, with Extensions of Population by Age and Sex to 2015," *Current Population Reports*, ser. 25, no. 381, 1967.

———: *Vital and Health Statistics*, ser. 20, no. 11, September, 1971; ser. 21, no. 20, December, 1970; ser. 21, no. 15, February, 1968; ser. 21, no. 16, September, 1968; ser. 21, no. 18, February, 1970.

———: *Vital Statistics Report*, vol. 15, no. 13, July 26, 1967; vol. 16, no. 11, supplement, Feb. 2, 1968.

———: *Vital Statistics of the United States, 1959*, vol. 1, 1959; *1968*, vol. 2, sec. 5, 1968.

U.S. Department of Labor: *1969 Handbook on Women Workers*, Bulletin no. 294.

———: "Dual Careers," *Manpower Research Monograph*, 1970, vol. I, no. 21.

U.S. Supreme Court: *Jane Roe et al. v. Henry Wade*, no. 70-18, Jan. 22, 1973; *Mary Doe et al v. Arthur K. Bolton*, no. 70-40, Jan. 22, 1973.

Valenti, C., C. C. Lin, A. Baum, M. Massobrio, and A. Carbonara: "Prenatal Sex Determination," *American Journal of Obstetrics and Gynecology*, vol. 112, no. 7, pp. 890–895, Apr. 1, 1972.

Vessey, M. P., and Richard Doll: "Investigation of Relation between Use of Oral Contraceptives and Thromboembolic Disease," *British Medical Journal*, vol. 2, no. 5599, pp. 193–199, Apr. 27, 1968.

——— and ———: "Investigation of Relation between Use of Oral Contraceptives and Thromboembolic Disease. A Further Report," *British Medical Journal*, vol. 2, no. 5658, pp. 651–657, June 14, 1969.

——— and Josephine A. C. Weatherall: "Venous Thromboembolic Disease and the Use of Oral Contraceptives," *The Lancet,* vol. 2, no. 7559, pp. 94–96, July 13, 1968.

Vessey, Martin P., Richard Doll, and Peter M. Sutton: "Oral Contraceptives and Breast Neoplasia: A Retrospective Study," *British Medical Journal,* vol. 3, no. 5829, pp. 719–724, Sept. 23, 1972.

Villee, Claude A. (ed.): *The Placenta and Fetal Membranes,* The Williams & Wilkins Company, Baltimore, 1960.

Vincent, Clark E.: "The Physician as Counselor in Nonmarital and Premarital Pregnancies," *Medical Aspects of Human Sexuality,* vol. 1, no. 2, pp. 28–38, October, 1967.

Wakin, Edward, and Joseph F. Scheuer: *The De-Romanization of the American Catholic Church,* The Macmillan Company, New York, 1966.

Wall, Roscoe L., Jr.: "Evaluation and Management of Infertility," *Clinical Obstetrics and Gynecology,* vol. 12, no. 4, pp. 851–926, December, 1969.

Wallace, Helen M. (ed.): "Human Reproduction Problems of the Adolescent," *Clinical Obstetrics and Gynecology,* vol. 14, no. 2, pp. 325–488, June, 1971a.

———: "Venereal Disease in Teen-agers," in Helen M. Wallace (ed.), "Human Reproduction Problems of the Adolescent," *Clinical Obstetrics and Gynecology,* vol. 14, no. 2, pp. 325–488, June, 1971b, pp. 432–441.

Wallach, Edward E.: "Breast and Reproductive System Effects of Oral Contraceptives," in Celso-Ramon Garcia (ed.), "Oral Contraception," *Clinical Obstetrics and Gynecology,* vol. 11, no. 3, pp. 623–752, September, 1968, pp. 645–668.

——— (ed.): "Dysfunctional Uterine Bleeding," *Clinical Obstetrics and Gynecology,* vol. 13, no. 2, pp. 361–488, June, 1970.

———: "Endocrinology of Ovulation," in Luigi Mastroianni, Jr. (ed.), "Ovulation," *Clinical Obstetrics and Gynecology,* vol. 10, no. 2, pp. 343–430, June, 1967, pp. 361–379.

Waller, Willard: *The Family: A Dynamic Interpretation,* rev. by Reuben Hill, Holt, Rinehart and Winston, Inc., New York, 1951.

Wallin, Paul, and Alexander L. Clark: "A Study of Orgasm as a Condition of Women's Enjoyment of Coitus in the Middle Years of Marriage," *Human Biology,* vol. 35, no. 2, pp. 131–139, May, 1963.

Walter, George S.: "Psychologic and Emotional Consequences of Elective Abortion," *Obstetrics and Gynecology,* vol. 36, no. 3, pp. 482–491, September, 1970.

Warrior, Betsy: "Man as an Obsolete Life Form," in Sookie Stambler (ed.), *Women's Liberation: Blueprint for the Future,* Charter Communications, Inc., New York, 1970.

Washington, Joseph R., Jr.: *Marriage in Black and White,* Beacon Press, Boston, 1970.

Weaver, Robert G.: "Scrotum and Testes," *Medical Aspects of Human Sexuality,* vol. 4, no. 10, pp. 124–143, October, 1970.

Weinstein, Eugene A.: "Adoption and Fertility," *American Sociological Review,* vol. 27, no. 3, pp. 408–412, June, 1962.

Weisman, Abner I.: "Open Legal Abortion 'On Request' Is Working in New York City, but Is It the Answer?" *American Journal of Obstetrics and Gynecology,* vol. 112, no. 1, pp. 138–143, Jan. 1, 1972.

Wershub, Leonard Paul: *The Human Testis: A Clinical Treatise,* Charles C Thomas, Publisher, Springfield, Ill., 1962.

———: *Sexual Impotence in the Male,* Charles C Thomas, Publisher, Springfield, Ill., 1959.

Westoff, Charles F., and Norman B. Ryder: "Methods of Fertility Control in the United States: 1955, 1960, and 1965," in William T. Liu (ed.), *Family and Fertility,* University of Notre Dame Press, Notre Dame, Ind., 1967, pp. 157–169.

Wharton, Lawrence R.: *The Ovarian Hormones,* Charles C Thomas, Publisher, Springfield, Ill., 1967.

Wile, Ira S., and Mary Day Winn: *Marriage in the Modern Manner,* Appleton Century Crofts, Inc., New York, 1929.

Wilkins, Lawson: *The Diagnosis and Treatment of Endocrine Disorders in Childhood and Adolescence,* Charles C Thomas, Publisher, Springfield, Ill., 1965.

Willocks, James, Ian McDonald, T. C. Duggan, and N. Day: "Fetal Cephalometry by Ultrasound," *Journal of Obstetrics and Gynecology of the British Commonwealth,* vol. 71, no. 1, pp. 11–20, February, 1964.

Willson, J. Robert: "Intrauterine Contraceptive Devices in Family Planning," in David Charles (ed.), *Progress in Conception Control 1967,* J. B. Lippincott Company, Philadelphia, 1967, chap. 9.

———: "Intrauterine Contraceptive Devices: Their

Effectiveness in Controlling Fertility and Their Effects on Uterine Tissue," *Pacific Medicine and Surgery,* vol. 73, no. 1A, pp. 44–51, February, 1965.

Winch, Robert F., and Robert McGinnis (eds.): *Selected Studies in Marriage and the Family,* Holt, Rinehart and Winston, Inc., New York, 1953.

Winokur, George (ed.): *Determinants of Human Sexual Behavior,* Charles C Thomas, Publisher, Springfield, Ill., 1963.

Work, Bruce, Robert B. Jaffe, Colin Campbell, and Walter Whitehouse: "A Technic of Intrauterine Transfusion of the Fetus," *Obstetrics and Gynecology,* vol. 27, no. 3, pp. 319–322, March, 1966.

Wu, Paul Y. K., and William Oh: "Management of the Newborn," in Allan G. Charles and Emanuel A. Friedman: *Rh Immunization and Erythroblastosis Fetalis,* Appleton Century Crofts, New York, 1969, chap. 14.

Wulff, George J. L. (ed.): "Forceps Delivery," *Clinical Obstetrics and Gynecology,* vol. 8, no. 4, pp. 893–913, December, 1965.

Wynn, Ralph M. (ed.): *Obstetrics and Gynecology Annual 1972,* Appleton Century Crofts, New York, 1972.

Yahia, Clement, and Melvin L. Taymor: "A 3-Minute Immunologic Pregnancy Test," *Obstetrics and Gynecology,* vol. 23, no. 1, pp. 37–40, January, 1964.

Yankowski, John S.: *The Yankowski Report on Premarital Sex,* Holloway Publishing Company, Los Angeles, 1965.

Yaswen, Gordon: *Sunrise Hill Community: Postmortem,* 2d ed. (mimeographed), Montague, Mass., 1970.

Yerushalmy, J.: "Infants with Low Birth Weight before Their Mothers Started to Smoke Cigarettes," *American Journal of Obstetrics and Gynecology,* vol. 112, no. 2, pp. 277–284, Jan. 15, 1972.

Young, William C.: "The Mammalian Ovary," in William C. Young (ed.), *Sex and Internal Secretions,* 3d ed., The Williams & Wilkins Company, Baltimore, 1961a, chap. 7.

———: "The Organization of Sexual Behavior by Hormonal Action during the Prenatal and Larval Periods in Vertebrates," in Frank A. Beach (ed.), *Sexual Behavior,* John Wiley & Sons, Inc., New York, 1965. chap. 5.

——— (ed.): *Sex and Internal Secretions,* 3d ed., The Williams & Wilkins Company, Baltimore, 1961b.

———, Robert W. Goy, and Charles H. Phoenix: "Hormones and Sexual Behavior," *Science,* vol. 143, no. 3603, pp. 212–218, Jan. 17, 1964.

Zartman, Edwin R.: *Science News,* May 21, 1966.

Zelson, Carl, Estrellita Rubio, and Edward Wasserman: "Neonatal Narcotic Addiction: 10 Year Observation," *Pediatrics,* vol. 48, no. 2, pp. 178–189, August, 1971.

Zipper, Jaime A., Howard J. Tatum, Mario Medel, Laura Pastene, and Mirta Rivera: "Contraception through the Use of Intrauterine Metals, I: Copper as an Adjunct to the 'T' Device," *American Journal of Obstetrics and Gynecology,* vol. 109, no. 5, pp. 771–774, Mar. 1, 1971.

Zipursky, Alvin, Janet Pollack, Bruce Chown, and L. G. Israels: "Transplacental Foetal Haemorrhage after Placental Injury during Delivery or Amniocentesis," *The Lancet,* vol. 2, no. 7306, pp. 493–494, 1963.

Indexes

Name Index

Abbey, H., 363, 479
Abbott, W. M., 169, 170, 475
Ackerman, N. W., 106, 475
Addison, R. G., 332, 492
Addition, H., 332, 492
Adler, A., 12, 291
Aitken, G. S., 335, 497
Albert, E. M., 264
Albrecht, R. E., 475, 476
Allan, M. S., 391, 475
Allen, F. H., Jr., 445, 446, 475
Anderson, A. B. M., 371, 499
Anderson, G. G., 350, 441, 475
Anderson, M. M., 441, 489
Andolšek, L., 409, 491
Andreas, C., 265
Andrews, R., 244, 478
Andrews, W. C., 414, 475
Arnstein, H. S., 474
Aronson, H. G., 475
Aronson, M. E., 324, 424, 475
Arrata, W. S. M., 352, 368, 475
Arthes, F. G., 413, 496
Arvay, A., 366, 493
Asai, J., 350, 492
Ashley, D. J. B., 355, 475
Averkin, E., 412, 483
Ayre, J. E., 411, 475
Aznar-Ramos, R., 412, 475

Baecker, J. M., 79, 493
Baer, J., 175
Baker, T. G., 352, 475
Bakker, C. B., 412, 475
Ballard, C. A., 441, 476

Ballard, F. E., 441, 476
Balswick, J. O., 41, 495
Banner, E. A., 476, 477, 486
Banowsky, W. S., 80
Barber, H. R. K., 415, 476
Bardwick, J. M., 12, 15–18, 35, 36, 44, 332, 476, 486, 489
Barglow, P., 367, 477
Barnes, A. C., 332, 476
Barron, D. H., 361, 476
Bartell, G. D., 109
Barton, J. J., 419, 476
Baum, A., 366, 499
Bauman, K. E., 73, 476
Beach, F. A., 476, 485, 491, 496, 501
Beacham, D. W., 409, 476
Beacham, W. D., 409, 476
Beam, L., 40, 480
Bearne, C., 482, 495
Bednarik, K., 33, 37, 241, 476
Beer, A. E., 398, 476
Behrman, S. J., 426, 476
Bell, E. T., 407, 412, 414, 422, 489
Bell, R. R., 41, 47, 476
Belliveau, F., 335
Belskie, D. A., 387
Bendel, R. P., 366, 478
Benirschke, K., 366, 487
Benjamin, H., 476, 488
Benson, R. C., 391, 476
Berlind, M., 357, 476
Berman, E., 417, 489, 490
Bernard, J., 44, 90, 92, 109, 161, 299, 476, 477, 490, 495
Bernstein, M. C., 223, 483
Bertocci, P. A., 80
Besanceney, P. H., 175
Bing, E., 480

Bird, C., 265, 299
Bird, L., 299, 335
Birnbaum, S. J., 379, 476, 497
Birnberg, C. H., 406
Bishop, D. W., 350, 476
Bishop, E. H., 476, 480, 483
Bishop, H. L., 446, 484
Blackmun, H. A., 430, 431
Blaine, G. B., 39, 476
Blandau, R. J., 355, 477
Blazer, J. A., 314, 328, 477
Blood, R. O., Jr., 56, 484
Bock, E. W., 475, 476
Boehm, B. R., 447, 477
Boggs, T. R., 477
Bosmajian, Haag, 265, 477, 484
Bosmajian, Hamida, 265, 477, 484
Boulton, M., 489
Bourke, G. J., 363, 477
Bourne, A. W., 364, 477
Bourne, J. P., 431, 432, 487
Böving, B. G., 415, 477
Bowes, K., 332, 333, 477
Bowes, W. A., Jr., 446, 477
Bowman, J. M., 446, 482
Boyd, N. R. H., 371, 478
Brant, H. A., 386, 488
Brasch, R., 189, 477
Breckinridge, S., 232, 477
Bremer, J., 28, 477
Brenton, M., 264
Brill, M., 176
Briller, S. W., 265
Brish, M., 484
Britten, F. H., 40, 477
Broderick, C. B., 322, 477, 490, 495
Bromley, D. D., 40, 477
Brotherton, J., 427, 477
Brown, B. A., 237, 477
Brown, E., 367, 477
Brown, W. J., 78, 79, 477
Bruce, J., 333, 477
Bruns, P. D., 446, 477
Buckle, A. E. R., 441, 489
Bulmer, M. G., 386–388, 477
Bunge, R. G., 426, 477
Burgess, E. W., 40, 56, 144, 477
Burnett, J. B. C., 409, 480

Butler, C., 409, 480
Butler, N. R., 363, 477
Buxton, C. L., 477, 482, 497

Calderon, J. J., 417, 490
Calderone, M. S., 76, 80, 396, 448, 478, 482, 495, 497, 498
Calhoun, D. W., 413, 480
Callagan, D. A., 363, 499
Callahan, S. C., 176
Campbell, A. A., 172, 402, 482
Campbell, C., 446, 501
Cantarow, A., 332, 494
Cantor, B., 442, 478
Carbonara, A., 366, 499
Carpenter, P., 446, 475
Carr, D. H., 427, 478
Carrington, E. R., 478, 492
Carter, H., 107, 155, 259, 260, 478
Cavanagh, J. R., 170, 171, 331, 478
Cawood, C. D., 68, 478
Cervenka, J., 366, 478
Chalmers, J. A., 375, 478
Chard, T., 371, 478
Charles, A. G., 443, 478, 501
Charles, D., 413, 414, 478, 487, 492, 500
Charney, C. W., 28, 478
Chaskes, J. B., 41, 476
Chin, J., 363, 478
Chown, B., 444, 501
Christensen, H. T., 40, 41, 43, 76, 77, 244, 478
Christenson, C. V., 482
Church, J., 497
Clark, A. L., 301, 306, 478, 500
Clark, J. H., 402, 479
Clark, L., 40
Clark, T. L., 444, 479
Clarke, C. A., 443, 445, 447, 479
Clayton, E. M., Jr., 444, 479
Cleckley, H., 127, 479
Clemens, A. H., 169, 479
Cohen, F., 443, 479
Comstock, G. W., 363, 479
Connell, E., 417, 479
Convers, D., 259, 479
Coppen, A., 332, 487

Coser, R. L., 479
Craft, I. L., 427, 477
Crampton, C. B., 389, 479
Crist, T., 72, 479
Csaop, A. I., 442, 479
Cuber, J. F., 149, 257, 479
Cudlipp, E., 265
Cunningham, G., 330, 490
Cutright, P., 75, 479

Dacie, J. V., 443, 444, 479
Dalton, K., 332, 333, 479
Davidsohn, I., 443, 479
Davis, C. D., 409, 480
Davis, H. J., 405–407, 479, 480
Davis, K. B., 40, 480
Davis, K. E., 41, 487
Davis, M. B., 370, 486
Day, B., 393
Day, N., 376, 500
de Alvarez, R. R., 386, 498
de Balzac, H., 283
Decter, M., 235, 236, 239, 265, 480
Deep, A. A., 427, 440, 480
De Lora, J. R., 109
De Lora, J. S., 109
del Solar, C., 474
Dewhurst, C. J., 27, 33, 480
Diamond, L. K., 445, 446, 475
Diamond, M., 29, 480
Dickinson, R. L., 40, 387, 480
Dick-Read, G., 379
Dightman, C. R., 412, 475
Di Saia, P. J., 409, 480
Doll, R., 411, 413, 499, 500
Dolman, H., 417, 499
Donald, I., 330, 359, 375, 379, 480
Donnelly, J. F., Jr., 363, 480
Douvan, E., 36, 476
Downs, J., 176
Drill, V. A., 409–411, 413, 480
Drose, V. E., 446, 477
Drucker, P., 388, 480
Drummond, I., 259, 480
Dubin, L., 328, 480
Dublin, L. I., 148, 480
Duffy, B. J., Jr., 172, 480

Duggan, T. C., 376, 500
Duvall, E. M., 473, 480
Dyrenfurth, I., 442, 478

Eastman, N. J., 379, 385, 388, 480
Eastman, W. F., 41, 73, 480
Ebbin, A. J., 363, 478
Eckerling, B., 444, 483
Eckstein, P., 409, 480
Edgren, R. A., 409, 480
Edwards, C. R. W., 371, 478
Ehrhardt, A. A., 28, 36, 492
Ehrlich, S. S., 197, 480
Ehrmann, W., 41, 42, 44, 45, 480, 494, 495
Eichler, L., 189–191, 480
Eisner, T., 420, 480
Ejlersen, M., 320, 481
Elias, J. E., 41, 47, 481
Elliot, J., 417, 499
Ellis, A., 489, 494
Ellis, V., 487
Emerson, T. I., 237, 477
Engelund, A., 415, 486
Engle, E. A., 353, 481
Ersek, R. A., 426, 481
Evans, B., 75, 76, 493
Evans, M. E., 444
Evans, M. M., 479
Ewing, J. A., 423, 487
Exner, M. J., 40, 481

Fagundes, W. B., 411, 475
Fairfield, R., 109
Falk, G., 237, 477
Falls, H. C., 376, 481
Farber, S. M., 264
Farris, E. J., 399, 481
Feinleib, M., 385, 496
Feldhaus, W. D., 444, 479
Feldman, J. G., 409, 481
Ferreira, A. J., 359, 364, 365, 481
Ferriss, A. L., 75, 232, 233, 481
Fields, C., 376, 481
Findley, P., 317, 481
Finegold, W. J., 425, 449, 481
Finger, F. W., 40, 481
Finkel, J., 388, 480

Firestone, S., 265
Fish, S. A., 444, 490
Fisher, S., 321, 481
Fitzgerald, G. R., 109
Fiumara, N. J., 80, 481
Fletcher, J. F., 65, 481
Flowers, C. E., 377, 445, 481, 486
Flowers, C. E., Jr., 377, 379, 481
Fluhmann, C. F., 331–333, 398, 481
Fontana, J., 388, 481
Ford, M. E. N., 246, 495
Fotherby, K., 409, 480
Fowler, C. R., 298
Fox, M. R., 440, 493
Foy, F. A., 167, 168, 170, 171, 481
Fraenkel, L., 397
Francisco, J. T., 70, 483
Freda, V. J., 447, 481
Freed, S. C., 332, 488
Freedman, A. E., 237, 477
Freedman, M. B., 41, 305, 481
Freedman, R., 172, 402, 482
Freeman, R. K., 324, 482
Freiser, S., 244, 478
Fremantle, A., 169, 171, 482
Freund, M., 426, 482
Friedan, B., 266
Friedman, E. A., 428, 433, 443, 447, 478,
    482, 501
Friedman, L. J., 327, 355
Friesan, R. F., 446, 482
Fromme, A., 109, 302, 482
Fujita, B. N., 41, 73, 74, 482
Furlong, W. B., 176

Gaddis, M., 392
Gaddis, V., 392
Gagnon, J. H., 482, 495
Galton, L., 78, 79, 482
Gambrell, R. D., 410, 482
Garai, J. E., 31, 482
Garcia, C., 55, 399, 409, 411, 412, 414,
    417, 482, 498, 500
Garcia-Bunuel, R., 417, 482
Gardo, S., 366, 493
Garvin, J. E., 333, 495
Geary, W. L., 471, 496
Gebhard, P. H., 56, 74, 301, 321, 482,
    488, 495

Genné, W. H., 84, 176
Gentry, W. C., 425, 487
Giese, H., 32, 482, 495
Gill, M. M., 332, 483
Gillespie, L., 363, 483
Gillett, P. G., 442, 483
Gillette, P. J., 449
Glass, R. H., 356, 483
Glazer-Malbin, N., 265, 484
Glick, P. C., 107, 155, 478
Glienke, C. F., 424, 475
Golden, B. A., 62, 211, 306, 309, 318,
    326, 329, 356, 483
Goldfarb, A. F., 415, 422, 484
Goldman, G. D., 27, 323, 483
Goldman, J. A., 444, 483
Goldsmith, S., 441, 483
Goldstein, H., 363, 477
Goldzieher, J. W., 409, 411, 412, 415,
    483
Gonzoga, F. P., 333, 497
Good, F. L., 171, 483
Goode, W. J., 176, 227, 264, 483
Goodlin, R. C., 330, 483
Goplerud, C. P., 386, 483
Gorbach, A., 330, 483
Gordon, A. I., 174–176, 483
Gordon, M., 223, 432, 434, 483, 497
Gordon, R. R., 27, 33, 480
Gorlin, R. J., 366, 478
Gorney, R., 332, 486
Goy, R. W., 28, 501
Graber, E. A., 415, 476
Granfield, D., 435, 483
Grant, A., 424, 483
Graves, L. R., Jr., 70, 483
Gray, M., 31, 483
Greaves, D. C., 367, 483
Green, M., 363, 497
Green, P. E., 367, 483
Green, R., 33, 484
Greenblatt, R., 484, 490
Greene, G. R., 413, 496
Greenhill, J. P., 18, 330, 332, 356, 357,
    359, 363, 367–369, 371, 373, 375, 376,
    379, 388, 397, 399, 424, 427, 440, 477,
    479, 481, 482, 484, 487, 489, 491
Greer, G., 266
Gregg, C. F., 40, 41, 43, 478
Grold, L. J., 85, 290, 484

Gruenberg, S. M., 474
Grunewald, H. A., 477
Gustafson, D., 444, 479
Gutierrez, R., 350, 489
Gutmann, D., 36, 476
Guttmacher, A. F., 330, 363, 365, 385, 484, 486, 495, 497
Guyton, A. C., 322, 351, 484

Haagensen, C. D., 320, 484
Hack, M., 484
Hacker, H. M., 237, 241, 265, 484
Hall, D. J., 41, 73, 490
Hall, R. E., 407, 483, 484, 493
Halpin, T. F., 446, 484
Hamblen, E. C., 332, 484
Hamblin, R. L., 56, 484
Hamilton, E. G., 447, 484
Hamilton, G. V., 40, 56, 485
Hampson, J. G., 32, 485
Hampson, J. L., 32, 33, 485
Häring, B., 173, 485
Harkell, R. L., 325, 485
Harper, F. V., 485
Harper, R. A., 289, 299, 320, 328, 485
Harris, D., 432, 434, 493
Harroff, P. B., 257, 479
Hart, H. H., 109
Hartman, C. G., 350, 351, 397–399, 402, 485
Haskins, A. L., 419, 485
Hastings, D. W., 335
Hatch, M. C., 359, 485
Hathorn, R., 176
Havighurst, R. J., 473, 485
Heer, D. M., 176
Helpern, M., 485
Herman, H. A., 425, 485
Hernton, C. C., 155, 485
Herpay, G., 366, 493
Hertig, A. Y., 386, 485
Herzig, N., 324, 485
Hettlinger, R. F., 80
Heyns, O. S., 379, 485
Hibbard, L. T., 440, 485
Higgins, D. H., 418, 485
Hill, R., 500
Hinman, F., 350, 489
Hobbs, L., 266, 321, 485

Hoffman, J., 332, 485
Hoffman, L. W., 233, 493
Hofmann, H., 80
Hohman, L. B., 40, 485
Holder, A. R., 435, 485
Hollender, M. H., 306, 485
Holt, J. G. H., 397
Holtzman, L., 438, 485
Holzman, G. B., 484, 486, 487
Hon, E. H., 370, 486
Horner, M. S., 36, 476
Horton, E. W., 442, 486
Hosoe, K., 350, 492
Houriet, R., 109
Howard, D. H., 56, 487
Howell, D. A., 445, 486
Hudson, C. N., 371, 478
Huffman, J. W., 486
Hunt, L., 332, 492
Hutchinson, D. L., 366, 486
Hyams, L. L., 330, 486
Hyatt, H. W., Sr., 362, 486
Hytten, F. E., 363, 364, 486

Iffy, L., 352, 368, 475
Illsley, R., 363, 486
Ingelman-Sundberg, A., 392
Ingraham, H. S., 431, 441, 486
Inman, W. H. W., 413–415, 486
Insler, V., 484
Iscoe, I., 233
Israel, S. L., 332, 367, 486
Israels, L. G., 444, 501
Ivey, M. E., 332, 486

Jacobs, R. I., 73, 496
Jacobs, W. M., 444, 479
Jacobson, B. D., 370, 486
Jacobson, I., 427, 440, 480
Jaffe, R. B., 446, 501
Janowsky, D. S., 332, 486
Jansson, I., 375, 490
Jensen, O., 237, 486
Jewelewicz, R., 442, 478
Johnson, E. W., 474
Johnson, V. E., 17, 30, 44, 57, 62, 63, 290, 301, 306, 310, 316, 320, 321, 323, 329, 335, 356, 403, 408, 486, 491

Johnson, W. L., 486
Johnston, R. A., Sr., 376, 494
Jolly, H., 19, 486
Jones, A. R., 446, 484
Jones, G. S., 332, 425, 493
Jones, H. J., Jr., 425
Jones, H. W., Jr., 27, 320, 321, 332, 486, 493
Josselyn, I. M., 33, 486
Jungck, E. C., 417, 487

Kaats, G. R., 41, 487
Kahn, J. B., 431, 432, 487
Kaltreider, D. F., 363, 494
Kane, F. J., 423, 487
Kanin, E. J., 41, 56, 68, 487
Kapstein, R., 176
Karim, S. M. M., 441, 442, 487
Karow, W. G., 425, 487
Kase, N. G., 356, 483
Kasirsky, G., 449
Katz, J., 12, 41, 487
Kay, C. R., 414, 487
Kaye, B. M., 362, 487
Keefer, C. S., 487
Kegel, A. H., 319, 487
Kellar, R. J., 485, 487, 491, 496
Keller, A. G., 191, 267, 498
Keller, D. W., 330, 483
Kelly, O. F., 171, 483
Kennedy, E. C., 48, 50, 80, 93, 439, 487
Kephart, W. M., 37, 487
Kesler, K. F., 363, 499
Kessel, N., 332, 487
Khudr, G., 366, 487
Kilgo, R. D., 90, 487
Kinch, R. A. H., 442, 483
King, K., 41, 495
King, R. C., 348, 487
Kinsey, A. C., 22, 40, 41, 56, 76, 488
Kirkendall, L. A., 45, 56, 58, 488
Kirshen, E. J., 442, 488
Kistner, R. W., 320, 333, 356, 357, 411, 414, 416, 422, 427, 449, 488
Klein, M., 428, 493
Klemer, R. H., 95, 285, 488
Knight, J. A., 367, 488
Knopf, O., 291, 488

Koedt, A., 321, 488
Kokken, S., 325, 488
Komisar, L., 266
Korn, H. A., 487
Kramer, R., 474
Kretchmer, N., 488, 492
Kreykamp, A. M. J., 176
Kroger, W. S., 332, 412, 488
Kuchera, L. K., 73, 418, 488
Kulka, E. W., 407, 489

Lachelin, G. C. L., 386, 488
Lader, L., 449
Lal, G. B., 25, 488
Lamb, W. M., 332, 488
Landis, C., 40, 488
Landis, J. T., 40, 489
Landis, M. G., 40, 489
Lanford, C. F., 363, 490
Larsson, C. M., 176
Lattanzi, E., 444, 499
Lav, H. L., 370, 489
Lawrence, G., 492
Leach, W. H., 183, 489
Leathem, J. H., 489
Lednicer, D., 480, 489
Legett, G., 356
Le Guerrier, J. M., 411, 475
Lehfeldt, H., 73, 407, 489
Lehrman, N., 335
Lein, J. N., 486
Lerner, S., 446, 484
Lesinski, J., 405, 406, 480
Levin, H., 464, 496
Levin, M. M., 417, 487, 489, 490
Lewis, E. C., 36
Lewit, S., 407, 489, 491, 498
Leyburn, J. G., 224, 489
Lidz, R. W., 412, 489
Liebmann, H. G., 407, 489
Liley, A. W., 445, 489
Liley, H. M. I., 393
Lin, C. C., 366, 499
Lindsey, B., 90
Linnette, E. H., 363, 478
Linton, E. B., 329, 489
Lippes, J., 407, 409, 481, 489
Lipton, M. A., 423, 487

Little, V., 386, 488
Liu, W. T., 489, 500
Lloyd, C. W., 150, 332, 333, 399, 423, 485, 486, 489, 491
Locke, H. J., 56, 489
Long, E. M., Jr., 329, 491
Longood, R. J., 431, 441, 486
Lopata, H. Z., 235, 240, 489
Loraine, J. A., 407, 412, 414, 422, 489
Lotvin, B. R., 417, 489
Loung, K. C., 441, 489
Lowrie, S. H., 76, 489
Lowsley, O. S., 350, 489
Lozoff, M. M., 487
Lucas, J. B., 78, 79, 496
Luce, G. G., 288, 490
Lucey, J. F., 446, 490
Lumkin, M., 418, 492
Lunenfeld, B., 484
Lurie, H. L., 477, 490

Maas, J. M., 409, 490
McCall, M. L., 391, 392, 490
McCammon, R. E., 407, 490
McCance, C., 41, 73, 490
McCary, J. L., 335
Maccoby, E. E., 464, 496
McConnell, R. B., 443, 445, 479
McDermott, S., 322, 490
McDonald, I., 376, 500
McDonald, R. L., 363, 367
MacDonald, R. R., 415, 490, 492, 497–499
Mace, D. R., 299, 324, 335, 449, 490
McElin, T. M., 333, 495
McGinnis, R., 501
McGuire, T. F., 306, 308, 321, 490
Mackenzie, J. M., 441, 490
McLarey, D. C., 444, 490
McLaughlin, H. B., 424, 495
McMahon, B., 385, 496
MacMillan, A., 393
Madison, P., 487
Madsen, M. K., 481
Maeck, J. Van S., 363, 490
Magoun, F. A., 109
Mahan, C. S., 322, 490
Malmström, T., 375, 490

Manabe, Y., 441, 490
Mandell, A. J., 332, 490
Mandell, M. P., 332, 490
Mann, E. C., 330, 490
Maqueo-Topete, M., 417, 490
Marcus, C. C., 482, 486, 491, 498
Marcus, S. L., 482, 486, 491, 498
Margolis, A. J., 391, 441, 483, 491
Margulies, L. C., 406, 407, 491
Markun, L., 236, 491
Markush, R. E., 413, 491, 493
Marmor, J., 61, 491
Martin, C. B., Jr., 329, 491
Martin, C. E., 56, 482, 488
Masi, A. T., 413, 496
Massarik, F., 75, 76, 493
Massobrio, M., 366, 499
Masters, W. H., 17, 30, 44, 57, 62, 63, 290, 301, 306, 310, 316, 320, 321, 323, 329, 332, 335, 356, 403, 408, 486, 488, 491
Mastroianni, L., Jr., 482, 483, 491, 500
Mayes, B., 362, 491
Mead, M., 90, 92, 109, 201, 491
Mears, D. L., 478
Mears, E., 409, 412, 491
Medel, M., 406, 501
Meissner, H. H., 77, 478
Melody, G. F., 332, 491
Melville, K., 109
Meyer, H. M., Jr., 363, 491
Meyer, M. B., 363, 479
Meyer, R., 417, 492
Millett, K., 11, 237, 266, 321, 492
Milliken, R. L., 202, 496
Mills, C. W., 46, 492
Milman, D. S., 27, 323, 483
Mishell, D. R., 406, 418, 492
Mitsuya, H., 350, 492
Moghissi, K. S., 441, 442, 492
Moloshok, R. E., 363, 492
Monahan, T. P., 257, 492
Money, J., 27, 28, 33, 36, 484, 492
Monif, G. R. G., 388, 481
Montagu, M. F. A., 18, 36, 146, 385, 492
Moore, B. M., 233, 495
Moreales, A., 422, 483
Morese, K. N., 363, 494
Morris, J. McL., 418, 492

Morton, J. H., 332, 492
Moses, L. E., 412, 483
Moyer, D. L., 350, 351, 355, 356, 406, 488, 492, 493
Mukherjee, T. K., 409, 480
Mulcahy, R., 363, 492
Munro, A., 492
Murdock, G. P., 1, 492
Murphy, J. F., 363, 492
Murray, R. R., 440, 492

Naftolin, F., 442, 488
Nanni, L. F., 413, 492
Nathanson, B. N., 440, 441, 492
Nelson, F., 432, 434, 493
Nelson, P. K., 324, 475
Neubardt, S., 74, 356, 405, 436, 492, 493
Neubeck, G., 109
Neumann, H. H., 79, 493
Nilsson, L., 359, 392
Niswander, K. R., 428, 493
Noonan, J. T., Jr., 167, 169–171, 434, 435, 493
Novak, E., 332, 493
Novak, E. R., 332, 425, 493
Nye, F. I., 233, 493

Ochsner, A., 363, 493
Odell, W. D., 350, 351, 355, 356, 493
O'Donnell, T. J., 435, 493
Oettinger, K. B., 77, 493
Oh, W., 445, 501
Ohly, J. I., 333, 497
O'Lane, J. M., 363, 499
Oliven, J. F., 150, 350, 351, 356, 403, 423, 493
O'Neill, W. L., 255, 493
O'Rourke, J. J., 415, 476
Osofsky, H. J., 440, 493
Osofsky, J. D., 440, 493
Ostergard, D. R., 361, 493
Otto, H. A., 109, 491, 493
Oven, A., 409, 491

Pace-Asciak, C., 442, 483
Packard, V., 41, 45, 80, 493
Page, E. W., 27, 333, 364, 400, 493
Pakter, J., 432, 434, 493

Palagi, R., 444, 499
Palti, Z., 422, 493
Pannor, R., 75, 76, 493
Papanicolaou, G. N., 410
Papp, Z., 366, 493
Parkman, P. D., 363, 491
Paschkiss, K. E., 332, 494
Pasnau, R. O., 439, 494
Pastene, L., 406, 501
Patner, A., 442, 478
Pavella, T. H., 155, 494
Payne, S., 425, 489
Peck, N. W., 40, 494
Peel, J., 405, 407, 409, 411, 494
Peretti, P. O., 41, 494
Perkins, H. F., 424, 494
Perry, E. J., 485, 494
Peterson, K. M., 40, 494
Peterson, W. F., 363, 412, 494
Phillips, C. A., 363, 490
Phoenix, C. H., 28, 501
Phythyon, J. M., 444, 479
Pillay, A. P., 494
Pilpel, H., 484
Pincus, G., 398, 410, 415, 482, 494
Pion, R. J., 73, 74, 482
Piver, M. S., 376, 494
Plateris, A., 259, 260, 478
Polk, B. B., 33, 494
Pollack, J., 444, 501
Pomeroy, W. B., 56, 482, 488
Pope Paul VI, 170–172, 494
Pope Pius XI, 169, 170
Pope Pius XII, 169, 171, 494
Porterfield, A. L., 40, 494
Potter, A. L., 494
Potter, E. L., 427, 494
Potts, M., 405, 407, 409, 411, 494
Powell, L. C., 417, 496
Preston, S. N., 413, 494
Price, D., 350, 494
Pritchard, J. A., 359, 494
Protos, P., 422, 483

Quay, P. M., 170, 494
Queenan, J. T., 443–447, 479, 490, 495

Raboch, J., 306, 482, 495

Raffin, M., 330, 483
Rajan, R., 440, 493
Rakoff, A. E., 332, 422, 483, 494
Ramsey, G. V., 233, 495
Randall, C. L., 428, 493
Reaney, B. V., 362, 487
Reeves, B. D., 333, 495
Reevy, W. R., 40, 495
Reiss, I. R., 44, 47, 48, 80, 84, 176, 495
Resnick, P. J., 437, 495
Reyner, F. C., 411, 475
Reynolds, E. O. R., 386, 488
Rice-Wray, E., 409, 411, 412, 415, 483
Richards, B., 414, 487
Richards, D. J., 409, 480
Richardson, S. A., 486, 495
Richter, L., 335
Riemer, S., 202, 495
Riley, G. M., 18, 150, 495
Rivera, M., 406, 501
Robertiello, R. C., 489
Roberts, G. F., 444, 495
Roberts, R. E., 89
Robinson, D. W., 332, 488
Robinson, I. E., 41, 495
Robinson, S. C., 412, 495
Rock, J., 176, 402, 424, 495
Rockwood, L. D., 246, 495
Rosenblatt, F., 420, 480
Ross, E. M., 363, 477
Ross, R. T., 40, 495
Roth, E., 363, 496
Rottenberg, I. C., 176
Roufa, A., 441, 490
Routtenberg, L. S., 183, 495
Rovinsky, J., 431, 432, 434, 439, 496, 497
Roy, D., 84, 496
Roy, R., 84, 496
Rubin, W. S., 449
Rubio, E., 363, 501
Rudikoff, E., 480
Rudolph, A. H., 79, 496
Rupp, J. J., 332, 494
Rushmer, R. F., 486
Russell, G. F. M., 333, 477
Ryan, K. J., 442, 488
Ryder, N. B., 500

Sadoughi, N., 28, 478

Safilios-Rothschild, C., 494
Salber, E. J., 385, 496
Salerno, L. J., 363
Salk, L., 474
Salley, H. E., 40, 494
Samenfink, J. A., 202, 496
Sandberg, E. C., 73, 496
Sanford, N., 487
Sartwell, P. E., 413, 496
Sauvage, J. P., 442, 479
Savel, L. E., 363, 388, 480, 496
Sawada, Y., 426, 476
Saxton, L., 496
Schaefer, G., 431, 433, 485, 486, 490,
    492, 493, 496, 497
Schaefer, L. C., 489
Schaffner, B., 40, 485
Scheel, C., 412, 483
Scheinfeld, A., 31, 146, 386, 387, 393,
    482, 496
Schellevis, L., 176
Scheuer, J. F., 172, 173, 500
Schneider, G. T., 471, 496
Schroder, R., 202, 496
Schroeter, A. L., 78, 79, 496
Schulman, H., 74, 436, 441, 493
Schumann, E. A., 360, 496
Schur, E. M., 80
Schwartz, A., 474
Schwarz, R. H., 427, 440, 496
Scott, J. S., 446, 496
Scott, L. S., 423, 496
Scott, R. D., 407, 496
Scott, W. W., 27, 320, 321, 486
Seaman, B., 335
Sears, R. R., 33, 464, 496
Sebba, H., 476
Segal, S. J., 496, 498
Seigel, D. G., 413, 491, 496
Seldin, R. R., 183, 495
Serr, M., 484
Seward, G. H., 487, 496
Sexton, P. C., 36
Seymour, R. J., 417, 496
Shader, R. I., 333, 497
Shafer, K. D., 496, 498
Shah, F. K., 363, 479
Shearman, R. P., 422, 497
Sherfey, M. J., 321, 497
Sherman, J. A., 34, 497

Sherman, J. K., 426, 497
Shiloh, A., 481, 482, 495, 497
Shipman, G., 244, 246, 497
Shnider, S. M., 481, 491, 497
Shulman, H., 379, 497
Simon, J., 173, 177, 497
Simon, P., 173, 177, 497
Simon, W., 482, 495
Singer, S., 487
Sjövall, E., 356, 403, 497
Skolnick, A. S., 265
Skolnick, J. H., 265
Sloane, R. B., 497
Smith, A., 414, 487
Smith, B. K., 233, 495
Smith, D. R., 350, 489
Smith, D. T., 493
Smith, H. E., 413, 496
Smith, R. A., 419, 497
Smithells, R. W., 363, 497
Soberon, J., 490
Sobrero, A. J., 335, 417, 497
Solerno, L. J., 497
Southam, A. L., 333, 407, 496–498
Speert, H., 330, 363, 497
Speroff, L., 350, 441, 475
Stambler, S., 497, 500
Stegall, H. F., 486
Stein, R. B., 33, 494
Steinhilber, R. M., 306, 308, 321, 490
Stevens, G., 485
Stewart, I., 332, 498
Stokes, W., 320, 328, 485
Stoller, R. J., 33, 497
Stone, A., 335, 356, 497
Stone, H. M., 335, 356, 497
Stone, L. J., 497
Stone, M. L., 363, 432, 434, 497
Stone, S., 418, 492
Strausz, I. K., 441, 497
Suarez, R., 28, 478
Sullenger, T. E., 497
Sullivan, J. J., 332, 492
Sumner, W. G., 191, 267, 498
Sutherland, H., 332, 498
Sutton, P. M., 411, 500
Suyama, K., 350, 492
Swyer, G. I. M., 386, 488
Symmonds, R. E., 419, 497

Taber, B. Z., 409, 412, 480, 483
Tanner, J. M., 359, 498
Tanner, L. B., 488, 498
Tatsuoka, R. Y., 488
Tatum, H. J., 406, 498, 501
Taussig, H. B., 363, 498
Taylor, E. S., 359, 445, 498
Taylor, G. R., 359, 498
Taymor, M. L., 370, 501
Terman, L., 40, 56, 498
Thomas, J. L., 169, 171, 498
Thompson, S. G., 375, 498
Thomson, A. M., 364, 486
Tien, H. Y., 244, 497
Tietze, C., 74, 404, 407, 409, 414, 424,
    484, 489, 491, 495, 498
Timmons, J. D., 386, 498
Tindall, V. R., 415, 498
Tobin, T. E., 169, 498
Toffler, A., 91, 92, 499
Tovell, H. M. M., 441, 490
Trace, R. J., 391, 392, 490
Trethowan, W. H., 367, 499
Troelstrup, A. W., 299
Trythall, S. W., 130, 499
Turchetti, G., 444, 499
Turnbull, A. C., 371, 499
Tyler, C. W., Jr., 431, 432, 487
Tyler, E. T., 417, 475, 499

Ulett, G. A., 332, 488
Underwood, P. B., 363, 499
Ushida, T., 350, 492

Valenti, C., 366, 499
Vande Wiele, R. L., 442, 478
van Noort, L. G. A., 176
Van Tienhoven, A., 420, 480
van Wagenen, G., 418, 492
Vessey, M. P., 409, 411, 413–415, 486,
    491, 499, 500
Villee, C. A., 27, 333, 362, 364, 400, 476,
    485, 493, 500
Villee, D. B., 27, 333, 364, 400, 493
Vincent, C. E., 500

Waehrer, H. Y., 265, 484
Wagner, N. N., 73, 74, 482
Wakin, E., 172, 173, 500
Walcher, D. H., 488, 492
Wall, R. L., Jr., 500
Wallace, H. M., 78, 500
Wallace, M. J., 172, 480
Wallach, E. E., 396, 412, 416, 500
Wallach, E. S., 476
Waller, W., 500
Wallin, P., 40, 56, 144, 301, 306, 477, 478, 500
Walter, G. S., 439, 500
Warren, C. P., 376, 481
Warren, M., 442, 478
Warrior, B., 238, 500
Washington, J. R., Jr., 156, 177, 500
Wasserman, E., 363, 501
Weatherall, J. A. C., 414, 499
Weaver, R. G., 150, 500
Weber, L. E., 393
Weinstein, E. A., 424, 500
Weisman, A. I., 431, 500
Wells, F. L., 40, 494
Wershub, L. P., 350, 500
West, L. J., 367, 483
Westerholm, B., 415, 486
Westoff, C. F., 500
Wharton, L. R., 18, 500
Whelpton, P. K., 172, 402, 482
Whitacre, F. E., 444, 479
Whitby, M., 409, 480
Whitehead, T. P., 409, 480
Whitehouse, W., 446, 501
Whitty, R. J., 363, 477
Wiederman, J., 426, 482
Wiest, W. G., 442, 479
Wile, I. S., 292, 500

Wilkins, L., 18, 500
Williams, L. H., 364, 477
Williams-Ashman, H. G., 350, 494
Williamson, R. C., 487, 496
Willocks, J., 376, 500
Willson, J. R., 405, 407, 500
Wilson, M. G., 363, 478
Wilson, R. H. L., 264
Winch, R. F., 501
Winn, M. D., 292, 500
Winokur, G., 27, 320, 423, 492, 501
Wirsén, B., 392
Wirsén, C., 392
Wolfe, L. S., 442, 483
Wood, H. C., 449
Work, B., 446, 501
Wu, P. Y. K., 445, 501
Wulff, G. J. L., 490, 501
Wylie, E. M., 449
Wynn, R. M., 476, 492, 501

Yahia, C., 370, 501
Yankowski, J. S., 41, 501
Yaswen, G., 88, 501
Yerushalmy, J., 363, 501
Young, W. C., 28, 33, 398, 422, 475–477, 494, 501

Zarrow, M. X., 402, 479
Zartman, E. R., 417, 501
Zelson, C., 363, 497, 501
Zimberoff, M., 376, 481
Zipper, J. A., 406, 501
Zipursky, A., 444, 501
Zuelzer, W. W., 444, 479

Subject Index

Abortion, 426–442
  and children, unwanted, 437
  conception control, effect on, 440
  deaths from, 432
  definition of, 426
  on demand, 429
  effects of, psychological, 439
  fetus, nature of, 433–436
  induction of, 440-442
    amnioinfusion, 441
    dilation and curettage (D&C), 441
    drugs, 440
    hysterotomy, 442
    illegal, 427–428, 432–433
    prostaglandins, use of, 441–442
    saline injection, 441
    self-induction, 440
    soap-suds douche, danger of, 440
    vacuum aspiration, 441
  law, liberalization of, 430
    in New York State, 430–432
  legal control of, 428–429
  male: responsibility of, 439
    rights of, 438-439
  reform, future of, 442
  on request, 428–432
    woman, rights of, 436–438
  silent, 427
  spontaneous, 426–427
    defective fetus in, 426–427
  Supreme Court decision, 430–434
  therapeutic, 428
  types of, 426–429
  voluntary, 429
Adoption, 447–448
  infertility, as cure for, 424
  and premarital pregnancy, 77

Adultery (*see* Extramarital sexual relations)
Adults, consenting, and premarital sexual intercourse, 51
Afterbirth, expulsion of, 377
Afterglow, 306, 323–324
Age:
  of female and premarital pregnancy, 76
  at first marriage, 107–108
    and divorce, 108
  mixed marriage, difference in, 148–152
Alcohol, effect on fetus, 363
Alternative life styles, 81–92
Ambisexuality and Women's Liberation Movement, 240
Amenorrhea, 19
American Association of Marriage and Family Counselors, 298
Amniocentesis and ascertaining sex of fetus, 366
Amnioinfusion abortion, as means of inducing, 441
Amnion, zygote, development from, 356
Amniotic fluid, function of, 361
Anesthesia:
  fetus, effect on, 363
  obstetrical, 377–379
Annulment, nature of, 251
Antagonistic cooperation, 267
Artificial insemination (*see* Insemination, artificial)

Ballottement, as sign of pregnancy, 369
Barr body, 366

Basal body temperature (*see* Temperature, basal body)
Birth control (*see* Conception control)
Birth rate, sexes, difference between, 23
Bisexuality and Women's Liberation Movement, 240
Braxton Hicks contractions, 368
Breast feeding, 385
   effect of oral contraceptives on, 410
   and menstruation, 385
   and pregnancy, 385
Breech presentation, 374

Caesarean section, 375–376
   sterilization during, 376
Campus marriage (*see* Marriage, campus)
Castration, 27–28
Catholic-non-Catholic marriage (*see* Marriage, mixed, Catholic-non-Catholic)
Cervical cap, as means of conception control, 404
Charivari, 192
Childbirth, 371–384
   afterbirth, expulsion of, 377
   breech presentation, 374
   Caesarean section, 375–376
   dry birth, 371
   episiotomy during, 375
   father in delivery room during, 391
   forceps, use of, 375
   hypnosis, use of, 379
   identification of baby, 376
   labor: duration of, 371
      stages of, 371–374
   lightening, 371
   menstruation after, 385
   molding of child's head, 374
   natural, 379
   pain of, 373
      relief of, 377–380
         decompression, 379
         hypnosis, 379
   pregnancy after, 385
   vacuum extractor, use of during, 375
   ventouse, use of during, 375
   version, 374

Children:
   in campus marriage, 208
   in Catholic-non-Catholic marriage, 167–168
   in communes, care of, 88
   and divorce, 257–258
      effects of, 262
   in mixed marriage, 156
   rearing of, 453–455
      discipline, 463–465
      needs of, 455–472
      stage-typical behavior, 460
   unwanted, and abortion, 437
Choice, freedom of, 50–51
Chromosomes:
   fluorescence of Y, in ascertaining sex of fetus, 366
   number of, 348–349
   and sex determination, 365
   and sex differences, 26–27
Cilia, and ovum transportation, 353
Climacteric, male, 150
Clitoris:
   location of, 316
   nature of, 319–320
   stimulation of, 319–320
   tumescence of, 320
Co-ed dormitories, 83
Coital postures, 325–326
Coitus interruptus:
   Catholic Church's attitude toward, 170
   conception control, as means of, 403
Coitus reservatus, conception control, as means of, 403
College marriage (*see* Marriage, campus)
Collusion and divorce, 262–263
Colostrum:
   after childbirth, secretion of, 385
   pregnancy, as sign of, 368
Communes, 86–89
   children in, 88
   sex and marriage in, 88
Communication:
   limitations on, 286–287
   in marriage, improvement of, 287–290
   between sexes, 287
Comparative rectitude and divorce, 263
Conception:
   meaning of, 395

Conception:
   orgasm, relation to, 306
Conception control:
   abortion, effect of on, 440
   cervical cap, 404
   condom, 404-405
   diaphragm, 403–404
   douching, 408
   experimental forms of, 417–418
   intrauterine device (IUD, IUCD),
      405–407
   intravaginal device (IVD), 418
   methods: comparative effectiveness of,
      420
      male, to be used by, 417
   oral contraceptives, 408–417
      action of, 409
      contraindications for, 410
      effects of: favorable, 415
         long-term, 415–416
         sociomarital, 416
      fertility, relation to, 411–412
      lactation, effect on, 410
      libodo, female, effect on, 412
      morning-after pill, 418
      and premarital sexual intercourse,
         416–417
      regimen of, 409–410
      side effects of, 411–412
         cancer, relation to, 411
         smoking, relation to, 414
         thromboembolic disease, 412–
            415
      types of, 409
   requirements of means of, 395–396
   sterilization (see Sterilization)
   users of, education of, 440
Condom:
   as means of conception control, 404–
      405
   and venereal disease, prevention of,
      79–80
Conflict in marriage, normal, 267–268
Consensus and wedding, 185
Consenting adults and premarital sexual
      intercourse, 51
Contraception, premarital intercourse,
      inadequate in, 72–74
   (See also Conception control)

Contraceptives:
   Catholics, use by, 172–173
   oral: Catholic attitude toward, 170–171
      and venereal disease, 80
Corpus luteum:
   formation of, 353
   hormones secreted by, 353, 396
Counseling:
   marriage adjustment, role in, 298–299
   quacks and charlatans, characteristics
      of, 298–299
Cross-dressing, 25
Cryobanking (see Sperms, frozen, banks)
Cryptorchidism, infertility, as cause of,
   423
Culture, internalization of, 30–31
Cystitis, honeymoon, 329

Date, qualities of, and choice of mar-
      riage partner, 120–121
Dating, 119–120
   during engagement, 141–142
   failure in, 119
   functional, 121
   and social change, 119–120
Death rate:
   decline of, and divorce rate, 255
   infant, and premarital pregnancy, 77
   maternal, 380–381
      and premarital pregnancy, 77
   sexes, difference between, 23
Decision-making, 51–54
Decompression, childbirth, as pain relief
      in, 379
Desertion and separation ratio, 253
Diaphragm, vaginal, as means of con-
      ception control, 403–404
Dilation and curettage (D&C), abortion,
      as means of inducing, 441
Diminishing returns, law of, and mar-
      riage adjustment, 297
Divorce:
   and age at first marriage, 108
   Catholic Church's attitude toward, 168
   and children, 257–258, 262
   collusion, 262–263
   comparative rectitude, 263
   and couple, effect on, 261

Divorce:
definition of, 250–251
grounds, 258–261
Hollywood, 252
law: Federal, 264
uniform, 264
before marriage: duration of, 256–257
mixed, 159–162
by mutual consent, 262–263
Nevada, 251–252
no-fault, 260–262
rate, 251–252
factors affecting, 254–256
failure, and extent of, 253–254
and premarital pregnancy, 77
recrimination, 263
and separation, 253, 257
spouse obtaining, 256
suggested remedies for, 262–264
Double standard, 55–56
Douching:
abortion, as means of inducing, danger, 440
conception control, as means of, 408
Drugs:
disorienting, and petting, 69
narcotic, fetus, effect on, 363
Dry birth, 371
Dysmenorrhea, causes of, 400–401

Education, mixed marriage, difference in, 158
Ejaculation:
orgasm, relation to, 305
of seminal fluid, 351
Embryo, early, sexually undifferentiated, 27
Engagement, 141–146
and premarital sexual intercourse, 65–66
Epididymis, 350
Episiotomy during childbirth, 375
Erection, failure to achieve, 18
Erythroblastosis fetalis (*see* Rh factor)
Estrogen:
corpus luteum, secreted by, 353
Graafian follicle, secreted by, 352, 396
Eunuch, 28

Extramarital sexual relations, as life style, 84

Fallopian tube and ovum transportation, 353–354
Family:
background, in mixed marriage, 157–158
development, 472–474
developmental tasks, 470–472
functions of, 451–453
changes in, 225–227
institutional aspects, 223–225
personality aspects, 225–227
life, pattern of, and married woman's employment, 235
life cycle, 470–474
Father:
childbirth, in delivery room during, 391
functions of, 390
role of, changes in, 227–228
Fear in marriage adjustment, role in, 290
Female:
orgasm, capacity and frequency, 17–18
puberty, changes at, 18–21
sex drive, nature of, 17–18
Femaleness, nature of, 28–29
Femininity:
continuum, as part of, 28
femaleness, relation to, 28–29
nature of, 28–29
Fertility:
drugs, 386, 422
menarche, relation to, 18
menopause, relation to, 422–423
Fertilization, nature of, 354–355
Fetus:
activities of, 359
development of, 356–359
factors affecting: alcohol, 363
anesthesia, 363
hormones, 363
maternal impressions, 364–365
mother: diet of, 364
smoking by, 363
structure of, 364
narcotic drugs, 363

Fetus:
　　placenta, development of, 364
　　pregnancy, duration of, 364
　　rubella, 362
　　thalidomide, 363
　　viruses, 361–362
　　heartbeat, as sign of pregnancy, 369
　　labor, role in initiating, 371
　　movement, as sign of pregnancy, 369
　　nature of, and abortion, 433–436
　　protection, food and oxygen supply,
　　　　360–364
　　responsibility for, 438
　　sex of: ascertaining, amniocentesis,
　　　　366
　　　　false tests, 365
　　　　fluorescence of Y chromosome, 366
　　　　sex chromatin, 366
　　weight gain of, 358
Fimbriae, 353
Finances in campus marriage, 203–205,
　　209
Focal points, marriage adjustment, role
　　in, 279–280
Folkways, conditioning, role in, 272–273
Follicle stimulating hormone (FSH) and
　　follicle formation, 352
Forceps, obstetrical, 375
Frame of reference, 286
　　and communication, 289
Freedom, sexes, difference between, 16

Gender:
　　orientation, predisposition at birth, 29
　　role, determination of, 32–33
Genes:
　　nature of, 348–349
　　and sex differences, 26–27
German measles (*see* Rubella)
Gonads and sex differences, 27–28
Graafian follicle:
　　formation of, 352
　　secretion of, 352, 396
Group sex, 84–86

Hemolytic disease of newborn (*see* Rh
　　factor)

Heredity and choice of marriage partner,
　　129–132
Hermaphrodite, 25
Homicide, sexes, difference between, 23
Homosexuality:
　　female (*see* Lesbianism)
　　as life style, 82–83
　　and sex, group, 85–86
　　visibility of, 48
Homosexuals, marriage of, 179–180
Honeymoon, 194–195
　　cystitis, 329
　　sexual problems, 318
Human chorionic gonadotropin (HCG)
　　and pregnancy tests, 370
Humanae vitae, 170
Husband:
　　mobility of, in campus marriage, 202–
　　　　203
　　role of, changes in, 227–230
Hymen:
　　condition of, as indication of virginity,
　　　　315–316
　　intact, and pregnancy, 355–356
　　nature of, 314
　　stretching of: in first intercourse, 314–
　　　　315
　　　　and premarital medical examination,
　　　　317
　　variation in anatomy of, 315–316
Hypnosis, childbirth, use in, 379
Hysterotomy, abortion, as means of in-
　　ducing, 442

Identity, transition in, at marriage, 197
Illegitimacy (*see* Premarital pregnancy)
Implantation of zygote, 355
Impotence, 18
Infatuation and love compared, 96–100
Infertility, 421–424
In-laws, marriage adjustment, role in,
　　295–296
Insemination:
　　artificial, 424–426
　　　　Catholic attitude toward, 171
　　　　frozen sperms used in, 425–426
　　　　nature of, 424
　　　　types of, 425

Insemination:
  and conception, 355–356
Intercourse:
  anal, 51–52
  homosexual, 51–52
  sexual, incomplete, and parthe-
    nogenesis, 355
Interstitial cells and testosterone secretion, 350
Intrauterine device (IUD, IUCD):
  conception control, as means of, 405–
    407
  expulsion of, 407
  failure rate, 407
  method of action, 405–406
  penetration of uterus by, 407
  side effects, 407
Intrauterine transfusion (*see* Rh factor)

Jealousy, marriage adjustment, role in,
  290–291
Jewish-non-Jewish marriage, 174–175

Labia, tumescence of, 316
Labor:
  duration of, 371
  false, 371
  induced, 359
  stages of, 371–374
Lactation (*see* Breast feeding)
Lacunae, 361, 396
Lanugo, 358
Laparoscopy, salpingectomy, as means
  of, 419
Law:
  abortion, liberalization of, 430
  marriage, 244
Least interest, principle of, and marriage
  adjustment, 296–297
Leisure time, use of, in marriage, 281–
  283
Lesbianism and Women's Liberation
  Movement, 240
Levirate, 189
Life expectancy, sexes, difference be-
  tween, 23
Lightening in pregnancy, 371

Love:
  and infatuation compared, 96–100
  marriage, as reason for, 93–94, 225–
    227
  misconceptions concerning, 94–96
  nature of, 93–94
  premarital sexual intercourse, as rea-
    son for, 64–65
  questions for self-analysis, 100–106
  and sex: combining, 18
    separation from, 18
Luteinizing hormone (LH), production
  of, 352

Male:
  erection, failure of, 18
  orgasm-ejaculation, threat of failure
    of, 18
  puberty, changes at, 18–21
  sex drive, nature of, 17–18
  sexual intercourse, need for, 57–58
Maleness, nature of, 28–29
Marital status in mixed marriage, difference in, 159–163
Marriage:
  absence of, factors affecting, 82
  adjustment in (factors affecting): ac-
    ceptance, 284–285
    before acquaintance, length of,
      121–123
    communication, 287–290
    conditioning, 270
    counseling, 298–299
    diminishing returns, law of, 297
    fear, 290
    focal points, 279–280
    in-laws, 295–296
    jealousy, 290–291
    least interest, principle of, 296–297
    leisure time, use of, 281–283
    money, use of, 280–281
    mores and folkways, 272–273
    motivation, 283–284
    negative adaptation, 272
    orgasm, female, 301, 305–307
    perspective, 276–279
    private worlds, recognition of, 285–
      287

Marriage:
  adjustment in:
    quarreling, 294
    sex, 301–334
  age at first, 107–108
    and divorce, 108
  apprenticeship, 90
  campus, 198–211
    child care in, 208
    drop out, 200–201
    finances, 203–205, 209
    grades, 202
    husband, mobility of, 202–203
    number of, 199
      two- and four-year colleges, 200
    parents: attitude of, 203, 208
      subsidy by, 204–205, 209
    planning, 205–206
    role reversal in, 206–207
    special stresses in, 206–211
    successful, making, 211
    wife, employment of, 208
  changes in, 225–227
  in communes, 88
  dissolubility of, 187–188
  duration of, 250
    before divorce, 256–257
  in earlier times in U.S., 223–225
  factors affecting: failure, publicizing
      of, 250
    law, 244
    obscurantism, 245–247
    premarital romance, 247–248
    preparation, lack of, 245
    sex, overemphasis on, 248
    stereotypes, 248–249
    tradition, 249–250
  group, 89–90
  homosexual, 83, 179–180
  launching, 179–211
    two-stage, 179
  love as reason for, 93–94, 225–227
  mixed, 147–175
    age difference, 148–152
      and menopause, 149–150
    Catholic-non-Catholic, 166–173
      children in, 167–168
      contraceptives, use of, 169–173
      divorce in, 168
      number of, 172

Marriage:
  mixed:
    Catholic-non-Catholic: preparation
        for, 173
      requirements for, 167
      sterilization, Catholic attitude
          toward, 171
      wedding, 168
    definition of, 147
    education, difference in, 158
    family background, difference in,
        157–158
    intelligence, difference in, 158–159
    Jewish-non-Jewish, 174–175
    nationality, difference in, 152–154
    previous marital status, difference
        in, 159–163
    race, difference in, 154–157
    religion, difference in, 163–175
    success in, 147–148
  multilateral, 89–90
  premarital sexual intercourse, effect
      on, 56
  proportion of population married,
      107
  rate, 106–107
  reasons for, 92–94
  renewable, 90
  repudiation of, 83–84
  roles, expected and played, 223
  as sacrament, 184
  secret, 192–194
  serial, 91–92
  successful, nature of, 213
  transition to, from singleness, 195–198
  triad, 89
  trial, 84, 90–91
  trio, 89
  troika, 89
  in two steps, 90–91
  unconsummated, 314, 328
Marriage partner:
  choice of, 119–146
  in earlier times, 224
Married couples:
  number of, 107
  number employed, 232
Masculine protest, 12
Masculinity:
  continuum, as part of, 28

Masculinity:
   maleness, relation to, 28–29
   nature of, 28–29
Masturbation and education for sexuality, 470–472
Mate swapping (*see* Group sex)
Maternal impressions, 364–365
Maternal mortality, 380–381
Maternity, early, 18–19
Meiosis, 349
Men:
   employment, choice of, 16
   position of, 241–242
   relation to status, women, and marriage, 242–243
Menarche, 18
   fertility following, 18
Menopause:
   fertility, relation to, 422–423
   in marriage with age difference, 149–150
   after ovariectomy, 423
Menstrual cycle, 396–399
   anovulatory, 397–398
   and breast feeding, 385
   intermenstrual bleeding, 399
   intermenstrual pain, 399
   irregularity of, 402
   length of, 397–398
   mid-month stain, 399
   ovulatory, 396–398
   and wedding date, 183
Menstruation:
   cause of, 396–397
   cessation of, as sign of pregnancy, 367–368
   after childbirth, 385
   ovulation, relation to, 398
   at puberty, 18–19
   sexual intercourse during, 329
Miscarriage (*see* Abortion, spontaneous)
Mitosis, 348–349
Mittelschmerz, 399
Mixed marriage (*see* Marriage, mixed)
Molding of child's head during childbirth, 374
Money, use of, in marriage, 280–281
Morality, new, 38–39
Mores, role in conditioning, 272–273

Multiple births, 385–389
   and fertility drugs, 422
   incidence of, 385–386
      Hellin-Zeleny principle, 385
   superfecundation, 387–389
   superfetation, 388–389

Nagging, nature of, 274–275
Negative adaptation, 272
Neonaticide, 437
Nidation, 355
Nocturnal emissions, 19–20

Obstetrician, choice of, 388–390
Oophorectomy, 28
Orchialgia, 68
Orgasm:
   capacity, sex difference, 20
   clitoris, role in, 320–322
   conception, relation to, 306
   female: capacity and frequency, 17–18
      faking of, 18
      lack of, 18, 301, 306
      marriage, success in, relation to, 301
   male, failure in, 18
   nature of, 306
   vagina, role in, 320–322
Ova:
   chromosomes in, 348
   life of, 353, 401
   production of, 352–353
   size of, 349–350
Ovariectomy, 28
   and female sex drive, 423
   menopause, relation to, 423
Ovaries:
   embryonic, relation to sexual differentiation, 27
   removal of, 28
   sex differences, relation to, 27–28
Ovulation:
   and basal body temperature, 399
   coitus-induced, 402
   hormones, relation to, 352
   menstruation, relation to, 398
   pain associated with, 399
   reflex, 402

Ovulation:
time of, ascertaining, 398–399
Ovum (*see* Ova)

Papanicolaou (Pap) smear, 410
Parents:
campus marriage: attitude toward, 203,
208
subsidy of, 204–205, 209
objections to choice of marriage partner, 138–139
overattachment to, 139–141
Parthenogenesis, 355–356
Paternity test, 71
Pelvic examination, importance of, 317–
318
Pelvis, pubic joint, relaxation during
childbirth, 374–375
Periodicity of sexual desire, 330–331
Petting:
consequences of, 67–68
definition of, 67
and disorienting drugs, 69
force, use of, by males, 68
sexes, difference between, 68–69
sexual intercourse, relation to, 51–52
terms for, 67
Phocomelia, 363
Placenta:
development from zygote, 356
and human chorionic gonadotropin
(HCG), secretion of, 370
maternal portion, decidua basalis, 360
nature of, 360–361
Polygamy, serial, 91, 252
Preejaculate, sperms in, 355, 403
Pregnancy:
abdominal, 357
and breast feeding, 385
after childbirth, 385
compulsory, 429–430
and corpus luteum hormones, 353
duration of, 359
and fetus, 364
ectopic, 357
false, 367
meaning of, 395
precocious, 18–19

Pregnancy:
premarital, 72–78
adoption of babies, 77
and age of female, 76
and broken engagement, 65–66
and contraceptives, nonuse of,
72–74
and divorce rate, 77
incidence of, 74–77
reasons for increase in, 75
infant death rate, 77
males involved, 76
maternal death rate, 77
prenatal care in, 77
pressure to marry, 75
risk of, in single unprotected intercourse, 74
sexual intercourse during, 330
signs of, 366–370
tests for, 370–371
tubal, 356–357
in virgin female, 355–356
woman's activities during, 391
Premarital medical examination, 317–318
hymen, stretching of, 317
Premarital sexual intercourse (*see* Sexual
intercourse, premarital)
Premenstrual syndrome, 331–333
accidents, relation to, 332
crime, relation to, 332
incidence, 332
suicide, relation to, 332
symptoms, 332–333
Premenstrual tension (*see* Premenstrual
syndrome)
Prenatal care and premarital pregnancy,
77
Progesterone, secreted by corpus luteum, 353, 396
Prostaglandins:
abortion, as means of inducing, 441–
442
nature of, 441
Prostate gland, secretion, and activity of
sperms, 351
Pseudocyesis, 367
Psychopathic personality, 126–127
Puberty, changes at, 18–21
Pubococcygeus muscle, 319

Quarreling, marriage, role in, 294

Race, difference in mixed marriage, 154–157
Rape:
    accusation of, and premarital intercourse, 70
    statutory, 70–71
Recrimination and divorce, 263
Reduction division, 349
Religion, difference in mixed marriage, 163–175
Remarriage:
    Catholic attitude toward, 188
    incidence of, 107
    Jewish attitude toward, 188
    Protestant attitude toward, 188
Repercussion, as sign of pregnancy, 369
Rh factor, 443–447
    and antibody formation, 444–445
    and erythroblastosis fetalis, 444
        treatment of: exchange transfusion, 445
            feeding baby, 446
            fluorescent light, use of, 446
            intrauterine transfusion, 445–446
            phenobarbital, use of, 446
    and hemolytic disease of newborn, 444
    and isoimmunization, 444–445
        prevention of, anti-D gamma globulin, 446–447
Rhythm (see Safe period)
Rhythm bodily, individual variation in, 288
Ring:
    engagement, meaning of, 142
    wedding, significance of, 190–191
Rubella:
    fetus, effect on, 362
    vaccination for, 362–363

Safe period:
    conception control, as means of, 402–403
    menstrual cycle, relation to, 401–402
Saline injection, abortion, as means of inducing, 441
Salpingectomy, 419–420

Salpingectomy:
    laparoscopy, as means of, 419
    reversal of, 419
Salting out (see Saline injection)
Scrotum:
    and location of testes, 350
    temperature in, 350
Semen (see Seminal fluid)
Seminal fluid:
    ejaculation of, 351
    prostate gland, secreted by, 350
    seminal vesicles, secreted by, 350
    and sexual stimulation, 322–323
Seminal vesicles:
    and seminal fluid, storage of, 350
    and sperm storage, 350
Separation:
    before divorce, 257
    ratio, 253
Sex:
    afterglow, 306
    change of, 25
    chromatin, 366
    co-marital (see Group sex)
    in communes, 88
    determination of, chromosomes, 365
    drive: difference between sexes, 17–18
        female, after ovariectomy, 423
    education (see Sexuality, education for)
    of fetus: ascertaining: amniocentesis, 366
        false tests, 365
        fluorescence of Y chromosome, 366
        sex chromatin, 366
        controlling, 366
    group, as life style, 84–86
    love, separation from, 18
    in marriage, 301–334
        adjustment in, 309, 333–334
        bodily exposure, 313–314
        husband: reactions, 309–311
            responsibility, 318–319
            understanding, 311–314
        mutuality of, 302–305
        success in, 306–309
        wife: reactions, 305–307, 311–314
            understanding, 309–311

Sex:
    nature of, 301–302
    overemphasis on, and marriage, 248
    ratio, 23–24
    variables of, 32
Sex differences:
    attitudes toward, 11–13
    birth rate, 23
    causes of, 26–33
    death rate, 23
    love and sex, separation of, 18, 43–45
    nature of, 14–26
    orgasm capacity, 20
    overlapping of, 14
    sex drive, 17–18
    sexual experience, frequency of, 20
    sexual intercourse, 22, 302–303, 319
    sexual stimulation, 322
Sexes:
    characteristics, blending and overlap-
        ping, 25
    classification, dissatisfaction with, 12
    communication between, 287
    complementarity of, 34–35
        and sexual intercourse, 302–303
    conflict between, attitude toward, 12
    equality of, 33–34
    marriage, roles in, 223
    married students, numbers of, 199–
        200
    similarities between, 26
Sexual dimorphism, 11
Sexual intercourse:
    acceptable behavior, 324
    dangerous behavior, 324
    difficulty in, 315
    female, reactions in, 326–327
    first, fear of pain in, 314–317
    freedom of choice, consenting adults,
        51
    frequency of, 328
    group sex, depersonalization in, 86
    honeymoon, problems on, 318
    incomplete, as means of conception
        control, 403
    male, need for, 57–58
    mechanical devices in, 325
    during menstruation, 329
    nature of, 51–52

Sexual intercourse:
    orientation, sexes, difference between,
        22, 43–45
    petting, relation to, 51–52
    positions (postures) in, 325–326
    during pregnancy, 330
    premarital, 39–67
        engagement as reason for, 65–66
        female: reaction to, 43–45, 58–59
            type involved, 50
        force, used by males, 68
        with inadequate contraceptive pro-
            tection: incidence of, 72–73
            reasons for, 73–74
        incidence of, 39–43, 47
            increase, reasons for assuming,
                47–50
        as learning experience, 61–62
        love, as reason for, 64–65
        male responsibility, 60–61
            and female: reaction to, 58–59
            relationship, 58–61
        marriage, effect on, 56
        meaning imputed to, 66–67
        paternity: accusation of, 71
            acknowledgement of, 71–72
        pregnancy, risk of, 72
        rape: accusation of, 70
            statutory, 70–71
        research findings, 40–41, 45–47
        risks in, 69–80
        sexes, difference between, 20
        testing female responsiveness, 62–64
        vaginismus in, 63–64
        veneral disease, 78–80
    reactions in, 323–324
    sexes, differences between, 319
    technique, 325
    woman, preparation for, 325
Sexual responsiveness:
    female, 327
    in premarital sexual intercourse, 58–59
Sexual revolution, 37–39
    nature of, 47
Sexuality, education for, 465–472
Sexually colored experience, 30–31
Situation ethics, 65
Smoking:
    by mother, effect on fetus, 363

Smoking:
    and oral contraceptives, relation to
        side effects, 414
Sperm banks (*see* Sperms, frozen, banks)
Sperms:
    activity of, and prostatic secretion, 351
    chromosomes in, 348
    during ejaculation, 351
    frozen: and artificial insemination,
        425–426
      banks, 426
    life of, 352, 401
    motility of, 350
    number of, 351–352
      reaching ovum, 354–355
    in preejaculate, 403
    production of, 350–352
    size of, 350
    storage of, 350
    uterus, entrance into, 352
Spermatozoa (*see* Sperms)
State-typical behavior, 460
Step mother, 162–163
Sterilization, 418–420
    during Caesarean section, 376
    Catholic attitude toward, 171
    effects of, ignorance of, 420
    salpingectomy, 419–420
    tubal ligation, 419–420
    vasectomy, 418–420
Suicide:
    premenstrual syndrome, relation to,
        332
    sexes, difference between, 23
Superfecundation, 387–389
Superfetation, 388–389
Swinging (*see* Group sex)

Temperature:
    basal body: charts, 400
      ovulation, relation to, 399
      pregnancy, as sign of, 369
    breast, pregnancy, as sign of, 369
Testalgia, 68
Testes, sex differences: relation to, 27–28
    removal of, 27 –28
    and sperm production, 350
    undescended, and infertility, 423

Testicles (*see* Testes)
Testosterone, 27, 350
Thalidomide, effect on fetus, 363
Thromboembolic disease:
    nature of, 412
    oral contraceptives, relation to, 412–
      415
Thrombophlebitis (*see* Thromboembolic
    disease)
Transsexual, 25
Transudation, vaginal, 316
Transvestite, 25
Tubal ligation, sterilization, as method
    of, 419–420
Tumescence of labia, 316
Twins, types of, 386
    (*See also* Multiple births)

Umbilical cord, development from
    zygote, 356
Unawakened females, 304

Vacuum aspiration, abortion, as means
    of inducing, 441
Vacuum extractor, childbirth, use dur-
    ing, 375
Vagina:
    foreign objects in, 471
    inflation, danger of, 324
    lubrication of, 316–317
    orgasm, role in, 320–322
Vaginismus, 63–64
Vas deferens and sperm storage, 350
Vasectomy, 418–420
    reversal of, 419
Venereal disease:
    asymptomatic cases, 79
    contagion of, 78
    incidence of, 78
      age group, 78–79
    and premarital sexual intercourse,
      78–80
    prevention of, condom, 79–80
    treatment of, 79
Ventouse, childbirth, use during, 375
Vernix caseosa, 358
Version, 374

Villi, 360–361
Virgin birth (*see* Parthenogenesis)
Virginity:
    loss of, female attitude toward, 60
    pregnancy in, 355–356
    in unconsummated marriages, 314

Wed, meaning of term, 189
Wedding, 83, 106–107, 168, 179–192, 250
    in Catholic-non-Catholic marriage,
        168
    ceremony, 183–188
    customs, 188–192
    date, and menstrual cycle, 183
    golden, number, 250
    homosexual, 83
    number of, 106–107
    silver, number of, 250
Widowhood, sexes, difference between,
    24
Wife:
    role, changes in, 230–231
    sex, reaction to, 305–307

Wife:
    swapping (*see* Group sex)
Withdrawal, conception control, as
        means of, 403
Women:
    employment of married, 231–236
        children, effect on, 232–233
        choice of, 16
        number of, 231–236
        problems resulting from, 232–236
    minority, treated as, 237
    periodicity of sexual desire, 330–331
    position of, changes in, 236–238
    relation to status, men, and marriage,
        240–241
Women's Liberation Movement, 238–240

Yellow body (*see* Corpus luteum)

Zygote:
    implantation of, 355
    potential of, 347